VICTIMS OF THE CHILEAN MIRACLE

EDITED BY PETER WINN

Victims of the Chilean Miracle

Workers and Neoliberalism in the Pinochet Era, 1973–2002

with a foreword by Paul Drake

Duke University Press · Durham and London · 2004

© 2004 Duke University Press

All rights reserved

Printed in the United States

of America on acid-free paper ∞

Designed by C. H. Westmoreland

Typeset in Quadraat

by Keystone Typesetting, Inc.

Library of Congress Cataloging-

in-Publication Data appear

on the last printed page of this book.

IN MEMORY

OF MY PARENTS, WHO

FOUGHT FOR LABOR RIGHTS

IN HARD TIMES, AND

FOR THE CHILEAN WORKERS

WHO STRUGGLED IN THE

FACE OF DICTATORSHIP AND

NEOLIBERALISM FOR THE RIGHT

TO SHAPE THEIR OWN

DESTINY

Contents

PAUL W. DRAKE

Foreword

Peter Winn and his coauthors have the audacity to challenge the most successful economic experiment in Latin America since the 1970s. They do so by
examining the human underside of the glowing aggregate data. While conced-
ing numerous vaunted achievements from 1973 to 1998, these scholars argue
that many workers in a wide range of sectors suffered from Chile's neoliberal
"miracle." They also contend that this market-oriented model had a differential
and sometimes worse impact on women. At the same time, they expose the
damage to the environment. This book is not, however, merely an exercise in
"victimology," for it emphasizes the agency and resistance of labor as well as its
mistreatment and misfortune.

Winn deserves credit for questioning the conventional wisdom about Chile's
economic triumphs. He also makes a valuable contribution by showcasing the
innovative and gracefully written research of a talented new generation of Chil-
eanists. Most unusually, he has produced a remarkably integrated, cohesive,
and coherent collection, not simply another patchwork of loosely related articles. Just as Chilean capitalists have imposed discipline on their workers, so
this editor has on his authors.

As the paragon of neoliberalism in Latin America, Chile is the crucial test case
for the consequences of those market-driven policies for the working class. It
has been hailed as the shining example not only for Latin America but also for
other parts of the world. If the "Washington consensus" on the free market has
produced economic and social well-being anywhere, it must be in Chile, which
has been on that path longer than any of its neighbors.

In the wake of the hemispheric economic downturn at the end of the 1990s,
discontent with neoliberal economics mounted throughout the region, but least
of all in Chile, which, despite declining from its earlier boom, continued to
outperform other countries. Moreover, rising disillusionment with open markets did not spawn any clear alternative formula, least of all in Chile, which

remained firmly committed to that approach. However rocky and uneven, that route to modernization had lifted the country to new heights. Instead of switching tracks, Chile, like the international financial institutions and many other nations in Latin America, pledged to adjust the model in order to pay more attention to poverty, inequality, and environmental degradation. Therefore this anthology arrives at a propitious moment, when Latin Americans are reevaluating the results of neoliberalism for the most vulnerable members of their populations, expressing dismay at the exclusion and deprivation of vast numbers of their fellow citizens, and groping for new solutions to social injustices, whether those remedies can be found within or outside the reigning paradigm.

In assessing the Chilean experience, it is important to highlight three distinctions: the conditions under the dictatorship versus those under the democracy, the absolute levels of income versus the relative distribution of income, and the impact on workers in general versus the impact on organized labor in particular. In the first case, it was no secret that workers bore the brunt of the repression and economic reorientation under Augusto Pinochet Ugarte (1973–90). What was more surprising was that they fared less well than expected under the democratic governments of the Concertación (1990 onward), whose takeover was a tremendous victory for the working class and its political allies. The authoritarian regime devastated labor by smashing political parties aligned with workers, shackling union activities, and imposing neoliberal economic restructuring. By contrast, the democracy liberated the political parties, relaxed the hobbling union legislation but only slightly, and continued the neoliberal model while improving many social aspects. Because the overwhelmingly negative authoritarian period has received more scholarly attention, this foreword will concentrate on the contradictory situation in the 1990s.

Despite shortcomings, the Chilean economic record of the last quarter century, especially since the return of democracy in 1990, attracted ardent defenders. Small wonder, since the 1990s combined spectacular stability, growth, and poverty reduction. Enthusiasts lauded the stunning overall statistics.* From 1990 to 1996, the economy grew at an annual average of over 7 percent, surpassing the rates under the military government. Unemployment and underemployment shrank. Meanwhile, inflation fell to single digits. Education, health, and life expectancy soared, as social expenditures per inhabitant escalated over 7 percent per year, with the most progressive allocation in Latin America.

*All the data in this essay are taken from Paul W. Drake and Iván Jáksic, eds., *El modelo chileno: Democracia y desarrollo en los noventa* (Santiago: LOM, 1999).

Unlike many other converts to the marketplace, democratic Chile not only spurred growth but also slashed poverty. From 1990 to 1996 the share of the population living in poverty plummeted from 39 percent to 23 percent (the resulting percentage ranked about in the middle among Latin American countries) and those in indigency from 13 percent to 6 percent. Nevertheless, hundreds of thousands of Chileans remained trapped in deplorable conditions, as this anthology underscores. Many workers made gains: from 1990 to 1996 labor productivity rose an annual average of 4 percent, employment 3 percent, and real wages 5 percent, while unemployment hovered between 6 percent and 7 percent. Nevertheless, even those who prospered still encountered exploitation in many ways, particularly in terms of wretched working conditions, such as insecure jobs, weak unions, and inadequate social services. In a poll in 1998, 53 percent of the population agreed that the economy had improved under democratic rule, but 83 percent said that their own lives had not gotten better. Politically, economically, and socially, many workers gained significantly from the return of democracy, but not as much as they had hoped.

While Chile's democratic presidents curtailed absolute poverty, they did not reduce inequality, a much harder task without massive government intervention that would violate the limits of the model. From 1990 to 1996 the share of national income of the poorest 20 percent of the population stagnated beneath 4 percent, while that of the richest 20 percent inched up from 56 percent to 57 percent. In other words, in 1996 the top one-fifth of income earners garnered fourteen times the income of the bottom one-fifth. Indeed, the distribution of income was one of the most unequal in the world. In Latin America, only Brazil was worse.

While some women toiled under the harsh regimen described in this book, others had trouble finding work at all. At 37 percent, female participation in the urban workforce registered one of the lowest in Latin America. Only Brazil exhibited greater salary discrimination than Chile, where women earned an average of 25 percent less than their male counterparts. Among union members in Chile, only some 21 percent were women.

When assessing the outcomes of Chile's economic policies, it is necessary to distinguish between their consequences for workers and for the labor movement. Among workers, there were, of course, winners as well as losers, supporters as well as critics of the hegemonic orthodoxy. Whereas the results for laborers varied across subgroups, the ramifications for organized labor were much more uniformly negative. Viewed as an impediment to the unfettered functioning of markets, unions were undercut first by the reign of terror of Pinochet and second by the exigencies of development spearheaded by the private sector. As this book reveals, unionists reeled from macroeconomic transformations such as privatizations, sectoral shifts away from manufacturing toward services, decentralization of production, and downsizing of a porous social safety net. They also lost ground due to changes at the workplace, notably mechanization, flexibilization, individualization of pay and perquisites, fragmentation of the workforce, precarious or temporary employment, subcontracting, long hours, onerous working conditions, and inadequate benefits. Unions were handicapped in resisting these changes because of legal and informal restrictions on labor rights and collective bargaining and because of lack of support from their historic political champions, even when they held power.

After recuperating briefly in the first flush of democratization, the proportion of workers involved in unions and collective bargaining diminished between 1992 and 1998. The percentage of workers in unions went from 14 percent in 1986 to 22 percent in 1991 and then 16 percent in 1997. The percentage of workers covered by collective bargaining went from 9 percent in 1986 to 14 percent in 1991 and then to 11 percent in 1996. In the 1990s the number of unions grew, while their average size shriveled. The emasculation of unionized laborers under the democracy as well as the dictatorship suggested that economic restructuring did them even more permanent harm than did authoritarian coercion. This impression was fortified by the international trend for trade unions to lose sway under globalization, almost regardless of the political regime. In the 1990s both of the traditional vehicles for working-class conquests in Chile—labor unions and political parties—lost relevance. They could no longer exert much leverage on a restrained state.

Along with laborers, Chilean environmentalists voiced frustration at trying to get the state to compensate for market failures. By contrast, business leaders and conservative economists averred that efficient market mechanisms inevitably entailed certain costs for nature as well as nurture, warning that excessive interference by the public sector would dampen prosperity. Defenders of the environment and labor failed to convince the government that rapid growth might be unsustainable when it damaged the country's natural and human resources.

This book focuses on those Chileans who gained relatively little from the economic juggernaut. At the beginning of the 21st century, the neoliberal regime faced two major challenges. Could it sustain growth, and could it provide better treatment to those who had been marginalized? Although neither challenge was easy, the record to date indicated that the prognosis for the first had to be more optimistic than for the second. Perhaps studies like this collection will inspire new strategies to wed growth with equity, or perhaps more likely, a successor volume in the near future will find little change.

La Jolla, California

Acknowledgments

This book emerged out of a panel of the same name at the Latin American Studies Association meetings in Guadalajara, Mexico. The enthusiastic response of the scholars—Latin American and North American—who attended the session motivated the presenters, Thomas Miller Klubock, Joel Stillerman, Heidi Tinsman, and myself, to write and publish this edited volume on the impact of the Pinochet dictatorship and the neoliberal policies it initiated and imposed on workers in different sectors of the Chilean economy. We want to thank all who attended that panel, in particular Paul Drake, who chaired it and generously agreed to write the foreword for this book, and Francisco Zapata, whose perceptive comments as discussant helped shape the revision of those presentations for publication.

Volker Frank, who attended that session, was inspired to join us and to offer his critique of labor policy under the Concertación governments of the 1990s as his contribution. At the suggestion of the readers for Duke University Press, we added chapters on workers in the forestry and fisheries sectors. We want to thank them for their helpful comments.

We are also indebted to many Chilean scholars for their work and their help. The authors of this book acknowledge their intellectual debts in their respective chapters. Here I only have space to pay tribute to a few scholars whose contributions have been more global: Tomás Moulian, whose *Chile actual* punctured the triumphalism of the "Chilean Miracle" and made it possible to discuss it critically; and the many scholars, analysts, and activists of the Programa de Economía y Trabajo (PET) over two decades, from Jaime Ruíz Tagle to Jorge Rojas, who began the study of the impact of the dictatorship and its economic model on Chile's workers when it was dangerous to do so and who helped give both workers and scholars the tools with which to understand the new situation of Chilean labor. We all stand on the shoulders of those who have gone before us.

At Duke University Press, Valerie Millholland has been both supportive and patient throughout the long gestation of this project and deserves a special vote of thanks. With her combination of intelligence and empathy, she has been an ideal editor. Justin Faerber kept this project on track, an often difficult task, and Alexis Wichowski Tobin constructed a unifying index out of the diversity of this multi-authored volume; my thanks to both of them. The financial support of the Tufts Faculty Research Fund for the preparation of the index is also greatly appreciated.

Finally, as editor of this volume and as author of three of its chapters, I want to thank the John D. and Catherine T. MacArthur Foundation for their generous support of my writing and the Social Science Research Council and the Fulbright-Hays Program for their generous support of my research.

I also want to thank Tom Klubock for his generosity in serving as the informal editor of my chapters and Sue Gronewold for her thoughtful comments as my "in-house" editor. My very special thanks to Ethan Winn for creating the map in record time.

Every one of the many hours spent on this book meant fewer hours that I could spend with my family. I want to thank them for their love and their forbearance. They are the "victims" of the "miracle" of this book's creation.

VICTIMS OF THE CHILEAN MIRACLE

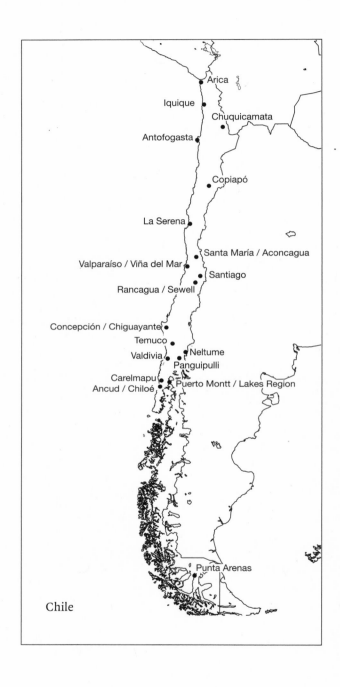

Arica

Iquique

Chuquicamata

Antofogasta

Copiapó

La Serena

Santa María / Aconcagua

Valparaíso / Viña del Mar

Santiago

Rancagua / Sewell

Concepción / Chiguayante

Temuco

Valdivia

Neltume

Panguipulli

Carelmapu

Puerto Montt / Lakes Region

Ancud / Chiloé

Punta Arenas

Chile

Introduction

"The Chilean miracle?" Luis Rodríguez gave me an ironic look. "What miracle?" he scoffed, pointing to the piles of garbage on the muddy path between the untidy rows of tin-roofed shacks that made up Las Turbinas, his shantytown community in Santiago, Chile's capital city. "There are two Santiagos," he exclaimed, with a wave toward the elegant neighborhoods in the foothills of the distant mountains, "and two Chiles: one rich, the other poor." Luis Rodríguez worked in the former but lived in the latter.

He was lucky, Luis affirmed. He had a regular job, unlike most of the young men in Las Turbinas, who survived as pickpockets or by selling crack. Luis was a construction worker in Las Condes, the richest county in Chile, a land of Mercedes and cellular phones, where one felt in the First World and people talked of "the Chilean miracle," the decade-long economic boom that had doubled Chile's national income by 1998 and made its neoliberal, market-driven economy the envy of Latin America and a model for others to emulate.

Luis Rodríguez was one of the millions of Chilean workers whose long hours and hard labor had made that "miracle" possible. To get to his job, he had to spend five hours a day six days a week on crowded buses, then work 10 hours a day, reaping as his share of the miracle a shack that he had built himself in the shadow of electricity pylons on land that flooded when it rained, amid the garbage, the rats, and the crime. "The miracle never reached *here*," he said with a bitter laugh. "We are *victims* of the miracle."

Rodríguez was not alone in viewing himself as a victim of Chile's neoliberal success story. Many of the workers interviewed by the authors of this book voiced similar views.

Together, their accounts of their experiences question whether Chile's workers have benefited from the boom—with its high growth rates and increased productivity—that their labor made possible. They also call into question the claims of the Pinochet regime to have created an economic miracle as well as the pledges of the democratic governments that succeeded it in the 1990s to promote growth with equity. At bottom, they pose the central questions of this book: Have Chile's workers paid the costs for their country's economic success? Were their interests sacrificed on the altar of neoliberalism? Are they victims of Chile's neoliberal "miracle"?

As the word neoliberalism suggests, this economic dogma looks back to the "liberalism" of an earlier era, in Chile's case, to the pre-1930s, with their monetarism, free trade, and laissez-faire state. Neoliberalism, however, is not merely a return to the past but rather an ideology that has applied "liberal" principles in the very different circumstances of recent decades.

The triumph of neoliberalism in Chile is part of a worldwide trend. Since the collapse of communism and the discrediting of statist economic alternatives, the economic gospel of the market has swept the globe. It has been embraced with particular fervor in places where it had been an ideological anathema only a short time before.

In Latin America, a region with a long history of consuming imported ideologies and also of pendulum swings in economic strategies, the extreme "neoliberal" version of market capitalism has triumphed even in the bastions of import substitution industrialization—Argentina, Brazil, Chile, Mexico—where the interests of the entrenched, inefficient industries that this economic strategy of protected industrialization created reinforced the ideology of nationalism and the politics of welfare that sustained it.

Viewed from the distance of the United States at the start of the 21st century, the hegemony of neoliberalism in Latin America may seem little more than a regional response to an economic globalization that has affected all regions of the world during recent decades. This globalization has increasingly integrated far-flung nations with very different histories, resources, and levels of development into a new international "economic order" dominated by the markets, bankers, and corporations of Europe, East Asia, and North America.

Within Latin America, however, the roots of neoliberalism seem more local and more specific, a reaction against the "failed" statist and protectionist policies of the past. Liberalism was held responsible for the region's deep crisis during the 1930s depression, which gave rise to import substitution policies. Their goal was self-sustained industrial growth and escape from a "dependence" on raw material exports and foreign markets.

For nearly half a century, import substitution—a strategy of accelerated industrialization with active government intervention through which Latin American nations sought to catch up with the developed world—seemed to be the solution. But what for the United States was a brief recession during the early

1980s, Latin America experienced as a profound crisis that cut far deeper and lasted far longer. The 1980s are known in Latin America as "the lost decade," in which economic growth stagnated, debts could not be paid, little foreign capital flowed to Latin America, and hyperinflation and high unemployment plagued the region.

The crisis of the 1980s sounded the death knell for import substitution industrialization, which was held responsible for the debacle. Although it meant surrendering nationalistic dreams of joining the ranks of the "developed" industrialized nations, country after country in Latin America has lowered its tariff barriers, opened itself to foreign investment, reduced the size of the state, privatized public sector companies and services, and embraced the market as the regulator of the economy and even the society.

Chile was the first major Latin American country to carry out this neoliberal transformation, and it has been both the most successful showcase for neoliberalism and the model for others—in Latin America and elsewhere—to emulate. Chilean neoliberalism was inspired by the theories of Chicago economist Milton Friedman, who argued that the market, not the state, should be the regulator of the economy, and later by the policies of Britain's Margaret Thatcher, with her privatizations of state enterprises and public services. In Chile, neoliberalism was introduced by the military regime as a reaction and solution to the grave economic crisis generated during Salvador Allende's "Chilean road to socialism" (1970–73), with its hyperinflation, consumer shortages, and public sector financial losses. It also represented a rejection and reversal of the interventionist state, protected industries, and deficit spending of the previous decades of stagflation and import substitution industrialization.

Neoliberalism was imposed by the Pinochet dictatorship during the late 1970s in a highly ideological version that made it a vehicle for an aggressive attack on Chile's workers and the labor rights they had acquired during decades of struggle. Neoliberal policies were an economic assault on the gains in wages, benefits, and working conditions that workers had won since the 1930s. They complemented Pinochet's violent repression of labor unions and worker activists, political attacks designed to disarticulate worker resistance to the dictatorship and to cow workers into a passivity that would enable the regime to impose neoliberal labor and economic policies that were prejudicial to worker interests. When in 1982 these policies led to Chile's worst economic crisis since the Great Depression, they were sustained by military bayonets, despite widespread social protests and political opposition.

A more pragmatic version of neoliberalism was introduced by the junta in the mid-1980s and promoted a remarkable decade of economic success for Chile, in which the country experienced its most sustained period of high economic growth (averaging 8 percent from 1988 to 1997) with low inflation in the 20th century.

Most striking is that since the restoration of democracy in 1990, Pinochet's neoliberal model has been maintained by the center-left governments of the Concertación coalition, which had criticized the model's high social costs, including deepening poverty and inequality, when they were in opposition to the Pinochet regime. It is precisely this neoliberal democracy of the Concertación government that has been promoted by the United States and international organizations as the model for other countries to emulate. Under the Concertación, not only did growth continue and foreign investment soar but both unemployment and poverty decreased, in part because of programs targeted at the poorest sectors of the population by center-left governments with greater social concern than the Pinochet dictatorship. It is little wonder that analysts as well as publicists have called this 11-year boom the "Chilean miracle."

Yet there was no comparable rise in real wages during this boom, despite significant increases in productivity and a work week that was among the longest in the world; nor was there the full recovery of labor rights that workers expected from the center-left democratic governments they supported. Most striking of all, there was no improvement in a maldistribution of income and wealth that had made Chile one of the most unequal countries in the world—a legacy of the Pinochet dictatorship that the Concertación criticized in opposition yet was unable or unwilling to change in government. At the end of the "miracle," one in five Chileans—some three million people—still lived in poverty and the country was still divided into "two Chiles."

During the heyday of the boom of the 1990s, Chileans were reluctant to examine the inequality and social costs of their economic miracle, particularly as it was intertwined with a transition to a still unconsolidated and incomplete democracy. But another cost of neoliberal policies, which had made Chile "one of the most open economies in the world,"[1] was heightened vulnerability to external economic shocks. The Asian financial crisis of 1997–98 put an end to the Chilean boom, and the Brazilian and Argentine crises that followed helped keep Chile in a long "crisis" of stagnation that continued into the new century, with growth falling to -1.1 percent in 1999 and unemployment rising to 10 percent by 2000 and 15 percent jobless in the Santiago metropolitan area, with similar statistics in late 2002.

The result has been an end to the triumphalism of the 1990s. Now that the shine is off the miracle, Chileans are more willing to listen to critical voices such as Tomás Moulían, whose book Chile actual, an attack on the selling of the transition and the 1990s as a successful model, has become a surprise bestseller.[2]

Our book aims to contribute to the growing debate on neoliberalism, the Pinochet dictatorship, and the restored democracy governed by the center-left Concertación coalition during the 1990s. It is unusual in that several authors from the differing perspectives of different academic disciplines and economic sectors focus on the same set of questions: What was the impact of the changes of the Pinochet era (1973–98) on Chile's workers? Did they pay the social costs of the military dictatorship, the transition back to democracy, and the neoliberal policies that reshaped Chile during this era? Have they been the "victims" of Chile's "miracle?"

To answer these questions, the contributors to this volume not only analyze government policies and statistics; they also explore changes in work processes and working conditions, labor relations, and labor politics, including repression and resistance in both places of work and communities. Moreover, most of the authors take a "bottom-up" approach to these issues, where previous scholarship has tended to remain at a national level in its analysis of policies and their consequences. The analyses in this book are grounded in original subnational case studies that include extensive interviews with workers and their leaders. This enables the authors to go beyond structures and statistics, policies and decrees to explore the experience of workers. The result is a more nuanced analysis of the impact of the changes of the Pinochet era. It also reveals the human face of these changes and the complex consequences and costs for Chile's workers, the great majority of its people.

Although they do not claim to be comprehensive, together these chapters span the productive sectors of the Chilean economy, including the principal export industries, the motor of the neoliberal economy. They include a traditional import substitution industry (textiles), based on imported inputs (both raw materials and energy); a manufacturing industry (metallurgical), based on Chile's natural resources; and the country's most important traditional export industry (copper). There are also chapters on three nontraditional export industries that have been showcases for the Chilean miracle: fruit, fish, and forestry.

While each of these chapters addresses the same general question—what has been the Chilean workers' experience of the Pinochet era and neoliberalism?— they do so in somewhat different ways. The authors give their own spin to that question, focusing on aspects that seem most germane to their case studies, and in the process consider an array of related issues such as consumer culture, gender relations, and environmental impact.

The chapter " 'No Miracle for Us' " surveys the history of the textile industry, a classic import substitution industry based on imported inputs, dependent on high levels of state protection, a bastion of the Left under Allende—and thus a vulnerable target of Pinochet's repression and neoliberal policies. In this chapter I explore the experience of both workers and entrepreneurs between 1973 and 2002—including issues of subcontracting, job quality, and the feminization of the workforce—and conclude that the whole industry was a victim of Pinochet-era policies but that textile workers bore the brunt of the costs. I stress as well the resistance of textile workers to these attacks on their jobs, wages, and working conditions, using both traditional and innovative strategies. At the end of the Pinochet dictatorship, their strategies seemed promising, as did a leaner and more modern textile industry. During the 1990s, however, a global structural and technological revolution in textile production brought the Chilean textile industry to its knees, pleading for a state aid that the Concertación governments refused to grant, citing neoliberal principles. By 2002 the Chilean textile industry seemed on its last legs, and its workers were lamenting that they were victims of the economic policies of the center-left democratic governments they had supported.

In "Disciplined Workers and Avid Consumers," Joel Stillerman analyzes the experience of the workers of Madeco, a metallurgical industry based on copper, Chile's chief natural resource. Madeco successfully adapted to neoliberal restructuring and emerged as South America's largest producer of metallurgical or other industries, a firm that exemplified the "Chilean miracle." Stillerman argues that it was Madeco's workers who paid for this corporate success in their loss of job security, wages, and benefits, in longer hours and speedups, with their intensified demands for higher productivity, and in the weakening of their union. He concludes that even relatively privileged workers in a successful industry were hurt by neoliberal restructuring but that the violent strikes of 1983 and 1993 demonstrated that Madeco workers resisted these losses with courage and consciousness. Stillerman reports as well on the increasing consumerism and indebtedness of Madeco workers—a pattern common to workers in other economic sectors as well—that, by the end of the Pinochet era, had undermined class solidarity and challenged the model of masculinity based on workplace and social solidarity.

"Class, Community, and Neoliberalism in Chile," by Thomas Miller Klubock, focuses on a more privileged group of workers, the miners of El Teniente, the world's largest underground copper mine, yet he comes to similar conclusions. State terror and economic "shock therapy," he argues, led to the fragmentation of community ties, political networks, and workplace cultures during the initial Pinochet decade. Copper miners continued to resist assaults on their wages, benefits, and organizations, drawing on traditions of union activism and political militancy. Moreover, their strikes and protests mobilized both a resurgent labor movement and the broader social protests against the Pinochet regime of the 1980s. Yet by the 1990s mechanization, downsizing, and cultural changes had undermined their workplace solidarity, weakened their class identity and unions, and disarticulated their communities. Klubock stresses as well the special issues for Chile's copper miners as workers in the largest remaining public enterprise, Codelco, which led to a "strategic alliance" with the Concertación managers enabling the state mining company to continue its economic success and giving the existing workers a measure of job security, though at the cost of jobs for their children.

In "More than Victims," Heidi Tinsman explores the experience of one of the least privileged groups of Chilean workers, the largely female seasonal workers in the fruit industry of the Aconcagua valley, the center of one of Chile's new export industries. Tinsman makes it clear that both male and female fruit workers were victims of Pinochet-era policies that displaced small farmers, forced men to work for minimum wage, and weakened the ability of rural unions to defend the incomes or working conditions of their members. But her interest is mostly in the seasonal women workers who constitute an overwhelming majority of the labor force in the new packing plants. Tinsman reveals the differential impact of neoliberalism on men and women and examines the changes in gender roles and relations that economic restructuring provoked. Her argument is complex: while they were exploited within the workplace—often working 15-hour days at low piece work rates in harsh conditions—the new incomes of these female workers increased their agency in their communities and homes. In particular, women's earnings lessened their dependence on and strengthened their bargaining power with their men and gave them the power to leave abusive relationships. The result was a complex and contradictory impact of Pinochet-era changes that left women workers *both* victims *and* beneficiaries.

"Shuckers, Sorters, Headers, and Gutters" also explores the feminization of a new export sector: fish and seafood. Rachel Schurman examines the experience of workers in the fisheries industry, including its many women workers, but adds an ecological analysis and a consideration of sustainable development in this sector. She traces these issues across two cycles that were shaped less by government policy than by Chilean ecology and the global political economy. The "wild fisheries" boom may have begun in response to neoliberal deregulation of the industry, but it ended because this unregulated exploitation led to species collapse by 1990. The boom in fish farming that succeeded it was running into both ecological and market problems by 1998, the end of the

Pinochet era. Workers paid the price of both booms and busts, Schurman concludes, in insecure short-term jobs, low wages, long hours, and bad working conditions. At bottom, she argues, Pinochet-era changes allowed employers to impose arduous work rhythms and to "shift the risk of natural resource-based production on to processing plant workers," while weakening the ability of these workers to defend their interests.·

In "Labor, Land, and Environmental Change in the Forestry Sector in Chile," Thomas Miller Klubock draws on his research on the forestry sector in southern Chile to explore the impact of neoliberalism on the environment, as well as on the sector's workers and on peasant communities in the area. The creation of tree farms producing fast-growing foreign species for wood pulp exports on lands that were occupied before by native hardwood forests and mixed farming was a signature Pinochet-era success story for private entrepreneurs and Chilean export earnings. But it was built on the intense exploitation of workers, who lost their previous levels of real wages, benefits, job security, working conditions, and representation at the hands of ruthless capitalists from Chile's elite, who took advantage of every loophole that Pinochet-era decrees and lack of regulation gave them. The result was soaring corporate profits and forestry exports—but at the cost of rising worker poverty, community disintegration, and environmental degradation of the world's largest temperate rain forest.

These six case studies are preceded by two introductory chapters written from a more general perspective. In the first of these chapters ("The Pinochet Era") I introduce the Pinochet era, which in effect lasted from the coup of 1973 well beyond his replacement as head of state in 1990 to Pinochet's retirement as armed forces commander in 1998—with a coda that extended Pinochet's era to his retirement from public life in 2002—outlining the principal features of the politics, economics, and labor policies that Pinochet instituted and contextualizing the case studies that follow. I stress Pinochet's political repression and his imposition of neoliberal economic policies and labor laws during the first decade of his rule and the Concertación government's failure to significantly alter these laws and policies during the 1990s. This chapter also explores the crisis of the 1980s and the transition toward democracy that followed. It examines the interaction between government policies, business decisions, and worker responses as a frame for understanding labor relations and contemporary Chilean history.

In "Politics without Policy," Volker Frank focuses on the final decade of the Pinochet era, when the transition to democracy and the governments of the center-left Concertación held out the promise of the creation of "social concertation," a "modern" system of consensual labor relations that would reform

Pinochet's probusiness labor code and create a more level playing field, while not returning to the pre-1973 state-centered system. But the labor law reforms of 1991 and 2001 were limited and social concertation never took hold. Frank concludes that the Concertación government gained most and labor least from these failed efforts at social concertation and that this failure is reflected in Chile's extreme inequality, despite a decade of economic growth and productivity increases. The failure to transform labor relations, he concludes, weakened unions, alienated workers, and doomed the Concertación government's public goal of "growth with equity."

Several of the later chapters call into question the neoliberal "miracle" itself, even in its signature industries. Thomas Klubock makes clear in his chapter on forestry workers that the much vaunted private sector "success" story in the forestry industry was at bottom a harvesting of prior public investment with heavy state subsidies, and at a high environmental cost. Rachel Schurman is equally skeptical of the neoliberal miracle in the fisheries sector, another Pinochet era showcase, but from a different standpoint. Like Klubock, she calls attention to the negative environmental impact of neoliberal policies. But her chapter also questions the sustainability of the neoliberal model in the fishing industry, with its high costs for both workers and the environment. The wild fishing phase, she concludes, led to the collapse of species after species in what had been very rich fishing grounds. Now, the attempt to replace wild fishing with fish farming is destroying the marine food chain and running into ecological, economic, and diplomatic problems that call the sector's future—and that of fisheries workers—into question.

Schurman's chapter—like Tinsman's on the fruit industry—also underscores the precarious character of export "success" in a globalized economy, where capital has no national loyalties, sourcing is global, and profit margins are often slim. Whether the product was grapes or salmon, Chilean "success" in export markets stimulated production for export in countries with even lower labor costs or other comparative advantages. As a result, supply soon exceeded demand and prices dropped to a point where they threatened Chilean profitability or competitiveness. In a globalized economy, today's miracle may be tomorrow's mirage. Workers in these industries might not understand all these global economic factors, but they experienced their negative impact in the form of lower wages, worse working conditions, and heightened job insecurity, as employers passed on their risks and costs.

Globalization and its impact on Chilean workers is a complex subject, which the authors have addressed in their own ways, relating their Chilean case studies to larger processes. My study of the textile and apparel industry (" 'No

Miracle for Us'"), for example, explores the geographic restructuring and production chains that have reshaped the sector worldwide. Stillerman relates his findings to the global debate about the impact of consumerism on worker identities and solidarity. Klubock, in his chapter on miners, finds similarities between miner strikes and rollbacks in Chile and the United States. His chapter on forestry workers, on the other hand, analyzes the use and abuse of subcontracting that has accompanied globalization in many areas of the world. Klubock shares with Tinsman and Schurman a focus on globalization and export worker vulnerability to market instability abroad that echoes experiences elsewhere, as well as an examination of the impact of globalization on gender relations, and environmental degradation.

I have left it to the contributors to discuss debates on these issues in their chapters as they deemed appropriate. It is worth noting here, however, that our critical analysis of Chilean neoliberalism is consonant with the growing global disenchantment with and criticism of the neoliberal "Washington consensus"—from the streets of Seattle to the pages of Nobel economist Joseph Stiglitz.[3]

Finally, a word about the title: this book asks if Chile's workers have been victims of its neoliberal economic miracle as a way of focusing debate on the impact of neoliberal policies on workers and on their social costs. In general, the authors share with many of the workers they interviewed the conviction that Chile's workers *have* been victims of the neoliberal restructuring of the economy and state: that they have not received a fair share of the benefits from the economic growth and productivity increases that their labor has produced and that they have had to bear a disproportionate share of the costs of this restructuring in their wages, working conditions, job quality, and labor relations. It also suggests that the impact of the cultural changes promoted by neoliberalism has been largely negative on worker sociability, lifestyles, and organizations.

Chilean workers, moreover, were also victims of General Pinochet's dictatorship. They were central targets of his political repression and suffered greatly from his state terror. They also paid a disproportionate share of the costs of his regime's regressive social policies. Workers and their organizations were also the primary targets of Pinochet's labor laws and among the biggest losers from his policies of privatization and deindustrialization. They paid the social costs as well of Chile's democratic transition within Pinochet's authoritarian constitution. Their socioeconomic aspirations were postponed in the interest of not jeopardizing the transition and their expectations of labor law reform were sacrificed on the same altar.

More than a decade of democracy and center-left governments has not altered neoliberalism's fundamentally negative impact on Chilean workers. In fact, viewed in historical perspective as part of the Pinochet era, the neoliberal democracy of the Concertación consolidated the neoliberal "revolution" that Pinochet began. It did this by conferring democratic legitimacy on the decrees that Pinochet had imposed by dictatorial fiat and by embracing and even extending many of his policy shifts. If Chile's workers have been victims of its neoliberal miracle, the Concertación governments must bear a significant share of responsibility for their fate.

These are conclusions that I—and my coauthors—have come to with reluctance. I was an international observer for the 1988 plebiscite that ended the Pinochet dictatorship, and I experienced firsthand the euphoria and expectations of those heady early days of the transition to democracy. Many of my friends have served in the governments and parties of the Concertación. They—and I—had hoped for a different ending to this story.

However, the fact that Chilean workers have been victims of Pinochet's dictatorship and neoliberal policies doesn't mean that they ceased to resist or that they have had no agency. On the contrary, the chapters on textile, metallurgical, and mining workers all underscore the resistance of workers to both the dictatorship and its neoliberal policies, often against great odds and at great risk. Moreover, during the Pinochet era, with its repression and restrictions on union activism, Chile's workers displayed great creativity in devising new ways to resist. They refused to eat at company cafeterias, took to the streets, mobilized sympathy strikes and social protests, and marched hundreds of kilometers to publicize their cause. They created new forms of organization, from lunch rooms and day care centers for the unorganized to new labor confederations, independent unions, and territorial federations inspired by the *cordones industriales* of the Allende era.

Nor was this resistance confined to the workplace or workers' issues. As Klubock's chapter on copper miners argues, it was Chile's workers who first raised the flag of political resistance against the dictatorship in the 1970s and sustained it during the years when political parties were banned. And it was the copper miners who mobilized the social protests and political opposition to the military regime in the 1980s to demand an end to Pinochet's dictatorship and the restoration of democracy and civil liberties. Labor initiated the transition to democracy that culminated in Pinochet's plebiscite defeat in 1988 and the inauguration of a democratically elected president in 1990.

Chile's workers may have been victims of Pinochet's dictatorship and neoliberalism, but they remained protagonists of their own and their nation's destinies. So, in asking if Chile's workers were victims of the neoliberal miracle, we are underscoring that despite their resistance and hard work they paid a disproportionate share of the costs and received fewer benefits from both the economic boom and the democracy for which they had struggled.[4]

This does not mean, however, that Chilean workers were just victims during the Pinochet era. The impact of neoliberal policies has often been complex and cross-cutting. As Tinsman and Schurman point out in their chapters about women workers in the fruit and seafood industries, their new incomes made women workers more independent and placed them in a stronger position to question patriarchal norms and insist on equality in their relationships with men and within their families.

The title we have chosen also problematizes the term "miracle." We question whether Chile's neoliberal boom—which may have had more victims than beneficiaries—should be regarded as a miracle. When confronted by such a claim, scholars and students should always ask: a miracle for *whom*—and at what cost?

In fact, few Chilean workers regard themselves as beneficiaries of the neoliberal miracle. Worker leaders and activists, moreover, were central targets of the military regime's state terror, whose goal was to intimidate them into passivity, in large part so that neoliberal policies could be imposed. Central to Pinochet's neoliberalism was a probusiness Labor Code that made workers easy to hire and fire and strikes difficult to win. The restoration of democracy in 1990 brought an end to state terror, a more labor-friendly government, and a minor reform of the labor laws. But the modifications to law and policy were slight, unions remained weak, and strikes few and far between. When, a decade after the 1988 plebiscite that restored democracy, Patricia Coñomon, a combative Communist labor leader, confessed that strikes were no longer in the workers' interest,[5] it was hard not to conclude that the military had succeeded in "disciplining" Chile's workers after all. In the interim, the market and the Concertación's neoliberal governments had completed what the military had begun. "Fear and consumerism," Coñomon maintained, were the regime's chief weapons against the workers.[6]

In 1998 Pinochet's retirement and arrest brought his era to a close and the Asian crisis brought Chile's economic boom to an end. The Argentine crisis of 2001–2002 and Pinochet's definitive retirement from public life during those years confirmed that both the economic miracle and his political career were history. Still, though the Pinochet era and the neoliberal miracle might be over, their impact on Chile's workers and their organizations remains. So does the question that informs this book: Were Chile's workers "victims" of its neoliberal economic "miracle"?

1 Andres Velasco, assistant treasury minister, quoted in Peter Winn, *Americas: The Changing Face of Latin America and the Caribbean*, 2d ed. (Berkeley: University of California Press: 1999), 198.
2 Tomás Moulían, *Chile actual: Anatomía de un mito* (Santiago: LOM, 1997).
3 See Joseph E. Stiglitz, *Globalization and Its Discontents* (New York: W. W. Norton, 2002).
4 Paul Drake, in an important comparative study, *Labor Movements and Dictatorships: The Southern Cone in Comparative Perspective* (Baltimore: Johns Hopkins University Press, 1996), concludes that the experience of the Chilean labor movement was in many ways similar to that of other Southern Cone labor movements during the dictatorships and democratic transitions of recent decades.
5 Patricia Coñoman, Santiago, interview of June 1997.
6 Patricia Coñoman, Santiago, interview of July 2002.

PETER WINN

The Pinochet Era

On the gray morning of 11 September 1973, I stared in disbelief from across the square as Chilean army tanks opened fire on the presidential palace of Salvador Allende, who had been elected as Chile's first Socialist president three years before. Later that day, from an apartment window high over Santiago, Chile's capital, I watched while Chilean air force jets bombed their nation's presidential palace, setting it on fire and bringing the Allende era—three years of grassroots democracy and political polarization, socialist reforms and economic dislocation, social revolution and class conflict—to an end.

That same night, on a grainy black-and-white television screen, I watched Chile's new leaders, the junta composed of the four armed forces chiefs headed by General Augusto Pinochet, proclaim their new era in harsh tones and rigid postures. One stressed their determination to excise "the Marxist cancer" from Chile's body politic. Another declared the need to erase the previous half century of Chilean history—a far-reaching counterrevolution that went well beyond reversing the radical changes of the Allende era. It implied rolling back as well the social reforms of the 1960s Christian Democrats and 1930s Popular Front, as well as the introduction of mass politics in the 1920s. The Pinochet era had begun, and it would be authoritarian.

It was also clear that this junta would not be a transitional, caretaker government, like those produced by military interventions in the past. What no one knew then—and few would have predicted—was that General Pinochet's dictatorship would last more than sixteen years and that he would remain head of the armed forces and a shadow over Chile's restored democracy until his retirement and arrest in England on charges of gross violations of human rights in 1998. This quarter of a century of Chilean history—from 1973 to 1998—is the subject of this book. General

Pinochet's stamp on those years is so great that it we will refer to it as the "Pinochet era."*

During this quarter of a century, Chile was transformed from one of South America's model democracies into its most notorious dictatorship, and then into a restored democracy limited by Pinochet's authoritarian constitution and continuing presence as armed forces commander. These same years also witnessed a dramatic and far-reaching economic transformation, as the Pinochet regime reversed Allende's advances toward socialism and decades of industrial protection and state intervention, replacing them with a neoliberal open economy and shrunken state, in which the market was the regulator of both economy and society.

These political and economic changes had major impacts on workers and their organizations. They had reached a zenith of power and influence under Allende but would struggle to survive under Pinochet, who would use repression, neoliberal labor laws, and the market to discipline Chile's workers and undermine their unions.

In response, Chile's workers employed both old and new forms of resistance, playing a key role in keeping the flame of opposition alive during the 1970s and mobilizing broader social and political protests in the 1980s. Although the restoration of democracy in the 1990s lifted the threat of repression and brought modest improvements in the country's labor laws, it did not alter Chile's commitment to neoliberalism or the hegemony of the market. The center-left governments that Chile's workers supported proved unable or unwilling to transform working conditions or labor relations, leaving labor unions weak and workers vulnerable and demoralized when the Pinochet era came to an end in 1998—a situation that the ensuing years did little to reverse.

*As Pinochet extended his era in public life until he resigned from the Senate and received immunity from prosecution for reasons of dementia in 2002, the authors of this volume have also extended their accounts to 2002. However, 1998–2002 was a coda in a very different key not only for General Pinochet but also for Chile's neoliberal economic "miracle." The Asian, Brazilian, and Argentine crises put an end to Chile's economic boom, replacing it with an era of recession and stagnation that Chileans called a "crisis." The era of Pinochet and the "Miracle" came to an end together in 1998, so we have concentrated our accounts on these years, with 1998–2002 as an epilogue.

The Allende government that Pinochet overthrew in 1973 had been elected in 1970 on a platform of pioneering a democratic road to a democratic socialism. His Unidad Popular (Popular Unity) coalition was a center-left alliance dominated by the Socialist and Communist parties, but including the centrist Radicals and Christian leftists, the culmination of decades of center-left coalitions stretching back to the Popular Front of the 1930s. Allende had been elected president with a narrow plurality of the vote in a three-way election, but claimed a mandate for change because of the endorsement of structural change by his Christian Democratic opponent, Radomiro Tomic, and his coalition's majority victory in the 1971 municipal elections.

Allende's "Chilean Road to Socialism" was a self-proclaimed revolution in democracy, whose goal was to prepare the way for a future Chilean socialism by winning an electoral majority for socialism and nationalizing "the commanding heights" of the economy. Populist benefits were thought to be key to winning votes for socialism, a political mix that characterized Allende's Socialist Party, reflecting a half century of populist politics in Chile. These benefits were encapsulated in the Popular Unity program's "forty points," populist promises that ranged from assuring a pint of milk a day to every child and a job to every worker to major expansions in public health, housing, and education.

Allende's "structural changes" were steps toward socialism. With unanimous congressional approval, his Popular Unity government expropriated the U.S.-owned copper mines that accounted for two-thirds of Chile's exports. Allende used Chile's stock market to purchase almost all of the country's banks. His government also acquired control of most of Chile's important industrial enterprises, using executive decree powers where their owners refused to sell. In addition, Popular Unity completed the agrarian reform begun by the Christian Democrats in 1967, transforming more than 4,400 landed estates into peasant cooperatives. Together, these enterprises formed the new "Social Property Area" (APS), conceived of as the nucleus of a future socialist economy. Most of these changes took place during Allende's first year in office, at the end of which he could claim: "We control 90 percent of what were the private banks. . . . more than seventy strategic and monopolistic enterprises. . . . We are *owners!* We are able to say: *our* copper, *our* coal, *our* iron, *our* nitrates, *our* steel; the fundamental bases of heavy industry today belong to Chile and the Chileans."[1]

These rapid advances toward socialism owed much to the support and actions of Chile's workers and peasants, who both spearheaded and accelerated Allende's road to socialism. In the process, they transformed themselves into protagonists of their own and their nation's destinies.

Under Allende, Chilean workers reached historic heights of income, status, and organization, and their representatives won unprecedented power and influence. The first year of Popular Unity government witnessed a 30 percent average rise in real wages, and a nearly 10 percent shift of national income from capital to labor. Although these gains eroded with the inflation of the following years, consumer shortages and rationing also had a leveling effect that sustained the increase in equality under Allende.

If their new spending power brought workers into the consumer market, their new power at their places of work altered their working conditions and self-image. Under Allende, over five hundred enterprises were nationalized—in many cases after being seized by their workers—and most experimented with worker participation in their management. Even those that remained privately owned and managed often had to accept worker watchdog committees at the level of both the enterprise and the factory floor.

Reinforcing this heady experience of workplace power, the self-styled "government of the workers" projected them as the protagonists of the "revolutionary process," an image echoed in the leftist media, with their frequent interviews with workers who were praised for their "class consciousness" and solidarity. Add to this the workers' own projection of their views, desires, and power beyond their factory gates and into the public spaces of streets, squares, and stadiums, and the surge in their self-image and status is clearly explicable. Marrying a worker and becoming a worker suddenly became desirable and dignified. Although the upper and middle classes might continue to scorn them as "rotos"—"broken ones"—now their disdain was mixed with fear. It was this fear that led some to bang on the barracks doors and many more to support a military coup that would destroy the democracy they prized.

For Chile's labor unions, the Popular Unity era marked the highpoint of their membership, representativity, influence, power, and organization. Their membership grew to 855,000 in 1972, roughly a third of the workforce. Their leaders were consulted on issues of national policy and shaped labor relations. Local leaders played crucial roles in the administration of the greatly expanded public and mixed sector of the economy. National leaders were named as ministers of labor and filled key government posts.

Moreover, although the Labor Code of 1931 remained in force, the way in which it was interpreted by a prolabor government tipped the balance of power in favor of workers and their unions, as the tripartite commissions that mediated and arbitrated labor disputes demonstrated. In industries such as the textile industry, a start was made as well on worker participation in sectoral planning, and the textile workers federation (Fenatex) won its historic goal of sectoral collective bargaining.

During the "October Strike" (Federacíon Nacional de Trabajadores Textiles) of 1972, when business elites sought to bring the economy to a standstill and force the government out, the workers mobilized to stalemate their strategy. At first they organized through their factories and their unions. But when these seemed insufficient, Chilean workers pioneered new forms of organization of a territorial character, such as the *cordones industriales*, which transcended the craft divides of Chilean labor unions to unite workers of the same industrial belt or geographic district. It was the cordones industriales that organized the defense of their areas during the conflicts of 1972 and 1973. The cordones, moreover, took advantage of these conflicts to advance their vision of revolution from below, pushing the seizure and socialization of factories well beyond the ninety-one enterprises on the government nationalization list.

These "revolutionary advances" both reflected and generated social tensions and political polarization. So did the growing economic dislocation epitomized by accelerating inflation, consumer shortages, and budget deficits, in large part a reflection of the huge increase in Chilean incomes under Allende and the limited resources with which to meet the resulting demand in a semi-developed economy subject to a credit blockade by a hostile United States.

The political consequence was an accelerating polarization of politics between the Popular Unity and its opponents. Although the Popular Unity increased its parliamentary support to 44 percent in the 1973 legislative balloting, the center-right opposition alliance, led by the Christian Democrats and Nationalists, controlled the Congress and used this control to block laws enabling and financing Allende's democratic road to socialism. When Allende resorted to controversial executive powers to implement his program, his opponents challenged their legality. The result was a political deadlock and constitutional crisis that Chile's political institutions proved unable to resolve. Increasingly, Allende's opponents took the growing political conflict to the streets—and to the army barracks—acting with the covert support of the United States, which provided both money and expertise to "destabilize" Allende's government.[2] As a consequence, Pinochet would claim that his military coup had the support of the majority of the Chilean electorate. Many of those who hailed the coup on September 11, 1973, however, regretted the break with Chile's democratic tradition, "something we Chileans were tremendously proud of."[3] Many more would be shocked and dismayed by its violence and human rights abuses and by the long years of military dictatorship that followed.

Although Allende's road to socialism was controversial and generated severe economic dislocations, social tensions, and political polarization, his term in office in many ways represented the apex of democracy in Chile. Under Allende, illiterates and eighteen-year-olds received the right to vote and the entire population was mobilized by the Popular Unity and its opponents. Grassroots participatory democracy was promoted in residential neighborhoods, and economic democracy—although imperfect—was created in Chile's larger workplaces through worker comanagement and in rural cooperatives that replaced the great landed estates of the past. Although the press and other mass media were partisan and polemical, all political views were represented. Allende's Chile was striking for its political pluralism and both representative and direct democracy. The contrast between the politics of Allende's and Pinochet's Chile could not be greater.

THE PINOCHET REGIME: INTERNAL WAR, 1973–1978

Within days of seizing power, the Pinochet junta suspended the constitution, and along with it all political rights and civil liberties. The press and mass media were censored. The parties that had supported Allende were banned, and even those of his opponents were suspended. All elections were prohibited, even in social organizations such as youth clubs and labor unions. Military officers were placed in charge of universities and many schools, whose faculty, student body, curriculum, and libraries were purged. The public burning of "subversive" books became a chilling symbol of Chile's new lack of freedom that evoked comparisons to Nazi Germany.[4]

Those first weeks also established the Pinochet regime's reputation for massive and extreme violations of human rights. Some 1,500 Chileans were killed, many executed, often without trials. Perhaps 100,000 were detained, often in sports stadiums or arenas, where they were interrogated and tortured. Thousands, including former cabinet ministers and legislators, party leaders, and union officers, were imprisoned in concentration camps on frigid Antarctic islands or in the burning deserts of the north. A notorious "Caravan of Death" was sent north by Pinochet to "review" and increase the sentences passed by military courts.

In 1974, Pinochet formed the DINA (Direccíon de Inteligensia Nacional) as his secret police. Hundreds disappeared into its torture chambers and were never seen again. Hundreds of thousands of Chileans fled into the supposed safety of foreign exile. But through Operation Condor, a secret alliance initiated by Chile among the region's military regimes and their intelligence services, the DINA was able to strike at Pinochet's enemies even in foreign countries. It assassinated his constitutionalist predecessor as army commander, General Carlos Prats, in Buenos Aires and Orlando Letelier, a former Allende ambassador and minister, in Washington.[5]

Chile's armed forces had intervened in politics during the 1920s and 1930s, but after that had created a tradition of being the nonpartisan guardians of its constitutional order. This doctrine survived the upheavals of the 1960s and the murder in 1970 of General René Schneider, the army commander whose name was associated with it, at the hands of rightist assassins linked to the CIA. A Chile shocked by this uncustomary political violence rallied around Schneider's successor, General Carlos Prats, who maintained the political neutrality of the armed forces until August 1973. By then, the armed forces had been politicized and a decisive majority of his generals favored a military coup to oust Allende. The Chilean army is a rigidly hierarchical organization in which only the commander can lead a coup. Knowing this, the coup plotters pressured Prats to resign.

Realizing that he could no longer command the loyalties of the armed forces, Prats resigned and advised Allende to appoint his army chief of staff General Augusto Pinochet to succeed him. Prats persuaded Allende that Pinochet was a soldier's soldier who would uphold the Schneider Doctrine and keep the plotters in line as he would enjoy the support of the apolitical officers in the army. One month later, Pinochet led the military coup that overthrew Allende and ended constitutional government in Chile.

To most political observers at the time, Pinochet seemed like an accidental and temporary leader of the military regime, one so uncharismatic and politically inept that he was sure to be replaced by a more polished and savvy general, such as coup plotter General Oscar Bonilla, aide-de-camp to the Christian Democratic ex-president Eduardo Frei. But Bonilla died in a suspicious crash and several other potential rivals either met early ends or decided to take early retirement. A year later, only Pinochet remained. Like his model General Francisco Franco, he had succeeded where more charismatic and talented officers had failed.

Although it is frequently grouped with the other Southern Cone military dictatorships of this era as a "bureaucratic authoritarian" regime, in part because of its alliance with civilian technocrats, the Chilean regime was fundamentally different. Where the Brazilian, Argentine, and Uruguayan regimes were governments of the armed forces as institutions, the Chilean was increasingly the personal dictatorship of General Pinochet. With the help of the DINA, the secret police he created to control his military rivals as much as his civilian enemies, the sixteen-year dictatorship would belong to Pinochet alone.

Pinochet gradually transformed a government of the Chilean armed forces, embodied in a four-man *junta de gobierno* in which the heads of the services sat as equals, into a personalistic dictatorship. Chilean social scientist Augusto Varas has called attention to the double distancing by which Pinochet accomplished this task.[6] First, he persuaded the other service chiefs to distance themselves from their services and to exclude their subordinates from deliberative roles in the military government. Then, in 1974, Pinochet, initially just the *first* president of the junta, became "Supreme Chief of the Nation," and "President of the Republic," relegating its other members to secondary roles. When air force commander Leigh objected to his concentration of power, Pinochet marginalized him. In 1978, he forced Leigh's resignation—and consolidated his own power—by surrounding the air force bases with army tanks and troops.[7]

Nor would there be a rotation of the presidency among army generals as in the other Southern Cone regimes. Pinochet would remain dictatorial president of the junta and then the republic until his defeat in a plebiscite of his own design in 1988. He would be the only military president and the era would bear his stamp and his name.

In the Pinochet era, Chile would become a byword for human rights violations, with more than 3,000 dead or disappeared and estimates of torture victims exceeding 100,000. Many of the victims were labor leaders and worker activists, whom Pinochet regarded as prime targets of his "internal war" of 1973–78.

Given their high degree of power and organization and their political role as the central social base of the Left, it was not surprising that Chilean workers and their organizations were viewed by the Chilean military as dangerous enemies to be neutralized during the coup and as central targets of the repression that followed. On the day of the coup, the headquarters of the CUT (Central Unica de Trabajadores) was one of the first buildings seized by the armed forces.

During the three days and nights of twenty-four-hour curfew that followed, I watched from my window while troops, aided by tanks and helicopter gunships, reduced the cordones industriales one by one. The CUT was banned, its properties confiscated, and its officers transformed from vaunted leaders to hunted "subversives."

In many factories, military intelligence interrogated the workers one by one, pressing them to inform on their coworkers, and especially on their leaders. The most militant activists disappeared, some to early graves or torture chambers, others to exile or the underground resistance. But even Christian Democratic union leaders like Manuel Bustos, the future head of a new national labor confederation, were detained and tortured.[8] In the state terror of those first months, worker leaders and activists were among those most persecuted and treated most brutally by the military.

The repression of unions and labor leaders would continue through 1978, basing itself on Decree-Law (D.L.) 198, which allowed the government to remove union leaders at will.[9] The union leaders who remained ran rump unions, without power to protect their members and with fear of even trying to do so.

In place of union democracy, Pinochet offered the workers labor gerontocracy: the oldest workers became union officers, usually company men or workers too fearful or feeble to do much more than hold informational meetings that no one attended, write minutes that nobody read, and administer declining social funds. Collective bargaining was banned, as were strikes and union elections. Military decrees also reduced by three-quarters the 130 federations and confederations affiliated with the now banned CUT and decimated the ranks of those that survived. In addition, the tripartite labor commissions were suspended, along with the state-led mediation boards.

The military regime might favor economic freedom for business, but not for workers. The junta set wages by fiat and its social politics were clearly regressive: prices were allowed to rise freely—the price of bread soared 1,000 percent in three months in late 1973—while wages were frozen. Under government controls, real wages fell precipitously between 1973 and 1975. Coercion would remain the centerpiece of Pinochet's labor policies until 1978, when the regime ended its "internal war" and set about institutionalizing itself.[10]

Within the severe constraints of political repression and antilabor policies, Chile's workers and their organizations struggled as best they could to defend their interests, knowing full well that it was probably a losing battle fraught with personal and collective risk. During the state of siege (1973–78), when labor rights and civil liberties were suspended and employer revenge was unbridled, resistance—a term interpreted loosely by Pinochet's security forces—could result in disappearance and death. Worker actions were mostly furtive—industrial sabotage, brief wildcat work stoppages, or innovative protests such as the *viandazos* of the copper miners that Thomas Klubock describes in his chapter, where El Teniente miners refused to eat at the company cafeteria.

Copper workers were among the minority of workers—textile workers at the Sumar plants were others—who were able to win wage increases through informal processes that bypassed the official ban on collective bargaining and mandated government control of wages.

During this most difficult period, workers strove to take advantage of any government opening, such as Pinochet's 1976 policy of meeting directly with worker representatives in an effort to create unions loyal to his regime. The textile workers of Panal, one of Chile's largest cotton mills, for example, used this as an opportunity—unsuccessful in the end—to try and convince Pinochet to return their factory to its paternalistic former owners, the Hirmas. During these years, the labor movement survived and restructured itself at the national level, where labor leaders continued to speak out in defense of worker interests and labor rights, and increasingly to criticize the regime's economic and labor policies and to form new organizations for that purpose.

In the wake of the 1973 coup, Christian Democratic leaders and rightist gremialistas[11] filled the vacuum created by the repression of leftist leaders. The initial stance of Christian Democratic leaders was to seek a dialogue with the government, stressing their anti-Marxist credentials and offering their conditional support to the regime. In January 1974, they joined together with the more independent gremialistas to form the Central Nacional de Trabajadores (CNT) as a replacement for the now banned CUT, which continued to rally leftist support in exile and to carry out a clandestine resistance in Chile.

This Christian Democratic strategy seemed successful in mid-1974 with the naming of General Nicanor Díaz Estrada as labor minister. Díaz, with the support of air force commander General Gustavo Leigh, promoted a program of institutionalization that sought to consolidate the support of the Christian Democrats and the creation of a labor movement supportive of the regime. This corporatist program included industrial protection, a new labor code in which the state would prevent employer abuses, "social projects" such as a worker's bank, a national training system, and a "social statute" for private enterprises.

The defeat of these initiatives—reflecting the opposition of Pinochet to Leigh, the security forces to any loss of power, and the neoliberal economists to an interventionist state—would spell the failure of Díaz and Leigh and their efforts to create a new system of labor relations. It would also lead to the alienation of the Christian Democrats from the regime and their gradual move toward an alliance with the Left, which in 1975 formed the Coordinadora Nacional Sindical (CNS) together with dissident Christian Democrats as a replacement for the now discarded CUT. Increasingly, the discourse of both the CNT and CNS was critical of working conditions and wages, of the denial of labor rights, and of the government's neoliberal economic policies and political repression. Their criticisms, together with the growing ascendancy of military hardliners and neoliberals in the government, put an end to Nicanor Díaz and the corporatist-conciliatory phase of the regime's labor policy.

Pinochet's close civilian collaborator, Sergio Fernández, became labor minister, and government policies turned more repressive and oriented toward the formation of a parallel proregime labor movement. In 1976, Pinochet began direct meetings with selected worker leaders in an effort to stem the growing convergence of Christian Democrats and leftists into an oppositional labor movement. At the same time, the regime initiated its neoliberal economic policies, including a new set of privatizations and lowered tariffs that detonated a wave of bankruptcies and lay-offs. These hard-line policies were accompanied by the open flouting of labor regulations by employers and a failure of state officials to enforce them. From labor's perspective, the return to the harsh repression of the postcoup period—with its persecution of the Left and use of D.L. 198 to remove combative labor leaders and replace them with proregime gremialistas— was the political precondition for Pinochet's imposition of a rigid neoliberal economic model on the backs of the workers. During 1976–77, this repression even reached independent and Christian Democratic labor leaders who had supported the coup, several of whom were sent into internal exile.

In response, Christian Democrat and leftist labor organizations came together to form the first mass labor opposition since the coup. The creation in mid-1976 of the "Group of Ten" by the leading Christian Democratic unionists and their critique of the social exclusion of the workers in the regime's policies added a deeper note to continuing conjunctural critiques of the junta. Although they maintained their separate identities, increasingly the stances of Christian Democratic and leftist labor leaders converged around an outspoken critique of the regime. By 1978, they were calling for a restoration of democracy and a respect for human rights. This process culminated on May Day 1978 in the first united public demonstration by opposition workers.

At the grassroots level, too, there was growing dissidence and open defiance, despite the risks. These ranged from the viandazos and sickouts of copper workers to slowdowns by port workers and a twenty-four-hour work stoppage at the Burger clothing plant in Santiago. Strike actions spread during 1977–78 to metallurgical, chemical, and transport workers, despite the regime's repressive measures. This resurgence of labor militancy represented not only resistance to the Pinochet dictatorship but a worker response to his neoliberal economic "shock treatment" as well.

The military junta may have known how it wanted to change Chilean politics when it seized power in September 1973, but it did not come to power with an economic vision of its own. Unlike the Brazilian or Peruvian armed forces, which had introduced courses on economic development into the curriculum of their academies, the Chilean military claimed no expertise in the area of economic policy.

The junta therefore looked to its civilian supporters for guidance. The one thing all agreed on was reversing Allende's steps toward socialism by reprivatizing the nonstrategic enterprises that he had nationalized, although even here there were disagreements on the scope and pace of these reprivatizations. The major structural change of this first phase was reprivatizing most of the more than five hundred enterprises nationalized by Popular Unity, as well as 3,700 agrarian estates, roughly a third of the properties expropriated under the Christian Democratic land reform law of 1967. This policy also meant taking power in the workplace and the marketplace away from labor and returning it to business. The first phase of Pinochet's economic policies would be the economic equivalent of internal war.[12]

Beyond that, there was little agreement in the Pinochet camp on economic issues. Within the opposition to Allende were a variety of competing economic models—and business interests—that ranged from the centrist developmentalism of the Christian Democrats with its mixed economy, directive state, and protected industries, to the rightist shrunken state and extreme free market capitalism of "los Chicago Boys," Chilean economists formed in a neoliberal mold at the University of Chicago by Milton Friedman and Arnold Harberger.[13]

At first, it was unclear which economic vision would win out. The issue was complicated by the rivalries among the armed forces and their top officers, each of whom had their favorite technocrat and policies.[14] Initially, the junta navigated a pragmatic middle course, the conservative promarket, but protectionist stance advocated by its business supporters. This gradualist approach was epitomized by Fernando Leníz of the Edwards financial group, who became economics minister, and Raul Saéz, the former Alliance for Progress guru and Christian Democratic minister. Saéz became the final arbiter of economic debates between the Chicago Boys, who argued for the rigorous implementation of their neoliberal model, and the civilians and military officers who worried about the social costs and loss of state control over the economy. Pinochet played the balancer, backing the Chicago Boy advisers in their insistence on a massive devaluation and a single exchange rate, but naming key army skeptics to a special advisory committee that would monitor the advisers.[15]

During these first years, the military regime focused on economic stabilization, dealing with Allende's legacy of hyperinflation, consumer shortages, and deficit spending by freeing prices and freezing wages and salaries, tightening the money supply, and reducing the government budget deficit by slashing social programs and public investment and employment. Consumer shortages ended as real incomes plunged and consumer demand fell, but at a high social cost. Workers complained of being reduced to a diet of "bread, tea, and onions."[16]

Although these measures lowered the inflation rate and fiscal deficit, they did not eliminate them, and led to plummeting real wages and soaring unemployment. The Chilean economy sank into a deep recession, a crisis that provoked a renewed debate over economic policy. By mid-1975, the crisis had become acute and the debate decisive. Pragmatic conservatism was not tough enough therapy, the Chicago Boys argued. Chile needed their stronger medicine to cure its economic ills. Sergio de Castro, the leader of the Chicago Boys, replaced Leníz as economy minister, with Jorge Cauas, a former Christian Democratic and World Bank technocrat who had moved closer to the neoliberals, as finance minister and economic czar.

As the day of decision approached, the Chicago Boys brought in their big guns, with Milton Friedman himself visiting Chile in 1975 and supporting their cause in high-profile public lectures and private meetings with Pinochet and his aides. In the final showdown, de Castro echoed Friedman's call for economic "shock treatment," while Cauas argued that stronger measures were needed to tame inflation once and for all and that the private sector had to be freed to restart growth. In response, Sáez warned of economic dislocation and social costs and argued for gradualism. In the end, it was Pinochet who decided for Cauas and de Castro, by "decision of the commander in chief," a formulation that ended debate within the hierarchical Chilean military.[17]

Why did Pinochet, who was obsessed with state control in the political sphere, choose an economic strategy that minimized the role of government? Why did he reject the views of Sáez that he had respected in the past, and decide for the Chicago Boys? The failure of the more gradualist and balanced policies that Sáez stood for was a prime concern. But Pinochet was as impressed by the Chicago Boys' arrogant certitude as by their arguments, and by the international assistance that their U.S. and multilateral bank connections seemed to promise. There were other factors as well that favored the Chicago Boys. Their stance as technocrats who were above politics and private interests—although bogus[18]—fit Pinochet's own self-image, as did their desire to make a "revolution" that would change Chile forever. Even their readiness to impose harsh measures on their people in order to "save" Chile matched the military's sense of mission, as did their identification of their measures with "efficiency" and "modernization."[19]

Sergio de Castro's determination to reverse "a half century of errors"[20] in Chile's economic policy, paralleled the junta's own resolve to reverse "the previous half century of Chilean history," with its mass politics and social reform.[21] In addition, the deindustrialization implicit in their economic model would undermine the Left's central social base, the industrial working class, who would be the chief victims of their neoliberal policies, punished for their leading role in Allende's democratic road to socialism—an appealing moralization of economic policy. Last, in embracing the reduced state, lowered tariffs, and market dominance recommended by Cauas and de Castro, Pinochet was also rejecting the more corporatist and protective policies promoted by the political parties he detested and by the air force commander, General Gustavo Leigh, who had emerged as Pinochet's chief rival within the junta.

By 1978, Leigh had been forced to resign, Chicago Boys filled the key economic policymaking positions, and their hegemony was reinforced by the support of a powerful business coalition and new military and civilian cabinet ministers, especially Sergio Fernández as interior minister and José Piñera as labor minister. Cauas, the former Christian Democrat, who believed in balance in economic policy, had lost out and left the Finance Ministry for the embassy in Washington, opening the way for de Castro to replace him as Pinochet's economic czar.[22] Also important were the "retirements" of "statist" officials and their replacement by neoliberals in key secondary positions such as the Corporación de Fomento (Corfo), which controlled the public sector enterprises, and Odeplan (Oficina de Planficacíon Nacional), which shaped public spending.[23] The Chicago Boys were now in a position to launch their economic "revolution."

With de Castro and his Chicago Boys in control, Chile embraced an extreme version of neoliberalism, which looked back to the laissez-faire state and free trade of the liberal era (1870–1930). This export-oriented economic model had lost favor in Latin America when liberal policies were blamed for the region's vulnerability to the depression of the 1930s. The economic "errors" that de Castro railed against had been committed in the service of the strategy of import substitution industrialization that emerged out of that depression experience. It was a model of protected industrialization with high levels of state economic intervention, including regulation of foreign trade, consumer prices, capital markets, and labor relations. Under de Castro, all this would change.

Tariffs, which averaged 94 percent in 1973, were cut to 10 percent by 1979. Public spending was slashed to one-half its 1973 level as a percentage of the GNP, amid a new round of privatizations. Prices were freed and the banking system and financial markets deregulated. A new probusiness labor code was decreed and social security was privatized.

At first, the results of the "Program of Economic Recovery" seemed more negative than positive. During 1975, industrial production fell 28 percent and the GNP 13 percent, the biggest drop since the 1930s, while unemployment soared to 17 percent. But slashed public employment and investment combined with a regressive new 20 percent value-added sales tax to turn a fiscal deficit into a surplus by 1979. Moreover, exports began to expand in 1976 and represented one-third of the GNP by 1979 and some US$4.7 billion in 1980, including $1.8 billion in nontraditional exports, such as fruit, fish, and forest products that had been virtually non-existent before the coup. Between 1976 and 1981, the economy grew at an average of nearly 8 percent annually, while inflation fell from 370 percent to 9.5 percent.[24] Chile's international reserves rose from only $167 million in 1973 to over $4 billion in 1980. Pundits hailed Chile as an "economic miracle" and de Castro as a miracle worker who had transformed a disaster into a success story in only five years. Neoliberalism's tough economic medicine seemed to work.

With the defeated Left no longer providing a security justification for military rule, the Pinochet regime shifted its claim for legitimacy to its economic success. Authoritarian rule became the precondition for economic transformation, with the Chicago Boys themselves affirming that "in a democracy we could not have done one-fifth of what we did."[25]

Although the Chicago Boys justified their policies with a discourse of liberty, they were not troubled by the contradiction of basing the economic freedom they promoted on the most dictatorial regime in Chilean history—or in denying workers the freedom to strike or bargain collectively. At bottom, the only freedom that they cared about was the economic liberty of those Chileans and foreigners with capital to invest and consume, and that "freedom," de Castro believed, was best assured by an authoritarian government and a passive labor force. In short, their notions of freedom were both selective and self-serving.[26]

So were the economic indicators they highlighted. By taking 1975, a recession year in which the Chilean economy declined by 13 percent, as the starting point of their analysis, the Chicago Boys obscured the fact that their "boom" was more a recovery from the deep recession than a new economic expansion. From 1974 to 1981, the Chilean economy grew at a modest 1.4 percent a year on average. Even at the height of the "boom" in 1980, moreover, effective unemployment was so high—17 percent—that 5 percent of the workforce were in government make-work programs, a confession of failure for neoliberals who believe in the market as self-correcting and who abhor government welfare programs. Nor did the Chicago Boys call attention to the extreme concentration of capital, precipitous fall in real wages and negative redistribution of income that their policies promoted, or their disincentives to productive investment.[27]

Instead, by 1979, de Castro was boasting that Chile would soon join the ranks of the developed countries. By then, Pinochet's advisers had persuaded him to end the state of siege, institutionalize his government, and formalize a new system of labor relations consonant with both authoritarian rule and neoliberal economics.

INSTITUTIONALIZING PINOCHET'S "REVOLUTION"

The decision to institutionalize the military regime reflected several mutually reinforcing factors. By 1977, the leftist guerrilla threat had been crushed and the major parties and movements of the Left decimated. In that same year, Jimmy Carter became president of the United States after a campaign in which he attacked his Republican predecessors for failing to defend human rights, with Chile as his example, promising that he would act differently. International criticism of the regime was growing, as were proposals for sanctions against it. In the view of Pinochet's advisers, it was time for him to win international acceptance as a legitimate ruler. They also urged Pinochet to institutionalize his rule in order to perpetuate his legacy.

In his July 1977 Chacarillas Plan, Pinochet gave Chileans a glimpse of his vision of their future, promising to replace his dictatorship with a "protected democracy." This was followed in March 1978 by an amnesty for political crimes committed since the coup. This decree-law was also a "self-amnesty," giving Pinochet and his subordinates immunity from prosecution for the many human rights abuses they had committed. It heralded the end of the state of siege and the reestablishment of a rule of law, however distorted in practice by authoritarian decrees, political police, torture chambers, and a judiciary complicit with the dictatorship. That same year saw a "plebiscite" on Pinochet's rule, but in an election with no opponent and no guarantees, in which voters had to choose between the Chilean flag or symbols of "anarchy." General Pinochet's "victory" in this bizarre balloting and his defiant response to international repudiation, won him few plaudits and little legitimacy.

Pinochet's more sophisticated political advisers urged him to institutionalize his legacy in a new constitution that would be difficult to alter after his rule and would make him a constitutional head of state. They were supported by the Chicago Boys, who feared that a future elected government would reverse economic measures taken by an illegitimate dictatorship and were convinced that the existence of a constitutional government, even an authoritarian one, would promote foreign investment. An unintended consequence of their opening Chile to global economic forces was Chile's increased dependence on global goodwill.

The result was the authoritarian constitution of 1980, which sought to create a "protected democracy" under military tutelage. It was written so as to be difficult to amend and designed to handcuff a future opposition government and frustrate the popular will. The 1980 constitution removed the military from civilian control, while submitting future elected governments to a military-dominated National Security Council with vague but broad purview. The Left was excluded from political participation. The Constitutional Tribunal was rigged to have a conservative cast, and a significant part of the Senate was to be appointed, not elected. Paradoxically, because Pinochet had the presidency designed for his own ambitions, his constitution created a presidency even stronger than under the 1925 constitution that Salvador Allende had used to advance his road to socialism. But the 1980 charter—which allowed Pinochet to be "reelected" in 1988 and remain president until 1997—banned measures against private property. Although important parts of the future political system remained to be spelled out in future decree-laws, the 1980 constitution was designed to produce a "democracy" limited both by military tutelage and Pinochet's authoritarian powers.[28] The rights it granted Chilean citizens were subordinated to the needs of "national security."

This authoritarian constitution was ratified in a referendum that left much to be desired, with opposition suspended, censorship in effect, vote rigging, and widespread fears that the ballot was not secret. But Pinochet could now claim legitimacy for his "presidency" and his decrees as head of state. With the election of Ronald Reagan as U.S. president that same year, he soon gained a measure of international acceptance as well. Moreover, with relatively minor modifications of some of its most egregious features during the transition to democracy, this constitution would remain in effect for the rest of the century. It is still Chile's fundamental charter today.

The Plan Laboral

These same years also saw the institutionalization of the regime's labor policies through a series of decree-laws known collectively as the Plan Laboral, which replaced the old precoup labor code and transformed labor relations in Chile. There were several reasons for the replacement of a labor policy of coercion by a new system of labor laws, and they all came together at the end of 1978. By then, the maintenance of a de facto system of labor relations grounded in "emergency measures" adopted in a "state of war" was difficult to justify. A new authoritarian labor code paralleled plans for a new authoritarian constitution, both reflecting the conviction that it was time to consolidate the Pinochet "revolution" by institutionalizing it.

The new "modern" labor code was also one of the so-called seven modernizations, through which Pinochet and the Chicago Boys sought to transform Chile. Others included the privatization of health care and social security, and the decentralization of education and local government. Although their purposes were diverse and their "modernity" can be questioned, together the "seven modernizations" added up to a profound transformation of Chilean economy, society, and culture, whose legacy would transcend the Pinochet era.

All had hidden economic and political agendas. The privatization of social security's immediate goal was to shore up capital markets through its transfer of worker savings to Chile's business elites.[29] The Plan Laboral was intended to definitively shift the balance of power in labor relations in favor of business and to weaken the workers and unions that formed the central political base of the Left.

The labor law reforms of 1979–81 also reflected the ascendancy of the Chicago Boys. By 1978, they were pressing for new laws that would bring labor relations in line with the neoliberal economic model in which the market, not the state, would regulate factors of production. At the same time, they wanted to reassure investors that the changes were permanent by embodying them in law and giving them institutional expression.

But what finally convinced the junta to replace its emergency decrees and crude repression with a new system of labor relations and determined its timing was international pressure. Leftist labor leaders in exile had long been campaigning for such international pressure to compensate for labor's weakness inside Chile—despite courageous worker resistance. U.S. support for Pinochet under Nixon and Ford and AFL-CIO anticommunism had combined with Christian Democratic conditional support to frustrate international solidarity. But, by 1978, the international context had shifted against Pinochet. The election of

Jimmy Carter as U.S. president on a human rights platform transformed Washington from ally to enemy, while the growing alienation of the Christian Democrats and the failure of the regime to create a new system of labor relations forced a shift in the AFL-CIO position as well. In this context, the return of repressive labor policies in 1978 was the final straw.

In October of that year, the regime threw down the gauntlet. It arrogated to itself the power to fire public employees without due process. It dissolved seven national labor federations, representing four hundred unions and 113,000 workers, and confiscated all their possessions. Then, without any warning, it decreed on 27 October that all unions in private enterprises would hold elections four days later, without any campaigns and with a ban on current officers or anyone who had participated in politics during the previous ten years.

Coming after an AFL-CIO mission in March 1978 that had warned Pinochet to restore labor rights or face international sanctions, the hard-line measures of October 1978 were a direct challenge to the U.S. labor confederation. They led the AFL-CIO to swing its considerable weight in the International Labor Organization (ILO) behind a boycott of Chilean exports and imports.

It was this threat to bring Chile's export-oriented economy to a halt that panicked Pinochet's economic team and led to promises to create a new system of labor relations, in return for a delay in the imposition of sanctions. On 26 December 1978, Jose Piñera, a Harvard-educated engineer closely linked to the Chicago Boys, was appointed minister of labor for that purpose. The Plan Laboral of 1979 would bear his name and their imprint.

Although the Plan Laboral superseded and replaced the Labor Code of 1931, it was not a unified code, but rather a group of related "decree-laws" proclaimed over the course of four years.[30] Together, they represented a neoliberal effort to bring labor markets and labor relations in line with the regime's market-dominated economic model. They also represented an effort to make permanent the subordination of Chile's workers and the weakening of their organizations.

The first and last of these measures, D.L. 2200 (1978) and Law 18,018 (1981), reshaped labor contracts so as to increase employer flexibility, decrease job security, and reduce labor costs. Although the worker was bound by the contract, the employer was allowed to modify it unilaterally in order to change job descriptions or workplace locations. Employers claimed they needed this power to use their personnel efficiently, but they would also use it to isolate union leaders and to "discipline" activists.

These decree-laws also ended job security for Chile's workers, allowing employers to fire workers without cause on thirty days' notice, or immediately by paying a month's wages, and limited the traditional severance pay arrangement of one month for each year of service to a maximum of five months, with no severance pay at all where the enterprise claimed dismissals were for "business needs"—a claim that penniless workers were ill-placed to contest in court. They also permitted businesses to pay apprentices and minors less than minimum wage and to force workers to work up to twelve hours a day without overtime pay, provided that their work week did not exceed forty-eight hours. Finally, these decrees eliminated most of the special rights enjoyed by pregnant or sick workers, as well as the employer contributions to union housing and social funds negotiated in the past.

A second group of decrees—principally D.L. 2756 (1979) and D.L. 3355 (1980)—recast Chile's labor organizations and limited their power to protect their members. They established four kinds of unions—enterprise, interenterprise, independent workers, and construction workers—only one of which, the enterprise union, could engage in collective bargaining. As Heidi Tinsman shows in her chapter, workers who could only form interenterprise unions could not defend their interests effectively.

Even the enterprise union, however, was a pale shadow of its predecessor, the old plant-level industrial union, which included all blue-collar workers once 55 percent of them joined it. The Piñera decrees forbade a closed shop, made union membership voluntary, and promoted the formation of multiple parallel unions within the same enterprise by allowing as few as twenty-five workers as long as they represent at least 10 percent of the labor force—blue- or white-collar—to form a union.

The Pinochet regime's goal of weakening worker organizations was clear as well in regulations making it difficult to present slates of candidates and to campaign for union office. It was also seen in provisions prohibiting employers from funding unions in any way, including—as in the past—paying the salaries of union officers whom the decrees allowed to work half-time so that they could attend to their union duties. In view of the poverty of Chilean workers, this prohibition denied in practice the right that the decree conceded in principle, weakening the union and its ability to represent its members in the process. Alternatively, it would require the levying of larger union dues, which would be a disincentive for poor workers to join. Piñera's antiunion bias was underscored as well by other provisions of these same decrees, which prohibited federations and confederations from bargaining for their members and reduced them to purely advisory roles in collective bargaining or labor conflicts.

Collective bargaining itself was the subject of D.L. 2758 (1979). This decree forbade industry-wide contracts, restricting collective negotiations to private sector enterprise unions. It also limited what could be a subject for bargaining by barring agreements that could circumscribe the freedom of the employer "to organize, direct and administer the enterprise." There could be no negotiation of worker participation in the management of the enterprise, nor of work rules on the factory floor.

Moreover, only the members of the union would be covered by its negotiated contract. As the decree permitted the formation of multiple unions within a single enterprise, employers who promoted a company union alternative could manipulate contract negotiations so as to undermine the independent union.

In addition, D.L. 2758 established a timetable for collective bargaining that assured that these negotiations—and potential conflicts—would be spread out, both to avoid economic problems and to prevent united worker actions that might be akin to a general strike, which the same decree also prohibited.

If anything, the decree's restrictions on the workers' right to strike was even more severe. Under the 1931 labor code, the right to strike was regulated by a bureaucratic process that distinguished between legal and illegal strikes and made it complex to strike. But there were no limits placed on the length of legal strikes, employers were prohibited from hiring replacements for striking workers, and strike-ending negotiations could provide for payment to workers for lost wages while the employer remained responsible for social security payments. There were also tripartite conciliation boards and employer lockouts were prohibited. Moreover, although collective bargaining and strikes by public employees were prohibited by law, they were permitted in practice. Under Pinochet, all this changed.

The 1979 decree discouraged workers from striking and made it very difficult for them to win a strike if they did stop work. It made striking workers responsible for both their own and their employer's social security payments. It also prohibited strikes by government employees or workers in enterprises that "provide services important to the public interest" or "whose stoppage might cause serious damage to the health or supply of the population, to the economy of the country or to national security"—as determined by the ministers of defense, labor, and economy.[31]

If workers went out on strike, their jobs were only guaranteed for fifty-nine days, after which the decree deemed them to have quit the enterprise voluntarily—that is, without the right to severance pay. After a month, the employer could break the strike by taking back individual strikers on the terms of the old contract. Throughout the strike, moreover, the decree empowered employers to hire replacement workers.

In effect, D.L. 2758 gave any employer who could withstand a fifty-nine-day work stoppage the power to defeat a strike. Because workers knew that they were discouraged from even going out on strike, they often felt forced to accept the contract their employer offered, even if it was a give-back contract that took away "conquistas" won in previous contracts and conflicts. This was particularly true in periods of high unemployment, as was the case under Pinochet, where workers feared not finding another job. After analyzing D.L. 2578 in theory and examining how it worked in practice, Jose Valenzuela and Guillermo Campero concluded in 1984 that "the right to strike does not exist in Chile."[32]

Another decree of the same era—D.L. 3648 (1981)—abolished the specialized labor courts, forcing workers to sue in regular courts where litigants and defendants were presumed to be equal. There judges lacked the specialized knowledge of the old labor courts and no longer had as part of their function to protect the workers from abuses by their employer.

At bottom, the Plan Laboral favored business by lowering labor costs; increasing flexibility in hiring, firing, and using workers; and decreasing the power of unions to promote and defend the interests of their members. In principle, it created a "free" labor market comparable to Chile's neoliberal market economic reforms. In practice, it left workers subordinated to both market forces and employers.

The Plan Laboral also superseded a tripartite system of labor relations in which the state regulated employers' fulfillment of their part and could balance the relative weakness of the workers with its own intervention. In its place Piñera created a system in which state labor inspectors were weak, specialized courts and mediation boards were abolished, and state officials lacked the power and means to intervene.

Taken together, these decrees replaced the Labor Code of 1931, which theoretically created a level playing field for labor relations, with one that was so tilted in favor of business that one labor leader later described it as "a labor code written by a businessman for businessmen."[33] With scant modification, this Plan Laboral would remain in force throughout the Pinochet era.

Although laws are important in shaping labor relations, also significant are the ways in which they are implemented and interpreted by government officials. Under Allende, these discretionary powers had favored labor. Under Pinochet, the Dirección de Trabajo, which was responsible for labor law enforcement, was purged and reduced in its budget and personnel.

Those inspectors who remained were overstretched and underpaid, which made them vulnerable to business maneuvers and bribes. Moreover, they were well aware of the regime's antilabor bias and that their own jobs were now as insecure as those of the workers who vainly looked to them for support.

The treatment of labor relations as internal security under the Pinochet regime, and the harsh treatment of those detained by the security forces, cast a sinister pall over worker efforts to fight for their rights, even those accorded to them under the new labor laws. The fifty-nine-day strike by the Panal textile workers in 1980 (see " 'No Miracle for Us' "), was one of the first and most combative of the work stoppages and protests against the new system by Chilean workers. Yet, government documentation of it cannot be found in the archives of the Labor Ministry, because it was removed and taken to the Interior Ministry, which was in charge of internal security. Nor was this an isolated case.

Also important to labor relations is the degree to which employers use their legal rights to discipline workers and weaken unions. The neoliberal economic policies pursued by the Pinochet regime forced Chilean enterprises to compete with foreign imports that enjoyed more advanced technology, lower labor costs, and more efficient management. Compelled to compete or go under, it was a rare Chilean entrepreneur or manager who did not take full advantage of the new labor laws to lower labor costs. In addition, the Plan Laboral enabled employers to act on the rage and desire for revenge many felt after the "worker power" of the Allende era.

Still, workers did not passively accept these attacks on their wages, working conditions, and labor rights. With the ending of the state of siege, the election of new union leaders, and the proclamation of the Plan Laboral, labor activism revived and spread. The Plan Laboral might create a labor relations playing field tilted against the workers and their unions, but it did establish a legal space for labor actions—from union formation and elected leaders to collective bargaining and strikes. Workers and their organizations took advantage of the space provided, probed for loopholes in the new laws, tested their limits, and subverted their purpose whenever possible—but always with the awareness that in standing up for their rights and defending their interests they might be risking their jobs, their liberty, and even their lives.

This determination of the workers to reassert their agency and subvert Pinochet's purposes was prefigured in October 1978 when the regime suddenly called for new union elections within seventy-two hours, with no campaigning and with former union leaders and activists barred from office. The goal of this manifestly unfair electoral procedure was to prevent the Left from reasserting its control of the labor movement, and to boost the chances of proregime gremialistas or company union leaders. Yet, despite these obstacles, workers found ways to identify candidates who would defend their interests and to inform other workers about for whom they should vote—whether by bathroom graffiti or cafeteria buzz. The result was generally a new union leadership that lacked the experience of the old but was similar in its center-left politics.

Pinochet's snap election failed to achieve its goal, frustrated by the creativity and consciousness of Chile's workers.

The same was true for the forced dissolution of the key leftist federations within the CNS—including the Federacion Minera (coal) and the Fenatex (textiles)—in 1978 and the confiscation of their properties and possessions. As one Fenatex leader explained, they immediately reinvented the Fenatex as a for-profit consulting firm—which the regime's probusiness stance legitimated—and sold their services to the new union leaders, providing them with the wisdom of experience that they lacked.[34] Moreover, new federations soon were created to replace those that had been banned, generally with leaders whose politics was similar to the old leaders.

Although none of the new groups could claim the comprehensive representativity of the pre-1973 CUT, together they spoke for the overwhelming majority of organized Chilean workers—and did so with increasing force. Moreover, in a situation where political parties were condemned to silence, union leaders and their organizations filled the vacuum, and pioneered the center-left alliance that would eventually oust Pinochet, a process made easier by the party associations of the principal national labor leaders who emerged under Pinochet—from Christian Democrats such as Manuel Bustos to Socialists such as Arturo Martínez. In effect, the CNS of the 1970s was the precursor of the Concertación political alliance of the 1980s.

Unions and their leaders were also active at the local level, as the chapters on the copper miners and textile and metal workers make clear. The new leaders (and old advisers) used the resumption of collective bargaining to press for a recovery of the wages and benefits lost during the preceding years, and despite the constraints of the new labor laws and economic policy many were successful in winning increases that exceeded inflation. Moreover, despite the difficulty of winning a strike under the new labor laws, seventy-four unions representing 26,648 workers did go out on strike during 1979–80.[35] These included a major textile strike in 1980, when the 1,500 workers of the Panal cotton mill struck for the maximum of fifty-nine days despite threats of job loss and disappearances, and during the following years a major copper miners' strike in 1981, when El Teniente miners struck for forty days in the face of government intransigence, and a fifty-nine-day strike of Madeco metalworkers in 1983. The Panal union also hosted a militant regional May Day rally in 1981, defying government bans.

In short, although Pinochet used force, decrees, and the market to depoliticize Chile's labor movement in the 1970s, he did not succeed. On the contrary, organized labor recovered its militancy and would emerge in the 1980s as the convener of a mass movement that transcended its ranks and crossed political and class lines. It would also serve as the catalyst for massive resistance to the regime, a resistance that during the economic crisis of the 1980s almost brought the dictatorship down.

FROM BOOM TO BUST: THE NEOLIBERAL CRISIS, 1981–1985

The 1980s promised to be the highpoint of the Pinochet regime but proved to be its last hurrah instead. At the start of 1981, the economy was booming and foreign capital was still flowing in. The new constitution lent Pinochet's personalist authoritarian rule legitimacy and institutionalized his "seven modernizations." The new Reagan administration offered Chile an end to its international isolation. Yet by 1982 the economy was in shambles and Chile in the throes of its worst economic crisis since the depression of the 1930s. A year later, massive social protests defied Pinochet's security forces, he was forced to negotiate with the political parties he had banned, and protesters raced through the streets of Santiago shouting: "He's going to fall!" By 1986, the Reagan administration had abandoned its support for Pinochet and was promoting a negotiated return to democracy.

It was the economy that collapsed first, and that was the biggest surprise. In 1979, Sergio de Castro was presiding over an "economic miracle" and boasting that Chile was on the verge of joining the developed countries. To further encourage foreign investment, the motor of the boom, he fixed the value of the Chilean peso at thirty-nine to one U.S. dollar—and kept it there. At the same time, capital markets were completely deregulated and unsupervised. With interest rates far in excess of prevailing international rates offered by Chile's deregulated financial sector, foreign capital poured in, making up for Chile's limited savings—and creating windfall profits for its bankers.

What followed was a speculative bubble that was hailed as an "economic miracle" until it burst in the 1981–82 bank crack that brought the deregulated Chilean economy down in its wake. The capital that had flowed into Chile was largely short-term speculative capital attracted by high interest rates, a fixed exchange rate and no regulation. It concentrated in the deregulated financial sector, producing a bubble in stock market and real estate values. Ample foreign capital fueled easy credit, which in turn financed an orgy of luxury imports and construction. Consumer goods imports grew by an astounding 40 percent per year between 1976 and 1981, while capital goods imports only expanded by 16 percent annually. In effect, the boom in Chile was being fueled by consumer spending that was sustained by foreign credits, not domestic savings. With

38 · Peter Winn

fortunes to be made in short-term speculations, comparatively little capital was invested in productive enterprises with longer gestation periods. As a result, the huge influx of foreign capital during this era did not lead to increased productivity or sustained growth.[36]

In addition, the full costs of the economic dislocations from the neoliberal economic shock therapy had still to be paid. One was deindustrialization, as Chilean manufacturers failed in the face of foreign competition or shifted to importing what they had previously produced in Chile. For example, Daniel Platowsky's family firm had assembled radios and televisions in Chile from imported parts. With the end of protection they would have to compete with these same products imported from Japan. "We did a calculation and began shutting down our assembly lines," he recounted. "We decided to import Panasonics instead. From an industrial enterprise we became a commercial enterprise."[37]

They were not alone. As the chapter " 'No Miracle for Us' " shows, many textile and clothing manufacturers closed their plants and imported similar Asian goods instead. They viewed this as a rational response to a situation created by adverse government policies, from the dismantling of protective tariffs to Sergio de Castro's overvalued fixed exchange rate, which in effect subsidized imports. Neoliberalism in Chile would mean plant closings and a loss of relatively well-paid industrial jobs.

Another cost was the growing financial difficulties of increasing numbers of Chilean manufacturers. The transformation of manufacturers into importers boosted unemployment and endangered the prosperity of their Chilean suppliers. Other Chilean manufacturers borrowed at high interest rates to purchase the modern technology that they hoped would enable them to compete with the flood of foreign imports. Still others ran through their reserves with the goal of riding out what they assumed would be a temporary policy shift. These indebted enterprises oriented to the Chilean market would be the first to fail when the economic crisis hit.

Another consequence of de Castro's neoliberal policies was Chile's growing negative trade balance—made worse by rising oil prices after 1979 and declining copper prices after 1980. It was covered for a time by the inflow of short-term foreign capital. But Chile's foreign debt soared from $5.6 billion in 1977 to $17 billion by 1983, 13 percent more than the country's GNP. When international interest rates rose in the 1980s, foreign capital flowed out of Chile as rapidly as it had arrived, while payments due on Chile's foreign debt rose precipitously. At the same time, the fixed exchange rate obscured a 30 percent decline in the real value of the Chilean peso, and became a destabilizing factor.

For Chile's financial sector, these developments spelled disaster. Highly leveraged and dependent on continual flows of foreign capital, it now paid the price for its orgy of unbridled speculation and unregulated imprudence. The bank crisis that began at the end of 1981 exploded in 1982. By 1983 a government hostile to regulation, let alone economic intervention, had to liquidate three banks, take over the administration of five of Chile's largest private banks, and have the Central Bank provide large credits to the rest to save them from bankruptcy—and this from a regime that had attacked the Allende government for its extensive credits to the public sector. With understandable irony, critics lampooned the "Chicago road to socialism."[38]

This socialization of private debts was both striking and unequal. By then, bad loans were four times as large as the capital of the biggest private banks. During this same time period, the Central Bank lost nearly half of its international reserves. The false boom of the seventies was over—and the all-too-real crisis of the eighties had begun.

This financial disaster detonated Chile's worst economic crisis in half a century. It was exacerbated by the extreme weakness and vulnerability of Chilean enterprises as a consequence of the Chicago Boys' neoliberal reforms and by their refusal to recognize the gravity of the crisis that they had caused until it was too late. With dogmatic arrogance, they insisted that there was no need for government intervention or policy changes because as a result of their neoliberal restructuring "the Chilean economy could count on self-corrrecting mechanisms to resolve any economic problem."[39] Foremost amongst those mechanisms was the fixed exchange rate. Not until June of 1982, with the economy falling apart and the automatic adjustment mechanisms ineffective, was the peso finally devalued.

Neoliberal apologists have tried to explain away the crisis brought by the imposition of neoliberal policies by ascribing it solely to Sergio de Castro's mistake in maintaining a fixed exchange rate for three years, or by attributing it to shifts in international prices and interest rates beyond their control.[40] But these apologia ignore the negative impact of other neoliberal policies, including problems inherent in their economic model.

More critical analysts have stressed the deregulation of financial and capital markets and the vulnerability of a neoliberal economy to external shocks.[41] Falling copper prices and rising international interest rates may have aggravated the instability produced by internal policies, economist Patricio Meller concludes, but they were less important than Chilean policy decisions that ignored the growing trade deficit and the speculative character of most of the foreign capital flows and much of the Chilean investment.[42] Also important, stresses Alejandro Foxley, was a privatization policy that promoted an increasing concentration of economic power in the hands of a few financial groups.[43]

Meller pointed as well to entrepreneurial inexperience as a factor in the crisis, arguing that the neoliberal model required Chile's entrepreneurs and managers to make decisions that nothing in their prior experience of a controlled and regulated economy prepared them for.[44] "It was a completely new system for Chilean businessmen," one leading entrepreneur recalled. "Suddenly we were confronted with a government that said: 'Señores, from here on, you are on your own. The state won't regulate anything.' It was a big shock."[45] Those who failed in the crisis were often the businessmen who could not adjust to the new system. Others were bankers or entrepreneurs who took advantage of their new freedom but did not manage it responsibly, riding a roller coaster of boom and bust.[46]

Analysts have also criticized the sequencing of the reforms and the "naïeveté" of the Chicago Boys for applying a simplistic "textbook" version of neoliberalism to a complex Chilean reality that was, as Ricardo Ffrench-Davis argues, "spectacularly different" from their assumptions. As a result, he concluded, their financial and external sector reforms were "at the heart of the economic crisis."[47] Beyond the technicalities of macroeconomic policy, critics also called attention to the dictatorship's ban on democratic discussion of its policies, which suppressed timely critiques.[48]

The causes of the crisis of 1982–83 might be debatable, but its gravity and consequences were clear. During 1982, Chile's GNP fell by more than 14 percent, while its real disposable GNP declined by 19 percent. The industrial sector contracted by more than 21 percent and construction by more than 23 percent. Bankruptcies tripled and many of the enterprises that survived did so in a weakened condition that would prejudice their futures. It was a crisis comparable to the Great Depression of the 1930s, which affected Chile more severely than any other country in the world.

Chile's workers, who had paid the social costs of the illusory neoliberal "miracle," now paid as well the highest price for the errors of their nation's military rulers and Chicago Boy technocrats and the imprudence of their country's capitalists. Plant closings and layoffs drove the effective unemployment rate above 30 percent, while real wages for those lucky enough to retain their jobs fell by nearly 11 percent in 1979–82 and by some 20 percent during the 1980s.[49] In addition, inflation jumped to over 20 percent in both 1982 and 1983, and the budget surplus gave way to a deficit equal to 3 percent of the GNP by 1983. By then, Chile's foreign debt was 13 percent higher than its GNP—and

Chile had joined Mexico, Brazil, and Argentina as prime examples of the "Latin American debt crisis"—although Chile's economy contracted 400 percent more in 1982–83 than the rest of Latin America.[50]

Elsewhere in Latin America, import substitution industrialization caught the blame for the debt crisis of the 1980s. In Chile, it was neoliberalism—the *opposite* economic model—that was responsible for the crisis. The questions in Chile were, would the regime fall as a consequence—as happened elsewhere—and would neoliberalism be jettisoned as a failed economic strategy?

In the end, the regime tottered, but did not fall—in part because it sacrificed Sergio de Castro and his extreme version of neoliberalism, bringing in new faces and a more pragmatic economic policy that resorted to heterodox measures to save the new economic orthodoxy. On 14 June 1982, the peso was devalued 18 percent—where the real loss of value over the previous three years was closer to 30 percent.[51] It would be the first of many departures from Chicago orthodoxy during the years that followed, as Pinochet and his economists struggled first to save his regime and then to restore economic stability and growth through a modified, pragmatic version of the neoliberal model.

Between 1981 and 1986, the Chilean peso was devalued by 80 percent. During 1982–84, import tariffs rose from 10 percent to 35 percent, to which were added antidumping surcharges of 20 percent on fifty different products when Chilean manufacturers accused foreign imports of being sold below cost. Interest rates were now "suggested" by the Central Bank, and dropped from 30 percent in 1982 to single digits by 1986. The private banks were bailed out by the government, which spent $6 billion in subsidies during 1983–85 (equal to 30 percent of the GNP!) but were made subject to strict government regulation designed to assure their solvency.[52] Controls were also placed on flows of foreign capital, and debt-asset swaps were legalized to encourage foreign investment at discounted prices in Chilean bonds, which could then be used to purchase shares in indebted enterprises.[53] The creation of a preferential dollar would linger for years, leaving subsidized Chileans indebted in dollars.[54] Together with austerity budgets that accompanied an International Monetary Fund (IMF) standby agreement, these measures drastically reduced Chilean imports, while increasing the competitiveness of the nation's exports, bringing the country's commercial account into balance. With the help of far larger public subsidies than under Allende, the banking system righted itself. By 1986, the economy had stabilized and the crisis was over, although many of its effects would linger for years, leaving a private sector debt overhang that would cause bankruptcies even a decade later.

The crisis of the 1980s may have posed a challenge to Chile's business elites, but it was their workers who bore the brunt of its consequences. The reaction of Chile's workers to the crisis, however, would shake the Pinochet regime. During 1980–82, there was growing frustration within the labor movement at its impotence under the new labor code, which increased with every failed collective bargaining. The failure of worker actions that remained within the new labor code built up pressure from below to go outside it. With the deepening economic crisis, this pressure cooker of worker discontent exploded.

In May 1983, in response to a decree abolishing the inflation indexing of wages in the middle of the economic crisis, the copper workers confederation stopped work and called for a movement of solidarity and protest that was adhered to by the urban middle class as well as by workers throughout the country. The success of this protest led to the creation of a new broader labor confederation, the center-left Comando Nacional de Trabajadores (CNT), as a successor to the CNS. The crisis also provoked an intensification of worker militancy at the grassroots level, from strikes focused on wages and working conditions to actions to avert plant closings or to force the government to keep bankrupt enterprises producing.

The success of the first protest also led to the decision to repeat the daylong protest in June 1983, which the CNT and other labor groups helped coordinate. Although labor participation declined in later protests and brutal government repression put even the militant copper miners on the defensive, the monthly protests continued, with the new social movements and the old political parties taking the lead. For the next two years, each month featured a day of protest when workers did not work, women banged empty pots, and shantytown youth fought police behind burning barricades. Soon, what had begun as a movement of social protest of economic crisis became a movement for the restoration of political democracy, a demand incorporated into the CNT's open 1984 letter to Pinochet, along with demands for the repeal of the Plan Laboral and an end to neoliberal policies.

The ratification of the constitution of 1980 had ended hopes of a peaceful transition back to Chile's pre-1973 democracy and forced Pinochet's opponents to contemplate extralegal routes. Now, the failure of Pinochet's economic policies and the massive popular protests created the possibility that Pinochet might be forced to resign and the military might return to their barracks. Unemployment, poverty, and hunger conferred a desperate courage on the protesters that even Pinochet's ruthless security forces could not control. The social protests, moreover, rocked Chile's image of stability and punctured Pinochet's aura of invincibility. The cries of "He's going to fall!" held out the hope that the mounting monthly crescendo of popular repudiation would weaken Pinochet and force him to resign.

In the end, however, Pinochet did not fall. He compromised, dissembled, and bought time to ride out the crisis, while repressing or dividing his opponents. But he was forced to fire his economic czar, modify his neoliberal policies, and accept the legitimacy of his democratic political opponents. His strategy of legitimating his regime through economic success had backfired. Pinochet did not know it, but the transition from his dictatorship to democracy had begun.

The Transition, 1985–1990

By 1985, the social protests had ebbed, the economy was recovering, and Pinochet's democratic opposition was in disarray. Pinochet was confident that he had survived the crisis. The Catholic Church, which had protected human rights and promoted the reorganization of civil society during the dark days of the dictatorship, kept hope of change alive by organizing civil society opponents to the dictatorship into a Civic Assembly. In 1985, the opposition came together on a "National Accord for Transition to Full Democracy," which called for an end to states of exception and political exile and a reversal of Pinochet's authoritarian constitution and neoliberal policies. But the opposition had little hope of implementing it or ousting Pinochet, who rejected the accord and cracked down on dissent.

In this context of widespread but frustrated opposition, the Communist party opted for armed struggle and assassination. A combination of factors impelled Chile's Communists to abandon their traditional commitment to the "democratic road." One was the brutal assault on their leaders and activists by Pinochet and his secret police. Another was their exclusion by the Christian Democrats from the opposition alliance. A third was the failure of less radical measures.

But also important was the Sandinista overthrow of the equally ruthless and repressive Somoza dictatorship in Nicaragua in 1979, by a combination of guerrilla forces and popular rebellion. Some Chilean Communists had participated in the Sandinista struggle and many others went into exile in Sandinista Nicaragua after their victory. In 1980, with the democratic road blocked by Pinochet's intransigence, the Communist party approved the creation of an armed affiliate, the Manuel Rodriguez Patriotic Front (FPMR), whose dramatic actions—from attacks on power lines and military installations to bank robberies and food distribution—were interwoven with the popular protests of 1983–85.[55]

The Communists supported the protests and as a result reaped youth support in the shantytowns—where the FPMR were viewed as heroes. The failure of the protest movement to oust Pinochet, however, removed the possibility of popular rebellion. The military's seizure of the armaments hidden in the northern desert for the FPMR weakened the alternative of guerrilla struggle. The option that remained was assassination, and in September 1986, the Manuel Rodríguez Front ambushed Pinochet's motorcade on a valley road near Santiago and narrowly missed killing him. This failure spelled the end of armed struggle as a realistic political alternative in Chile.

The following year, a new U.S. ambassador, Harry Barnes, pushing a new Reagan policy of orchestrating a democratic transition before Pinochet went the way of Somoza and Communists took over Chile in his wake, helped persuade Chile's center-left democratic opposition to accept the only mechanism left to them: the plebiscite on Pinochet's continued rule that his 1980 constitution had set for 1988. It was a difficult decision: the opposition doubted its fairness, and contested it would mean accepting the legitimacy of Pinochet's constitution and decrees as president. If they won, a contested presidential election would be held in 1989; but, if they lost, Pinochet would be president for another eight years. It would be a referendum on Pinochet's rule—"sí" or "no"—an all-or-nothing political gamble.

It was a gamble that Pinochet was willing to take because he was convinced that he would win. He controlled the mass media, the levers of government, and the public purse strings—all of which could help swing an election. He could tar his opponents with the brush of "communism" and frighten Chileans by warning them of a return to the "chaos" of the past. He was sure that he was both indispensable and popular. Moreover, by 1987, when rising prices for Chilean exports provided an external boost, the economy had recovered its dynamism. Wages were rising and unemployment declining, as was labor militancy and popular protest. Pinochet could run as the architect of Chile's economic success.[56]

Pinochet's confidence in his plebiscite victory reinforced the fears of his democratic opponents that it would be another fraudulent electoral ritual as in 1978 and 1980. Their doubts led to a deeper U.S. involvement. In return for the Center-Left's participation in the plebiscite, the United States agreed to press the Pinochet regime to suspend censorship, give the opposition media access, allow exiles to return home and permit foreign electoral observers. Washington also agreed to help Pinochet's opponents with funds, expertise, and computer equipment, which would allow them to create a parallel vote count. It would not be a level playing field, but they stood a chance to win, if they remained united and campaigned well.

The result was the Concertación por el No, a center-left alliance of sixteen parties, with Christian Democrats and Socialists at its core. It triumphed against all odds in the plebiscite of 1988 and then went on to win the presidential elections of 1989, 1993, and 1999–2000, as well as all the congressional elections held during the course of that decade.

In this process of political transition, Chile's workers and unions played a significant but secondary role, after leading the opposition to Pinochet during the preceding decade. In retrospect, the labor movement's mobilization of the social protests of 1983–85 was its high watermark in the Pinochet era. Unlike Solidarity in Poland, it did not continue to lead the struggle for democracy, in part because it lacked a dominant charismatic labor leader like Lech Walesa.[57] Another factor was the regime's severe repression of the labor leaders and activists whom they saw as responsible for the social protests, beginning with the leaders who were sent into internal exile and the jailing and firing of copper workers, which forced the key miners' unions to focus on the defense of their own, instead of the national movement they had catalyzed.

Also important was that the broader social movement that the labor movement mobilized, with its base in the unemployed youth of the urban shantytowns, was more radical in its tactics than the unions. Individual workers continued to play important roles in their neighborhoods, but as burning barricades and nocturnal battles with security forces came to symbolize the protests, the labor leaders could no longer control them or speak for them.

Most important of all, the broad social protests in a situation of severe economic crisis, created a space for the reemergence of the political parties and the need for such legitimate political interlocutors on the part of the regime that had previously banned them. As a consequence, it was the old political parties— especially the Christian Democrats and the Socialists, the core of the electoral alliance against Pinochet during the 1980s and of the center-left Concertación governments of the 1990s—that led the transition to democracy, relegating the labor leaders who had made their reentry possible to the second rank.

In part, this reflected the fact that, for all their talk of autonomy, Chile's labor leaders continued to be representatives of their parties. Their high political profile before 1983 reflected the inability of party leaders to participate openly in politics during the first decade of the Pinochet dictatorship. Once their party leaders resurfaced, labor leaders subordinated themselves once again to party discipline and hierarchy. In part, too, it reflected the failure of the social protests to actually bring about Pinochet's fall from power, leading to a negotiated transition within Pinochet's authoritarian 1980 constitution in which the politicians and parties played the leading role.

In that elongated process of transition, the continued importance of labor leaders like Manuel Bustos and Arturo Martínez was signaled by their continued targeting by the regime for prison or internal exile. Increasingly, however, union leaders refocused locally on labor issues and nationally on their own unification across party lines, culminating in the creation in May 1988 of a new labor confederation—a new CUT (Central Unitaria de Trabajadores) to replace the old CUT Pinochet had dissolved[58]—parallel to the Concertación por el No in politics, but including Communists as well.

This formation of a new CUT was a labor victory over the Pinochet regime that had dissolved the old labor "central" in 1973 and tried to keep the labor movement divided ever after. But, in reality, the new CUT was very different from the old. This was signaled by its declaration of principles, which omitted traditional statements about class struggle—despite two decades in which class conflict had shaped the lives of Chilean workers. This change reflected both years of regime propaganda and the ascendancy of the Christian Democrats within the CUT, as within the Concertación, replacing a Communist–left Socialist axis with their own alliance with Socialist moderates. Significantly, the first head of the new CUT, Manuel Bustos, was a Christian Democrat, whereas the old CUT had been headed by a Communist. These shifts reflected the increased strength of the Christian Democrats, the weaker position of the Communists, and the "renovation" of the once Marxist-Leninist Socialists, and their transformation into European-style social democrats. They also revealed the rising importance of white-collar workers and the decline of industrial unions within Chile's labor movement, itself a reflection of the deindustrialization under Pinochet.

One way in which the new CUT was similar to the old, however, was in its domination by the political parties. Although one of the lessons unionists claimed to have learned from their analysis of what went wrong in the 1970s was to avoid the subordination of labor leaders to their parties (and there was much brave talk about the need for labor autonomy), when the delegates to the CUT were chosen, the parties imposed their choices, often over labor leaders with greater legitimacy among the workers. It was a sign of things to come in a situation where the CUT was formed from above through a political accord that paralleled the formation of the Concertación, and where the Chilean labor movement was weak at the grassroots level and dependent on outside financial and political support. The political party ties that had helped sustain the Chilean labor movement during the dark days of the postcoup era and renew it after 1978 would limit it during the transition of the 1980s.

During the 1980s, however, the Chilean labor movement slowly rebuilt, adding members and organizations. Between 1982 and 1987, the number of local unions nearly quadrupled, increasing their membership from 85,727 to 221,642, and the number of federations and confederations tripled. But only 10.5 percent of the workforce was unionized in 1988, less than a third of labor's height of power in 1972, when 855,000 workers were organized. In 1987 only 422,000 workers were union members, half the number of 1972.[59] Only mine workers maintained their traditionally high (65 percent) levels of organization.[60] In addition, where the new labor laws restricted effective unions, workers experimented with new forms of organization, such as the "House of the Temporary Worker" discussed in Heidi Tinsman's chapter.

During the late 1980s unionized workers did win real wage increases that made up for some of their earlier losses, but the recovering economy had as much to do with these gains as union militancy, and the same was true for the drop in unemployment to 11 percent. By 1988, the average real wage had returned to 1980 levels, but it was still well below 1970 levels. Moreover, in 1986, some 37 percent of the labor force worked in the informal sector, where wages were lower and benefits often nonexistent. Many worked for minimum wage, which in 1988 provided only half of what an average family required to live decently—and a fifth of the workers didn't even earn that. A survey at the time of the CUT's founding concluded that nearly half of Chileans lived in poverty.[61]

Yet Chilean workers were optimistic as the Pinochet dictatorship came to an end in 1990 and expectant that a restored democracy led by the center-left coalition that they had supported would transform their lives. Even shantytown dwellers who had not worked in a decade identified themselves as "working class" and expected the return of democracy to lead to their own return to the active workforce. Even unionized workers with prized industrial jobs were underpaid and overworked and looked to the advent of a center-left democratic government to remedy their union's weak bargaining power and to restore their lost labor rights. The Concertación took over the presidency in 1990 amid expectations of change that would be hard to fulfill.

The 1988 plebiscite was a devil's bargain, whose consequences the Concertación had to face even before Patricio Aylwin became Chile's first democratically elected president since Salvador Allende in 1990. The plebiscite had enabled the Concertación to end the Pinochet dictatorship, but in return for accepting Pinochet's authoritarian constitution and decree-laws. In its wake, the Concertación negotiated with the junta modifications in the 1980 constitution that repealed the exclusion of Marxists from politics and made the constitution somewhat easier to amend. They also won a reduction in the number of appointed senators and an even balance between military and civilians in the National Security Council. But they were not able to put an end to these and other "authoritarian enclaves"—such as the independence of the military from civilian control. Nor, despite a decade of decisive electoral triumphs, would the Concertación enjoy a majority in the Senate that would allow it to pass laws without the consent of its rightist opponents. Pinochet's "designated senators" and undemocratic electoral law continued to frustrate the popular will and limit Chile's restored democracy, underscoring its limits. The Concertación's decisive victory in the plebiscite of 1988 made it clear that the center-left alliance would win both the presidential and congressional balloting in 1989. As a consequence, Pinochet decided not to run for president himself but to use his final months as president to decree laws that would hamstring his opponents, even if a majority of the electorate supported them. The most important of these measures was a unique undemocratic binomial electoral law, which created two-member congressional districts, with both seats contested in the same balloting. Political parties or electoral alliances could run two candidates for these seats, but to elect both they had to more than double the vote of their opponents. This meant that if the Concertación candidates for the Senate in a district received 60 percent of the vote and their rightist opponents only 30 percent—a decisive victory in any country—each slate would elect one senator. During the 1990s, in combination with the nine appointed senators, this skewed electoral system meant that a string of Concertación majorities at the polls translated into a senate controlled by the rightist minority. In addition, the Concertación was confronted by a judiciary and government bureaucracy packed by Pinochet with his own adherents. Moreover, the Right enjoyed a near monopoly of the press and media that grew as the decade advanced.

As a consequence, a decade of Concertación governments would not greatly alter the policy course set by Pinochet—whose presence dominated the era until his retirement from the army and arrest in 1998 and continued to cast a pall until his resignation from the Senate and withdrawal from public life in 2002, in exchange for immunity from prosecution for human rights abuses. Nor were these the only ways in which the 1990s continued to be the "Pinochet era." General Pinochet may have ceded the presidential sash to a civilian opponent, but he continued to cast an authoritarian shadow over Chile's restored democracy, underscoring its limited character.

Pinochet might not be president to 1997, as he had planned, but he remained commander of the armed forces until he retired in March 1998 as captain general at the age of eighty-two—long after the mandatory retirement age for military officers. As head of the armed forces, moreover, he not only insisted on control of military affairs but also did his best to shape other policy areas while zealously defending military prerogatives. In a major comparative study of democratic transitions in Latin America and both Southern and Eastern Europe, Juan Linz and Alfred Stepan conclude that no other military retained as many prerogatives after the restoration of "democracy" as the Chilean armed forces. As a consequence, they warned, Chile's democracy was not fully consolidated.[62]

Nor did Pinochet hide his continued political presence. If anything he exaggerated it for effect. On 11 September 1990, he warned that he would lead another coup if conditions warranted it. In 1993, when investigations into an arms procurement scandal implicated his son, Pinochet ordered combat-ready troops and tanks into the streets for an "exercise." Two years before, when the bipartisan Rettig Commission issued its report documenting human rights abuses under the dictatorship, Pinochet denounced it as a "sewer" and warned of dire consequences if the government "touched a hair" of any of his people. Throughout the Aylwin presidency, Pinochet maintained an army "shadow cabinet" that acted as a political pressure group.

In response to these threats, Patricio Aylwin maintained the dignity of his office but often backed down in practice for the sake of social peace—or out of fear of endangering the transition to democracy. As a result, Aylwin was unable to fulfill his promises of constitutional and institutional reforms that would reverse Pinochet's authoritarian legacy, including his self-amnesty. The exception was a law on local government replacing Pinochet's appointed mayors with elected mayors and councilors. Aylwin was also able to win tax increases targeted for social spending for the poor, as well as legislation creating an environmental protection agency, an indigenous development commission, and a cabinet-level agency focusing on women's issues. In addition, he passed a labor law reform that somewhat improved severance pay, collective bargaining, and union organization and made progress on human rights issues, poverty, and foreign policy. But most of his agenda was blocked by the rightist majority in the Senate. Still, Aylwin finished his term with the economy booming and handed over the sash of office in 1994 to his elected civilian successor, Eduardo Frei, son of a former Christian Democratic president, and the second Concertación president.

Frei was elected with one of the biggest pluralities of the century, but did little with this political mandate. A less able and dynamic president than Aylwin, he made little progress in pushing the Concertación's agenda of constitutional and institutional reforms, although his defense minister was able to neutralize the National Security Council as an instrument of military tutelage. By jailing the ex-head of the DINA for his role in the 1976 assassination of Orlando Letelier in Washington, Frei advanced the causes of justice and human rights, but this success was undercut by his efforts to end other human rights prosecutions and his acceptance of Pinochet's becoming an unelected senator-for-life after his retirement as armed forces commander in March 1998.

For Pinochet, this was his final triumph over the civilian democrats whom he despised. It embarrassed Chilean democracy, and the willingness of the Concertación to accept this solution enabled Pinochet to reinvent himself as an avuncular patriarch. Only Pinochet's arrest in England seven months later freed Chile from his grip, if not from his shadow. In its wake, human rights re-emerged as a central unresolved issue, the Chilean judiciary reclaimed its autonomy, and the new armed forces commander, General Ricardo Izurieta, gradually distanced himself and his institution from the captain general. Still, only the retirement of Pinochet from public life in 2002 in exchange for immunity from prosecution finally brought "the Pinochet era" to an end. By then, Ricardo Lagos had become the first Socialist president of Chile since Salvador Allende, a seeming shift to the left within the Concertación that masked an underlying continuity in policy.

During the 1990s, moreover, despite the restoration of democracy and a decade of center-left governments, there was more continuity than change in economic policy and labor relations. The privatization of social security and health care was continued under the Concertación, and the privatization of state enterprises was extended further, as were neoliberal tariff and exchange rate policies. Labor law reform was limited and the government stance on labor relations was a studied neutrality that left business in command. In the end, the Concertación did more to legitimate and consolidate Pinochet's economic and social "revolution" than to reverse it.

This was true as well in the realm of values and culture. Pinochet's efforts to replace Chile's culture of solidarity with one of individualism and consumerism finally triumphed in the 1990s, when incomes doubled, consumer credit spread, and even the "self-employed" poor began to think of themselves as "micro-empresarios" who could start their own tiny business. Increasingly, workers were left to confront their social problems—illness, retirement, education—as individual consumer choices within the marketplace, not as objects of social solidarity or collective action. Ironically, this hegemony of the market as the regulator of society and culture would take place under democratic governments led by political parties of the Center-Left that had always decried such capitalist values.

Nor can the responsibility for the consolidation of these changes be laid purely at Pinochet's door or blamed solely on his constitution or institutional legacy. These profound changes reflected as well the Concertación's own embrace of Pinochet's neoliberal ideology, as well as the individualism and consumerism that informed them and the economic and social policies that flowed from them. The result would be a "neoliberal democracy."

In economic terms, this period began in 1987, when the Chilean economy recovered its dynamism and began to grow again. Buoyed by high export prices, record foreign investment, and pragmatic economic policies, the Chilean economy would continue to grow for the next eleven years at an unprecedented annual average rate of 7.8 percent—and did so with low inflation rates.[63] It was the longest period of sustained growth with low inflation in modern Chilean history. If there was a neoliberal economic "miracle" in Chile, it was this post-1986 boom—most of which took place under the center-left democratic governments of the Concertación—and not the more hyped false boom of the Chicago Boys of 1977–81, whose excesses played a central role in the crisis of 1982.

Moreover, if any group of economists can claim to have made an economic miracle in Chile, it was the center-left economists of the Concertación, not the Chicago Boys. Despite the need to slow down the economy during 1990–91 to avoid accelerating inflation—a legacy of Pinochet's election year populism—during the seven years that followed, the Concertación governments presided over an economic expansion that averaged 7.7 percent a year, while lowering inflation to only 6.1 percent annually. During this time, moreover, unemployment also dropped to 6.1 percent, tariffs fell to 11 percent, and foreign investment rose from $885 million in 1990 to $5.8 billion in 1997. Most remarkable of all, through targeted social spending within the context of this economic boom, the Concertación was able to halve the 1988 45 percent poverty rate bequeathed by Pinochet, while balancing the budget and lowering inflation to single digits. Now that was a "miracle."

This economic growth of the 1990s was a *neoliberal* success story, even though the Concertación modified some neoliberal principles in practice and infused their policies with a measure of social and environmental concern absent under the Pinochet dictatorship. To the surprise of many—both among its supporters and opponents—the Concertación governments opted to retain the very Pinochet economic model that its chief economic policy maker, Alejandro Foxley, had criticized for its economic and social costs when he was in opposition.[64]

There were several reasons for this policy decision by the center-left coalition, and they were mutually reinforcing. One was the analysis by their social scientists that the coup of 1973 and the dictatorship that followed reflected the decision of business elites to call in the military, because they could not protect their core interests under Chile's radicalized democracy. The lesson that the Concertación drew from this analysis of the breakdown of democracy in the 1970s was that to avoid its repetition in the 1990s it was necessary to reassure business that its interests would be protected under Chile's restored democracy, which business elites had fought out of fear in the plebiscite of 1988—and to demonstrate that their interests would even be promoted under a center-left government, which they had opposed in the presidential election of 1989. At a minimum, this argument ran, business elites had to be neutralized and their alliance with the military broken for Chilean democracy to be consolidated.

There was also another powerful reason, the Concertación's economists argued, to shape economic policies that would reassure business. In the post-communist world of the 1990s, where neither socialism nor state capitalism was a viable alternative, the Concertación could only succeed if the private sector—Chilean and foreign—invested in Chile. The consolidation of democracy, therefore, depended on the collaboration of business interests. That would only happen if they felt confident that their investments were both safe and profitable.

This was particularly difficult to demonstrate by a coalition government that included Allende's Socialist party, whose last term in office in the early 1970s—with its frozen prices, runaway inflation, and seizure and socialization of enterprises—was still a traumatic memory in the minds of Chilean business. "This government had to convince business that they were really in favor of the economic system," stressed Chamber of Commerce president Daniel Platowsky.[65] This was even true for the Christian Democrats who dominated the first Concertación administrations, whose ranks included many who had favored a mixed economy in the 1960s, when the Frei government had promoted a strategy of protected industrialization and land reform, with an active government role in the economy and populist social policies.

With the fading of socialism, "populism" emerged as the new ideological enemy, a populism that the Concertación both feared being accused of and was determined to avoid at all costs. Foxley was "determined to break the populist cycle, in which a government is elected on promises to satisfy unmet social demands but in doing this undermines its budget, generates inflation, erodes incomes and is overthrown—two years of euphoria and fifteen years of penance!"[66] This thinly veiled critique of the Allende government underscored the extent to which the "lessons" of the past shaped the policies of the Concertación in the 1990s, as they did the fears of Chile's business community, who "worried about what democracy would bring."[67]

Because of these concerns, Foxley went out of his way to reassure the business community that their property rights were safe, that the neoliberal macroeconomic model would be maintained, and that the rules of the economic game would not change. In addition, the Concertación was persuaded to continue Pinochet's neoliberal policies by a calculation that Foxley put succinctly in explaining why he maintained in office an economic model that he had criticized in opposition: "We have already paid the social costs of these neoliberal policies, so we might as well enjoy their economic benefits."[68]

Those economic benefits did not extend to Chile's manufacturing industries, which had to confront intensified Asian and Latin American competition without the government assistance that they had expected from an elected, center-left government. On the contrary, under the Concertación, the tariff rate fell from 15 percent to 11 percent in 1997, with a projected 6 percent tariff rate by 2004. The result was a continuation of the deindustrialization begun by Pinochet. By 1998 there was little left of the textile industry, which had once been the second largest industrial sector in terms of employment in Chile.

The Concertación even proved willing to throw the overheated economy they inherited from Pinochet into recession in 1990 in order to avoid the risk of inflation (Chile's chronic economic disease, and the ailment most associated with democratic governments in the past). The political goal of the Concertación's economic policies was to demonstrate that a center-left democratic government could be a reliable steward of the neoliberal economic model and not end in economic "chaos," even that it could administer the model more efficiently.

The Concertación did take steps to ameliorate some of the worst social costs of the model, particularly the high poverty rate that it had generated. In return for the Concertación's embrace of the neoliberal model and a balanced budget, the rightist majority in the Senate and the business interests they represented agreed to $500 million in new taxes to be devoted to social spending on the poor. The Aylwin government targeted the bulk of this spending on the poorest of the poor, the 25 percent of the population classified as destitute in 1988, through rent and utility subsidies and increases in pensions and the minimum wage. But its major stress was on promoting the economic expansion that would put the poor back to work. Together with the near full employment from a booming economy, these measures would halve poverty rates in Chile during the 1990s, reducing them to roughly 22 percent by 1998.

But the Concertación's economic miracle also had its costs. Environmental degradation was one. Foxley himself recognized that the market was not very efficient when it came to protecting the environment, but the Concertación's efforts to remedy this were more rhetorical than real. The political power of business interests in Congress combined with the Concertación's reluctance to antagonize business in general and foreign investors in particular to limit the effectiveness of environmental protections that on paper seemed modeled after the United States.

As a result, environmental degradation kept pace with economic growth. As the chapters on the fruit, forestry, and fishing industries reveal, the new export sectors that were trumpeted as the great neoliberal success stories were developed at a high environmental cost, with long-term negative implications for sustainable development and a harsh impact on workers and residents of the production zones.[69]

Heightened vulnerability to external shocks was another cost of the neoliberal model. The Concertacion might boast that Chile was "one of the most open economies in the world,"[70] but this export orientation and lack of protection also had its flip side. This vulnerability became clear when the discovery of a poisoned Chilean grape in Philadelphia in 1989 sent the fruit industry into a tailspin, as did the decision of the European Union a few years later not to buy Chilean apples in order to protect their own inefficient orchards.

Even more serious and long lasting were the ripple effects of the Asian financial crisis of 1997–98, the Brazilian crisis of 1998–99, and the Argentine crisis of 2001–2 on Chile's economy. Its growth slowed, reaching recession levels in 1999, and unemployment soared into double digits by 2001, with 15 percent out of work in Gran Santiago.[71] Together these crises brought the Chilean "miracle" to an end and showed how wrong was the Chilean boast "Adios a America Latina"—"Goodbye to Latin America"—with its claim that Chile was the "fifth Pacific tiger" and had left typically Latin American economic problems behind. It was absurd to claim equality with a Taiwan or Korea—with their steel, electronics, and autos—on the basis of exports of copper, fruits, fish, and forest products with little value added in Chile to the raw material. At bottom, neoliberal Chile had diversified its export economy, adding new products and new markets, while maintaining the same dependence on natural resource exports to foreign markets and the vulnerability that such a system creates—a situation that has been typical of Latin America through most of its history. As a result the Pinochet era ended as it began: with an economic crisis.

In 1998, moreover, some three million Chileans still lived in poverty, despite the longest period of steady economic growth without inflation in modern Chilean history. In addition, the high levels of indebtedness of many low-wage Chilean workers meant that poverty statistics understated the numbers of Chileans whose take-home pay left them below the poverty line.

At the end of this unprecedented stretch of prosperity, moreover, there was no improvement in the stark inequities that had made Chile one of the most unequal countries in the world, reversing the dramatic increase in equality achieved under Salvador Allende. In 1972, Chile was the second most equal country in Latin America; by 2002, it was the second most unequal country in the region. It was the Concertación that had accused Pinochet of dividing the country into "Two Chiles"—one wealthy and First World, the other poor and Third World—with his neoliberal policies. Yet, in eight years of prosperity it had done little to reverse this negative redistribution of wealth and income. If anything, the distribution of income was worse in 1998 than it had been in 1990— and the half decade of economic stagnation that followed did not improve this situation.[72] Instead, the Concertación held out the hope that in the long run its increased investment in education might have that effect, although the inequalities of educational quality and opportunity in Chile called that hope too into question.

In part, this failure to alter the distribution of wealth and income reflected the Concertación's neoliberal embrace of limited government and the market as the regulator of the economy; in part, it stemmed from the Concertación's weak support for labor law reform and its refusal to jeopardize the cooperation of business interests by pressing on them the concerns of their workers. Instead it pressured Socialist and Christian Democratic labor leaders to contain the demands of their working-class constituents "for the sake of democracy." As a result, worker wage gains lagged behind productivity increases and inequality did not diminish. Moreover, as Volker Frank shows in his chapter, this reluctance of the Concertación to pressure Chile's business community would doom its efforts to create a "modern" system of labor relations shaped by "social concertation"—social pacts and consultation on the European model.

For a periodization based on political history, 1990 is the great divide, the year that Pinochet handed over the presidential sash to an elected civilian, Patricio Aylwin, whose election he had opposed. From the perspective of many of Chile's workers, this political transition, while significant, was less important than the underlying continuity in economic policy and labor relations during the 1990s.

Despite its leading role in the fight against the dictatorship and its seeming success, the Chilean labor movement that emerged from sixteen years of Pinochet's dictatorship was weak at both local and national levels. It was constrained by the Plan Laboral, the neoliberal economy, and arrogantly aggressive business practices, and it was in need of state and party support if it was to level the labor relations playing field. Moreover, both workers and employers expected the Concertación to restore the balance in labor relations by tilting toward labor.

As Volker Frank argues, these needs and expectations would fly in the face of the Aylwin government's vision of modern labor relations, sound economics, and transition politics. Labor leaders were persuaded by their political parties to postpone their demands so as not to jeopardize the democratic transition and to accept a policy of social concertation that business then refused to embrace. Even labor's focus on changing the Pinochet labor laws was doomed to frustration in the face of business and rightist opposition and lukewarm government support.

Subordinating themselves to parties that failed to support worker demands, labor leaders increasingly lost legitimacy in the eyes of their own mass base, and the new CUT sank like a stone: by 1997 its authority was so weak that it could not mobilize more than five thousand workers on May Day, the historic Day of the Worker. By then, the most militant activists were experimenting with alternatives to the CUT: independent unions and local federations inspired by the *cordon industrial* of the Allende era.[73]

Chilean labor leaders also confronted a new working class during the 1990s, the product of the economic, social, and cultural changes of the Pinochet era. Economic restructuring had led to a rise in subcontracting and temporary labor, with production chains buying from smaller, unregulated informal-sector shops. Neoliberal laws gave employers the flexibility to hire and fire to change the conditions and character of their labor force.

As the chapters in this book make clear, one result was a marked decline in job quality. The number of stable, unionized industrial jobs declined, while insecure, nonunion jobs increased, many of them in precarious sweatshop conditions. Even in the prosperous metallurgical industry, Joel Stillerman concludes in his chapter, job security became a thing of the past. Long work hours were another characteristic of the 1990s. The Chilean work week was the longest in the world,[74] with many people working sixty hours a week or more, as my chapter on textile workers concludes.

These changes in the job market shaped a new working class. It was younger, with a majority who had never experienced the heady days of the Allende era, a generational shift accelerated by the policy in many industries not to hire workers who were over thirty years old. These younger workers had spent their entire lives in the Pinochet era and were influenced by its individualism and consumerism, as the chapters by Stillerman and Klubock stress.

Their adult lives, moreover, had been lived under the Concertación. They were distant not only from the radical politics of the Allende era, but from the class solidarity and consciousness that had sustained the resistance to the dictatorship during the 1970s and 1980s as well. They were more likely to identify with MTV's transnational youth culture than with the Chilean class culture of the past and to be apolitical or alienated from the leftist politics of their parents. In short, they represented a neoliberal working class who were more likely to act as consumers than as citizens—or as "class-conscious" workers. The emergence of this neoliberal working class was one of the chief preoccupations of labor leaders in the 1990s and one of the most profound changes of the Pinochet era. Ironically, it was the Concertación that was responsible for the consolidation of this central project of the dictatorship—the hegemony of the market in Chilean culture and society.[75]

The 1990s also revealed a more female workforce, reflecting a gender shift that paralleled the rise of informality and temporary work in both industry and agriculture. By 1990, almost 30 percent of Chilean women worked outside the home, whereas only 22 percent had in 1970; this trend accelerated in the 1990s, rising to nearly 40 percent by 1998—a reflection of both economic restructuring and changing household economies.[76] The feminization of the labor force in the textile, seafood, and fruit industries was striking. Most stunning of all was the gender shift in the countryside, where women had only rarely worked outside the home before 1973 and where four-fifths of the labor force had been composed of permanent workers. In the 1990s, more than three-quarters of the rural labor force was composed of temporary workers, half of whom were female, led by the seasonal women workers in the fruit-packing houses, the central subjects of Heidi Tinsman's chapter. Some of these women workers, as Heidi Tinsman demonstrates, were combative and active in unions. Many more—especially single mothers—were too preoccupied with the daily struggle to support their families to participate, especially when union activism might risk their jobs. Moreover, many women worked in informal-sector shops that were unregulated and too small to be organized under Chile's labor laws. They were unable to defend their interests, let alone demand their rights.

It was little wonder then that the return of democracy in the 1990s brought no upsurge in labor militancy. The decline of strike activity during the 1990s that Volker Frank chronicles, however, was less a sign of worker satisfaction than of labor weakness and worker alienation in a context of increased personal indebtedness, decreased union power, and a government that was unable or unwilling to defend their interests. Under these circumstances, many union leaders ceased to view the strike as a viable weapon of the workers.[77]

Social concertation, the center-left coalition's new model of "modern" labor relations, would prove a recipe for labor union weakness and worker vulnerability. Chile's workers would become victims not only of the Pinochet dictatorship that they had fought against but of the center-left democracy that they had fought—and voted—for.

In 1999 and 2000, most Chilean workers voted once again for the presidential candidate of the Concertación. The election of Ricardo Lagos in 2000 as the first Socialist president since Allende renewed the hopes of many workers that their turn had finally come. But midway through Lagos's six-year term in office, it seemed as if these hopes too were doomed to disappointment. Although Lagos made labor law reform a priority, he found himself opposed by Christian Democratic neoliberals within his coalition as well as by the Concertación's rightist opponents. In the end, he had to settle for a weakened reform, which Volker Frank concludes made little difference to wages, working conditions, or labor rights. Labor unions remained weak under Lagos and workers without bargaining power.

These weaknesses were exacerbated by the economic stagnation of 2000–2003, a reflection of economic downturns in Chile's major markets—Japan, Europe, and the United States—and crises in its neighbors, particularly Argentina. If Chilean businesses had been unwilling to share their profits more equitably during the long economic boom, they were unlikely to grant large real wage increases during a prolonged period of recession and stagnation. As a consequence, although Lagos had run for president on a platform promising "growth with equality," the first half of his presidency had been characterized by "stagnation with inequity."

It was little wonder that Chilean workers became alienated from the Concertación, nor was it surprising that parties of the Concertación such as the Socialist party ceased to mobilize what had been their central mass base. Fearful of a mobilization that might lead to "populist demands" that could endanger the neoliberal model, the Socialist party allowed its mass base to atrophy and became a party of political elites who focused on the tactics of politics and the posts and influence this brought. The result was a distancing of the political elite from the supporters whose struggles had brought them to power and a political demobilization that paralleled the demobilization of Chile's workers. What Pinochet had not succeeded in imposing with state terror, the Concertación accomplished with its neoliberal democracy.

In the end, the final "democratic" decade of the Pinochet era was as important as the preceding fifteen years in establishing his legacy. When the Concertación won the presidency in 1989, both workers and their employers expected the elected center-left coalition to reverse the neoliberal policies and probusiness labor relations that the Pinochet dictatorship had imposed by force. Its failure to do so consolidated this Pinochet "revolution" and left Chile's workers at the mercy of their employer and the market, which the Concertación allowed to "discipline" them. The chapters that follow explore the consequences of this complex history for Chile's workers and their organizations and analyze their experience of the long Pinochet era.

NOTES

1 Salvador Allende, speech in National Stadium, Santiago, Nov. 4, 1971. Quoted in Peter Winn, *Weavers of Revolution: The Yarur Workers and Chile's Road to Socialism* (New York: Oxford University Press, 1986), 227–28 (my translation).

2 Although much rumored at the time, knowledge of the U.S. covert war against Allende was greatly expanded by the postcoup investigations of the U.S. Senate Intelligence Committee, whose report *Covert Action in Chile, 1963–1973* (Washington, D.C., 1975), documents a decade-long pattern of covert interference in Chile's internal affairs to prevent Allende from coming to power and to undermine his government and project once he became president. U.S. tactics included supporting both civilian opponents and military plotters and in CIA "dirty tricks" designed to persuade apolitical military officers to overthrow Allende. More recently, declassification of documents by the Clinton administration has deepened our understanding and broadened the dimensions of U.S. involvement both in the destabilizing of the Allende government and in the consolidation of the Pinochet dictatorship. See Peter Kornbluh, ed. *The Pinochet File: A Declassified Dossier on Atrocity and Accountability* (New York: New Press, 2003, chaps. 2 and 4).

3 Alicia Romo, quoted in Peter Winn, *Americas: The Changing Face of Latin America and the Caribbean*, 2d ed. (Berkeley: University of California Press, 1999), 323. Romo would become Director of Industry and Commerce for the Pinochet regime.

4 After witnessing one such book burning in front of my building, I searched the embers to see what was so offensive to the military as to require public burning. In addition to works of Allende and Marx, the burned books included the love poems of Pablo Neruda and U.S. social science texts, many of them of a conservative cast, but written in English. Also destroyed was a cassette of Beethoven's Ninth Symphony, with its "Ode to Joy" celebrating universal brotherhood. The book burnings, censorship, and purges made clear that the military intended to carry out a cultural counterrevolution as well, one that would reverse the internationalism of the previous era and replace it with a narrow provincial nationalism based on military mythology.

5 Operación Condor and the Prats assassination are subjects of ongoing investigations in Chile, Argentina, and Spain. The best source on this still unfolding story is the website of the National Security Archive—http://www.gwu.edu/7Ensarchiv/latin_america—which posts recently declassified documents. For the Letelier case, see John Dinges and Saul Landau, *Assassination on Embassy Row* (New York: Pantheon, 1980). For Operación Condor, see John Dinges, *The Condor Years* (New York: New Press, 2004).

6 Augusto Varas, *Los militares en el poder: Regimen y gobierno militar en Chile, 1973–1986* (Santiago: FLACSO, 1987).

7 The eight senior air force generals refused to replace Leigh as head of the air force in solidarity and protest. General Fernando Matthei finally accepted the post, but the air force remained alienated and Matthei would play a key role in forcing Pinochet to recognize his plebiscite defeat in 1988. For lucids account of the Pinochet-Leigh conflict, see Pamela Constable and Arturo Valenzuela, *A Nation of Enemies: Chile under Pinochet* (New York: W. W. Norton, 1991), 64–69; and Veronica Valdivia, *El golpe después del golpe: Leigh vs. Pinochet, 1960–1980* (Santiago: LDM, 2003).

8 Miguel Vega, president, Contevech (Conferacíon de Trabajadores Textiles y del Vestuario de Chile), Santiago, interview of July 1988; Manuel Bustos, president, CUT, Santiago, interview of July 1989.

9 Decree laws were edicts approved by the junta, which acted as the four-man "legislature" of the military dictatorship.

10 The one exception to this reliance on coercion during the initial five years of military rule was the abortive effort to create a corporatist labor relations system promoted by air force chief General Gustavo Leigh and labor minister General Nicanor Díaz Estrada in 1974–75 that is discussed in greater detail below.

11 *Gremialistas* were rightists who theoretically believed in workers' having organizations—*gremios*—that were independent of political interests, reflecting the neocorporatist ideology of *gremialismo* promoted by Jaime Guzmán, a key ideologue of both the Allende opposition and the Pinochet regime. In practice, they were partisans of the military dictatorship.

12 Although statistics vary, a study of privatizations based on the archives of the Corfo, the government development corporation that controlled the public sector under

Allende, concluded that in 1973 the Corfo controlled 596 enterprises, some 526 of which had entered the state sector since 1970. Of these, 120 had been reprivatized by April 1974 and another 205 by April 1975, when a civilian Chicago Boy took over the Corfo. See Dominique Hachette, "Privatizaciones: Reforma estructural, pero inconclusa," in La transformación económica de Chile, ed. Felipe Larraín and Rodrigo Vergara (Santiago: CEP, 2000), 115–19. For a more detailed analysis of privatizations and their relationship to the military and their mentalities, see Veronica Valdivia, "Estatismo y neoliberalismo: Un contrapunto militar, Chile, 1973–1979," Historia (Santiago) 34 (2001): 194–214. Valdivia stresses the strength of statist ideas within the military during this first phase of the regime, as well as a concern for worker participation in the privatized enterprises within a significant sector of military officers. See also her El golpe despúes del golpe, chap. 3.

13 For an account of these views and personalities, including a history of the formation of the Chicago Boys, see Juan Gabriel Valdés, Pinochet's Economists: The Chicago School in Chile (Cambridge: Cambridge University Press, 1995), especially chaps. 1 and 5–11. For a more recent work that examines as well the gremialista influence on the military's economic policy and the regime's treatments of different groups of economists, see Carlos Huneeus, El régimen de Pinochet (Santiago: Sudamericana, 2001), chap. 7. For an analysis of the rival business interests and coalitions that sought to shape the Junta's economic strategy, see Eduardo Silva, The State and Capital in Chile: Business Elites, Technocrats, and Market Economics (Boulder: Westview, 1996), chaps. 3–5. For a self-justifying account by the key Chicago Boys, see Sergio de Castro, ed., El ladrillo: Bases de la política económica del gobierno militar chileno (Santiago: CEP, 1992).

14 Ten economists, most of them neoliberals, had been asked in late 1972 to prepare a plan for a postcoup economic policy for the navy, which was initially in charge of the economy for the junta. Coordinated by Roberto Kelly, a retired navy officer who would become head of Odeplan, the planning ministry, they created a promarket strategy known by its code name El Ladrillo, the Brick. Even earlier, during 1971–72, aided by funds from the CIA, another group of economists of similar bent had prepared a post-Allende program for the Sofofa (Sociedad de Fomento Fabril), Chile's manufacturers' association. Most of these economists, including the key Chicago Boys, would later be prominent policymakers under the junta. See Valdés, Pinochet's Economists, chap. 11.

15 This Comite Asesor de la Junta de Gobierno (hereafter, advisory committee) included officers who described themselves as "social democrats." Its initial policy statement, "Líneas de acción de la Junta de Gobierno de Chile" of 10 March 1974, still supported a mixed economy, with import substitution industries at its core and regional integration as its foreign economic policy. ("Líneas de acción de la Junta de Gobierno de Chile," in Primer año de la reconstrucción nacional [Santiago, 1974]. For an analysis of this document and its authors that relates both to the formation of their generation of officers, see Valencia, "Estatismo y neoliberalismo," 187–88, 195–98.)

16 Hernán López, Yarur, S.A., private communication, December 1974.

17 Arturo Fontaine Aldunate, Los economistas y el presidente Pinochet (Santiago: Zig-Zag, 1988), 87–101. This formulation was important because Pinochet's own military

advisory committee supported Saéz and the gradualist position in this debate. But, for military officers who owed their positions to Pinochet, hierarchy and loyalty trumped ideology. (See Valencia, "Estatismo y neoliberalismo," 188–93, 209–10.)

18 For an analysis of the rightist politics of the principal Chicago Boys, see Huneeus, *El régimen de Pinochet*, 395–98. Huneeus also reveals their personal gains from their privatization policies (476–85). Eduardo Silva stresses the alliance of the Chicago Boys with "a core of radical internationalist conglomerates with a heavy concentration in liquid assets" that had been expanded by the influx of petrodollars after 1974. In particular, he identifies the B H C (Banco Hipotecario de Chile) and Cruzat-Larraín groups as the greatest gainers from the neoliberal triumph, with the Edwards and Matte economic groups shifting from their traditional orientation to domestic markets in time to jump on the neoliberal bandwagon (see Silva, *State and Capital in Chile*, chaps. 5–6). Sergio de Castro was a close friend of Manuel Cruzat and on the board of directors of Edwards' group enterprises both before and after his government posts (Silva, *State and Capital in Chile*, 140).

19 For an account relating these neoliberal claims to preexisting military values, see Valencia, "Estatismo y neoliberalismo," 215–26.

20 Quoted in Constable and Valenzuela, *Nation of Enemies*, 186.

21 General Gustavo Leigh, air force commander, Junta de Gobierno, national television address, 11 September 1973.

22 Fontaine Aldunate, *Los economistas*, 125–28. Only Codelco, the nationalized copper enterprise that owned Chile's biggest mines, resisted this tide of neoliberalism under a shrewd nationalistic army office. Colonel Gastón Frez carried the day with Pinochet in favor of leaving Codelco under state control by arguing its strategic importance to Chile and tarring the privatization of the copper mines as "unpatriotic" (Constable and Valenzuela, *Nation of Enemies*, 189). By 1980, only 23 strategic industries, including energy and telecommunications, remained in the public sector. But, because Codelco was so large, despite the privatization campaign and the Chicago Boys' neoliberal ideology, three-quarters of Chilean enterprises by value were still in state hands, and Cauas's notion of a mixed economy still prevailed. (See also Hachette, "Privatizaciones," 115–18.)

23 See Valdivia, "Estatismo y neoliberalismo," 199–213, 225–26; Valdivia, *El golpe después del golpe*, chap. 4; and Huneeus, *El régimen de Pinochet*, 406–23.

24 Although the Chicago Boys were ultimately successful in controlling inflation, it took eight years—and the failure of several stabilization programs at an elevated social cost—before they ended double-digit inflation. Unregulated prices, a controlled money supply and reduced public deficits did not succeed until combined with a fixed exchange rate during 1979–81. In other words, the stabilization programs they prescribed not only were not miraculous—they were not successful. Patricio Meller has offered an intriguing explanation, centered around the inflationary effects of the deregulation of the financial sector and international capital flows. The former led to high interest rates that increased prices, the latter to easy credit that greatly expanded the money supply and consumer spending. See Patricio Meller, *Un siglo de economía política chilena (1890–1990)* (Santiago: Andrés Bello, 1996), 191–92.

25 Quoted in Meller, *Un siglo*, 195. My translation.

26 For a fuller discussion, with revealing quotes, see Constable and Valenzuela, *Nation of Enemies*, 187–88.

27 In a lucid critique of Chilean neoliberalism, Ricardo Ffrench-Davis concluded: "In synthesis, the neoliberal experiment generated a society with increased inequality in many areas . . . It deepened the problem of unemployment notably, discouraged investment, and in general, privileged speculative tendencies instead of activities that would lead to increases in productivity and Chilean capital formation" (Ricardo Ffrench-Davis, *Entre el neoliberalismo y el crecimiento con equidad: Tres décadas de política económica en Chile* [Santiago: Dolmen, 1999], 91.). My translation.

28 Later decree laws specified that 28 percent of the Senate would be "designated," including four retired military officers named by the National Security Council. This antidemocratic measure was complemented by Pinochet's unique binomial electoral law, which established two-member congressional districts, in which to elect two deputies or senators from the same district, a party or electoral alliance needed to double its opponent's vote—a difficult feat—or else the opponent received an equal number of seats in the congress. Together, these Pinochet measures preserved rightist control of the Senate up to the end of the century, despite a decade of majority victories by his center-left opponents in legislative elections.

29 D.L. 3500 (1980) privatized the social security system, replacing a public pool of money in which current workers helped pay for retirees with individual retirement accounts managed by private profit-seeking enterprises—the AFP (Administradoras de Fondos de Pensiones). The goal was to allow a worker to retire with 70 percent of his/her salary, with the government responsible for topping it up if it did not work that way. Although much has been made of this reform in Chile and abroad, its efficacy as a retirement system is as yet unproved, as workers have yet to accumulate the thirty years required to retire in the AFP system. In 1980, however, its primary goals were to reduce government social spending and to shore up capital markets. Yet recent studies suggest that it has led to government social security expenditure deficits between 1981 and 1998 that are more than double—5.7 percent vs. 2.4 percent of the GDP—the level of 1974–1980. The privatization of social security, however, has been far more successful for the development of capital markets in Chile, although that was not an avowed goal of the original project. In effect, this decree transferred worker savings in the form of social security contributions from the public to the private sector, making them available to the country's economic groups for investment. Given the oligopic concentration of wealth and corporate control under Pinochet, this meant handing the forced savings of workers over to Chile's most powerful capitalists.

The AFPs then played an important—but perverse (from the workers' perspective) role—in the second wave of privatizations in the 1980s. The AFPs used the forced worker savings they controlled to purchase large shares of such "strategic" public enterprises as the electricity companies, whose privatized management then fired workers in the interest of maximizing profits. The AFPs' participation in these privatizations, moreover, allowed the regime to claim they were examples of its "popular capitalism," as the workers whose savings they used were "owners" of the shares—although they had no say over how they were voted or how their money was invested. Worse still, these privatizations were unregulated, so that the executives of the public enterprises, many of them regime economists, controlled the private companies through preferential shares that excluded workers who bought shares from voting rights and monopolized the benefits of privatization in their own hands. (For a more detailed account of the uses and abuses of the social security "modernization" in Chile, see Huneeus, El régimen de Pinochet, chap. 9.)

30 Most of these dictatorial decrees were from 1979, under labor minister Jose Piñera, but the earliest dated from 1978 and the last from 1981.

31 Guillermo Campero and José A. Valenzuela, El movimento sindical en el regimen militar chileno, 1973–1981 (Santiago: ILET, 1984), 145. My translation.

32 Campero and Valenzuela, El movimiento sindical, 145. My translation. I am indebted to Campero and Valenzuela for their detailed analysis in chapter 2 of the decrees that comprised the Plan Laboral.

33 Arturo Martínez, then vice president, CUT, Santiago, interview of July 1991.

34 Mario Rodriguez, Santiago, interview of August 1989.

35 Campero and Valenzuela, Movimiento sindical, 298.

36 For a trenchant critique of the Chicago Boys' neoliberal policies that concludes that the boom's high growth rate itself reflected consumer spending on foreign imports purchased on credit, see Ffrench-Davis, Entre el neoliberalismo, 74–84.

37 Quoted in Winn, Americas, 194.

38 Brian Loveman, Chile: The Legacy of Hispanic Capitalism, 3d ed. (New York: Oxford University Press, 2001), 293.

39 Quoted in Meller, Un siglo, 220. My translation.

40 See, for example, Fontaine Aldunate, Los economistas, 156, 164.

Chile's terms of trade did deteriorate 20 percent during 1981–82, equal to 3 percent of the GNP, with the price of copper dropping $0.32, a loss of $800 million in export earnings. At the same time, the rise in international interest rates did increase the country's foreign debt payments from 20 percent of exports in 1978 to 50 percent of export earnings in 1982. Rising interest rates and declining copper prices reflected oil price hikes and global recession, both decisions Chile could not control. But what intelligent policymaker would assume that oil prices would never be raised, that international interest rates would always be low, and that the world economy would never again enter into a recession? Yet these are the assumptions implicit in the decisions of the Chicago Boys and their banker friends and business collaborators. Moreover, while "not negligible," conclude Sebastián Edwards and Alejandra Cox, external factors "were not the dominating force" and "the drying up of foreign capital flows . . . was to a large extent a reaction on behalf of international bankers to the deteriorating domestic conditions and to the policy mistakes." Monetarism and Liberalization: The Chilean Experiment (Cambridge, Mass.: Ballinger, 1987), 196. The best recent analyses from the Right avoid having to explain the crisis altogether by taking the entire Pinochet era, from 1973 to 1998 as their unit of analysis. See, for example, most of the essays in *La transformación económica de Chile*, ed. Felipe Larraín and Rodrigo Vergara (Santiago: CEP, 2000).

41 This is the conclusion even of mainstream economists sympathetic to liberal reforms. Barry Bosworth, Rudiger Dornbusch, and Raúl Labán conclude that while the Chilean crisis "was partly the result of a combination of several external shocks . . . the effects of external developments was exacerbated by the mishandling of several domestic policies," including the fixed exchange rate and wage indexation, but also "the sweeping opening of the capital account at the time of the boom; the radical liberalization of domestic financial markets without the provision of proper regulations and controls," and a rigid belief in the "automatic adjustment" mechanism of the market. *The Chilean Economy: Policy Lessons and Challenges* (Washington, D.C.: Brookings Institution, 1994), 8–9.

42 Meller, *Un siglo*, 204–11.

43 Alejandro Foxley, *Experimentos neoliberales en América Latina* (Mexico City: Fondo de Cultura Económica, 1988), 87–91. By December 1982, the two most powerful economic groups controlled 30 percent of the capital and 42 percent of the credit of the financial sector. Foxley's critique is shared by Edwards and Cox (*Monetarization and Liberalization*, 98–101). For even more critical analyses of "radical neoliberalism" and the concentration of wealth and economic power, see Silva, *State and Capital in Chile*, chap. 6; and Fernando Dahse, *Mapa de la extrema riqueza: Los grupos económicos y el proceso de concentración de capitales* (Santiago: Aconcagua, 1979).

44 See, for example, Meller, *Un siglo*, 323–24.

45 Daniel Platowsky, quoted in Winn, *Americas*, 193.

46 For Patricio Meller, the crisis was a "high cost apprenticeship" that argues against the wisdom of rapid structural reforms and deregulation (Meller, *Un siglo*, 323.)

47 Ffrench-Davis, *Entre el neoliberalismo*, 72.

48 See, for example, Edwards and Cox, *Monetarism and Liberalization*, 175–205; and Bosworth, Dornbusch, and Laban, *The Chilean Economy*, 8–9.

49 By October 1983, more than half a million Chileans, some 14 percent of the labor force, were enrolled in two government make-work programs that paid less than the minimum wage. Most were in PEM (Programa de Empleo Mínimo), which had been started in 1975 to deal with the unemployment generated by that crisis. But almost half were in the POJH (Programa de Ocupacíon para Jefes de Hogar), a program for heads of households begun the year before to help Chileans to deal with the current crisis. (For annual statistics on the PEM and POJH, see Loveman, *Chile*, 293, table 10-6.)

50 The GNP in Chile fell 14 percent during 1982–83 versus a 3.5 percent drop in Latin America as a whole (Ffrench-Davis, *Entre el neoliberalismo*, 83–84).

51 Meller, *Un siglo*, 216–17.

52 Small and medium-size businesses were also afforded government relief, although not on the scale of the bank bailout.

53 The "second round" of privatizations undertaken in the 1980s were significantly

different from the first round of the 1970s. They included strategic state enterprises, such as the power and telephone companies, including enterprises that had not been nationalized under Allende. They also included the banks and other enterprises that the government had bailed out and taken over during the crisis of 1981–83. A large number of these were sold off—at a fraction of their asset value in a procedure that often lacked transparency—and handed over to leading economic groups or their former executives, many of them Chicago Boy economists with government connections.

To counter the expected criticism, these privatizations were presented as part of a new strategy of "popular capitalism," which would make Chile a nation of "owners." In fact, only small numbers of Chileans became significant owners of these newly privatized firms, those who had access to the necessary financial resources. Those workers who did buy shares in their enterprises—as happened in Chilectra—were manipulated by the former executives who reserved the voting shares and control of the company for themselves. To save its public relations image of "popular capitalism"—and both to give the privatized social security firms something to invest in and to mobilize the capital needed to privatize these public enterprises—the AFPs were allowed to buy large holdings in these privatized companies. The government then claimed that all the workers whose savings were in these AFPs were in effect "owners" of these companies. This effort at spin control was unsuccessful, especially as the AFPs were run by the same class of executives that ran the companies, did not consult the workers on policy issues, and did not object when workers were then fired by these newly privatized firms in the name of efficiency and profit maximization. Had the worker social security accounts remained under the control of their organizations, which then invested in these privatized companies and received seats on their boards of directors in recognition of their sizable holdings, it could have yielded a very different result (one that might have justified the notion of a popular capitalism), but that was clearly not the intent of the Pinochet regime or its Chicago Boy advisers and publicists. For a lucid account and analysis of this second round of privatizations, see Huneeus, El régimen de Pinochet, chap. 9.

54 Also important in the recovery of the Chilean economy were large loans from multilateral funding agencies. Having embraced Chile as their model of structural adjustment, the IMF and World Bank were unwilling to abandon the Pinochet regime to its fate. The new loans that they provided Chile during the crisis were both crucial in themselves and a signal to foreign bankers and investors. See Meller, Un siglo, 236–40.

55 The Chilean Communist Party has always denied that the FPMR was its creation or its "brazo armado." Formally, all it did was to approve "all forms of struggle." The discourse surrounding this shift of party line and the appearance of the Frente in 1983, as well as the Communist origins of FPMR members and especially the strong presence of the children of party leaders in the FPMR left a contrary impression. In effect, both Communists and their enemies understood the FPMR to be the armed wing of the party during the 1980s. (The history of the FPMR has yet to be written.

For a start, albeit partial and partisan, see César Quiroz, "La política de la rebelión popular de las masas," in *Por un rojo amanecer: Hacia una historia de los comunistas chilenos*, ed. Manuel Loyola and Jorge Rojas [Santiago: Valus, 2000], 247–58; and Ricardo Palma, *Una larga cola de accro: Historia del FPMR, 1984–1988* [Santiago: LDM, 2001].)

56 Pinochet also expected to reap political benefits from his "popular capitalism," which in theory had assured a broad diffusion of ownership of the enterprises privatized during the 1980s in the wake of the crisis, creating a "nation of owners." This second round of privatizations differed from the first in that it included strategic enterprises, many of them profitable, such as the utility companies, as well as many formerly profitable enterprises such as the banks bailed out in the crisis. In reality, the number of new shareholders was so low that the government never released the statistics. The privatizations were carried out in ways that lacked transparency, subsidized with tax benefits and the purchases of shares by the wealthy, and benefited most the former executives of the state-owned enterprises (many of them neoliberal colleagues of the government officials who controlled the privatizations) and the AFP, the privatized social security enterprises, who were the major Chilean source of savings in the wake of the crisis. The regime had to resort to the sophistry of claiming that the ownership of shares by the AFP in effect represented the distribution of shares to the workers of Chile. In fact, it represented their double victimization: their savings were used without their approval to privatize public firms, whose managers then often fired large numbers of workers in the name of efficiency and profit maximization. (For a trenchant analysis of the privatizations of the 1980s and their relationship to the privatization of social security, see Huneeus, *Regimen de Pinochet*, chap. 9.)

57 A 1988 poll of Santiago workers showed that only one labor leader—Manuel Bustos—was recognized by more than 6 percent as "the best national leader," and even Bustos received little more than a third of the support of those polled. Alan Angell, "Unions and Workers in Chile in the 1980s," in Paul Drake and Iván Jaksic, *The Struggle for Democracy in Chile, 1982–1990* (Lincoln: University of Nebraska Press, 1991), 362.

58 The new CUT was formally the Central Unitaria de Trabajadores where the old CUT had been the Central Unica de Trabajadores, but this legal difference did not obscure the claim of continuity and restoration implicit in the acronym, which was all anyone used.

59 This figure included some 20 percent of industrial workers, but less than 4 percent of service workers, who represented over 28 percent of the labor force, nearly double that of industrial workers (Angell, "Unions and Workers," 360–61). It was lower than 1981, when 12.1 percent of the labor force were union members. See PET, *Economía y Trabajo en Chile: Informe Anual 6* (1995–96), 286, table 23; and Constable and Valenzuela, *Nation of Enemies*, 227, 243.

60 Angell, "Unions and Workers," 360–61. The unionized included some 20 percent of industrial workers, but less than 4 percent of service workers, who represented over 28 percent of the labor force, nearly double that of industrial workers.

61 PET survey cited in *La Epoca* (Santiago), 22 October 1988. See also Angell, "Unions and Workers," in Paul Drake and Iván Jaksic, eds., *The Struggle for Democracy in Chile*, rev. ed. (Lincoln: University of Nebraska Press, 1995), 189–90, for an analysis concluding that the Pinochet regime manipulated the minimum wage, so that by 1988 it was only half of what a family needed to meet basic needs. Even studies by proregime economists reached similar conclusions about poverty levels (See Constable and Valenzuela, *Nation of Enemies*, 232).

62 Juan Linz and Alfred Stepan, *Problems of Democratic Transition and Consolidation: Southern Europe, South America, and Post-Communist Europe* (Baltimore: Johns Hopkins University Press, 1996), 204–21. These military prerogatives included (1) the unremovability of the commanders of the armed forces who sat on the National Security Council and who chose appointed senators, removing civilian authority over key promotions, retirement of officers, military curricula, and doctrinal publications, and (2) permanent entitlement to 10 percent of the earnings of the state copper corporation, a military budget the size of the high 1989 budget, and the receipts from the sales of military property. For a theoretical analysis of military prerogatives, see Alfred Stepan, *Rethinking Military Politics: Brazil and the Southern Cone* (Princeton: Princeton University Press, 1988), 93–127.

63 Although the high government spending of the Pinochet regime for the elections of 1988 and 1989 boosted inflation to 26.0 percent in 1990, under the Concertación it would fall to 12.2 percent by 1993 and to 6.1 percent in 1997. In the recession that followed, inflation fell still further, and stood at 3.4 percent in October 2002 (Chile, Instituto Nacional de Estadísticas, "Indice de Precios al Consumidor").

64 See Foxley, *Experimentos neoliberales*, chaps. 3–7, for a detailed exposition of this critique, which was made repeatedly in newspapers and mass media during the plebiscite campaign of 1988.

65 Quoted in Winn, *Americas*, 196.

66 Quoted in Winn, *Americas*, 196.

67 Daniel Platowsky, Quoted in Winn, *Americas*, 197.

68 Quoted in Winn, *Americas*, 195.

69 That these environmental costs are systemic in neoliberal Chile is shown by Rayén Quiroga and Saar van Hauwermeiren, eds., *The Tiger without a Jungle: Environmental Consequences of the Economic Transformation of Chile* (Santiago: Instituto de Ecología Política, 1996).

70 Andrés Velasco, assistant treasury minister, quoted in Winn, *Americas*, 198.

71 Chile, Instituto Nacional de Estadística, "Encuesta Nacional de Empleos."

72 See Chile, Mideplan, Casen household surveys for 1990 and 1998. They are also summarized in Loveman, *Chile*, 347, table 11–11. The worsening of income distribution traced in these surveys was not great—the lowest three deciles' share of monetary income dropped by 0.1–2 percent—but Chile's failure to improve its income distribution significantly during its long economic boom, despite low unemployment and high rates of job creation, is both striking and troubling. Loveman provides further support for this analysis from another viewpoint—a 1999 marketing survey that contrasts the top decile's $8,000 per month family income and luxurious

lifestyle with the bottom decile's $250 per month family income and indigent life style (Loveman, Chile, 346, table 11-9). Data for 2000 showed that the poorest decile's share of the national income had declined from 1.4 percent to 1.1 percent since 1990. Another study of income distribution concludes that income distribution improved between 1987 and 1992, but worsened thereafter and worsened still more during the economic downturn of 1998–2002, and suggests the importance of rates of unemployment and women in the workforce as explanatory factors. See Osvaldo Larrañaga, "Distribución de ingresos: 1958–2001," in Reformas, crecimiento y políticas sociales en Chile desde 1973, ed. Ricardo Ffrench-Davis and Barbara Stallings (Santiago: LOM/Cepal, 2001), 306–25.

73 For a more detailed analysis of labor unions in the 1990s, see Volker Frank's account in chapter 2.

74 A comparative study by a Swiss investment bank concluded that workers in Santiago work more hours annually—2,244 hours—than in any other major city in the world. By contrast, in Europe the average work year is under 1,600 hours (La Tercera, 22 July 2001).

75 Eugenio Tironi was one of the first to call attention to these changes in Chilean society and mentality. His analysis is summarized and updated in El cambio está aquí (Santiago: La Tercera-Mondadori, 2002).

76 Teresa Valdes and Enrique Gómez, coordinators, Latin American Women: Compared Figures (Santiago: FLACSO, 1995), 69: "Percentage of Women in the Economically Active Population, 1950–1990"; and Loveman, Chile, 337.

77 Patricia Coñoman, president of the Contextil and then CUT secretary for international relations, interview of June 1997.

VOLKER FRANK

Politics without Policy: The Failure of Social
Concertation in Democratic Chile, 1990–2000

As many Latin American nations continue their difficult task of economic reform and democratic consolidation, scholars of the region are often applying a
similar conceptual framework in their studies of these countries. This has
furthered our understanding of the economic, social, and political processes at
hand. In particular, since the mid-1980s we have seen a burgeoning of literature[1] focusing on *social concertation* as the much proclaimed "magic formula" of
newly elected democratic regimes to achieve sustained economic growth with
political stability. It is often pointed out that what many of these countries
shared was the perceived need to establish some type of consensus among
different social classes over the desired type of capitalist democracy. Otherwise,
these governments feared, they would not be able to solve many of the problems
that they had inherited from the 1980s or earlier decades and that came to
dominate their agenda by the late 1980s (problems such as increased poverty,
high inflation, and heavy foreign debt). This attempt at "class consensus" or
"class compromise" is far from novel, nor is it exclusively a Latin American
phenomenon.[2] But, in one form or another, and with different degrees of
success, countries such as Argentina, Brazil, Mexico, and Chile pursued social
concertation during the 1990s.

This chapter illuminates the Chilean version of social concertation by critically examining the roles played by labor (more specifically, the national union
confederation CUT, the Central Unitaria de Trabajadores), business (more specifically, the top national employer association CPC, the Confederación de la
Producción y del Comercio), and the first three democratically elected governments of Patricio Aylwin (1990–94), Eduardo Frei (1994–2000), and Ricardo
Lagos (2000–). The Chilean version of social concertation is often referred to as
the "outstanding success story" in the region, but a critical analysis reveals its
limitations and shortcomings. The development strategy pursued by the new

democratic governments—the so-called growth with equity model—has serious tensions between its sociopolitical dimension and the underlying neoliberal economic policies. More specifically, I argue that, due to the state's and capital's unwillingness to grant labor a larger role in the formulation and implementation of reform programs, labor has reaped few, if any, benefits from social concertation.[3] My research lends support to those who argue that Chile continues to follow an aggressive, market-driven, individualistic, and inegalitarian model of development,[4] despite a decade of center-left democratic governments pursuing policies of social concertation.

A FEW WORDS OF CAUTION

This chapter is not about the accomplishments since the return to democracy in Chile. Instead, it seeks to present a more critical perspective on developments that took place during the 1990s. Because the primary focus of this chapter is the failure of social concertation among state, capital, and labor, it is necessary, first, to examine the core piece of the democratic government's labor policy, that is, the reform of the Pinochet labor legislation. Second, it is important to look at state-labor-capital relations, which were shaped by but which also in turn influenced governmental policy making, though capital's ability to shape the outcome was superior to labor's. Third, it is necessary to explain the whys and hows of this unequal influence.

Yet social concertation, and whether it failed or succeeded, is not the whole story. As an attempt to combine a return to democracy with economic reform in order to achieve a form of "sustained development" that included not just economic but also social development,[5] it should be seen within the larger perspective of a particular moment of political economy. How much participation—especially in a social and economic sense—are elites willing to concede the working classes?[6] In a context of democratization, the Chilean political and economic elites were more worried about threats to capital accumulation and governability than they were interested in labor's participation. To be sure, while most workers and union leaders welcomed a return to democracy, and were moderately optimistic about chances for economic improvement, none had any illusions that the new democratic state would attempt to return to the failed socialist experiment of 1970–73. Therefore most workers and unionists were quite realistic and understood that the new democratic state would not favor workers *more* than capitalists. Their hope was that in democracy, economic and political elites would be willing to *negotiate* the creation of an industrial relations system that would facilitate workers' attempts to move toward a "balance of power" and a level playing field.[7] The reform of the Pinochet labor legislation, a new approach to labor policies, and new state-labor-capital relations, were all regarded by labor as important elements of Chile's new democracy—a democracy not only characterized by procedures but also by substance, a sense of justice and fairness.

The buzzword of the latest phase in the transformation of Chile's economy is labor market flexibility. Although an integral part of the economy—at least since 1979 with the reform of the labor legislation—labor flexibility has only become a contested notion since the early 1990s. In part, this reflects the return to democracy, in part the Chilean government's attempt to accomplish two things at the same time: sustained economic growth and a deepening of democracy.

The Chilean version of labor market flexibility is built around three inter-related concepts: labor cost flexibility, employment flexibility, and collective bargaining, which is a crucial variable that can mitigate the effectiveness of the first two variables. Thus employment flexibility requires sufficient freedom for employers to hire and fire workers without having to face resistance in the form of effective union opposition. The current labor legislation gives employers that freedom. Flexibility in terms of labor costs can also be obtained by other means, such as use of part-time workers and subcontracted and temporary workers, who do not always enjoy the same benefits as full-time workers. Flexible working hours is a key element of employment flexibility.

Defenders of the Chilean model argue that the neoliberal changes brought about by Pinochet have resulted in a modernization of the entire economic structure. Yet they have not led to more modern industrial relations for Chile's workers, despite increases in productivity and in the quality of production. On the contrary, the modernization of the economy was made possible in part because new production techniques employed by companies make frequent use of their authoritarian control over the labor force, including the use of such strategies as subcontracting of workers, scarce participation of workers in enterprise decisions, and frequent rotation of personnel.[8]

Chile's extreme labor market flexibility also had negative consequences for the government's "growth with equity" model. Since 1990 inequality consistently worsened, despite the fact that poverty rates decreased. Moreover, there is evidence that productivity growth outpaced real wage growth by as much as a ratio of 3:1 in 1993 and 5:1 in 1997.[9] In addition, a substantial number of the Chilean labor force receives wages and salaries that are only slightly above the minimum wage. By official standards, this does not make them poor, although it is hard not to regard as poor those who have to live in Chile on $300 per month. In addition, an important percentage of the poor are working poor. The problem is therefore that "the labor market itself is one of the factors reproducing poverty."[10] Thus what took place in the 1990s was an ever increasing tendency to substitute permanent contract workers with temporary or subcontracted labor, a lowering of income for the total labor force, a decrease in fixed individual incomes for Chile's workers, and an increase in incomes tied to productivity gains, bonuses, and other "incentives."

Because for Chile's workers social concertation was a failure, the current character of Chile's industrial relations system renders unrealistic labor's hopes to see growth with equity in the near future. If this scenario continues (and it is unlikely that the current Lagos government can or will do much to change it), Chile's success story will have come at a heavy cost to its workers. The implications are clear and already evident: with an economic model that is basically neoliberal in nature, many new democracies in Latin America put their nations on a path that increasingly falls short of more substantive social development.[11]

For Chile, this also entails the continued absence of a more modern industrial relations system, the affirmations of its new democratic governments to the contrary. While it may not be possible for Chile to produce industrial relations systems such as those in northern Europe, what might have been possible in the 1990s in Chile was a more modest attempt at institutionalizing state-labor-capital relations and an industrial relations system that seeks to extend basic labor rights to more workers and unions. My idea of "modern" is neither new nor extreme: collective bargaining (including unions' greater input in collective bargaining on issues of flexibility, competitiveness, and job security), protection from abusive employers, sick leave, decent working conditions or at least fair remuneration for tough working conditions, and investment in human capital. Many of these issues were posed, but few of them materialized, perhaps most notably the new unemployment insurance, which would only materialize in April 2000. Thus, as Chile enters the 21st century, many of its workers wonder whether they are not headed toward 19th-century Manchester, England.

AFTER THE TRANSITION:
THE FIRST DEMOCRATIC GOVERNMENT UNDER AYLWIN

The Chilean labor movement had ample reasons to look favorably toward cooperation with and participation in the first democratic government headed by Patricio Aylwin. The labor movement had played a crucial role not only in what

Guillermo O'Donnell, Philippe Schmitter, and Lawrence Whitehead have called the "resurrection of civil society" but also in helping political parties overcome their disagreements and ideological differences, which paved the way for victory in the 1988 plebiscite confrontation between Pinochet and a united opposition front of political parties and the labor movement.[12] Thus the labor movement quite rationally assumed that, given its important role in the return to democracy, it would maintain if not *increase* its participation in social and economic policy making. Such hopes were by no means exaggerated. The incoming Aylwin government itself had promised labor organizations a new industrial relations system in which labor was to play a fundamental role as "equal partner alongside with employers." In fact, the coalition government promised to "stimulate a social concertation . . . between employers and workers . . . so that policies [which labor and employers themselves propose] will be considered legitimate by all groups and [in this way] conflicts can be limited."[13] Thus the new government had called for the creation of a social concertation that would enable the country to pursue a "simultaneous commitment to economic growth and social justice."[14]

For such a concerted effort at "growth with equity" to happen, however, the government needed to reform the labor legislation that was inherited from the Pinochet regime and that severely restricted the unions' collective bargaining power as well as their ability to organize workers into their organizations at all levels of the Chilean union structure, including the intermediate-level organizations such as federations and confederations. One should not forget that the national union organization CUT (Central Unitaria de Trabajadores) had been outlawed by the Pinochet regime, and its top labor leaders (people such as Manuel Bustos and Arturo Martínez) had been repeatedly subjected to persecution and internal exile. Thus the new government also needed to include in the reform of the labor legislation a clause that legalized the new CUT, formed in August 1988. Yet the focus of the coalition government's growth with equity strategy resided not only in the reform of the labor legislation; in fact that was only one—albeit crucial—element of its vision. The thrust of the government's development strategy resided in three fundamental yet interrelated concepts: economic growth, social justice, and worker participation.

At the time, it seemed as if the government was seriously committed to realizing these goals. Barely one month into the new democratic regime (April 1990), the country's most powerful employer association, CPC, the national union organization CUT, and government representatives signed a historic "framework" agreement, the so-called Acuerdo Marco.[15] The most significant aspect of this agreement resided in labor's explicit recognition of private enterprise as the principal and legitimate agent of economic growth.[16] However, despite the acknowledgment of employers' legitimate interests, the Acuerdo did not pretend to create social peace between the bargaining sides. Rather, it stated that existing conflicts would be resolved at the enterprise level, where unions and employers would "assume a fundamental role in the modern enterprise, [and] value the initiative, the capacity and the efforts of the work force."[17] Thus labor-management relations acquired a new meaning as negotiations were considered to be the crucial instrument for accomplishing one's objectives in a consensual way.[18] The Acuerdo also represented the government's new perception of the "role of the state," that is, while it would continue to participate in some areas—for example, in setting the minimum wage—its role in the economy (and more specifically in the industrial relations system) would be much more limited. Thus the first Acuerdo Marco stated that the state should "promote direct negotiations between labor organizations and employers," but otherwise it "should not intervene unnecessarily in their affairs."[19]

In addition to the declaration of these principles, the Acuerdo included a series of initiatives to which the participants committed themselves. Although no specific timetable was set, all three sides (government, employers, and labor) agreed to initiate common projects for vocational training, occupational health and occupational hazards prevention programs, unemployment programs, and wage policies, among others.

Looking back from the vantage point of the early 21st century, there is reason to believe that it was the Concertación government that benefited most from subsequent Acuerdos Marco in 1992 and 1993. In bringing employers and workers to the bargaining table, the Aylwin government was widely perceived as the actor sine qua non of redemocratization. This added to the almost unprecedented popularity the government enjoyed not just among one sector of Chilean political society (as was the case for the Left during Allende) but among the vast majority of Chileans. Employers also gained legitimacy in the eyes of the general public by participating in the Acuerdos Marco and thereby were able to shed their image as being antidemocratic.[20] For workers and the labor movement, however, the Acuerdos were increasingly mere symbolic meetings, that is, a show of goodwill instead of an opportunity to make progress on substantive issues that included the minimum wage, the labor reform, its participation in that reform, relations with employers, and more.

To be fair, the Acuerdos did produce some tangible results for Chilean workers. The minimum wage was raised by 17 percent (real terms) in the first Acuerdo Marco,[21] and was once again raised by approximately 15 percent (again in real terms) in the 1992 agreement. One should keep in mind that despite these gains, the vast majority of CUT-affiliated workers make more than the minimum wage,[22] although their contract demands often took the increase in the minimum wage as a reference point. Moreover, the CUT and its workers have historically shown solidarity toward the large number of workers in the informal economy who were paid minimum wage.[23] Therefore my major reason for arguing that the government benefited so much from the Acuerdos Marco (and labor so little) stems from the impression—shared not only by many labor leaders but also by some government representatives—that more than anything else, the value of these agreements resided in the fact that they had come about at all. For despite all the good intentions that employers and the government indicated, labor organizations became increasingly disillusioned with the annual signing of "big agreements," which in reality meant little or nothing to the majority of organized workers.[24]

What is worse, the agreements had little impact in terms of improving labor-management relations at the plant level,[25] although that had been a major objective of the Acuerdos. Neither did the agreements have any noticeable consequence in terms of producing more bilateral or trilateral talks (not to mention *permanent institutional arrangements*) that would focus on issues the CUT was *very* interested in, and to which both employers (CPC) and the government had committed themselves at the signing of the first Acuerdo: issues related to vocational training, unemployment and health insurance, productivity, economic integration, and most important of all, agreements over the need to reform the labor legislation inherited from the Pinochet regime.

The discrepancies between the promise and discourse of the first democratic government and the reality of labor policies and industrial relations hindered an outcome more favorable to labor's interest. Hence the first democratic government's "social concertation program" may have been doomed to failure from the very beginning as the following section makes clear.

THE 1991–1992 REFORM OF THE LABOR LEGISLATION UNDER AYLWIN

The new laws that were instituted during the Aylwin reforms pertained primarily to the termination of contract and collective bargaining.[26] These laws were important for all types of union organizations in Chile,[27] but they carried the most significant consequences for the plant-level union. So it is this type of union that will receive most of our attention. The 1991–92 reform left intact the basic union structure that was established through the Plan Laboral in 1979.[28]

The legislation did not go back to the original design of the first labor legislation of 1924, which divided unions into professional and industrial unions.

The law concerning termination of contract established a new requirement for employers in case they wanted to dismiss workers. This was important for both collective bargaining and ordinary periods in which the rank and file simply participate in the workforce. The 1979 law (concerning nonbargaining periods) had given employers the right to fire workers without having to give any justification. An employer would simply deliver the dismissal order to the employee and pay him/her a compensation equaling no more than five months of wages (article 155f). Employees could dispute the legality of the dismissal and make an appeal to the local labor inspectorate, which would then investigate the rightfulness of the decision. Notice, however, that even if the state determined that the firing was not justified, the employer could not be forced to rehire the employee; instead, he/she would merely have to pay an additional amount of compensation. The new law (article 19010) of 1991–92 forced the employer "to justify" in written form the dismissal and increased the time period for which severance compensation is paid to workers. While the Plan Laboral had a ceiling of five months (one month of compensation per year worked), the new limit after the Aylwin reform was now 11 months. The same follow-up conditions as in the 1979 law applied if an employee should contest the firing.

The most important of all changes that were made in the 1991–92 reform was the new law on collective bargaining.[29] To begin with, it continued to limit collective bargaining to only a small minority of the Chilean labor force. Public employees and those workers whose firm is more than 50 percent owned by the state were prohibited from collective bargaining. Moreover, dating back to the 1924 legislation, only plant-level unions have the right to collective bargaining. This ban on collective bargaining included many transitory unions that were created by the 1979 changes, such as the unions of port, construction, and agricultural workers. Many workers had been complaining throughout the first four years of the Aylwin presidency that the 1991–92 reform had done nothing to improve their situation. Port worker unions and agricultural unions are a good case in point because they both belong to very important sectors of the Chilean economy—agricultural exports now make up the second largest commodity after copper—and port workers are crucial in a country whose export economy depends on the functioning of its ports. The Aylwin government's refusal to include other union categories in the reform package was probably based on the fear of giving these unions a powerful weapon that would enable them to strike at harvest time and thereby pose a major threat to the economy.

This possibility was never admitted, but it is clear that higher agricultural wages or a prolonged strike of agricultural workers and/or port workers could put Chile's export economy in a difficult situation.[30]

The cornerstone of the new laws on collective bargaining, and thus in a way of the entire Aylwin reform, is the employer's last offer to the union. According to the new law, if this offer included (a) identical stipulations as those of the old contract and (b) a wage readjustment of at least the inflation level, the employer had the right to replace striking workers from the first day (article 157). Although the new law stated that those who participate in collective bargaining could not be fired 10 days prior to the presentation of the union's new demands until the signing of the new contract (article 85), in practice, from the moment a strike begins, workers do not know whether or not they will be able to keep their jobs, and it may not be of much help to know that they have the option of crossing the picket line after the 15th strike day. Should, however, the employer's last offer not have included criteria (a) and (b), he/she could only replace strikebreakers after the 15th day, and workers could start reintegrating themselves into the workforce after the 30th day. But even if the workers were to opt for crossing the picket line, the employer has the right—regardless of the type of offer he/she makes—to reject those workers and continue to rely on his/her strikebreakers (article 159). By law, every worker who has participated in a strike should, after having been replaced by strikebreakers, be allowed to return to the workforce once the strike was over. In practice, however, this is not what happens. The new law simply required employers "to justify" the dismissal of a worker. This is usually done by arguing that it was "necessary" for business reasons.[31] We should also remember that an employer's decision cannot be contested. He/she can only be forced to pay additional compensation. Thus employment protection during strikes is effectively eliminated by the employer's unrestricted power to fire workers. However, the new collective bargaining law eliminated the maximum strike duration, which was 60 days under the 1979 legislation. The new law thus made it once again possible for Chilean workers to stage an indefinite strike. Undoubtedly, this enhanced the unions' bargaining power somewhat, which was why employers staunchly opposed the reform, fearing that an unlimited strike would put the enterprise at the mercy of their unions.[32]

Both the Acuerdo Marco and the reform of the Pinochet labor legislation were crucial elements of the first democratic government's agenda for democracy. Yet according to the leaders of the Chilean labor movement, neither the Acuerdo nor the reform accomplished its goal. So it is worth looking at factors that may help explain this failure. Such an exploration takes us beyond the discussion of specific labor policies and into a brief analysis of "social concertation" as understood by the first democratic government. This is important because it was Aylwin's government that laid a new foundation for state-labor-capital relations, whereas the subsequent governments of Frei (1994–2000) and Lagos (2000–) merely pursued the same objectives. That is why the tripartite relations among labor, business, and the government did not get any better than they were in 1992.

IMPLICATIONS OF HISTORIC AND POLITICAL
LESSONS FOR THE FIRST DEMOCRATIC GOVERNMENT'S
FORMULA FOR SOCIAL CONCERTATION

The intellectual origins of social concertation in Chile go back to the late 1970s and early 1980s,[33] when influential political leaders—mostly Christian Democrats and Socialists—began to think about a possible transition to democracy. These reflections included a critical assessment of conditions that had contributed to the demise of Chilean democracy. The breakdown of a broad-based consensus among political, economic, and social actors was believed to be the origin of the national crisis and the traumatic events of 1973. It followed from this diagnosis that a return to democracy and its governability would require the reconstruction of a "big consensus" within Chilean society. Such a consensus should not be based solely on the mutual recognition of all sectors and agents of society; it should also be capable of creating mechanisms that would allow the channeling of disputed interests within recognized and agreed-on institutions.

The emphasis on consensus and on the autonomy of civil society, the conductive role of the state, and other similar notions are all elements of the particular lessons these leaders had drawn from the authoritarian regime, and from the factors that had led the country into this traumatic experience. In short, at the source of democratic failure was the perceived breakdown of national consensus. From the 1920s until the breakdown of democracy in 1973, the role of the state increased steadily and no single class was able to gain complete control over it, for which reason it was called the "compromise state" ("estado de compromiso").[34] Thus the remarkable aspect of 20th-century Chilean history is that democracy remained stable and even succeeded in incorporating more classes into political and economic participation, despite strong underlying class conflicts. One of the important factors that allowed for this peaceful articulation of different societal interests lay in the role of the Chilean legislature.[35] It is from this reading of history that the leaders of the center and left political parties drew their conclusion about the requirement of a stable democracy. Chile needed to become a society based on a broadly shared consensus and for that to endure it was imperative that socioeconomic actors themselves participated directly in the creation of the necessary institutions with which to channel social demands. That would help reduce conflicts between them, avoid a need for the state to assume once again its historic role as arbitrator—which would have then transferred social conflicts into a struggle for state power—and make civil society stronger and more autonomous.[36]

The recognition of different interests in society, and new institutional arrangements with which to safeguard these, was a necessary first step for laying the basis of a new national consensus. Yet the government's formula also had a neoliberal dimension. Specifically, the Chilean economy would remain open as it had been for many years. It would be regulated by market forces, rather than, as in the pre-Pinochet past, by a powerful interventionist state, and it would continue to place great emphasis on export capabilities. In that way, Chile could continue to modernize its economy and increase its productivity as well as its competitiveness in global markets. In sum, the government's formula for social concertation envisioned a state that would modify the legal institutions inherited from the Pinochet regime in accordance with negotiations between workers and employers. Otherwise, the state would not interfere in labor-management relations because of lessons drawn from the past.

Hence, in the "program" elaborated during the first six months of 1989, the member parties of the then so-called Coalition of Parties for Democracy (during and after the plebiscite campaign known as "Concertación") laid down their ideas concerning the social, political, and economic bases of the next democratic regime. "Without economic growth," it was stated, "some can only win if others lose"[37] and a redistribution of the nation's wealth is not possible. However, growth should also be an "integrative area which will permit the channeling of conflicts of interests between distinct social strata." The development of the country was perceived as a "simultaneous commitment to economic growth and social justice."[38] The program placed great emphasis on showing that employers and workers would be the major economic agents. Hence the program mentioned once again the importance of "stimulating a concertation . . . between employers and workers . . . so that policies (which they propose) are considered legitimate by all groups, and conflicts can be limited. . . . The state should promote concertation by fostering instances where different organizations can have contact."[39] In contrast to labor organizations, which had hoped that in a future democratic regime the state would play a considerably *stronger* role, the program made clear that the intentions of the political leaders of the Concertación government were different. Hence the role of the state was often described by top political party leaders as "conductive," "configurative," or "protective." In Alejandro Foxley's own words, the future government needed to "decongest the state."[40] Thus, by taking the state out of industrial relations as much as possible, the government hoped that employers and labor organizations themselves would agree on the state's role for the first time in Chile's history and build a much more friendly relationship with each other.

STATE-LABOR SOCIAL CONCERTATION

The first Acuerdo Marco stated that the initiation of permanent bilateral and trilateral commissions was a way to arrive at more substantive discussions concerning the institutionalization of new industrial relations. Taking the agreement at its word, the CUT sent a letter to the Aylwin government in early July 1991 requesting a specification of the policy areas in which labor organizations would either simply be informed, or consulted, or allowed to participate in the political decision-making process. The CUT's letter continued by stating that because of labor's "co-responsibility in the transition process, its participation" (in the elaboration of policies) was "justified."[41] The CUT emphasized that it wanted to develop a specific agenda and define concrete areas such as those first indicated in its December 1990 program and requested once again participation in the creation of a national investment fund, vocational training, and other social programs. Many CUT leaders believed that behind the government's vague response to their requests was an unwillingness to give labor a greater role in the elaboration of joint policies. Perhaps it is an exaggeration to argue that labor organizations were purposely excluded, but it is the case that the CUT was unable to convince the government to include topics of particular interest to labor in the negotiations.

The government's unwillingness to involve labor organizations more in the elaboration and implementation of labor policies goes a long way toward explaining why union leaders accomplished relatively little in terms of concerted actions. It does not completely answer why union leaders insisted so much on the state's participation in trilateral negotiations nor why the government was increasingly less inclined to get involved in such negotiations. Therefore, in order to better understand labor organizations' expectations for concerted action in the new democratic regime, it is important to point out that the type of talks and commissions initiated with the new democratic government resembled much more the character of Pinochet's trilateral commissions (whose task it was to study and propose only) than those created earlier under Eduardo Frei (1964–70) and Salvador Allende (1970–73), which had a binding character. Both the Pinochet regime and the new democratic government were pursuing similar objectives with the trilateral commissions. Both attempted to limit labor organizations' participation to a necessary minimum, which was accomplished by depriving the commissions of the power to devise binding policies. In this sense, the new democratic government repeated a historic precedent first set by the Pinochet regime in 1974.

Yet the CUT leaders were not only disappointed over the government's position on tripartite agreements. The government's reluctance to institutionalize and/or participate in tripartite commissions came as a result of the perceived new role of the state. As mentioned, in Chile's new democracy, the state is no longer perceived as the historic mediator between antagonistic class interests. Instead, social actors are called on to reach consensual agreements themselves without recurring to the state. The government's idea of social concertation was a result of its reading of twentieth-century Chilean history and, more specifically, its interpretation of the historic role of Chile's political system leading to the breakdown of democracy. Thus the political leaders of the government believed that by transferring the level of conflict resolution as well as decision making downward to the social actors themselves, another overload or erosion of the political system could be avoided.[42]

The strengthening of social actors may have been the *intention* of the Concertación government, but this is not what has actually happened.[43] Thus another reason for the CUT's disappointment with the Aylwin government relates to its conceptualization of socially concerted action and the degree to which social actors have in fact the freedom to elaborate policies on their own and how much the government is willing to grant them some participation in the implementation of these policies. The government's recognition of the CUT as the sole national labor organization was a political move to guarantee this organization's monopoly of representation for Chilean workers, but the government has not been willing to share decision making with the CUT, not even specifically in relation to labor policies, despite the close political relationship between CUT leaders and the parties of the Concertación.

Throughout the period of the Aylwin government, relations between labor and employers increasingly worsened due to the continued disagreements between the two sides. No advances were made beyond promises of goodwill and symbolic agreements already laid out in the first agreement in 1991. Chilean workers and organized labor continued to be troubled by tremendously adverse working conditions that were necessary for the survival of the neoliberal model put in place by the Pinochet regime. What is therefore important to mention as well are aspects that the reform of the labor legislation was never meant to touch on, although labor leaders did express their concern to government representatives at the time the reform was elaborated and have continued to do so ever since. I refer to transformations of the firm that were initiated by the middle and late 1970s. After their dismal experiences with the Allende regime, employers initiated a systematic process of production rationalization or, as some authors put it, embarked on the "neo-Taylorist road to modernization."[44] This entailed, among other things, the dismissal or relocation of workers within the same factory, the subcontracting of parts of the labor force, and the creation of so-called production chains whereby large and highly competitive firms were linked to medium and small firms that were mostly nonunionized and hence also employed cheap(er) labor. The imposition of the draconian labor legislation in 1979 can be seen as a functional element of these production changes insofar as it allowed and even encouraged the creation of parallel unions as well as the formation of so-called negotiating groups within the same firm, all of which severely restricted unions' collective power and thus created the legal basis on which employers could then deepen the rationalization process throughout the 1980s. All of these elements remained in place and continued to put limitations not just on organized labor but perhaps even more on nonunionized workers.[45] In fact, what workers witnessed in the 1990s was an intensification of the production process along with a *decline* in job security, work benefits, and participation in management decisions.[46] In essence then, Chilean labor witnessed a paradoxical situation: while outside their workplace they saw a return of democracy (they could vote, they no longer had to fear the police, etc.), inside their firm they continued to be subjected to the same if not worsening authoritarian working conditions.

In light of these conditions, it was difficult for labor to remain optimistic about its capacity to convince either the government or employers to return to the bargaining table and thus despite the Acuerdos Marco (the last to be signed was in 1994) and the reform of the Pinochet labor laws, for the Chilean labor movement, the Aylwin government came to a disappointing close and the first attempt at social concertation ended with meager results. To argue, however, that the government had attempted to preempt any changes in order to maintain a weak labor movement would be an exaggeration. The intention of the Aylwin government was *not* to totally thwart social concertation. Yet one cannot but help interpret the repeated and much publicized interruptions in the dialogue between the CUT and the Labor Ministry[47] as being symptomatic of the whole process. Thus what was lacking was a political will to move from political rhetoric to concrete policies via new state-labor-capital relations.

In retrospect, many efforts appear to have been more signs of goodwill than a concrete attempt at articulating more modern and ultimately more equitable labor relations. Perhaps the clearest, though by no means only, evidence to support this argument is the limited reform of the labor legislation. Thus a preliminary conclusion is that social concertation in Chile during Aylwin's government served different interests; perhaps most important on the government's agenda was the concern for governability and political stability during the first four years. But undoubtedly, the Aylwin regime also pursued an economic policy that was similar to the neoliberal model put in place by the Pinochet dictatorship. Foxley was right in 1990 in warning "the people" that the Concertación government was not going to repeat mistakes of the past and was not going to pursue populist policies. The government did promise, however, to reduce poverty, and that was accomplished.

Yet one cannot help but notice the strange alchemy of a center-left coalition government in pursuit of neoliberal policies *and* growth with equity and the fact that the magic formula to accomplish this was social concertation between state-labor and capital. Could this have worked? Were there not inherent tensions if not "contradictions" in this development strategy?[48] Some authors have pointed out that a center-left coalition government may have been destined to excessive consensus politics, which in turn radically diminished the Socialist and Christian Democratic parties' ability—or willingness—to offer more substantive if differing political, economic, and social viewpoints. Hence the great historic conflict between Chile's Center and Left was terminated, but at the cost of renouncing ideological differences that in the past constituted an "important engine for change"[49] and that brought about considerable socioeconomic progress, particularly for the urban working classes and rural poor. Thus, in light of the Aylwin government's interest in internationalizing the economy, its desire to increase competition, and its repeated calls for the need to rationalize production with more flexible and more aggressive production techniques, many labor leaders openly questioned how "the people could win."[50] Many believed that workers were unable to improve wages if their collective power and bargaining rights were so restricted and if employers had much more power than unions.[51]

For organized labor, social concertation was—and still is—perceived as a potentially fruitful attempt at growth with equity—that is, more equitable labor relations that would allow workers to participate in the gains of a growing economy. For employers, the idea of social concertation was—and still is—synonymous with a free market economy (the neoliberal model), hence their insistence throughout the 1990s on no "artificial" state intervention into the workings of market forces, on the one hand, and, on the other, their rejection of labor's demand for more equal participation in the management of the enterprise. Much of CPC's support of social concertation was therefore mere discourse. What really drove many employers to the bargaining table was their determination to preempt a labor legislation that would in their view prevent them from remaining competitive through low labor costs and extremely flexible and deregulated production systems. This strategy seems to have worked. Many Chilean employers were quite satisfied with the Aylwin government and had no complaints.[52] In fact many believed that a more conservative government (presumably a center-right coalition) would not have performed as well in economic terms, precisely because it would have faced a stronger opposition from labor and also from political parties of the Left.

As the following section attempts to show, neither the Frei nor the Lagos governments were any more successful than Aylwin in accomplishing this goal. Hence in terms of labor policies, there is little that differentiated one democratic government from the other . There is also little to indicate that after 1994, employers—and more specifically the largest employer association, the CPC—altered course with regard to its relations with unions and its commitment to create more equal and better relations with their workers. From 1992 to 2002, labor organizations have expressed the same demands: more participation in enterprise decisions and a more profound change in the labor legislation. Labor organizations then and now wanted to see a concerted effort at implementing growth with equity in Chile. Yet what many labor leaders seem to have seen was simply one side of the coin: economic growth, but no equity.

I begin with a brief account of the efforts at labor reform in Chile that culminated during the first year of the Lagos government (2000–2001). In a subsequent section I will show how the combination of weak labor reform and high labor market flexibility had adverse effects on labor organizations and their ability to reap greater benefits throughout the 1990s.

LABOR POLICY UNDER FREI (1994–2000)
AND LAGOS (2000–)

Throughout the 1990s the Concertación governments made the same claim. Aylwin's electoral platform stressed that "social justice, equity, and participation are obstructed by current labor institutions. These institutions put workers in a gravely unprotected situation. These institutions also prevent the constitution of strong and representative unions, as well as the development of an equitable and fair collective bargaining for labor."[53] Four years later, President Frei declared: "Labor policy constitutes an essential component of the modernizing dimension of the country, in a context of deepening democratization and socioeconomic development with equity and stability." He also stated that "[we] have two fundamental challenges with regards to labor policies: to contribute to a solid strategy of equitable socioeconomic development and productive modernization; and to guarantee the participation and active and permanent contribution of social actors in the design, implementation, and results of these policies."[54]

The fact that a full four years later, that is, *after* the reform of the labor legislation during Aylwin and one presidential term[55] into democracy, Frei thought it was necessary to reiterate a commitment to create "a more equal process of social and economic development" as well as his confession that his government had *yet* to "face the challenge to develop a modernizing strategy" with regard to labor policies, is a good indication of the government's own assessment of its progress along these lines. Yet such recognition came very late and already "well into the game." Moreover, Frei's language, and the vision (or reality) of state-labor-capital relations it entailed, constitutes an important *element of continuity* among all three governments (including that of Lagos). As will be shown, by 2001 the labor reform—once heralded as the core instrument to foster new state-labor–relations—had come to a dead end. It was now largely ignored by the media, no one in Congress was willing to give it any serious thought, employers were convinced that the economy and thus also workers could only benefit from a flexible labor market, while the Lagos government believed that much was accomplished with labor reform in Chile. The only group insisting that this could not be the end of it was the CUT. A quick review of what happened to some of the more important elements of the labor reform between 1994–2001 follows below.

Partially as a result of the realization that the Aylwin reform was indeed insufficient, and partially as a result of the CUT's criticism of the reform, the Frei government promised further changes that would be closer to labor organizations' expectations.[56] Only three days after assuming office, the government announced the ratification of Law 19.269. For the first time in Chile's history, public employees' associations were officially recognized as unions by granting them legal status within labor law. Prior to that, these groups (for example, teachers' and state employees' associations) had always enjoyed ambiguous legal status: de jure, they could not act as if they were unions—so any strike would be illegal—but de facto they had always done so. In addition to obtaining official union status, by the end of 1994, these "new unions" were granted the right to create "paritary commissions" on hygiene and safety issues (Law 19.345) and a year later they obtained the right to bargain collectively. In addition, the Frei government intended to make other amendments to the Aylwin reform.[57]

The guiding principle of the new proposal put forward by the Frei regime was to move toward a "protective" labor market.[58] Therefore, its reform proposed to amplify collective bargaining: working conditions, productivity goals, and negotiations with regards to issues such as product quality, and incentive pay could be included in collective bargaining. The Aylwin reform did not provide any room for such union initiatives and had left them up to the employer's goodwill. In short, under the proposed Frei reform, flexibility would have been more negotiated, not simply imposed by one side. This would have been quite significant, since any discussion concerning productivity was anathema to employers. However, quite contradictory to the first point, greater union input in collective bargaining would only be possible if both sides agreed to it. Unions could not force employers to include any of these themes in collective bargaining.

Another provision of the proposed Frei reform would have given so-called transitory unions the right to bargain collectively. In 1994 many of these unions could only present a written proposal but could not legally negotiate new terms. This new law would have been particularly relevant for construction workers and many of the mine workers who move from one place to another to set up the huge infrastructure to be used for mining. This law would have given workers a much desired weapon to defend themselves against the increasing use of temporary contracts in such important sectors as mining, agriculture, construction, and ports.[59]

Very importantly, Frei's proposed reform would have made it impossible for employers to replace striking workers. If passed, this provision would have put pressure on employers to come to an agreement with workers. The Aylwin law allowed employers to replace strikers from day 1, provided they had offered a new contract at 100 percent of the inflation rate. This new provision still would have given employers that option, but it also would have brought workers' economic demands into the negotiating realm more forcefully. Another provision stipulated that all workers engaged in collective bargaining would be protected up to thirty days after the bargaining, a ruling that would have given workers more employment protection.

Finally, the Frei proposal also included a stipulation that the employer must justify his/her position with regard to the union's demands. In other words, the employer could no longer simply reject union proposals; instead, the employer would have been forced to share much more information about the firm with the labor force. This projected new law did not stipulate precisely what kind of information the employer would have had to reveal however, so the employer would still have been able to exclude any item from the discussion that he/she deemed "confidential."

In sum, this new reform project sought to expand the scope of labor reform in democratic Chile and can therefore be seen as an attempt to move slightly away from a more flexible labor market regulation toward a more liberal and protective legislation. The state would have assumed a more protective role for labor interests and rights by specifically anchoring new, or expanded rights, in the labor code. Yet to a considerable degree these new rights were simply a frame of reference and would not necessarily have regulated outcomes, as demonstrated by the new collective bargaining law. This law would have given workers a reasonable assurance that they have at least certain minimum rights.[60] Direct negotiation between union and employer would have remained an important aspect of this new labor reform and this may have buttressed exactly the kind of labor-capital relations the first Aylwin government envisioned, as outlined in the first Acuerdo Marco.

Yet, because of strong employer opposition and the strength of probusiness parties in Congress, the entire Frei reform project to the labor legislation was rejected in Congress. The only consensus reached between government and opposition was with the so-called Arrate-Thayer agreement of 1997, which came as a result of two years of painful debate and a rejection of the reform proposal in the Senate in 1995. In 1997 the lower House of Congress passed a reform package but it was once again rejected in the Senate. After that, the reform proposal moved to a mixed Senate commission where, following the Arrate-Thayer agreement, the government was now willing to make major concessions to an intransigent political Right.[61] Even so, no agreement was reached and the reform remained stuck in a Senate committee until December 1999, when Frei wanted to see some concrete results prior to his departure. He reintroduced the reform project to the Senate where it was rejected for the third time. Thus the Frei government was not able to make any progress whatever in what constituted the core of its labor policy.

During his presidential campaign Lagos had already announced that he intended to bring the reform of the labor legislation to a successful end. Unlike Frei's proposal, which had included a dozen or more aspects, Lagos and his incoming labor minister, Ricardo Solari, focused on a handful of issues, most importantly the right to collective bargaining for transitory and interenterprise unions and the prohibition for employers to replace striking workers. In fact, Lagos and Solari felt so optimistic about chances for reform that after only one week in office they announced their determination to have what they considered the major remaining elements of the reform ratified by Congress within two months. Yet, aware of the history of labor reform in democratic Chile, the government also proceeded with caution. Part of the strategy was to bring employers and unions back to the bargaining table (the so-called Mesa de Dialogo). Instead of trying to push the reform through Congress—an unsuccessful approach taken by Frei in his last months in office—Lagos and Solari announced that if disagreements emerged, aspects of the reform could always be dealt with separately.[62] Yet Solari also made it clear that he was not willing to cede on a few crucial issues that the government considered "nonnegotiable." Among these were the prohibition on replacing striking workers.

Yet anyone who closely followed the political developments over the next year would come to the conclusion that there were no nonnegotiable issues for the government. Thus, two months later (May 2000), two important aspects of the reform package had been dropped, and neither the CUT nor the CPC had any idea that this was going to happen. What is more, by early July Solari declared that his government did not intend to "push" for a quick approval of the reform and that the prohibition on replacing striking workers—an aspect of the reform considered "nonnegotiable" in March—"was far from being the principal issue of the labor reform."[63] He also indicated the government's desire to see further progress with the reform through the Mesa de Dialogo (i.e., in direct negotiations between the CUT and the CPC). The government's inability to send clear signals as to which road it favored to take with the labor reform (i.e., either Congress or the Mesa de Dialogo) did not go down very well with business and opposition leaders. For example, by late August, Sofofa (Sociedad de Fomento Fabric) president Felipe Lamarca strongly criticized the government by arguing that "the signals [we receive] are wrong, and the policies incorrect."[64] He called on Lagos to give the private sector a clear definition of what the government intended to do with regard to the labor reform. And even though the government promised to accelerate the process, the offensive against the labor reform continued. Less than two weeks later, leaders of top employer and finance organizations such as the agricultural association SNA, the CPC, commerce, banking, and construction, met with Lagos and his team of ministers to inform them that the labor reform constituted "a change in the rules of the game [that would only] produce uncertainty and obstruct hopes for economic recovery."[65] The following day, Solari told the press that the meeting with business leaders had been "frank, open, and cordial." Furthermore, he announced that the government would drop "the more complex issues of the labor reform,"[66] including the prohibition on replacing striking workers. He did not address the issue of whether this dramatic turnaround came as a result of business pressure, though it seems highly likely that it did.

Over the next six months, the Senate's Labor Committee was busy fine-tuning the labor reform, so that by late March 2001, the government announced that the reform package was ready to be submitted to the entire Senate. And while some disagreements between the government and the opposition remained, the issue that had always divided them was now resolved: employers could continue to replace striking workers, but they would have to pay a small fine for doing so. Neither the CUT nor business leaders were happy with this outcome. Arturo Martínez believed that "in the end, pressure from employers and the Right convinced the government to soften the crucial aspects of the reform, these reforms do not help us." Eugenio Velasco, president of the Chamber of Construction, did not address what amounted to a major victory of employers, that is, their continued right to hire workers during a strike. Instead, he chose to point out that the 30-day job protection during collective bargaining introduced new rigidity into the labor legislation.[67]

In light of the constant pressure business exerted on the government, the Concertación was beginning to show some signs of fatigue as well as serious internal divisions, not just over the labor reform but also over the perceived need to do something about the state of the economy. Reports in September 2000 that unemployment was still at 10.2 percent came as a shock to Lagos and the Concertación.[68] Therefore, over the next two weeks, the government was busy trying to mend fences with members of the coalition. After a retreat Lagos held with all the senators of the Concertación, Senator Carlos Ominami (Socialist Party) announced that "the Concertación decided to end internal quarrels (especially those over the labor reform) and to seek the largest consensus possible." He also admitted that the current economic scenario had something to do with the government's decision to speed up the consensus finding by stating that "it is reasonable that during these times we prefer to have agreements (within the coalition)."[69] Interestingly, President Lagos did not even mention the labor reform in his important 21 May 2001 address,[70] a further indication that the government did not expect any major surprises from Congress. Indeed, on 11 September 2001, the Senate finally approved the labor reform.

It took the Lagos government exactly 18 months to end the reform of the labor legislation. This is not too long, but if one considers the fact that in many ways the process had started in March 2000, it would seem that 11 years of labor reform is excessive. Let us quickly look at some aspects of the reform.

As mentioned, the employers' right to replace strikers from day 1 of the strike is maintained provided they offer a wage rise at the level of inflation. Should an employer replace strikers, he/she has to pay a fine of approximately $100, payable to every worker that is replaced.[71] Employers have to reveal at least three months prior to collective bargaining "all necessary information" that unions or negotiating groups require in the preparation of their new contract demands. Specifically, unions have the right to request from the employer finance statements, including labor costs of all departments. The employer also has to hand over information with regard to investment plans. Although somewhat vague (and employers can therefore find ways to circumvent it), this stipulation does provide unions with better insights into their company's finances, though it still does not give unions greater input in collective bargaining. There is some improvement in employment protection, for collective bargaining as well as for regular employment periods. Should a labor court decide that a dismissal was not justified, the worker or the employee has to be reinstated. Previously, the employer had to pay severance but could not be forced to rehire the worker. All workers involved in collective bargaining now enjoy one month's job protection from dismissal once the new contract is signed.[72] The maximum period of severance pay remains at 11 months, but with the new reform it must be paid in one lump sum and can no longer be paid over an extended period of time. The minimum number of workers or employees required for companies to be forced to comply with Chilean safety and hygiene regulations was lowered from 25 to 10. Starting in 2005, weekly working hours will come down to 45, currently at 48. Extraordinary hours must be agreed on with a written contract. The contract cannot exceed three months but can be renewed by mutual agreement. Finally, the new legislation states that all part-time work enjoys the same rights as full-time work, including pay, minimum pay, social security, holidays, safety, and hygiene. This last point is indeed a major improvement compared to the previous scenario, in which employers frequently used workers for part-time jobs by way of subcontracting. At the same time, however, employers rejected the idea of granting part-time labor a contract; they opposed the idea that any limited contract should become a permanent contract the second time it is signed between the same parties. It remains to be seen whether this new law will limit employers' ability to fire workers before their contract expires, only to then hire them again as if they were really "new" workers—that is, workers that had never before worked for that company. In this way, employers may no longer be able to avoid paying benefits such as unemployment insurance or severance pay. Abuses of this sort were rampant in Chile. Many people were informed during their morning shift that—due to the needs of the firm—they are fired. In the afternoon, however, they were informed that they should nevertheless return during the next few days because the possibility existed that the firm could need them again.[73] And since temporary workers were not allowed to unionize, the new law may change that as well, and perhaps we shall see some efforts of Chilean workers to create new unions.

Finally, though not a part of the labor reform, in April 2000 the Lagos government introduced a new system of unemployment insurance, which Congress approved on 13 April 2001. This, too, was a long time in the making, as plans for an unemployment insurance had first emerged in 1992. Neither Aylwin nor Frei were able to make progress, but after nine years, the CUT and the CPC finally agreed with the proposals introduced by Lagos. After one year of debate, Congress ratified the new law. Unemployment benefits are paid for a maximum of 12 months. They are financed by the employer, the worker, and the state.[74]

COMPARING CHILEAN LABOR LEGISLATIONS

To give the reader a larger perspective by which to assess labor reform during the 1990s, it is useful to briefly present a historic trajectory of Chilean labor legislation.

In addition to severely restricting unions' ability to defend workers' interest by making use of the strike weapon, the Plan Laboral of 1979 also drastically limited the scope of collective bargaining by making subject to negotiations only the initial wage readjustments, the time period for inflationary adjustments (usually every three to four months), and the levels of inflation adjustments. Unions were strictly prohibited from including other topics in the negotiations that pertained to the "organization, direction, and administration of the firm" (article 82). Such narrowly defined collective bargaining had not always existed in Chile. In fact, the pre-1979 legislation allowed unions to discuss promotions, work crews, machinery, and other production-related issues.[75] What is more, the state was much more involved in industrial relations. For instance, between 1968 and 1974 trilateral commissions[76] fulfilled an important function. In the aftermath of the military coup, the Pinochet regime canceled the trilateral commissions' binding character and gave them only "advisory" status.[77]

Prior to 1973, the state also exercised an important role in other areas. For example, labor legislation stipulated that if the union staged a legal strike, the firm was not allowed to continue production.[78] Moreover, employers were not allowed to hire a new labor force. The freedom for employers to continue production during a strike was established only with the 1979 legislation, as could have been expected. And while the legislation prior to the Plan Laboral also included incentives for workers to disaffiliate themselves from their striking colleagues, it made their reinstatement to the workforce once the strike was over obligatory for employers (article 348). In sum, the changes brought about by the new labor legislation of 1979 put great limitations on workers' ability to negotiate favorable contracts with their employers, forced them to follow extremely complicated and narrowly defined bargaining processes, and decreased their opportunities for creating a strong network of organized unions.

The Aylwin labor legislation has important differences and parallels to the first labor laws enacted after 1924 and to the 1979 Plan Laboral of the military regime. First, one of the fundamental reasons for reforming the labor laws in the 1990s was to institutionalize a legitimate legislation that would help avoid a dangerous polarization of antagonistic interests that separated employers and workers. Fearing (or perhaps knowing) that employers would not fundamentally alter their behavior toward workers and unions without the control of the state, government authorities in 1924 as well as in 1979 and during the 1990s were fully aware that labor unions, then and now, would sidestep the legal constrictions and attempt to defend their interests and demands by other means. Hence the 1991–92 Aylwin reform was also an intent by the new democratic government to create an instrument that would allow the state to regulate and oversee labor-management relations despite the government's statement to the contrary (i.e., the "decongestion" of the state). The primary purpose was to obtain, or to induce, social peace. The greater the legitimacy of the labor laws, the greater the likelihood that employers and unions would abide by them, and the better the chances for peaceful coexistence.

Second, there are also interesting aspects that separate the new legislation (Aylwin's and Lagos's) from previous ones. The 1924 laws were enacted by the

Alessandri regime under pressure from rebellious military officers who were not so much interested in solving the social question as in improving their own lot and in depriving the hostile working classes of a fertile soil for their increasing agitations. The Pinochet regime decreed the laws in 1979 under an authoritarian regime. This leaves the reforms of the 1990s as the only ones implemented during a democratic regime. This distinction makes them all the more meaningful. The 1924 and certainly the 1979 legislation were created in the spirit of acquiring more state control over the laboring classes, limiting their capabilities of disturbing or threatening social peace, and, most important, reconciling their perceived hostile interests by integrating them into an institutionalized system of labor-management relations. The 1990s legislation presumably intended to open up a very closed and unequal industrial relations system to *strengthen* workers' organizations and to make this system fairer and more equal. Thus, from a historical perspective, the 1990s reforms to the labor legislation included elements that were difficult to reconcile with each other. The dilemma for the new democratic governments was therefore, on the one hand, to rewrite labor laws that would maintain state control over the organized working classes and, on the other, to receive employers' and workers' legitimate recognition and support for social concertation and to provide workers with a more effective weapon to defend their interests.

EXPLAINING THE FAILURE OF
SOCIAL CONCERTATION IN CHILE

As mentioned, some of the reasons why the Lagos government did not push for a more extensive labor reform had to do with continued employer resistance to the labor reform. Up until late 2000 employers believed that a reform of the Pinochet labor legislation was not good for the economy or their interests. Throughout the decade they were successfully defending their interests, at times walking away from the bargaining table, at times threatening the government, or workers, with the need to fire workers, and at times willing to make concessions. It is clear that, on balance, they got most of what they wanted within a context of slowed economic growth. CPC president Lamarca quite eloquently combined employers' defense of their interests with a subtle warning to the government and workers when, a few months into the Lagos presidency, he stated that "what the country and investors today need is [not a labor reform] but certainty and security with the rules of the games otherwise we are going to have a problem that is going to affect the way the entire country acts."[79] Perhaps it is an exaggeration to argue this, but for the most part, the worldview of employers, and especially those employers organized under the CPC, has not yet made the transition from Pinochet to democracy. Many continue to blame socialism and communism and the organized working class for bringing the country to the brink of civil war in September 1973, and many share a firm belief that it was Pinochet's neoliberal economy that rescued the country from Marxism and put Chile on the road to international economic success. In the end, employers were quite successful in convincing all three democratic governments that a reform of the labor legislation should under no circumstances go "too far" in the wrong direction. The fact that Lagos attempted another labor reform in the aftermath of the Asian crisis of 1997–98 and in the middle of an economic recession may have given employers additional arguments against the reform. Yet it is not clear that low labor costs and extremely flexible labor markets are a better recipe for economic reactivation than the increased purchasing power of the working classes leading to increased consumer demand. Moreover, if employers indeed thought that labor reform was bad during or after an economic recession, why did they oppose it during eight years of unprecedented economic growth?

Yet employer resistance alone does not account for the governments' inability to produce a labor reform akin to the one promised to labor in 1989. The political Right (Renovación National [RN] and Unión Democrata Independiente [UDI]), long an ally of Chile's capitalists,[80] along with influential conservative academic think tanks and a conservative media, have also been quite successful in creating a public discourse that complicated the Concertación's scenario and put it often on the defensive. Part of the political Right's strength derived from Pinochet's electoral system as well as the designated senators and so it was able to retain control of the Senate up until Lagos. The Right worried that a center-left government might attempt to revive its old relationship with the organized working class. These phantoms of the past help explain why many employers and many politicians within the UDI and the RN distrusted the government, and why they maintained a consistent antilabor attitude throughout the 1990s. What employers and the political Right have in common is a shared sense of history and an almost religious conviction that they were called on to defend Pinochet's legacy.[81] Yet even if the Right was a strong and recalcitrant political opponent, it does not mean that it was unyielding on all policy issues. For example, the UDI and the RN agreed to the early tax reform of March 1990, and they also agreed to important constitutional changes.[82] If the Concertación could bring the opposition to compromise on some issues, why did it fail to convince the Right and employers that a more profound labor reform was possible? In light of these important concessions, I argue that while historic and ideological aspects are a *necessary* element in the explanation of failed labor reform, they are not *sufficient* to account for the whole story.

By the time Lagos and Solari attempted further changes in early 2000, the Concertación government could no longer count on unconditional support from within its own ranks. Specifically, the Christian Democratic party was beginning to side with the opposition and feared that an additional reform would jeopardize a badly needed economic recovery. It believed that the creation of jobs along with employers' freedom to hire and fire workers, was more important than employment security, which in their view added excessive rigidity to the labor market. Some of this dissent within the Concertación had already emerged at the end of the Frei presidency, when some Christian Democratic senators opposed Frei's attempt to revive the reform.[83] It is thus quite ironic that at a time when the Concertación finally could legislate further reforms—for the first time since 1990 it enjoys a majority in the Senate—internal divisions made such change unlikely. For it was not the Christian Democratic party alone that began to question the merits of further labor reform. Lagos's own camp, the Left (Party for Democracy [PPD] and the Socialist party [PS]), showed signs of strain between those who still favored a reform and those who sided with the Christian Democrats. Thus, the official position of the Concertación today (2002) is that Chile needs to create a stronger economy capable of moving beyond the simple export of raw materials and many Concertación politicians have joined ranks with the moderate Right (Renovación Nacional) in their belief that the challenges Chile faces in an open and highly competitive environment can only be met if current labor market conditions prevail. So long as this labor market produces more jobs and relatively low labor costs, a weak labor movement may be an acceptable price to pay.

Any attempt to account for failed labor reform should mention the lessons drawn from the transition to democracy during the first democratic decade. In 1990 members and leaders of the Concertación believed that social concertation was fully compatible with the lessons they had learned from that history. In fact, social concertation was *necessary* to implement their new vision of a peaceful, consensual, and prospering society. However, the limits of labor's participation were not clear in 1990, though what was clear was the fact that Pinochet's constitution and the binomial majoritarian electoral system had given the opposition in Congress veto power to bloc any attempt to legislate "too much participation" for the labor movement. This uncertainty was not perceived as a threat to democracy. Quite the opposite, if labor and capital were able to build consensual relations, it would only help build trust, give capitalists confidence to invest, and avoid excessive labor strife of the sort witnessed between 1970 and 1973.

Thus to the Concertación governments a modern industrial relations system was primarily understood as being instrumental in character, a means to an end, with the end being the ability to avoid social conflicts. In many central and northern European countries, labor-capital relations are relatively consensual as a result of an industrial relations system that gives both sides great decision-making power, including on such important aspects as education of the work-force, national wage guidelines, retirement, and health benefits. Moreover, in Europe unions enjoy an enormous amount of collective bargaining power, and capital is willing to share information with workers. In Chile, by contrast, state-labor-capital relations were not able to move in any significant way beyond the level of intentions. Yet none of the democratic governments saw it that way. For, as long as labor and capital were willing to maintain a minimum of dialogue (which they did), and as long as the country was not plagued by too many strikes (it was not), the Concertación had little to worry about, and thus it would not share labor's demand to make more substantive progress. If consensus was already attained, what else was there to do?

This minimalist conception of an industrial relations system was well ex-pressed by then labor minister René Cortázar in 1991.[84] By that year's end, the CUT had already complained to Aylwin that it was deeply disappointed over the level of labor participation. Thus, looking back at the year and the apparent progress of state-labor-capital relations, Cortázar stated that "last year we dis-cussed readjustments. . . . This year we'll add unemployment insurance. In this way, we are establishing procedures to accomplish participation."[85] Yet the CUT and the CPC disagreed with the government's assessment, arguing that what happened was anything but participation, let alone the accomplishment of concrete goals. As one adviser to the CUT argued, "There has not been on part of the government a clear decision to grant . . . room for decision making. Moreover, there is a tendency to reduce the concept concertation to what has been produced in practice: a mixture of partial and strictly instrumental results, with a vague notion of dialogue which assimilates social concertation to the 'politics of agreement.' "[86] This understanding of social concertation was first articulated by Cortázar, then continued by Arrate under Frei and by Solari under Lagos.

A final factor that accounts for the democratic governments' merely instru-mental view of industrial relations[87] has to do with their excessive concern for consensus, which is in turn related to the structure of government set up in

1990.[88] The so-called supraparty governments of Aylwin, Frei, and Lagos enjoyed unprecedented autonomy from and influence over the coalition's political parties, another reflection of the lessons learned from the past, when the state was often held hostage by the party or party coalition in power. Aylwin, Frei, and Lagos all agreed that party political differences should be kept out of the executive as much as possible. Thus the subordination of political parties to a strong government produced a handful of key political players who enjoyed great decision-making powers and who shared a belief in pragmatic, non-ideological, and efficient "priority politics."[89] To the degree that the labor reform produced tension among state, labor, and capital, instead of consensus, it gradually lost relevance in the governments' agenda. What surprises a bit is that the governments got away with this strategy in a country where labor parties have a historic record of defending workers' interests. Yet the concerns of the labor movement were not irrelevant to the parties of the coalition. Precisely because the labor movement had played a supportive role in defeating Pinochet, it was not considered a "risk factor" by the incoming Aylwin government and the political parties of the Concertación. Therefore, while the social question was important to Christian Democrats and Socialists, it was not a particularly worrisome concern. What worried them more were the political Right and business, because the opposition by those two centers of power in Congress and their refusal to invest in the economy could seriously jeopardize the transition to democracy. This in turn could produce a degree of political and social instability, which the armed forces under Pinochet—himself a vital ally of the Right and capital—might interpret as a return to the days of August–September 1973 and might once again perceive as the need to "rescue" the country from itself.

These contingencies played an important role in the approach that political parties and their leaders would take to labor, to labor policy, and, importantly, to employers. It helps explain why the labor movement only occasionally—though quite tellingly at crucial political moments—showed up on the Christian Democrats' and Socialists' radar. I refer to the important union elections during the 1990s. During CUT congresses in 1991, 1996, and 1998, all parties of the Concertación attempted in one way or another to influence election outcomes. To a large degree they were successful if only in preempting undesirable outcomes.[90]

In sum, the major reasons for the failure of the labor reform in Chile and thus also for failed social concertation during the 1990s must be found in a combination of factors: First, employers' staunch opposition to the reform and their lack of interest—or need—in fostering better relations with workers; second, the political Right's support of employers as well as its fear and distrust of a strong labor movement; third, the Concertación's inability and unwillingness to push for a deepening of social concertation as promised in 1989 and repeatedly mentioned throughout the 1990s.

THE LABOR MOVEMENT EXPERIENCE IN DEMOCRATIC CHILE, 1990–2000

It should be stated at the beginning that it is not possible to look at a 10-year period and speak of one single experience. The Chilean labor movement has a complex structure. It includes various levels (from shop floor to CUT), important sectors of it are not even under the jurisdiction of the Labor Ministry, and so forth. Moreover, aggregate data on union membership, strikes, and the like are insufficient indicators of how workers "really do" and inadequately reflect their experience during the past 10 years.[91] In what follows I shall try to keep the statistical evidence to a minimum and make use of it only where relevant.

STRUCTURAL CHANGE AND INDUSTRIAL RELATIONS: SUBCONTRACTING AND TEMPORARY WORK

According to statistics from the Chilean Labor Directorate (DT) and PET (Programa de Economía y Trabajo) union affiliation consistently increased since the middle of the 1980s until 1992, after which it began to level off, with no significant increase in union members thereafter, although the number of unions continued to rise throughout the 1990s. See table 1.

It is interesting to note that between 1984 and 1995 the number of unions continued to rise in all economic sectors despite important economic changes that occurred in the same period. In 1995 the manufacturing sector was still by far the one with the most unions (3,424),[92] followed in second place by commerce (1,987), then transportation (1,953). The sector that showed the biggest growth rate was agriculture, having been able to more than double the number of unions by 1995 (from 765 to 1,787). Mining ranked close to the end of the list (445), though the number of unions alone may tell us little about the strength of these unions, which have historically been regarded as the strongest sector of Chilean organized labor. This is more readily apparent by taking into consideration not just the absolute number of unions in a sector but the rate of unionization per sector (number of union members over number of employed labor

Table I. Unions and Rate of Affiliation, 1986–2001

Year	Number of Unions	Union Members	Waged Labor Force	Rate of Affiliation
1986	5,391	386,907	2,717,500	14.2%
1987	5,883	422,302	2,798,500	15.1%
1988	6,446	446,194	2,944,900	15.2%
1989	7,118	507,616	3,019,600	16.8%
1990	8,861	606,812	3,063,100	19.8%
1991	9,858	701,355	3,134,600	22.4%
1992	10,756	724,065	3,295,400	22%
1993	11,389	684,361	3,472,500	19.7%
1994	12,109	661,966	3,422,700	19.3%
1995	12,715	637,570	3,482,610	18.3%
1996	13,258	655,597	3,713,080	17.7%
1997	13,795	617,761	3,787,650	16.3%
1998	14,276	611,535	3,758,600	16.3%
1999	14,652	579,996	3,786,680	15.3%
2000	14,724	595,495	3,750,270	15.9%
2001	15,134	605,363	3,763,980	16.1%

Source: Dirección del Trabajo, *Informes de conflictividad: Serie años 1989–2000, huelgas legales en negociaciones colectivas*. Santiago: Dirección del Trabajo, Departamento de Estudios, 2002.

force in sector). Thus by far the leader in terms of affiliation was mining (at 65.7 percent), followed by utilities (gas, electricity, water; 49 percent), transportation (40.9 percent), manufactures (28.3 percent), commerce (20.1 percent), financial services (14.2 percent), agriculture (13.5 percent), and construction (13.4 percent).[93]

From this angle, one could make the argument that the "strongest" sector of the Chilean labor movement is mining, followed by transportation and manufacture. This is, by and large, a reasonable conclusion, though it omits a few considerations that complicate this assessment. Take for example, construction. By rate of affiliation, this sector ranked eighth, which would make it a rather weak sector of the labor movement. In addition, due to Chile's labor laws, union workers in the construction sector are considered "temporary unions" and thus do not have the right to bargain collectively.[94] Any strike is considered illegal and can be severely punished, such as by firing all the labor force or those perceived to be the agitators. And yet throughout the 1990s this sector was considered one of the strongest together with manufacture and mining. Why? The unions in the construction sector, particularly those in the Santiago area, had well-organized federations that were not divided politically and a radical leadership critical of the Concertación governments. Historically, the Communist party was the strongest party in the construction sector (and important in mining and manufacture). So what makes these unions so strong? In part it is their radical politics. Unlike many union leaders that are closer ideologically or politically to the Concertación governments, these leaders have maintained their "political autonomy." In fact, they had even criticized the Pinochet regime as early as 1973 and continued their protests with little change in language since 1990.

At first sight, it may look as if mining is "in good shape."[95] After all, these unions managed to affiliate close to two-thirds of the labor force in the sector. What has not been mentioned, however, is that historically, that sector's affiliation was *even higher* (86.6 percent in 1992 and 80.2 percent in 1990). Thus what happened in mining was a decline of the organized labor force: between 1988 and 1994 the sector suffered a 15 percent loss in its affiliation, while agriculture gained more than 6 percent and construction 8.3 percent. Between 1988 and 1995, mining lost more than 6,500 union members. Therefore, in terms of union strength, the question is which factors (political autonomy, increased affiliation, legal status, etc.) matter most for which economic sector and particularly for which specific union within each sector? One thing is certain, however: during the 1990s it became increasingly difficult for unions to recruit and keep rank-and-file members. In light of the fact that employment in mining increased slightly, this decline is all the more important.

Mining has become one of the leading sectors in the use of temporary work, subcontracting, and even employment without contract. For example, a study published by Mideplan (Ministerio de Planificación y Cooperación) indicates that by 1996–97, approximately 22.3 percent of the salaried labor force was employed without contract (it should be added that the bottom 20 percent of the income ladder make up almost 40 percent of noncontract labor).[96] Moreover, statistics can hide important differences between economic sectors and between individual firms of differently sized labor forces. For example, the 1994 Casen survey[97] reported that the manufacturing sector had on average 14 percent of its labor force without contract, although, again, within the sector significant differences exist as well, in some cases reaching 24 percent and more than 31 percent in others.[98] The percentage of workers without contract is consistently high for agriculture and fisheries (36 percent), although construction, a sector that has grown consistently throughout the 1990s, also employs a significant part of its labor force without contracts (approximately 27 percent).

A survey conducted by the Dirección del Trabajo in the Santiago metropolitan area shows that among those firms that make use of subcontracting (roughly half of those interviewed), mining was the leading sector. A full 80 percent of these employers stated that they made use of it. The comparative percentage for manufacture was 47 percent.[99] Subcontracting has increased more moderately in the Gran Minería, but that has probably something to do with the fact that most of this division is state-owned. The reader should be informed that subcontracted workers can unionize only in unions *exclusively* for subcontracted labor, and workers have made use of this right but have often faced opposition from employers. Employers frequently intimidate workers who are interested in forming such unions and often have to deal with tremendous organizational difficulties in getting the rank and file together at the same firm at the same time. This is why subcontracting companies were not shy in promoting themselves as "union-free" companies to potential clients.[100]

A WEAK LABOR MOVEMENT, FEW ECONOMIC GAINS

As mentioned, in Chile, collective bargaining is a very complex institutional arrangement, not only separating unions into those that can and cannot bargain collectively but further separating those who *can* bargain collectively into those who have the legal right to strike and those who do not (i.e., *contrato colectivo* and *convenio colectivo*). In practice, under a convenio arrangement, the union simply accepts the employer's last offer. Thus, while at first glance it may seem "normal" that approximately 75 percent of all organized Chilean workers have the right to strike, this picture quickly changes when we take into consideration this difference. Thus, at any moment during the 1990s, only about 7–12 percent of *all* employed workers in Chile could bargain collectively.[101] Moreover, while among enterprises with 50 or more workers, roughly 36 percent could bargain collectively, in enterprises with less than 50 workers—the typical Chilean size—that number was 1.3 percent. It is also interesting to point out that the number of contracts as well as the number of workers covered under this type of collective bargaining (as compared to the "convenio" type) started to decline in 1994. This could indicate that with the end of the labor reform under Aylwin, or, to be precise, with no hopes in sight that Aylwin and labor minister René Cortázar might include the provision that would make it more difficult for employers to replace strikers, many unions may have begun a trend to opt for a convenio rather than a contrato. Though this leaves the union in a weaker bargaining position, since a convenio does not entail any real collective bargaining or the right to strike, it also makes the union appear less aggressive, and this may increase employers' willingness to compromise.[102] But all of this is very uncertain—a point made by CUT leaders to all three democratic governments.

An interesting way to reveal unions' weak bargaining position is to look at the wage increases they were able to obtain from employers. See table 2.

Table 2 shows that the number of unions involved in collective bargaining increased with the return to democracy. There was a big difference between the 1980s and 1990s in terms of the number of collective bargaining rounds. This is in itself a positive change. However, there was little change in terms of "the deal" unions were able to strike in collective bargaining. To begin, there was a tendency toward shorter readjustment of wages for inflation periods, and that is a good sign as well. During the 1980s, the average period spanned six to seven months, whereas in the 1990s, the average readjustment period shortened by about one month. Yet the average future wage increase has been consistently below the inflation rate. This does not mean that unions could not obtain wage raises equal to or even higher than inflation during collective bargaining. It does mean, however, that as inflation persists, automatic wage readjustments were below the inflation rate. This put enormous pressure on the union to obtain a relatively high initial wage rise that is "sufficiently" above inflation so that over the course of a two-year contract inflation will hopefully not be able to catch up with their wages. In practice, initial raises varied by economic sector. Statistics from the Dirección del Trabajo show the following results for the years 1997–98 (July–June): Manufacture: increase from 1.68 percent to 1.77 percent; agriculture: decrease from 1.99 percent to 1.77 percent; mining: decrease from 1.56 percent to 0.57 percent; utilities: decrease from 1.56 percent to 1.19 percent; construction: decrease from 1.36 percent to 0.52 percent; commerce: decrease from 1.15 percent to 0.90 percent; transport: decrease from 1.29 percent to 0.42 percent.[103] Hence not all economic sectors were able to obtain initial wage increases above the inflation rate. In fact, miners, construction workers, and commerce and transportation workers who negotiated contracts between July 1997 and June 1998 witnessed a slow but steady erosion of the initial wage rise. These examples show that the increase in wages was often just barely above the inflation rate, and if the future readjustment is taken into consideration, wages

Table 2. Collective Bargaining: Number of Unions, Future Wage Increases, and Wage Readjustment Periods, 1985–1997

Year	Number of Unions Involved in Collective Bargaining	Future Readjustment (% of inflation)	Readjustment Periods (months)
1985	1,417	91.56	7.12
1986	1,039	95.27	6.75
1987	1,749	96.75	7.02
1988	1,319	98.75	6.49
1989	2,342	99.49	6.14
1990	2,420	99.16	6.03
1991	2,905	99.44	6.15
1992	2,809	99.65	5.90
1993	3,043	99.90	6.01
1994	2,716	99.78	6.13
1995	2,762	99.78	5.88
1996	2,550	99.84	5.69
1997	2,774	99.92	6.03

Source: Patricio Frías, "Perspectiva del estado de las relaciones laborales en Chile: Del gobierno autoritario a la transición democratica." Santiago: Dirección del Trabajo, Departamento de Relaciones Laborales, 1998.

continued to be right at the level of the inflation rate. These numbers, admittedly only samples, refer specifically to unionized workers but should be kept in mind when considering statistics on the labor force in *general*. Here, the picture is slightly different. Real wages during the 1980s were at about 85–92 percent of the 1970 level. Around 1990–91, they began to show improvement: 96.9 percent in 1991, 101.3 percent in 1992, 105 percent in 1994, 109 percent in 1995, and 117.4 percent in 1996.[104] This generally positive trend varied again by sector. Compared to their 1980 levels, in 1995, manufacture was at 111 percent, utilities at 103 percent, construction at 113 percent, commerce at 112 percent, transportation at 108 percent, finance services at 107 percent, but mining only at 99.3 percent. Real wages in mining were actually high in 1989–92 (average 120 percent of 1980 levels) but then dropped precipitously in 1994 to 99.2 percent. It is very likely that during the 1990s, real wages improved for most workers.

However, the improvement was not big, and there was, as noted, variation across sectors. One could argue that the economic crises witnessed in Brazil, Argentina, and Chile in the aftermath of the "Asian crisis" of 1997–98 had something to do with the poor showing of real wage increases for Chilean workers. But all the statistics cited point to a consistent and hence more important long-term trend: for organized labor, wage increases tended to be uncomfortably close to the level of inflation. Therefore, combining initial and future readjustment levels depicts a less favorable but more precise image than the one given by statistics on improvements in real wages for all workers. The meager results are an important corrective to aggregated statistics and should be taken as a reason for concern, particularly with regard to conflicts between unions and employers, a point to be made in what follows.

Even though collective bargaining is generally thought to be a very important aspect of industrial relations, we have seen that, when measured by its size (i.e., the number of workers and unions involved) and by its effectiveness (i.e., the type of economic deal it affords unions), the Chilean case cannot easily be categorized as either significant or effective. This is not to say, however, that collective bargaining and industrial relations cannot be effective in other ways, for example, in the prevention of open industrial conflict (strikes) or employers' ability to deal with a "radical" labor force. Based on what we have seen about labor reform in Chile, it should come as no surprise that during the 1990s, the country witnessed few strikes. See table 3.

According to the figures in table 3, there was a decrease in the number of strikes after 1993, which was the first year of the new labor reform. The number of strikes leveled off in subsequent years to a low of 108 in 1999 and 125 in 2000. Strikes lasted on the average 12 days, which is not a particularly long period. But this may have more to do with union finances or other issues than with the nature of the conflict that caused the strike to emerge in the first place. Better information is needed to make more precise arguments with regard to strike behavior during those years. In general, however, there was a relative labor acquiescence in democracy and a low level of open conflicts between unions and employers.

Yet this labor peace of the last decade may also be more a result of unequal relations of power between union and employer than a reflection of genuine consensus between both sides. To recall, even though the Lagos government promised that it would make it more difficult for employers to fire workers, this is not what happened, as my discussion of the 2001 labor reform has shown. Thus employers still have the right to replace a striking labor force provided they offer wage readjustments at least at the level of inflation, for which the

Table 3. Number of Strikes, Strikers, Average Size, and Average Duration, 1983–2000

Year	Number of Strikes	Number of Workers Covered by Contract	Number of Workers on Strike	Average Workers per Strike	Average Strike Length in Days	Average Days per Worker per Strike
1983	36	n.a.	3,571	99	13	n.a.
1984	38	n.a.	3,595	95	12	n.a.
1985	42	n.a.	8,532	203	21	n.a.
1986	41	n.a.	3,940	96	15	n.a.
1987	81	n.a.	9,913	122	14	n.a.
1988	72	n.a.	5,645	78	14	n.a.
1989	101	140,426	17,857	177	16	2,956
1990	176	138,478	25,010	142	15	1,393
1991	224	200,482	46,215	206	12	3,276
1992	247	157,944	26,962	109	12	1,355
1993	284	175,966	25,098	112	12	1,393
1994	196	156,125	16,209	83	13	1,171
1995	187	145,958	24,724	132	12	1,872
1996	183	157,565	25,776	141	10	1,282
1997	171	129,628	19,278	108	10	1,198
1998	121	112,829	12,608	104	10	1,021
1999	108	97,461	10,667	99	12	956
2000	125	119,388	13,227	106	9	914

Source: Dirección del Trabajo, *Informes de conflictividad: Serie años 1989–2000, huelgas legales en negociaciones colectivas*. Santiago: Dirección del Trabajo, Departamento de Estudios, 2002; Patricio Frías, "Sindicatos en la transición: En la busqueda de una nueva identidad." In *Economia y Trabajo Informe Annual, 1993–1994*. Santiago: pet (1994): 55–73; Patricio Frías, "Perspectiva del estado de las relaciones laborales en Chile: Del gobierno autoritario a la transición democratica." Santiago: Dirección del Trabajo, Departamento de Relaciones Laborales, 1998.

right to replace strikers became a nightmare for unions. Throughout the 1990s Chilean employers not only replaced and ultimately fired strikers; they also made use of their legally guaranteed right to fire workers if it was in the "need of the firm."

Thus the labor law makes it very easy for employers to invoke that prerogative and to get rid of union members who participate in a strike. Union leaders often point out that employer abuse in firing workers is still very prevalent, while employers tend to defend themselves by arguing that since the firm is their property it is their right to do whatever they want with it. Given the character of the new labor laws created since 1990, collective bargaining (and strikes) are still seen by many union leaders as an ineffective weapon.[105] Data published by the Dirección del Trabajo in 1996 confirm workers' fears that the new labor laws do not really protect their right to collective bargaining. A survey conducted among union leaders representing more than 5,500 firms found that a full 32.2 percent of all workers who participated in collective bargaining—and not in a strike—had been fired by their employers not more than three months after the negotiation. Among those firms in which more than 70 percent of the labor force participated in collective bargaining, 40 percent of the labor force was fired after the first month simply because they participated in collective bargaining, a legally guaranteed right, though a right many employers continue to see more as a threat to private property and respond to accordingly.

Finally, collective bargaining is not only a rare and oftentimes inefficient if not dangerous instrument for unions, it is also of very limited scope. Again, only Frei attempted to "open up" collective bargaining somewhat to include other issues, while neither Aylwin nor Lagos were willing to move beyond what was inherited from Pinochet's Plan Laboral. From the beginning in 1990 the CUT favored a more open negotiation that could also include aspects such as informing the unions about the financial situation of the firm. Union leaders attempted to convince employers that it was also in their interest to share vital information with the union. After all, it would help unions to make more "realistic" wage demands that would diminish the risk of ruining the firm financially.

The idea to open collective bargaining by sharing more information with unions would make sense from a perspective that attempts to improve labor relations. Among others, more information shared should help improve trust among the sides, it should allow for more effective collective bargaining,[106] and it should give the union more opportunities to participate in the life of the firm. However, employers' continued categorical rejection of any chances for increased participation of the union in enterprise decision making can be illustrated by the fact that just in 1994 more days or workers' hours were lost to work-related accidents—which worker participation could reduce, though that would entail including the matter in collective bargaining agreements—than to strikes.[107] Thus the 1990s have not seen any fundamental change in the way employers approach collective bargaining. Therefore, there has also not been any change in the unions' ability to use collective bargaining as an effective tool to raise wages or to improve working conditions.

THE LABOR MOVEMENT'S
APPROACH TO SOCIAL CONCERTATION

In the last part of this discussion it is necessary to focus a little more on the Chilean labor movement itself. This is in part a result of my conviction that it would be inaccurate (and unfair) to solely blame the new Chilean governments and the employers for the dismal results of social concertation. Chilean union leaders, too, are in part to be blamed for the outcome. Perhaps the most important questions to ask are these: Why did the CUT lend itself to agreements such as the Acuerdo Marco when in fact these were mostly symbolic and had little concrete benefits for the CUT and its affiliated workers? Why did the CUT not pressure the government and/or the employers for more concessions with regard to social concertation in general and the reform of the labor legislation in particular? Can we deduce from the outcome, and the CUT's criticism of it, that the labor movement had attempted all it could but had indeed been unable to prevent the outcome? What are the consequences of failed social concertation for the CUT and the labor movement?

Why the CUT consented to the symbolic agreements is easy to answer with hindsight. At the time, that is, barely three months into the first democratic regime, it seemed that these agreements could really be the beginning of new industrial relations in Chile. In addition, these agreements should be seen in their historic moment, that is, given the CUT's role in the demise of the authoritarian regime and the return to democracy, its leaders had reason to believe that the CUT was indeed going to play a major role in the democratization period. This aspect cannot be separated from yet another historic dimension, that is, the close relationship between the labor movement and the political parties that came to power in 1990. Thus, CUT leaders had reason to believe that their historic allies were serious in their promises and "speaking the same language" in terms of establishing concerted action in Chile.

The earliest sign that things were not going to go that easily for the CUT in the new democracy was the result of the December 1989 elections, in which, because of Pinochet's designated senators and the binominal electoral system, the rightist opposition obtained a majority in the Senate. Hence CUT leaders understood that the coalition government needed to "rationalize its agenda,"[108] particularly with regard to the labor reform, otherwise there may not have been any reform at all. Most of the top leaders in the CUT therefore went along with this interpretation of the political reality at the time. As far as the elaboration of the labor reform is concerned, the CUT and the CPC did originally sit down to negotiate a revision, but they soon ran into an impasse. Fearing that its plans for "democracy on the installment plan" might be delayed (or derailed), the government was quick to take the reform out of the hands of the CUT and the CPC and decided unilaterally to take it to Congress, where a quicker compromise solution was worked out within approximately one year.

As to why the CUT did not pressure the government into more concessions: the political-ideological identification of the CUT leadership with the political parties in government (all of which are traditional allies of the labor movement) led these leaders to identify too much with the success of the Aylwin government, even if that meant—paradoxically—a loss for their organization.[109] Some commentators have interpreted this as a situation in which "the leadership of the trade union movement has willingly become 'labor lieutenants of the capitalist class' and "an instrument of the Aylwin government."[110] Arguments such as these are not without some truth. Undoubtedly the CUT leadership was too much under the influence of political parties, yet I would argue that the leadership was not a mere "transmission belt" for political parties. The leadership had more autonomy than some observers might think (though the CUT had less autonomy than its leadership wanted us to believe).[111]

Therefore, while political identification with the Concertación parties may count as a reason, there may yet be another ideological factor at work here. The union leadership, too, has learned from its past. This explains why the CUT leadership insisted so much on consensus and cooperation, rather than, even when necessary or appropriate, dissent and confrontation.[112] Moreover, the CUT may have been unwilling to pressure for more concessions, but it was also unable to do so because it lacked the necessary strength to pressure the government and/or the employers into a deepening of concerted action. This inability was also due to a structural problem related to the very decentralized nature of Chilean unionism. Top-down decisions are difficult to impose, a fact that never escapes employers or the government. Therefore the CUT could not simply call for strikes, unless these were meant to be illegal. Few if any plant-level leaders, however, were willing to risk having their rank and file fired. That left massive mobilizations as the only alternative. Yet the CUT knew full well, at least until

1994, that few plant-level unions would heed its call for protests. Hence, from a strategic perspective, it would have been extremely unwise to call for mobilizations. This explains why the CUT leadership threatened to but never actually called on its rank and file to protest. In essence, it was a strategic game played between the CUT and the government. On the one hand, as long as the CUT did not have to prove that it was weak, it could continue its threats, which the government knew were just that. Yet, on the other hand, it was also in the government's interest to somehow respond to these threats so as not to force the CUT into revealing its weakness, since that would have entailed a political cost for the government and in all likelihood would have forced it to come to the rescue of its historic ally. That in turn would have forced it to make concessions to employers as well, or otherwise be accused of once again committing historic mistakes and, what is perhaps worse, losing the little influence that the government had over business.

Ultimately, the CUT never succeeded in finding a solution to this dilemma. Thus, at the end of the decade, it took a precipitous dive in terms of its relevance as an important player in the new democracy. Between 1990 and the end of the decade, the CUT continuously proposed initiatives, such as a new unemployment insurance, reform of health care, and of course the labor reform. At times, the CUT managed to mobilize workers to stage massive mobilizations, such as those that took place on 11 July 1994 (Dia de Dignidad, to protest the slow progress in the labor reform), 23 October 1995 (Dia de Dignidad del Trabajador Publico, to protest the conditions of public employees for which almost 400,000 workers and employees took the streets), 4 November 1997 (to protest the deadlocked negotiations over the labor reforms and unemployment insurance), and 20 November 1997 (to protest privatizations). The issue here is not so much the CUT's ability to mobilize workers to protest. The numbers show that the CUT was able to do that. The problem is rather of a qualitative nature. The CUT needed to make use of extraordinary steps such as a call for national strikes in order to be considered a serious player, but once the call was made, it was unclear how to make further progress. Often, the CUT walked away from the bargaining table feeling empty-handed because its proposals were rejected. On top of this, the CUT could make only sporadic use of threats, since a more frequent call to mobilizations would have resulted in a poor(er) turnout and thus would have weakened even further the CUT's ability ("poder convocatorio") to mobilize its members (the 1997 protests were disappointing since fewer than expected workers showed up). The risk of diminishing returns became a reality, yet the CUT leadership had no ready-made recipe to deal with this. Instead, it adopted a dual discourse (and few actions), swinging pendulum-like between open confrontation and cooperation with government and business. Ultimately this turned into a series of "missed opportunities"[113] and a loss of "negotiating space" in which to maneuver.

This outcome was not inevitable. But the CUT would have had to rely much more on organization building to avoid such a result. Early in the Aylwin government the CUT announced that it hoped to have 1 million members within a couple of years. This was by no means unrealistic, but in order to reach that number, the CUT would have had to more than double its membership. The circumstances to do this were unusually favorable: a growing economy, the euphoric climate among a majority of the population, the presence of a labor-friendly government, the national attention to the "social question" in general and to the "labor question" in particular. Yet the CUT failed to reach its goal; in fact, by the end of 1992, the increase in membership had already slowed down and by mid-decade, membership began to decrease. This is all the more dramatic if we compare CUT membership rates to plant-level unions and especially to federations and confederations. Both in terms of rank-and-file membership and number of unions, the labor movement grew throughout the decade. Rank-and-file affiliation and number of federations more than doubled, and the number of confederations and membership increased by no less than a third between 1990 and 1995. Most important, during the second half of the decade, public sector unions maintained a high profile of protest and staged numerous illegal and legal strikes in 1996 and 1997.[114] One of these unions, the Colegio de Profesores, staged a national mobilization in 1996 that was so impressive that observers compared it to ones "the country had not seen since the days of Allende."[115]

Consequently, while intermediate and low-level union organizations were able to grow spectacularly, the CUT enjoyed a brief period of growth, which then quickly declined. Outside Santiago, the CUT was unable to establish a national presence. The CUT has headquarters in many regions, but in most cases these regional organizations exist on paper only. Moreover, the CUT remained a financially poor organization whose leadership could not afford to work full-time for the organization (though this is in part also a result of the legislation that does not provide the CUT with member fees). This condition was thus both a cause and a consequence of the CUT's failure to strengthen its organizational reach. The CUT has not been able to convince its affiliates to increase their membership dues, though it did make an attempt at the 1991 Congress. Many affiliates pay, but many do not; few union officials oversee the payment system and nobody enforces it. This organizational weakness has had far-reaching negative consequences. Paradoxically, CUT leaders, particularly

Manuel Bustos and Arturo Martínez, tended to complain about a labor movement that was unwilling to "fight" ("entreguismo") and that had no clear strategies, though as I argued elsewhere this was an erroneous assumption.[116] Rather than reflecting the reality of plant-level unions, this false impression reveals the degree of "distance" that the leadership had put between itself and its followers, who increasingly perceived the CUT as "too political, not willing to fight, and elitist."[117]

CONCLUSIONS

This chapter examines the decade-old experience of the Chilean labor movement in the new democracy. I argue that Chile's version of social concertation has failed and that as a result the labor movement has not become an equal partner in a new industrial relations system. The limits of the 1990s experiment are particularly evident in the new and not-so-new labor legislation that was the stated centerpiece of state-labor-capital relations. All three democratic governments—those of Aylwin, Frei, and Lagos—proclaimed that the success of the new democracy hinged to a very large degree on the ability to create, through concerted action among state, labor, and capital, a fairer and more equal industrial relations system, but none of the three delivered it. Although employer intransigence and weak government support played a role, I also argue that the failure to accomplish a deepening of democracy—particularly in its social dimension—reflected labor's own behavior during the first democratic decade. Specifically, the top leaders of the CUT were unable to subordinate their political identification with the Concertación to the more important organizational needs of the labor movement. Such "ordering of the political affairs" might have resulted in a greater ability to win concessions from employers and the governments, and it might have allowed the CUT to remain the important social and political actor it was in the years just prior to 1988.

It is premature to write off the CUT completely. To the degree to which it remains an important political-electoral ally of the Concertación, political parties may be well advised to occasionally "check back" with their unionists. If that check can take place in a more constructive way than the one demonstrated during union elections of the 1990s, so much the better for the labor movement and the parties. But for better or worse, the CUT is not synonymous with the labor movement. Depending on the kind of organization (federation, public sector unions, or plant-level unions), the 1990s witnessed some successes, particularly in the form of new unions that can bargain collectively or go on strike. But overall, the experience of most workers and unionists in the new democracy has been disappointing. For, regardless of some modest economic gains that were made by one or the other sector, for most workers, relations with employers are precarious. Fear and authority rather than trust and participation characterize labor relations. Working conditions are such that uncertainty, pressure, and a constant willingness to make concessions prevail rather than a feeling of respect for workers' contributions. In short, the quality of a worker's work life in Chile's new democracy leaves much to be desired and may be lower today than it was in 1990. What is all the more worrisome is the degree to which politicians of the Concertación increasingly share the same language with the political opposition and employers—as they have done over the past four years, even though the supposedly prolabor Lagos assumed the presidency in 2000. Hence, to no one's surprise, there is much talk in Chile today of "growth," and few remember that it once was a discourse of "growth with equity."

By far the most important factors responsible for failed social concertation are the employers' staunch resistance to modify the existing industrial relations system and the inability or the unwillingness of the new democratic governments to get them to do so. In the eyes of many employers, and particularly those of the CPC, the 1990–92 changes to the Pinochet labor reform were unnecessary and threatened the very survival of private enterprise. Little has changed since those days. The return to democracy has not meant a greater willingness on the part of employers to grant labor more participation in the enterprise. The Chilean employer's limited commitment to more democracy in the factory or nationwide has important implications for our understanding of transitions and democratization. Evidence from the Chilean case shows that a deepening of democracy—O'Donnell's second transition—may not be possible if important sectors of society oppose it. Moreover, short of nationalizing the economy (which is completely unlikely), there is little the government may be able to do. In other words, democracy without "semidemocrats" may be possible and even sustainable in the long run. As neoliberal ideology finds more and more supporters among Chile's governments, there are fewer and fewer voices calling for some "intervention" in the economy.

But this is not exactly the Chilean scenario. In Chile, for the most part, government representatives have praised employers' "commitment to progress" and have by and large ignored labor's complaints. Due in large part to its interpretation of twentieth-century Chilean history and the breakdown of democracy, the Chilean political elite has been quick to embrace an idea of sociopolitical and economic development whose two pillars are growth and equity. In that, politicians of the Concertación and leaders of the labor movement are speaking the same language. But the CUT and the governments have pursued different objectives. This, too, has important implications, as the Chilean case demonstrates the degree to which former Socialist labor parties can "renovate" themselves to embrace capitalism at the cost of labor. Moreover, if new democratic governments are not seriously committed to improving a "balance of power" that favors one side, democratic institutions may be undermined and actors may diminish their allegiance to democracy. This disloyalty to democracy acquired dramatic proportions in Chile's past and ultimately produced a society so polarized that democracy could not be sustained. Therefore, the current industrial relations system in Chile has a potential for social and political instability. Although Chile is being touted as the model to follow, other countries in the region may therefore question the wisdom of following the failed Chilean version of social concertation.

NOTES

The author wishes to acknowledge Peter Winn and Joel Stillerman for their careful reading and useful commenting on earlier versions. I also wish to thank Edward Epstein and two anonymous readers for their comments on the original version. None of them bear any responsibility for the shortcomings this chapter may have.

1 The list is too long to do justice to those who have written on the subject. See for example Louis Carlos Bresser-Pereira, Jose María Maravall, and Adam Przeworski, *Economic Reforms in New Democracies: A Social Democratic Approach* (New York: Cambridge University Press, 1993); James Petras, Fernando I. Leiva, and Henry Veltmeyer, *Democracy and Poverty in Chile: The Limits to Electoral Politics* (Boulder: Westview Press, 1994).

2 This is not the place to compare these more recent attempts at social concertation with earlier experiences of "corporatism," "neocorporatism," or similar versions of concerted action as witnessed both in Europe and Latin America. For a rich discussion of empirical and theoretical issues of these cases, see, among others, Philippe Schmitter, "Modes of Interest Intermediation and Models of Societal Change in Western Europe," in *Trends toward Corporatist Intermediation*, ed. Philippe Schmitter and Georg Lehmbruch (London: Sage, 1979), 63–94. See also Wolfgang Streek "Organizational Consequences of Neo-Corporatist Co-operation in West German Labor Unions," in *Patterns of Corporatist Policy-Making*, ed. Georg Lehmbruch and Philippe Schmitter (Beverly Hills: Sage, 1982), 29–81.

3 In the following, I shall use "social concertation," "socially concerted action," and "concerted action" interchangeably.

4 Huber and Berensztein call this the neoliberal model (as compared to the social democratic model). Bresser-Pereira, Maravall, and Przeworski (in *Economic Reforms in*

New Democracies) express a similar idea in their notion of the neoliberal "Washington" approach (as opposed to the "pragmatic" or, once again, social democratic approach): Evelyn Huber and Sergio Berensztein, "The Politics of Social Policy in Chile, Costa Rica and Mexico: Crisis and Response," paper presented at the 19th Latin American Studies Association (LASA) Congress, 28–30 September 1995, Washington, D.C.

5 See here also O'Donnell and his argument on the "second transition to democracy": Guillermo O'Donnell, "Transitions, Continuities, and Paradoxes," in *Issues in Democratic Consolidation*, ed. S. Mainwaring, G. O'Donnell, and J. S. Valenzuela (Notre Dame: Notre Dame University Press, 1992), 17–56.

6 See here Dietrich Rueschemeyer, John Stephens, and Evelyn Huber, *Capitalist Development and Democracy* (Chicago: University of Chicago Press, 1992).

7 It would be difficult to find any capitalist democracy where the organized working class enjoys *as much power* as capitalists. Investment and income policies remain clear prerogatives of the capitalist class and are *sometimes* subject to union negotiation and/or state intervention. But if anything, the departure of Keynesian policies and the arrival in the 1980s of neoliberal economics has buttressed the power of the capitalist class even more. I therefore urge for caution in the use of "balance of power."

8 See Gonzalo Herrera, "Tendencias del cambio tecnológico en la industria chilena," *Economía y trabajo: 5o informe anual*, 1994–1995 (Santiago: PET, 1995), 75–94. The emergence of more informal relations between labor and capital has led some authors to argue that the "organic relation" between capital and labor is showing signs of a new characteristic, a "new matrix of power" accompanied by the total absence of state regulation and illustrative of an "effective reorganization of the political and economic system." Quoted from Alvaro Díaz, *Restructuring and the Working Classes in Chile: Trends in Waged Employment, Informality, and Poverty, 1973–1990*, Discussion Paper 47 (Geneva: UNRISD [United Nations Research Institute for Social Development], 1993), 14. Numerous studies in Chile highlight the degree to which the emphasis on flexible labor markets has led to precarious employment conditions that in turn have become a normal feature of the Chilean labor market. See Mideplan/Casen, "Encuesta de caracterización socioeconómica nacional 1996," quoted in Rafael Agacino, "Cinco ecuaciones 'virtuosas' del modelo económico chileno y orientaciones para una nueva política económica." *Economía y trabajo: Informe anual*, 1995–1996 (Santiago: PET, 1996), 57–84.

9 Figures are from Casen (1994), quoted in Jaime Ruíz-Tagle, "Desarrollo social y políticas publicas en Chile: 1985–1995," *Economía y trabajo: Informe Anual*, 1995–1996 (Santiago: PET, 1996), 7–56. Agacino reports that in 1995, productivity grew nationwide by 7.4 percent while real wages only grew by 4.1 percent. Between 1990–94, the figures were 4.4 percent and 3.9 percent respectively. See Agacino, "Cinco ecuaciones 'virtuosas,'" 57–84. The 5:1 ratio is reported by Cristián González, "Notas sobre empleo precario y precarización del empleo en Chile," *Economía y trabajo: Informe Anual*, 1997–1998 (Santiago: PET, 1998), 51–88.

10 See Agacino, "Cinco ecuaciones 'virtuosas,'" 6.

11 Agacino ("Cinco ecuaciones 'virtuosas,'" 63) argues that in Chile "the economy and those who run it, will sooner rather than later manage to totally subordinate workers' needs to the exigencies of the modern factory." One need not project too much into the future, however, to be skeptical about Chile's success. Public opinion surveys taken by CERC (Centro de Estudios de la Realidad Contemporanea) in the 1990s consistently show that a majority of Chileans believe that the economic system is "unfair," that the government should "do a lot more" about workers' rights, and that a majority of Chileans are "not satisfied" with democracy.

12 For a more full discussion and bibliography, see Volker Frank, "Plant-Level Leaders, the Union Movement, and the Return to Democracy in Chile," Ph.D. diss., University of Notre Dame, 1995.

13 CPD (Concertación de Partidos por la Democracia), *Programa de Gobierno* (Santiago: CPD, 1989), 11.

14 CPD, *Programa de Gobierno*, 12.

15 Early success in signing agreements on fundamental issues such as the Acuerdo Marco were made possible by bilateral conversations that had taken place between the CUT and the CPC *independently* of any initiatives of the then Concertation of Parties for Democracy. Trilateral negotiations between the CUT, the CPC, and the government only began thereafter, at the closing of the "transition" period between the December 1989 elections and the March 1990 inauguration of the new democratic government. See Ciasi (Centro de Investigación y Asesoría Sindical), "Minuta de Discusión con el Gobierno sobre Participación Sindical," photocopy, July 1991.

16 Thus, this recognition marks a renunciation of one of labor's historic objectives, the annihilation of capital. This is one reason why the Acuerdo had such a strong symbolic value for employers as well.

17 CUT, CPC, and the Government of Chile, *Acuerdo Marco* (Santiago: CUT, 1990), 4.

18 This agreement emphasized a need for consensus and the "historic opportunity . . . for Chile to develop in equity and democracy." See CUT, CPC, and the Government, *Acuerdo Marco*, 2–3.

19 CUT, CPC, and the Government, *Acuerdo Marco*, 5.

20 See Malva Espinosa and Laís Abramo, *Los empresarios en la transición democrática* (Santiago: ILET, 1992).

21 In addition to the increase in the minimum wage, that Acuerdo also resulted in an increase of pensions and family subsidies of 10.6 percent and 25 percent, respectively. These were important gains for all workers.

22 Likewise, CPC-affiliated enterprises are big and usually pay higher wages and salaries than the minimum wage. Even Conupia, the association of small and medium-sized enterprises that participated in the third Acuerdo Marco, stated that its affiliates consider the minimum wage issue not relevant.

23 In a survey conducted by this author among 294 plant level leaders, they were asked whether the rise in the minimum wage would have any influence on their collective bargaining with employers. Only 19 percent said they took the minimum wage level into consideration. See Frank, "Plant-Level Leaders."

24 CUT vice president Arturo Martínez put it this way: "If there is no discussion on substantive issues, consensus does not serve much, and the demonstration of big agreements becomes useless." Quoted in El Diario, 3 March 1992.

25 A majority of the plant-level leaders I surveyed did not know about the Acuerdos Marco.

26 In the following, particular attention will be paid to the most important dimension of the reform: collective bargaining. Of necessity, many details of the complex Chilean labor legislation had to be omitted. A much more detailed discussion of the entire reform process, including political negotiations among labor, employers, and government representatives, is given in Frank, "Plant-Level Leaders."

27 At the top of the vertical structure are the national organizations, at the intermediate level are the confederations and federations (and some national unions), and at the bottom are the base-level unions, which come in four variants: The plant-level unions, the interenterprise unions, the transitory unions (such as construction), and the independent unions.

28 Peter Winn's introductory chapter in this book discusses important changes brought about by the Plan Laboral and how it affected the labor movement.

29 An important qualifier is in place. In Chile, collective bargaining can take place in two different ways. Unions can either have a collective contract ("contrato colectivo") or a collective agreement ("convenio colectivo"). Only the former is considered by unions to be a real bargaining process because they can reject the employer's offer and threaten with a strike. In a convenio, the employer simply presents unions an offer which they either accept or don't (article 127). In this type, there is no negotiation, the union does not have the right to strike, and no contract is signed. Transitory unions, such as construction, have convenios, but consider these, as many leaders have told me in interviews, "negotiations without any real strength." See Victor Maturana, "Y los trabajadores . . . ¿cuando?" Revista Cambio, no. 7 (Sept.–Oct. 1987): 18–23. Some agricultural unions also have convenios, but they have the additional impediments that (a) the employer can reject the union's demand for contracts (article 93) and (b) the union can only propose to bargain during June, the off-season for agricultural products (article 93).

30 The reader is reminded of the damage done to the Chilean grape industry by the discovery of a handful of bad grapes by U.S. customs in the late 1980s and a subsequent though brief U.S. embargo on Chilean grapes.

31 The law leaves the employer a great deal of leeway to justify the dismissal. One of their options is to simply invoke "the firm's need" ("necesidad de la empresa"). See Law 19010, article 3.

32 Daniel Platovsky, an influential member of the CPC and past president of Chile's Chamber of Commerce, commented that the indefinite strike "can become a weapon to expropriate the firm, (because) every time (the strike) occurs, the employer can be deprived indefinitely of the possibility to make the (firm) function." Quoted in Espinosa and Abramo, Los empresarios en la transición democrática, 64.

33 It is impossible to confirm when the idea of a "Chilean social concertation" was "born." My argument is based on the reading of literature that conveys the idea that

around this time political, intellectual, and labor leaders began to think about necessary paths to return to democracy.

34 This notion is from Tomás Moulían, "Desarrollo político y estado de compromiso: Desajustes y crisis estatal en Chile," *Colección Estudios Cieplan*, no. 8 (1982): 43–53.

35 The "responsive performance" of the Chilean political system is mentioned in Arturo Valenzuela, *The Breakdown of Democratic Regimes: Chile* (Baltimore: Johns Hopkins University Press, 1978), 18–19.

36 In this context it is interesting to mention the Popular Unity government of President Allende, where a Socialist and Communist coalition attempted—against a staunch center and right opposition in Congress—to create in Chile a socialist society. Thus, the continuation of the "Parties for the No" to the "Parties for Democracy" reflects another dimension of the learning process of the Chilean political class. They seemed to have learned, among other things, that political stability is not served well by radical minorities in Congress attempting to transform an entire society.

37 CPD, *Programa de Gobierno*, 11.

38 CPD, *Programa de Gobierno*, 12.

39 CPD, *Programa de Gobierno*, 25.

40 Alejandro Foxley, "Bases para el desarrollo de la economía chilena: Una visión alternativa." *Colección Estudios Cieplan*, no. 26 (1989): 175–186.

41 Ciasi, "Minuta de Discusión con el Gobierno," 1.

42 Yet the primary failure of the political system did not reside in the legislature itself, but in the politicians and parties that slowly drifted apart and ultimately beyond the borders of democratic consensus. See Valenzuela, *The Breakdown of Democratic Regimes*.

43 Mario Alburquerque, a former CUT advisor and as such a participant in most negotiations with the Aylwin government, hypothesized that the transfer of socioeconomic decisions from the state to social actors becomes more attractive (and hence more likely) if the decisions themselves become more important to the actors. See Mario Alburquerque, "El sindicalismo en el primer año de gobierno democrático," Serie documentos Ciasi 9 (Santiago: Ciasi, 1991), 13. Bresser-Pereira, Maravall, and Przeworski make the same point: "Democratic institutions can be consolidated only if they offer the politically relevant groups incentives to process their demands within the institutional framework" (*Economic Reforms in New Democracies*, 5).

44 Javier Martínez and Alvaro Díaz, *Chile: The Great Transformation* (Washington, D.C.: Brookings Institution; Geneva: UNRISD, 1996), 72.

45 This is particularly the case for temporary workers such as those in construction and agriculture (especially fruit production), and for those employed in fishing, forestry, mining, and garment manufacturing. See again Martínez and Díaz, *Chile: The Great Transformation* (1996): 70–74.

46 See also the chapters by Winn, Klubock, and Stillerman in this volume.

47 Such as in 1991, 1992, and just prior to the first massive street demonstrations in July 1994 and later that year in November.

48 See here Petras, Leiva, and Veltmeyer, *Democracy and Poverty in Chile*, 94.

49 Manuel Antonio Garretón. *Hacia una nueva era política: Estudio sobre las democratizaciones* (Mexico City: Fondo de Cultura Economica, 1995).

50 The slogan of the incoming Aylwin government was "Gana la gente"—the people win.

51 This assessment stems from survey results taken in 1992 by this author. Surveys taken by the Dirección del Trabajo in 1995 and 1998 confirm my results.

52 See Ernest Bartell, "Business Perceptions and the Transition to Democracy in Chile," working paper 184 (Notre Dame: Helen Kellogg Institute for International Studies, University of Notre Dame, 1992). When asked about their experience with the new Concertación government, and the presumably new economic policies, many employers simply responded with "Changes, what changes?"

53 See CPD, Programa de Gobierno.

54 Segundo Gobierno de la Concertación, "Un gobierno para los nuevos tiempos: Bases programáticas del segundo gobierno de la Concertación," n.d.

55 To be precise, the transition government's term was only four years, while Frei's and Lagos's terms reverted back to the historic six-year period.

56 See Segundo Gobierno de la Concertación, "Un gobierno para los nuevos tiempos."

57 The relationship among the labor movement, employers, and the Frei government has been discussed at greater length in Volker Frank, "Labor Movement Strategies in Democratic Chile, 1990—2000," unnumbered working paper (Notre Dame: Helen Kellogg Institute for International Studies, University of Notre Dame, spring 2000).

58 See Maria Lorena Cook, "Toward Flexible Industrial Relations? Neo-liberalism, Democracy, and Labor Reform in Latin America," Industrial Relations 37, no. 3 (1998): 311–37.

59 See Fernando de Laire, La trama invisible o los claroscuros de la flexibilidad: Producir, construir y proveer servicios bajo jornadas excepcionales en la minería privada y en sus eslabonamientos de subcontratación, Cuadernos de Investigación 8, (Santiago: Dirección del Trabajo, 1999).

60 For example, flexible contracts (subcontracting) without suspension of collective bargaining rights, flexible working hours with guaranteed proportional remuneration, and minimum and maximum hours. See Diego Lopez, "El proyecto de reforma laboral: Avances y desafíos," Economía y Trabajo: Informe Anual, 1994–1995 (Santiago: PET, 1995), 95–114.

61 See for example Manuel Razeto "El proceso de reformas laborales. Itinerario, enseñanzas y propuestas para el mundo sindical," Revista de Economía y Trabajo (Santiago: PET, 2000): 177–225.

62 Small and medium employers were very concerned about wage costs. The government was willing to offer them a special package and to discuss unemployment insurance separately.

63 La Tercera, "Gobierno no adelantará: Envío de la reforma Laboral," www.LaTercera.cl, accessed 6 July 2000.

64 La Tercera, "Empresarios piden definición al gobierno," www.LaTercera.cl, accessed 31 August 2000.

65 La Tercera, "García recibe a empresarios en nuevo intento por despejar dudas," www.LaTercera.cl, accessed 8 September 2000.

66 See *La Tercera*, "Gobierno retira temas."

67 See *La Tercera*, "Incertidumbre mundial despejó reforma laboral," *www.LaTercera.cl*, accessed 23 March 2001.

68 The more "liberal" group within the coalition (which included the Finance, Economy, and Labor Ministries) took the figure as a "wake-up call" and increased pressure on Lagos to give up his support of the more "social democratic" sector within the Concertación. Given the economic crisis, this latter group would have liked to see more rather than less state involvement; among others they argued for increased social spending and opposed further privatization. Lagos opted to support the "liberal wing" for which he was strongly criticized by N. Eyzaguirre, a member of his own party, the PPD. See *La Tercera*, "Lagos opta por liberales en la Concertación," *www.LaTercera.cl*, accessed 10 September 2000.

69 See *La Tercera*, "Incertidumbre mundial."

70 Commemorating the Combate Naval de Iquique, the president traditionally addresses Congress and the Nation, similar to the state of the Union address here in the United States. See *La Tercera*, "La moneda busca cerrar el capítulo de la reforma laboral," *www.LaTercera.cl*, accessed 25 May 2001.

71 The fine is indexed at 4 UF (Unidad de Fomento).

72 To recall, the Frei government attempted to include this in its reform.

73 I heard this story in countless conversations with friends and colleagues during my visit to Chile December 1998–January 1999 and again during January 2001.

74 Based on a worker's average income over the previous 12 months, employers pay 2.4 percent and the worker pays 0.6 percent. The state also contributes, but the amount it pays varies.

75 J. Samuel Valenzuela, "Labor Movement Formation and Politics: The Chilean and French Cases in Comparative Perspective," Ph.D. diss., Columbia University, 1979, 257.

76 A good historic review of these is given by Lara Hugo Yanes, *Las comisiones tripartitas*, Serie documentos 4 (Santiago: Ciasi, 1990). These tripartite commissions lasted for two years, were paritary (three representatives), and had binding character. Prior to ratification in Congress, any new project had to be approved by an absolute majority. The task of these commissions was to prevent, or solve, labor conflicts through the creation of sector wide norms. Any side could initiate the creation of such commissions. In many interviews, union leaders remembered these commissions and expressed hope for their return. One should also not forget that the CUT itself pushed for their reintroduction. These commissions should *not* be confused with sector-wide agreements between a few union confederations (such as COMACH, FONACC) and their respective employers during the late sixties and early seventies, which are briefly discussed in Alan Angell, *Politics and the Labour Movement in Chile* (London: Oxford University Press, 1972).

77 Their purpose was to simply study economic conditions and make proposals to the labor ministry—which was under no obligation to act on the recommendations of these commissions. They only had a duration of two years, their permanent status

was canceled, and they were called into session only when it seemed necessary. Workers and employers could delegate four representatives; the government appointed one president who had also four votes. This system was once again slightly changed in 1977 before it was dissolved two years later.

78 Valenzuela, "Labor Movement Formation and Politics," 151.

79 See La Tercera, "Ministro Solari expone contenidos de la reforma laboral," www.La Tercera.cl, accessed 14 September 2000.

80 See Guillermo Campero, Los empresarios chilenos en el regimen militar y el post plebiscito (Santiago: ILET, 1989); Fernando Dahse, El mapa de la extreme riqueza: Los grupos económicos y el proceso de concentración de capitales (Santiago: Aconcagua, 1979); Carlos Huneeus, "La nueva derecha en el postautoritarismo en Chile: La Unión Democrata Independiente (UDI)," unnumbered working paper (Notre Dame: Helen Kellogg Institute for International Studies, University of Notre Dame, 2000); Pilar Vergara, Auge y caida del neoliberalismo en Chile (Santiago: FLACSO, 1985).

81 They may have also simply turned on their TV sets. Talk of globalization was everywhere, and was there any government in the 1990s which dared to reject neoliberal economics?

82 This has been brilliantly analyzed in an article by Andrés Allamand, "Las paradojas de un legado," In El Modelo Chileno Democracia y Desarrollo en los Noventa, ed. Paul Drake and Ivan Jaksic (Santiago: LOM, 1999), 169–90.

83 One of the opponents of the Frei reform was Jose de Gregorio, minister of mining, economy, and energy in the Lagos government.

84 Quite tellingly, his 1993 book—presumably a reflection of the labor reform while he was labor minister—mentions nothing of the great conflicts between labor, capital, and the state. Instead, it is mostly a reiteration of the Concertación's success and the challenges that lie ahead.

85 Quoted in Frank, "Plant-Level Leaders." Emphasis is mine. As we have seen, unemployment insurance would come much later, in 2000.

86 Alburquerque, "El sindicalismo en el primer año," 13.

87 All industrial relations systems have an instrumental dimension, but they are also designed to accomplish substantive goals.

88 Ministerial positions were carefully allocated, reflecting only in part electoral strength. Ministries were also perceived as teams, with the top two positions going to members of different parties, in the majority of cases the DC, PS, or PPD.

89 See Huneeus, "La nueva derecha en el postautoritarismo en Chile." See also Claudio Fuentes, "Partidos y coaliciones en el Chile de los '90: Entre pactos y proyectos," in El modelo chileno democracia y desarrollo en los noventa, ed. Paul Drake and Ivan Jaksic (Santiago: LOM, 1999), 191–219.

90 See Frank, "Labor Movement Strategies in Democratic Chile."

91 Even authors who are critical of Chile's new democratic governments tend to infer the labor movement experience either from aggregate data (e.g., strikes, number of unions, etc.) or from contextual variables (e.g., wage level, economic growth, etc.) that ignore important characteristics about the Chilean labor movement itself. See

for example Patrick Barrett, "Labour Policy, Labor-Business Relations, and the Transition to Democracy in Chile," *Journal of Latin American Studies* 33 (2001): 561–97. Elsewhere (Frank, "Labor Movement Strategies in Democratic Chile,") I have shown that labor movement strategies and hence a big part of the labor movement's experience in the 1990s is a result, first and foremost, of how labor leaders "deal with" and then respond to a set of circumstances, including, very importantly, not only economic variables (wages) but also political and legal aspects. The last section of this chapter elaborates on this important point.

92 All statistics are from PET, *Informe anual*, issues for 1996, 1997, and 1998.

93 Unfortunately, while data exist on membership, there are no data as to the rate of affiliation of public sector unions.

94 These unions have the right to a convenio colectivo, a crucial distinction made by Chilean labor law, as explained earlier.

95 I have discussed developments in Chile's mining sector at greater length in Frank, "Labor Movement Strategies in Democratic Chile." I also refer the reader to Klubock's discussion of the mining sector in this volume.

96 See Agacino, "Cinco ecuaciones 'virtuosas,' " 61.

97 Ibid.

98 See González, "Notas sobre empleo precario," 51–88. See also Rafael Agacino, Cristián González, and Jorge Rojas, *Capital transnacional y trabajo: El desarrollo minero en Chile* (Santiago: LOM, 1998). See also Klubock's chapter in this volume.

99 See Dirección del Trabajo, *Sindicalismo en la empresa moderna: Ni ocaso, ni crisis terminal*, Cuaderno de Investigación 4 (Santiago: Dirección del Trabajo, 1997), 28.

100 Magdalena Echeverría, Valeria Solis, and Verónica Uribe-Echevarría, *El otro trabajo. El suministro de personas en las empresas*, Cuadernos de Investigación 7 (Santiago: Dirección del Trabajo, 1998), 119–91.

101 See Dirección del Trabajo, *Sindicalismo en la empresa moderna*, 30; and Rodolfo Bonifaz, "Comentarios de los actores sociales al proyecto de ley que modifica el codigo del trabajo en materias de negociación colectiva y otras," unpublished document. Photocopy.

102 See here Victor Maturana, "Primer semestre 1991: Más huelgas, pero más cortas," unpublished document (Santiago: Ciasi, 1991), 91.

103 See Dirección del Trabajo, *Informativo del departamento de las relaciones laborales de la Dirección del Trabajo para organizaciones sindicales, empresas y usuarios en general* (Santiago: Dirección del Trabajo, 1998).

104 PET, *Informe anual*, 1998, 276

105 A national survey conducted by the Dirección del Trabajo in 1992–93 found that 63.8 percent of interviewed plant-level leaders believed that there was no adequate legislation to protect employment or to protect unions against "unfair" employer practices; 55.8 percent responded that the strike was not an effective weapon. See Dirección del Trabajo, *Como operan las normas de negociación colectiva y de organizaciones sindicales*, Cuaderno de Investigación 1 (Santiago: Dirección del Trabajo, 1995), 45, 53.

106 Admittedly, it may also backfire, and unions may also go on strike based on im-

proved knowledge of their firm's financial situation—but then again the strike itself is a risky decision and many union leaders were aware of the dire consequences a strike may have for the rank and file who goes on strike.

107 Dirección del Trabajo, *Temas Laborales: Año* 1, no. 4 (Sept. 1996): 38.

108 Expression used by CUT vice president Maria Rozas in an interview with this author, 1992.

109 Bustos himself admitted in an interview with this author (1992) that "there is still too much political pollution in the CUT."

110 Petras, Leiva, Veltmeyer, *Democracy and Poverty in Chile*, 121–23.

111 This was very evident during all union congresses held throughout the decade. In 1991, 1996, 1997, and 1998, top union leaders were more concerned about political coalitions and behind the scenes deals than about the current state of union affairs. Or, to be more precise, the top leadership believed that union problems could be solved with the "right political deal."

112 The CUT leadership continues to suffer from this contradictory position. For example, when the labor reform was finally ratified in September 2001, Arturo Martínez stated that "it signifies a way to find once again common ground with the Concertación over something that *strengthens* the CUT and the Chilean workers. With a fairer labor legislation we can now help build Chile" (emphasis is mine). See *La Tercera*, "Rápida aprobación de reformas laborales por el Senado," *www.LaTercera.cl*, accessed 11 September 2001. The CUT's pamphlet, entitled "Las reformas laborales," published in September 2001 and signed by Martínez, states that "this labor reform is insufficient and we maintain that there is still much to be done." See CUT, *Las reformas laborales: Un desafío para los trabajadores* (Santiago: CUT, 2001).

113 I thank Mario Alburquerque and Hermann Schink for clarifying this for me.

114 See Patricio F. Frías, "Perspectiva del estado de las relaciones laborales en Chile: Del gobierno autoritario a la transición democrática" (Santiago: Dirección del Trabajo, Departamento de Relaciones Laborales, 1998).

115 Frias, "Perspectiva del estado," 33. A number of things explain the success of public sector unions. Importantly, many of their leaders are either Communists or, if they identify politically with any of the Concertación parties, they do not let their political sympathies trump their loyalties to the union. Similarly, some unions in mining and agriculture have also been successful in terms of recruiting new members as well as gaining important concessions from employers.

116 Frank, "Labor Movement Strategies in Democratic Chile."

117 Personal interviews with union leaders Cabrera and F. Castro, 1992. See also Gonzalo Falabella, "Reestructuración y respuesta sindical: La experiencia en Santa Maria, Madre de la Fruta Chilena," *Economia y Trabajo* 1, no. 2 (1993): 239–61. It should be pointed out, however, that the CUT leadership is not a unitary body. The *consejo ejecutivo* has 45 members who represent different political tendencies, and who disagree over union strategies. It would not be precise to assume that this group of leaders always agrees with the top CUT leadership (basically the president and all vice presidents). The consejo voiced skepticism toward the CUT's top leadership as early as in 1991.

PETER WINN

"No Miracle for Us":
The Textile Industry in the Pinochet Era, 1973–1998

Radomiro looked far older than his fifty years, prematurely aged from too many years running too many textile looms—and too many months of unemployment, worrying about how to feed his family. It was mid-1998, soon after General Pinochet's retirement as armed forces chief brought his era to an end. We were talking about Chile's neoliberal "miracle," the decade-long run of high economic growth with low inflation that had begun under the Pinochet dictatorship and continued under the center-left government that had succeeded him in the restored democracy of the 1990s. Yet, despite this boom, Radomiro had lost his job, his factory was closed, his future was uncertain at best. "Miracle?" he asked rhetorically. "There was no miracle for us."[1]

It was a judgment with which many textile entrepreneurs and managers would have agreed. Although the focus of this chapter, as in the book as a whole, is on the impact of the neoliberal model on the sector's workers, where the textile industry was concerned there were many who considered themselves victims by 1998. Looking at the Pinochet era as a whole, it could be argued that the Chilean textile industry—not just its workers—was a victim of the neoliberal "miracle." Its workers, however, were *doubly* victimized, both by neoliberal policies and their employers' response to them. Most of this chapter tells their story.

THE CHILEAN TEXTILE INDUSTRY BEFORE PINOCHET

As in most countries, textiles was one of Chile's oldest and most traditional industrial sectors, with a history stretching back into the 19th century.[2] For most of the 20th century it remained more important for its output and job creation—textiles employed more manufacturing workers than any other sector—than for its quality or productivity.[3] In the mid-20th century, it was a typical "import substitution" industry, prospering because of high levels of protection, despite low levels of productivity, technology, and managerial efficiency, with its high costs passed on to the captive Chilean consumer. It was also a highly concentrated industry, dominated by a handful of large mills and a few Arab-Chilean families—Yarur, Sumar, and Hirmas—with traditional family firms hidden behind a modern corporate façade.

Yet, under the Popular Unity administration, the textile industry became a vanguard of the Left's efforts to construct a "New Chile." Textile mills were the first Chilean-owned factories seized by their workers and textiles was the first industrial sector to be largely nationalized by the Allende government and incorporated into the new "social property area." It was in the socialized textile sector that the Popular Unity's experiment in worker comanagement—the workplace form of its democratic socialism—was inaugurated first and taken the furthest. It was among textile workers too that the Popular Unity parties found some of their strongest bastions of support. Textile workers and their leaders were frequently sought out and quoted in the media of the era. Textile workers benefited from major increases in real wages, and their unions won the coveted right to sector-wide collective bargaining. To many Chileans, the textile industry was a symbol of Allende's "democratic road to socialism."

But the textile industry also came to symbolize many of the problematic aspects of the "revolutionary process." Its labor-intensive mills absorbed too many unemployed workers. Although production remained high, it could not keep up with the increased incomes and demand of the Allende era, and textiles were among the most visible consumer shortages—and black market goods— of 1972–73. Frozen prices and rising costs translated into financial losses, which the nationalized banks covered, adding to accelerating inflation and ballooning corporate debt. Worker power was at times abused, with absenteeism and low productivity leading Allende himself to spend three days in 1973 at the Sumar mill, underscoring the special responsibility of textile workers in self-managed enterprises. The high degree of politicization within the textile industry also had its flipside: a sectarian politics that divided the Left and alienated the Center. For all these reasons, by the 1973 coup, the textile industry and its workers had become targets of rightist attacks.

It was also a target of its former owners, some of whom provided financial backing for the rightist paramilitary groups that helped create the climate of violence that justified the military coup. For Chile's textile entrepreneurs, the Popular Unity era was traumatic. Many of them had their factories requisitioned and run by the government, often after these had been seized by their workers, itself a conflictual experience that realized their worst nightmares. But even those entrepreneurs who retained their textile mills spent the Allende years fearful that their factories would be seized and socialized, despite government assurances to the contrary. These fears led them to grant their workers outsize increases in wages and benefits, in order to avoid a labor conflict that might provoke such steps. Many felt constrained to accept worker "vigilance committees," which acted as watchdogs over their management of their mill. As most Chilean textile enterprises were family firms run in a patrimonial manner, these "revolutionary advances" struck at the heart of the owner-managers' sense of their own prerogatives. Within a market in which demand outpaced supply—a reflection of the Popular Unity's massive redistribution of income—private textile firms were often highly profitable. But this neither won the Allende government entrepreneurial support nor elicited reinvestment. Instead, textile entrepreneurs complained about the insecurity of property, the loss of control over their workers and work process, and the uncertainty of "the rules of the game." All three would be central concerns of entrepreneurs under the military regime.

THE TEXTILE INDUSTRY UNDER PINOCHET

After the 1973 coup, the textile industry became an early focus of the regime's privatization policies.[4] The first sector to be nationalized, it was now the first to be privatized. Almost all the textile enterprises taken over by the Popular Unity were returned to their former owners by 1976. The condition was that they assume the considerable debts contracted under state administration. The mill owners accepted this condition, confident that in their experienced hands their enterprises would generate the profits to service these debts. But they were also counting on the Pinochet regime's returning to the pre-1970 rules of the economic game, maintaining high protective tariffs and favorable exchange rates while giving them a degree of control over a cowed and passive labor force that had not existed for many decades. They were correct in their assessment of the dictatorship's social politics but mistaken in their expectations of its economic policies.

The introduction of the neoliberal economic model after 1975, therefore, was a shock to the textile industry's capitalists. They were accustomed to levels of protection that had enabled them to operate inefficiently and pass on their high costs to the consumer. Between 1973 and 1982, however, tariffs on textile imports fell from 100 percent to 10 percent while exchange rates ceased to offer effective protection to national production and, after 1979, even provided incentives to substitute imported for Chilean goods. The problems confronting Chilean textile entrepreneurs as a result of this opening-up of the economy were compounded by the low international textile prices of the era. As a consequence of this combination of factors, the cost of imported textiles dropped by two-thirds between 1974 and 1982. By then, imported textiles accounted for a record 30 percent of the Chilean market—and there was 35 percent idle capacity in the local textile industry. The problems of Chilean textile entrepreneurs, already beset by sharply lower product prices and fierce foreign competition, were compounded by stagnant domestic demand, itself a reflection of the lowered real wages and high unemployment produced by the economic model, with periods of deep recession that made planning difficult and large inventories risky. The peculiarities of the local capital market under the regime's extreme version of neoliberalism, in particular the sharp difference between low international interest rates and high domestic rates, provided further advantages to importers, while raising the cost of local borrowing to onerous levels.[5]

Together, these factors prejudiced the profitability of the Chilean textile industry and threatened the viability of even the largest and wealthiest enterprises. It also presented a challenge that few Chilean textile entrepreneurs, accustomed to operating in a different economic universe, were prepared to face, but one that they all had to confront, irrespective of their resources, political influence, or previous market position. It required not only changes in production but also a transformation in business culture. Those who could not adjust did not survive.

Many of the mill owners who failed did not take the new rules of the game seriously, believing that they were too "un-Chilean" to last.[6] But the Pinochet regime stayed the neoliberal course that had been prescribed as harsh but necessary economic medicine by its "Chicago Boy" advisers, who had been educated in the extreme neoliberal economics taught by Milton Friedman and Arnold Harberger at the University of Chicago. In the past, the textile industry had enjoyed government protection because of its large number of workers, sizable output—accounting for 7 percent of the GDP in 1970—and political influence. Now, it had lost its political influence, and none of the other rationales counted for much with the Chicago Boys, who tended to see the textile industry—a high-cost, uncompetitive industry, dependent on government protection and political influence—as a prime example of what was wrong with the Chilean economy. Sergio de Castro, the key neoliberal policymaker, told a group of textile entrepreneurs in the late 1970s that there was no rational reason for a textile industry to exist in Chile. Two decades later, few textile mills remained.

Although each firm responded somewhat differently to the new situation, the common denominator was a search for ways to rationalize production and lower costs. Some made efforts to reduce energy costs or shifted to lower-cost imported yarns. For most Chilean textile entrepreneurs, however, the most important economy was the lowering of their labor costs, through sharp cuts in real wages, a substantial reduction of the labor force, and a more productive and flexible use of the remaining workers. These economies were made possible by the newly permissive labor policies and decrees of the military regime, which undermined the power of unions to protect the interests or jobs of their members and made it both easy and cheap to fire workers. The new Labor Code also eroded the previous limitations on the length of the workday and work week and gave employers new flexibility to switch workers from job to job, shift to shift, and even from plant to plant. This flexibility was central to the productivity gains that textile managers sought from their smaller workforce, through increased workloads and more efficient organization, as well as through the acquisition of new technology.[7]

The purchase of imported machinery at a time of declining profits required the investment of additional capital or the contracting of new debts. It was just one of the financial pressures that textile owners had to confront during this period, when most were operating at a loss. As time went on, those who were unable to reduce their costs sufficiently fell increasingly into debt, which further burdened their finances with onerous interest payments in an economy where interest rates could exceed 25 percent. The number of bankruptcies in the textile sector grew, including some of the largest and most important enterprises. When the bank crack of 1981–82 put an end to the prospect of further loans and the economic crisis that followed depressed consumer demand, the number of bankruptcies soared, until nearly half (45 percent) of all textile enterprises had failed. For Chile's mill owners, the crisis of 1981–83 was as traumatic in its own way as the Popular Unity period of 1971–73 had been.

Yet more than half the textile firms in Chile did survive the crisis. The reasons why some textile firms survived where others failed are complex, but there were certain common denominators. In general, the successful textile entrepreneur was a cautious innovator, like Fuad Garib, the most successful mill owner of the Pinochet era, who upgraded his machinery but did so gradually and without going heavily into debt. Those who survived the crisis were generally those who also resisted the temptation to invest heavily in real estate or other ventures outside their area of expertise during the speculative boom of the preceding years. Almost all had reduced costs in general and labor costs in particular. At bottom, successful firms maximized their productivity and efficiency and mini-mized their financial costs and risks.[8]

Those who survived to mid-1983 benefited from the modification of the policies that had aggravated their situation. When the economic crisis became acute enough to cause a political crisis, the regime's neoliberal economic prin-ciples were compromised in the interest of political expediency. The exchange rate was allowed to rise, ending the "negative protection" that had encouraged imports at the cost of local production. Textile tariffs were raised 20–30 per-cent, with surcharges on imports where there was evidence of dumping subsi-dized imported goods at below cost or other forms of unfair competition. Taken together, these measures represented an effective protection of over 35 percent that enabled the more efficient Chilean textile mills to enlarge their market share and survive an economic crisis that had depressed local consumer demand.[9] Gradually, the crisis eased and consumer demand revived, as did a more competitive Chilean textile industry.

By 1990, when Pinochet handed over his presidential sash to Patricio Aylwin, his elected civilian successor, the textile industry seemed prosperous and profit-able, able to maintain its domestic market share and even to export some of its products. Investment and employment was growing in an industry that con-tinued to upgrade its machinery and had begun to attract foreign capital, as the 1987 purchase of Textil Viña, a major cotton textile mill, by the Saudi Bin Mafouz group attested.

Although many factors contributed to this new competitiveness and profit-ability, the most important were lowered labor costs and increased productivity, 1970s strategies that intensified further during the 1980s. The production of the Sumar mills, for example, had not changed significantly since 1970, but the number of workers producing that same quantity of cloth dropped from 2,600 workers in 1970 to 1,800 by 1988.[10]

Equally striking was the sector's low real wages, which dramatically altered the Chilean textile industry's competitiveness internationally. A 1984 study of 100 textile-producing countries found that Chilean labor costs were the seventh lowest—one-tenth the cost of textile labor in Italy or Japan, one-quarter that of Mexico, one-third that of South Korea, and one-half that of Tunisia or Turkey. Even textile workers in India and the northeast of Brazil received higher wages and benefits.[11] At bottom, what transformed the Chilean textile industry from an inefficient industry requiring high levels of protection in order to survive into a prosperous and competitive industry was its lowered labor costs and in-creased labor productivity. The Chilean textile industry had restructured itself on the backs of its workers.

Chilean textile workers paid the costs of their industry's new competitiveness in reduced real wages and raised production norms. It was their increased efforts and decreased real earnings that made possible the industry's turn around in the 1980s. But what did that experience do to—and for—them? And what were the lessons that they drew from it?

THE WORKERS' STORY[12]

Chile's textile workers were affected by many of the same events and processes as their employers—the Popular Unity, the military coup, the neoliberal model, the crisis of 1981–83. But their experience of this history was different, as were the lessons that they drew from it. If the coup ended their dreams of transcendence and the neoliberal model threatened their jobs, the crisis menaced them with a permanent loss of livelihood.

For most textile workers the trauma was not the Popular Unity period, but the coup that brought that era to an end, and especially its repressive and regressive aftermath. In the wake of the coup, most of the "revolutionary" leaders of the textile workers disappeared, some to unmarked graves, jails, or concentration camps, others to exile or the underground resistance. Moreover, when the textile factories resumed production, it was under military administration and with soldiers patrolling the plants. Authoritarian management and industrial discipline were reimposed at the point of a bayonet, and few workers dared to protest. Some feared for their lives or liberty; many more feared for their jobs. Military intelligence officers interrogated the workers one by one, pressing them to inform on each other and then firing those considered to be leftist activists. The dismissals often continued after the mills were returned to their former owners, at first for political reasons or for personal revenge, but, with the recession of 1975, for economic motives as well. The unions, decimated by their leadership losses, intimidated by the repression, and proscribed by military decree from collective bargaining, strikes, or other militant actions, were incapable of defending their members' jobs, wages, or working conditions. With wages frozen and prices rising rapidly, living standards fell precipitously, even for those fortunate enough to keep their jobs. By 1975 many were reduced to a "diet of bread, tea, and onions."[13]

The rigorous imposition of the neoliberal economic model after 1975 soon threatened their job security too. The economic "shock treatment" may have been difficult for textile entrepreneurs to adapt to, but it was the workers who bore the brunt of their response in lost jobs and raised work norms. The increased workloads the mill owners hailed as a commendable increase in labor

ry

productivity, managerial efficiency, and economic rationality was experienced by their workers as a speedup backed by the threat of dismissal and chronic job insecurity.

This process and these fears culminated in the crisis of 1982–83. For many workers, the failure of the firm for which they labored was the most traumatic experience of all. In part, this was because of its sudden finality: at one blow everyone's job was wiped out, without recourse or appeal. In addition, a firm's bankruptcy often meant dismissal without severance pay and could mean a loss of unfunded pension annuities as well, or at best a long legal battle to recover them, one that unemployed workers could ill afford. Moreover, even if new owners took over the factory, the law did not require them to hire back the old workers, and if they did, the new labor laws stripped rehired workers of their seniority and their past levels of wages and benefits.

What made the crisis of 1982–83 particularly terrifying was the failure of so many textile enterprises at the same time, including some of the largest, wealthiest, and oldest firms in the industry. If they could go bankrupt, then no textile enterprise—or job—was safe. Moreover, the prospect of the entire industry going under threatened textile workers not just with a temporary job loss but with a permanent loss of livelihood. This meant that even for those who worked in enterprises that did not fail during the crisis, it was a sobering experience, which led them both to count their blessings and not take anything for granted, more especially as many of these firms survived by laying off personnel during the crisis. Suddenly, all their jobs were precarious, and textile workers seemed an endangered species.

Even before the crisis, most mill owners took full advantage of the regime's probusiness Labor Code. The crisis only exacerbated this tendency of textile enterprises to become mean as well as lean. At many mills, sweatshop conditions prevailed, wages were low, and management was authoritarian, even tyrannical. The lesson that the neoliberal model and the crisis had taught these entrepreneurs was that in order to survive and prosper in so competitive a market, they had to extract the maximum from their workers. This was particularly true of the smaller, less modern mills, which competed with their more mechanized and efficient rivals "by exploiting their workers more," one bitter worker activist complained.[14] Others took advantage of the Labor Code to replace veteran workers with ill-paid apprentices, or to hire workers on short-term contracts.

Workers might resent these conditions, but they often felt powerless to oppose them. Informers and the threat of dismissal kept even alienated and discontented workers in line, and the absent or weak union, assisted by a labor code that prohibited the union shop, made strikes difficult to win and dangerous to attempt and workers easy to hire and fire. Some employers took advantage of the new Labor Code's ban on collective bargaining to divide and conquer the workers through individual contracts whose differences reflected "loyalty" more than skill or production. "It is in the industrialist's interest to maintain such big differences," explained one veteran woman worker in a small mill, because "the more united the workers are the more problems he will have."[15] It was easy to discourage worker participation in a union that could win few concessions and offer few benefits. In many mills, workers were afraid to participate actively in their union—or even to join one—for fear of being fired. In one factory where the union had won 100 percent wage increases during the Allende era, veteran union leaders lamented that their goal during the Pinochet era was merely to survive.[16] Their feeling of powerlessness underscored the weakness of organized labor even within the economically improved and politically liberalized Chile of 1986–89.

Although the unequal advantages that the new labor code granted business were a major reason for this worker fear and union weakness, the antilabor social politics of the regime played an important role as well. In part this was because even with a labor code designed to enshrine the regulatory power of the market, the way in which the state implemented and enforced its provisions still had a significant impact upon labor relations. The mill owners who hired workers cheaply on successive short-term contracts of questionable legality did so with the knowledge that such practices would not be questioned by government labor inspectors. Workers who asked their leaders whether the labor code specifically sanctioned an action before agreeing to participate in it were reflecting their awareness that the Pinochet government was likely to use the full rigor of the law against workers who acted in defense of their interests. Moreover, even though the arbitrary actions of the secret police diminished in the last years of the dictatorship, they did not disappear, nor did their internalized legacy. Fear of becoming a target of repression still exercised a chilling effect on both workers and their leaders.

This effect was compounded by the regressive character of the regime's economic and social policies. With so many people unemployed and poverty so widespread, even ill-paid and ill-treated workers were afraid of losing their jobs or of taking actions that might jeopardize them. The impact of the existence of a "reserve army" of the unemployed upon textile workers is seen in the response of one mill owner to a demand for increases in the exceedingly low wages he paid his workers. Turning down this union request, he told his workers that those who wished to leave were welcome to go, as there would be 10 applicants for their jobs, at even lower wages.[17]

What made the threat of job loss particularly terrifying to older workers was the growing tendency of textile industries, particularly those investing in new technologies, to not hire workers who were over 30 years old. If workers lost the jobs they had, therefore, they might never get another one in the industry, raising the specter of permanent unemployment, the fate of many of their neighbors in the shantytowns where most textile workers lived. Moreover, cutbacks in government welfare programs meant that there was not much of a safety net to support those who did lose their jobs.

It was a situation that explained as well the reluctance of apprentices and other younger workers to get involved: for many this was a unique chance to secure a regular factory job, a definition of success in their social world. The seeming lack of "class consciousness" in young workers that veteran activists complained of in 1989 reflected this personal priority, as well as their parents' desire or desperate need that they contribute to the family's inadequate income.[18] Sixteen years of official propaganda promoting individualism and decrying collective consciousness also took its toll. Women workers, many of whose men were absent or unemployed, often felt constrained by being the sole support of their family. For other workers, the need to work 12-hour days and weekends in order to make up for their low wages and pay their high debts discouraged active union participation and militant action. The result was a legalistic mentality, an apparent passivity, and a seeming lack of class solidarity and consciousness that weakened many textile unions from within.

Yet it would be an error to leave the impression that the traumatic events through which textile workers lived during 16 years of dictatorship left all of them fearful and passive, and all of their unions weaker and less militant. On the contrary, important groups of textile workers—generally but not always from the larger enterprises—emerged from the trials and tribulations of the 1980s with increased self-confidence, more powerful organizations, and greater optimism. In part, their survival reflected the fact that they had lived through these hard times, and that the worst days—in both economic and political terms— seemed past. The resurgence of the economy and labor unions during the years that followed the crisis was another source of optimism. But their confidence also reflected their own experience during the preceding years of active protagonism. They might be victims of the dictatorship and its neoliberal policies, but they still retained their protagonism, as the example of the Machasa workers demonstrates.

Machasa had been formed in 1980 by the Yarurs, Chile's leading family of textile entrepreneurs, as a merger and restructuring of three bankrupt cotton textile enterprises that had been among the largest and most important in Chile before the military regime. Two of these enterprises—Yarur and Caupolican— had been Yarur family firms before 1970 and had been returned to their control by the military regime. The third, Panal, had formerly belonged to the Hirmas, another leading Arab-Chilean textile family, but it had been sold by them to the Allende government, and for that reason was not returned to them by the junta, despite a personal appeal to Pinochet by the firm's workers. Instead, after administering the enterprise for several years, the military government sold it in 1978 to the Galmes group, owners of a leading department store, Almacenes París. All three enterprises were burdened by heavy debts, compounded by the cost of machinery imported to shore up their competitive position in the face of cheaper foreign textile imports. None of the enterprises had recovered from the shock of the opening of the economy, with its elimination of protective tariffs on textile imports.

Panal had, in addition, just suffered a traumatic strike of 59 days. The strike had begun as the first big show of textile worker resistance since the coup; it was one of the first major industrial strikes of the Pinochet era and was viewed widely as a symbolic struggle. It ended with the government retaking control of the Panal mills, canceling the contracts of all the workers, and breaking the union. Many Panal workers believed that the regime's motives were political and that the firm's merger into Machasa was the instrument chosen for that purpose, so as to give economic cover to a political act.[19] The Yarurs did in fact close the Panal plants and fire most of their workers, after shifting their most modern machinery and most skilled workers to the Yarur mills.

The Machasa merger also gave the Yarurs greater freedom in dealing with the wages and working conditions of the labor force at their old enterprises, so the merger was fraught with anxiety for these workers as well. Yet it held out hope for saving their factories from closing and their jobs from disappearing. In the end, these hopes proved illusory. Despite a $40 million loan from the Banco del Estado, Machasa declared bankruptcy in 1981, threatening its remaining 3,000 workers with the definitive loss of their jobs.

But that is not what happened, and the workers themselves were largely responsible. Instead of passively accepting their fate and resigning themselves to the loss of their jobs, they pressured the military government to retake control of the bankrupt enterprise and keep its factories producing under state administration. Given the regime's commitment to privatizing the economy and its antilabor social politics, this seemed a quixotic request at best, and a dangerous strategy at worst. But the Machasa workers persevered, going public with their campaign in street demonstrations and media interviews that recalled the Popular Unity era.

In the end, the Pinochet regime, faced with the embarrassing prospect of publicly insisting on increasing the number of the unemployed by another 3,000—and adding 15,000 people to its poverty rolls—at a time of grave economic crisis and growing social unrest, did the unthinkable: it accepted the failure of one of its touted privatization efforts and transformed Machasa into an "economic unit" under state administration, an action which froze the jobs of Machasa workers, giving them job security at a time of national economic uncertainty. The workers of Machasa had succeeded not only in saving their jobs but in pressing an unsympathetic military regime to decree state control over a private industry in violation of that regime's economic policies and ideological tenets.

Nor was that all. During the years that followed, Machasa workers also secured a major role in deciding to whom their enterprise should be sold and won payment of their accumulated annuities for years of service before the sale took place. Moreover, from the new owners of the enterprise, they were able to win the rehiring of all the Machasa workers at a similar salary scale, as well as the continuation of their union and its leftist leadership, despite Pinochet-era labor laws that allowed the new owners broad discretion in these areas.

During the three years that followed, the Machasa workers built on these "conquests," gaining further improvements in wages, benefits, and working conditions, while developing a cooperative relationship with the new managers that included worker participation in problem solving on the factory floor and something approaching the "social concertation"—consultation and consensus—at the plant level that the center-left democratic governments of the 1990s would promote as their vision of a "modern" labor relations. In 1989 Machasa workers were by far the best paid in the textile industry.

The Machasa workers could not claim all the credit for these advances. They were fortunate that their new managers saw themselves as leading a "labor relations revolution" in Chile, and that their new owners were millionaires who viewed Machasa as a flagship enterprise that could win them coveted status as modern industrialists.[20] But this does not negate the self-image of Machasa workers who saw themselves as protagonists of their own destiny, whose efforts since 1982 played a central role in their surviving the crisis that bankrupted their firm and in winning them a favorable situation during the years that followed. Their confidence in their own agency and unions reflected this belief.

The experience of the crisis of the 1980s also brought home to the workers who remained employed in the textile industry the realization that the profitability of the firm for which they worked was in their own self-interest and could not be taken for granted. This was a lesson that for many was a new departure from a Marxist-inflected vision of class conflict, opening up the possibility of a new era of cooperation between capital and labor, based upon a common concern for the survival and thus the competitiveness of their enterprise. At Hitega, for example, worker gratitude to owner Fuad Garib for successfully piloting their enterprise through the crisis and doing it without large layoffs would translate into labor relations free of strikes or other major conflicts.

This was also clear at the large Sumar mill, where Christian Democrat union leaders forged a cooperative relationship with owners and managers that survived strikes and the jailing of Manuel Bustos, a Sumar union leader who emerged in the 1980s as a national leader of Chile's labor movement. Even when Bustos was sent into internal exile by the regime, the Sumars continued to pay his salary, talk about the need for "modern" labor relations, and work with plant-level leaders to implement them.[21]

But few textile entrepreneurs were as far-sighted as the owners and managers of Machasa, Hitega, and Sumar. More typical of the sector was Tejidos López, a smaller weaving plant in Santiago, and the comparison to Machasa is instructive.

Where Machasa's 2,600 workers tended modern machinery that was periodically upgraded, López's 70 workers labored at machines that had not been changed for more than a quarter of a century. At Machasa, workers were encouraged to participate in the improvement of the work process, in contrast to the authoritarian, even despotic, manner in which Tejidos López was run. Machine operators worked hard at both factories, but Machasa's earned an hourly rate plus an incentive bonus for exceeding production norms, while Lopez's worked for a piece rate that was stacked against them. The average wage at Machasa in 1989 was more than four times the minimum wage, plus overtime and production bonuses. At López, many machine operators earned only the 14,000 pesos per month minimum wage, and most earned close to the industry average of 17,000 pesos per month. The difference in fringe benefits and job quality was equally stark. Workers at both enterprises had unions led by militant leaders, but Machasa's had won favorable contracts and the power to resolve worker problems, where López's struggled to survive and could do little for their members. Not surprisingly, the López worker leaders seemed both less optimistic and more embattled, viewing labor relations in traditional class conflict terms, where Machasa's spoke of a new "modern" vision of cooperative labor relations. The conditions at López would become the norm during the decade that followed.[22]

Nor was Tejidos López the worst in the industry. Union leaders spoke of small sweatshops where conditions and wages were even worse. At Bichara, workers were forced to resort to a wildcat strike to protest sexual harassment by supervisors. Moreover, the Instituto Textil, the sector's business association, itself complained of the "unfair competition" and violation of the labor code and safety regulations by recently arrived Korean textile entrepreneurs, whom they charged with locking their workers in for 12-hour shifts.[23] The emergence of a new "putting-out" system, with mostly women workers slaving over rented machines in their home for ill-paid piece work, often helped by their children—in violation of both Chilean labor laws and international conventions—added yet another variant. All these workers were in the same industrial sector, but the enormous differences between their wages and working conditions testified to the fragmentation within the Chilean working class by the end of the Pinochet regime.

Chilean workers were divided by many factors, beginning with their workplaces. But, even among textile workers, the fragmentation of the working class was notable—in work and wages, living standards and lifestyles, consciousness and politics. The work and lives of textile workers differed according to the size of their factory, the modernity of its machinery, and the policies of its management; but they also depended upon the length of their contract, the security of their job, and the nature of their work. Generations and gender created other divides, as did ideology and political partisanship. Some were paid by piece work and some by the hour, but most were paid badly and lived in poverty.

The Contevech (Confederation of Textile and Clothing Workers), the chief textile union confederation, calculated in late 1988 that a family of five in Santiago needed an income of some 70,000 pesos a month in order to live decently. By those standards only Machasa workers were doing well. Most textile workers were at the other end of the salary scale, with the industry average of some 17,000 pesos described as "una miseria" by more than one worker.[24] At those wage levels, the necessity for spouses or adolescent children to work as well was overwhelming. Even so, workers spoke of a diet composed largely of bread and tea, onions, rice, beans, and eggs, with a *puchero* [stew] of "just bones" or organ meats as a feast dish, where in the past they used to eat an *asado* [roast]. The decline in worker living standards over the preceding sixteen years was underscored by the weaver who explained that workers used to eat two big meals a day, but were now reduced to one.[25] In some cases, even this meal—of pasta, beans or rice, and an egg—could not be counted on. Where women did not work, as was the case of two clothing machine operators whose wives were at home taking care of young children, if their output in a month was insufficient to earn them a bonus, "they simply did not eat, they went hungry."[26]

The low wages of textile workers were compounded by the deep cuts in social spending under Pinochet. Workers lived in terror of illness, because the national health service (SNS) now charged for medicines, needles, and other aspects of medical care. For most textile workers, a serious illness meant going into debt, as they had no savings to draw on. During the 1980s, moreover, finance companies began to press loans and charge cards on workers, even sending agents to their factories to hawk them, then garnishing their wages when they missed a payment. Also common was borrowing from a local storekeeper, who extended credit at interest rates of up to 50 percent per year. Once in debt, workers whose low wages rarely covered their family's needs found it difficult to escape the circle of poverty that enclosed them.

This was reflected in worker lifestyles as well. Most textile workers lived in suburban shantytowns distant from their factories, and even if they had a transportation allowance, it only covered half their commuting costs. The high cost of housing forced young married workers to live with their parents, while their low wages made it difficult even for single workers to spend much on entertainment. Most textile workers earned incomes that left them below the poverty line in 1989, despite long hours of hard work. Above and beyond the divisions that separated them was the fact that they belonged to the working poor, part of the more than 5 million Chileans who lived in poverty, despite the "success" of the neoliberal economic model and the prosperity of Chile's elite and upper middle class. For textile workers, employment was no guarantee of prosperity. On the contrary, the recovery of the industry after 1982, based upon their low wages, condemned most textile workers to a poverty that falling unemployment rates and a rising national income had not altered by 1989. They were living symbols of the "two Chiles" into which Pinochet's neoliberal policies had divided their country.

This situation reflected weaknesses in the labor movement as well as government policies. The fact that many local unions were unable to protect the interests of their members was also due to the inexperience of their leaders and activists, itself a reflection of the Pinochet repression and banning of experienced activists from the precoup era. At the same time, the division of Chile's textile unions into rival confederations dominated by the Christian Democrats and Communists, the Contevech and the Contextil (Confederation of Textile Workers), respectively—a partisan division that reflected Chilean politics of the era—weakened the authority and influence of their national leaders.[27]

This formation of parallel confederations within the textile sector was at odds with the active support that both organizations had given to efforts to unite the Chilean labor movement nationally. Textile union leaders and activists played an important role in the recomposition of the labor movement after the 1973 coup and the dissolution of the CUT (Central Unica de Trabajadores), the old national labor confederation. They participated in the creation of the Coordinadora Nacional Sindical (CNS), the first national workers' organization under the military regime to fight for labor and economic and political rights, contesting the dictatorship's hegemony with the "Pliego de Chile" (Demands of Chile) of 1980. Textile unions were also prominent in the formation of the Comando Nacional de Trabajadores (CNT), which organized the demonstrations that detonated the social protests of 1983–85, which doomed Pinochet's authoritarian political project and set the stage for the transition to democracy. In 1988 textile union leaders spearheaded the reunification of the organized working class in a new CUT (the Central Unitaria de Trabajadores), and Manuel Bustos, vice president of the Contevech and a Sumar worker, was elected as its first president, after playing a prominent leadership role in the CNS and CNT. Although personal and political factors were important in Bustos's selection as head of Chile's new national labor confederation, the relative strength of the textile unions—the third largest group of organized workers after the miners and the bank employees—also played a part.

With one of their own as Chile's top labor leader, textile workers expected to have their voices heard and their concerns raised at the highest levels of national politics, more especially as the new Concertación government, elected in 1989, would be led by their political parties. After their difficult experience of the preceding decades, it was a major reason why they approached the restoration of democracy in 1990 with optimism.

Textile entrepreneurs shared this optimism but for different reasons. They were convinced that the changes in the industry induced by the neoliberal model and the crisis made it more competitive, with more efficient machinery, a more productive workforce, lower labor costs, higher quality products, and better management. Their concern was that neoliberalism be maintained.

Historical experience also shaped the attitudes and demands of textile workers and their leaders, but in a different mold from that of their bosses. The workers were acutely aware of what they had lost—in real wages, living standards, working conditions, and the power to influence them. Although few expected miracles from a transitional democratic government, most expected progress in all these areas.

Textile union leaders, however, were conscious that they had emerged from the 16 years of military rule with weakened unions, a reduced membership, and lessened political influence. These realizations shaped their demand for the restoration of lost "conquests" and a more equal distribution of the industry's profits. They also underlay their priorities: modifying the probusiness Labor Code and reducing unemployment, viewed as a way both to eliminate the "reserve army of unemployed" that was keeping wages depressed and to enlarge their unions. By increasing union membership, they hoped to increase their political influence while helping to overcome the fragmentation of their worker base.

At the same time, the crisis and resurgence of their industry since 1982 led most textile workers to see the private ownership of their mills as proper, the profitability of their firms as in their own interest, and cooperative labor relations as desirable. The renewed profitability of textile enterprises in the late 1980s, however, led workers to demand that they receive a more equitable share of the profits earned from their labor.

As a result, even left Socialist and Communist leaders accepted capitalist ownership of their mills and did not expect the advent of an elected center-left government to mean a return to socialism. Moreover, most textile workers were open in 1989 to the creation of a new, more cooperative pattern of labor relations, even to something akin to "social concertation," at both the local and national levels. This meant that Chile's transition to democracy carried with it as well a rare opportunity to transcend the class conflict that had historically shaped its labor relations—if business was willing to embrace a new vision and meet labor halfway.

In 1989 this seemed unlikely. There were some forward-looking mill owners in the textile industry, including some of the most successful, who were willing to admit that the Pinochet Labor Code was biased toward business, that a more "modern" vision of Chilean labor relations was needed, and that wages and benefits should be raised. But they were in the minority, and even this minority was convinced that the competitive advantage that the Chilean textile industry enjoyed from having low labor costs had to be maintained.

Most textile entrepreneurs were not only reluctant to modify the Labor Code, but were also also determined to take full advantage of its provisions to maximize their profits at their workers' expense. They were also resistant to any "concertation" within their firm or to sectoral collective bargaining. In part, this was because they rejected any worker say in the management of their enterprise, as well as any "political" intervention in the economy.

But mostly, their opposition reflected their fear that such an accord would raise their labor costs, restrict their utilization of their workforce, and undercut their ability to compete. The dominance of these views within business circles was indicated by the opposition of the Instituto Textil, the industry's business association, to collective bargaining above the enterprise level.

The inauguration in 1990 of a democratically elected civilian government, therefore, raised expectations—and anxieties—throughout the textile industry. The workers, who had struggled for this restoration of democracy, led by their parties, expected that both the labor and economic policies of the new Concertación government would reflect their interests. Their hope was the fear of their employers. But, both textile workers and mill owners shared the belief that with democracy restored and an elected center-left government, led by Christian Democratic and Socialist parties that had always supported national industries, the hard years were behind them and a new era of prosperity and government assistance was at hand.

NEOLIBERAL DEMOCRACY AND THE TEXTILE INDUSTRY

If textile entrepreneurs and workers were expecting the new democratically elected civilian governments of the left-center Concertación to promote and protect Chile's textile industry, they were doomed to disappointment. If anything, the economic policies of the Aylwin and Frei governments were less protective of the textile industry than the Pinochet regime had been since the crisis of the early 1980s. In the wake of the crisis, the Pinochet government had raised textile tariffs to 20 percent, only to have the Concertación reduce it to 10 percent.[28] Equally important to the textile industry, if less visible, was the favorable exchange rate of the late 1980s, which added significantly to the effective protection that the textile industry enjoyed. Under Concertación rule the exchange rate was altered to favor exports, and mill owners calculated that during the 1990s these measures lowered the cost of imports by as much as 40 percent. The third aspect of the protection that the textile industry had secured during the final years of Pinochet's rule was countervailing duties in cases of dumping by foreign rivals. These too were weakened under the Concertación, to such an extent that by 1998 entrepreneurs had ceased to count on them—or even apply for them.[29]

Ironically, the authoritarian Pinochet regime also proved more willing to violate its professed neoliberal principles on an ad hoc basis than its democratically elected successors. When Textil Viña needed a loan to pay its crisis-driven debts in 1985, its union leaders went to Admiral José Torribio Merino, the head of the navy, and he intervened to make sure that the State Bank (Banco del Estado) granted it. For Merino, Viña del Mar was the navy's turf and its flagship industries were his clients, whose interests he would protect.[30] When Machasa tried the same tactic under the Aylwin government, the elected civilian leaders, even when they were of the same party as the union leaders, were unwilling to intervene, pointing to neoliberal principles and a fear of setting precedents to justify their inaction.[31]

If anything, the close political ties between government and union leaders seemed to make it more difficult for the textile industry. It was true that Christian Democrat and Socialist labor leaders had greater access to policymakers from their party, but this did not necessarily translate into greater influence *over* policy. In fact, this closeness often worked the other way: government leaders used party ties to persuade union leaders not to rock the boat and party discipline to impose their priorities on them.[32]

At bottom, these priorities were sustaining the neoliberal model, with its open economy and noninterventionist state, that the Concertación had inherited from the Pinochet regime. What made the civilian government's adherence to that model even more rigid than its military predecessor was the desire to demonstrate that an elected government of the center-left could resist "populist" pressures, that it would not compromise "sound" economic principles for "political" interests. The Concertación was also determined to hold the line on inflation, the most traumatic memory of the last civilian government—and the last to include Socialists.

So was the Central Bank, which enjoyed considerably autonomy due to Pinochet's reforms and played the key role of technical secretary on the interministerial commission that ruled on requests for countervailing antidumping duties. Cheap foreign imports kept inflation low, and that—not helping national manufacturing industries—was the chief concern of the Central Bank and the Finance Ministry, the most powerful economic ministry in the government, which was headed by Christian Democrats, the coalition's dominant party.

Textile entrepreneurs and union leaders got a more sympathetic hearing at the Ministry of Economy, where the Socialists reigned, but it was the weaker ministry and the Socialists the weaker party during the 1990s. As a result, the only government help offered to the textile industry by the Concertación was a plan to subsidize training programs by making them tax deductible. But most textile entrepreneurs didn't want to "waste" their money on training. When only Machasa agreed to make the necessary investment to qualify for the tax deduction, the government withdrew the offer, arguing that to subsidize only one firm would be favoritism—a charge that would not have stopped the military regime. Taken together with the fear of setting a precedent that other industries could then cite, these mutually reinforcing rationales justified a policy stance that both textile entrepreneurs and worker leaders perceived as unhelpful, myopic, or hostile.[33]

What made this hands-off stance on the part of the Concertación government particularly damaging to the Chilean textile industry was the "revolution" in textile technology, production, and marketing that took place during the 1990s. Weaving was a case in point: with shuttleless looms leading the way, weaving technology advanced with accelerating speed, so that at Hitega in 1997, the same number of workers as in 1974 produced more than six times as much cloth.[34] Computerization brought another revolution, requiring expensive investments that many Chilean firms were unable or reluctant to make. Hitega was one of the rare Chilean mills to computerize its design operations, but no Chilean enterprise could match the computerized Swiss spinning mill run by a single worker, whose job was merely to monitor the screens.

This technological revolution meant that much of the expensive investment in modern machinery by Chilean mills in the 1980s was rendered obsolete, in many cases before it had been amortized. It also meant the need for new rounds of increasingly expensive investments in imported machinery to keep up with international rivals, and in a context where that same tough competition kept textile prices low, along with the profits that had to finance those purchases of cutting-edge technology.

This intensified international competition reflected both changes in traditional textile exporters and the emergence of new nations as major textile exporters, part of a globalization of production that transformed the industry worldwide. During the 1990s China consolidated a position as the world's largest textile exporter, using both unpaid prison labor and ill-paid women and rural workers. Yet by 1998 the Chinese textile industry itself was laying off millions of workers, in order to confront competition from newer Asian textile exporters, from Turkey to Vietnam.[35] Older textile exporters survived by withdrawing from the mass textile market and finding market niches, as Italy did with its designer mills. Increasingly, however, cloth and clothing designed in Europe and the United States was manufactured elsewhere, usually far away, in a country where labor was cheaper, labor laws less protective, and unions weaker. At bottom, the textile "revolution" of the 1990s represented a geographic reorganization of both labor and production on a global scale—a restructuring that soon affected Chile's textile and garment industry.

It meant not only cheaper yarn, cloth, and clothing imports from a widening group of countries. Increasingly, Chilean firms themselves utilized these new patterns of global sourcing. Marcelo Calderón, a leading owner of textile and clothing plants in Chile, but also of a chain of clothing stores, resisted his aides' advice to shut down his Chilean mills and import everything he sold, as he had done during the crisis of the 1980s. Calderón valued his image as an industrialist, which his purchase of Machasa in 1986 had established, but chronic red ink persuaded him to sell Machasa in 1993, and by 1998 he had established a relationship with a Chinese textile mill that produced fabrics according to his designs at a fraction of the cost of his Chilean plants. During the 1980s quality control in Chinese mills was unreliable, and the cloth that arrived was often different from what had been ordered. But by 1998 quality control was much improved and the fax machine and the Internet made it possible to control design and, together with international courier services, to secure "just-in-time" delivery.[36]

The result was the creation of international production chains, stretching across oceans and continents, in which manufacturing was broken down and each step subcontracted to where it was least expensive. At the top of the chain was a manufacturing giant, or, in Chile, a department store or clothing store chain that dominated marketing at home and shaped production both at home and abroad. At the bottom of the chain might be a Santiago sweatshop or a mother slaving over a rented sewing machine in a shantytown shack. All along the chain, however, the demand was for lowered costs and cutthroat price competition.[37]

As a result, Chile's textile entrepreneurs confronted a new and more difficult situation than a decade before. "In the 1980s you could compete internationally on the basis of *either* cheap labor *or* cutting-edge technology," explained one of Chile's most knowledgeable textile managers. "In the 1990s you have to have *both*."[38] But in the 1990s Chilean wages were relatively higher than its Asian or Latin American rivals (such as Mexico or Brazil), a reflection of its higher exchange rate and economic prosperity. At the same time, its textile technology, while modern, generally lagged behind its Asian and European competitors. Nor could it reach the economies of scale of China, Pakistan, or Brazil.

In the face of this rapid and massive "revolution" in the global textile industry, the refusal of the Chilean government to aid its national textile industry was equivalent to a death knell. "We underestimated the speed and scope of change in the international textile industry," one top government official, who had advocated modest relief measures, later confessed ruefully.[39] "We were taken by surprise." But this unanticipated crisis did not lead the Concertación governments to intervene and protect Chile's textile producers. Other nations that were committed to open markets—including the United States, Mexico, and Brazil—found ways to protect their textile and garment industries from the full brunt of this global race to the bottom. But Chile's Concertación governments of the 1990s prided themselves on being the most open economy in the world and perhaps felt insecure in their neoliberal credentials. So they allowed the Chilean textile industry to fend for itself.

As a result, the Chilean textile industry could only compete in certain market niches, whether at home or abroad. In export markets, it did best where bilateral treaties afforded privileged access, as in Machasa's export of denim to Colombia. At home, Chilean manufacturers did best in lines and in markets where quality counted for more than cost and knowledge of national idiosyncrasies for more than machinery. Yet even here, inexpensive imports could undermine a seemingly well-designed production strategy. Machasa's efforts to have its Santiago plant reach economies of scale by concentrating all its production on sheeting failed when an importer brought in Pakistani sheets at less than half the price. Machasa might claim that its sheets were higher quality, but where the price differential was so great, Chilean consumers were willing to take the risk.[40]

This was part of a restructuring of the Chilean textile and clothing market that crystallized in the 1990s. Another segment of the market was used clothing, donated by individuals in Europe and North America, then sold by charities to jobbers who then resold the clothing to importers and wholesalers in poorer countries with open economies such as Chile, where they were retailed in special shops or street fairs. Although used clothing imports leveled off in the 1990s, they still represented the biggest share of imported clothing by weight, if not by value, depriving Chilean textile and clothing manufacturers of a sizable traditional market.[41]

Even more important was the new dominance of department stores and chain stores such as Falabella or Johnson, which bought at home or abroad depending on price, timing, or style in an unpredictable pattern that changed from season to season. The result for Chilean manufacturers was a volatility of demand, in which the dominance of the large stores meant either feast or famine, as they could take the entire production of a small plant one season and order little or nothing the next.

This volatility of demand was exacerbated in Chile's open economy by the imported effects of foreign crises in the 1990s. The causes of financial crises in

Asia, Mexico, or Brazil might have nothing to do with the Chilean textile industry, but their results included lowered demand in Chile's domestic and export markets and lower-priced exports from crisis-ridden producers. By late 2002 the Chilean miracle of high growth was a memory, replaced by an economic stagnation that successive external crises had extended through four of the preceding five years.

What made this difficult situation worse for many Chilean textile enterprises was that they confronted it from weakened positions. Many were saddled with high levels of debt, some from the crisis of the 1980s, others from the purchase of cutting-edge machinery during the years that followed. Textil Viña's balance sheets suffered from both sources, but it was only one of several Chilean mills in the 1990s with a debt overhang that turned operating profits into financial losses. It would close in 1998.

Machasa, which followed an old Chilean entrepreneurial tradition in taking advantage of a "good deal" by buying the used machinery of a closed U.S. plant, paid the price of this Pyrrhic bargain in lost time and production and in being saddled with machinery that was outdated before it was installed, yet whose considerable costs remained to be paid out of the profits that this second-hand machinery made more difficult to obtain. Machasa was not the only Chilean textile manufacturer to buy used machinery instead of cutting-edge technology and then find itself at a competitive disadvantage when confronted by the textile revolution of the 1990s.

Textil Viña and Machasa, two of Chile's foremost mills, were also weakened by the long-term impact of innovations that seemed cutting edge when introduced in the 1980s. Textil Viña pioneered a fourth shift at the end of the decade, so as to keep the factory working 24 hours a day, 365 days a year, and thus extract maximum output from its expensive imported machinery. The introduction of a fourth shift provoked a costly strike in 1989, but a decade later its chief cost was in wear and tear on the machinery and an overproduction that could not be marketed. Machasa, under its new owners in the late 1980s, was proud of its large and well-funded human resources department, generous benefits, and good labor relations. During the 1990s, however, what had been praised as a "modern" enterprise structure was blamed for high labor and administrative costs and rising financial losses.

Although each Chilean textile enterprise had its unique history, culture, and characteristics, what all shared was the need for a strategy with which to confront the worldwide textile revolution of the 1990s, within a neoliberalism that denied them aid from their government. The enterprises that were most successful in adjusting to the new situation were those led by owners or managers who read the changed global and local context correctly, understood its implications for their firm, and had the vision, resources, power, and flexibility to transform their mills accordingly—despite the difficult global context.

Flexibility was the new watchword. For most Chilean textile firms this meant commercial and product flexibility, on the one hand, and a more flexible use of their labor force, on the other. Enterprises varied their sourcing, mixing imports and subcontracting with the products of their own mills to adjust to changes in relative prices at home and abroad. Few Chilean textile mill owners, however, adopted flexible specialization, a common successful strategy elsewhere.[42]

An exception was the most successful, Fuad Garib, who was both owner and manager of his mills, which gave him the power to make the necessary changes. During the 1990s he transformed Hitega into what he termed "a service enterprise." From selling its own designs on the open market, Hitega became a manufacturer that responded to customer orders. This required lowering its turnaround time from 120 days to 60 and then 45 days, so as to offer rapid response and just-in-time delivery. It also meant computerizing his design department and building in the flexibility to create designs in the customer's image and adjust the mill's looms to work on a new cloth order without delay, while maintaining a quality control and customer relations that rivals could not match. Hitega could do that, Garib insisted, because it was a small firm with fewer than 300 workers, even in 1997. He had avoided the inflexibility he felt was inherent to large firms such as Machasa or Textil Viña. In 1998 his three textile mills together comprised the largest textile enterprise in Chile, but Garib ran them as separate medium-sized enterprises, with the flexibility he saw as crucial to survival in the altered textile world of the 1990s.[43]

The large mills that Garib dismissed as "dinosaurs" tried a different strategy. Machasa and Textil Viña both brought in professional managers with visionary plans for transforming their enterprise. Samuel Puentes, whom the new owners of Machasa hired in 1986, brought with him a "modern" style of labor relations that approached social concertation, complete with worker consultation, quality circles, and generous benefits administered by a large human resources department, a dramatic change from the authoritarian, top-down management under Yarur. The new owners of Textil Viña took a different route, hiring Hugo Grisanti in 1989 to transform an indebted and inefficient enterprise into a lean and mean textile complex, working around the clock 365 days a year, and managed in an authoritarian, top-down style that took full advantage of the Pinochet labor laws to undermine the unions and extract the maximum from each worker.

Both models failed in the 1990s. Ironically, when this became clear, their owners reversed their strategies. In the 1990s Textil Viña hired Samuel Puentes to humanize what Hugo Grisanti had wrought by fiat and to win the cooperation of the unions and their workers in the difficult struggle to survive. And Machasa hired Grisanti to dismantle the costly system of labor relations and social concertation that Puentes had established in an effort to transform Machasa into a low-cost enterprise capable of meeting the challenges of the 1990s. Yet by 1998 neither Puentes nor Grisanti were heading major textile firms, and neither Textil Viña nor Machasa were success stories.

As the Pinochet era came to an end, Textil Viña was liquidated and sold to become a shopping center selling mostly imported goods. By then, Machasa had closed its Santiago plant and was laying off workers in its Chiguayante plant, which would soon be sold to a Brazilian rival. The two flagships of the Chilean textile industry had become two more victims of the neoliberal economic miracle—despite its new democratic politics.

During the years that followed, years that closed one century and opened another, the few Chilean textile enterprises still afloat tried to adjust to extended hard times. Successive economic crises in Asia, Brazil, and Argentina kept the Chilean economy stagnant and internal demand for textiles depressed. "You have to eat, but you don't have to buy new clothes," a leading business spokesperson explained with a shrug.[44] The Brazilian and Argentine crises also sharply reduced Chilean textile exports to what had been their biggest markets.

At the enterprise level, the costs of these crises were personalized as firms tried to adjust to them. Argentina's economic collapse in 2001–2 cost Artela more than $1 million in uncollectable sales and its innovative general manager his job. Pollak adjusted at the expense of its workforce, downsizing by one-third and closing its dyeing plant.[45]

Increasingly the fate of Chile's textile industry seemed to depend on foreign events and decisions beyond its control. Increasingly the hopes and fears of Chile's textile entrepreneurs revolved around free trade treaties negotiated with other Chilean economic sectors in mind. When President George W. Bush won fast-track negotiating authority in 2002 and used it to negotiate a free trade treaty with Chile, excited Chilean textile entrepreneurs began to have visions of a piece of the huge U.S. market. But recent studies of the North American textile and garment industry under NAFTA (North American Free Trade Association) suggest that those dreams may not be fulfilled, as compared to the better founded expectations of Chile's wine and fish industries.[46]

The prospect of a free trade treaty with the European Union awakened other fantasies, but the head of Chile's textile business association was well aware that a European niche market was a window that would close when Eastern European nations entered the European Union in 2004 and was pessimistic that Chilean entrepreneurs would move fast enough to take advantage of this moment of opportunity.[47]

Moreover, if free trade treaties with the United States and Europe fuelled Chilean textile dreams, the negotiation of another free trade treaty in 2003—with South Korea—was its entrepreneurs' nightmare, threatening to finish off what was left of the Chilean textile industry. But this was a treaty that Chile's powerful export sectors strongly backed, leaving the textile industry to lobby for a longer adjustment period for its overmatched sector—at bottom a delay of a death sentence.

Even in a crisis, an entrepreneurial genius with vision like Fuad Garib could find a way to survive, even profit—making up in Mexico what he lost in Argentina, searching for a European niche before Eastern Europe filled them all, while maintaining a premium Bolivian market share based on his reputation for quality textiles. But increasingly Garib was the exception that proved the rule, and with his retirement in sight, it was unclear that his family firm would be in hands as skilled in the future. His withdrawal from the industry might be yet another sign and symbol of its approaching end.

TEXTILE WORKERS AND
THE "MIRACLE" OF NEOLIBERAL DEMOCRACY

The changes for Chile's textile workers that followed this restructuring after 1990 were profound. Although the number of workers employed in the textile-clothing sector as a whole remained relatively stable through 1996, there was a dramatic loss of jobs in the large textile mills, either because they closed down or because they reduced their labor force and subcontracted labor-intensive operations in order to avoid bankruptcy, become more competitive, or increase profits. Simultaneously, the number of jobs swelled in smaller plants and workshops, many of them in the unregulated informal sector. At bottom, this was a gendered shift of jobs from unionized, male textile workers earning relatively high salaries and benefits, to nonunion, female garment workers earning low wages (often minimum wage or a piece rate pegged to the minimum wage) with few or no benefits in unregulated sweatshops.[48]

What this structural shift meant for textile and garment workers was a sharp drop in "job quality," which involves much more than the wage a worker earns. It encompasses monetary and nonmonetary benefits, job security, contractual status, social protection, working hours, and working conditions, including the physical working conditions, organization, and intensity of work, as well as worker participation in setting working conditions. The interest/monotony of work, along with the opportunities for personal and professional development, the ethical and moral context of the work, and the social status it confers are other dimensions of job quality. Recently, the ILO (International Labor Organization) has bundled these concerns into the concept of "decent jobs," which includes a respect for core labor standards, many of them similar to these dimensions of job quality.[49]

Job security was a casualty of the restructuring brought by globalization and neoliberalism that textile and garment workers worried about almost everywhere in the industry. Downsizing and plant closings were the biggest complaints, but the hiring of temporary workers on short-term contracts and subcontracting of labor-intensive operations were often the causes. The upshot was a marked insecurity with respect to both income and regular jobs during the 1990s.[50]

The stress on managerial "flexibility," moreover, meant a growing insecurity among workers as to what their job was and the declining participation of workers or their representatives in shaping working conditions. For textile workers this meant an increase in work intensity and working hours (including overtime and weekend work) that left women workers in particular complaining about exhaustion, pain, and chronic ailments.[51]

For many workers, the most onerous part was overtime. Rather than hire more workers and pay more benefits, many enterprises preferred to press their reduced workforce to work more hours than the already long 48-hour week mandated by Chilean labor law. Workers were asked to work extra hours during the week or on Sundays or holidays and felt that they could not say no. There were too few textile jobs, and it was too easy to fire workers under Chilean labor law. Their jobs were too precarious to run the risk. In addition, given the low wages and high debts of many textile workers, once workers became accustomed to earning the money from extra hours, they were often hard pressed to stop working overtime. During the economic downturn after 1998, moreover, firms started offering 20 percent production bonuses for a doubling of output, a production that could only be reached by working overtime and weekends.[52] The result was work weeks that could exceed 60 hours—and that sometimes reached 75 hours.[53] At bottom, those textile firms that survived the shakeout of the 1990s profited from the exploitation and self-exploitation of their workers.[54]

The shift of jobs through subcontracting from large, formal-sector mills to smaller sweatshops and home work, moreover, meant a marked decline in job quality. Informal-sector firms were largely unregulated and for the most part did not comply even with the minimal labor standards of Chile's neoliberal legislation. Few workers in these small plants had written contracts, and those who did generally were forced to sign contracts that said they would be paid at the minimum wage, but then were paid at a piece rate that encouraged self-exploitation. This method of payment understated their income for social security purposes and diminished the tax costs to the owner. Long working hours and a lack of job stability and social benefits were endemic throughout the informal sector of the industry. The physical conditions of work were also far worse in the informal sector, with inadequate heating, lighting, and ventilation, little regard for workplace safety, and worker complaints about physical ailments that reflected high work intensity and low ergonomic values. Bathrooms were also inadequate, lunch rooms largely absent, and day care facilities non-existent, even where mandated by law.[55] The mostly women workers also had to cope with verbal, physical, and sexual abuse by owners and managers. A media exposé of Santiago's notorious Patronato garment district in 1997, in conjunction with the government Labor Office (Dirección de Trabajo), raised Chilean awareness of the problems, but in the absence of decisive government regulation by a deliberately underfunded labor inspectorate (Inspección del Trabajo), changed little for the workers in this sector.[56] Neoliberal Chile might style itself a "Pacific tiger," but where the garment industry was concerned it resembled a Central American sweatshop.[57]

These deficiencies and abuses, together with a desire to be able to look after their children and an income insufficient to cover the costs of day care, led a growing number of women in the 1990s to work at home for piece rates on leased sewing machines. Home work did give them the ability to arrange their time so as to be able to tend to household tasks and monitor children, but at the cost of self-exploitation and a work week that could exceed 70 hours. In an image that evokes the preindustrial era—yet which, like sweatshops, seems to be an integral part of contemporary capitalism—other family members often worked alongside the women in an effort to make ends meet and pay off the leased machines, including children, in violation of international accords and Chilean law. More than a quarter of the sector's home workers earned less than minimum wage. As most of them lived in shantytown dwellings with poor light and ventilation and without the safety regulations of a factory, the health costs and risks were often great, as were the social costs to family life. Overall, the job quality of home work was even worse than in Chile's garment industry sweatshops.[58]

Yet, as bad as the lowered quality of jobs was for the textile and clothing

workers who had them, it was better than unemployment. The most catastrophic consequence for Chilean textile workers resulting from the transformation of their industry was the loss of their jobs, whether it was due to the
closing of their mill, or because they were laid off or were downsized as part of
cost-cutting to make the enterprise more competitive or more profitable. Even
here there were differences. Workers laid off because of a downturn in demand
might be rehired once business picked up again. Workers who were downsized
faced a more difficult prospect but might hope to receive a good reference from
their old employer and find a new job in the industry. Most difficult of all was
the situation of workers whose mill closed down, because the large numbers
who would be looking for alternatives made the prospects of finding another
job poorer—and because the restructuring of the industry meant that there were
fewer textile mills, fewer jobs at those mills, and more workers competing
for them.

A worker's prospects of finding a new job varied with age, skill, and geography. In general, older workers (and "older" could mean as young as 30) faced a
more difficult task, as many employers wouldn't hire them. Skill was a more
complex factor. A textile worker might be highly skilled on a particular machine
—a loom for example—but these skills did not easily transfer to another industry. A mechanic or electrician, on the other hand, had a skill that could win a job
outside the textile industry.

A government retraining program could help a weaver gain a skill that might
be transferable, but these programs were regarded as jokes by the workers who
had experienced them. Veteran weavers, for example, were offered retraining as
road construction workers, a job that paid half their previous salary and did not
utilize a lifetime of painfully acquired skills and experience.[59]

Geography, too, affected a worker's possibilities of finding a new job. In a
small company town like Chiguayante or in a provincial city like Viña del Mar
that had lost its industrial base, a former Machasa or former Textil Viña worker
might have a difficult time finding comparable employment. In Santiago, on the
other hand, Machasa workers faced the closing of their plant with confidence
that they could find other jobs. Yet Chiguayante and Viña del Mar were communities where workers had homes, lifestyles, and social networks that they
prized. Relocation in search of uncertain and ill-paid employment meant adding a further cost to the loss that they had already suffered.

To many workers, this new "crisis of the 1990s" was like "the crisis of the
eighties all over again."[60] In reality, for textile workers it was worse. The 1980s
crisis was a recession so deep that it seemed like a depression, but it was a
general crisis of the Chilean economy. Once the economy recovered—with gov-

ernment help—employment in the sector rose.[61] The crisis of the nineties in the textile industry took place in the midst of the longest period of sustained growth with low inflation in modern Chilean history. Moreover, it was a *structural* crisis, from which there would be no recovery—unless the government intervened to protect the industry, which it refused to do. During the prosperity and low unemployment of the mid-1990s, this starker reality was softened by the existence of alternative jobs, if not always for a comparable wage or in the same industry or region. In 1998, however, the boom ended and unemployment rose, as did worker anxiety over job insecurity and comparisons to the 1980s.[62]

During the years of economic downturn that followed, the crisis spread to the garment industry, which increasingly had to compete with Asian imports and depend on department and chain stores that insisted on lower prices and the return of unsold merchandise. In response, clothing plants reduced their workforce still further and pressed those who remained to work harder for longer hours for less pay. Labor "rationalization" became a permanent feature in both the textile and garment industries. As a result, although Contextil in 2002 contained the same number of local plant unions as in 1997, the number of its members had plummeted by two-thirds, from 15,000 to 5,000. In the textile and garment industry as a whole, the labor force had been reduced to an estimated 80,000 by 2002, not including home workers.[63]

Fear of job loss and plant closings also weakened worker power in the workplace. The inability to say no to a management demand for overtime work, no matter how unreasonable it might be, was only one instance of the more generalized loss of power that textile workers experienced in their mills. "Flexibilization"—allowing management to move workers from task to task, section to section, shift to shift, or plant to plant—was a central employer demand, embodied, as we have seen, in the Pinochet Labor Code and not modified under the Concertación. But even where contracts forbade the practice, neither workers nor their union representatives felt in a position to protest. Where jobs were perceived as precarious and job security as the top priority, fear of firing inhibited workers from defending themselves. The same was true in the face of Labor Code violations and arbitrary or abusive behavior by supervisors on the factory floor.

This worker loss of power was clear as well at the bargaining table. It was most dramatic where workers felt compelled to give in to management demands for givebacks, as was the case with Machasa workers, who had been the highest paid and most empowered in the industry in the 1980s. In a 1993 cost-cutting move, they were asked to accept reductions in wages and benefits and threatened with the closing of their plant and loss of their jobs if they refused.

In the end, workers at Machasa's Santiago plant refused to agree to givebacks and the plant was closed, while workers at Machasa's Chiguayante plant did accept them and their plant continued to operate, but with a reduced workforce as well as lower wages and benefits and a military martinet as manager.[64] In the 1990s it seemed as if even formerly combative textile workers and their unions had lost the protagonism of the past.

The powerlessness that textile workers felt in the 1990s as a result of precarious jobs in an unprotected industry in a globalized economy led many to lose self-confidence and self-esteem as well. This loss of agency under the restored democracy they had fought for and the center-left governments they had voted for was particularly ironic when compared to the intense activism that textile workers had retained in the 1980s in the face of a repressive dictatorship and economic crisis.

There were exceptions to this rule, and some of them were surprising. In 1992 workers at Artela, a profitable medium-sized mill that had not had a strike for decades, stopped work to protest abusive foremen and went on to win a big strike. As a consequence, worker and union militancy increased during the 1990s and Artela's owners chose a new manager known for his skill in labor relations and preference for social concertation.[65]

But strikes were few and far between in the Chilean textile industry in the 1990s.[66] The labor laws were stacked against them, and both jobs and mills were too precarious. The Christian Democratic leaders of the Contevech advised their local leaders not to run the risk of confronting management.[67] Even a combative Communist like Patricia Coñoman, the head of the Contextil and its representative at the CUT for much of the 1990s, who had fearlessly led both strikes and protests under the dictatorship, was convinced by 1997 that "the strike as a weapon no longer serves the interests of the workers"—although she was hard put to discover a more promising alternative.[68] Five years later, she confessed to not knowing what to advise local union leaders.[69] The Christian Democrat–led Contevech seemed to have accepted the gradual demise of the industry and was focusing on job retraining.[70]

It was this kind of pessimism and passivity on the part of national and regional labor leaders within the CUT that led Artela workers at the close of the Pinochet era to take a leading role in forming an independent county-wide labor federation that cut across craft lines. At bottom, it was an effort to adapt the militant *cordon industrial* model of the Allende years to an era in which traditional trade unionism did not seem to work.[71] By then, the shift in power at most of Chile's textile mills seemed irreversible.

It was evident in the production sections, where management was authoritarian and worker participation in shaping working conditions absent. It was apparent at the negotiating table, where the bargaining power of the workers was limited. And it was all too clear in the low wages that Chile's textile and garment workers took home in return for their increasingly hard and long labor.

To live decently in the 1990s, a family of five needed an income of at least double the minimum wage. But unless more than one family member worked, most textile and garment workers did not come close to that standard and most earned at or near minimum wage. By 2002 the situation had worsened and in order to live decently both mother and father also had to earn the production bonuses that many enterprises offered as an incentive for its workers to work overtime and weekends, saving them the costs of hiring more personnel and paying them benefits. Moreover, as many workers were deeply in debt, once their debt payments were discounted—often directly from their pay—even though they earned a decent salary on paper, their "real" take home pay was close to the minimum wage, which left them close to the poverty line.

This was particularly true in the smaller textile mills and in the sweatshops and home workplaces that dominated the garment industry. Yet these were the sectors that experienced the greatest job growth in the 1990s as a result of the structural shift in the textile and garment industries in Chile, with chains of production controlled by department stores or clothing store chains that subcontracted labor-intensive operations to small, low-cost, unregulated plants.

Taken together, these changes added up to a sharp decline in job quality during the 1990s in the textile and clothing sectors. In general, work weeks were longer and work rhythms more intense. Fewer workers had written contracts. Physical working conditions were worse, in terms of noise, space, safety, light, and ventilation. Moreover, workers had less say over their working conditions and fewer had unions to represent them or much social protection in case of illness, pregnancy, dismissal, or retirement. Few had opportunities for continuing education or training. Nor were their jobs and incomes secure. In different ways, therefore, work in the textile and garment industries had become "precarious."

As a result, by 1998 far fewer textile and clothing workers had what the ILO considered "decent jobs." As a group, the workers of the sector had not benefited from Chile's decade of steady economic growth with low inflation. On the contrary, many felt that they had paid the costs of that "miracle," even that they had been sacrificed on its altar: angry sentiments that worsening conditions during the economic downturn of 1998–2002 only deepened.

Many also felt betrayed by the parties of the center-left Concertación that they had supported and counted on to support them in return. Some even felt disillusioned with the democracy that they had fought to restore during the 1980s, yet that they felt had not fulfilled the hopes and expectations that accompanied its restoration. "We were better off under Pinochet," one embittered Textil Viña employee affirmed as he faced the loss of his job and livelihood.[72] Few textile workers were willing to agree that they were better off under Pinochet, but many attested to feeling disillusioned with a democracy that "had benefited the bosses, not the workers" and that had left intact the antilabor laws and neoliberal policies of the dictatorship.[73] Several union leaders who were members of the parties of the Concertación and had in the past campaigned hard to put them in power, confessed to me that they were among the nearly 40 percent of Chilean voters who refused to register or cast blank or spoiled ballots in the December 1997 congressional elections. "I did it as a protest," one explained, adding that many workers he knew had done the same.[74] It was a protest that raised questions about the sustainability of Chile's neoliberal democracy—and underscored the costs to textile workers of the country's neoliberal economic policy.

TEXTILE WORKERS AND THE CHILEAN "MIRACLE"

For the Chilean textile industry, the Pinochet era was one of crisis, resurgence, and renewed crisis. It was a saga of survival and success, but also of bankruptcy and failure. In 1982 most textile enterprises were either bankrupt or on the verge of failing; by 1989 the crisis was over, and the survivors were optimistic about the future under a restored democracy led by a center-left government. Yet in 1998, at the end of the Chilean miracle and the Pinochet era, there were few textile enterprises left and fewer still that were prosperous—a decline that the economic downturn of 1998–2002 only made worse. The democratic governments of the Concertación had proved even less protective of the Chilean textile industry than the Pinochet dictatorship in the face of a globalization that resembled a race to the bottom. The Concertación had completed what the Pinochet dictatorship had begun, and Sergio de Castro's neoliberal vision of the end of the Chilean textile industry had become prophecy.

In place of the large, protected Chilean textile industries that Pinochet had inherited in 1973 was an international chain of production that stretched from large Asian mills to small Chilean sweatshops and poor women working on rented sewing machines in their shantytown homes. Although the overall employment in the industrial sector that the ILO defines as "textiles and clothing" did not decline dramatically in absolute terms before 1998, it accounted for a far smaller share of an enlarged Chilean labor force. Moreover, there had been a dramatic restructuring within the sector, a gendered shift from male textile workers earning high wages in large, unionized mills to female garment workers earning low wages in small, unorganized sweatshops. During the years of economic downturn that followed the end of the Chilean boom, however, the crisis spread to the garment industry as well. Overall, between 1990 and 2002, the industry estimates its job loss as 30,000 to 40,000 positions, or 25–33 percent of its workforce.[75]

The implications for Chile's textile workers were severe. Many of them lost their jobs and careers; most of those who retained their jobs lived in fear of being fired or of their enterprise closing down. Not only were their jobs more precarious, they had also experienced a decline in the quality of their jobs, whether measured by wages and benefits, work hours and work intensity, or working conditions and participation in decision making. Although there were exceptions, this process was accompanied by the declining power of textile workers and their organizations in collective bargaining and on the factory floor. As a result, textile workers labored harder and for longer hours, in worsened conditions, and for wages and benefits that did not reflect their increased productivity and often did not exceed the minimum wage. It was hard to disagree with the ex-Machasa worker who—like most textile workers I interviewed—concluded: "We [textile workers] were *victims* of the Miracle."[76]

NOTES

1 Radomiro Ferrer, Viña del Mar, interview of July 1998. Except where people interviewed were public figures, I have changed their names to protect their privacy.

2 For a more detailed description of the Chilean textile industry before Pinochet, see Peter Winn, *Weavers of Revolution: The Yarur Workers and Chile's Road to Socialism* (New York: Oxford University Press, 1986), chaps. 1–2 and 13–18, on which this section is based, except where otherwise noted.

3 In 1968, for example, the textile industry employed one-fifth of the industrial labor force and (together with clothing) accounted for 15 percent of industrial production. Augusto Aninat, "Sector textil: Transformaciones y potencialidades," table 4, "Significado del sector textil, 1960–1973," in Aninat et al., *La industria chilena: Cuatro visiones sectoriales* (Santiago: Centro de Estudios del Desarrollo, 1986), 283.

4 Unless otherwise noted, the sources for this section are the interviews with more than 50 textile entrepreneurs, managers, and economists that I conducted between 1988 and 1998, and the reports and statistics of the Instituto Textil de Chile.

5 Aninat, "Sector textil," 250–63.

6 Fuad Garib, Santiago, interview of August 1988.

7 For a more detailed account of the Plan Laboral, see Peter Winn's chapter "The Pinochet Era," and Guillermo Campero and José A. Valenzuela, *El movimiento sindical en el regimen militar, 1973–1981* (Santiago: ILET, 1984), chap. 3.

8 Fuad Garib, Santiago, interview of August 1988; Augusto Aninat, Santiago, interview of August 1988.

9 Aninat concluded that by 1984 the effective protection for textiles was 37.1 percent and for consumer goods was 36.1 percent (Aninat, "Sector textil," table 18, "Protecciones efectivas para el sector textil," 258).

10 Manufacturas Sumar, S.A., *Memoria*, no. 50 (April 1988); Miguel Vega, Santiago, interview of July 1988; Roberto Sumar, Santiago, interview of August 1988.

11 Aninat, "Sector textil," table 39: "Costos laborales hilandería y tejeduría, 1984," 285.

12 Except where noted otherwise, this section is based on over 100 interviews with textile workers and their leaders conducted between 1988 and 1998. I want to thank them for sharing their experiences with me. I am also indebted to the authors of the PET studies on the Chilean textile industry—Patricio Frías, Magdalena Echeverría, Gonzalo Herrera, Christian Larraín, and Rafael Agacino—who, while writing for worker and union leaders, blazed a research trail that I have followed. See Patricio Frías, Magdalena Echeverría, Gonzalo Herrera, and Christian Larraín, *Industria textil y del vestuario en Chile*, 3 vols. (Santiago: PET, 1987); and Rafael Agacino, *Evolución económica reciente de los sectores textil y del vestuario, 1986–1990* (Santiago: PET, 1991).

13 Hernán López, private communication, Santiago, January 1975.

14 Renato Baéz, Santiago, interview of July 1988.

15 Lucía Bonilla, Santiago, interview of July 1988.

16 Oscar Godoy, Santiago, interview of July 1988.

17 Lucía Bonilla, Santiago, interview of July 1988.

18 Renato Baéza, Santiago, interview of July 1988.

19 Orlando Serna, Santiago, interview of August 1988.

20 Alejandro Fridman, general manager, Machasa, Santiago, interview of August 1988; Raimundo San Martín, human resources manager, Machasa, Santiago, interview of August 1988.

21 Roberto Sumar, Santiago, interview of August 1988; Miguel Vega, president, Contevech, Santiago, interview of July 1988.

22 Lucía Bonilla, Santiago, interview of July 1988; Manuel Robles, Santiago, interview of August 1988.

23 Mario García, manager, Instituto Textil de Chile, Santiago, interview of July 1989.

24 Mario Sepúlveda, Santiago, interview of July 1988.

25 Ernesto Robles, Santiago, interview of July 1988.

26 Lucía Bonilla, Santiago, interview of July 1988.

27 The Contextil is the successor confederation to the Fenatratex. It was formed in 1983 by Communist and Socialist labor leaders who were unhappy with Contevech's pragmatic orientation and its largely Christian Democratic leadership. Its late foun-

dation reflects the initial reluctance of the Left to take actions that might imply acceptance of the legitimacy of the new Labor Code. Its late start and promotion of strikes that workers could not win weakened it during the 1980s, when the Contevech was by far the stronger confederation. During the 1990s the Contevech's closeness to the Concertación government was at first a benefit and then a burden, as worker disillusionment set in, leaving the more combative Contextil as the confederation of choice for many.

28 Together with antidumping countervailing duties, the Pinochet protection of the Chilean textile industry in the mid-1980s exceeded 30 percent in many cases. By 1988, with the industry resurgent, this combination of tariffs had been reduced to 20 percent, which was still double what the level of protection had been 10 years before—or would be a decade later (Mario García, manager, Instituto Textil de Chile, Santiago, interview of August 1988).

29 Fuad Garib, president, Hitega, Santiago, interview of March 1997; Gustavo Soria, general manager, Machasa, Santiago, interview of June 1997; Mario García, Santiago, interview of August 1988.

30 Luis Ramírez, president, Sindicato 2, Textil Viña, Viña del Mar, interview of June 1997.

31 Juan Carlos Poblete, director, Machasa-Santiago Union, Santiago, interview of June 1991; Juan Carlos Ramos, ex-president, Machasa-Santiago Union, Santiago, interview of June 1998.

32 Juan Carlos Ramos, Machasa, Santiago, interview of June 1998; Miguel Vega, Santiago, interview of July 1997.

33 Gustavo Soria, Santiago, interview of June 1997; Gonzalo Sepúlveda, general manager, Textil Viña, Santiago, interview of June 1997; Luis Ramírez, president, Textil Viña, Sindicato 2, Viña del Mar, interview of June 1997; Juan Carlos Ramos, ex-president, Machasa–Santiago Union, Santiago, interview of July 1988.

34 Fuad Garib, Santiago, interview of March 1997.

35 I am grateful to Sue Gronewold for sharing with me her research in Shanghai. By 2001, the New York Times was reporting that China's "financially troubled" textile industry had "laid off about 1.4 million cotton workers since 1998" (New York Times, 18 March 2001, 8).

36 David Lerman, Confecciones Calderon, Santiago, interview of June 1997; Fuad Garib, Santiago, interview of March 1997.

37 For a more detailed analysis of production chains in the Chilean textile industry, see Gerhart Reinecke, "Inside the Model: Politics, Enterprise Strategies, and Employment Quality in Chile." Ph.D. diss., University of Hamburg, 2000, 202–23.

38 Gustavo Acuña, general manager, Artela, Santiago, interview of August 1997.

39 Alberto Saéz, Santiago, interview of June 1997. As this interview was not for attribution, I have changed the name of the interviewee.

40 Hugo Grisanti, former general manager, Machasa and Textil Viña, Santiago, interview of July 1997; Gustavo Soria, Santiago, interview of June 1997; Juan Carlos Ramos, Santiago, interview of July 1998.

41 Mario García, Santiago, interview of August 1997.

42 For a more detailed analysis of flexibilization and the Chilean textile industry, see Reinecke, "Inside the Model," 185–201.

43 Fuad Garib, Santiago, interview, March 1997.

44 Mario García, president, Instituto Textil de Chile, Santiago, interview of August 2002.

45 Mario García, Santiago, interview of August 2000; Patricia Coñoman, president, Contextil, Santiago, interview of August 2000.

46 Mario García, Santiago, interview of August 2002; Estrella Díaz, Dirección del Trabajo, Ministerio del Trabajo, Santiago, interview of August 2002; Gary Gereffi, David Spener, and Jennifer Bair, eds., *Free Trade and Uneven Development: The North American Apparel Industry after* NAFTA (Philadelphia: Temple University Press, 2002). This book's analysis of winners and losers in the textile and garment industry concludes that NAFTA impelled a new regional division of labor that favored the producers with lowest costs and proximity and easy transport to U.S. markets, as well as those clustered in an industrial center with a preexisting manufacturing tradition in apparel and a dynamic group of entrepreneurs. These characteristics have turned Torreón in northern Mexico into the "jeans capital of the world" (207), which attracted further investment that has deepened and consolidated its dominant position in the region, discouraging the growth of other centers. This regional restructuring of the North American apparel industry has made Mexico the United States's leading supplier, while confining Central America and the Caribbean to peripheral *maquiladora* assembly roles. There is little reason to believe that these logics of regional restructuring would favor the Chilean textile and garment industry.

47 Mario García, Santiago, interview of August 2002.

48 See Reinecke, "Inside the Model," 162–63, tables 5.2–5.4. The Encuesta Nacional Industrial Anual for 1980 yielded a total of 47,512 workers in the textile and garment industries, of whom 29,506 worked in the textile sector and 18,006 in the garment sector. In 1996, the textile-garment total was 49,118, but the textile sector was reduced to 25,644 workers, while the garment sector had grown to 23,474 workers. The employment survey—carried out in households, not workplaces and thus able to get at unregulated informal economy enterprises as well—by the same National Statistics Institute (INE) suggested that total employment in the industry in 1996 was 80,029, with 49,837 in the garment sector and 30,192 in the textile area. But all of these worked in enterprises with more than 10 employees. When the self-employed (mostly homeworkers) and those who worked in enterprises with fewer than 10 employees were added in, the number of workers in the industry rose to 152,538, with 106,909 in the garment sector and only 45,629 in the textile sector. Most of the women employed in the industry worked in these smaller enterprises, while most of the men worked in enterprises with 10 or more employees (Reinecke, "Inside the Model," tables 5.2–5.4).

49 For a general discussion of job quality and its application to Latin America in the 1990s, see Ricardo Infante, ed., *La calidad del empleo: La experiencia de los países latinoamericanos y de los Estados Unidos*, 2d ed. (Santiago: ILO, 2000), chaps. 1–2. For an application of these concepts to Chile, see Reinecke, "Inside the Model," 135–50.

50 See Ximena Díaz and Sonia Yáñez, "La proliferación del sistema de subcontrataciones en la industria del vestuario en Chile come fuente de la precarización del empleo femenino," working paper (Santiago: Centro de Estudios de la Mujer [CEM], 1998).

51 See Ximena Díaz and Norah Schlaen, La salud ignorada: Trabajadores de la confección (Santiago: CEM, 1994), 97–149.

52 Patricia Coñoman, president, Contextil, Santiago, interview of August 2002.

53 I am grateful to Ximena Díaz and Julía Medel for sharing with me the unpublished CEM survey of and interviews with clothing workers in small shops and homeworkers.

54 Reinecke concluded that longer working hours and increased work intensity did not translate into higher productivity in the smaller subcontracted enterprises because they did not have modern technology (Reinecke, "Inside the Model," 224).

55 Chilean labor law required an employer to provide day care where there were more than 19 women working at the enterprise. In the largely female clothing industry, employers evaded this requirement by limiting the size of their labor force, subcontracting, or simply ignoring the requirement, counting on poor or corrupt regulation, or on claiming ignorance if caught.

    None of the employers I interviewed in the Patronato garment district had day care centers, even when they admitted to having more than 19 female employees. Nor did women employed in the sector attest to the presence of day care centers in their workplace. The lack of day care centers was often cited by women as a reason they preferred home work. The larger CEM survey of women workers in the garment industry supports these conclusions. See for example, Ximena Díaz, Julia Medel, and Norah Schlaen, Mujer, trabajo y familia: El trabajo a domicilio en Chile (Santiago: CEM, 1996).

56 I am grateful to the Comedor Acogedor del Patronato for sharing their video copies of these television reports of October 1996 with me. Their analysis and conclusions were confirmed by my interviews with María Estér Feres, Directora del Trabajo, Santiago, interview of June 1997; Sandra Leal, Comedor Acogedor, Santiago, interview of July 1997; Felisa Garay, Comedor Acogedor, Santiago, interview of July 1997; and Patricia Coñoman, president, Contextil, Santiago, interview of June 1997.

57 For an interesting discussion of the origins of the term "sweatshop" and the problems involved in defining and describing it, see Daniel Bender, "Sweatshop Subjectivity and the Politics of Description and Exhibition," International Labor and Working-Class History 61 (spring 2002), Sweated Labor: The Politics of Representation and Reform, 13–23. The realization that sweatshops are not a vestige of an earlier time, but part and parcel of 20th-century capitalist globalization is clear both in Carmen Teresa Whelan's article on the garment industry in the Caribbean and New York, "Sweatshops Here and There: The Garment Industry, Latinas, and Labor Migrations," International Labor and Working-Class History 61 (spring 2002): Sweated Labor: The Politics of Representation and Reform, 45–68; and in Jefferson Cowie's review essay, "A Century of Sweat: Subcontracting, Flexibility, and Consumption," International Labor and Working-Class History 61 (spring 2002): Sweated Labor: The Politics of Representation and

Reform, 128–140, which discusses recent books about garment workers in sweat-shops in Los Angeles, El Paso, New York, and Paris, and stresses that modern sweatshops are not just plants with substandard working conditions but rather the result of the subcontracting at the heart of the globalization of textile and clothing production. A recent book that addresses those issues is Miriam Ching Yoon Louie, *Sweatshop Warriors: Immigrant Women Workers Take on the Global Factory* (Cambridge, Mass.: South End Press, 2001).

58 In addition to my own interviews, this analysis is based on the far larger group of interviews done for the CEM study on home work, whose conclusions confirm my own. See Díaz, Medel, and Schlaen, *Mujer, trabajo y familiae*.

59 Luis Ramírez, president Sindicato 2, Textil Viña, Viña del Mar, interview of June 1997.

60 José Pinto, Textil Viña, Viña del Mar, interview of July 1997.

61 Reinecke, "Inside the Model," 162, table 5.2: "Employment in textile and garment establishments of 10 and more workers, 1980–1996."

62 José Pinto, Textil Viña, Viña del Mar, interview of July 1997.

63 Patricia Coñoman, president, Contextil, Viña del Mar, interview of August 2000. Her estimate for 1997 was 120,000 workers in the sector.

64 Antonio Cañulado, president, Machasa-Santiago Union, Santiago, interview of December 1997; Juan Carlos Ramos, ex-president, Machasa-Santiago Union, Santiago, interview of August 1998; Ruben Muñoz, president, Machasa-Chiguayante Union 2, Chiguayante, interview of August 1998; José Cid, director, Machasa-Chiguayante Union 2, Chiguayante, interview of August 1998; Eduardo Mora, ex-president, Machasa-Chiguayante Union 2, Concepción, interview of August 2000.

65 Gustavo Acuña, general manager, Artela, Santiago, interview of August 1997; Isaac Motles, president, Artela, Santiago, interview of September 1997.

66 A long, bitter strike in 2001 at Pollak—one of the largest remaining mills with one of the most militant unions—could not stop a one-third reduction in its workforce, although it was able to win concessions for those workers who remained (Patricia Coñoman, Santiago, interview of August 2002; Mario García, Santiago, interview of August 2002).

67 Octavio Paéz, Contevech, Santiago, interview of March 1997.

68 Patricia Coñoman, Santiago, interview of June 1997.

69 Patricia Coñoman, Santiago, interview of August 2002.

70 Oscar Padilla, Contevech, Santiago, interview of March 1997.

71 Lautaro Vásquez, Artela Union officer, Santiago, interview of August 1997.

72 José Muñoz, Viña del Mar, interview of June 1997.

73 Andrés Lorca, Artela, Santiago, interview of August 1997.

74 Juan Carlos Muñoz, Santiago, interview of August 1998.

75 Mario García, president, Instituto Textil de Chile, Santiago, interview of August 2002. These estimates do not include homeworkers.

76 Alberto Robles, Santiago, interview of December 1997.

JOEL STILLERMAN

Disciplined Workers and Avid Consumers:

Neoliberal Policy and the Transformation of Work and

Identity among Chilean Metalworkers

The health consequences for those who work long hours are disastrous. One worker in shipping and receiving doubled his standard output, forcing his workmates to do the same in a sort of Olympics of production. He's suffering the consequences today: he fell into a depression and is off the job. He went so far as to say, "I sit in my living room and I see my boss in front of me." . . . The more hours you work, the more money you make, but your quality of life declines when there's no time to spend with your family, relax, play sports, or attend cultural events.[1]

Madeco, S.A. (Manufacturas de Cobre, Sociedad Anónima), the Southern Cone's largest copper products manufacturer, experienced spectacular growth during the Pinochet dictatorship and subsequent civilian administrations. In 1979 the junta sold the state-owned firm to the Luksic Group, one of Chile's most prosperous family-owned business conglomerates. After surviving the 1981–83 crisis, when many firms folded, Madeco aggressively expanded and modernized operations by acquiring domestic and foreign competitors, issuing stock on the New York Stock Exchange, and investing in new machinery. Madeco exemplified the "Chilean miracle."

As the introductory epigraph suggests, however, there are two sides to the coin. In tandem with the dictatorship's broader goals, Madeco's managers believed they had to discipline and remold workers in order to achieve this success. Management, and in particular the retired military official who served as personnel manager, systematically purged Marxist militants, tried to short-circuit the powerful blue-collar union, undercut workers' shop floor solidarity, and shifted resources from workers to managers and stockholders.

I examine these processes of political repression, wage and benefit cuts, and work intensification that made Madeco's success possible. How did workers experience and respond to these assaults on their economic power, political sympathies, and collective identities? More important, how did Madeco's transformation affect its workers' precoup solidaristic culture? Madeco's modernization, while it provoked tenacious resistance, ultimately eroded working-class solidarity. In the process, political terror and industrial rationalization reworked the relationships between production, consumption, and social identities.

Madeco is a compelling case for examining these processes because of the blue-collar union's militant traditions. Before 1973 Madeco workers were among the highest paid industrial workers in Chile, consistently elected leftist union leaders, worked to build the labor movement, and actively supported the socialist Popular Unity government. The union held one of the most militant strikes during the dictatorship and helped rebuild the labor movement from the grass-roots. The dictatorship and subsequent civilian administrations fundamentally challenged these radical traditions.

Madeco's recent history highlights the contradictory effects of industrial restructuring on a group of relatively privileged workers. Beginning in the mid-1970s with the opening of the Chilean economy, Madeco's managers rationalized production in piecemeal fashion through wage and benefit reductions, work intensification, and the promotion of worker competition. Rationalization also included massive layoffs during the 1981–83 economic crisis and targeted dismissals of union activists. During the 1990s the incorporation of more advanced machinery and computerized monitors extended these processes. Work intensification interacted with the growing availability of consumer credit, more sophisticated marketing, and global retailers' entry into Chile. This interaction promoted a vicious circle of overtime work, conspicuous consumption, and debt for many workers. The new consumerism undermined work and union solidarity among many, while union activists defended collective forms of consumption and a specific model of masculinity they associated with class solidarity.

In February 1993 workers responded to this last wave of rationalization and benefit cuts throughout the dictatorship by holding a violent strike to maintain their right to sue management for underpayment of a share of profits. The union won its principal demand, but management had already changed the rules of the game by luring half of the white-collar staff and a few blue-collar workers into company unions. For the first time since the blue-collar union's 1945 inception, management had broken its monopoly over blue-collar workers, raising serious questions about the union's future.

The Madeco case encourages us to supplement existing findings regarding managerial restructuring in Chilean workplaces. Scholars note that workplace restructuring has led to work intensification and reduced real wages without significant technological upgrades, new product designs, or effective job training.[2] This work has not explored how these managerial practices may generate significant shop floor conflicts and strikes. At Madeco, work intensification and managers' contempt for workers' ideas led to a blue-collar revolt. This case points to the limits of Chilean managers' efforts to restructure workplaces without engaging in some sort of social contract with the workforce.

The experiences of industrial restructuring at Madeco and other Chilean firms are part of a global story of the erosion of the post–World War II class compromise. Beginning in the 1970s managers have experimented with new, more efficient forms of workplace organization: industrial districts composed of small flexible firms, team-based production, and the reduction of buffer inventories. Scholars debate whether these industrial changes are liberating or increasingly exploitative.[3] However, researchers on both sides of this debate agree that global market competition drives these firm-level changes. The Madeco case, in contrast, demonstrates that national political regimes and legal institutions profoundly shape industrial change.

Madeco workers' resistance to managerial authority also challenges the view that shantytown protest eclipsed union activism under the Chilean junta.[4] In contrast, I show that the experience of many Madeco workers in these same protests informed their resistance to managerial authority and participation in the 1993 strike. Hence the protests influenced the character of young people's workplace resistance after they entered factories in the mid-1980s.

Finally, Madeco workers' adaptation to and criticisms of new consumption-based lifestyles challenge the common perspective that globalization leads to the homogenization of local cultures.[5] Others criticize this view by showing that globalization often provokes nationalist or ethnic responses. In contrast to these critiques, I found that working-class Chilean men have reacted to the entry of new consumption-based lifestyles by defending their class identity and masculinity.

This chapter traces Madeco's transformation under the dictatorship through three distinct phases. From 1973 to 1978 political terror, existing labor law, and traditional management attitudes conditioned and limited managerial efforts at industrial restructuring. During the second phase, from 1979 to 1986, new owners adopted a different managerial vision and exploited the advantages the new labor laws offered. The third period, extending to today, witnessed the firm's transformation into an economic group and the partial implementation of internationally recognized flexible management techniques. This last wave of modernization has challenged workers' traditional controls over production volume, attitudes about shop floor solidarity, consumption patterns, and gender identities. Workers responded to these challenges in the 1993 strike, whose consequences may threaten the union over the long term.

Since its origins in 1944 Madeco has been Chile's largest copper manufacturer. At its main Santiago location,[6] the firm consists of two adjacent plants: a wire mill, where workers fashion copper wire and cables; and a brass mill, where they make sheets, tubes, pipes, and profiles from copper and copper alloys. Each mill supplies different markets, is subject to distinct market cycles, and has different labor processes.[7] Madeco was founded in 1944 as a family-managed firm with state support through investment and loans. In 1958 the state sold its share in the industry. Nine years later, General Cable (U.S.A.) and CEAT International (Italy) came to dominate the firm through a joint venture to build a telephone cable plant in Antofagasta near the Chuquicamata copper mine. In 1971, as part of the Allende administration's policy of creating a social property area, the state development corporation (Corporación de Fomento, Corfo), took over management of the firm in collaboration with worker production committees and bought 21 percent of its shares. Less than a year later Corfo negotiated an option to buy 42 percent of the shares owned by the two foreign enterprises and took physical possession of those shares.[8]

Madeco's founders, the Simonetti brothers, were paternalistic managers who benefited from significant state subsidies and tariff protection. The brothers allowed workers to adopt internal subcontracting (hiring family members) and established an internal labor market permitting considerable upward mobility. In 1966 two professional managers took over the firm and began Madeco's first effort at rationalization, provoked by the loss of key subsidies and economic stagnation. From 1966 to 1971 the firm's executives sought to shift some productive functions in cables to the new plant in Antofagasta, reduce personnel in Santiago, and increase skill levels among blue-collar workers and middle management. State administration of Madeco from 1971 to 1973 reversed these cost savings as personnel increased and work discipline declined under worker-state comanagement.

Prior to the 1973 coup the Madeco blue-collar union became one of the strongest in the metallurgical sector, and workers there earned salaries and benefits well above the average for industrial workers. The union had strong ties to leftist parties, spearheaded organizing campaigns among other unions in the San Miguel municipality, where the union is located, and contributed leaders to the national metalworkers' federation. The Madeco union hall became a center of neighborhood social and political events, and the union organized an array of services and activities for members and their families: a school and a health clinic, sports clubs, political debates, and a library, as well as consumer and housing cooperatives. In short, the Madeco union was economically and politically strong, as well as a rich center of working-class and neighborhood sociability.[9]

Repression with a Human Face, 1973–1978

Madeco faced serious financial problems after the Popular Unity period, which, combined with monetary devaluations and the elimination of price subsidies, forced the new general manager (who had been production manager from 1966 to 1971) to think on his feet. Madeco's ambiguous ownership status and its substantial debt meant that its executive had neither the decision-making authority nor the cash to invest in labor-saving machinery.[10]

While these economic imperatives and constraints acted as important guides to managerial policy, political terror against the Left also played a crucial role. A retired army official, Jaime Deischler, served as personnel manager from 1967 until 1992, when it was discovered that one of the Pinochet intelligence service's most brutal interrogators, Osvaldo Romo, had worked at Madeco on company salary in 1974 to identify and detain subversives. Deischler terrorized and humiliated workers and tried to neutralize the blue-collar union, the oldest and most militant in the firm. Thus management implemented each reform with a veiled or explicit threat of dismissal or imprisonment to back it up.

Beginning in 1973 management reduced the workforce through two mechanisms. First, Deischler fired many political militants and others he simply disliked for alleged "subversion." Second, from 1973 to 1978 the personnel manager weeded out many more through "voluntary retirement," where management offered workers increased severance payments in exchange for their agreement to leave.[11] Though the workforce declined from 2,050 in 1973 to 1,085 in 1978, the firm did hire new workers during the finance- and import-driven boom beginning in 1976. Management sought workers with recommendations from military officials, incorrectly assuming that this was a guarantee against troublemakers.

By requiring a high school education for new staff, preferably in trade school, management boosted workers' educational levels, and homogenized their skills. One brass mill worker describes the older workforce he found in 1976:

"When I was hired, most of the guys were real country boys [bien huasitos]. They were sort of illiterate, and they really liked to use their strength. They would pick up one 25-kilo copper bar in each hand and pass them to each other. I was a little skinny guy and could barely pick up one of them."[12] Though they increased educational demands for new recruits, management maintained the internal labor market during this period, thus lending a certain continuity to the workforce.[13] Finally, during the 1970s, management began to subcontract ancillary functions (carpentry, plumbing, painting, etc.) to dismissed employees from these sections.[14]

Management's adoption of new payment schemes meant tremendous losses in workers' earning power. Because collective bargaining was illegal, the firm was unable to rescind workers' contractually and legally guaranteed salaries and benefits. The only way to change payment schemes was to make informal agreements with management-appointed union leaders. To make it a little easier to swallow the bitter pill of wage rollbacks, management offered workers a lump sum in exchange for accepting the new payment formulae. However, placed in a broader context, a single payment could not compare to workers' loss of a significant benefit. As a former long-term leader argues, "No one gives away something for nothing. So in order for management to take away workers' production incentives, they had to pay them a lump sum. . . . People accepted the payment because it helped them satisfy an immediate economic need. So it wasn't really an exchange; it was a trick designed to take away the benefits workers had fought for and won during the preceding period."[15]

Madeco workers had negotiated one of the best union contracts in the country prior to the coup, and thus the stakes of such changes were high for both managers and workers. In September 1974 Madeco workers earned nearly double the average industrial workers' wage.[16] Thus management made two efforts to attack blue-collar workers' main sources of income: production incentives and profit sharing.

In 1976 management replaced production incentives specific to individual machines or work sections and all other productivity-based payments with a uniform monthly bonus based on tonnage produced in each plant. This meant that blue-collar workers, who often earned more than administrative and maintenance personnel because of their productivity bonuses, saw their salaries reduced, while administrative and maintenance personnel now earned a production bonus based on their higher salary scales: the relative earning power of the two groups was reversed.[17]

The second bonanza for management concerned profit sharing. In contracts negotiated prior to the coup, blue-collar union members had won 15 percent of the firm's annual profits for the members (the law required firms to pay 6 percent), as well as vacation, Christmas, and Independence Day bonuses. In 1977 management convinced the union leaders to fuse these separate benefits into a lump sum equaling three monthly base salaries paid quarterly: "The leaders at that time wanted workers to receive a guaranteed payment because the firm had declared losses in the preceding years. The leadership feared that [because the company was not generating profits] workers would lose their monthly profit-sharing payment."[18]

While this decision seemed sensible at the time, it was a serious error over the long term because the firm became profitable again by the end of the decade. Although the leaders' decision to accept this massive payment reduction seems surprising, we need to remember that the junta had appointed them. They had not been elected and had few opportunities to consult with their constituents because union meetings were under military surveillance. Without rank-and-file input and pressure, appointed leaders were more susceptible to persuasion or coercion from the personnel manager.

Beyond the layoffs and payment cuts, management also began to demand worker speedups. In the wire mill, this process began in 1976:

> Ricardo Ruff, who began as supervisor of the hot rolling mill department, began moving up the ladder, until he became plant superintendent. He gained management's favor by taking two or three loyal workers and placing them in different sections: they were like his "top ten." They would go in and work incredibly fast, report on anyone who couldn't keep up the pace, and then [those slower workers] were promptly sacked. He particularly enjoyed doing this on vacation, when everyone was away. He would take a few guys and run the machines in the whole plant, showing that it could be done. When people saw what was going on, they started working faster. That's when the race began, when Ruff destroyed workers' natural movement of resistance, their attempt to control work rhythms. That's how he turned one worker against another.[19]

Paradoxically, while these brutal wage cuts, attacks against the Left, and work speedups were occurring, management solicited workers' suggestions on how to make machines more cost-efficient, offering them prizes for successful ideas and high productivity: "Management had contests back then to see who could come up with new ideas. I still have the certificates they gave me for my inventions somewhere. You see, I'm about the most comfortable guy you'll meet. If I can figure out a way to pick up that rock without exerting any effort, you can be sure I'll do it. So, I came up with a lot of ideas."[20] In a peculiar nod to Japanese managers' use of workers' suggestions to improve products and processes,

Madeco managers made a virtue of necessity, as there was no money for large-scale machinery innovations. During the 1990s executives would experiment with other Japanese-style production techniques such as multitasking and the use of line workers in quality control. However, in the nineties, management explicitly rejected worker participation in production decisions.[21] While the firm did not adopt Japanese concepts systematically during either period, managers seemed more interested in worker ideas during the 1970s, when political terror was at its zenith, than during the 1990s, as Chile returned to civilian rule.

"Professionalism" and "Lite" Production

In late 1979 after the state had considerable difficulty selling its de facto majority interest in Madeco, the Luksic family bought a controlling stake in the company.[22] The Luksics had begun in car sales and mining in the late 1950s, expanded to fisheries and coal mining in the 1960s, and sold almost all of their enterprises during the Popular Unity era. The group gained a reputation for buying apparently unprofitable enterprises, cutting administrative and payroll costs, and rapidly turning the companies around. Their shrewd investment style helped them weather the 1981–83 economic crisis. By 1978 the Luksic Group was the fourth largest conglomerate in Chile, and by 1993 the family held the third largest fortune in Latin America and 97th largest in the world, with over $4 billion in assets.[23]

With the firm's privatization, the Luksic Group made much more serious efforts to raise productivity and harness control over hiring and firing. The Luksic family replaced Fernando Pérez with a former CEAT manager, Tiberio Dall'Ollio. In addition to CEAT's recommendation of Dall'Ollio, we can speculate that Luksic hired the Italian executive rather than one of their own managers because of his experience in the copper-manufacturing business and training with an Italian multinational. Moreover, by hiring Dall'Ollio, Luksic could receive technical assistance from CEAT while maintaining control over Madeco, a pattern he adopted in other partnerships with foreign corporations.[24]

Dall'Ollio took advantage of new provisions in the labor law permitting massive layoffs for "business reasons" as a way to reduce costs and attack union leaders (elected beginning in 1979) and activists. Management's strategy from the late 1970s, and more strongly after the 1983 strike (discussed below), was fourfold: fire union activists, offer blue-collar members incentives to join the white-collar union (which included skilled workers and office employees), manipulate the white-collar union leaders, and attempt to fire or bribe blue-collar union leaders to quit (union leaders can only be fired through a court proceeding unless they relinquish their job security [*fuero sindical*] out of court).[25] Efficiency and union busting went hand-in-hand.

The feasibility of massive layoffs as of 1981 interacted synergistically with another legal innovation, employers' ability to move workers from one machine to another and to alter their job descriptions: "I started working in 1981, and by the time I arrived, the helpers and quality control inspectors on each machine had been eliminated. Each machine operator had to load his raw material and tools, as well as focus on quality."[26]

In 1979 the Luksics ended the practice of hiring family members of existing staff and began to hire food service, security, construction, and cleaning staff through personnel agencies.[27] An even more significant change was the elimination of the internal labor market for blue-collar workers. In the past, when foreman or middle-management positions were vacated, blue-collar workers were eligible to compete for these jobs.[28] However, the elimination of upward mobility for blue-collar workers coincided with the retention of most foremen who had begun as blue-collar workers. Because blue-collar workers hired after 1975 were required to have a high school education, during the 1980s new recruits were often better educated than their immediate supervisors. Likewise, many foremen adopted an authoritarian style under Deischler's leadership. Hence after 1979 blue-collar workers resented foremen's ham-fisted supervisory style and the fact that they could not become foremen even though they felt more qualified than their superiors. These tensions would later affect Madeco's efforts at organizational change, as I explore below.

Blue-collar workers faced additional obstacles to upward mobility. Though management requires that blue-collar recruits have a high school education with a specialization in machine maintenance, very few of these newer workers ever make it off the shop floor into the machine shop. Many who joined the firm in the 1980s had to begin work before they had completed their high school education because of economic hardship during the 1981–83 crisis. Thus workers at Madeco lost the opportunity to enter into higher-paying jobs appropriate to their level of education. As Madeco's only major competitor in wire production, Cocesa (Cobre Cerrillos, Sociedad Anónima), had an agreement with the firm not to accept former Madeco employees, the latter had few exit options from the company. One worker commented, "If you leave Madeco, you have to get into another line of work, like taking care of the kids, for example [laughs]. If I work 10 years as a machine tender at Madeco, I can't get a job outside as a mechanic because my school training is obsolete. I can't go back to school to get my diploma because I can't afford it and can't schedule it because I work rotating shifts. I'm certainly not going to go work somewhere else for 100,000 pesos a month [about $250] when I make 300,000 here. I'm stuck."[29]

Further fine-tuning of payment forms translated into decreasing worker compensation for rising productivity. First, in 1980 management set a cap on the productivity incentive at 50 percent of base salary (there had formerly been no limit on the payment), with the commitment to increase the incentive immediately should productivity exceed this level. However, they did not raise the cap to 60 percent of base salary until 1994. Furthermore, while production consistently went beyond the cap, the incentive itself was never recalculated: workers were hardly compensated for hefty productivity increases that have continued to today. Second, during the economic crisis of 1982, the company forced workers, under protest, to give back their quarterly profit-sharing payments because the firm had registered losses that year. Third, after a 59-day strike in 1983, discussed below, management lowered base salary scales for blue-collar union members, a move that was only reversed in 1989.[30]

Much of Madeco's profit increases during this period resulted from wage cuts and work intensification, rather than installation of labor-saving machinery. The Luksics dropped any pretenses to seeking workers' opinions in the mid-1980s, preferring to crack the whip. This change in approach reflected the high unemployment rates of the 1981–83 crisis, labor law provisions making dismissals inexpensive, management's efforts to harden lines of occupational stratification, and the firm's attacks on union activists who led a two-month strike in 1983. Managerial attitudes and the firm's economic and legal environment militated against forging a partnership with the workforce.[31]

Becoming a Chilean Tiger:
International Expansion and Flexible Production, 1986–1996

In 1986 the Luksic Group appointed as general manager Carlos Vicuña, a high-level executive at Madeco. During his tenure, he carried out the group's strategy of technological modernization within the firm, expansion in Chile, and acquisitions in neighboring Latin American countries. The group took similar actions in its beer, pasta, and aluminum operations during the same period. Madeco began to buy other enterprises and created its own new firms in the mid-1980s. After an unsuccessful joint venture in Beijing, Madeco bought smaller competitors in Chile, such as the tube and coin-blank manufacturer, Armat.

Then, beginning in the early 1990s the company bought analogous firms in

Argentina, Peru, and Brazil. The group's international acquisitions reflected its assessment that by expanding market share in neighboring countries and diversifying its product base, Madeco would be less dependent on a given product's market cycles or Chile's small domestic market. This strategy also took advantage of privatization waves in these countries, mimicking the family's previous strategy in Chile. Currently, Madeco owns 50 enterprises, many of which are holding companies, distributors, or consulting firms. It forms one of the key chess pieces in the Luksic empire and is far larger now than it ever was as a domestic monopoly industry.[32] Madeco financed these acquisitions and machinery purchases through debt and stock issues (American depository receipts, or ADRs) on the New York Stock Exchange and in Chile, raising over $90 million in 1993.[33]

In addition to these machinery upgrades and new acquisitions, management began to utilize some elements of Japanese-style management practices. This adoption of the "Japanese model," as noted in my introduction, came in the context of global changes in the organization of enterprises. While some believe these changes increase workers' job satisfaction,[34] others emphasize cost-cutting and work intensification.[35] While each of these positions anticipates relatively uniform patterns of management response to heightened competitive pressures, evidence on a variety of local cases suggests that the degree to which managers may permit worker participation in production decisions reflects the character of national collective bargaining institutions and the degree of union power in specific countries.[36]

The Madeco case supports the view that the specific social and institutional contexts of countries affect how managers adapt the Japanese model. Chilean managers adapted the Japanese model within the specific legal and political context of the Pinochet dictatorship. Hence, unlike Japan, where employers compensated core workers for increased productivity and attention to quality, no such quid pro quo was adopted in Chile, as legal changes facilitated layoffs and the threat of repression by military authorities always loomed behind management demands. Moreover, because the Pinochet dictatorship viewed worker comanagement as one of the "errors" of the Allende administration, it was unlikely that managers would look to increasing worker participation in management decisions via Japanese-style work teams as a viable option.[37] Indeed, because class conflict was so intense under Allende, managers attempted to reassert control over workers under the dictatorship, as noted above. Hence Madeco's managers applied those elements of Japanese management concepts that increased productivity without threatening their control over the workforce.

From 1990 to the present Madeco began to deploy Japanese-style production techniques such as "just-in-time" and total quality management.[38] The former technique seeks to reduce finished-goods inventories in order to cut in-process costs and dead time, forcing workers to identify and correct bottlenecks on the shop floor; the latter tries to incorporate workers' suggestions to increase quality. Requiring workers to play a greater role in programming and quality control in itself implies an increase in work intensity, as job responsibilities expand beyond strictly productive activities. In addition, the elimination of buffer stocks places greater pressure on workers because they must fill product orders on time regardless of accidents, machine breakdowns, errors, and so on. The increasing pressure on workers resulting from just-in-time has led some to describe the technique as "management through stress."[39] Moreover, just-in-time and total quality management introduce greater job rotation—often termed multi-skilling—as production is reoriented around teams defined by product line rather than process. Management's solicitation of workers' ideas and criticisms to increase efficiency and quality is the cornerstone of these two techniques.[40]

Like many other Chilean firms,[41] Madeco has implemented these techniques in authoritarian fashion, increasing work intensity while in fact discouraging, ignoring, or punishing workers who offer suggestions about how to increase efficiency or quality. For management, those elements of Japanese techniques that boosted productivity and improved quality were useful. However, any technique that undermined the authority of upper or middle management was suspect.

Systematic implementation of these techniques would require extensive investment in worker training and decentralization of authority. Such policies would reverse management patterns that had been so effective during the 1980s. Greater investment in training would tie management more closely to a specific set of workers. However, executives found the threat of dismissal useful in counteracting union activism and improving work discipline. Conversely, workers who received extensive training might leave the firm to take a better job elsewhere.[42] Furthermore, by increasing blue-collar workers' authority on the shop floor, management would undermine foremen's monopoly on power. Foremen, though often undereducated, had been very useful in pressuring workers to increase productivity, as noted below. Indeed, several workers note that until 1998 (when many older foremen were given early retirement), most foremen had 20 years of tenure and were thus accustomed to abusing their authority as was the norm under the dictatorship—some even had direct links with military intelligence.[43] Madeco adopted those elements of Japanese techniques that allowed them to increase quality, reduce stocks, and move products to market more quickly without upsetting the rigid hierarchy and employment insecurity that had underwritten the firm's rising profits over the preceding years.

Managers' unwillingness to include workers in efforts to improve product and process has limited these techniques' success. One worker in shipping and receiving describes how these policies actually function: "The programming is lousy here. We fill about 35 percent of orders on time. A lot of times we have orders that are two months early, while others are late. The general manager meets with us every year and says, 'We need to improve quality, cleanliness, and the timely completion of product orders,' but that's as far as it goes. They sent a few workers to a quality control course, but then when those workers rejected a defective order, the quality control staff that make the final decision let it go anyway. Why bother?"[44]

While these techniques may not have led to improved coordination of production and line worker involvement in quality control, they certainly boosted worker productivity. The introduction of computerized monitors in the early 1990s is a case in point. The monitors record when a machine is down, forcing workers to account for any lost time: "Before, you could fudge the data if you took a break, because you wrote down a time log; now you can't, because you punch your data in the computer when the shift begins, so it's all recorded."[45] The use of computer monitors has allowed management to virtually eliminate downtime in some sections: "You have to struggle to get permission to go to the bathroom."[46] In a sardonic cartoon in the union's magazine, a shipping and receiving worker hopes that the union will win disposable diapers in the next contract.[47]

Increased work rhythms and productivity demands have fostered greater competition among workers:

> When a worker arrives, he is given three months' probation. In order to get a permanent contract, he works like crazy. Once he has permanent status, they move him up two pay scales. However, in order to get to the highest scale on his machine, it may take two or three years. So he produces more to try to convince management to move him up. The older worker sees him, and says to himself, "If I don't speed up, this guy might steal my job." And there you have it, the Olympics of production.[48]

New recruits are particularly eager to maintain their positions at Madeco because the company still pays above-average industrial wages. For example, in 1995 the national average blue-collar wage was 141,591 pesos per month, whereas most Madeco workers earned an average of 250,000 pesos per month.[49]

Older workers face a different problem: if they are dismissed, they face age discrimination in the labor market and have few marketable skills because of the limited number of firms in this sector.

New machinery has also increased job rotation: "Each of the guys in my section can operate four or five machines, so when there's no work on one, they have to move to another." Another worker had a more somber view of job rotation: "They want us to be polyvalent workers, so that we know how to do everything. For them, it would be best if we were robots that you could just plug in and they started working."[50]

In addition to these demands for time economies, management pressures workers to put in extensive overtime hours. Throughout the 1990s a significant minority of workers toiled for 12, 14, or 16 hours per day for extended periods of time.[51] While overtime certainly results from the firm's increasing orders during the boom and its attempt to work with a lean "head count," foremen sometimes "fabricate" overtime to pad their own salaries.[52] Instead of hiring additional staff, management sets two rather than three shifts in some sections. This strategy allows the firm to increase the workday from eight to 12 hours, extend the work week to seven days during peak periods, and reduce work hours during slack periods without the expense of maintaining a larger staff.

Until 1994 overtime was essentially obligatory, though the law prohibits employers from requiring workers to continue for more than two hours beyond their regular shift.[53] Some of those who worked extensive overtime hours began to develop physical and psychological ailments:

> I remember a few years ago I was working overtime constantly. I broke records. I used to work and all I would think about was the next order I needed to fill, not what I was doing. One day, I was taking the bus to work, and I realized I was squeezing my bus receipt between my fingers—I was suffering from what I would call "acute work stress." I'm lucky I realized, because I could have gone off the deep end. I cut back my hours, relaxed, spent more time with my family, and recovered. But some people don't realize, and get into trouble. One time, we finished the night shift and went out for a drink. One guy was asleep, and all of a sudden, he started acting like he was soldering. My buddies looked at him, puzzled; and I said, "I know what's wrong with him, he's overworked." I woke him up, and he had no idea what had happened.[54]

Throughout the early 1990s the blue- and white-collar unions reported that several workers suffered physical and psychological illnesses and accidents from overwork, leading to hospitalizations, long periods of convalescence, and in some cases, dismissal.[55]

Madeco's technological modernization and entry into world-class status in the last decade has increased the precariousness and intensity of work in unprecedented ways. New machinery permitted managers to further break down old job demarcations, ushering in the "polyvalent" worker; and the authoritarian application of Japanese production concepts such as just-in-time and total quality management has translated into greater work effort rather than higher-quality production based on worker initiatives and suggestions.

Work and Consumption

The increase of overtime work in the late 1980s and 1990s, coinciding with Chile's sustained economic boom, further eroded workers' traditional efforts to control work intensity, output, and the length of the working day. Workers traditionally had implicit assumptions about acceptable levels of work effort and overtime that management gradually eroded during the dictatorship. These assumptions were linked to disdain for individuals that worked faster or longer than the group accepted.[56] Today, active union members vehemently criticize workmates who join the "Olympics of production" and assimilate the dominant model of upward mobility. Likewise, they criticize themselves for acceding to management's demands for excessive overtime. Their scorn for *amarrillos* (company loyalists) and self-criticism represent a multistranded moral and gendered discourse about work, consumption, and the relationship between the two.

The moral and gender dimensions of this discourse center on ideas about loyalty toward fellow workers, self-sufficiency, appropriate gender roles, class loyalty versus upward mobility, and collective versus individual models of consumption. These ideas and debates have intensified in recent years due to heightened shop floor competition and overtime work as well as shifting characteristics of Chile's retail and consumer credit infrastructure.

We can better understand union members' current concerns about "consumerism" by placing them in the context of the consumer behavior of previous cohorts of Madeco workers, national-level changes in retailing and credit in Chile since the late 1970s, and comparative scholarship regarding the effects of globalization on the identities and practices of local populations.

Prior to the 1973 military coup, and continuing to some degree until the early 1980s, blue-collar workers at Madeco enjoyed an array of collective forms of consumption resulting from state policies, management policies, and union demands or initiatives. Approximately 300 Madeco workers and their families rented and later purchased town homes in a housing block constructed by management in response to a 1943 law requiring large employers to invest 5 percent of profits in worker housing. Moreover, hundreds of Madeco workers formed and managed several housing cooperatives. Management purchased large stretches of land, and workers received mortgages through a government program to purchase individual plots and construct their own homes there.

Until the early 1980s union members ran a consumer cooperative in the third floor of the union hall. They could purchase household appliances at wholesale prices through the coop from Madeco's sister firm, Mademsa, and pay for them in installments. The union also ran a medical and dental clinic for members. As noted earlier, the union organized an array of sports and cultural and political activities for union and community members at the union hall. Finally, in the mid-1960s the organization built a summer resort on the coast that members and families visited during their vacations.[57]

Notwithstanding the strongly "collectivist" character of these phenomena, during the 1960s, as Madeco employees earned the highest wages among industrial workers in the country, they also set consumption trends for other workers in their southern Santiago community. As one veteran leader recalls of the 1960s: "When color TV first came to Chile around 1960, if you looked at the roofs of the town homes in the Madeco housing block, they all had antennas. If you observed the Mademsa houses down the road, not all of them had antennas."[58]

Some families were also able to maintain two homes—one in the Madeco housing block and the other either in the housing cooperatives or elsewhere: "I lived in the Madeco housing block until 1971. Since I was a white-collar worker, I had applied for a mortgage through the white-collar workers' pension fund [Caja de Empleados Particulares]. Even though I was purchasing my place [in the Madeco block], the fund gave me an apartment in Providencia [a middle-class area in eastern Santiago], so I moved, and some of my kids stayed here at the housing block. Thanks to Jehová there are a lot of us—we have 11 children."[59] Many workers were able to purchase cars prior to the coup.[60] Finally, Madeco workers had a reputation for being particularly well-dressed.[61]

Prior to the 1973 coup, then, Madeco workers were status-conscious and enjoyed a higher-than-average standard of living for industrial workers.[62] However, their prosperity resulted from contractual guarantees as well as cooperative institutions and coexisted with workers' enforcement of strong informal collective controls on work pace and intensity.[63] After the 1973 coup, management's erosion of those controls, wage and benefit reductions, massive layoffs, and promotion of rate busting (individual efforts to produce more than one's coworkers) radically limited workers' ability to achieve a satisfying standard of living without competing among themselves and contracting high-interest debt.

The changes on the shop floor during the 1990s coincided with shifts in Chile's retail and credit infrastructure with origins in the late 1970s. Trade liberalization in the 1978–83 period facilitated increasing consumption of imported consumer durables. This was so because the relative prices of imported electronics and autos had decreased in relation to food and social services. Purchase of these goods was facilitated by the expansion of consumer credit. Moreover, the emergence of large supermarkets and malls followed a longer tradition of nationally owned department stores.

In the 1990s the reemergence of the debt-financed consumption of imported prestige goods among broad portions of the population became a topic of popular and scholarly debate. While consumption levels declined during the 1981–83 recession, from 1985 to 1995 purchases of consumer durables increased faster than nondurables or services for all social classes, but for largely the same reasons as they had a decade before. The chief difference during the 1990s is that increasing luxury consumption reflected, in part, growing wages across all social classes (though they did not return to their 1974 level until 1992).

These trends have coincided with growing use of department store credit cards. During the mid-1990s, the most indebted groups were the middle and upper-middle class, while the working class had the fastest growth in indebtedness. Moreover, shopping malls and big-box supermarkets have expanded throughout Santiago's periphery during the 1980s and 1990s, reducing sales in corner stores and traditional shopping districts.[64]

These broader changes in Chile's retailing infrastructure are emblematic of global shifts in commodity flows, retailing, and credit most commonly associated with the international diffusion of U.S. consumer lifestyles via fast-food franchises, shopping malls, popular music, and media images. While some accounts view this phenomenon as a process of "Americanization" or cultural imperialism, locally based empirical studies take a more complex view of the consumer behaviors and identities of specific populations. Some observe nationalist reactions to perceived "attacks" on local culture, others examine how consumers integrate foreign commodities and retail forms into local cultural contexts, while a third group explores how global commodities and images become the raw material through which ethnic diasporas or local populations develop transnational identities (either viewing themselves as part of international subcultures or reimagining "lost" national cultures).[65]

My examination, while indebted to the last-mentioned focus on local understandings and uses of global goods and services, focuses on how Madeco union activists have sought to defend a masculine and class-based identity against what they perceived as new models of individualism ushered in by Chile's changing retail infrastructure. They counterposed class-specific communal forms of consumption to the individualism they viewed as inappropriate for workers. Hence, analogous to responses to global retailing that focus on national or ethnic identity, Madeco union activists have reacted in class terms, albeit with some ambivalence, to Chile's new retail infrastructure. This reaction reflects the continued (if transformed) salience of class identities in Chile and the fact that these responses emanate from work and union contexts.

This class-based critique of consumerism is manifest most clearly in relation to the rising availability of formal credit. Workers' increasing use of credit cards has provoked significant debate and concern among union activists. Lower-income Chileans have traditionally accumulated debts, particularly to local grocery stores. However, in the 1990s, as department store credit cards were made increasingly available to lower-income groups, workers quickly became credit junkies. Union leaders have found that indebted workers feel compelled to work extensive overtime on a regular basis in order to satisfy credit payments. This makes them more beholden to employers, gives them less time to participate in union activities, and makes them less willing to threaten their good relations with the boss.[66] During the mid-nineties, credit card salespeople sometimes offered free cards to Madeco workers at the plant's entrance.[67] One Madeco worker commented, "I think 95 percent of the workers in my section have debt problems."[68]

Union members have developed a complicated set of ideas and behaviors in response to work intensification and new forms of debt-financed consumption, all of which valorize autonomy, class loyalty, and a particular form of masculinity. These ideas emerge from their critiques of fellow workers who succumb to management's prerogatives. For example, management successfully purged union activists in the telephone cable section during the 1980s, and the workers there are known for always working overtime and accepting management authority. Union activists comment that workers in the section "bow down their heads," "put up with anything," "are the foremen's favorites [regalones]," and "run around snitching on workers who don't work at top speed."[69] Describing workers as "regalones" conjures the image of the spoiled child who has gained the parent's favor. This image of currying individual favor with superiors through obedience is diametrically opposed to the image of strong, masculine workers who resist management.

Ideas regarding trust are related to the preceding resistance/passivity dichotomy. Many union activists complained that both new recruits and older workers were untrustworthy. One older worker, hired during the 1960s, complained: "In my section, one guy produces 1,500 tons per month and another makes 1,300 in order to earn production bonuses, while we had previously agreed to limit output to 1,000. I told them that we all need to produce 1,000 so we don't give more power to the owners, but they don't listen because they're fags [maricones]. The only thing they care about is living it up."[70]

Another worker, hired during the mid-1980s, commented, "I can't talk about union stuff on the job. All of the people in my section are fags [maricones]—they're worthless. Management fired all of the good people in 1987–88. The new people will only participate in the union if they have friends there or to get material benefits."[71] Finally, a third worker, hired during the late 1980s, commented,

> There are four older guys in my section. One is OK—he does his job, doesn't complain about anyone. The other three stink—they're always too eager to work. The three have been working for 20 years; the other guy has been here for 30. The foreman has their home phone so he can call them on Sundays if he needs someone, and then they show up. I'll never give my foreman my telephone! He has no business calling someone at home. These guys have no life outside the factory. We went out on strike [see below], and I was still working because I wasn't on vacation yet [the strike ended at the beginning of the summer vacation season]. Because of the strike, there was a lot of work, so management called up 20 guys and they had the entire plant running! They called Catalan from my section, and I saw him when I arrived at work. It really hurt me because we had just been on strike. So the bosses have them all set up: they work overtime when they feel like it, they work on good machines that always have orders, etc.[72]

All of these quotes depict company loyalists as untrustworthy. The first testimony's use of the term maricon, common in many other discussions on this theme, is revealing. While this slang term literally means "fag," Chileans often use the term to criticize dishonest and disloyal individuals. By using the term in this context, Madeco workers suggest that those who violate the collective trust of their coworkers and accede to management's demands are simultaneously antiunion and not "real men." Being a "real man" means standing up to management and remaining loyal to workmates. Only "weak" men, whose sexuality is thus suspect, would betray their workmates by acceding to management demands.

In addition to the sexual connotations in these criticisms, they point to union activists' notions about appropriate levels of work effort, the value of reciprocity in the workplace, and workers' need for autonomy from employers. These related issues take on an ethical tone in some testimonies: "When new people arrived with a gung ho attitude about work, we began to lose the spirit of trade unionism. These people who—by their own free will or because of management pressure—start to take on new tasks or multiple jobs have no moral values."[73] Thus, respecting appropriate limits to work reflects union activists' sense of class loyalty, masculinity, and ethical standards.

Union activists link many workers' more individualistic behavior in the workplace (rate busting, extensive overtime, accession to managerial authority) to their consumption patterns. Thus, in their view, company loyalists' penchant for overtime work finds its counterpart in an imbalance between work and appropriate forms of consumption. Activists' critique of "consumerism" focuses on three dimensions: its corrosive effects on workplace and union solidarity, its superficiality, and its indication of excessive ambition.

Union activists see overtime work, debt, and consumerism as connected. Thus their criticisms of those who work excessive overtime are not only comments about their behavior at work; they also focus on many workers' adoption of individualistic models of consumption. Many company loyalists (particularly younger workers) put in extensive overtime hours to purchase and/or service debt for flashy consumer items: "They need to make sure their house looks beautiful outside, but they don't even have a place to die. They need to have the latest model car, so all they think about is getting to work early to find a parking space." The implications of this work-consumption pattern for class solidarity are obvious: "The union complained a while back about compulsory overtime, but a group of people wrote letters to management saying that they didn't care what the union said, they wanted to work 12-hour days, that their families would starve to death if they couldn't work seven days, and the company needs them to work overtime. I talked with one of these guys once, and all he talked about was his cable TV, his car, etc."[74] Thus, many union activists observe new patterns of conspicuous consumption that depend on both the easy availability of credit and overtime work. These interrelated phenomena all undermine workplace solidarity by breaking down collective controls over the work process and rejecting collective efforts to improve living standards.

Activists not only criticize company loyalists' seduction by debt and ostentation, they criticize themselves for developing similar problems. Many active union participants have also fallen under the spell of credit. Some employ a discourse of vice to describe their debts: "It's a vice that we Chileans have. We like to spend more than we have."[75] They see profligate spending as an addiction that could be overcome through self-control. Activists also have ambiguous attitudes regarding overtime. Many want to have the right to say no to overtime work without risk of reprisal: "I have to work on Saturdays because my boss decided there's no overtime in my section, and I need the extra money to pay my bills."[76] Those who use the discourse of vice also criticize union members who consistently work overtime: "Guido says he needs to work overtime, but that just helps the firm. Juan moonlights as a home repairman if he needs extra money. That way he doesn't depend so much on management."[77]

The issues of credit, overtime, and dependence on management are also bound up with male workers' conceptions of gender roles. Madeco workers almost exclusively maintain their households with one income. This phenomenon contrasts with national trends of increasing female workforce participation during the 1980s and 1990s.[78] The endurance of the male breadwinner model is due to the fact that Madeco still offers wages that are far higher than the average industrial pay. Even though they could supplement their wages with their spouses' income—and many wives have training as schoolteachers or in other professions—husbands work extra hours to make sure that their wives don't work. Why? "I want my wife to stay home and take care of the kids, because otherwise her relationship with them might be too distant. Besides, the kids might be molested at a day care center"[79]; "Being poor, we kind of look down on ourselves. We assume that the women we marry are poor like us and don't have a great educational background. What options does that give them? Working as a waitress, in a topless bar, at a massage parlor, or as a maid."[80] Union activists articulate several rationalizations for resisting their wives' entry into the workforce.

Ironically, while union activists do not want their wives to work and may work extensive overtime hours to keep them at home, they often blame their wives for pressuring them to earn greater income to buy consumer goods or nonessentials: "Workers' wives and kids watch TV, they talk to their neighbors, and become jealous if they don't have the same things. Then the kid says, 'Daddy, I want some Reebok or Nike shoes.' "[81]

Marital tensions surrounding women's entry into the labor force and the alleged effects of TV advertising and peer pressure on family members are compounded by union activists' group consumption rituals. Union activists, in contrast to amarrillos, have developed rituals of group sociability, centered in the union hall. For most special events—holidays, sports games, and farewells—workers assemble at the union hall for barbecues. Additionally, small groups gather informally to watch soccer games or relax at the end of the week with food and drink. In addition to being fun, activists use these events to recruit new adherents. As one activist comments, "Since many workers are reluctant to go to the union hall, you need to prepare some food and drinks to get them to participate."[82] Finally, these events allow workers to escape from work and family commitments in an all-male environment: "The other day, I was working the graveyard shift and after getting off, we went to the union to prepare seafood stew. We were there until late, and my wife went to the clinic looking for me. Velásquez screwed me over when he told her I was there. He shouldn't have done that. I went straight home."[83]

Union activists reaffirm their masculinity both by socializing with other men and by showing their workmates that they are independent from their wives. When workers' spouses call them or come to look for them at the union, their workmates jeer at them, calling out, "She's controlling you." Thus, in criticizing conspicuous consumption, union activists are also defending a collective model of consumption that simultaneously reinforces informal group solidarity, masculinity, and autonomy. Interestingly, a foreman from the brass mill gained notoriety by holding barbecues every time workers in the section broke production records.[84] While ostensibly similar to union activists' gatherings, this activity has a different function: to cement worker loyalty to management.

The contrast between collective and individual models of consumption reflects attitudes regarding status aspirations. Union activists criticize rate busting, overtime, and debt because they undermine work place and union solidarity. They also value their male-centered rituals of consumption over models of conspicuous consumption. These views point to ideas about consumption practices as markers of social class. Many expressed disdain for amarrillos' status competition with neighbors: "This guy bought this expensive dog. It's like a rich person's dog. He's become bourgeois [emburgesado]. He wants to live like a rich man, but he's a worker."[85] Another activist comments, "If you keep a tight budget, you don't need to work overtime. That's why I say the human quality of Madeco workers isn't what it used to be. Guido works overtime because his wife wants to have a higher standard of living that isn't appropriate for a worker."[86]

Union activists draw a sharp line between appropriate levels and types of working-class consumption and those that belong to other, higher social classes. They point to a more general problem regarding class-specific lifestyles. By seeking the badges of middle- and upper-class identity through individual strategies of upward mobility, workers may cease to identify with their own social class, eroding the ties of trust and solidarity that go along with specific forms of workplace and leisure time behavior. Thus activists adopt what Pierre Bourdieu calls "a taste for the necessary" while they watch their workmates try to emulate middle- and upper-class lifestyles. His observations about French workers are relevant in Chile today: "The dominated only have two options: loyalty to self and the group . . . or the individual effort to assimilate the dominant ideal, which is the antithesis of the very ambition of collectively regaining control over social identity."[87]

Union activists' struggles to retain a class identity in the domains of work, union, and leisure are riddled with contradictions. As noted above, many workers who criticize others' upwardly mobile goals themselves participate in Chile's new retail and credit infrastructure to varying degrees. As workers are inevitably exposed to retailers' and creditors' promotion of conspicuous consumption, it would be unrealistic to expect them to totally reject new products and lifestyles. Moreover, as their regular salaries no longer allow them to live as prosperously as previous cohorts of workers, overtime or moonlighting are the only ways to supplement their base income.

Given these structural factors, it is significant that union members struggle to maintain what they view as an appropriate balance between work and leisure as well as class-based forms of consumption. This finding supports scholarship that finds locally specific reactions to and uses of imported commodities and lifestyles, rather than supporting conceptions of Americanization or cultural imperialism. In the Chilean context, these findings qualify the popular view that Chilean workers have fully succumbed to the lure of creditors and marketers.[88] While Madeco activists are ambivalent about their relationship to the new credit and retail infrastructures, their ideas and practices point to the stubborn persistence of working-class lifestyles and identities.

The greater availability of consumer credit, imported consumer goods, and aggressive marketing has interacted with changes in the workplace to promote challenges to traditional notions about the relationship between work, consumption, and gender. While workers hired since the late 1980s adopt individualistic strategies of upward mobility in the workplace and engage in conspicuous consumption, union activists seek to retain collective controls over work pace and group consumption rituals. Activists' critique of upwardly mobile workers is simultaneously a defense of class solidarity and specific forms of masculinity cultivated through trust relationships in the workplace and male-centered group leisure activities. These challenges to old forms of workplace organization and group association would provoke open resistance during the early 1990s.

This detailed discussion of industrial rationalization at Madeco is deceptive insofar as it does not incorporate workers' considerable shop floor and union resistance to these two decades of labor intensification and salary declines. Madeco workers conducted a 59-day strike in 1983 in response to massive layoffs and nonpayment of *gratificaciones* (profit sharing). The strike followed several years of clandestine union organizing. It gained national attention because it occurred during the 1981–83 crisis, and prodemocracy activists viewed it as a challenge to the Plan Laboral. While the strike was defeated and management purged over 100 strike activists, Madeco leaders became prominent activists in the Santiago labor movement during the 1980s. Though management ran roughshod over the union during the 1970s and 1980s, the union became a symbol of resistance to management and the dictatorship for many Santiago activists.[89]

A decade later, in 1993, pay reductions negotiated in the mid-1970s and the work intensification of the late 1980s and 1990s fueled a violent strike. In order to understand how and why open resistance emerged, it is first necessary to discuss the consequences of managerial repression against the union after the 1983 strike and the political experiences of workers hired during the 1980s.

In addition to the dismissal of over 100 strike activists, management continued targeted attacks against wire mill activists throughout the 1980s. Why did they target the wire mill rather than the brass mill? First, they sought to remove Héctor Velásquez, a wire mill worker who served as union president during the period. As noted above, the law stipulates that union leaders can only be fired through a court proceeding. Though Deischler tried this, and even attempted to frame Velásquez in 1984 by planting a bomb outside the firm and then calling in the police to arrest, interrogate, and torture him, Deischler was unable to build a defensible case against the leader. Given that they could not fire him, management dismissed his coworkers. Talking about the incident more than a decade later, Velásquez notes: "Personally, this produced a very difficult situation for me. I had to isolate myself at work, because anyone who talked to me got burned."[90]

Another reason why management targeted wire mill union members was that the wire mill had a larger pool of activists than the brass mill: "There are always more people willing to collaborate with the union in the wire mill. They're predisposed to do the methodical work on committees and to run for office.

The guys in the brass mill are more combative, more ready to fight, but they don't produce as many leaders."[91] Yet another possible explanation for these distinct managerial strategies in the two plants is their different markets. The wire mill produces almost exclusively for the domestic market and faces two local competitors. The brass mill, by contrast, has a monopoly on the local market and exports to over 30 countries.[92] The brass mill is therefore less vulnerable to local business downturns, and thus workers' jobs are more secure there. Additionally, work in the brass mill is more physically taxing and pays less than in the wire mill, and workers there toil in teams in several sections, rather than on individual machines. Teamwork gives brass mill workers more power at the point of production and makes increases in individual job responsibilities more difficult to impose.[93] It is thus likely that because wire mill workers were more dispensable and had fewer tools for shop floor protest, they recognized that their only protection was through union activism. In contrast, brass mill workers have more options and face fewer risks for resistance on the shop floor and therefore see sustained union activism as less essential.

Given that the wire mill hosted the prime pool of activists, and management did everything in its power to eliminate this group, the union faced a chronic shortage of viable leadership candidates. Although Velásquez continued serving until his 2003 death, and Guillermo Gómez, another 1983 strike activist from the brass mill, served until 1989, the leadership was plagued by a series of bad apples beginning in the late 1980s. In 1988 Mario Muñoz, a wire mill worker and the union's secretary, was fired when guards caught him stealing from the firm.[94] In 1991 José Oviedo, a brass mill worker and union director, stole union funds and negotiated his retirement without advising the other union leaders.[95] Petty corruption was the order of the day. The ongoing purges of union activists after the 1983 strike made it risky for workers to become union leaders. Many who participated in committee work to gain experience risked dismissal. Moreover, union leaders who were not continually reelected would likely be fired—the law does not protect them from dismissal after they leave office. The corrosive effects of ongoing repression demobilized activists, and thus the few who did decide to run for office were inexperienced, largely unaccountable to the inactive membership base, and not necessarily committed to the union. These conditions facilitated the increase in corruption.[96]

The leadership crisis did not place a damper on union activism, however, as rank-and-file members became increasingly restive. Workers hired during the 1980s had a set of social and political experiences that made them prone to react to the firm's most recent modernization. Though they were often new to trade unionism, some had parents who had been union leaders and leftist militants.[97]

Others had been political militants and activists in the shantytown protests of 1983–86. A wire mill activist comments, "I participated in the protests during the mid-1980s. I was a kid. I wasn't married, so I didn't have any major responsibilities. . . . We used to risk everything. We used to get in a van and pass out pamphlets promoting the party line."[98] An activist from the brass mill reinforces the link between the protests and the strike: "We liked to go out and protest in the streets. Then, when we came to work at Madeco, they would force you to do overtime, and you couldn't say 'I don't want to.' We weren't used to being bossed around like that."[99] Another wire mill activist recalls his exposure to extreme poverty during the mid-1980s:

> [In 1985–86] there were a lot of people that didn't have any food to throw in the pot. I was working as an assistant for a truck driver that delivered processed meat and sausage to Pudahuel [one of Santiago's poorest municipalities]. I saw homes without bathrooms and people cooking with wood. I was only 19 then. I stole sausage from the truck and gave bags of it to people—they were so thankful. You need to live through those kind of things to really feel them. I realized that there were people much worse off than myself.[100]

Madeco workers hired during the 1980s had become politicized during the protests. They learned direct action tactics and became sensitized to the intense social inequalities brought about by the 1981–83 economic crisis, and they valued the freedom and power they felt in the streets. These styles of mobilization, social values, and principles conflicted with the rigid hierarchy of Madeco. The conflict between workers' political experience and values and the firm's authority crystallized in the 1993 strike.

System Breakdown

In the context of the rapid changes in the labor process, a crisis in union leadership, and the coming of age of a new cohort of workers, conflicts over the firm's overall model of authoritarian modernization crystallized over two issues: overtime payment and profit sharing. In 1991, with their lawyer's assistance, the union learned that management had systematically underpaid workers for overtime, excluding the production incentive, higher hourly rate for the night shift, and other contractual obligations from payment. In other words, workers were not even paid the fixed incentive set in 1980 that in itself did not compensate them adequately for radical production increases. The union sued management for repayment of lost hours in 1994 and accepted an out-of-court settlement in 1995.[101]

However, both the union and management were unable to compromise over the issue of quarterly payments based on profits. As noted above, in 1977 management eliminated workers' contractual guarantee to 15 percent of the firm's net profits and holiday bonuses, replacing them with quarterly bonuses (gratificaciones). Since the 1931 labor law, workers had been guaranteed 6 percent of their employers' profits, though Madeco workers had negotiated a higher sum. Even after the replacement of profit sharing with quarterly bonuses, the union found that the firm was only paying part of the 30 percent of net profits it owed the workers under the 1977 pact.

In mid-1992 the union filed two suits against Madeco for underpayment of quarterly bonuses based on the firm's profits from 1989–91. Significantly, the historically more conservative supervisors' union initially suggested the lawsuit; the white- and blue-collar unions quickly joined them in the endeavor. With contract negotiations pending for the end of the year, management refused to negotiate salary issues unless the union dropped the suit and agreed to rewrite the section in its contract on quarterly bonuses, thereby eliminating the legal grounds for its suit.

As the battle lines were drawn in mid-1992, overtime work became a flashpoint for intra- and interclass conflict. In June union members voted to halt overtime to prepare for the strike, sparking sharp criticism from management. Union activists may have initially felt emboldened to take this step when they learned that the firm's notorious personnel director would retire the following month. After two weeks passed, some union members questioned the decision to suspend overtime. While some argued that the union had halted overtime too early (since the contract negotiations would not begin until December), others contended that union members should not become too dependent on overtime, and that the union would appear weak if they resumed overtime work. The internal fissures over work effort and consumption became intertwined with debates over union strategy.[102]

As tensions increased between management and the blue-collar union, the supervisors' union dropped the suit and negotiated a contract. When management offered a vacation bonus to those who would sign away rights to pursue the suit and join newly created nonunion negotiating groups, half of the white-collar union (all of its office staff) left their organization. Many who fled did not realize that a smaller severance payment and more excuses for dismissal were hidden in the fine print of their new contracts. The blue-collar union stood firm and refused to accede to management's ploy.[103]

Ironically, the firm did not attempt to challenge the blue-collar unions' monopoly over the workforce until the return of civilian rule. They had had the legal right to set up parallel unions since 1979, but up until 1992, management had not gone that far. As noted above, the personnel manager had used other means to intimidate and neutralize union members short of organizing company unions. This new strategy was far more dangerous to the unions, as it promised to institutionalize informal divisions between union activists and company loyalists.

Why did management make this drastic decision in 1992? Labor reforms after the democratic transition had created new legal opportunities for workers unavailable during the junta, including the right to sue for nonpayment of profits. Workers' legal rights did not fundamentally threaten management before 1990. With the lawsuit, Madeco could lose about $10 million. Perhaps more important, the company and their peers likely feared that the suit could serve as a precedent. Two years later, when the Supreme Court ruled in the union's favor, William Thayer, a conservative senator designated by Pinochet, argued that "the ruling could have devastating social and economic consequences."[104] These fears were borne out when the union at Alusa, a Madeco subsidiary, sued Madeco for underpayment of gratificaciones.[105] Though $10 million might not represent a huge loss for Madeco, the potential losses in other suits for both Madeco and other enterprises could be substantial.

As the strike loomed on the horizon, management fired two workers who spoke up at union meetings.[106] These acts of intimidation added to union activists' broader sense of injustice. First, they were suspicious of management's unwillingness to simply fight the case out in court: "If they thought they were right, why didn't they just settle in court? Because they tried to block the suit, it looked like they were hiding something, and that made us more certain that we were right."[107] Union members reasoned that if management was trying to hide something by avoiding a court battle, they had probably cheated on the quarterly bonus as well.

At a deeper level, members were disgusted that after all of their sacrifices to adapt to increasing work demands in the last years, they had been cheated out of a share of the profits, while management and stockholders received handsome rewards: "You see the firm become more and more profitable, and we're stuck in the same place, without any kind of compensation or gratitude for all the extra responsibilities we've assumed and the resulting productivity increases."[108]

While strikers were certainly willing to take on the firm, many younger workers feared the financial consequences of a long strike. One participant comments, "During the first few days, the strike was no problem. Later, people started feeling uncertainty and desperation. . . . We were really down by the second week. Everyone wanted to go on summer vacation—we thought the strike would only last a week."[109] It is likely that because of many workers' debts, activists were enthusiastic about the strike but also unwilling to carry it out to its "final consequences," unlike the two-month strike of a decade before. Prior to contract negotiations four years later, one worker commented, "Increasing consumerism is the reason why everyone wants to have early contract negotiations this year. They're afraid to go on strike because of the financial hardships it implies."[110] Workers were "fired up," but consumer debts limited their staying power.

Activists adopted the visual style and ethos of the 1983–86 protests. They tooted on cornets, banged on garbage cans, pelted vans transporting strikebreakers with rocks, and fought with the police. The union's leadership, older leaders, and management had not anticipated the level of violence and bravado witnessed during the strike. One veteran of the 1983 strike commented, "I never imagined younger workers would go on strike. I thought they were more anti-union, but they were really committed."[111] Union leaders were equally out of sorts: "We knew that a peaceful strike wouldn't work, so our goal was to intimidate management. . . . We had a group that got together at night and cut the electricity, flattened truck tires in the warehouse, and blocked strikebreakers' entry to the firm. Most of the leaders had no idea about this. We had a sort of parallel organization of rank-and-file workers from both plants that planned these sabotage actions."[112] The executives were indeed intimidated: "Management never imagined that the strike would be so violent. They were shocked."[113] The strike's violence sparked the memories of the handful of workers who hailed from the 1950s: "During the strike, the older guys told us about the 1960 strike, when they threw flour on strikebreakers to identify them, and then followed them onto buses and beat them up."[114]

The conflict itself only lasted ten days. Strikers astutely planned a march to the presidential palace just when American and European investors were visiting the firm, housed in the Hotel Carrera across the street (also owned by the Luksic Group):

> The most important event was when we marched at La Moneda. Since investors were staying across the street, management agreed that afternoon to drop its demand that we withdraw the lawsuit. We met with a staff person at the Ministry of Interior. Our wives and kids marched there with us. At first, we thought the police wouldn't let us march, so we arrived in small groups. The police surrounded us, spoke with our lawyer, and allowed us to continue if we weren't violent or disrespectful. All the press covered the march.[115]

The strikers had found the firm's Achilles heel: if they could threaten the stock offering in the United States (presumably the issue discussed with the investors), then they could twist management's arm. While this action was obviously a strategic success, it must be placed in a broader context. Just as strikers used their repertoire of action developed during the 1983–86 pro-democracy protests, the symbolic power of actually marching in front of the presidential palace after seventeen years of dictatorship should not be under-estimated. As one young striker characterized the conflict as a whole, "Boy, people really fought in that strike. It was like saying, 'Now we're in democracy!' It served as an example for the youth."[116] Schooled in the cauldron of anti-dictatorial protest, this strike's younger protagonists displayed their particular conception of democracy during this brief conflict.

With the strike's successful conclusion, union members won their right to continue the case, and two years later, the Supreme Court ruled in their favor. However, the firm used dilatory appeals to avoid payment until 2002. The strike did have immediate reverberations in the workplace. A week after the strike, a protest in both plants won a dismissed worker's reinstatement.[117] When management offered nonstrikers a 100,000 peso bonus, brass mill workers who were emboldened by the preceding protest overturned their lunch trays in a *viandazo*.[118]

Management responded decisively to the cafeteria protest: "Management thought, 'If we don't reestablish discipline now, it will cost us more later.' So they organized a military operation with ambulances, detectives, two busloads of police, and vans to prevent any conflict."[119] The company fired more than 40 workers after the protest. Leadership was again caught off-guard by the rank-and-file's initiatives. While an inexperienced union leader noted that he had casually mentioned to other workers on the street that maybe they should protest the bonus, he acknowledged that he should have raised the issue in a union assembly. The other leaders were equally befuddled.

Union members who recall the incident blame the leaders for not anticipat-ing and defusing the event. The 40 who were sacked had to agree to retire voluntarily in order to be eligible to receive severance payments and avoid facing criminal charges for property damage.[120] The firm, still reeling from the strike, hired a psychologist to study the reasons for the bad "labor climate." He found that workers were unhappy at the firm, saw no opportunities for training, and felt there was no communication between workers and management. In re-sponse, the general manager began Monday morning breakfast chats with workers in different work sections, but most workers were afraid to speak because their immediate supervisor was present: they anticipated they would be fired if they complained.[121]

After the strike, management continued targeted layoffs against union activists in the wire mill. In 1995 the company eliminated 60 workers from the brass mill's aluminum section and relocated approximately 10 more to other work sections. In mid-1998 Madeco also moved the brass mill casting shop's 40 workers to a new plant located a few miles south of Madeco's headquarters. The elimination of an entire product line substantially reduced the number of union members, while movement of part of the workforce to a more distant location promises to further fragment workplace based solidarities by reducing the day-to-day interactions between casting shop workers and their other brass and wire mill counterparts.[122]

Though the loss of union members and separation of work sections diminished the union's power, the creation of company unions did not noticeably affect the blue-collar union. The organization's losses to the blue-collar company union were very small. After losing 60 workers from the aluminum section, the union only lost 20 members to the blue-collar company group, leaving them with 340 members in 1996. The union later lured some of these workers and new hires into their organization, boosting their membership to 358 in 1998. Over the long term, the blue-collar union has lost more members because, beginning in 1983, management successfully lured skilled workers into the white-collar union.

In contrast to the blue-collar union, the white-collar and supervisory unions lost 307 members, virtually gutting their organizations. We should keep in mind, however, that the white-collar and supervisory unions have historically been weak organizations that management often used against the blue-collar union. Therefore the white-collar and supervisory company union may not be as much of a threat against the blue-collar union as it first appears.[123]

Since office workers were the main white-collar group that left their union in 1992, the remaining members of the white-collar union are skilled manual workers who could potentially be classified as blue-collar. Because most of the blue-collar union's losses in membership have been to the white-collar union, they have adopted two strategies. First, as noted above, they have called on blue-collar workers in the company union to return to the blue-collar union, with modest success. Second, they have officially proposed to merge the blue- and white-collar unions in an effort to prevent management efforts to split the two unions in contract negotiations. Thus, while the blue-collar union activists do not anticipate being able to reverse the mass exodus of office and supervisory workers from their unions, they believe the unification of blue- and white-collar workers in one organization could potentially reverse management's counter-attack against the unions in response to the lawsuit on gratificaciones.[124]

In addition to a declining workforce and divisions between organizations, leadership corruption continued after the strike. In 1994 four of five leaders were caught defrauding the union's medical insurer. One of the three was not reelected and negotiated a handsome severance package with the firm in exchange for relinquishing his job security protection (fuerosindical). Surprisingly, members reelected the three brass mill leaders found guilty in this scandal. Two of them subsequently retired, gaining substantial severance packages. The remaining perpetrator stepped down a few years later. Finally, in 1998 the treasurer elected after the 1994 scandal was caught having embezzled a large sum from the union. He resigned after the union sued him for theft. In subsequent elections, Velásquez, the only veteran leader who did not succumb to corruption, assumed the treasurer position and produced monthly reports on the union's budget during his tenure in that position until late 2003.[125]

We can understand this rise of union corruption as an acceleration and intensification of the above-noted processes begun in the late 1980s and as a result of management's attacks against the union in the context of the 1993 strike. The reelection of corrupt officials (all from the brass mill) seems to respond to increased hostility between brass and wire mill workers since the strike, as there are a greater number of blue-collar company union members in the wire mill.[126] Brass mill workers, who outnumber their counterparts in the blue-collar union, may have placed both workplace and personal loyalties above ethical concerns. In contrast, leadership corruption provoked distrust and demoralization among many wire mill activists. Some express great disappointment in their leadership.[127] The rise in corruption reflects the gradual erosion of work-based and union solidarity since the 1993 strike, and is part of a 30-year process of working-class transformation in which the state and managers effectively undermined leftist parties, union organizations, and a working-class culture with roots at the beginning of the 20th century. Corruption is one symptom of a cultural, ideological, and organizational crisis among working people.[128]

Post-Boom Madeco

Until the end of 1998 management continued its authoritarian model of work organization. The union complained that while Deischler had retired in 1992, the foremen who had loyally worked as his lieutenants over the previous two decades maintained their authoritarian style.[129] By mid-1997 management still insisted on an explicit policy of firing rather than relocating workers who contracted illnesses or suffered injuries on the job.[130] While we might imagine that the new plant would provide better working conditions, this was not the case: workers in the new casting shop complained about labor intensity, contamination, illnesses, and contractual violations through inadequate payment.[131]

The tide did seem to turn in May 1998, when Tomas Jiménez, Deischler's right-hand man, retired as chief of industrial relations. By the end of the year, the company had changed the legal status of Madeco's headquarters. It became an affiliate of the Madeco group, and its top executives moved up to manage the group as a whole. With the organizational shake-up, management fired almost all of the old foremen, and workers immediately noticed a change in atmosphere, particularly less persecution of union activists.[132] As part of this management reorganization, Madeco hired Albert Cussen, a former executive from Chile's state-owned copper mines, as CEO of Madeco, to replace Carlos Vicuña, who became a board member on a large energy company.[133]

The dismissal of foremen appears to form part of upper management's strategy to streamline middle and upper management, while integrating Chile's Madeco plant with the firm's growing multinational empire. However, company records do not identify the rationale behind the move. These changes coincided with the Asian crisis so that as orders declined, many anticipated layoffs at year's end. The end of the boom coincided with the apparent end of Madeco's old style of management.

The management shake-up could not protect Madeco from the effects of the Asian crisis, the gradual economic meltdown of the Argentine economy, financial weakness in Brazil, and the blue-collar union's persistence in demanding their court settlement. From 1999 to the present, Madeco has had a series of financial problems. In 1999 the firm lost $100 million, and the following year it lost $29 million.[134] In 2000 the firm closed some of the Argentine plants it had purchased a few years prior in order to offset the previous year's losses.[135] By the end of 2001 Madeco had hired a New York investment bank, Salomon Smith Barney, to restructure its debts of $325 million. In this context, the firm's shares on the New York Stock Exchange (ADRs) had fallen in value to $0.75 per share. According to a New York Stock Exchange rule, firms whose shares fall below $1.00 for more than 30 days can no longer be traded on the exchange. To respond to both the debt and low share price, in July 2002, Madeco issued $90 million in equity. However, by late September 2002, except for the Luksic Group, few other shareholders bought additional stock, forcing the firm to enter new negotiations with creditors and placing it in a very precarious financial position.[136] At this juncture, Cussen left the firm, and Tiberio Dall'Olio returned to steer the ship. As Héctor Velásquez assessed the situation in September 2002, "Now the whole possibility of shutting down the Santiago plant will be discussed once again. It's a very grim situation."[137]

The final resolution of the union's class action suit occurred in the context of the firm's severe financial problems. While the company effectively evaded paying the settlement through several legal appeals, by August 2001 the union had finally received a court order to seize firm assets if it did not pay the settlement. In response, management argued that paying the settlement would leave it with insufficient funds to pay August salaries and the quarterly share of profits to all Madeco employees. As many union members were hired after the 1989–91 period covered by the lawsuit, they stood to suffer economically even though they would not benefit from any settlement. In contrast, many workers who had resigned or had been fired were still part of the suit and thus had a stake in receiving the settlement regardless of the firm's economic situation.

Because of pressure from union members who were not part of the suit and feared for their jobs, the union called for the removal of the order to seize Madeco's assets and began negotiating a settlement. Dissatisfied with the firm's offers, all of the participants in the suit rejected them. In November management struck back, firing all participants in the suit from the white-collar union (which, through the union's attorney's efforts, were reincorporated into the suit) and threatening to fire all of the participants in the blue-collar union.

After joint protests in front of the firm, management reopened negotiations, and rehired the dismissed workers. As a consequence, the union agreed to a formula in which the firm would pay 60 percent of the money it owed in four annual installments, but only to workers who leave or have left the firm. Hence, management was effectively able to convert the settlement into a supplemental severance payment, thereby spreading its costs over time. While the blue-collar union had succeeded in unifying blue-collar, white-collar, and dismissed workers, the ultimate settlement favored management.[138]

The pattern of conspicuous consumption among some workers declined as the Chilean economy slowed down. By 1999 more costly purchases such as a car or home, as well as use of department store credit cards, were only possible while overtime work was plentiful. Families were much more pragmatic in their purchases (adjusting aspirations downward with real purchasing power declines), and consumption decisions were shaped by negotiations between men and women over purchasing priorities as much as by peer pressure or advertising and marketing.[139]

The 1993 strike demonstrated hidden tensions in Chile's "miracle." Younger workers held cultural and political resources from the previous decade that they deployed in a guerrilla war against the firm in response to systematic underpayment and ever heightened work pressures. However, this strike also represented a crisis of unionism on a deeper level. The disjuncture between union leaders and the rank and file and employers' ability to continue layoffs without a response resulted from the union's leadership crisis. A shortage of committed leaders and a legacy of petty corruption delegitimized most current leaders. These shifts forced inexperienced union activists to take matters into their own hands, with problematic results for the organization and its members. The firm's precarious position after the boom forced the union to accept a smaller legal settlement and led workers to take a more pragmatic approach to consumer behavior.

CONCLUSIONS

Madeco managers have subjected workers to successive wage cuts, benefit rollbacks, as well as increased job responsibilities and work effort over the last three decades. These measures have undermined workplace solidarities in two ways: they have promoted shop floor competition and interacted with the rise of formal credit, advertising, and foreign retailers to encourage a new model of debt-financed conspicuous consumption (even if this model was contested by some and only economically feasible during the boom). A new cohort of workers who had participated in the 1983–86 protests has reacted to systematic underpayment and management's efforts to extend work effort to its physical limits by holding a violent strike whose reverberations echoed throughout the following year. Workers hired in the mid-1980s have developed their own strategies and repertoires of action during and after the strike because of their distance from a leadership plagued by petty corruption scandals. In addition to purging strike activists after a cafeteria protest, management took an unprecedented step against the union by creating parallel nonunion organizations, but with little success.

Through this analysis of industrial innovation and worker resistance, I have focused on the interrelations among work, consumption, and identity. In contrast to most discussions of industrial restructuring focused exclusively on managerial initiatives, I argue that Madeco workers both resisted the managerial offensive through the 1993 strike and accommodated the new model of production by enduring speedups and overtime. Union activists were complicit in these managerial offensives by working overtime in order to prevent their wives' entry into the workforce. Worker responses reshaped managerial strategy, most notably in the 1998 dismissal of veteran foremen. While management may have had its own reasons for sacking the foremen, the strike and subsequent resistance likely indicated to them that retaining this cohort of supervisors would only generate further conflicts and thereby undermine firm efficiency and stability.

The findings also support arguments emphasizing the influence of political and institutional factors in shaping the character of managerial action. Unlike Japan or northern Europe, where corporatist institutions at the firm or national level promoted worker participation in decision making, Chile's experience of dictatorship and radical free market labor reforms militated against the creation of a new "social contract" between management and labor. The ease with which employers could dismiss workers, and managers' fear that worker initiative would bring a return of worker comanagement under Allende, discouraged managers from providing workers with an active role in fine-tuning production as in Japanese or northern European factories.

My analysis of new consumption practices and the moral debates that surround them builds on recent discussions of consumption in global context. First, it finds that, in addition to national and ethnic identities, class and gender can also function as bases of resistance to perceived cultural homogenization associated with new retail and credit infrastructures. Madeco workers counterposed their communal and masculine forms of consumption to the increasingly individualistic model of consumption they observed among coworkers and lurking within themselves.

Second, this chapter represents one effort to identify the links between the spheres of production and consumption, parting from the tendency in much scholarship to view consumption as increasingly divorced from work-centered identities and practices.[140] In the Madeco case, work intensification and the declining authority of informal work groups over individual behavior (itself due to the weakening of the unions) laid the groundwork for new consumer behavior. Hence, changes in retail and consumer credit as well as shifts in work organization reinforced one another, rather than being entirely separate processes.

While the "Chilean miracle" engendered the collective belief that Chile would soon rival the Asian "tigers," the 1998 Asian crisis and 2001 unraveling of the Argentine economy represented wake-up calls. As unemployment mounted, workers' debt-driven fantasies of upward mobility succumbed to pragmatic attitudes regarding consumption. The end of the boom placed Madeco in a precarious situation, forcing the firm to unload many of the assets acquired during the 1980s and 1990s and placing its future solvency in doubt. If the boom had only intensified work while offering few rewards, what would the recession bring?

NOTES

The author wishes to gratefully acknowledge funding for portions of this research provided by the University of Arizona Foundation and the vice president's Office for Research. Additionally, I wish to thank Kim Iden for research assistance with this chapter. Finally, I would like to thank three Duke University Press anonymous reviewers, in addition to Volker Frank and Peter Winn, for valuable comments on earlier drafts of this chapter.

1 "Los peligros de la productividad," *Crisol* 14, no. 10 (September 1996): 3–4.
2 Examples include Fernando Leiva and Rafael Agacino, "Mercado de trabajo flexible, pobreza y desintegración social en Chile, 1990–1994," working paper (Santiago: ARCIS, 1994); Mario Castillo et al., "Reorganización industrial y estrategias competitivas en Chile," in *Estabilización macroeconómica, reforma estructural, y comportamiento industrial*, ed. J. Katz (Buenos Aires: CEPAL, 1996), 223–57; Alvaro Díaz, "Chile: Dinámica de largo plazo en el cambio tecnológico de una empresa metalmecánica," working paper 135 (Santiago: Sur, 1992); Magdalena Echeverría and Gonzalo Herrera, "Innovaciones en la empresa y situación del trabajo: La visión sindical," working paper 97 (Santiago: Programa de Economía del Trabajo, 1993); Enrique Errazuriz et al., *Huachipato, 1947–1988: De empresa pública a empresa privada* (Santiago: PET [Programa de Economía del Trabajo], 1990); Jorge Katz and Héctor Vera, "Evolución histórica de una planta metalmecánica chilena," paper presented at the conference "Productividad, cambio tecnológico, y sistemas innovativos en América Latina en los años 90," sponsored by CEPAL/CIID, UNU/Intech (Marbella, Chile, 1995); Javier Martínez and Alvaro Díaz, *Chile: The Great Transformation* (Washington, D.C.: Brookings Institution, 1996); Peter Winn and Maria Angélica Ibañez, "Textile Entrepreneurs and Workers in Pinochet's Chile, 1973–1989," Institute for Latin American and Iberian Studies, Latin America papers 15 (New York: Columbia University, 1990); Mario Castillo and Raúl Alvarez, "El liderazgo en las grandes empresas en Chile," in *Grandes empresas y grupos industriales latinoamericanos*, ed. W. Péres (Mexico City: Siglo XXI, 1998), 285–332; and Lucio Geller and Claudio Ramos, *Chile: Innovaciones en la empresa industrial metalmecánica, 1990–1995: Programas y resultados de la gestión de productividad*, working paper 54 (Lima: International Labor Office, 1997).
3 I review these debates in some detail below.
4 See Phillip Oxhorn, *Organizing Civil Society: The Popular Sectors and the Struggle for Democracy in Chile* (University Park: Pennsylvania State University Press, 1995); Cathy Schneider, *Shantytown Resistance in Pinochet's Chile* (Philadelphia: Temple University Press, 1995).

5 I review discussions of consumption in a global context in detail below. Useful overviews of the broader debate on globalization include Mauro Guillén, "Is Globalization Civilizing, Destructive or Feeble? A Critique of Five Key Debates," *Annual Review of Sociology* 27 (2001): 235–60; David Held, Anthony McGrew, David Goldblatt, and Jonathan Perraton, *Global Transformations: Politics, Economics, and Culture* (Stanford: Stanford University Press, 1999); Anthony Giddens, *Runaway World: How Globalization Is Reshaping Our Lives* (New York: Routledge, 2000); Michael Burawoy et al., *Global Ethnography: Forces, Connections and Imaginations in a Postmodern World* (Berkeley: University of California Press, 2000).

6 Madeco diversified into aluminum processing in the late 1950s, and purchased a number of related copper-processing industries beginning in the late 1980s: Manufacturas de Cobre, S.A. (Madeco), *Memoria anual* (Santiago: Madeco, 1945–97).

7 The wire mill is more dependent on infrastructural development tied to state investments (telecommunications, electrification, and high-tension wires for mining), while the brass mill supplies the construction industry: Raskill Information Services, *The Economics of Copper*, 3d ed. (London: Raskill 1984).

8 Manufacturas de Cobre, S.A. (Madeco), *Memoria anual*, 1944–1978.

9 Joel Stillerman, *From Solidarity to Survival: Transformations in the Culture and Styles of Mobilization of Chilean Metalworkers under Democratic and Authoritarian Regimes, 1945–1995*, Ph.D. diss., New School for Social Research, New York, 1998.

10 Interviews with Fernando Pérez, production manager from 1966–71 and general manager from 1973–78, 29 November and 6 December 1994; and Enrique Tassara, Madeco board member, 1973–78, 17 January 1995. Pseudonyms used where requested by interviewee appear as first name only.

11 I discuss this phenomenon in great detail in Joel Stillerman, "The Paradoxes of Power: The Unintended Consequences of Military Rule for Chilean Working-Class Mobilization," *Political Power and Social Theory* 12 (1998): 97–139. It was less expensive for Madeco to offer employees a "buyout" than to fire them, because the law stipulated that the firm must pay double severance pay if it fired workers without due cause (unless management could demonstrate that the worker was a Marxist militant). Employers also could not fire more than 10 workers per month without biministerial approval prior to the Plan Laboral.

12 Interview with Angel, 17 November 1996.

13 Group discussion with wire mill workers, 8 November 1996.

14 Some of those laid off formed cooperatives and continued to work for the firm as outside contractors. There is little additional information available on this group, though it appears they were a small, highly skilled segment of the work force. It is unlikely their dismissal had a significant effect on union affiliation, especially compared to the massive workforce decline due to layoffs of political militants and voluntary retirements, as noted above. Management may have rehired these workers as subcontractors to take advantage of their skills without paying them the same benefits as unionized workers. Interview with Oscar Quezada, 12 June 1994.

15 Interview with Héctor Velásquez, 1 January 1995. Velásquez was a Madeco union

leader beginning in 1981, served as president from 1983–91 and 1995–98, was director from 1992–94, and treasurer from 1999–2003, when he died at age 52.

16 Alicia Tortora and Susana Villacura, "Sistematización de práctica efectuada en Manufacturas de Cobre S.A., Madeco," report on BA practicum, Department of Social Work, Universidad Católica de Chile (June–October, 1974), 24; Dirección de Estudios, Banco Central de Chile, *Indicadores económicos y sociales, 1960–1988* (Santiago: Banco Central, 1989), 212.

17 Santiago, Chile, Segundo Juzgado de Letras del Trabajo, "Demanda laboral por reliquidación de pagos de horas extraordinarias" (16 May 1994); interview with Angel, 17 November 1996; Stillerman, "The Paradoxes of Power"; "Los peligros de la productividad."

18 "Gratificaciones: Esta vez hubo justicia," *Crisol* 13, no. 5 (May 1995): 4; Stillerman, "The Paradoxes of Power."

19 Interview with Héctor Velásquez and Chico Castro, 7 November 1996. The firm seems not to have pursued this strategy until much more recently in the brass mill: interviews with Tonio, 13 November 1996, and Arturo, 21 November 1996. I discuss the reasons for this difference below.

20 Interview with Angel, 17 November 1996; interviews with Fernando Pérez, 29 November and 6 December 1994, and Tonio, 13 November 1996; "Madeco continua premiando a sus obreros," *Madeco informa* (December 1979): 10.

21 On this aspect of Japanese management, see, for example, James P. Womack, Daniel Roos, and Daniel Jones, *The Machine That Changed the World* (New York: Rawson Associates, 1990).

22 Manufacturas de Cobre, S.A. (Madeco), *Memoria anual, 1980*.

23 "La Saga de los Luksic," (four-part series) *Qué pasa* (9, 16, 23, and 30 October 1993); Baring Securities, "Chile Company Report: Madeco, S.A." (Santiago: Baring, 20 April 1995), 6.

24 "La Saga" (16 October 1993), 39–40; interview with Fernando Pérez, 6 December 1994.

25 Interview with Héctor Velásquez, 16 March 1995.

26 Interview with Luís Muñoz, 6 November 1996; Hector Velásquez and Chico Castro, 7 November 1996, Tonio, 13 November 1996, and the wire mill workers, 8 November 1996 made the same point.

27 Interview with Hector Velásquez and Chico Castro, 7 November 1996.

28 Stillerman, "The Paradoxes of Power"; interview with Tomás Jimenez, former personnel manager at Madeco, 7 April 1994.

29 Interview with Manuel, 14 November 1996. This view was expressed universally by informants hired after 1984.

30 "Gratificaciones"; "Los peligros de la productividad."

31 Stillerman, "The Paradoxes of Power."

32 Manufacturas de Cobre, S.A. (Madeco), *Memorias anual* (Santiago: Madeco, 1986–1997); "Madeco expects to increase income by 42%," *CHIP News* (14 January 1997); "La saga de los Luksic."

33 "US $ 90 millones sumó el aumento de capital completado por Madeco," El Mercurio, 25 August 1993, D5.

34 Michael Piore and Charles Sabel, The Second Industrial Divide: Possibilities for Prosperity (New York: Basic Books, 1984); and Womack et al., Machine That Changed the World, articulate this perspective.

35 See Bennett Harrison, Lean and Mean: The Changing Architecture of Corporate Power in the Age of Flexibility (New York: Basic Books, 1994); John Tomaney "A New Paradigm of Work Organization and Technology?" in Post-Fordism: A Reader, ed. Ash Amin (Oxford: Blackwell, 1994), 157–94; Mark Elam, "Puzzling out the Post-Fordist Debate: Technology, Markets, and Institutions," in Amin, Post-Fordism, 71–98.

36 See Thomas Kochan, Russell Lansbury, and John MacDuffie, eds., After Lean Production: Evolving Employment Practices in the World Auto Industry (Ithaca: Cornell University, ILR Press, 1997); Sanford Jacoby, ed., The Workers of Nations: Industrial Relations in a Global Economy (New York: Oxford University Press, 1997).

37 Interview with Enrique Tassara, 17 January 1995.

38 Baring Securities, "Chile Company Report: Madeco, S.A.," notes the reduction of inventories in several product lines. Vicuña told union leaders the firm sought to adopt total quality management in early 1994 in order to satisfy the demands of European customers for defect-free products: Sindicato 1 Madeco, Asamblea general de socios (13 March 1994). In many conversations, union members noted the implementation of these two models.

39 See Harley Shaiken, "Advanced Manufacturing and Mexico: A New International Division of Labor?" Latin American Research Review 29, no. 2 (1994): 39–71.

40 On the definitions and uses of just-in-time and total quality management, see Makoto Kumazawa, Portraits of the Japanese Workplace: Labor Movements, Workers, and Managers (Boulder: Westview, 1996).

41 For discussions of the authoritarian adoption of Japanese management techniques in Chilean firms, see works cited in note 2 above.

42 Interview with Tomás Jimenez, former industrial relations manager, 7 April 1994. Jimenez intimated that he was concerned that excessive training might lead workers to resign by stating, "If a mechanic asks me to pay for an accounting class, I won't accept it." While an absurd example, it points to management's reluctance to offer training beyond the bare minimum. Many blue-collar workers complained that management refused to send them to training courses. See interview with Humberto, 7 January 1994.

43 Discussions with wire mill workers, 8 November 1996, and group discussion with brass mill workers, 25 November 1996.

44 Interview with Hector Velásquez and Chico Castro, 7 November 1996. Echeverría and Herrera in "Innovaciones en la empresa y situación del trabajo" and Castillo et al. in "Reorganización industrial y estrategias competitivas," note that in Chilean firms, the use of work teams or quality circles seldom extends below middle managers.

45 Group discussion with brass mill workers, 25 November 1996. Wire mill workers made similar observations.

46 Group discussion with brass mill workers, 25 November 1996.

47 *Crisol* 14, no. 10 (September 1996): 5.

48 Interview with Héctor Velásquez and Chico Castro, 7 November 1996.

49 INE (Instituto Nacional de Estadísticas), *Compendio estadístico, 1995* (Santiago: INE, 1995); interviews with Héctor Velásquez and Chico Castro (7 November 1996), brass mill workers (25 November 1996), and Manuel, 14 November 1996.

50 Both quotes from a discussion with wire mill workers, 8 November 1996.

51 "Editorial," *Crisol,* 12, no. 5 (July 1994): 4–5.

52 "Los peligros de la productividad."

53 Republica of Chile, *Código del trabajo* (Santiago: Editora Jurídica Publigráfica, 1992), 17–18; interview with José Pérez Concha, white-collar union leader, 3 June 1994. Many informants echoed this observation.

54 Interview with Carlos and Samuel, 29 October 1996.

55 " 'Exitos' que llevan al fracaso: Manía del trabajo," *Crisol* 10, no. 2 (November 1992): 18; "Condiciones de trabajo y salud de los trabajadores," *Crisol* 12, no. 5 (October, 1994): 5–7; "Los peligros de la productividad"; interview with José Pérez Concha, white-collar union leader, 3 June 1994.

56 Interview with Daniel, 5 February 1994; group conversations with older, younger, and retired workers, 24 July and 5 August 1994.

57 Stillerman, *From Solidarity to Survival*, chap. 2.

58 Interview with Marcos Medina, 15 July 1999.

59 Interview with Mario Ariarrán, 22 December 1993. Residents at the Madeco housing block were renters until 1969, when the union made an agreement with management permitting workers to purchase the homes. See Stillerman, *From Solidarity to Survival*, chap. 2.

60 Interview with Medina, 15 July 1999. During fieldwork from 1993 to 1995 and subsequent one- or two-month visits to Chile, I also observed many retirees arriving to meetings in cars.

61 Interview with J. R. Valenzuela, 29 December 1993. Valenzuela is a lifelong resident of San Miguel, the southern Santiago neighborhood where Madeco is located. He worked briefly in Mademsa and has published two novels concerning the community.

62 Their disposable income and status-conscious lifestyles resemble those of copper miners: Thomas Klubock, *Contested Communities: Class, Gender and Politics in Chile's El Teniente Copper Mines, 1904–1951* (Durham: Duke University Press, 1998), chap. 6.

63 See Stillerman, *From Solidarity to Survival*, chap. 6.

64 For these general trends, see: Gonzalo Cáceres, and Lorena Farías, "Efectos de las grandes superficies comerciales en el Santiago de la modernización ininterrumpida, 1982–1999," *Ambiente y Desarrollo* 15, no. 4 (1999): 36–41; Hernán Frigolett and Alejandra Sanhueza, *Evolución del gasto del consumo de los hogares en Chile, 1985–1995* (Santiago: Ministry of Planning, 1999); INE, *V Encuesta de Presupuestos Familiares, 1996–1997: Versión resumida* (Santiago: INE, 1999); Consumers International, *Cambios en los patrones de consumo y sustenabilidad en Chile* (Santiago: Consumers International, 2000); Mariana Schkolnik, *Transformaciones en las pautas de consumo y políticas*

neoliberales. Chile: 1974–1981 (Santiago: PET, 1983); Cámara de Comercio de Santiago, *Deudas de consumo consolidadas por estrato socioeconomico* (Santiago: 1995). Tomás Moulián's critique of contemporary consumer culture in Chile has attracted wide popular interest and resonates with frequent news accounts on the topic. See Tomás Moulián, *Chile actual: Anatomía de un mito* (Santiago: LOM Ediciones, 1997) and *El consumo me consume* (Santiago: LOM Ediciones, 1998).

65 For discussions of global retailing as Americanization, see Benjamin Barber, *Jihad vs. McWorld: How Globalism and Tribalism Are Reshaping the World* (New York: Ballantine Books, 1995); George Ritzer, *The McDonaldization Thesis: Explorations and Extensions* (London: Sage, 1998), chaps. 6 and 7. For an interpretation of these changes as examples of cultural imperialism, see Leslie Sklair, *Sociology of the Global System*, 2d ed. (Baltimore: Johns Hopkins University Press, 1995), chap. 5. For analyses of nationalist reactions to foreign goods, see Richard Wilk, "Food and Nationalism: The Origins of 'Belizean Food,' " in *Food Nations: Selling Taste in Consumer Societies*, ed. W. Bellasco and P. Scranton (New York: Routledge, 2002), chap. 6; Lauren Derby, "Gringo Chickens with Worms: Food and Nationalism in the Dominican Republic," in *Close Encounters of Empire: Writing the Cultural History of U.S.–Latin American Relations*, ed. G. Joseph, C. LeGrand, and R. Salvatore (Durham: Duke University Press, 1998), 451–96. Discussions of how local populations appropriate and integrate foreign commodities and retail styles into local cultural contexts include Daniel Miller, *Modernity: An Ethnographic Approach. Dualism and Mass Consumption in Trinidad* (Oxford: Berg, 1994), and *Capitalism: An Ethnographic Approach* (New York: Berg, 1997); William Roseberry, "Americanization in the Americas," in *Anthropologies and Histories: Essays in Culture, History, and Political Economy* (New Brunswick: Rutgers University Press, 1991), 80–124; James L. Watson, ed., *Golden Arches East: McDonalds in East Asia* (Stanford: Stanford University Press, 1997); and David Howes, ed., *Cross-Cultural Consumption: Global Markets, Local Realities* (London: Routledge, 1996). Works that examine how local populations and émigré diasporas use commodities and media images to construct long-distance national, ethnic, and cultural identities include Néstor Garcia-Canclini, *Consumers and Citizens: Globalization and Multicultural Conflicts*, trans. George Yúdice (Minneapolis: University of Minnesota Press, 2001); Arjun Appadurai, *Modernity at Large: Cultural Dimensions of Globalization* (Minneapolis: University of Minnesota Press, 1996); and Rudi Colloredo-Mansfeld, *The Native Leisure Class: Consumption and Cultural Creativity in the Andes* (Chicago: University of Chicago Press, 1999).

66 Union leaders at the Huachipato steelworks make a similar observation in Errazuriz et al., *Huachipato*, as does Moulián, *Chile actual*.

67 Interviews with Manuel, 14 November 1996, and Tonio, 13 November 1996.

68 Interview with Hector Velásquez and Chico Castro, 7 November 1996.

69 Interview with Carlos and Samuel, 29 October 1996; interview with Hector Velásquez, 6 January 1999.

70 Interview with Daniel, 5 February 1994.

71 Interview with Manuel, 14 November 1996.

72 Interview with Carlos and Samuel, 29 October 1996.

73 Interview with Arturo, 21 November 1996.
74 Both quotes from interview with Carlos and Samuel, 29 October 1996.
75 Discussion with wire mill workers, 8 November 1996.
76 Discussion with wire mill workers, 8 November 1996.
77 Interview with Cicero, 10 November 1996.
78 Martínez and Díaz, Chile, 105.
79 Interview with Cicero, 10 November 1996.
80 Discussion with brass mill workers, 25 November 1996.
81 Interview with Manuel, 14 November 1996.
82 Interview with Cicero, 10 November 1996.
83 Interview with Carlos and Samuel, 29 October 1996.
84 "Peligros de la productividad," 3.
85 Interview with Carlos and Samuel, 29 October 1996.
86 Interview with Cicero, 9 November 1996.
87 Pierre Bourdieu, Distinction: A Social Critique of the Judgment of Taste, trans. Richard Nice (Cambridge: Harvard University Press, 1984), 384.
88 See Moulián, Chile actual: Anatomía de un mito and El consumo me consume.
89 Stillerman, "The Paradoxes of Power."
90 Interview with Héctor Velásquez, 24 November 1996.
91 Interview with Héctor Velásquez, 24 November 1996.
92 Salomon Brothers et al., Prospectus: 3,937,500 American Depositary Shares, Representing 39,375,000 Shares of Common Stock: Madeco, S.A. (New York, 7 May 1993).
93 Interviews with Carlos and Samuel, 29 October 1996, and brass mill workers, 25 November 1996.
94 Sindicato 1 Madeco, Asamblea general de socios, 14 January 1988.
95 Sindicato 1 Madeco, Asamblea general de socios, 31 May 1991.
96 Interview with Leonardo, a former union employee and activist, 23 March 1995.
97 Interview with Arturo, 21 November 1996, discussion with brass mill workers, 25 November 1996.
98 Interview with Manuel, 14 November 1996.
99 Discussion with brass mill workers, 25 November 1996. All workers hired during this time remembered participating in the protests.
100 Interview with Héctor Velásquez and Chico Castro, 7 November 1996.
101 Interview with Héctor Velásquez, 24 November 1996.
102 Sindicato 1 Madeco, Asamblea General de Socios, 6 and 16 June 1992.
103 Interview with José Pérez Concha, 3 June 1994; Sindicato 1 Madeco, Asamblea extraordinaria, 28 May 1992; "Cuanto vale la demanda por gratificaciones," Crisol 10, no. 2 (November 1992): 3–8.
104 "Senador Designado, William Thayer, dice que el fallo puede tener 'efectos devastadores,' " Crisol 31, no. 5 (May 1995): 6.
105 Field notes, 15 July 1999.
106 Sindicato 1 Madeco, Asamblea general de socios, 8 July 1992; "Conversando con: Julio Martínez," Crisol 10, no. 2 (November 1992): 13–14.
107 Interview with Arturo, 21 November 1996.

108 Interview with Tonio, 13 November 1996.
109 Interview with Héctor Velásquez and Chico Castro, 7 November 1996.
110 Interview with Tonio, 13 November 1996.
111 Interview with Luís Muñoz, 6 November 1996.
112 Interview with Arturo, 21 November 1996.
113 Interview with Tonio, 13 November 1996.
114 Interview with Tonio, 26 January 1995.
115 Interview with Angel, 9 November 1993.
116 Discussion with brass mill workers, 25 November 1996.
117 Interview with Héctor Velásquez, 6 January 1999.
118 A form of protest that copper miners in the Chuquicamata mine made famous in one of the first public labor protests under the dictatorship in 1977. See Gonzalo Falabella, "La diversidad en el movimiento sindical chileno bajo el régimen militar," in Sindicatos bajo regimenes militares: Argentina, Brasil, Chile, ed. Manuel Barrera and Gonzalo Falabella (Santiago: CES, 1990).
119 Interview with Héctor Velásquez, 6 January 1999.
120 Sindicato 1 Madeco, Asamblea general de socios (8 and 16 April 1993); interviews with Manuel, 14 November 1996, and Arturo, 21 November 1996.
121 "Psicólogo y psicosis: Apareció el resultado de la encuesta de los psicologos de la U.C.," Crisol 12, no. 5 (July 1994): 13–14; interview with Angel, 17 November 1996.
122 Sindicato 1 Madeco, Asamblea general de socios, 5 January 1995 and 25 September 1998; field notes, 1 February 1995.
123 Stillerman, From Solidarity to Survival; phone communications with Héctor Velásquez, 25 March 1996 and 30 September 2002; Sindicato 1 Madeco, Asamblea general de socios, 31 January 1993; Sindicato 1 Madeco, S.A., Convenio colectivo; Sindicato 1 Vigencia: 10 de noviembre 1999–31 de enero del 2002 (Santiago: November 1998).
124 "Editorial," Crisol 15, no. 11 (May 1997), 2–3.
125 Interview with Hector Velásquez, 6 January 1999; Sindicato 1 Madeco, Asamblea general de socios, 7 August and 25 September 1998.
126 Interview with Arturo, 21 November 1996.
127 Interview with Carlos and Samuel, 29 October 1996. Others express similar sentiments.
128 Stillerman, From Solidarity to Survival; Moulián, El Consumo me consume.
129 "Madeco: Farol de la calle, oscuridad en la casa," Crisol 12, no. 4 (January 1994): 6–8.
130 Sindicato 1 Madeco, Asamblea general de socios, 24 July 1997.
131 Sindicato 1 Madeco, Asamblea general de socios, 25 September 1998.
132 Interview with Samuel and Héctor Velásquez, 6 January 1999.
133 "Cussen to Leave Codelco for Madeco," Santiago Times, 10 June 1999 (www.santiago times.cl).
134 "Madeco Improves Its Results but Records Losses," Santiago Times, 9 March 2001 (www.santiagotimes.cl).
135 "Argentine Subsidiaries Assist Madeco Recovery," Santiago Times, 14 November 2000.

136 David Roberts, "Madeco H1 loss shoots up 88%," *BNAmericas.com Metals News*, 29 August 2002; "Madeco missing capital increase target," *BNAmericas.com Metals News*, 26 September 2002.

137 Héctor Velásquez, phone communication, 30 September 2002.

138 Héctor Velásquez, phone communication, 30 September 2002.

139 Joel Stillerman, "Gender, Class, and Generational Contexts for Consumption in Contemporary Chile," *Journal of Consumer Culture* 4, no. 1 (2004).

140 While this is a general trend, exceptions include Bourdieu, *Distinction*; Ben Fine and Ellen Leopold, *The World of Consumption* (London: Routledge, 1993); and Moulián, *El consumo me consume*.

THOMAS MILLER KLUBOCK

Class, Community, and Neoliberalism in Chile:
Copper Workers and the Labor Movement During the Military
Dictatorship and Restoration of Democracy

In April of 1983 the Chilean copper miners' confederation (the Confederación de Trabajadores del Cobre—CTC), representing 26,000 copper workers and under independent leadership for the first time in a decade, called for a general strike in Chile's copper mines and for a day of national protest against the dictatorship of Augusto Pinochet. On 11 May, tens of thousands of workers and urban poor (*pobladores*), responding to the copper miners' call, came together to demand a return to democracy and to protest the military regime's neoliberal economic policies. A month later, workers in El Teniente, the world's largest underground copper mine, paralyzed production for twenty-four hours in an illegal strike. The CTC declaration and the strike in the El Teniente mine placed the copper miners in the leadership of opposition to Pinochet and at the forefront of the reinvigorated national labor movement.[1] These May 1983 protests led to a three-year period of civil unrest that forced the military regime to negotiate with representatives of the democratic opposition.

The transition to democracy in Chile after 1989, however, did not satisfy mine workers' demands. Miners confronted center-left coalition governments (the Concertación de Partidos por la Democracia—Coalition of Parties for Democracy) committed to maintaining the military regime's free market policies and to modernizing Chile's copper production by restructuring the large state-owned mines (nationalized in 1971 by the government of Salvador Allende) and promoting foreign investment in new mining enterprises. Despite a strike in 1991 aimed at recouping losses incurred during the dictatorship, miners have been unable to effectively challenge the neoliberal economic model, the incremental privatization of the copper industry, and the reorganization of production in the state-owned mining sector. Unlike 1983, when workers drew on a resilient labor culture and underground political networks to forge their opposition to the dictatorship, by the early 1990s structural economic and social changes initiated during military rule had transformed the nature of work and community life, undermining the foundations of miners' militant working-class identity.

The case of the El Teniente miners provides a number of insights into the history of workers during the Pinochet dictatorship and the transition to democracy, a period defined by economic restructuring and the intensification of Chile's integration into the global economy.

First, El Teniente offers an important example of the effects of violent state repression and free market economics on an industrial working-class community, even one as strategically well placed and historically privileged as the copper miners were. Historically, wages were higher and unions stronger in the copper industry than in other industries, so that many social scientists have considered the copper miners a labor aristocracy. Yet the formation of a permanent working-class community in the copper mining camps after 1930, stimulated by the corporate welfare programs of the Anaconda and Kennecott copper companies and the nationalist and populist policies of the Chilean state after 1930, broke ground for labor relations in urban areas. In Santiago, textile and metallurgical companies employed paternalist labor policies similar to those of the North American copper companies. Anaconda and Kennecott also led the way in building housing projects for workers and their families and provided incentives and benefits that, combined with social legislation passed after 1938, established "the family wage" and created the conditions for the formation of stable families and working-class neighborhoods alongside the industries developed during the process of import substitution.[2] In the copper-mining camps, as in the city, strong community networks shaped a vibrant working-class culture and political identity tied to the leftist parties.[3] After 1973 in the mining camps, as well as in urban industrial neighborhoods, the combination of state terror and economic "shock therapy" led to the fragmentation of these community ties, political networks, and workplace cultures.

Second, the copper miners' work actions and mobilizations between 1977 and 1983 illustrate the ways in which labor protest against authoritarianism was woven out of traditions of union activism and political militancy that a decade of dictatorship could not eliminate. The case of the El Teniente miners demonstrates the importance of organized labor and industrial workers and miners to the civilian opposition to the Pinochet regime that erupted after 1983. In the copper mine, traditions of union militancy were driven underground but survived to provide copper workers with clandestine networks for organizing and expressing opposition to the regime and for maintaining workers' notions of class and community. Years of organizing, strikes, and mobilizations inside and outside unions by mine workers preceded the three years of popular insurgency known in Chile as "las protestas."[4] While most analysts have focused on the role of pobladores in the protests in terms of the emergence of a "new" historical actor and type of social movement, the case of El Teniente demonstrates the importance of workers and the labor movement to the building of civilian opposition to the Pinochet dictatorship.

Third, the El Teniente miners' experiences under the center-left democratic governments of the Concertación reflect the problems confronted by workers and organized labor during the transition to and restoration of democracy. Despite the central role played by the labor movement in the opposition to the Pinochet dictatorship during the 1980s, the position of Chile's workers has been weakened by the maintenance of political institutions, laws, and economic policies inherited from the dictatorship and unmodified under the democratic governments due to the opposition of a congress in which senators appointed by Pinochet have blocked efforts at reform. Despite their strategic location in the national economy and role in the transition to democracy, copper miners, like workers throughout Chile, have been unable to translate the incremental democratization of the political system into social and economic improvements or the strengthening of their unions. By the 1990s what political repression could not accomplish, structural economic change had begun to produce in the mining community. Workplace solidarities, community ties, and political networks that were once the basis of miners' powerful class identity and collective actions were disrupted by new labor systems, flexibilization, downsizing, the growth of cultures of individualism and consumerism, and the fragmentation and dispersal of residential neighborhoods. The case of El Teniente illuminates the effects of globalization and economic restructuring on working-class communities and organized labor throughout Chile.

Finally, as workers in Chile's largest state-owned company, the Corporación del Cobre (Codelco), and the most important industry in the national economy, miners confronted a series of unique challenges during the 1990s. First, how could they defend a state-owned industry against the incursions of foreign investment in the context of an economic model that privileges privatization and the liberalization of trade and investment without the political support of the government or its constituent parties? Second, what role would miners' unions and workers play in the new management programs designed to make Codelco internationally competitive while maintaining its status as a state-owned enterprise? Finally, could mine workers rebuild a shared sense of class and union solidarity in the context of new management strategies designed to reduce costs and increase production and workers' weakened position vis-à-vis the copper company in a democracy still limited by the legacies of authoritarian rule?

Before 1973 the El Teniente copper miners' unions and the CTC, representing workers in Chile's largest copper mines, had enjoyed a privileged position in terms of government support and recognition. Because earnings from taxes on copper exports composed the bulk of Chile's foreign revenues (close to 90 percent by 1971), beginning in the 1930s, miners occupied a strategic role in the national economy and their unions employed a great deal of leverage within the prevailing system of state-administered labor relations. Copper workers' unions were able to press the state to intervene in labor conflicts in order to maintain labor peace and high levels of production in the mines and were thus able to wrest substantial gains in wage levels and benefits from the North American companies that owned the mines. In addition, miners were able to identify their strikes and demands with Chile's national interests and with efforts to exert Chilean control over the foreign-owned mines and could thus call on national support in their conflicts with the foreign companies.[5] Nationalism became a primary mode of asserting working-class radicalism in the copper mines.

After 1938 the El Teniente mining community was integrated into a state-directed corporatist system of labor relations. With support from the state the miners were able to elect independent union leaders and build powerful unions led by members of the Communist party (PC) and Socialist party (PS). Communist party activists helped to organize miners' independent union movements during the 1930s, and both leftist parties provided crucial support to the miners' organizations during strikes and collective bargaining between the North American copper companies, the unions, and the state. Leftist senators and deputies frequently made speeches in Congress defending the copper miners against the North American company, echoed the miners' call for nationalization of the mines, and heralded the miners' strikes as part of a broader nationalist project to recover what Salvador Allende called "el sueldo de Chile" (Chile's wages). Strikes in the copper mines contributed to the 1966 decision of the Christian Democratic government of Eduardo Frei to "Chileanize" the country's copper mines by purchasing majority ownership from the Anaconda and Kennecott copper companies. And in 1971 the mines were nationalized outright by Allende's socialist Popular Unity government.

Workers in the Kennecott Copper Company's El Teniente mine were also able to take advantage of the company's need for a stable and skilled labor force and capacity to pay high wages relative to other sectors of the economy. In response to traditions of labor mobility and working-class effervescence that hampered production in the mine from 1904 to 1919, during the 1920s the North American company began to offer high wages and social welfare benefits in order to secure a reliable and trained labor force. Kennecott's Chilean subsidiary, the Braden Copper Company, used high wages, production bonuses, and welfare benefits to induce workers to stay on the job in the mine, marry, and form families in the camps. The company paid a periodic cost-of-living raise and a family allowance that gave married workers with children special bonuses. The company also built schools for workers and their children and provided cultural and social activities for the mining community. In addition, in almost annual strikes between 1938 and 1973 the miners won the right to health care, job security, hiring preference for their (male) children, and pensions, along with respect for job classifications and improvements in work conditions. The mining company offered male workers the possibility of approximating a middle-class lifestyle by maintaining their families on a single "family wage" that was significantly higher than salaries in other industrial sectors.

Despite high wages relative to other Chilean workers and the company's social welfare system, miners nurtured a combative culture of opposition to company authority. Work in teams (cuadrillas) created tight bonds of solidarity among miners who shared a common interest in meeting production quotas in order to earn bonuses. In addition, the constant danger of accidents in the mine drew workers within teams together and established ties based on their mutual reliance for survival. Like miners around the world, El Teniente copper workers elaborated an intensely masculine work identity based on their capacity for hard and dangerous physical labor in the mine. Pride in physical strength and the skill required to perform jobs inside the mine and its concentrating and re-fining plants laid the basis for the miners' sense of dignity and autonomy and produced a defiant and challenging attitude toward company authority; fights among workers and with foremen and supervisors were frequent, as were wildcat strikes and stoppages.

The miners' ties of workplace solidarity were reinforced by the tight links between the mining community and the mine. Until the late 1960s most El Teniente copper miners lived in isolated camps high up in the Andes. In these camps, the miners and their families forged a resilient community and class identity that lent strength to their struggles with the North American company. Their shared experiences in mining camps dominated by a single company fostered a sense of collective interest and antagonism to a common enemy. Recreation, education, the cost of living, housing, and health care were controlled by the company and were linked to miners' wages and work in the mine. Miners' wives participated in strikes, walked picket lines, and organized women's committees and cost-of-living committees. The gendered division of labor in the camps, promoted by the copper company and male workers alike, assigned women to the domestic sphere and defined their social role in terms of marriage and motherhood. As housewives, their responsibility for their families' welfare threw them into conflict with the company and placed them at the side of their husbands, on whose wages and benefits they depended during strikes.

MILITARY REPRESSION AND
THE NEOLIBERAL ECONOMIC MODEL IN THE COPPER MINES

The 1973 military coup initiated profound changes in the lives of the El Teniente copper miners and their families. Military officers took control of the mine's administration. Hundreds of leftist activists were fired, and many were arrested and tortured. Some members of El Teniente's administration appointed by Salvador Allende's socialist Popular Unity (UP) government (1970–73) and prominent members of the UP parties and union leaders were sent to concentration camps and then into exile. While union structures in El Teniente remained nominally intact, the military exercised a firm control over union leaders and activity within the unions remained dormant until the 1980s. As in other sectors of the economy, union elections were prohibited, union leaders were appointed by the regime, and collective bargaining was suspended.

A 1973 strike against the UP by El Teniente's white-collar workers (empleados) led by Christian Democratic party (PDC) and rightist gremialista (guild or trade) union leaders, with the support of the Chilean right and the United States Central Intelligence Agency, had earned the miners a certain level of approval in the eyes of Chile's new military rulers. Therefore, repression in the mine was not as harsh as in Santiago's militant industrial belts (cordones industriales) and urban factories that had been nationalized after workers' takeovers (tomas). The PDC had made inroads in copper miners' empleado unions during the late 1960s and had challenged the traditional hegemony of the Communist and

Socialist parties, which retained their base in the large blue-collar workers (*obreros*) unions.[6] In addition, a small number of ostensibly "nonpolitical" gremialista union leaders who viewed unions as professional associations or interest groups occupied leadership positions in the unions of empleados. The importance of copper production to the economy and the national symbolic and institutional weight of the copper miners' unions also impeded the implementation of more repressive actions in the mines. The regime initially hoped to use union leaders in the copper industry who had opposed Allende's UP government to manufacture the appearance of labor support for military rule. Thus, two weeks after the military coup, Pinochet traveled to El Teniente to meet with the wives of workers who had struck against the Allende government in order to demonstrate the regime's sympathy for "nonpolitical" and "nonsubversive" forms of organized labor.[7] A number of Christian Democratic and "independent" gremialista leaders were appointed to head El Teniente's unions.

During the first years following the military coup, the Pinochet regime also experimented briefly with nationalist and corporatist labor policies under the direction of some members of the military, particularly the new minister of labor General Nicanor Díaz Estrada and air force commander General Gustavo Leigh.[8] The regime sought to establish "direct" channels of communication with independent nonleftist and Christian Democratic union leaders. In 1974, for example, Díaz met with the regime-appointed leaders of the CTC to discuss their concerns about the military junta's labor policy. The general assured the CTC leaders that the government would respect miners' "derechos adquiridos" (acquired rights) but informed them that the regime would continue to suspend collective bargaining in order to combat inflation and because "75 percent of the union leaders are in place since 11 September 1973, but we can't trust all of them because there still remain some bad habits in terms of public order . . . and we must understand that the rules of the game are no longer what they once were."[9] The new military rulers appointed Guillermo Santana, a Christian Democrat with close ties to the AFL-CIO's anticommunist American Institute for Free Labor Development (AIFLD), itself linked to the CIA, to head the CTC. In 1974, Santana visited Washington at the invitation of AIFLD to speak on "the actual conditions of unionists in our country and the new avenues that have opened between the workers and the government."[10]

The regime drew on the support of Guillermo Medina, a leader of one of El Teniente's empleados unions with ties to the CIA, in order to claim the support of organized labor and the copper workers for the dictatorship. Medina acted as a gremialista union leader, with ties neither to the left-wing parties that dominated El Teniente's blue-collar unions, nor to the Christian Democratic leaders, whose base of support lay in the smaller white-collar unions. Medina had played a central role in the 1973 strike against the UP and, following the coup, was the only labor leader to be appointed to the regime's "Council of State." Throughout the period of Pinochet's rule, Medina met frequently with Pinochet, his ministers, and the military officers placed in charge of the national copper company to discuss issues that related to workers' demands in the copper sector. In addition, Medina was employed by the military regime as an unofficial spokesman for organized labor during discussions of national labor policy. In 1974 Medina organized a rally in El Teniente to support the minister of mining's threat to suspend copper exports to Great Britain in response to its criticisms of the military regime's human rights abuses.[11]

By 1975 the military government began to direct its repressive apparatus even at Christian Democratic union leaders in El Teniente and the CTC who were trying to organize a limited amount of autonomous union activity and to enter into collective bargaining with Codelco. The regime had begun to consolidate its rule and to plan a long-term project for the complete transformation of the nation's political and socioeconomic structures according to the radical neoliberalism of "los Chicago boys," a group of economists trained in the United States. After 1975, PDC political leaders and labor leaders who had supported the coup and who had hoped to carve out some space for unions under military rule, as well as to build Christian Democratic control of the labor movement, felt the brush of repression, and many were arrested and sent into exile. Only rightist union leaders loyal to the Pinochet regime, such as Medina, and "nonpolitical," regime-appointed leaders maintained their positions at the head of the miners' organizations.

As oral histories with mine workers testify, the decade following the military coup was defined by intense repression and a generalized climate of terror and fear. Miners no longer attended union assemblies, met in groups, or talked openly with one another. One worker recalls, for example, that "participation was braked because when someone spoke in the union, when they noted that he was making a demand for something, he was detained the next day."[12] Another miner remembers that until 1980 unions had to request police permission to hold assemblies and that police were sent to watch over union meetings.[13] At work, supervisors and foremen ruled with an authoritarian discipline that earned them the name "gringos chilenos" and the reputation of being worse than North American bosses. Supervisors (often appointed from the ranks of the military) and mine foremen frequently violated job classifications and forced workers to do extra jobs and work overtime without pay. As one miner said, "The situation deteriorated as to work conditions. Abuses by *jefes*, lack of respect for the workers and threats. The jefes drive us hard, as they say. They swear at us and treat us with arrogance: if you don't do this job you're fired. And go complain to the union. They don't respect the classifications. The jefe says: you have to do this job, and you have to do it. . . . They punish you for every slip up and order you to do dangerous jobs."[14]

Union leaders were chosen by Codelco and the government and were widely perceived to be the agents of the dictatorship. Miners reported that spies denounced workers who talked politics or spoke at union meetings to the company administration and police. They only went to the union hall to take out loans, visit the dental clinic, or receive benefits.

The miners' close bonds of workplace solidarity began to erode under the pressures of fear and repression. As one miner remembers: "I would say that everyone sought refuge; they kept quiet. . . . Often the workers didn't even greet one another out of fear. You saw it everywhere. You were walking and sometimes you bumped into someone who crossed the street to avoid contact, conversation, or greeting."[15] Another remembered that "you couldn't give your opinion, it was an atmosphere in which you couldn't work peacefully, where you couldn't talk to anyone, everyone was mistrustful."[16] Describing the deterioration of union life, one worker noted that "union members don't participate, they don't go to meetings. There's no trust. If you express your opinions, in two minutes they know in the office. The guys don't risk it, don't support the union leaders. They stay quiet, at home, in their car, and they take care of their jobs."[17]

The military repression of organized labor and the Left was exacerbated in El Teniente, as in other working-class communities in Chile, by the regime's economic policies, which reduced job security, wages, and benefits. El Teniente's military administration attempted to cut production costs in the copper industry by lowering workers' wages, limiting their benefits, reducing employment, and subcontracting many of the jobs not directly related to production. The suspension of collective bargaining and independent union activity led to a significant decline in workers' real wages following the coup. Between late 1973 and May 1983 real average wages dropped by 32.6 percent in El Teniente, considerably reducing production costs for Codelco, since wages and benefits constituted close to half the company's operating budget.[18] Codelco also cut costs by reducing workers' benefits. El Teniente workers no longer had access to free medical attention and health care from the company, a benefit they had won from Kennecott in the 1920s and a basic necessity in an industry where work-related injuries and illnesses proliferated. By the late 1970s El Teniente miners had to pay 50 percent of their medical costs, and for some procedures up to 90 percent, to private health care organizations. As union leaders noted, workers who suffered accidents on the job often fell deeply into debt in order to pay for medical treatment. To pay for health care, workers took out loans from the company or went to "officialist" union leaders for help in acquiring credit from the company or from banks. Miners noted a deterioration in the quality of the medical care they received. As the miners' paper put it in 1985: "It's a demonstrable fact that with the creation of the Fusat [El Teniente's health maintenance organization], the provision of health care to the workers and their family members has suffered a considerable deterioration of quality and quantity. This is demonstrated by the hundreds of demands and debts that pressure the workers."[19]

In an industry where work accidents were frequent and silicosis a common problem, private health organizations frequently refused to classify workers' injuries and illnesses as job-related. In 1983 one union leader noted that "our most serious problem right now is medical attention. Many people have had work accidents, and they haven't received good care."[20]

The privatization of Chile's social security system also undermined the miners' economic security. While the North American company and then the state under the U P government had provided workers pensions, now workers had to contribute to private financial groups that managed pension funds. Some miners who had little experience with finance and investment lost their pensions, which had been invested in precarious investment firms that went out of business during the economic recession that began in 1982. The privatization of social security and health care left workers vulnerable to the whims of the market and many deeply indebted.

Housing payments exacerbated this situation. Before 1973 copper workers lived in housing provided by the company in the mine's camps or in housing subsidized by the state and the company in Rancagua, the city below El Teniente. By the mid-1970s most El Teniente workers lived in housing developments in Rancagua built according to plans elaborated by the North American company and the Christian Democratic government of Eduardo Frei (1964–70) in 1966. Under the Popular Unity government of Allende the state assumed all of the costs for supplying miners housing after the nationalization of the mines in 1971, but after the military coup in 1973 workers had to take on financial responsibility for their homes, adding rents and housing payments to their ever increasing debt burdens.

The regime's 1979 Labor Code also took away many of the economic gains that the El Teniente miners had won from the North American copper company and that had been guaranteed by the state. The Labor Code established a number of laws that severely limited workers' organizations.[21] Industry-wide federations such as the CTC, which had won legal status after a general strike in the copper industry during the 1960s, were given no legal standing and could not represent workers in collective bargaining. Many workers in "industries whose paralyzation would damage the supply of goods to the population, the economy, or national security," like copper, could not go on strike. Employers were given the right to hire replacement workers during strikes. After 60 days on strike, workers were required either to return to work and accept the conditions offered by the employer or to leave the company. The introduction of the new Labor Code eroded the once strong position of miners' unions and transformed their relation to the state.

The introduction of new machinery in the mine after 1980 also rendered copper workers' livelihoods more precarious. While most of the labor involved in building tunnels and extracting mineral before 1980 was labor-intensive—drilling, placing charges, shoveling ore into cars—new machines transformed the nature of work in the mines and reduced the company's labor requirements. As one miner remembers: "Where the miner drilled and then blasted—a lot of that was done with physical force like with the shovel, today they have huge mechanical shovels. Before you needed a bottle of oxygen, of gas . . . you had to carry it on your shoulder—today this is transported by a vehicle; today they are trying out machines that do everything the miner used to do. . . . The machine drills into the hill, deposits the explosive. . . . That means a reduction in personnel."[22]

In the mine, new equipment and tractors (the "jumbos" and LHDs—load, haul, dump) were used for drilling and shoveling, diesel-powered transportation was introduced, and new mechanized operating systems were installed. In the foundry and mill, the company introduced the automation and the simplification of tasks through the use of machinery and computers. Mechanization led to changes in job classifications and pay systems as well. In 1987 a company committee completed a reorganization of job classifications to fit the realities of new work systems. As a union bulletin put it, "with the modernization the company has experienced, incorporating new more advanced technologies, job classifications have suffered extra burdens in terms of duties, responsibilities, and obligations; but this hasn't been compensated for in money for the worker."[23] The paper pointed out that workers had learned new skills and taken on new responsibilities and tasks, leading to an increase in production, with no change in the system of payment. The paper noted that the new organization of job classifications introduced by the company actually led to a decrease in remunerations for most workers and that there was a "crisis of discontent among the workers" for the decline in income as well as "the exhaustion and physical damage caused by the unchecked increase in work."[24] The use of new technologies led to increased production, lower costs, a reduced labor force, and record earnings for Codelco, despite the steadily dropping price of copper on the world market. In 1982, for example, the price of copper dropped from 73 to 62 cents a pound on the world market, yet the company still earned 50 percent more than it had in 1981. In 1974 Codelco employed 32,849 workers; in 1981, 27,900; and by 1982, 26,387. In addition, the cost per worker declined by 16 percent just between 1981 and 1982, due to the intensification of work, salary reductions, and mechanization.[25] Between 1982 and 1983, real wages declined by 6 percent in El Teniente and, with the use of new machinery in the mine and foundry, led to a reduction in the cost of production by 27.6 percent.[26]

Through the use of subcontractors (*contratistas*) the military administration began to privatize many "support" above-ground functions and even some activities directly related to production inside the mine. New construction and expansion projects were given to private firms, thus diminishing the significance of El Teniente's organized workers. By 1986 over half (5,200) the total workers employed by El Teniente (8,250) worked for nearly 200 private contractors. These firms paid workers roughly half the wages earned by miners employed by the national copper company, provided no benefits, and offered little job security. Workers' efforts to unionize these small companies were easily thwarted.[27]

Before 1973 children of El Teniente workers could depend on a steady job in the mine. Most miners had been born and raised in the mining camps, and a career as a miner and a healthy pension were viewed as a right guaranteed by the paternalist labor system established by the North American copper company during the 1920s. Under the military regime, neither the miners nor their children had a secure future in El Teniente, since subcontractors were able to take advantage of an ever increasing pool of urban unemployed. The growth of subcontracting temporary jobs to replace permanent Codelco workers led to the miners' sense that their employment was increasingly precarious. Workers in the small private firms enjoyed no job security and none of the benefits and bonuses that Codelco's workers had won in strikes and contracts since the 1930s. The living and work conditions of subcontracted workers resembled those of workers during the first decades of the 20th century. By the 1980s many mine workers had family members and friends (often former El Teniente employees) working at temporary jobs for the contratistas.

The difficulty of living and working conditions for workers in private sub-contracting firms was symbolized by the fact that they were lodged in barracks in the old mining camps built by the North American companies, whereas workers employed directly by Codelco lived in private homes and apartments in the city. In 1990 a parliamentary delegation visited the old camps. In a description that harkened back to the early 1900s, Héctor Olivares, a deputy and former El Teniente union leader from before 1973, told the press that he had seen the miserable conditions in which the contratista workers lived in the camps: "living 30 or 40 workers to a room, the lack of ventilation and bathrooms, and the absence of recreational facilities." A second parliamentary visit in 1994 noted that the 5,000 contratista workers labored 12-hour days and received significantly lower pay for the same jobs performed by workers employed by Codelco.[28] That year just over a quarter (26.8 percent) of workers in Codelco's large copper mines were employed by subcontractors.[29]

In 1987–88 the union Sinami and the national construction workers' union held the first meeting to discuss unionization of the 8,000 workers in private firms in Codelco mines. Fittingly, their demands echoed the first efforts to organize copper workers after the First World War: legal guarantees against the firing of union leaders, a common strategy of the contratistas, passes for union leaders to enter work sites and the mine, and the establishment of a minimum wage. In addition, the unions noted that workers in the subcontracting firms toiled in notoriously substandard and dangerous conditions without the necessary protective gear and equipment. In 1991 a similar union drive led by the Sindicato Interempresa de Trabajadores Contratistas del Cobre (Siteco) added pensions, an end to the companies' blacklists, and better living conditions in the camps to these petitions.[30] The ability of the contratista workers to make demands on the company was limited, however, by their "temporary" status. Mass dismissals of workers from different subcontracting companies undermined the strength of the unions and their leverage in negotiations with El Teniente's management. In 1990, for example, 2,300 workers from two different private companies lost their jobs. According to Siteco, over 30 percent of these workers had labored for more than four years in El Teniente. The following year, the end of a contract with two other large private firms led to the dismissal of 2,600 workers.[31] The weakness of the contratista unions was made clear when, in 1995, a new administration in El Teniente appointed by the Concertación government of Eduardo Frei, closed down the union hall, refused to grant passes to union leaders to enter the mine (rights won in 1991), and cut wages for subcontracted workers.[32]

Thus, first the military dictatorship and then the Concertación governments removed many of the pillars of the North American copper company's corporate welfare policies and dismantled the state-directed system of labor relations, destroying the foundation of the miners' cohesive community. As the case of subcontracted workers illustrates vividly, the military regime's political and economic policies recreated the conditions of the early 20th century when unions were banned or controlled by the company and workers enjoyed few legal guarantees. Rights to a family wage, job security, work bonuses, and benefits had enabled workers to commit to a lifetime of work in El Teniente and had led them to marry and form families in the camps, ensuring the reproduction and training of the labor force as generations of miners' sons followed their fathers into the mine. The military regime eliminated the economic and social securities that had been the foundation of the stable labor force and community in the El Teniente mine, leaving miners and their families vulnerable to the vicissitudes of life in the city and in a globalized market economy.

THE REORGANIZATION OF AN
INDEPENDENT LABOR MOVEMENT, 1977–1982

Despite the police state built by the Pinochet dictatorship during the 1970s, the El Teniente miners mounted a series of challenges to the authority of the company. Traditions of labor activism and political militancy in the Communist and Socialist parties, as well as in the Christian Democratic party, established the basis for underground organizing in the mine and in workers' neighborhoods and helped workers rebuild a sense of community and class identity. While the nature of work inside the mine and community life outside the mine in the city of Rancagua shifted during the 1970s, traditions of union and political activism provided networks that allowed mine workers to contest many of the changes that had begun to unsettle their lives. In 1977, following the regime's rejection of efforts by PDC union leaders to negotiate a new contract, miners engaged in a "viandazo" in which workers boycotted the mess halls to symbolize their protest of working conditions. Months later, over 70 percent of the El Teniente workforce engaged in a wildcat strike in response to the dismissal of opposition union leaders. A clandestine leaflet that circulated inside the mine read: "Nobody works the second of the month . . . because we are earning a pittance. Because we have nothing to put in the lunch box." The pamphlet attacked union leaders as "traitor puppets, a troop of sellouts" and called for a strike and a "return to the struggle against the common misery."[33] "Read it and pass it along," the pamphlet stated. The following year, workers in both El Teniente and the northern Chuquicamata mine engaged in another stoppage, again resulting in a wave of dismissals by Codelco. Workers organized these movements at soccer matches, over lunch in the mess hall, on the buses going up to work, and in the mine's changing room, where word of stoppages and clandestine pamphlets and leaflets were distributed. In general, these movements were led by workers outside the company-controlled union. As one worker remembered:[34]

> The movement was formed out of sight of the union leadership, because at that time the workers didn't trust the union leaders, because they hadn't been elected. . . . [It] was organized by the workers in the cage, in the train, they threw clandestine pamphlets. . . . The leaders began to make demands before the trains left, because there's a strategic point where all the workers put on their work clothes, they change clothes and get on the train—when the time came to get on the train and they were conversing and the train would leave and they wouldn't go up to the mine."[35]

After the 1977 strike in El Teniente, over 80 miners were fired and four union leaders were arrested and two sent into internal exile.

The strikes in the copper mines during 1977 and 1978 represented the first labor actions in Pinochet's Chile and occurred at the height of political repression. For the miners, the strikes signified the revival of decades-old traditions of labor militancy and the inauguration of a period of slow rebuilding of an autonomous labor movement in the copper industry. Oral sources recall that the workplace actions brought militants of the Christian Democratic, Communist, and Socialist parties together in common opposition to the military regime for the first time and initiated a process of winning back the unions from regime-appointed leaders.[36] At the national level, this newfound political unity was reflected by the revitalization of the national labor movement with the founding in 1978 of the Coordinadora Nacional Sindical (CNS) by Socialist, Communist, and Christian Democratic union activists.

The implementation of the new system of labor relations in 1979 under the Pinochet Labor Code provided the workers with new opportunities for organizing. Union elections and collective bargaining were legalized, and, despite restrictions on union activity, workers took advantage of this new institutional space to build independent unions and to remove union leaders loyal to the regime. El Teniente workers began to establish internal "commissions" to examine the corruption and mismanagement of officialist union leaders. As one worker recalled, "Inside the mine the workers began to circulate a petition to censure the union leaders. A ton of workers signed this list and they presented it to the authorities, and three or four days later the workers who were presenting the demands were fired." In the Caletones foundry, an opposition union leader recalls, "Workers formed an investigative commission, established by law, and this commission was accused of political activity and everyone was fired."[37] A 1984 CTC report reviewing the history of the struggles to win back the unions from regime-appointed leaders noted that "many workers have been fired to this day for having wanted to censure union leaders named by decree by the authorities of the government. . . . More or less 30 workers have been fired" for trying to investigate the actions and corruption of officialist union leaders.[38]

The investigative commissions provided the basis for a new union movement in the copper mines, and when union elections were held for the first time between 1980 and 1982, opposition leaders, mostly from the Communist and Christian Democratic parties took control of the unions and the CTC. At the national level, in 1982 the regime-appointed head of the CTC was replaced with an elected union leader from El Teniente, Emilio Torres, and Guillermo Medina was removed from his position at the head of the umbrella organization ("La Zonal") of El Teniente unions and replaced with Eugenio López, a worker who had been active in the movements of the late 1970s. Both Torres and López were militants of the Christian Democratic party. Militants of the Communist party were also elected to the CTC's national leadership, including Manuel Rodríguez, newly elected president of the El Teniente foundry workers' union (the Sindicato Industrial Caletones).

The workers who helped organize the first strikes and opposition movements within the El Teniente union were "old-timers" and younger workers who had profiles as political and union activists and who had escaped repression after 1973, despite their militancy in leftist parties and the PDC. They were known by other workers as combative and articulate, and they drew on the authority conferred on them by the miners' history of struggle to lead the new movements. As one worker recalled:

> I think at this time there was a terrific participation of the El Teniente old-timers. . . . The old-timers were the most enthusiastic. . . . They guided the young kids, gave the young kids incentive. . . . It's that the old guys came with a combative mentality, those old-timers that I'll tell you were those that hadn't known how to read and write and they arrived with the *puro ñeque no ma'* [just their force]. . . . It was the old-timers who gave it spirit. . . . Their presence outside of the house in the street was meaningful. The old guy went out in the street with his cigarette and with this he was demonstrating that "here I am and I'm with you" . . . and maybe that bravery was transmitted to [the others] by the old-timers.[39]

Often these workers were children of miners, had grown up in the mining camps, and had begun work in El Teniente during the 1950s, 1960s, or early 1970s. They had close contact with the mine's traditions of labor activism, but had been either too young to suffer dismissal and repression after the 1973 coup or had escaped because they hadn't occupied posts as union leaders or in the local leaderships of the leftist political parties.

Workers who spoke out against the regime and organized protests had the experience of militancy in political parties and often had the support of these parties. In this sense, their election and the protests they led were linked to the clandestine networks of the outlawed leftist parties and the PDC. One PS activist remembers, for example, the election of a Socialist union leader in 1981: "He was a man who had come out of clandestinity, because I'll tell you that he had worked clandestinely. . . . We all worked clandestinely for his candidacy, and I was detained precisely because they knew that I was one of those who supported him."[40] Before the 1973 coup the union leader had been a Socialist provincial delegate for the CUT. Political militancy won workers recognition and trust from other workers. Workers tended to vote for militants of the leftist parties and the PDC who worked actively and, at times, openly against the dictatorship. Thus one Communist union leader elected in 1981 recalls that "the workers knew me since before '73 because I was a candidate before '73—if I had been elected that time before '73 I would have been fired. . . . Everyone knew my way of thinking. . . . This is because the workers in this union are very old . . . with many years working. . . . This is how they knew me for my militancy in the Communist party."[41]

Members of the Communist, Socialist, and Christian Democratic parties held underground meetings at soccer matches, on buses, in taxis, or walking in small groups on the street. They distributed pamphlets and organized stoppages, slowdowns, and viandazos by word of mouth. Often, the opposition leaders elected after 1980 emerged with the support of these underground networks. As one leftist union activist recalls, "Communists and Socialists were elected. . . . There was an underground, clandestine [organization,] . . . leaders who worked clandestinely . . . speaking on the buses, small groups in the strike committee that was the school . . . you could speak at work and had the opportunity to talk on the bus—in the train—in the cafeteria, that's how the new leaders became known."[42]

Another miner remembers that

> people began to organize, I would say, clandestinely, because in the first place we knew who we were—those who were on the left knew who we were, so we began

to act with a lot of fear, but we began to create an organization. The parties began to organize themselves as we went along meeting, and we began to lose fear, and we went along talking to one another and holding clandestine meetings. . . . Here I would say that politically we worked together, with Christian Democrats, with Radicals, with Socialists, with Communists.[43]

With the unions under the control of the regime, the opposition parties provided an important resource for organizing. The work stoppages and protests of the late 1970s, one union activist remembers, "were directed by the popular parties; they were the initiators of the struggle . . . because the union leaders were still those that the dictatorship had imposed."[44] These leftist networks organized small acts of protest. He recalls:

> One year we went clandestinely to the cemetery No. 2 here in Rancagua, the 4th of September, the historic day when they held elections in Chile. So we said "the 4 at 11 in 2"—no one knew where it was, and we put a floral arrangement as homage to Allende and we made speeches and sang the socialist Marseillaise. . . . We were a few brave ones, thirty people, and the youth wrote graffiti in the cemetery—it was very quick, very committed people. . . . We held meetings in cars, walking along a group of leaders would hold a meeting, or we would hold meetings in a restaurant seated having a soda, very camouflaged meetings.[45]

The success of the grassroots opposition movement between 1977 and 1982 in wresting control of the El Teniente unions from "officialist" leaders did not, however, translate into results during collective bargaining with Codelco. Like workers in other industries between 1979 and 1982, copper miners found their position during negotiations and strikes undermined by the regime's Labor Code. Two years of collective bargaining and strikes in urban industries and the copper mines ended with few favorable results for workers. Nationally, workers won some wage increases, but these did little to make up for increases in the cost of living and the radical decline in real wages since 1973. Overall, by 1979 real wages had dropped by an average of 10.7 percent since 1969, while in the mining sector they had fallen 22.2 percent. The average wage increase of 7.2 percent (9.5 percent in the copper sector) during the first year of collective bargaining (1979–80) did not remedy workers' declining standard of living. During the second round of collective bargaining (1980–81) average wage hikes decreased to between 3 and 4 percent of workers' real wages.[46]

For the first time since the coup, workers could strike legally. However, the Labor Code rendered the strike a limited tool at best, and most strikes ended in defeat before the 59-day limit it imposed. During the first two years of collective bargaining there were 102 strikes in Chile involving 44,955 workers. In El

Teniente in 1981, 8,230 workers struck for 48 days, having demanded a 10 percent wage increase and having rejected the company offer of 2 percent. The strike ended when the miners' unions agreed to the company offer. In 1982, in response to the economic crisis, a new labor law eliminated automatic cost-of-living raises for all workers, one of the copper workers' most cherished conquests, dating back to the 1930s. The reality of the new labor legislation was made clear to El Teniente miners when, after 59 days on strike, 1,700 workers in the Caletones foundry who had petitioned for a 10 percent raise were forced to return to work and accept their previous contract—gaining no raise at all—which meant the loss of the long-established cost-of-living raise in a country with a long history of inflation. In addition, the foundry workers, like all workers in El Teniente, lost their right both to company-paid medical care and production bonuses that had been part of collective contracts for decades.[47] The lack of success experienced by miners' unions during collective bargaining in 1981–82 reflected a national reality for the labor movement. While unions requested an average of 23.1 percent in wage increases, employers offered only 4.4 percent. On average, strikes resulted in raises of 6.1 percent over the two years.[48] The wages lost to workers during the strikes outweighed the minimal increases they could win through negotiations with employers. In general, in the most important strikes, workers were forced to return to work with little gain after the 59-day strike limit expired.[49] While before 1973 the miners' unions had stood apart for their strength and capacity to wrest wage hikes and benefits from the North American copper companies, by the early 1980s they had lost their leverage, and the guarantees that had allowed copper workers a privileged place in the Chilean workforce had been dismantled.

The reanimation of El Teniente's unions between 1977 and 1982 coincided with a general rebuilding of the Chilean labor movement during the period following the institutionalization of the military regime's Labor Plan. Traditions of labor militancy and political networks served as the vehicle through which workers won control of El Teniente's unions and replaced regime-appointed union leaders. As in other industries, however, mine workers found that traditional forms of workplace-based labor action, collective bargaining, and the strike were ineffective. Whereas before 1973 mine workers' unions had enjoyed a privileged position in relation to the state, the two-year period of collective bargaining made clear that workers in the mining sector had lost their leverage when confronted with a dictatorship intent on dismantling corporatist structures, restricting union activity, and reorganizing the economy according to the dictates of free market economics.

The loss of crucial benefits during the strikes and collective bargaining in

Chile's copper mines represented a trend in the international copper industry. In 1983 workers in Phelps Dodge's Arizona mines engaged in a year-long strike in response to the company's decision to break the unions and eliminate automatic wage increases in the context of world recession and declining international copper prices. The loss of the strike was part of a general recasting of labor relations in the United States during the Reagan administration and the destruction of the close-knit mining communities in the U.S. Southwest. Thus the Chilean copper miners confronted global changes in labor relations that refracted in Chile during the country's intensified integration into the international economy and the implementation of neoliberal economic reforms.[50]

ECONOMIC CRISIS AND POPULAR PROTEST, 1983–1986

In 1982 the military regime's economic model entered a period of prolonged crisis that lasted until 1986. The collapse of the "economic miracle" of the late 1970s led to three years of protests and social mobilizations aimed at bringing down the dictatorship and instigated by the CTC's call for a day of national protest on 11 May 1983. The CTC's declaration, issued at its annual congress in Punto de Tralca, constituted one of the first broad challenges to the dictatorship's repressive policies and economic model and signaled the rebirth of a civilian opposition to the dictatorship rooted in the social movements of workers and the urban poor. As a union publication put it, "The day of national protest represented without any doubt the most significant political event that the Military Government has had to confront."[51] The CTC's announcement at its annual conference in Punta de Tralca stated that "our problem is not one law more or less . . . but a complete economic, social, cultural, and political system that has us smothered and bound. The moment has come to stand up and say ENOUGH."[52] The CTC's call for a national protest received an unexpectedly widespread response, as urban working-class neighborhoods all over Chile exploded banging empty pots (caceroleos), blowing horns, burning tires, and erecting barricades in the streets.

The CTC's statement reflected the failures of the opposition labor movement to wrest gains from employers during collective bargaining between 1980 and 1982 as a result of the restrictions imposed by the regime's Labor Code. In the context of intense military repression and the weakness of traditional means of organized pressure like the strike, the CTC viewed nation-wide protest to be the only viable form of opposition to the regime. Instead of a movement located at the level of the workplace, the CTC envisioned a national alliance with other workers and opposition sectors, including students, the Catholic Church, the middle class, and the human rights movement as the best response to regime repression. The protest, rather than the strike, would serve workers better, since the Labor Code made striking a no-win situation. The CTC perceived workers' problems as going beyond individual firms to the entire political and economic system.

The copper miners defined the protest of May 1983 as part of a general critique of the regime's neoliberal economic policies. In congresses in 1982 and 1983, the CTC released lengthy analyses of the Labor Code and the model of "los Chicago boys," which they linked to the dictatorship's political repression. In 1982 the CTC congress issued a detailed examination of workers' many losses under the Labor Code and concluded that "the Labor Code . . . permits the strengthening, accumulation, and concentration of economic power in Chile. And today this economic power imposes its decisions and has the power to obligate us to work in the conditions it decides, assuring the functioning of the economic model."[53] The CTC declaration emphasized that a national movement to oppose the economic system of the dictatorship was necessary because traditional forms of workplace-based action were no longer feasible: "During each collective negotiation union leaders have found that they have been able to gain little or nothing. . . . They have come to realize that companies present their own petitions to the unions, protected by the criminal laws of the Labor Code, which permit every kind of excess on the part of the companies and place every kind of limitation on the workers."[54]

The CTC provided a critique of the regime's economic policies and explained how neoliberalism had led to the economic crisis of the 1980s, arguing that the existence of the model depended on "maintaining workers disorganized, restricted, and crushed by regressive labor legislation." The report assailed the regime's plans to confront the economic crisis by slashing workers' wages, eliminating cost-of-living raises, and inviting foreign investment in a privatized copper industry, against the will "of all Chileans who once said yes to the nationalization of copper."

The copper miners were well situated to lead labor and civilian protest against the dictatorship. Unlike workers in other industries, they had managed to maintain their union structures and occupied an essential position in the export economy at a time of severe economic crisis. Both their relative security and threats to this same security placed the copper miners in a unique position to organize opposition to the dictatorship. By 1983 economic restructuring and recession had begun to erode the many material benefits and securities copper workers had won over the years. Following the failures of collective bargaining and strikes to defend wages and benefits, the El Teniente miners began to look for new forms of protest. As one miner said, "The guys were tired of losing and losing their conquests without daring to raise their voices, permanently threatened with unemployment and by the private contractors."[55] Another miner noted that "over time the worker saw that his conquests were being erased—the most important conquests, the production bonus, bonuses for [work-related] sicknesses. We lost the cost-of-living raise and hospital benefits."[56] Workers also complained of conditions in the workplace where "the situation has gotten a lot worse. Abuses by bosses, lack of respect for the workers, threats."[57]

In addition, while El Teniente miners had their jobs, many saw family members and friends fall into unemployment. Jobs in the mine were replaced with temporary jobs in subcontracting firms that often hired former El Teniente workers. One miner commented, "We aren't asking anything for ourselves. You realize what the situation is like in your family. Because you have brothers, brothers-in-law, fathers . . . who are unemployed. We are asking for work, and democracy."[58] As the Chilean economy took a nosedive after 1982 and unemployment rates reached more than 30 percent, miners began to share the day-to-day struggles of their jobless neighbors and relatives. No longer living in isolated mining camps, miners increasingly came to inhabit urban spaces where they constructed new forms of identity linked to the struggles of the poor and unemployed.

Following the 11 May protest, copper miners in the CTC helped organize a new national labor organization, the National Workers' Command (CNT), to direct and coordinate the protests and to support labor conflicts. The CTC's president in 1983, Christian Democrat Rodolfo Seguel, an El Teniente worker, became president of the CNT. For the next three years, despite continued repression in which opposition union leaders suffered dismissal and arrest, the miners continued to organize strong opposition to the military regime. Every month protests were held in Rancagua, and the CTC became a focal point for the reorganization of the labor movement. For the second national protest in June 1983, the CTC organized a general work stoppage in the copper mines. On 17 June, over three-quarters of the workers in El Teniente (between 85 and 95 percent) and Codelco's smaller Salvador and Andina mines participated. Intimidated by the massive military presence in the mine and its camps, workers in Chuquicamata did not participate in the work stoppage.[59]

The regime countered the protests and strike in the copper mines with severe repression. The copper mines were militarized, and union leaders, including the majority of the CTC's national council, were arrested for "inciting the stoppage" and for "organizing meetings to bring down the government." After another work stoppage to support the jailed CTC leaders, over 5,000 workers were fired, although this number was later reduced to 633, including 33 union leaders. Of these dismissals, 114 workers were fired without compensation (most from El Teniente), while the rest were forced to quit "voluntarily" with compensation, rather than simply being fired without any kind of compensation. A small number of workers were rehired after signing statements agreeing to cooperate with the company.[60]

In Rancagua, El Teniente's major union, the Sindicato Industrial Sewell y Mina, with over 4,000 members, set up a soup kitchen (olla común) for the families of fired workers with the help of neighborhood committees and organizations from the city, including small businesses in the central market and the taxi drivers' union. A number of union activists and fired workers engaged in a hunger strike, while workers and their families held demonstrations to protest the repression unleashed against the miners' unions. In October 1984 the miners organized a march from Rancagua to Santiago to demand the rehiring of union leaders and workers and to call for democratization. Union leaders and copper miners, many accompanied by their families, were confronted by police who arrested a number of union leaders once again. Protesters, including women and children from miners' families, were dragged onto police buses and beaten. Many of the marchers took refuge in Rancagua's church. Despite this repression, workers held a mass assembly in the union hall in Rancagua and reorganized the "march" to Santiago in taxis, buses, and by train. When the miners finally arrived in Santiago at a demonstration organized by the Santiago Popular Youth Organizations, they were applauded enthusiastically by 45,000 protesters, representing an important alliance between the labor movement in the copper mines and the popular protests in Santiago's working-class neighborhoods.[61]

The Sindicato Industrial Sewell y Mina came to play a central role in Rancagua and in the province-wide popular organizing that defined the period of the protests. One worker remembers, "It began with copper, with the copper workers' leaders, those who directed the protests and leaders from the neighborhoods where the families of the copper workers lived, this is where the cacerolazo protests began." Another worker recalls:

> The unions said that they were going to do a caceroleo protest at "such and such time," and that news was spread throughout all Rancagua in hours. . . . Everyone conversed. It was a great thing because when you took a collective taxi, the bus, or wherever, and everyone talked, and whoever didn't know listened to the person that was in front or the person behind—at this time there's going to be a cacerolazo. . . . Also we came up with a way of honking our car horns that had a

meaning—*y va a caer, y va a caer* [he's going to fall, he's going to fall]—then we left off for a bit and then kept going gradually, and you noticed that wherever you went, downtown, in every neighborhood . . . some people even rang doorbells like that—y va a caer, y va a caer.[62]

The hall of the Sindicato Industrial Sewell y Mina became a meeting place for organizations all over the city, including political parties and national and provincial labor organizations. The copper workers' unions formed a regional labor federation, the Comando Provincial de Trabajadores Cachapoal, and held organizational meetings for the unemployed, Codeju (Youth Defense Committee), the Youth Command for Democracy, taxi drivers, and other local unions.[63] When the hall filled, the street in front was closed off and speakers made speeches from a balcony on the second floor of the union's building. At times these meetings and demonstrations sparked violence from military police. On one occasion the union hall was machine-gunned. Although no one was killed, bullet holes pockmarked the building's walls.

For the copper miners, the most powerful symbol of the neoliberal economic model was the regime's strategy of stimulating foreign investment in new copper-mining ventures as an alternative to expanding production in the state-owned mines. Because they labored in the most important state-owned sector of the economy, had fought for decades against North American companies, and had phrased their labor struggles in the language of nationalism, the copper miners were well positioned to challenge the model of economic restructuring based on privatization and foreign investment. The miners perceived the nationalization of the North American–owned mines in 1971 to be the result of decades of strikes, and they saw the incremental privatization of the industry envisioned by the regime's economists in a new 1983 Mining Law as a major threat both to the industry and to their welfare. In its 1983 declaration the CTC concluded that Chile's copper industry was in crisis in 1983 because the regime had drained the state companies of capital and had invested little in modernization and expansion in order to justify the liberalization of investment in the mining sector. The union called for increased investment in Codelco's mines instead of privatization. As the producers of Chile's major resource, miners had led the struggle for nationalization of the copper mines in 1971. Now, the CTC argued, they had the "moral authority" to represent the demands of all of Chile for democracy and an end to the neoliberal experiment. Defense of the nationalized mines represented a major challenge to the free market model and allowed miners once again to link their material workplace-related demands to a national alliance in support of the state-owned copper industry. In strikes against the North American copper companies miners had invoked the interests of all of Chile and made their struggles national struggles. Now they reconfigured their radical nationalist rhetoric linking their specific petitions to national demands for democracy, human rights, and social justice.

In December 1983, seven months after the first protest, the CNS organized a demonstration against the regime's Mining Law. Despite the presence of military police in the streets, union, leftist, and Christian Democratic activists filled Santiago's Teatro Caupolicán to demand an end to efforts to privatize the copper industry.[64] The event reflected the significance of nationalism to working-class demands and to the rejection of the regime's economic model. In addition, it demonstrated that the political opposition, organized labor, and copper miners shared a common antagonism to privatization programs. The protest linked the rejection of the economic model and the demands for democracy. Prominent Christian Democrats such as Radomiro Tomic denounced the fact that the law took copper policy out of the hands of the Chilean state and placed it in the private sector, placing the interests of transnational corporations over national sovereignty. Christian Democratic party and National Labor Command (CNS) leader Manuel Bustos stressed that the Mining Law "traffics with our dignity as a free and sovereign nation." He also extolled the unity of the opposition parties in the demonstration as an example for the struggle for democracy. For Bustos, the struggle against the privatization of the copper industry would be the "great flag of the people's unity," linking the struggle against the law to the struggle for a democracy that "is not just political freedom, but very concrete things: bread, work, clothing, housing, health care, education, and respect for all essential rights." In 1987 the secretary general of the CTC, Omar Tapia, echoed Bustos when he argued that "the defense of copper is closely tied to the struggle for the restoration of democracy; the privatizing strategies of the regime originate in the current economic model. A change in this model will only be possible when Chile reconstructs democracy."[65]

FROM LABOR ACTION TO POPULAR PROTEST:
NEW STYLES OF COLLECTIVE ACTION IN EL TENIENTE

Despite the central role of the miners' unions and the opposition parties in the popular insurgency of the early 1980s, the protests were not traditional miners' strikes. Rather than workplace-focused movements restricted to the mine and the mining community, like miners' strikes before 1973, these were movements organized in neighborhoods and aimed at bringing down the dictatorship. The

11 May mobilizations sparked a new form of political protest that included the union and work-related struggles but that was located outside the mine as part of a broader struggle for democracy. The neighborhood became a central space for organization because of the many unemployed and fired miners and because of the authoritarian conditions within the mine. Neighborhood committees began to form ollas comunes to help feed Rancagua's unemployed and the many miners fired because of their participation in opposition politics and labor protests. In workers' neighborhoods, miners and their families banged on empty pots, built barricades in the streets, and burned tires. Leftist activists, groups affiliated with the Catholic Church, youth organizations, and human rights organizations played a role in these protests against the dictatorship and the disasters of the regime's economic model.

As in the rest of Chile's poor urban neighborhoods, women played a crucial role in these community organizations and began to assume a new political position in the movements for democracy. Asserting their rights as mothers to fend for their families, they began to organize communal soup kitchens and women's committees and to participate actively in the monthly protests. The miners' union organized a permanent soup kitchen in the union hall where fired workers and their families could receive three meals a day. Miners' wives formed women's committees that organized medical care, clothing, and food for workers' families. One women noted that "before, I was a housewife and nothing else. I had never even gone to the *centros de madres* [state-sponsored mothers centers]. But the day came when there was nothing to put in the pot. And the only possibility for eating, above all for the little kids, is through the organization with others who are also affected, looking for community support."[66]

Another woman, the wife of a foundry worker, who later worked clandestinely as a Communist party militant, remembers that after the June 1983 strike women organized community kitchens to feed unemployed and fired miners and their families:

> First came those who were doing the hunger strike, women, and we began to organize a soup kitchen. . . . We had the support of the community, especially the people from the marketplace. . . . Every day the wives of the people who were on strike came; we formed a women's committee, and we began to have cultural activities in order to make money because there were many basic needs. . . . The *compañeros* in Rancagua gave a lot of support, and we became a homogenous group, men with women, it was a very rich experience. The *compañeras* of the workers gave classes to the children. . . . It was a very exciting thing where you saw the active participation of women.[67]

As miners' wages deteriorated and as they lost their benefits, and as many fell into unemployment, women began to look for jobs outside the home. In the city, unlike the mining camps, women had greater opportunities for work, and by the early 1980s many miners' wives were looking for jobs throughout the local economy, as teachers, office workers, and saleswomen, as well as in commerce and the informal market. The economic crisis of the early 1980s, the deterioration of miner's wages and benefits, and growing unemployment, due partially to mass dismissals after the 1983 strike, undermined the family wage established during the 1930s and propelled many women into wage labor for the first time signifying an important change in the organization of miners' households.[68]

The copper miners' movements during the 1980s brought together traditional forms of labor organization and political militancy around workplace-related issues with new styles of popular protest and mobilization. Rather than two disparate spheres of political resistance to authoritarian rule, the miners' strikes, marches, and demonstrations combined workplace-based forms of organization, clandestine left-wing networks, and neighborhood-based movements that included workers' families, students, taxi drivers, the unemployed, and members of the urban informal sector.

The dislocation of the miners' traditional community and their integration into city life made the combination of these forms of struggle necessary. Miners could no longer depend on the strength of the unified and homogenous community of the mining camps. Similarly, the reorganization of the labor systems and repressive conditions inside the mine and the increasingly precarious nature of their employment meant that miners had to look to new forms of mobilization and alliances outside of the workplace with other urban working-class groups, often unemployed or intermittently employed, family members, and neighbors. The central role of women in the protests of the 1980s was symptomatic of changes in the structure of workers' families and community and of new forms of neighborhood-based social mobilization.

THE MINERS, ORGANIZED LABOR, AND THE TRANSITION TO DEMOCRACY

By 1986 the Pinochet regime had managed to defeat the insurgent movements for democracy with a policy that combined violent repression of the labor and popular social movements with negotiations with some members of the opposition, particularly leaders of the Christian Democratic party and "renovated" sectors of the Socialist party. After 1986 the labor movement in El Teniente, like the popular social movements for democracy throughout Chile, suffered a general debilitation. The transition to democracy would be negotiated from above by the leadership of the political parties and workers, and organized labor would have little role in determining the shape of the new political order. In El Teniente, repression had begun to take a toll on the union movement. Many of the union leaders who led the protests and first strikes were arrested and fired. Even in the early 1990s, many had yet to be rehired by the company. In 1986 a young leader of the Sindicato Industrial Caletones was kidnapped by the secret police, the C N I (Center for National Intelligence), brutally tortured, and forced to sign a fake confession to the possession of explosives. That same year the CTC headquarters and union leaders' houses were searched by the police, a number of union leaders were detained and beaten, and in Chuquicamata during a protest four union leaders and 130 workers were attacked by military police and then arrested.[69] In 1986 the CTC denounced the fact that Codelco, colluding with the Dirección General del Trabajo, had refused to recognize independent union leaders, closed union bank accounts, and pressured workers to replace the union leaders who had led the strikes and protests of the early 1980s. The CTC reported that in the workplace "the abusive and humiliating treatment by supervisors who act with arrogance against workers hasn't changed; they even threaten workers with dismissal for the sole fact of going to union assemblies and raising their voices to defend their conquests and benefits."[70] The miners' unions, debilitated by regime repression, approached the years of democratic transition from a weakened position.

By the late 1980s the copper miners had come to understand that a return to democratic rule was the precondition for any change in labor relations. Thus in 1988 the CTC supported the campaign for the "no" in the plebiscite called by Pinochet. The CTC called on all copper workers to vote "no" and established committees at the level of local copper unions to work on the campaign. The CTC was, however, suspicious of Pinochet's willingness to relinquish power and convinced of the likelihood of fraud. Thus it noted that the plebiscite alone would not lead to democratization. Rather, the CTC declaration noted that "only the struggle and mobilization of the immense majority of the people . . . can create the conditions for the recuperation of democracy."[71] Local union leaders and militants from all the opposition parties threw themselves into the campaign for the "no." In El Teniente, the newsletter of the Sindicato Industrial Sewell y Mina published a list of union leaders and their votes, including the few "sí" votes (six out of 30) of pro-Pinochet leaders who had remained at their posts in some of the unions, and celebrated the victory of the "no" with a special edition whose headlines shouted: "Not even bullets could silence us. The NO above all is a great victory for the working class."[72] The CTC also participated in the formation of a new national union federation, the Central Unitaria de Trabajadores (CUT) in August of 1988 and supported a national general strike of the CUT to demand the freedom of internally exiled labor leaders Manuel Bustos and Arturo Martínez following the plebiscite in April of 1989.[73]

Despite the copper miners' role in the movements for democracy during the 1980s and in driving the military dictatorship to pursue negotiations with opposition leaders, the transition of the 1990s did not fulfill their early expectations or remedy their losses under the dictatorship. The democratic government of Patricio Aylwin was constrained by legislation and institutions imposed by the Pinochet regime. In the copper industry, the Concertación did try to repair years of neglect of Codelco by initiating strategies to modernize the state-owned mines, stimulate foreign investment in new mines, and embark on expansion programs in Codelco-run mines based on joint ventures with private investors. The government's efforts to make Codelco into a modern and internationally competitive business, however, implied new company strategies toward labor relations and imposed limits on workers' petitions.

During the first years of democratic rule, the miners saw few of their demands resolved. In 1991, 7,500 miners in Chuquicamata and 8,500 miners in El Teniente engaged in two of the first and most important strikes during the transition. In both strikes, characterized by marches, demonstrations, and conflictive negotiations with Codelco's new administrators, the miners' unions sought to win back losses that they had incurred during the 17-year dictatorship, particularly in terms of real wages. As one El Teniente union leader said, "We only want to recuperate the lost buying power of our salaries, because of the loss of automatic cost-of-living raises."[74] For the miners, the strikes represented an attempt "to make democracy a reality in the mine." In addition, they linked the strikes to the broader labor movement, arguing that they represented a test case for labor relations during the transition to democracy. As one Chuquicamata union leader argued, "We aren't only negotiating for Chuquicamata and Codelco, we're doing it for all the workers of the country. If they manage to step on Chuqui, what will happen in the rest of the country? If they crush us, what will happen to the construction workers, the seasonal fruit workers, and other sectors with less organization and less negotiating power?"[75] In addition, as during past conflicts the miners invoked nationalism as they defined their strikes in opposition to the government's privatization programs.

The combative tone of the 1991 strikes and protests in the copper mines reflected workers' perception that democratization had brought few real changes.

The strikes also represented the new administration's commitment to modernizing Codelco's mines after years of neglect by the military regime. For El Teniente's new managers, workers' demands constituted an obstacle to reorganizing labor systems, reducing costs, and downsizing. Making the mine internationally competitive, they argued, required sacrifices from the workers. Holding the threat of an eventual closing over the workers' heads, mine administrators demanded that workers commit to lowering costs and increasing production. Union leaders denounced Codelco authorities as worse than the supervisors appointed by the dictatorship in their determination to modernize the mining companies at the expense of the workers. In his written account of the strike, one El Teniente union leader asked,

> Did we win or lose with these new señores [new Codelco executives]. . . . For many it's the same honey but with different bees. . . . Have we made progress with these new executives? The response that every worker has and says openly: Today we are worse off than before! . . . To be objective and honest, our union with the administrators who represented the military regime had won a space that cost a great deal through protests, mobilizations, and stoppages. Today, we have lost these spaces, and we workers have gone back a step. We haven't progressed, . . . while the company advances step by exhausting step toward modernity.[76]

During the strikes, workers noted that conditions inside the mines had changed little and that they continued to receive abusive and dictatorial treatment from supervisors, linking the system of political authoritarianism to the conduct of labor relations:

> For 16 years the workers of this mine had to support a system of autocratic administration, in which they violated the rights of the workers through unjust treatment and arbitrary dismissals, in which the opinion of the workers was not heard . . . the regional union movement was decapitated and many leaders persecuted. . . . After one year of democracy in Chile, we have been able to confirm, to our dismay, that in the interior of this mine, at many levels they maintain the same schemes of vertical command as in the past.[77]

Workers condemned Codelco administrators and supervisors left over from the dictatorship and, in the case of Chuquicamata, accused certain supervisors of having ties to the dictatorship's intelligence police, the Center for National Intelligence (CNI).[78] Workers noted the lack of change in labor relations in the mines: "When in every section we ask that they fix something, there are supervisors who tell us: Didn't you like voting for Don Pato? [President Patricio Alywin] Go ask him or put up with it."[79] The slogans shouted by thousands of El Teniente miners during marches, mocking the Concertación's electoral slogan

"La alegría ya viene" (Now comes happiness), summed up this general senti-ment: "La alegría ya llegó, del minero se olvidó" (Happiness has already come, but they've forgotten the miners) and "La alegría que venía era para los de arriba" (The happiness that came was for the upper class).

During the strike the copper miners no longer enjoyed the support of the national political parties of the Concertación. From 1983 to 1986 they could claim that their struggles were identified with national movements for human rights, democracy, and labor rights, just as before 1971 they had been able to articulate their interests in the language of nationalism and identify their strikes with the interests of the country in opposition to North American capital's control of the copper industry. After 1989, however, their strikes and move-ments were interpreted by the governing center-left coalition as threatening the interests of all Chileans in a smooth transition to democracy and a stable economy. The parties of the Concertación placed pressure on union leaders to resolve the strike. Thus, one El Teniente union leader recalls that during the strike "the parties of the Concertación . . . met and developed agreements to apply a hard hand to union leaders and to apply the law in its maximum rigor."[80]

As the North American mining companies had done during strikes since the 1930s, the government attempted to portray copper workers as a privileged labor aristocracy, defending old and outdated economic privileges and threat-ening Chile's economic well-being and thus the stability of Chile's process of democratization, because of their high wages and benefits relative to other workers. In a speech to Chuquicamata workers President Patricio Alywin at-tempted to discredit the miners' petitions by defining them as a "privileged" group. As one union leader noted,

> This word that has been used politically against us [in the past], it was the first blow that we received and nothing less than the president of the republic, for whom we were the first to open a path for him to arrive where he has. . . . I think that the copper workers don't deserve such a label, because . . . the producing man gives his life and builds the patria for all Chileans, because the deaths because of work accidents and work-related illnesses are many, because the natu-ral illnesses because of the hard work are many.[81]

A Chuquicamata miner said: "You can't imagine the pain it provoked to hear President Alywin, for whom I voted, say that I'm privileged. Here we sell our health at a low price. Here [in the mining camps] everything is expensive. You see how inhospitable the landscape [of the northern desert] is."[82] In El Teniente, miners carried placards with the phrases "Is silicosis a privilege?" and "47% with silicosis is not a privilege." One worker pointed out that "the useful life of a worker is 15 years. A worker who enters at 23, at 38 no one will give him work."[83]

Responding to the accusations that copper miners constituted a "labor aristocracy," an El Teniente union leader noted the miners' sense that they had played a key role in the struggles for democracy, had paid the cost of their strikes in repression, and continued to suffer difficult working conditions: "Our organization protected all the democratic sectors during the dictatorship; it also paid high costs in the dismissals of workers, in the strikes of 1977—when nobody did anything against the dictatorship—in 1981 and 17 June 1983. Now we're disappointed. . . . Working conditions are very difficult for us. We have 35-year-old workers with silicosis, with back problems, with arthritis already."[84]

As workers pointed out, while the company had introduced new technologies in the mine, these had not reduced workers' job-related physical problems. Many workers, particularly older miners, continued to suffer from silicosis, and the workers who operated the tractors and drilling machines in the mine developed back and spine problems that limited their working lives. Extremes of cold and hot temperatures inside the mine contributed to bronchial problems, arthritis, and rheumatism. Workers also continued to be killed inside the mine. Between 1987 and 1991, 12 workers died in accidents. In 1991 an estimated 870 El Teniente workers were qualified by the company as "unproductive" because of physical disabilities.[85]

El Teniente's new administration sought to pare down the labor force by offering early retirement to older miners and workers who suffered job-related illnesses. This 1989 plan for trimming the labor force of older workers also caused discontent during the 1991 strike. A union leader noted, "Today in this new administration they are offering the Special Retirement Plan to the workers, and if they don't accept it they tell them they will fire them anyhow because they are unproductive. Such are the contradictions of life; what the dictatorship wasn't capable of doing, today, in democracy, they threaten and commit all kinds of abuses."[86]

Despite the strike and union opposition, by the mid-1990s the company had succeeded with its incentives to older workers to retire and had reduced El Teniente's workforce to just over 7,000 from 8,500 in 1991. Between 1990 and 1996, Codelco's entire labor force declined from 27, 421 to 18, 879 workers.[87]

The 1991 copper strikes were settled with wage hikes (average raises of 6 percent in El Teniente and 9 percent in Chuquicamata) that represented only moderate gains after years of losses. The new contracts also included bonuses for increased output and reduced costs, representing the new administration's determination to link wage increases to productivity gains and lowered production costs. The confrontational bargaining posture assumed by the company represented a turning point in labor relations. In the future, miners would have to negotiate in the context of a company intent on reducing its workforce and expenses and introducing new work systems and technologies in the mine. Competition with transnational companies operating in Chile and abroad placed limits on workers' petitions and reshaped labor relations in the state-owned mine.

By the early 1990s copper miners' strategic location in the economy and their corresponding capacity to place pressure on the state declined as copper's share of export earnings fell from around 90 percent in 1973 to just above 40 percent, and Codelco's share of national copper production declined because of the development of new multinational companies. Miners' unions no longer carried the clout they once did. Workers in the state-owned mines began to compete with new and modern foreign-owned northern copper mines working veins with higher copper content. In 1994, Codelco accounted for only 52.8 percent of national copper production, while private mines, many owned by transnationals, produced 47.2 percent of Chile's copper.[88] The military dictatorship had not returned the large copper mines to their former North American owners. Instead, it pursued a policy of incremental privatization. While certain members of the military and Codelco authorities had advocated investment in the expansion of Codelco's productive capacity during the 1970s, the regime's free-market economists rejected this position and sought instead to limit the size of the state sector and promote foreign investment in the copper industry.[89]

Codelco was enormously profitable after 1973 because of increased labor discipline, the reduction in costs due to the contraction of real wages, and an increase in production based on expansion programs initiated during the late 1960s. Yet investments in the mines by the state were limited to levels only high enough to maintain existing levels of production. In addition, the military regime sought to milk Codelco's profits, reaping the benefits of investments made under the governments of Frei and Allende and diverting 10 percent of Codelco's earnings to the armed forces (a disincentive to privatization) while fomenting foreign investment in new, privately owned mining enterprises.

The 1974 Decree-Law 600, the Statute of Foreign Investment, gave a series of guarantees and incentives to foreign investors, including a fixed rate of 49.5 percent taxation on gross profits for ten years (before 1971 the North American copper companies had been taxed at around 70 percent), no restrictions on the repatriation of profits, a system of accelerated depreciation of equipment and machinery, and the right to deduct from profits losses during the first five years.[90] The regime's 1983 Mining Law reaffirmed these policies by establishing a principle of "nondiscrimination" against transnational companies in relation to Chilean companies in the mining sector and reiterating the guarantees on taxation rates and the repatriation of profits established in Decree-Law 600.[91] During the 1980s, transnational companies, most owned by oil companies, began to sign contracts to explore and exploit Chilean copper reserves, among them Disputada de Las Condes (owned by Exxon),[92] Quebrada Blanca (owned by Falconbridge Superior Oil), and, most important, the gigantic open-pit northern mine, La Escondida (owned by the Broken Hill Company of Australia, Rio Tinto Company of Great Britain, the Japanese Escondida Corporation of Mitsubishi, and the International Finance Corporation), which went into operation during the early 1990s. La Escondida began to produce copper at levels similar to El Teniente at a low cost of production (44 cents per pound) and export the copper to foundries in Japan, West Germany, and Finland.[93] Between 1986 and 1996 an average of 60 percent ($7.7 billion) of direct foreign investment in Chile was in mining activity.[94]

Thus by the early 1990s Codelco's mines had to compete directly with new transnationally owned Chilean mines employing more modern technologies and working copper with a higher content at a lower cost. Transnational companies also operated under privileged circumstances in Chile. A 7 October 1997 article in the Wall Street Journal celebrated the profitability and low taxation rates of private copper mines in Chile, noting that the copper mines in the private sector—60 percent of Chile's $7,300 million of copper exports in 1996—paid $270 million in taxes, while Codelco, which represented the rest, paid the government $1,500 million. The article noted that Exxon's Disputada de Las Condes had never paid any taxes to the Chilean government in its 15 years of production.[95] While a company like La Escondida paid a maximum of 35 percent in taxes, Codelco paid a minimum of 55 percent, not including the 10 percent given to the military.[96] In general, taxes on mining profits in Chile were the lowest in Latin America at 15 percent. Escondida extracted copper with a content of 2.8 percent, while Codelco's Chuquicamata's content was just over 1 percent. Finally, La Escondida exported its copper as concentrate to foundries abroad for refining, reducing the value added to the product in Chile prior to exportation.[97] A quirk in the military's mining legislation made it more profitable for companies to export unrefined copper by providing tax breaks for "medium-size" mines that produced only a certain amount of refined copper. Large mines won "medium" status and tax breaks by refining their copper abroad. While in 1970 only 3 percent of Chile's copper exports were of unrefined ore, in 1998 this figure had risen to 33 percent.[98]

As Codelco sought to modernize its mines and make them internationally competitive, workers confronted new limits on their demands. Codelco administrators sought to reorganize work systems, incorporating methods used by transnational companies, including work circles and new programs for worker training and participation. In exchange, they sought the early retirement of many older and incapacitated workers and greater management flexibility in assigning tasks and jobs and organizing the system of production. Following the 1991 strike, El Teniente's labor force declined by over 10 percent over the next four years, reducing workers' leverage during strikes and producing a sense of insecurity among workers. This anxiety about job security was exacerbated by the company's efforts to overcome perceived inefficiencies in the production process by redesigning the system of job classifications, remunerations, and production incentives in the mine, concentrating plant, and foundry. In addition, as Codelco's share of national copper production and national exports decreased, miners' strategic position in the economy was undermined, reducing their strength during collective bargaining and their capacity to place pressure on the state through strikes. At the national level, the miners unions received little political support from the parties of the Concertación governments of Alywin and Frei, which sought to boost production in Codelco and to increase private investment in new copper mines.

MINERS AND THE TRANSITION TO DEMOCRACY: CHANGES IN COMMUNITY, WORK, AND WORKING-CLASS CULTURE

By the 1990s mine workers confronted an enterprise intent on modernizing without the support of traditional workplace and community solidarities. The structural changes under way since the 1970s had begun to break apart the community and work identities that had been the pillars of miners' militant working-class politics. While during strikes and protests in 1977, 1978, 1981, 1982, 1983, and 1991, mine workers had mobilized traditions of union activism and political networks to build opposition to the dictatorship, by the 1990s changes in the national economy and in the mine introduced under the Pinochet dictatorship had transformed workers' sense of class identity and commitment to labor politics. State terror and neoliberal economic policies combined to reshape the nature of unionism, work, and community among miners and their families. The dismantling of the material securities that miners had enjoyed since the 1940s and that had kept them and their families committed to life and work in the mining camps was exacerbated by the cultural transformations wrought by the pressures of repression, the modernization of production in the mine, and the market economy.

Inside the mine and its plants, mechanization and the reduction of the labor force disrupted the organization of miners' work teams and eroded workplace solidarities. The introduction of computer-controlled processes and automation, as well as the use of new sophisticated machinery for both extracting and processing ore in the mine, concentrator, and foundry affected groups of workers that had been the core of union activism and militancy in the past. These tended to be the oldest and least educated workers, many of whom had grown up in the camps or who had spent their lives in El Teniente and who were steeped in the mine's labor traditions. Older workers who had learned their skills on the job and who had engaged in semiskilled tasks were replaced with machines or by specialized workers who operated new complex machinery. Whereas the workers' skills, particularly within the mine and the foundry, had provided the basis for a sense of occupational pride, autonomy, and self-assertiveness that underpinned their workplace militancy and challenging attitude toward company authority, mechanization and new "flexible" labor systems in which workers performed different jobs led to a breakdown in work identities.

Through the 1970s workers had learned their skills at work and ascended a complex hierarchy from unskilled work as day laborers to more skilled and higher paid jobs. In addition, while they were subject to the authority of supervisors and company management, company authority had been mediated, as well as implemented, by work crew leaders and foremen, many of whom had begun as workers themselves. Workers, crew chiefs, and foremen had a great deal of power in decision making within the labor process, and their authority was based on years of work experience. Younger workers learned their jobs through older workers in a system that resembled apprenticeship. That many workers were children of workers represented the generational passing down of knowledge about work, job skills, and union culture. By the 1980s old-timers had begun to retire from the mine, and the importance of on-the-job training in the mine was reduced. Whereas experience transmitted from worker to worker had been central to learning skills, increasingly the knowledge necessary to perform jobs was imparted by technicians and administrators, and new workers came to the mine with higher educational backgrounds and training, often from technical schools. The company's educational requirements for new workers began to include some time spent at a vocational school. The role of the work crew leader or foreman, often an older worker, in teaching new workers skills was greatly diminished.

In part, this change in work culture was produced by the company's plans for flexibilization or "Reconversión Laboral." Beginning in the 1990s under the administrations appointed by the democratic governments, the company sought to promote a new system of work in which workers would perform different jobs on a rotational basis, allowing the company freedom to assign workers to jobs outside their classifications. In 1995 the general manager of El Teniente argued that workers in the privately owned copper mines were "polyfunctional" and performed a number of different jobs allowing for greater productivity and flexibility. Whereas in El Teniente, for example, an LHD operator worked four hours per shift, in Disputada las Condes they operated 7.5 hours a shift since, during breaks, other workers—as with the hammer operators and truck drivers—replaced the LHD operators in a rotational system. Respect for job classifications had been won by El Teniente miners in strikes during the 1940s and had represented an important means of limiting management's prerogatives in the workplace. In addition, bonuses and wage levels had been pegged to specific jobs, and workers had developed a sense of occupational pride based on the particular skills and jobs they performed.

While El Teniente's management proposed new training programs and programs for worker participation in decision making to assist workers in acquiring "polyfunctionality" and in increasing production and reducing costs, the unions and workers viewed the plan for Reconversión Laboral as a potential threat to wages, bonuses, and to guarantees that workers had won decades ago. In addition, the plan envisioned early retirement for older workers and workers with health problems. For one union leader, the company's modernization program served as a "pretext to dismiss workers and lower salaries. The unions lose their strength with the mass dismissals."[99] In 1998 union leaders continued to denounce the lack of respect for job classifications: "They take workers out of their shifts with illegitimate pressures, threatening them with letters and notes from the office for demanding their legitimate right to have their job description respected." A union leader pointed out that the system of Reconversión Laboral had never been agreed to by the unions, despite the company's claim to the contrary.[100]

Finally, mechanization also disrupted miners' workplace traditions of solidarity. Miners' militant work culture and combative union politics had been founded in the bonds of mutual reliance forged at work in teams within the mine. Workplace ties provided the basis for traditions of collective action both during frequent wildcat stoppages and organized strikes. However, mechanization led to an increasingly heterogeneous and differentiated workforce and undermined the culture of the work teams that had provided the conditions for a tremendous unity among workers. Workers, better educated, working in safer and improved conditions due to the introduction of new machinery, increasingly approached their jobs as individuals.[101] In oral histories, older workers and union activists tended to lament the lack of consciousness and militancy of younger workers who had come of age during the dictatorship and who, they believed, had lost touch with the miners' labor traditions. Older miners who had grown up in the El Teniente camps in mining families, they argue, were responsible for the reorganization of the labor movement in the mines during the 1970s and 1980s. A union leader noted:

> The old worker, the worker with many years in the company is conscious and trusts leftist union leaders. . . . The young workers don't have much militancy, they haven't struggled, they haven't suffered what the old ones have suffered, the persecutions, they haven't suffered the great strikes of this mine which had distinguished itself by having many strikes, long strikes. . . . It hasn't cost the young workers what it cost the old workers. . . . There were great struggles, great strikes to win what we have now and they don't understand this.[102]

Symptomatic of the disarticulation of miners' community and workplace solidarities was the diminished role of the union in the lives of workers and their families. While the unions had provided central spaces for cultural and political activity in the mining camps, workers' relationship to unions had changed by the 1990s. They no longer lived close to the union, and the union halls in Rancagua were separated from the workplace. In addition, sports clubs and social clubs, which had been organized by workplace and closely tied to the unions, also began to witness declining participation. Workers no longer spent their leisure time in the union hall.[103]

The weakening of the miners' unions began during the repression of the strikes and protests of the early 1980s. During the 1981 strike, a number of workers fled the opposition-led unions to other El Teniente unions led by officialists in order to receive the bonuses these unions had won by signing new contracts in line with the company's offer. Throughout the 1980s workers joined unions directed by leaders who could negotiate one-time bonuses, granted by the company as a way of preempting the collective bargaining process and conflicts with the unions. Between 1984 and 1986, for example, the company was able to impose a wage freeze in exchange for a one-time bonus during negotiations prior to the legally mandated collective bargaining of a new contract. Workers, saddled with debt and reeling from the economic crisis, saw the bonuses as temporary relief from creditors and as an alternative to sacrificing wages during strikes that were unlikely to produce favorable outcomes. In addition, many new workers who entered the mine during the 1980s lacked direction and leadership from the unions. The workplace no longer constituted a school in which new workers were educated in El Teniente's union traditions. Union leaders noted that younger workers failed to appreciate the decades of struggles and strikes that went into winning bonuses, benefits, and wage increases and complained that workers no longer went to the union hall or to meetings.[104] According to some workers, many union leaders responded by devoting their time to "individuals, not social groups" as they sought to solve the problems of individual workers in order to win an electoral base. The membership of the Sindicato Industrial Sewell y Mina, El Teniente's largest, oldest, and historically most combative union, dropped from over 3,000 in 1991 to 1,500 in 1998 due to the many early retirements of old-time miners, reductions of El Teniente's labor force, and workers' flight to other unions, often empleados unions run by nonleftist leaders.

The erosion of workplace solidarity and union culture in El Teniente was exacerbated by the changes in community life and the separation of workplace and neighborhood. Oral histories describe the general disintegration of miners' community and culture that occurred during the parallel move to a market economy and to the city below the mine during the 1970s and 1980s. El Teniente miners traveled one hour by bus every morning from the city of Rancagua to reach the mine. While the culture and experiences of the mine infiltrated all areas of everyday life in the camps and workers' barracks, in the city miners' neighborhoods and communities were integrated into the broader urban environment. Miners and their families were exposed to a broad spectrum of cultural activities and influences. They watched television for the first time and participated in the cultural life of the city and the world of mass communication. Their children attended public schools, housing was urban and privately owned, and the city provided alternative forms of recreation, theater, music, cinema, newspapers, and magazines. For workers and their families involvement in urban society represented a new world of possibilities and the fulfillment of a long-term demand: "Life in Rancagua is totally different; in the camps we were marginalized from many things, marginalized from culture, from recreation, from sports, marginalized from everything. . . . There was one theater, but we were obliged to see the movie that was shown there. But in the city there are four or five theaters, and you choose. Before we didn't even have television."[105]

But city life also disrupted their traditional social networks. In oral histories, workers and their family members describe the cultural transformations that occurred as the mining camps were broken up with an almost unanimous nostalgia for a sense of lost community. The barracks that had been a central space in the camps where miners' families came together were replaced by individual homes and apartments. Workers now lived dispersed around the city in different neighborhoods. One woman noted, for example, how she no longer saw her friends and neighbors or spent time at the miners' union hall, which had operated as a community center in the camps: "I still see my neighbors and friends, but now we don't do the things we used to do, and life has separated us here [in the city] politically, we've become distant from one another, because in the camp above we didn't notice our differences, we all went to the union, but here no. For many the husband goes to the union, but many women no longer go."[106]

Similarly, a miner described how "above [in the mining camps] the workers lived in more of a community, there was more unity, the unions were stronger because everything was right there, the camp, life in the camp; it's different below [in the city]."[107] One former El Teniente worker noted how individualism in the city had reduced the strength of the union:

> Leaving the camps for the city dispersed the workers and made them apathetic. . . . The worker didn't go to the union hall afterward . . . because of the comfort of the house, the television, the children maybe; in contrast in Sewell it wasn't like this. . . . The men went to the union, and the union hall filled up every time there was an assembly. . . . Now in Rancagua the worker has his video player and he watches videos and he doesn't go to the union hall for assemblies. . . . In Sewell we didn't have to tell workers that there were assemblies, the worker knew. . . . Everyone communicated the information—the worker knew, and went to the union hall.[108]

In terms of cultural life, union leaders pointed out that the consumption of popular cultural products disseminated by the mass media contributed to an undermining of workers' class identity. The community, political, and union networks that had served to communicate news and information in the camps were replaced by radios and televisions. With the Left silenced and repressed by state terror during the 1970s and 1980s, the news, politics, and entertainment that workers absorbed were generated by the dictatorship or imported from abroad and received through official and approved newspapers and television, often consumed in the privacy of the home. As one miner noted, "The problem was that the workers received only what the dictatorship said, nothing else, since there was no opposition or freedom of expression. So all the propaganda, on the radio, TV, newspapers was the dictatorship's—everyday you saw the same thing."[109]

Workers and union leaders also noted that the miners' culture of workplace and community solidarity had been undermined by the spread of a culture of consumerism stimulated by economic policies that encouraged the importation of cheap foreign manufactured goods. By the late 1970s Rancagua's stores were flooded with consumer items that were made available to workers through the extension of credit, and many miners fell quickly into debt. The new culture of consumption fomented by the neoliberal economy along with the proliferation of media such as cinema and television transformed workers' relationship to the union and the company. The mine's administration and the workers' union now often operated as credit agencies; workers began to look to union leaders who, through their contacts, could arrange loans. Union leaders organized a base of support around their ability to get individual workers credit and advances from the company.

Union activists lamented the growth of consumerism among miners and the ways in which miners began to see the union as a source of credit and material benefits, rather than as an instrument of struggle.[110] One CTC report described, for example, how "the dictatorship imposed an economic system on Chileans, designed by the Chicago School, of the free market, with which they imposed on Chile consumerism that poisoned us with autos, color TVs, sophisticated electronics equipment. Economic groups made money with banks, finance groups, and mutual funds that flourished like mushrooms in support of this sinister and shady system."[111] Similarly, according to a group of El Teniente workers, under the dictatorship "came consumerism . . . electro domestics, stereos, color TVs, all these things. . . . Finance groups were created, the guys began to take out loans, so they had more and more economic problems every day because they owed so much."[112] Other union leaders noted that by the 1990s, with the easy availability of credit, many workers fell into debt and that debt reduced workers' willingness to risk their jobs or lose wages during strikes: "They tried to make the workers stop going to the union, to change their consciousness, so that they didn't worry about shared problems . . . and they showed the workers a bunch of things, and the workers were tempted— they bought things that they couldn't afford with credit, by quotas. For the government and for the company, the indebted worker is a worker who is not going to have any possibility of struggling for his things, for his wage."[113]

With the liberalization of the economy workers increasingly approached issues crucial to their well-being as individuals. Whereas before health care, housing, and pensions had been the subject of collective community movements in the camps in conflicts with the mining company and the state, now each worker struggled on his or her own to adjust to the realities of the market, which was precisely the goal of the regime's "modernizations." Struggling with debt reduced workers' capacity to view their economic problems as shared social problems. Union leaders often found that their jobs consisted mainly of helping workers deal with the many bureaucratic procedures required by banks, pensions funds, health care firms, and loan agencies. According to union activists and miners, the system of the loans provided by the company and the union in El Teniente eroded miners' traditions of militancy and combativeness and fomented individualism. They noted that workers only went to the union hall to solicit loans from union leaders. The atomization of the miners' community because of political repression under the dictatorship was thus reinforced by the move to the city, miners' forced entrance into the market economy, and the consumer culture fomented by "los Chicago boys."

CONCLUSION

From the founding of large-scale mines by North American capital at the beginning of the century through the 1970s, the Chilean copper industry was enormously profitable. Low labor costs, innovative methods of production introduced by Kennecott and Anaconda, and high grades of ore made Chile the most important supplier of copper to the world market. The industry's profitability allowed the North American copper companies to provide high wages and benefits and copper's strategic role in the national economy enabled workers to exert tremendous leverage during collective bargaining and strikes and to pressure the state to intervene on their behalf. By 1973 miners' unions were the most powerful in Chile, and workers had made significant improvements in their standard of living compared with the first decades of the century. The labor movement in the mines was strengthened by a workplace culture defined by solidarity within work teams, a defiant attitude toward company authority, and by the close ties among miners' families in the camps. Like mining communities around the world, El Teniente was known for its militancy and solidarity. After 1930 strikes in El Teniente played a major role in national political events and in the movement to nationalize the North American mines.

After 1973 the mining community experienced dramatic changes. Repression decapitated El Teniente's unions, drove political activity underground, and created a general atmosphere of fear. The new military administration established an autocratic system of labor relations in which workers' job classifications were systematically violated and in which labor discipline was enforced with an iron fist. The regime's austerity programs and economic "shock treatments" caused workers to lose a number of benefits and their real wages fell drastically. Temporary workers employed by private subcontractors began to replace permanent Codelco workers. By the 1980s miners and their families had begun to experience job insecurity and a lowered standard of living. In 1977 and 1978 mine workers organized the first strikes against the Pinochet dictatorship in Chile, drawing on clandestine political and labor networks to build a grassroots worker opposition outside of the unions, which were controlled by the regime-appointed leadership. This underground labor movement provided the foundation for workers to win back control of the unions with the institutionalization of the Labor Code in 1979. When union elections were reinstated, workers voted for leaders from the opposition Christian Democratic, Communist, and Socialist parties, who had stood out during the movements of the late 1970s and who were known for their political militancy. In El Teniente, the dictatorship was unsuccessful in eradicating workers' political and labor traditions. After the failures of collective bargaining between 1980 and 1982 to restore workers' lost wages and benefits, the newly independent miners' unions and the national leadership of the CTC spearheaded the national protests and labor opposition against the dictatorship from 1983 to 1986.

Ironically, during the transition to democracy after 1988, workers' capacity to confront changes in labor relations and to make demands on the state-owned copper company was diminished. Changes introduced under the military regime and the effects of repression began to take their toll. The regime had neglected the state-run copper mines and promoted private and foreign investments in new and modern mining enterprises. The democratically elected government of Patricio Aylwin inherited a state mining company debilitated by lack of investment and by the military's policy of draining copper revenues to fund its own budget. In El Teniente, the mine's administrators sought to lower costs and to boost production by reducing the labor force and introducing new management schemes, work systems, and technologies, many copied from their private competitors. For workers, the company's strategies for modernizing El Teniente and making it competitive with the modern transnational companies operating in Chile threatened basic guarantees they had won through strikes since the 1930s. Combined with mechanization, changes in work systems and the retirement of older workers began to transform work and workplace culture, undermining traditions of labor militancy in the mine.

The 1991 strike represented a major turning point in the history of labor relations in El Teniente. While the strike had involved traditional forms and styles of mobilization and militancy, the outcome had been far from favorable for workers, despite gains in wages and benefits. The end of the strike brought a redefinition of the terms in which labor relations would be cast in the future. The company proposed a "Strategic Alliance" of unions and company management in reducing the labor force and increasing productivity. In exchange for job stability, the unions would work with management to come up with ways to reduce costs and increase productivity. For the workers, the Strategic Alliance represented a guarantee that the company would remain in the hands of the state and that their jobs would be protected. In addition, the Strategic Alliance offered the possibility that through the unions workers would be able to participate in decision making over strategies for modernizing the copper company. Labor relations would no longer be an exercise in conflict channeled through the institutional framework of collective bargaining. Rather, workers would participate with management in establishing El Teniente's international competitiveness. While a number of union leaders rejected the plan and refused to sign on, the Strategic Alliance was put into effect in the mid-1990s. Yet, by 1998 union leaders were attacking the Alliance as a means for the company to reduce its workforce. As one union leader noted in 1998, "The last reconversión laboral meant trauma, camouflaged firings, and discontent for many workers. The most worrying is that it increased a growing job insecurity."[114] That same year the president of the Sindicato Industrial Sewell y Mina, Etiel Moraga, noted that Codelco had pressured unions to sign onto the Strategic Alliance "to reduce the workforce [and] increase production with fewer workers." He argued that the company continued to ignore the excessive workload forced on miners and the medical problems created by work in the mine and its plants.[115] With their unions in a weakened position and the Strategic Alliance imposing pressures to reduce the workforce and increase productivity in the name of making El Teniente viable as a state-owned enterprise, the copper workers had little leverage in negotiating better work conditions and salaries.

The 1998 Asian economic crisis placed additional pressures on Codelco and its workers. As world demand for copper fell and prices steadily declined, Codelco's plans to modernize and become internationally competitive were placed on hold. As prices for copper dipped to historic lows of $0.75 a pound from $1.09 a pound in 1990, the state mining company halted new projects to expand production in new and existing mines and to invest in mines in Africa.[116] The effects of the Asian crisis were compounded by Chile's radical increase of copper production, which also drove international prices down. With more than 35 percent of world production (similar to OPEC's 38 percent share of world oil production), increases in Chilean production, especially in the private sector, had a significant impact on prices. Between 1989 and 1998 privately owned companies increased their production of copper from 365.6

million tons to 2,262.9 tons, and Codelco's participation in national copper production fell from 75.3 percent to 38.27 percent.[117] While exports of copper increased by 76 percent between 1995 and 1999, the actual value of copper exports fell from $6,431 million to $5,889 million owing to falling prices (prices for copper fell from $1.40 a pound in 1995 to 62.5 cents in 1999).[118] Owing to privatization and the free fall of world copper prices, while the state had earned 65 cents for every pound of copper exported in 1989, in 1999 it earned only 3 cents per pound, and—even worse—its share of copper exports had declined from 50 percent to 5.[119]

During the late 1990s and early 2000s the Strategic Alliance signified an exchange in which the unions linked support for the expansion and modernization of Codelco to the stability of their jobs, wages, and benefits. The unions viewed support for the state-owned mining sector as essential to the defense of the workers' own position, especially when confronted with the expansion of the private sector in the mining industry. In 1999 the copper miners' union argued that "it is of primary importance to maintain a vigilant attitude and permanent mobilization to confront the constant efforts of private economic concerns to 'jibarizar' [reduce the size of] and legally privatize Codelco."[120] For the miners' unions, reform of the laws handed down by the dictatorship that discriminated against Codelco and favored private mining companies would be the major struggle of the late 1990s and early 2000s. The unions cast their lot with Codelco's plans to expand investment and modernize, denouncing the unequal taxation of Codelco (especially the 10 percent of earnings that went directly to the military) and the state's constriction of investments as a response to post-1998 budgetary crises.

Union leaders lamented the rupture in the generational passing down of knowledge about work and labor traditions and younger workers' lack of class consciousness. Changes in the organization of the labor process and work relations and the paring down of the labor force weakened the unions' bases in workplace solidarities. This transformation in the labor force was exacerbated by the move of the mining community from the old camps to the city of Rancagua. The separation of miners' neighborhoods from the workplace and the integration of workers and their families into urban life disrupted community networks that had provided miners' unions strength during conflicts with the company. The regime's privatization policies threw working-class families into the urban market economy, making them responsible for health care, pensions, housing, and education—benefits that had been provided by the company before 1973—thus promoting an individualist approach to social problems and a general sense of anxiety and insecurity. The growth of a culture of consumerism and the spread of mass popular culture contributed to this individualism and to the fragmentation of workers' community and class solidarities. New forms of leisure, recreation, and consumption undermined old community institutions such as sports teams and social clubs that had been pillars of union activity. The unanimous nostalgia for life in the camps expressed by older workers and their family members in oral histories represented a sense of lost community ties and isolation in the city. By the 1990s copper miners' unions approached conflicts with Codelco management over changes in the labor process, wage and bonus structures, and job security with unions that were weaker than those that led the protests of 1983. Miners' numbers had been reduced by downsizing and their capacity to place pressure on the state and build alliances with political parties was considerably diminished by the shrinking role of copper and Codelco in the national economy.

With the 2000 election of former Socialist Ricardo Lagos, who maintained the policies of his Concertación predecessors in the copper industry, and ineffective reforms of the Labor Code in 2001, the El Teniente copper workers confronted the challenge of rebuilding a strong union movement that could effectively participate in shaping the organization of labor relations in the state-owned mine. The miners faced the pressure of ensuring the profitability of the state-run mines in competition with private transnational companies operating in Chile and abroad, while defending their wages, benefits, and work guarantees. Could the state-run company, still producing half of Chile's copper, provide an alternative to the privatizing schemes of neoliberal reformers? What role would workers and their unions play in building a state-owned company that competed with privately owned transnational companies in the global capitalist economy? By the beginning of the 2000s the pressures to make El Teniente competitive in order to maintain its state-owned status and in order to protect jobs imposed limits on the demands workers could make and on the militancy of the unions.

As Codelco attempted to expand and become transnational itself, with investments in mining enterprises abroad, workers have also had to rethink the meaning of nationalism and class solidarity. The radical nationalism and anti-imperialism that structured miners' labor politics before 1973 is no longer as effective in sustaining their class identity and no longer serves as a vehicle for national alliances. In addition, the local community identity that had shaped miners' class politics in the mining camps has given way to workers' diffuse participation in city life and a mass culture that itself is increasingly transnational. The physical spaces that demarcated miners' community and class identities before 1973 have "melted into air" during the process of restructuring and the intensification of Chile' integration into the global economy.[121] Now that miners and their families inhabit a world no longer defined by the boundaries of the mine and its camps, the question will be how to rebuild a class identity that will allow them to confront the profound changes wrought by this latest phase in the modernization of capitalist production in the export sector.

NOTES

1 Confederación de Trabajadores del Cobre, "Memoria," Congreso ordinario, Punta de Tralca, 1983.

2 Karin Alejandra Rosemblatt, *Gendered Compromises: Political Cultures, Socialist Politics, and the State in Chile, 1920–1950* (Chapel Hill: University of North Carolina Press, 2000).

3 For workers in the textile industry, see Peter Winn, *Weavers of Revolution: The Yarur Workers and Chile's Road to Socialism* (New York: Oxford University Press, 1986). For metal workers, see Joel Stillerman, "From Solidarity to Survival: Transformations in the Culture and Styles of Mobilization of Chilean Metalworkers under Democratic and Authoritarian regimes, 1945–1995," Ph.D. diss., New School for Social Research, 1998.

4 Recent research has shown that urban industrial workers organized an independent and militant union movement between 1980 and 1982 in Chile. See, for example, Stillerman, "From Solidarity to Survival: 'Dando la Pelea Hasta el Final.' Metal Workers' Resistance in Authoritarian Chile, 1976–1983," paper presented at the 13th Annual Latin American Labor History Conference, Duke University, 1996; Guillermo Campero and José Valenzuela, *El movimiento sindical en el régimen militar chileno, 1973–1981* (Santiago: ILET, 1984); Manuel Barrera, Helia Henriquez, and Teresita Selamé, *Sindicatos y estado en el Chile actual* (Santiago: Centro de Estudios Sociales, 1985); Manuel Barrera, "Consideraciones acerca de la relación entre política y movimiento sindical" (Santiago: Centro de Estudios Sociales, 1988); Jaime Ruiz-Tagle, *El sindicalismo chileno después del Plan Laboral* (Santiago: PET, 1985); Manuel Barrera and Gonzalo Falabella, *Sindicatos bajo regimenes militares: Argentina, Brasil, Chile* (Santiago: Centro de Estudios Sociales, 1990); Manuel Barrera and J. Samuel Valenzuela, "The Development of Labor Movement Opposition to the Military Regime," in *Dictatorship and Oppositions: Military Rule in Chile*, ed. J. Samuel Valenzuela and Arturo Valenzuela (Baltimore: Johns Hopkins University Press, 1986); and Alan Angell, "Unions and Workers in Chile During the 1980s," in *The Struggle for Democracy in Chile, 1982–1990*, ed. Paul W. Drake and Ivan Jaksic (Lincoln: University of Nebraska Press, 1991).

5 For a history of copper miners before 1973, see Thomas Miller Klubock, *Contested Communities: Class, Gender, and Politics in the Chilean Copper Mines, 1904–1951* (Durham: Duke University Press, 1998).

6 For an account of this strike, see Sergio Bitar and Crisostomo Pizarro, *La caída de*

Allende y la huelga de El Teniente (Santiago: Ediciones del Ornitirrinco, 1986). The Chilean labor code divided blue-collar workers (*obreros*), who engaged in mostly manual labor, from white-collar workers (*empleados*), who worked in offices and performed work of a more technical nature. Empleados' and obreros' unions often negotiated separate contracts and had access to different benefits and wage structures. In El Teniente, the PDC controlled most of the mine's small empleado unions during the late 1960s and during Allende's government, while the PS and PC continued to dominate the obrero unions. The 1973 strike was largely the result of the activities of PDC activists and the empleado unions who opposed the UP. During the strike, the obrero unions mostly continued to work and to support the UP.

7 For Pinochet's visit to El Teniente and Rancagua see the company newspaper *El Semanario de El Teniente*, October 1973.

8 The nationalist Díaz was replaced in 1976 by Sergio Fernández who later became minister of the interior in 1978 and one of the most outspoken and radical ideologues of the Pinochet regime and neoliberal economic policies.

9 CTC, Consultivo Nacional, 15–18 October, 1974.

10 Quoted in Carlos Bongcam, *Sindicalismo chileno: Hechos y documentos, 1973–1983* (Santiago: CELA, Spanga, S.E., 1984), 109.

11 Bongcam, *Sindicalismo chileno*, 94. Reinaldo Jara, interview of December 1973, Santiago. I want to thank Peter Winn for sharing his interview with me.

12 Member of the Sindicato Industrial Caletones, interview of July 1991, Rancagua. I conducted interviews with workers, ex-workers, union leaders, and political activists in Rancagua and Santiago between 1989 and 1998. In one case, cited in this chapter, an interview was performed by my research assistant, Paola Fernández, under my direction. As guaranteed to those interviewed, their testimony is anonymous.

13 Former El Teniente union leader and labor activist, interview of 2 March 1992, Rancagua.

14 *Informe del Cobre*, December 1983.

15 Former El Teniente union leader and labor activist, interview of 2 March 1992, Rancagua.

16 Interview, workers of the Sindicato Industrial Caletones, 1991, Rancagua.

17 Quoted in Mario Alburquerque, Fernando Echeverría, Oscar Mac-Clure, and Eugenio Tironi, "La acción sindical en los sectores metalmecánico y cuprífero: Informe de Investigación," working paper (Santiago: SUR-CEDAL, 1987), 28.

18 CEDAL, "Confederación de Trabajadores del Cobre: Antecedentes descriptivos" (Santiago: CEDAL, March 1985), 24.

19 *Voz del Minero*, October 1985. Also see, for example, *Voz del Minero*, June 1984 and June 1988.

20 *Informe del Cobre*, June 1983.

21 For an analysis of the Labor Plan see *Análisis* (July 1979).

22 Former union leader, Sindicato Industrial Sewell y Mina, interview of 25 November 1992, Rancagua.

23 *Avanzar*, August 1987.

24 *Avanzar*, August 1987.

25 CEDAL, "Confederación de Trabajadores del Cobre: Antecedentes descriptivos" (Santiago: CEDAL, March 1985), 24.

26 *Informe del Cobre*, June 1983.

27 For a discussion of private contractors in the copper industry see, CTC, Congreso Ordinario, "Memoria," 26–28 July 1982. Also see CTC, Congreso Ordinario, "Memoria," 10–12 January 1986, and "Memoria," 6–8 March 1987; and *Voz del Minero*, December 1985.

28 Rafael Agacino, Cristián González, and Jorge Rojas, *Capital transnacional y trabajo: El desarrollo minero en Chile* (Santiago: PET/LOM, 1998), 173–74.

29 Agacino, González, and Rojas, *Capital transnacional y trabajo.*

30 Agacino, González, and Rojas, *Capital transnacional y trabajo,* 193–206, 216. For a list of demands by the contratistas' union, see also the newsletter of the Sindicato Interempresa de Trabajadores Contratistas del Cobre, División El Teniente, "Siteco," *Contratín* (May 1990).

31 Agacino, González, and Rojas, *Capital transnacional y trabajo,* 198.

32 Agacino, González, and Rojas, *Capital transnacional y trabajo,* 204.

33 Bongcam, *Sindicalismo chileno,* 169.

34 Former El Teniente union leader and labor activist, interview of 2 March 1992, Rancagua.

35 The massive elevator that carries workers to tunnels inside the mine.

36 For accounts of the strike, see *El Rancagüino*, 4–12 November 1977 and 24 November 1977. Also see *El Mercurio*, 4–8 November 1977.

37 Union leader, Sindicato Industrial Rancagua, interview of 18 March 1991, Rancagua.

38 CTC, "Memoria de Rodolfo Seguel Molina," 9–11 January 1984, Santiago.

39 Union leader, Sindicato Industrial Rancagua, interview of 18 March 1991, Rancagua.

40 Interview, former El Teniente union leader and labor activist, 2 March 1992, Rancagua.

41 Union leader, Sindicato Industrial Coya y Pangal, interview of 26 March 1991, Rancagua.

42 Interview, member of the Sindicato Industrial Caletones, July 1991, Rancagua.

43 Former El Teniente union leader and labor activist, interview of 2 March 1992, Rancagua.

44 Former El Teniente union leader and labor activist, interview of 2 March 1992, Rancagua.

45 Former El Teniente union leader and labor activist, interview of 2 March 1992, Rancagua.

46 Vicaría de Pastoral Obrera, Arzobispado de Santiago, Informe de Trabajo no.7, 1981, "Balance de dos años de negociación colectiva." Also see *Páginas sindicales* for these years. In addition, see Ruiz-Tagle, *El sindicalismo chileno después del Plan Laboral;* and Barrera, Henríquez, and Selamé, *Sindicatos y estado en el Chile actual.*

47 See *Informe del Cobre*, January 1983.

48 Vicaría de Pastoral Obrera, "Balance de dos años."

49 *Páginas sindicales*, January 1981.

50 Jonathan D. Rosenbaum, *Copper Crucible: How the Arizona Miners' Strike of 1983 Recast*

Labor-Management Relations in America (Ithaca: ILR Press, 1995); and Barbara King-solver, Holding the Line: Women in the Great Arizona Mine Strike of 1983 (Ithaca: ILR Press, 1989).

51 Informe del Cobre, June 1983.

52 Informe del Cobre, June 1983.

53 CTC, Congreso Extraordinario, Antofagasta, 1982; Congreso Ordinario, Punta de Tralca, 26–28 July 1982; Congreso Ordinario, Santiago, 9 January 1984.

54 CTC, Congreso Extraordinario, Antofagasta, 1982.

55 Informe del Cobre, December 1983.

56 Interview, workers of the Sindicato Industrial Caletones, July 1991, Rancagua.

57 Informe del Cobre, December 1983.

58 Informe del Cobre, December 1983.

59 Informe del Cobre, December 1983.

60 Análisis 6, no. 61, 2–16 August 1983; CTC, "Memoria de la Presidencia Nacional," Rodolfo Seguel Molina, Rancagua, 10–12 January 1986.

61 La Voz del Minero, November 1983, April 1984, June 1984, October 1984.

62 Union leader, Sindicato Industrial Rancagua, interview of 18 March 1991, Rancagua.

63 Interviews, various former and current union leaders, Sindicato Industrial Sewell y Mina, 1990–1992.

64 For a description of the demonstration see Análisis 6, no. 70, 6–20 December 1983.

65 Revista de los Trabajadores del Cobre 1, no. 1, December 1987.

66 Informe del Cobre, December 1983.

67 Interview of 4 April 1992 (with the assistance of Paola Fernández), Rancagua.

68 For studies of women's participation in the pobladores' movements of the early 1980s in Santiago, see Cathy Schneider, "Radical Opposition Parties and Squatter Movements in Pinochet's Chile," in Alvarez and Escobar, The Making of Social Movements in Latin America; Patricia Chuchryk, "From Dictatorship to Democracy: The Women's Movement in Chile," in Jane S. Jaquette, The Women's Movement in Latin America: Participation and Democracy (Boulder: Westview Press, 1994); and Catherine M. Boyle, "Touching the Air: The Cultural Force of Women in Chile," in Viva: Women and Popular Protest in Latin America, ed. Sarah A. Radcliffe and Sallie Westwood (London: Routledge, 1993).

69 CTC, Memoria del Consejo Directivo Nacional de la CTC, Congreso Ordinario, Rancagua, 10–12 January 1986.

70 CTC, Memoria del Consejo Directivo Nacional de la CTC, Congreso Ordinario, Rancagua, 10–12 January 1986.

71 Revista de los Trabajadores del Cobre, April–May 1988.

72 Avanzar, November 1988.

73 Revista de los Trabajadores del Cobre, April–May 1989.

74 El Siglo, 28 July–3 August 1991.

75 El Siglo, 30 June–6 July 1991.

76 Domingo Quinteros Tamayo, Memoria testimonial: Año 1991 (Rancagua, January 1992), 7–8.

77 Quinteros, Memoria testimonial, 35.

78 *Punto Final*, July 1991.

79 *Análisis*, 8–14 July 1991.

80 Quinteros, *Memoria testimonial*, 13.

81 Quinteros, *Memoria testimonial*, 22–23.

82 *Análisis*, 1–7 July 1991.

83 *El Siglo*, 30 June–6 July 1991.

84 *El Siglo*, 4–10 August 1991.

85 *El Siglo*, 11–17 August 1991; Quinteros, *Memoria testimonial*, 132.

86 Quinteros, *Memoria testimonial*, 127.

87 Agacino, González, and Rojas, *Capital transnacional y trabajo*, 150.

88 Agacino, González, and Rojas, *Capital transnacional y trabajo*, 65–66.

89 This is based on the analysis of Carlos Fortín, "The Copper Policy of the Chilean Junta," working paper 76 (Washington, D.C.: Latin America Program, Wilson Center, May 1980), 3.

90 Fortín, "The Copper Policy of the Chilean Junta."

91 For an analysis of the mining law see *Análisis* 4, October 1981.

92 Exxon purchased the mine in 1976 as part of a general strategy of penetrating the production and marketing of copper and diversifying its operations in order to reduce dependence on oil production. The company bought copper mines in Chile, the United States, and Canada. Exxon also obtained coal, uranium, and iron mines.

93 *Revista de los Trabajadores del Cobre* 1, no. 6, July–August 1988.

94 Agacino, González, and Rojas, *Capital transnacional y trabajo*, 65–66.

95 Quoted in Agacino, González, and Rojas, *Capital transnacional y trabajo*, 52. See also 17–18.

96 Agacino, González, and Rojas, *Capital transnacional y trabajo*, 70.

97 *Revista de los Trabajadores del Cobre* 1, no. 1, December 1987; *Análisis*, 20–26 May 1991.

98 Juventudes Comunistas de Chile, "A 30 años de la nacionalización del cobre chileno," 2001.

99 *Visión Sindical* 1, no. 1 (Rancagua, 1996).

100 *La Opinión de los Trabajadores* (Rancagua, July 1998).

101 See Oscar MacClure Hortal and Ivan Valenzuela Rabi, "Conflictos en la Gran Minería del Cobre, 1973–1983," working paper (Santiago: CEDAL, May 1985), 104–8 for a discussion of these changes in workplace conditions, as well as my discussion of work and the production process in *Contested Communities*.

102 Interview, union leader, Sindicato Industrial Coya y Pangal, 26 March 1991, Rancagua.

103 See MacClure and Valenzuela, "Conflictos en la Gran Minería del Cobre, 1973–1983."

104 Former union leader and El Teniente worker, interview of 25 June 1999, Rancagua.

105 Member of the Sindicato Industrial Caletones, interview of July 1991, Rancagua.

106 Interview of 12 July 1992 (with the assistance of Paola Fernández), Rancagua.

107 Union leader, Sindicato Industrial Sewell y Mina, interview of 25 November 1991, Rancagua.

108 Former union leader, Sindicato Industrial Sewell y Mina, interview of March 1992, Rancagua.

109 Former union leader, Sindicato Industrial Sewell y Mina, interview of March 1992, Rancagua.

110 Union leader, Sindicato Industrial Rancagua, interview of 18 March 1991, Rancagua.

111 CTC, Congreso Ordinario, Santiago, January 1984.

112 Workers of the Sindicato Industrial Caletones, interview of July 1991, Rancagua.

113 Union leader, Sindicato Industrial Coya y Pangal El Teniente, interview of 26 March 1991, Rancagua.

114 La Opinión de los Trabajadores, September 1998.

115 La Opinión de los Trabajadores, September 1998.

116 In 1970 copper prices were $5,629 dollars per metric ton. By 1998 they had dipped to $1,558 dollars per metric ton. See, for example, "Chile's Copper Giant 'Paralyzes' Growth Plans," Miami Herald, 25 January 1999.

117 Federación de Trabajadores del Cobre, "Los trabajadores del cobre aceptamos los desafíos de tiempos de crisis," 24 April 1999.

118 Orlando Caputo, "Visiones Económicas" (Santiago: ARCIS, May 2000/2002).

119 Caputo, "Visiones Económicas."

120 Federación de Trabajadores del Cobre, "Los trabajadores del cobre aceptamos los desafíos."

121 Marshall Berman, All That Is Solid Melts into Air: The Experience of Modernity (New York: Penguin Books, 1982). The phrase is from Karl Marx and Friedrich Engels, Manifesto of the Communist Party.

HEIDI TINSMAN

More Than Victims: *Women Agricultural Workers*

and Social Change in Rural Chile

Dictatorship in Chile had dire and dramatic consequences for the rural poor, particularly for rural women. Thanks to the excellent scholarship of many academics and activists—primarily Chileans who bravely labored in Santiago during the 1980s—we have a detailed, if devastating, narrative about the impact of neoliberal economics and authoritarian rule on the countryside.[1] It is a story about the material and political disenfranchisement of *campesinos* (peasants): the termination of an agrarian reform that had dismantled Chile's hacienda system and redistributed land to campesinos, the crushing of rural labor unions and political organizations, the replacement of state-managed development with market-driven models, the emergence of a highly profitable and intensely exploitative fruit export industry, the conversion of peasant farmers into impoverished wage laborers, and the death of Popular Unity socialism as well as of the Chilean state's long-standing commitment to deliver social justice to the poor. Although Chile's dictatorship ended in 1990, its legacy hangs heavy in the air; and as Chile prides itself on having one of the most market-driven economies in the world, its agricultural prowess still rests mightily on the exploitation of women.

The story of Chile's encounter with neoliberalism has a familiar ring to those now accustomed to current debates over late 20th-century capitalist globalization and the crushing poverty of so-called Third World countries. In the export-oriented economies that characterize this phenomenon, women workers are often the majority and almost always the fastest-growing sector of the labor force. Women sew Levis jeans in Guatemala, wash IBM computer chips in the Philippines, assemble RCA televisions in Indonesia, process broccoli and strawberries in Mexico, stitch Nike tennis shoes in Indonesia. As with Chile under military rule, most of these workspaces are in countries with authoritarian governments that overtly repress independent labor movements. However,

Chile's experiment with neoliberal capitalism began earlier than most other currently existing models and was far more extensive and intensive in its scope and depth of restructuring. Indeed, Chile became a model on which many other neoliberal reform projects were based.

Starting in the mid-1970s, while most developing nations were pursuing semiprotected and state-managed growth, the military junta headed by General Augusto Pinochet aggressively courted foreign investment and slashed tariffs. In the countryside, his actions transformed a mixed economy of private haciendas, state-managed farms, and peasant holdings that once produced grain and vegetables for domestic consumption into a high-tech agribusiness that exported grapes and peaches to the North Atlantic countries and Japan. By 1980 Chile's fruit-producing region closely resembled central California in its level of technological inputs and methods of agribusiness management. By 1987 Chile's international fruit sales grossed almost a half billion dollars and the Wall Street Journal hailed the fruit industry as proof of Chile's economic miracle.

But as scholars and activists were quick to point out, for Chile's rural laborers, such changes were miserable, not miraculous. Campesinos lost access to land and became more dependent on wage labor.[2] They built makeshift squatter settlements, without potable water or electricity, on the hills that peered over into the recently privatized and fenced orchards.[3] Agricultural work became highly insecure, as the permanent work campesinos had formerly enjoyed on state-managed farms gave way to seasonal jobs lasting between three and six months. Wages plummeted to $1.00 a day, well below the low minimum wage established by the military junta.[4]

Worker compliance was ensured through repression and fear. The regime's 1979 Labor Code eradicated most of the political leverage the Chilean working classes had won since the 1920s.[5] In the countryside, it strangled the rural organizing efforts begun under the agrarian reform of the 1960s, which had unionized over a quarter of a million campesinos by 1973.[6] The new legislation so greatly restricted organizing requirements and labor actions that it effectively made campesino unions illegal. The military "disappeared" and tortured thousands of labor leaders and political activists, many of them campesinos.[7] It outlawed left-wing political parties and took over neighborhood associations, women's organizations, and youth clubs.

This was a drama that prominently featured women. Indeed, studies of rural women have been central to analyzing and representing the dire circumstances of dictatorship as a whole.[8] According to the prevailing narrative, economic hardship and the fruit industry's demand for cheap and plentiful labor pushed campesina housewives and daughters out of their homes and into temporary wage work. Employers such as Dole and Standard Fruit joined new Chilean companies in recruiting masses of female laborers for orchard work and fruit-packaging jobs, to which women's supposedly nimble fingers and docile temperaments were thought to be particularly well suited. By the mid-1980s women comprised nearly 40 percent of the fruit industry's estimated 300,000-member labor force and a majority of its packing plant workers. Most women labored in fruit-packing plants, cleaning, weighing, and packaging grapes, apples, and peaches. A smaller number found work in orchards or vineyards in gender-specific tasks such as pruning and staking.

Scholars and activists have written in detail about the hardship that these new female workers suffered, giving special emphasis to women's unique exploitation *as women*. Throughout the 1970s and 1980s the *temporeras* (temporary workers) worked 10 to 16 hours a day during seasonal peaks, without job security, overtime pay, or vacations. They earned miserable piece rates and labored standing, with few breaks. They became sick from pesticides and toxic gases, miscarried fetuses, and gave birth to deformed babies. They were subjected to humiliating pregnancy tests by employers, fired when a pregnancy was discovered, and forced to endure sexual harassment and abuse by supervisors. They returned exhausted from work to additional daily labors of cooking and cleaning. Children went unattended while mothers worked. Women's relations with spouses and male family members became tense and combative because of poverty, women's need to work, and the reality that husbands and wives rarely saw each other. Such conflict, in turn, contributed to increased male home-abandonment, a rise in the number of female-headed households, and heightened domestic violence. Beyond such "family strife," scholars have noted that women's agricultural employment during dictatorship went hand in hand with a host of economic maladies: substandard wages, heightened male unemployment, the replacement of permanent jobs with temporary ones, and rural workers' inability to challenge employer authority. Although not explicitly "blaming" women for such resulting distress, it often is implicitly assumed that women were successfully used or manipulated by employers to depress wages and deter worker militancy.

This prevailing view of rural women's work during Chile's dictatorship is problematic, and I propose an alternative framework for considering what is at stake in discussions about gender, work, and authoritarianism. While recognizing the tremendous value of (and my own personal debt to) past studies on women's incorporation into the fruit export industry, I am critical of the resistant tendency within much of existing scholarship to view women workers chiefly as victims, and rather passive or complicit victims at that. However unwittingly, this view builds on the notion that men are somehow sturdier than women when it comes to weathering extreme exploitation or that it is more appalling to underpay and overwork women than men.

Feminist scholarship has made the crucial point that women *are* inserted into capitalism differently and unequally from men because of women's domestic responsibilities and the replication of gender hierarchies within the workforce: women can be, and often are, exploited "more" than men. Yet in much of the literature about Chilean temporeras, the theoretical and political points about "double burdens" and "sexism" have been taken by scholars to be unchanging *facts* about women's essential vulnerability in the workplace, rather than as points of departure for asking how and why male dominance is replicated. This is not merely condescending in its implication that women "are more easily exploited" than men. It perpetuates the notion that men, not women, should be the "real" workers or that at least men should be employed "first." As Susan Tiano has noted precisely in her book on Mexican maquiladoras, writings about the exploitation of women workers still "gain [their] emotional impact from the horror of women taking men's jobs"; and, I might add, from the sad spectacle of men becoming unable to support wives and families.[9]

Essentialist notions about gender and work have compounded a second problem in the existing literature: the tendency to examine women's work in vineyards and orchards as a simple matter of labor exploitation and personal distress and, therefore, as a perfect example of the dictatorship's moral bankruptcy. Thanks to enduring notions about female vulnerability and the desirability of a stable, well-paid force of *male* laborers, "suffering women workers" have come to represent regime injustice in one of its most despicable forms. The problem isn't that women did not suffer as temporeras—they did, and mightily. Rather, the problem is that this formulation has encouraged the collapsing of an understanding of "women's work" and "working women's lives" with the term "exploitation." With a few important exceptions, this has prevented any consideration of the positive effects that female wage work, despite its exploitative nature, may have had on other spheres of women's lives. There has been little room for an exploration of how wage work impacted women's understandings of themselves, negotiating power with the family, or willingness to challenge labor exploitation or authoritarianism. Closely linked to this, the literature on temporeras frequently assumes that what came *before* women's incorporation into export capitalism was necessarily better in all aspects. Last, and perhaps most fundamental, "gender analysis" has been limited to rural women alone. The failure to undertake a similar consideration of how dictatorship transformed men and men's understanding of their lives has made it difficult to see the changes *for* women as intimately wedded to changes *in* men. Or, in other words, it has prevented an attention to how military rule impacted rural patriarchy.

Based on research conducted on Aconcagua Valley, one of Chile's most productive and lucrative agricultural areas and a center of its grape industry, I argue that the processes that brought women into the rural labor force as fruit workers during military rule had an extremely complicated and contradictory impact on women's lives.[10] Not all changes amounted to exploitation. After 1973 women fruit workers also came to have significantly more agency within their local communities and, in particular, an improved relationship to male authority within the family. Women's wage work and the very structure of the fruit industry lessened women's material and social dependence on men. It gave women greater bargaining power in their relationship to male family members, more respect for the contributions they made to household maintenance, and, in many cases, the ability to leave (or threaten to leave) abusive situations.

Women also assumed unprecedented leadership in activist struggles against individual employers and the military regime as a whole. Rural women denounced the dictatorship's economic model and human rights abuses and were at the forefront of reviving and reshaping the agenda of the rural labor movement. In the last years of authoritarian rule in the late 1980s, a vocal minority came to insist that a successful democratic transition required economic justice and gender equality. Although in the 1990s all fruit workers would continue to face exploitation and obstacles to collective empowerment, women and women's demands became central to the organizational goals of a struggling labor movement.

In many cases, developments in rural Chile mirrored transformations taking place in gender dynamics, employment patterns, and political movements elsewhere in the country during military rule. In urban areas, women's part-time and informal labor also became crucial to family survival as tariff reform decimated domestic industries, expelling tens of thousands of men into the ranks of the un- and underemployed. Middle-class families similarly came to rely on women's extra-household labor as salaries were slashed and the welfare state dismantled: throughout the 1970s and 1980s female participation in white-collar work and the professions swelled. Women's greater participation in the workforce, together with a rising number of female-headed households nationally, generated some of the same struggles over gender entitlement in the cities as they did in rural areas. Moreover, as was the case in rural Chile, urban women's heightened economic responsibilities were related to a significant role played by women (both poor and middle class) in prodemocracy struggles.

To note such "gains" is *not* to suggest that military rule or exploitative capitalist relations were in some simple sense "good" for women. They were not. Rather, I argue that *some* gender hierarchies can be softened at the same time that life, as a whole, is experienced by women (and men) as more oppressive. We need to grasp the simultaneity of gender exploitation and erosions of certain forms of patriarchy without mechanically attributing one to the other. In other words, it is crucial to separate the question of why women come to exercise more authority in some realms of their lives from the issue of what authoritarian regimes and neoliberal economic projects impose. The historical contradictions that enable resistance to emerge from oppression—or that simply ameliorate certain hierarchies or forms of suffering—should not be conflated with the structures of oppression themselves. Few scholars argue that the militant labor movements that have arisen in mining industries across the world are an indication of how good capitalist relations have been for men mining West Virginian coal, Chilean copper, or South African gold. Instead, they attribute labor's actions (often in heroic terms) to male workers' own responses, tenacity, and ingenuity.

Where appropriate, we should be able to draw similar conclusions about women. It is crucial for both intellectual and political reasons to maintain the analysis of exploitation: Chilean authoritarianism clearly coerced women; women were exploited and suffered under these arrangements. But there are equally compelling intellectual and political reasons not to reduce our evaluation of gender and women to the sum of that coercion. The relation between capitalism and gender is as contradictory for women as it is for men; female agency must not be confused with employer and regime intentions; and narratives that reinforce sexist paradigms defeat the purpose of challenging oppression.

REASSESSING THE LIVES OF CHILEAN FRUIT WORKERS

In the lush Central Valley province of Aconcagua, one hundred kilometers north of Santiago, the immediate impact of dictatorship hit campesino men harder than it did women. Dictatorship changed rural men's ability to be manly men in ways that both male and female campesinos had come to see as right and natural. In particular, authoritarian politics and neoliberal economics dealt a powerful blow to the material and political gains that poor rural men had made during the agrarian reform.

Between 1964 and 1973 the Chilean state and a newly emergent rural labor movement championed a brand of campesino masculinity that emphasized rural men's personal autonomy, political combativeness, and the ability to support one's wife and children. Led first by a reformist Christian Democratic government (1964–70) and greatly accelerated by Allende's socialist administration (1970–73), the agrarian reform aimed to turn Chile's infamously unproductive haciendas and appalling rural poverty into a socially just, modern economy. Transforming illiterate and supposedly servile peasant men into assertive citizens and able producers was central to this project. Campesino men were encouraged to demonstrate their worthiness as future stewards of the land by participating in strikes, standing up to the boss, and exercising leadership and responsibility in their own home. Although procapitalist Christian Democrats and Popular Unity socialists clashed over issues of private property, both defined the male-headed nuclear family as a cornerstone for building a new society. Both proclaimed that they would "give land to the *man* who works it," and both distributed land almost exclusively to "heads of household" (almost always defined as men).[11] Catholics and Marxists alike spoke of the agrarian reform as turning campesino "children" into "*real men*," so that each campesino might become "his own *patrón* [boss]."[12]

Dictatorship made the realization of such male agency and patriarchal duty absurd. With the emergence of the fruit export industry, not only did the rural man not become his own patrón but he acquired a new employer-boss who controlled workers with impunity. By the late 1970s a majority of campesino men were dependent on badly paid, temporary jobs in orchards and vineyards to which they had no property claims.[13] Making matters worse, the repression of rural unions smashed the political vehicles by which working-class men had challenged the authority of elite men. The militant strikes and massive land occupations that had characterized the agrarian reform disappeared overnight, as did the decidedly proworker stance of labor tribunals and government bureaucrats. Repression eliminated the social spaces in which campesino men had fostered a sense of masculine camaraderie and male class militancy. Police sacked rural union halls and set fire to banners that had hung on estate walls proclaiming liberated territory. As one elderly campesino man bluntly summarized the impact on rural manhood, "[The dictatorship] broke us and reduced us to infants."[14]

For most men, such infantilization was closely linked to the impact of the military regime's economic policies on campesino gender roles, particularly on notions about male responsibilities and entitlements within the family. Loss of land, combined with a heightened dependency on inadequate cash wages, meant that men's earnings were no longer enough to sustain wives and children. Compounding this assault on male breadwinning was the fruit industry's demand for women's labor. The agrarian reform's ideal of men providing for wives and children withered as thousands of adult women, almost half of whom were married and over the age of 30, entered Aconcagua's paid labor force as temporeras.[15]

Women's work as temporeras profoundly altered the meaning of rural manhood and the basis of male dominance as they had been materially and socially defined prior to 1973. Rural women had always worked, but the meaning attached to women's work as temporeras represented a sharp break from that of the past. Prior to the agrarian reform, the Aconcagua Valley, like most of the Chilean countryside, was dominated by vast haciendas, owned by a few families and worked by a semipeon labor force. Throughout the late 19th and early 20th centuries, large numbers of women worked on haciendas as milkmaids but had lost such permanent employment with the mechanization of dairying in the 1930s.[16] On the eve of agrarian reform, most rural women's work took place in and around the campesino household and family plot.[17] Women fed and clothed families, raised chickens, sold homemade cheeses, and took in outside laundry. Women also plowed, planted, and harvested in family subsistence plots; a few hundred seasonally worked for wages on the large estates during harvests.[18] All of these labors were recognized as productive and crucial to family survival. However, such work was also seen as distinct from and secondary to that of men. Women's work was usually unremunerated, home-based, and "for the family" (or somebody else's family). In contrast, men comprised over 96 percent of the permanent wage earners and share-cropping tenants who labored on the haciendas and were credited with their production.[19]

After 1964 the agrarian reform reinforced the home-based nature of women's work and gave it a more explicitly domestic, and nonproductive definition. The state sponsored craft and sewing projects meant to help women contribute to family income but promoted them by stressing how they would *not interfere with* female responsibilities for children and housekeeping. Women were also encouraged to assume more responsibility for managing household budgets, a role that implied certain female rights to male wages and authority over expenditures. Agrarian reform programs benefited women, but they reserved the program's most important aims of empowering workers and redistributing land for rural men.

Dictatorship and export capitalism changed all this. Wage work, itself, became redefined. Temporary jobs, inadequate wages, and the inability to overtly challenge employer authority stripped paid agricultural work of the positive, empowering, and *male* associations it had had during the agrarian reform. Agricultural work was no longer touted as a means by which campesinos asserted a mature masculinity but instead came to represent the degradation of men and the exploitation of women. Breaking still further with the agrarian reform's ideal of men providing for women, the new fruit work suggested new forms of gender parity in hardship. Paid work was now something that both men and women did. The realities of poverty implied that women and men needed to share the monetary burden of sustaining households and identify with each other's common experiences of abuse in the workplace.

These changes in the meaning of work and gender responsibility challenged men's former sense of authority over women. During the last decades of Chile's latifundia society, over 80 percent of rural women eventually married, and many of those who did not migrated to towns and cities.[20] Within the campesino household, husbands, fathers, brothers, and uncles exercised considerable control over wives and other female family members. Men regulated women's extra-household activities, determining at what age daughters were withdrawn from school and whether wives took occasional paid work as domestic servants. Women did not routinely handle money or determine household budgets. Men made most family purchases and often marketed women's home-made crafts, intentionally limiting wives' and daughters' contact with other men.[21] Men even exercised considerable authority over women's tasks in and around the household. Because men labored both on hacienda properties and on family subsistence plots inside these estates, they worked in close proximity to female family members, even though male and female work was gender-specific.[22]

The agrarian reform altered, but did not fundamentally upset, these arrangements. Sexual divisions of labor became more clear-cut and social spaces more separated: men worked on newly received plots of land or state-managed farms and spent less time at home because of frequent educational seminars and political meetings. Meanwhile, women's energies were channeled into becoming modern housewives who fed children balanced meals and skillfully made family clothing on state-donated sewing machines.[23]

Despite (or precisely because of) the growing distance between men's and women's lives, the agrarian reform emphasized principles of gender harmony and cooperation. Men and women were to see each other as partners in the joint project of community uplift and class struggle. The rural labor movement encouraged women to join picket lines and union marches in special female auxiliaries. State-run literacy and adult education programs admonished husbands, as one manual put it, "to respect the vital roles that women play as home managers and educators of children," and to communicate more openly with their women "so that wives can appreciate their spouses' daily routines."[24]

To a certain extent, the celebration of gender collaboration validated women's opinions and roles and suggested limits to men's unilateral action without female consent. This was particularly true of Chile's first national family planning program. Begun in 1964 with heavy financial backing from the Rockefeller Foundation and U.S. Alliance for Progress, family planning programs emphasized men and women's mutual responsibilities as parents and the need for spouses to cooperate with each other in raising children.[25] Yet despite the meaningfully positive changes for women accompanying the ethos of gender cooperation, the agrarian reform steered clear of measures that directly threatened the principle of men's authority over women. Family planning programs focused almost exclusively on married couples and made a woman's access to contraceptives contingent on her husband's consent. As a result, by the early 1970s less than 10 percent of rural women reportedly used medical methods of birth control.[26] The directive that men should better cherish and esteem their wives did not change the policy focus on empowering male workers or the assumption that the reconstituted campesino family would be headed by men. Women remained largely excluded from membership in unions and state-managed farms, both of which were over 95 percent male. Men continued to be women's ticket to participating in the fruits of land reform. The agrarian reform uplifted women, but it made certain that men were lifted higher.

With the onset of military rule, campesino men's authority and sexual privilege were called into question. The repression of rural labor unions, the decimation of male earning power, the humiliation of relying on women's wages, and the specific rhythms of the fruit industry combined to undercut the agrarian reform's ideal of masculine agency. For one, women's work as temporeras lessened men's ability to monitor or control women's whereabouts and schedules. Women's shifts in the fruit-packing plants began in the early afternoon with the first delivery of harvested fruit and ended as late as 4:00 A.M. the following morning. In contrast, most male fruit workers labored in orchards and vineyards between the hours of 7:00 A.M. and 6:00 P.M. This meant that most working women labored in physically separate spaces from most men, and that women worked at night while their menfolk labored in the day. It also meant that men were expected to take on at least minimal responsibility for child care and food preparation during women's absences.[27]

Men also ceased to control the size and spending of household budgets. Most women insisted on retaining control over at least part, if not all, of their own wages and on their right to make basic purchases for themselves and their families.[28] This gave women relatively greater authority within their households and in their relationships with men than had been possible prior to and during the agrarian reform. It was not that wage work automatically shifted gender relations. Rural women had always made vital financial contributions to the family, and during the agrarian reform the numbers of campesinas in Aconcagua who worked for wages on a temporary basis had significantly increased.[29] What was different about women's work as temporeras after 1973 was the fact that cash wages were increasingly becoming the only means by which large numbers of rural people survived, and men's and women's earning power and contributions to the household had become roughly parallel. Significantly, during the harvest season, women often earned more than men on a monthly basis. Although men's temporary jobs lasted on average three months longer than did women's, the fact that women's packing plant work paid piece rate while men's orchard work paid by the day often allowed women to pull in higher wages during seasonal peaks.[30]

Another crucial factor driving the changes in the value attached to women's work and the leverage it commanded was new patterns in rural consumption. During military rule most of rural Chile, particularly areas dominated by fruit export industries and wage economies, became firmly integrated into a growing consumer culture with a distinctly urban accent. Throughout Aconcagua, grocery stores competed with, and often replaced, peasant markets as the primary place to purchase foodstuffs. By 1980 most campesinos bought cheap, ready-made synthetic clothes and rubber shoes at town retail outlets and in second-hand stores. Street vendors in village plazas hawked nail polish, tin combs, plastic jugs, and nylon curtains. Thanks to low tariffs and new marketing strategies, even imported radios, tape players, and televisions were offered to rural workers on lay-away plans. But despite the veneer of prosperity, consumerism was usually more symptomatic than ameliorating of rural poverty. Campesinos' loss of land drove the heightened dependency on store-bought clothes and food, and the expense and poor quality of the latter often resulted in malnutrition. Lay-away plans for electronic appliances and furniture usually saddled the poor with crippling debts.

Women fruit workers were the crucial players in this new consumer reality, and they actively used consumption in their negotiations within the rural family. Building on the idea promoted during the agrarian reform that rural women should oversee household budgets and expenditures, temporeras ventured into town centers on their days off from work to grocery shop or to select a husband's work shirt. This implied men handing over a portion of their wages to women and ceding to women's unchaperoned trips. It also involved women deciding when and how to spend their own wages. Buying school uniforms for the children or a pot for the kitchen with one's own wages allowed women to affirm their importance to household maintenance in the monetary terms that were becoming increasingly valued in a market-driven consumer economy. Likewise, women's willingness to make purchases without prior male approval signified women's growing sense that wage work implied certain rights to make (at least some) decisions independent of male authority. Women's occasional purchases for themselves—a blouse, some stockings, an Avon lipstick—symbolized something still bolder: women's claim to male workers' long-standing practice of spending wages for personal "indulgence."[31]

Women's new understandings of themselves as wage workers, together with the positive value that women attached to their work, challenged past notions of why men rightly exercised authority over women. "Worker" could no longer be the basis for an exclusively masculine identity, nor could "wages" be a central means by which men ensured female loyalty and dependence. As one temporera, María Toledo, explained in an interview, if women worked under conditions similar to those of men, they were entitled to similar privileges, even if that encroached on male terrain and prerogative.

> You see . . . now [women] work as a big group of women, apart, in the packing [plants]. This is what bothers men. Because now women . . . have the same conditions that men have always had—telling jokes, having a good time, gossiping about problems at home. . . . A man feels bad. [And] women begin to like their own money and like the fact they often earn more than men. [A woman] likes to buy herself things as was never possible before, and men begin to feel displaced, unnecessary.[32]

Closely linked to the perception that men were becoming less materially important to women was a suspicion that women workers were becoming sexually promiscuous. As the previous arrangement of male breadwinning gave way to notions that men and women did similar work, had similar material responsibilities to the family, and that women spent their own wages. Ideas that women needed their husbands less—or needed men less as a whole—took on the near hysteria language of social crisis: married women (about 45 percent of temporeras) were said to be having affairs, unmarried women were thought to be becoming unwed mothers at alarming rates, and all women were said to be in danger of engaging in prostitution.[33]

Although most alarm assumed women's liaisons with men, there was also anxiety about women's relationships with other women. In oral histories, women frequently remarked on men's hostility to the female world of the packing plant.[34] Men complained that their wives preferred to spend time with "gossips and shrews" (female coworkers) rather than with their families; that they picked up "bad habits" like smoking, spitting, and wearing halter tops; and that they were becoming sassy and insubordinate at home.[35] In at least a dozen interviews with temporeras who were married or cohabiting with male partners, women reported that men forbade them to go out socially with other temporeras because, as one woman recalled her husband's rationalization to her, "You [will] forget the duty of your sex [to the home]."[36] For single and adolescent women, socializing among women was less restricted and often looked on as "normal" peer gatherings. Still, with activities like dancing, which were socially coded as sensual and therefore as heterosexual, single women's preference for one another drew male ire. Norma, an 18-year-old temporera who lived with her mother, recalled in an interview that when she danced with female coworkers at parties, men sometimes jeered them as "ugly" and "macho."[37] Although according to oral histories, male anger and defensiveness did not involve accusations that women's relationships with one another were explicitly sexual, this does not mean that such relationships did not exist.[38] In any case, the threat that women's homosocial world posed was clearly sexual in nature. Men labeled women's intimacy with each other ugly, macho, rude, promiscuous, and unfeminine and juxtaposed this to the "natural inclination" of the female sex to *desire* to be with husbands and children.

Concern about changes in the social proclivities and sexual lives of temporeras was not entirely unfounded. Women fruit workers *did* spend more time with one another and enjoyed it. In interviews both for this study and for others, women almost unanimously agreed that one of the most satisfying things about fruit work was the friendships made with other women and the break from domestic routine and isolation.[39] As María Toledo stressed, now women worked apart from men, in big groups of women telling jokes, gossiping about neighbors, and sharing problems at home.[40] To be sure, they also quarreled and competed with one another, teaming up in strategic alliances and cliques. But women sought out their coworkers at social events such as birthdays and public dances and occasionally ventured out together on their own to window shop for shoes and buy children's school supplies.

Temporeras were also in more intimate contact with men, although much of it was unwelcome. Sexual coercion, abuse, and harassment were commonplace in both the packing plants and the orchards. Distance from the male-headed household hardly guaranteed women freedom from male sexual authority. Yet coercion by social superiors was not new, and many temporeras insisted that the dynamics of the packing plant were far more benign than the sexual violence and vulnerability their mothers experienced as domestic servants and peons on the great haciendas predating the agrarian reform. What was "new" after 1973 was a recognition that women's proletarianization had altered women's (sexual) relationship to family spaces (their own or someone else's).

Some women also consented to involvement with male supervisors and low-ranking packing plant employees. Such agreements were circumscribed by coercion and necessity, but they could also be gambles for benefit, protection, favor, or thrill. While adolescent women were the most likely to become involved in highly unequal and dangerous relationships with supervisors, married and older single women tended to pursue liaisons with near peers among the small groups of male permanent workers employed at the packing plants.[41] Romantic opportunities ranged from casual flirtation to full affairs, and the cash wages received by both male and female workers encouraged an abundance of weekend, heterosexual mingling at dance functions, village plazas, and soccer games.

Heterosexual relations were facilitated by the increased availability of birth control. Although abortion became more heavily persecuted during dictatorship, the military regime expanded on the family planning programs begun during the agrarian reform. Such policy resulted from the junta's own investment in projecting Chile as a modern nation. By 1986 almost 30 percent of women between the ages of 15 and 45 used some form of birth control, most commonly an IUD.[42] In rural areas dominated by the fruit industry, this created a paradox. At the same time the control of women's sexuality was becoming more intimately bound up in labor control strategies such as sexual harassment and mandatory pregnancy tests, rural women became more able to control reproduction and to engage in sexual encounters without overtly risking pregnancy.

Whatever the extent of temporeras' intimate and sexual relationships outside marriage, *perceptions* about female sexuality had most certainly altered. The sheer *possibility* that women might seek male company outside the family gaze suggested to many rural people, male and female, that most women did. Distinctions between the positions and desires of married women and those of single women tended to blur, and all temporeras were seen as potentially sexually deviant. This image reflected new fears about the weakened ability of parents and husbands to regulate women's sexual lives. Yet beyond perception, it also pointed to a concrete willingness by some temporeras to define codes of female behavior that qualified and sometimes rejected the agrarian reform's ideal of female chastity and fidelity. In oral histories, temporeras often defended women's extraconjugal sexual activities as justified compensation for the lack of respect, affection, and fidelity they received from their own husbands. As Elena Muñoz, a 35-year-old temporera, recalled of her own experience,

> If [a man] is in bed and [his wife] is not there, because she's working, he gets suspicious, he wonders about who she could be with. In my case, Pedro always, always makes me have [sexual] relations with him when I get home from a shift, no matter how exhausted I am, or if I say no. It's a way of testing where I've been. . . . Men worry about women having affairs, even though men often take advantage of a woman's absence . . . to cheat on her. . . . You know, there can be a case of a good woman, who works very hard, who maybe is forced to look for affection in the packing [plant] because her husband is always cheating on her.[43]

Elena's account simultaneously defended women's behavior and condemned male authority and duplicity. While recognizing that Pedro's suspicion (and abusive sexual surveillance) of her was rooted in a real increase in working women's sexual opportunities, her counter that it was still usually men who had affairs underscored the injustice of Pedro's actions at the same time it justified the conditions under which a respectable woman might have an affair. This both legitimated the decoupling of marriage and sexual activity (under specific circumstances) and challenged the assumption that husbands always deserved sexual loyalty from wives.

Importantly, both the erosion of men's sexual authority and women's entrance into wage work blatantly contradicted the military regime's ostensible goals. Throughout the dictatorship, the junta aggressively promoted a cross-class gender ideal in which men worked to support families while women stayed at home caring for children.[44] The sacrificing Mother became the female counterpart of the patriotic male Soldier, and both were celebrated as the foundation of national progress and social peace. The regime launched elaborate programs, most notably a revamped version of the mothers centers of Chile, now headed by Pinochet's wife, which instructed women in the arts of homemaking and preached that a woman's true worth lay in her self-abnegation and maternity.

The dictatorship's gender ideal diverged significantly from that promoted during the agrarian reform. Although the agrarian reform also celebrated women's home-based roles, it had seen women's civic education and political activism on behalf of male unions and political parties as a crucial part of being a good helpmate. In contrast, the military insisted that women were naturally *apolitical* and that it was this lack of interest in "dirty politics" that made women so moral. It is also important to note that although both the agrarian reform and the military regime sought to improve men's ability to provide for dependent wives and children, the reform-minded Catholics and Marxists of the agrarian reform years were far more successful at achieving the domestic ideal. Ironically, the dictatorship championed its particularly patriarchal domesticity at the same time that its economic policies made it difficult for poor men to keep wives at home.

Rural men did not easily accept changing gender relations. As I have argued elsewhere, authoritarian rule corresponded to a significant leap in reported incidences of wife beating among the rural poor.[45] In the Aconcagua Valley district of San Felipe, the number of formal complaints of wife beating filed in criminal court jumped from an annual average of 10 in the 1960s to an average of 50 in the 1980s.[46] Even after accounting for region's 40 percent population increase between 1970 and 1982, these numbers suggest a meaningful increase in women's willingness to formally challenge such violence, but may also indicate that such violence had become more pronounced.[47]

Certainly the reasons *why* men beat their wives had changed. During the agrarian reform, wife-beating cases overwhelmingly involved men's insistence that wives, by definition, owed them exclusive sexual and domestic services on demand. Men physically disciplined wives for supposed flirtations with other men, for withholding or being unable to have sex, and for failing to complete specific household duties. A second major factor in cases of wife beating was a woman's objection to a husband's sexuality infidelity: men beat women for complaining about their extramarital affairs. Although the very actions by which women "provoked" male rage indicate that women understood gender rights and obligations in ways that differed from those of men, women's overt material dependence on men and the agrarian reform's affirmation of male agency and authority made it difficult and rare for women to overtly challenge men's social and sexual dominance.

In contrast, during military rule, wife beating became increasingly mediated by men's heightened economic vulnerability and the ways in which women's employment threatened male authority. During the 1970s and 1980s conjugal conflicts that ended in men's violence against women frequently involved fights over money, particularly male objections to women's insistence on controlling their own wages and female accusations that men were not financially contributing enough to the household. Extramarital affairs also continued to be a central theme in cases of wife beating; however, now this involved men's complaints of women's infidelity and sexual independence. Above all, women's increased willingness to challenge past notions about male right and female obligation placed men on the defensive and provoked retaliation from spouses who felt it necessary to defend an insecure dominance. Women's assertiveness flowed both from an access to wage labor (which, however inadequate, had lessened women's overt material dependency on men) and from women's insistence that men owed women respect and parity for their roles as economic providers.

Paradoxically, men's violence against women stemmed from causes both nurtured and undermined by the dictatorship. The military regime's own patriarchal discourse and use of brutality to repress civilians bolstered long-standing notions about the appropriateness of husbands' physically disciplining wives. At the same time, men who beat their wives over money or supposed sexual liaisons were responding to the ways in which the regime's economic policy had eroded the very basis of men's previous material and sexual dominance over women. As historian Steve Stern has argued recently, violence against women may be most intense where the rules of male dominance have been most profoundly challenged.[48]

During military rule, husbands also abandoned wives with greater frequency. The percent of rural homes headed by women reached a record high of 30 percent in the mid-1980s.[49] On one hand, male abandonment was fueled by unemployment and low wages; yet both of these realities were inseparable from the more basic fact of men's feelings about such circumstances. As in male rationales for wife beating, men's reasons for leaving wives were intimately tied to outrage and shame over the fruit economy's assault on past ideals of male independence and (benevolent) authority over women. As one man poignantly explained his reasons for abandoning his spouse in an interview: "Before, I could hold my head up and place money on the table. Now, I must watch my wife [working] and my children going hungry."[50] But women also left men, most commonly because of abuse and/or alcoholism, and not all pursued a replacement.[51] Others simply never married. Wage-earning opportunities in the fruit industry allowed women to more independently sustain themselves and their children (however miserably) in ways that had been far less available a generation earlier.[52] Although households headed by women were invariably more impoverished than households containing two working spouses, both household types suffered poverty; and for some women, the absence of male authority compensated for the absence of male wages.

Yet rural women and men were not always in conflict. Their joint work experiences in the fruit industry fostered a sense of shared exploitation and struggle. If the new necessity of female wage work upset past notions about male prerogatives, it could also lead men to grudgingly approve of, or even deeply admire, women's labor and effort. Along with producing raw antagonisms over gender, the fruit industry fostered new types of collaboration, solidarity, and camaraderie. At times, this could lead men to accept a more assertive female subjectivity.

Contrary to widespread and enduring beliefs about female docility, particularly that of rural women, temporeras in Aconcagua played important roles in resisting both economic exploitation and authoritarianism. One of the first open displays of antiregime protest in the countryside was the all-female managed olla común (common pot, the rough equivalent of a communal soup kitchen).[53] The olla común involved women pooling the food rations of individual families in order to collectively provide more substantial meals to entire groups of families, workers, and neighbors. It required substantial organization and cooperation. Women took turns gathering firewood, planning menus, collecting ingredients, cooking stew, cleaning pans, and serving daily rations. The olla común was often cooked outdoors on open fires big enough to heat large kettles, although sometimes local churches and private Catholic schools offered their kitchen facilities for such purposes.

The olla común was usually started to meet immediate necessities but quickly developed into a place of political activism.[54] The inadequacy of the fruit industry was always a topic of conversation among the women while they peeled potatoes and ladled out portions. The ollas comunes were also intentionally created in public spaces—village plazas, major crossroads, churchyards—where they were a spectacle that symbolically denounced the failure of both the fruit industry and, by inference, the military regime to provide adequate levels of subsistence. That the olla común emphasized the traditional role of women cooking for husbands and children made their indictment all the more stinging since the regime's patriarchal discourse promised to ennoble Chilean mothers and families. In the context of dictatorship these were political acts.

Rural women also came to critique authoritarianism and neoliberal economics through new types of involvement with the Catholic Church. During the 1970s and 1980s, the Catholic Church in Chile advocated an activist role for clergy and laity in ameliorating what it called the devastating material, psychological, and spiritual consequences of poverty and lack of democracy. Mirroring the diverse and sometimes contradictory role of the church throughout Latin America, Catholic activities in Chile ranged from distributing charity to encouraging political challenges. Sometimes providing the first would spark the second, quite against the intentions of a Catholic sponsor. In other instances, progressive Catholics, inspired by the egalitarian and emancipatory tenets of liberation theology, explicitly fomented collective critiques of dictatorship.[55]

The participants in, and objects of, church actions were disproportionally female. The church distributed food to women in poor families and organized the first common pots.[56] It was largely women who attended church-sponsored workshops on sewing, gardening, and animal husbandry that aimed to provide alternative types of income generation during periods of unemployment. Women also comprised a majority of those who became involved in the Bible-study sessions, catechist organizations, and parish discussion groups that embraced varying degrees of radical Christianity.[57]

Progressive Catholic activities had a profound and often empowering impact on rural women. Although the Church's antipoverty programs tended to reinforce women's family-based roles, they also offered women an implicit critique of the fruit export industry. Progressive ecclesiastical groups pushed such criticism still further by stressing the contradiction between the Gospels' message of liberation and the authoritarian conditions of dictatorship. Importantly, progressive catechist and Bible-study groups often pointed to family situations in order to illustrate wider national political processes. The suffering and disenfranchisement of the campesino household symbolized what was morally indefensible about Chile as a whole.[58] Such pedagogical linking between the personal and the political had a particular significance for women. As authoritarianism was proclaimed unjust and sinful on both national and local levels, women employed new political and moral languages to critique their relationships to men. In oral histories, numerous women who belonged to a progressive catechist group in the Aconcagua town of Santa María remembered weekly meetings more as times of intense reflection about their marriages than as conversations about God or Chile. Discussions about "the state of the family" could raise heated debates about spousal fights over money, the negative impact of women's work schedules on children, and incidences of wife beating. It was not uncommon for women to criticize male authority as a form of authoritarianism. As 50-year-old Sonia Gutiérrez succinctly recalled in an interview, "I figured we already had trouble in Santiago [with Pinochet], I didn't need a dictator in my home."[59]

Beyond critiquing regime responsibility for poverty and family dynamics, women questioned authoritarian arrangements in the fruit export industry. As the excellent studies of Ximena Valdés and Gonzalo Falabella have shown, temporeras regularly challenged employer prerogatives in the packing plants.[60] Both individually and collectively, women petitioned bosses for higher wages and better hours, traded information on who was a "good boss," covered for one another if a coworker fell sick or needed to look in on her children, and engaged in small acts of sabotage. In the mid-1980s, temporeras in Aconcagua carried out several successful lightning strikes—temporary, collective work stoppages at peak times in which workers demanded (and received) specific improvements. Finally, in 1989, the dictatorship's last year, temporeras in the Aconcagua town of Santa María surmounted the prohibitive obstacles imposed by the military's Labor Code by joining with male temporeros and some permanent workers to form the first union of temporary and permanent fruit workers in Chile. Women comprised over half of the union's 500-plus membership, and two women served on the five-person executive council.[61]

Labor activism in Santa María signaled temporeras' engagement with Chile's broader oppositional political culture, not just a reaction to specific grievances with the fruit industry.[62] The 1980s was a decade of repeated violent confrontation between the military regime and its increasingly united critics. Following a 1983 strike by copper miners, Chile's labor movement began regrouping and coordinated numerous general strikes and protests.[63] Labor was joined by a mass movement of urban shantytown and slum dwellers as well as by university students and oppositional political parties.[64] From the countryside, temporeras joined in with work stoppages, the olla común, and catechist organizing. In the mid-1980s, rural labor activists from across the center-left political spectrum began gesturing toward the need to formally organize temporeras. Under the auspices of the church, they jointly hosted a series of workshops that brought together scores of women workers (including at least three from Santa María) to discuss problems and strategies related to the fruit industry.[65] Throughout 1988, as part of the organizing that culminated in the Santa María union, temporeras actively canvassed fellow workers to vote against Pinochet in the national plebiscite that helped pave the way for the transition to democracy in 1990.[66] The regime lost the plebiscite in large part because it received fewer votes from women and from new export-processing zones such as Aconcagua than it expected.

Women played major roles in forming the Santa María union and shaping its strategy. Such agency was enabled by women's specific understandings of their needs as women workers as well as by past organizing experience. Significantly, crucial support for the union was initially provided by an activist priest and a nonprofit worker education center headed by a prominent member of the reformed Socialist party.[67] This meant that women had contact with a broader national network of professionals and labor activists and that many women had already run common pots, participated in progressive catechist groups, and attended workshops on labor rights.[68] Women brought the concerns and lessons learned in these other forums to bear on the new union. For example, they stressed the importance of non-workplace-based issues such as housing, food, education, and health care to labor struggles.[69] Temporeras also raised issues specific to the situation of women: excessive hours, night shifts, lack of day care, pregnancy tests, and sexual harassment. Finally, women insisted on the importance of gender equality within the union. Drawing on the democratic language of antidictatorship struggles, they argued that women's prominence within the fruit industry should be reflected in female representation and leadership within the union. Making specific links between personal and national forms of oppression, they called for greater male respect for working women and criticized the machismo of husbands who refused to allow their wives to attend union meetings.[70]

The Santa María union challenged the entrenched patriarchy of the rural labor tradition. In the 1960s and early 1970s the agrarian reform's massive organizing of campesinos had denied women membership, celebrated a decidedly masculinist union culture, and limited female activism to being helpmates for male protagonists. Temporeras changed this. They criticized union sexism and insisted on women's inclusion not only as members but as leaders. They redefined labor issues to include a host of new concerns, both inside and outside of the workplace, that specifically affected women workers. Finally, women suggested that combating male dominance within the working-class community should be a central part of the union's struggle.

Women's demands were conditioned by the experience of surviving and contesting dictatorship—in packing plants, church meetings, at home. Yet they were also deeply rooted in the working-class radicalism of the agrarian reform. Worker equality, class solidarity, and social justice had been the foundational principles of campesino mobilization in the 1960s and early 1970s. If they had addressed women only as men's dependents, the overall goal of social uplift was still something rural women had supported. Neither women's practice of forming common pots for political purposes nor female support for unions began with dictatorship. Both dated from the agrarian reform when women fed striking workers and carried picket signs for a wide array of leftist and Catholic organizations. Under the conditions of dictatorship, the worker egalitarianism of the agrarian reform resonated especially strongly for the rural poor. As women became temporeras in the fruit industry, it became a legacy to which they could directly lay claim. Women made connections between their current situation and an older political culture that stressed justice, solidarity, and equality. Women lay claim to a labor movement that had previously excluded them and in doing so redefined that movement for their own times.

Life is still hard in rural Chile. High hopes that fundamental structural and political changes in the economy would follow Pinochet's formal exit from power were almost immediately quelled by the compromises that Chile's new civilian leaders deemed necessary to undertaking a stable transition. Since March 1990 the governing Concertación coalition of Christian Democratic and Socialist parties has largely accepted the neoliberal economic framework bequeathed to them by the military. In the countryside, fruit exports remain the backbone of the economy. Free markets and cheap labor continue to be the bait for luring much desired foreign investment. Rural labor unions, although formally recognized as a partner in rebuilding democracy, have been held at a careful distance and sternly warned against the dangers of unsettling the peace through strategies that might give an impression of class conflict. Workers still live in poverty conditions.

Yet there have been significant changes. Although rural men and women continue to rely on the fruit export industry, we should not underestimate the importance of no longer living under overt authoritarianism. Country towns have elected leaders not military appointees, soldiers no longer make routine visits to vineyards and packing plants, permits are not required for public meetings, and there are no night curfews. Agricultural wages, although still insufficient, have risen from approximately $1.00 to $2.00 a day in the mid-1980s to between $6.00 and $8.00 day in 1999 and as high as $11.00 a day in 2002, thanks to long overdue hikes in the government-mandated minimum wage.[71] Special government programs have been created to help the rural poor buy government-subsidized homes and receive small start-up loans for income-generating projects or "minibusinesses" such as raising winter tomatoes and selling alcoholic beverages.[72]

Reforms made to the military's restrictive 1979 Labor Code in the 1990s have mandated overtime pay and worker compensation for job terminations predating contract expirations, eased restrictions on union formation, and relegalized and relegitimated labor confederations at the national level.[73] Legislation drafted in 2001 expanded the minimum length of temporary work contracts and introduced incentives for employers to provide off-season job training to rural workers. During the last decade, the Santa María union has been joined by several other unions that include fruit workers: according to union leaders, the number of organized temporeras reached 7 percent in 1998.[74]

There have also been some expanded work opportunities for temporeras/os.

In the mid-1990s many men and women began increasing the length of their employment in the fruit industry by migrating to different zones for different planting and harvest cycles. For example, workers in Aconcagua who can count on local employment between November and March can work the additional months of September and October by traveling north to Copiapó for an earlier grape season; they can work through April and May if they travel south for the apple harvest. Although migrant agricultural labor has a long history in Chile (including in the fruit industry), most migrants traditionally have been men. Today, significant numbers of migrant workers are women, thanks to the expansion of packing plants and more liberal attitudes about the appropriateness of women working away from home. Migrant labor can bring significant financial gains. Not only do migrants double their time of employment, but demand for labor has helped elevate wages. In 2002 temporeras from Aconcagua reported that they could earn almost 50 percent more than the minimum wage outside their own province.[75]

But however meaningful these changes, the basic tenets of neoliberal capitalism remain intact. Fruit workers' labor is still cheap and expendable, and their ability to challenge employer prerogatives remains extremely limited. Well-intended promises by politicians and reformers to diversify agricultural production (with longer and more staggered employment possibilities) have generated little more than a handful of greenhouse pilot projects. While the increase in migrant labor has expanded the number of months temporeras/os can find work, it has had a stiff social cost. Women (and men) are compelled to leave children behind to be raised by relatives, and the extensive time that many spouses spend apart has strained marriages. Temporeras/os also suffer from bodily injury and disability from the repetitive nature of most tasks. It is unclear whether many of these workers will be physically capable of laboring in the fruit industry past their forties; thus the lack of alternative forms of rural employment makes their futures uncertain. Moreover, fruit production has declined since the early 1990s, thanks to drought, soil mismanagement, and a dangerous level of indebtedness among growers. Beginning in 1998 the economic crisis in Asia dealt an additional blow, further depressing production and raising regional seasonal unemployment to almost 20 percent in 1999.[76] The impact of Argentina's 2002 economic collapse remains to be seen.

Reforms made to the 1979 Labor Code were careful not to extend unionization rights to temporary workers in their own right; unions continue to be required to have a minimum of permanent workers who negotiate on behalf of temporary workers. Collective bargaining is still not a guaranteed right, and, where it is permitted, there are restrictions on when it can take place and for how long. As a result, almost all improvements in rural living conditions since 1990 have resulted from government initiatives, not grassroots pressure. Although the national labor movement has influenced reforms, many temporeras/os attribute positive changes to individual employers not unions. There are new rural unions, but the vast majority of fruit workers remain unorganized, and their ability to directly insist on the redistribution of profits or to determine their working conditions is practically nil.

Rural unions have been less than aggressive. The leadership of the largest campesino unions—including those affiliated with the left-leaning Worker-Campesino Unity confederation (UOC), to which the Santa María union belongs, and three of the four other main campesino confederations—is closely tied to political parties belonging to the governing Concertación coalition and has been unable, if not unwilling, to rock the boat. Reflecting the labor movement's organizational weakness as well as a sincere belief that strengthening support for the current government is the best immediate hope for pursing the much needed constitutional and legal reforms (and for preventing a presidential victory by the Right), most rural labor leaders see worker organizing as a means to push and support government-initiated reform rather than to confront employers directly or to overtly challenge government policy. One important exception to this cautionary line is that of the Communist confederation, El Surco, which has been quite vocal at national meetings and in the press about the limitations of market-driven development but whose organizing strength as been hampered by the same limitations as the more progovernment confederations.[77]

Yet, despite its limited gains, the rural labor movement continues to push for change and the struggle is far from over. One of the areas where the expectations raised by prodemocracy movements of the late 1980s have been most realized and long lasting has been the inclusion of women's demands and women's leadership in union structures. There are now formal women's departments in each of Chile's major rural labor confederations (affiliated respectively with the Communist, Socialist, Christian Democratic, and Worker-Campesino Unity parties) as well as several umbrella organizations that coordinate jointly sponsored actions among the distinct confederations. In 1993 the major labor confederations hosted the first National Meeting of Temporeras in Santiago, a three-day conference that brought together over 200 campesina leaders and activists for the explicit purpose of discussing temporeras' mobilization and leadership within the labor movement. The meeting's agenda included seminars and presentations on such things as women's conditions within the packing plants, the impact of women's work on the family, machismo within the labor movement and the family, and the need for better housing, education, and day care.[78] Subsequent meetings were held in 1995, 1997, and 1999, and the proceedings of each have been important to elaborating the strategy and goals of individual confederations. Since 1999 the government has sponsored regional advisory councils known as "rural tables," on which temporeras serve with labor leaders and representatives of women's nonprofit organizations to instruct the government on gender-specific needs.

The rural labor movement has also become more inclusive of ethnic-based demands. In 1997 Chile's four rural labor confederations joined forces with indigenous rights groups, as well as with small-farmers associations and cooperatives that include significant numbers of Mapuche Indians, to hold the first National Congress of the United Movement of Campesino and Ethnic Groups (Mucech), an organization which is now the primary national umbrella for all campesino and rural indigenous labor and land struggles. The initial weekend conference took place with great media fanfare at the former Congress building in Santiago, assembling over 500 elected delegates, roughly a quarter of whom were women. Women speakers—both indigenous and nonindigenous—were on half of the panels, addressing a wide range of issues from all temporary workers' inadequate pay to Mapuche farmers' need for formal land titles.[79] The integration of indigenous claims into the rural labor movement harkens back to the 1964–73 agrarian reform years, when Mapuches played a prominent role in rural labor politics, but it more immediately reflects the post-1990 emergence of a successful effort by Mapuche organizations to articulate a broad platform of ethnic cultural autonomy, antiracism, and control over community resources. Reflective of this push, a labor law reform bill aimed at temporary fruit workers that went before Congress in 2002 explicitly outlawed discrimination against employees of indigenous heritage.

The Santa María union has provided an important model for these developments. Not only was it the first union of temporary fruit workers and first rural union to substantially involve women, but its model for organizing under authoritarian rule has continued to be relevant to the enduring neoliberal conditions of civilian rule. In particular, the Santa María union's practice of organizing around non-workplace-based issues such as housing, food, and day care (as opposed to wage hikes and the length of shifts) has had certain advantages under a Labor Code and political climate that continues to disproportionally favor employers. Women delegates from the Santa María union have been repeatedly invited to make presentations at national meetings; Olga Gutiérrez, the union's former secretary, has served in the Santiago-based national Women's Department of Mucech since 1994 and became national treasurer of the UOC confederation in 2000.[80] In June 1996 the Santa María union organized over 70 women from the Aconcagua Valley to attend a ceremony launching a government-sponsored "Equal Opportunity Program for Women," disrupting the meeting as they marched into the hall with banners and chants calling for "equality for campesinas."[81] The action was more a display of power than dissent. They applauded the government's plan to establish a special committee on rural women and took credit for a document that committed the government to promoting equal pay, increased pensions, and an end to sexual harassment in the workplace. As Olga Gutiérrez commented, "The goal [of the labor movement] is to get government to finally push for what we want."[82]

Certainly there is a long way to go. The rural labor movement is weak and market prerogatives are the rule. If temporeras look to the state as their strongest ally (as well as a more effective target of their organizing efforts than employers), the government has alternately lacked the power and the will to fundamentally alter their conditions. Even the 2000 election of a Socialist president, Ricardo Lagos, has done little to alter the governing coalition's commitment to export-oriented free trade and fiscal policies in line with IMF and World Bank expectations. Despite gains from the time of military rule, rural incomes in fruit-producing areas—the most basic marker of temporeras' (and temporeros') well-being—remains at near poverty levels. The handful of day care centers that have opened since 1990 have been employer-government initiatives and fall far short of need and legal mandate.

But rural women are still there, protesting the inadequacies of the fruit industry and insisting on being part of a solution. In contrast to the way middle-class and professional women were marginalized within Chilean political parties and civilian government after 1990, women fruit workers' participation and leadership within the labor movement have been institutionalized in unprecedented ways, however constrained the movement is as a whole.[83] To be sure, campesino confederations and most rural unions are still male-dominated institutions where "women's issues" are often ideologically and organizationally differentiated from the more universal (male) "workers' issues." Nonetheless, women's very presence is a radical departure from the pre-1973 labor movement, and the incorporation of demands and strategies forged by women workers signals a long-lasting change and model for future organizing.

Beyond the realm of formal labor politics, there have been enduring changes within the rural family and in women's subjectivities. Men and women continue to share the burdens and responsibilities of wage work, necessitating at least minimum changes in gender divisions of labor at home and giving women a sense of pride and ownership in their roles as breadwinners. Women continue to control their own wages, negotiating an ever expanding consumer society and making connections between earning power and personal autonomy.[84] Civilian rule has not "returned women to the home" (never an accurate rendering of campesina women's roles to begin with) nor restored the pre-1973 affirmation of male privilege and authority over women. Neither have rural women wanted this. While deploring the continuance of low wages, absence of day care, and long shifts, their demand is for better working conditions and more available employment, not the shutting of fruit-packing plants or return to subsistence farming by male-dominated families.

The difference is crucial. Neoliberal capitalism has not been liberating for rural women, nor do women see it as such. It is not poverty jobs that give women more bargaining power within their families, but women's access to work and wages *on a par with that of men*. It is not the state terrorism of dictatorship nor the strangled labor reforms of civilian rule that have helped women organize, but women's ability to lay claim to new languages about democracy as well as to the utopian labor tradition of the 1960s and early 1970s that had previously been reserved for men. Rural women are not merely fodder ravaged by capital. They are surely victimized, but they are not passive victims. In Chile patriarchal structures were foundational to the architecture of state and employers' power under the dictatorship; yet rural women came to challenge significant forms of male dominance and to construct new types of community with each other. This was not automatically *caused* by capitalist exploitation and regime oppression. Rather, it sprang from the new meanings attached to women in their capacity as workers. These meanings were (and continue to be) created by negotiations between women and men over past and present gender responsibilities and entitlements; and they are generated by survival struggles within and against the conditions of political and economic oppression. They are struggles that continue.

NOTES

1 There is a substantial literature on the impact of military rule and neoliberal economic policy on the Chilean countryside. Major works include Sergio Gómez and Jorge Echenique, *La agricultura chilena: Dos caras de la modernizacion* (Santiago: CIREN, 1988); Sergio Gómez, *Politicas estatales y campesinado en Chile, 1960–1989* (Santiago: FLACSO, 1989); María Elena Cruz and Cecilia Leiva, *La fruticultura en Chile despues de 1973: Una area privilegiada de expansion del capitalismo* (Santiago: GIA, 1987); Jaime Crispi, "Neoliberalismo y campesinado en Chile," working paper 5 (Santiago: GIA, 1981); Lovell Jarvis, *Chilean Agriculture under Military Rule* (Berkeley: University of California Press, 1985); Arturo Saez, *El empresario fruticola chileno, 1973–1985: Uvas y*

manzanas, democracia y autoritarismo (Santiago: SUR, 1986); Daniel Rodríguez and Silvia Venegas, De praderas a parronales (Santiago: GEA [Grupo de Estudios Agrarios], 1989); Silvia Venegas, Una gota al día . . . un chorro al año: El impacto social de la expansión frutícola (Santiago: GEA, 1992); Cristobol Kay and Patricio Silva, eds., Development and Social Change in the Chilean Countryside (Amsterdam: CEDLA, 1992); Patricio Silva, "The State, Politics, and Peasant Unions in Chile," Journal of Latin American Studies, no. 20; Gonzalo Falabella, "Trabajo temporal y desorganizacion social," Proposiciones 18 (1988): 251–68.

2 The findings of scholars on the impact of neoliberal capitalism on peasant communities is consistent with the findings of other scholars on other regions. See Richard Franke and Barbara Chasin, Seeds of Famine: Ecological Destruction and the Development Dilemma in the West African Sahel (Totowa: Allanheld Publishers, 1980); J. C. Cambranes, Coffee and Peasants: The Origins of the Modern Plantation Economy in Guatemala (Stockholm: SAREC, 1985); Marilee Grindel, State and Countryside: Development Policy and Agrarian Politics in Latin America (Baltimore: John Hopkins University Press, 1986); Robert Williams, Export Agriculture and the Crisis in Central America (Chapel Hill: University of North Carolina Press, 1986); Jeffrey Gould, To Lead as Equals: Peasants and Land Struggle in Nicaragua (Chapel Hill: University of North Carolina Press, 1992).

3 Cruz and Leiva, La fruticultura en Chile.

4 During the 1980s, temporeros/as earned between one and four U.S. dollars daily. The earning power of temporeras and temporeros is greatly debated given the fact that most women and some men earned piece rate and employers did not pay (or divulge the amount of) standard wages. However, most investigators and all campesino labor confederations argue that temporeros/as earned only slightly above the official minimum monthly wage. Since men averaged between six and nine months of employment annually and women averaged between three and six months annually, both men and women faced chronic unemployment that pulled the annual value of their wages below that of the annual minimum wage (INE [Instituto Nacional de Estadísticas], Estadísticas laborales [Santiago: INE, 1982 and 1985]).

5 The 1979 Plan Laboral dealt a devastating blow to all unions, but particularly to rural unions. Under the new law, collective bargaining could be conducted only on the basis of the enterprise, not on the basis of the comuna (county) or across industry sectors. Federations and confederations could no longer represent workers from multiple unions. Most devastating, unions had to have a minimum of 25 permanent workers. Temporary workers could not form unions by themselves and could be represented in collective bargaining processes only indirectly through the agreements worked out by permanent workers. Union members lost the right to canvass in the workplace and to protection from arbitrary firings and were explicitly forbidden to participate in "unpatriotic" or "subversive" activities. The law made it legal for employers to hire replacements for striking workers, and strikes were limited to a maximum of 60 days. See Jaime Ruíz-Tagle, El sindicalismo chileno después del Plan Laboral (Santiago: PET [Programa de Economía del Trabajo], n.d.).

6 In 1962 the number of unionized rural workers in Chile was less than 2,000. Between 1967 and 1968 the number of rural union members registered at the Ministry of

Labor jumped to 76,000, and by early 1973, that had soared to over 225,000 (Luís Salinas, *Trayectoria de la orgnización campesina* [Santiago: AGRA, 1985]). For a history of the rural labor movement during the 1960s and early 1970s, see Almino Affonso, Sergio Gómez, Emilio Kline, and Pablo Ramírez, *Movimiento campesino chileno*, 2 vols. (Santiago: ICIRA, 1970); Brian Loveman, *Struggle in the Countryside: Politics and Rural Labor in Chile* (Bloomington: University of Indiana Press, 1976); and Heidi Tinsman, "Unequal Uplift: The Sexual Politics of Gender, Work, and Community in the Chilean Agrarian Reform," Ph.D. diss., Yale University, 1996.

7 The Chilean government's official truth and reconciliation committee places the number of disappeared at roughly 3,000; however church and human rights advocates estimate that the number is far higher, over 10,000. See Peter Winn, *Weavers of Revolution: The Yarur Workers and Chile's Road to Socialism* (New York: Oxford University Press, 1986).

8 Scholars who labored in Chilean think tanks and nonprofit organizations throughout the years of military rule were the first to point out the connections between Chilean agriculture's astounding new profitability and the exploitation of women. Social scientists such as María Elena Cruz, Sergio Gómez, Jorge Echenique, Cristobal Kay, and others argued that Chile's fruit industry relied on campesinos' loss of land and dependence on wages, both of which forced unprecedented numbers of campesina peasant women into the labor force. Scholars such as Daniel Rodríguez, Sylvia Venegas, Ximena Valdés, Gonzalo Falabella, and others added to this thesis by providing detailed documentation and descriptions of women's work. They asserted that the high seasonal demand for female workers flowed from ideas about women being particularly adept at detail work and notions that women were more manageable than male migrants from other parts of the country. All agreed that the speed and extent of women's employment was unprecedented.

See Cruz and Leiva, *La fruticultura*; Gómez and Echenique, *La agricultura chilena*; Gómez, "Políticas estatales y campesinado"; Crispi, "Neoliberalismo y campesinado en Chile"; Kay and Silva, eds., *Development and Social Change*; Silva, "The State, Politics, and Peasant Unions in Chile"; Rodriguez and Venegas, *De praderas a parronales*; Venegas, *Una gota al día*; Saez, *El empresario fruticola chileno*. For works specifically on gender, see Ximena Valdés, *Mujer, trabajo, y medio ambiente: Los nudos de la modernización agraria* (Santiago: CEM, 1992); Ximena Valdés, "Feminización del mercado de trabajo agrícola: Las temporeras," in *Mundo de mujer: Cambio y continuidad* (Santiago: CEM, 1988); Ximena Valdés, "Entre la crisis de la uva y la esperanza en crisis," paper presented at the 47th American Congress, New Orleans, July 1991; Ximena Valdés, *Sinópsis de una realidad oculta: La trabajadoras del campo* (Santiago: CEM, 1987); Ximena Valdés, "Una experiencia de organización autónoma de mujeres del campo," *Cuadernos de la mujer del campo* (Santiago: GIA, 1983); Gonzalo Falabella, "Trabajo temporal y desorganización social," *Proposiciones* (Santiago: SUR Profesionales, 1988); María Soledad Lago and Carlota Olavarría, *La participación de la mujer en las economias campesinas: Un estudio de casos en dos comunas frutícolas* (Santiago: GIA, 1981); Pilar Campana, "La problemática de la organización de la mujer rural en Chile," *Agricultura y Sociedad*, Santiago, May 1987; Julia Medel, Soledad Olívos, and

Verónica Riquelme, *Las temporeras y sus visión del trabajo* (Santiago: CEM, 1989); Verónica Oxmán, "La participación de la mujer campesina en organizaciones," unpublished paper (Santiago: ISIS, 1983).

9 Susan Tiano, *Patriarchy on the Line: Labor, Gender, and Ideology in the Mexican Maquila Industry* (Philadelphia: Temple University Press, 1994).

10 Fieldwork for this project was conducted between 1991 and 1993 with the generous support of the Social Science Research Council and the Inter-American Foundation. My research included archival and published materials as well as numerous interviews. I conducted oral histories with 95 campesino/a workers, labor activists, political leaders, government officials, and Catholic clergy and laypeople. During a brief research trip to Chile in 1997, I conducted an additional 10 interviews.

11 See Patricia Garrett, "Growing Apart: The Experiences of Rural Men and Women in Central Chile," Ph.D. diss., University of Wisconsin-Madison, 1978; Valdés, *Mujer, trabajo, y medio ambiente* and *Sinópsis de una realidad oculta*. These findings are consistent with a general tendency of agrarian reform projects throughout Latin America (Cuba and Nicaragua, partially excepted) to give land only to male household heads. See Carmen Diana Deere and Magdalena León, eds., *Rural Women and State Policy: Feminist Perspectives on Latin America* (Boulder: Westview Press, 1987).

12 Periodical literature from the agrarian reform, analyzed in Heidi Tinsman, "Masculine Militants and Feminine Helpmates: Gender and the Rural Labor Movement," in "Unequal Uplift," chap. 3.

13 After 1973 over a third of the land expropriated during the agrarian reform was immediately returned to its original owner. Campesino cooperatives and state-managed estates were dismantled and sold off at market prices to the most able buyer. A minority of campesinos who did receive land parcels under the junta's modest redistribution program lost their farms because of lack of credit and capacity to compete with large growers. Specifically, in the Central Valley province of Aconcagua, 35 percent of reformed-sector lands were immediately returned to their former owners, 55 percent were parceled out to individual campesinos, and 10 percent remained in the hands of the state. Due to lack of credit and technical assistance up to 55 percent of those campesinos had lost their land by 1984 (*Censo agropecuario*, 1974–1975 and 1984–1984; and "Inscripciones de CORA [La Corporación de informa agraria]," Bienes Raices [Notary Records], San Felipe, and Los Andes.) Similar national figures are estimated by Jarvis, *Chilean Agriculture under Military Rule*; and by Gomez and Echenique, *La agricultura chilena*.

14 Oral history of Armando Gómez, Putaendo, 14 June 1993. For reasons of privacy, all names of cited informants have been altered.

15 By 1979 an estimated 4,000 women in the Aconcagua Valley worked in packing plants during the December–April harvest season. By 1988, this number had climbed to 6,000. Estimates are calculated from production levels of individual packings, recorded in *Directorio agro-industrial frutícola de Chile* (Santiago: CIREN, 1979, 1983, 1984, 1988, 1993). To date, there is no published statistical record of the number of temporeros/as by region, province, or comuna in Chile. These estimates were calculated by dividing a packing plant's total annual production by a modest

estimate of the average production level of individual workers. These figures may significantly underestimate the number of women employed.

16 Ximena Valdés, *La posición de la mujer en la hacienda* (Santiago: CEM, 1988); Garrett, "Growing Apart."

17 X. Valdés, *Mujer, trabajo, y medio ambiente*; Garrett, "Growing Apart."

18 In the 1964–65 agricultural census for Aconcagua, 551 women were listed as seasonal laborers and 113 as permanent workers (INE, *Censo agropecuario: Aconcagua, 1964–65*).

19 INE, *Censo agropecuario: Aconcagua*, 1954–55 and 1964–65.

20 In Aconcagua province, fully 80 percent of rural women between the ages of 30 and 50 were married, and 6 percent lived in common-law marriages (INE, Cuadro no. 5, *Censo de población: Aconcagua* [Santiago: INE, 1960]).

21 This is a principal argument that I develop in my book, based on oral histories and judicial records. See Heidi Tinsman, *Partners in Conflict: The Politics of Gender, Sexuality, and Labor in the Chilean Agrarian Reform, 1950–1973* (Durham: Duke University Press, 2002). Also see Heidi Tinsman, "Esposas golpeadas: Violencia domestica y control sexual en Chile rural, 1958–1988," in *Diciplina y desacato: Estudios de genero en la historia de Chile, siglos XIX y XX*, ed. Lorena Gody, Elizabeth Hutchison, Karin Rosemblatt, and Soledad Zárate (Santiago: SUR/CEDEM, 1995); Heidi Tinsman, "Household Patrones: Wife Beating and Sexual Control in Rural Chile," in *The Gendered Worlds of Latin American Women Workers*, ed. Daniel James and John French (Durham: Duke University Press, 1997).

22 Tinsman, "Household Patrones."

23 The primary vehicle for organizing women toward these ends was the state-sponsored mothers centers. For a description of mothers centers' goals and activities, see Edda Gaviola, Lorella Lopresti, and Claudia Rojas, "Los centros de madres: Una forma de organización para la mujer rural," unpublished manuscript, (Santiago: ISIS, 1988); Teresa Valdés, María Weinstein, María Isabel Toledo, and Lilian Letelier, "Centros de madre, 1973–1989: Solo disciplinamiento?" working paper 416 (Santiago: FLACSO, 1989); Garrett, "Growing Apart." Also see various reports on mothers' centers in the periodical literature, including *Campo Nuevo*, May, June, November, December 1968; *La Nación*, 3 January 1966, 3; 2 July 1966, 4; *El Trabajo*, 1 July 1969, 7; 23 May 1970, 6.

24 "Marco nacional de programación" (Santiago: INDAP, 1968), 9–10; "Primer reunión nacional de institutos públicos y privados sobre el desarrollo de la comunidad," Consejo Nacional de Promoción Popular, 1968, 22.

25 "APROFA: Diez años de labor," *Boletín APROFA* (Asociación de Protección de la Familia) (August 1972): 6–7; "Síntesis historica de la planificación familiar en Chile" (Santiago: Aprofa, 1974). Also see Heidi Tinsman, "Family Health and the Politics of Birth Control," in "Unequal Uplift," chap. 6.

26 *Estadísticas APROFA* (Santiago: Aprofa, 1990).

27 Various oral interviews. Other scholars of women's work in the fruit industry have also argued that there have been some very minimal changes in men's responsibility for child care and meals. See Gonzalo Falabella, "Historia del Santa María sindicato

inter-empresa de trabajadores permanentes y temporeros," unpublished paper (Santiago: Mancomunal, 1990); Falabella, "Organizarse y sobrevivir: Democracia y sindicalización en Santa Maria," paper presented at the 47th American Congress, New Orleans, July 1991; Valdés, "Entre la crisis de la uva y la esperanza en crisis."

28 In almost all of the 95 interviews and oral histories I conducted, both women and men claimed the that women who worked as temporeras exercised at least some control over their earnings. This ranged from keeping a small, token allowance for purchasing "household needs," to guarding all wages and spending some of them on "personal" items like clothing, makeup, and food. Many interviewees also maintained that the rural poor's heightened reliance on wages corresponded to women, rather than men, taking primary responsibility for household budgets. This involved men's handing over (at least part of) their wages to women.

29 In Aconcagua, the number of women employed in paid seasonal agricultural work leaped from 551 in 1964 to 2,011 by 1974 (Cuadro 6.3 *Censo agropecuario: Aconcagua, 1964–1965*; and Cuadro 11.A, *Censo agropecuario: Aconcagua, 1975–1976*). Most of these jobs entailed harvesting fruits and vegetables on both state-managed farms and privately owned estates and farms. Yet this had not fundamentally challenged ideas about male authority over women in the family. Moreover, in oral histories conducted for this study as well as the prescriptive literature of the time, women were overwhelmingly referred to as "nonworking housewives."

30 Various oral histories. Also see Constance Newman, "How Are Piece Rates Determined? A Micro-Level Analysis of Piece Rates in Chilean Table Grape-Packing Sheds," Ph.D. diss., University of California-Davis, 1994; Cecilia Montero, Lovell Jarvis, and Sergio Gómez, eds., "El sector frutícola en la encrucijada: Opciones para una expansión sostenida," working paper 112 (Santiago: Cieplan, 1992).

31 Most women insisted that they used their wages to "make purchases for the family, especially the children." They defended their right to such agency by stressing the virtue of their spending choices in contrast to what they saw as men's tendency to spend their wages on alcohol, gambling, and occasionally other women. However, several women, particularly younger adolescent women and single women, "admitted" that they occasionally spent wages for personal luxuries. They defended such actions as *deserved* both because the women had earned their own money and, again, on the moral grounds that their personal consumer choices were less harmful and abusive to others than were men's.

32 Oral history of María Toledo, Santa María, 26 October 1992.

33 Fears about necessary connections between women's wage work and prostitution closely echoed the rhetoric of early 20th-century labor leaders and social reformers. See Elizabeth Quay Hutchison, "El fruto envenenado del arbol capitalista: Women Workers and the Prostitution of Labor in Urban Chile, 1896–1925," *Journal of Women's History* 9, no. 4 (1998): 131–52.

34 Various oral histories, including Rita Galdámez, Santa María, 20 April 1993; and María Toledo, Santa María, 26 October 1992.

35 Oral history of Elena Muñoz, Santa María, 31 May 1993.

36 Various oral histories, including Sonia Gutiérrez, Santa María, 14 June 1993.

37 Oral history of Norma Cárdanes, Santa María, 10 March 1993.

38 At the time these interviews were conducted in the 1990s, rural Chile, like many societies (particularly Catholic ones), had strong taboos against same-gender sex. But whereas sexual intimacy or sex between men was frequently referenced or used as a metaphor for other (negative) power relations; the same was not true for sex between women. Yet whereas other authors (Gutman, Lancaster) have taken the absence of a discussion about sex between women to be an actual absence of such sex, I would argue strongly against such a conclusion. Societal and Catholic taboos surrounding the female body, including and combined with an explicitly phallo-centric discourse about all sexuality, militate heavily against interviewees feeling comfortable (or even able) to discuss female sexuality in ways that are not already heterosexual.

39 Several studies on temporeras use oral histories and interviews in which a majority of temporeras discuss how fruit work is a welcome break from housework and a chance to make friends (Silvia Venegas, *Una gota al día . . . un chorro al año*; X. Valdés, *Mujer, trabajo, y medio ambiente*; X. Valdés, "Feminización del mercado de trabajo agrícola"; X. Valdés, "Entre la crisis de la uva y la esperanza en crisis"; Falabella, "Trabajo temporal y desorganización social"; Medelet al., *Las temporeras y sus visión*).

40 Oral history of María Toledo, Santa María, 26 October 1992.

41 Various oral sources.

42 According to the Chilean affiliate of International Planned Parenthood; 27.3 percent of Chilean women between the ages of 15 and 45 used contraceptives in 1985 as compared to 13.7 percent in 1970 (*Estadísticas* APROFA [Santiago: Aprofa, 1990]).

43 Oral history of Elena Muñoz, Santa María, 31 May 1993.

44 For work on the military's policy toward and discourse about the place of women in society, see Lisa Baldez, "In the Name of the Public and the Private: Conservative and Progressive Women's Movements in Chile, 1970–1996," Ph.D. diss., University of San Diego, 1997; Margaret Power, "Right-Wing Women and Chilean politics: 1964–1973," Ph.D. diss., University of Illinois-Chicago, 1997; Valdés et al., "Centros de madre, 1973–1989"; María de los Angeles Crummett, "El poder feminino: The Mobilization of Women against Socialism in Chile," *Latin American Perspectives*, no. 4 (1977).

45 Tinsman, "Esposas golpeadas" and "Household Patrones."

46 The number of formal charges of wife beating filed by women at the local district criminal court in San Felipe leapt from an annual average of 10 in the 1960s to an annual average of 35 in the mid-1970s to an annual average of 50 in the 1980s ("Registro de Crimenes," Juzgado de Crimen, San Felipe). See Tinsman, "Esposas golpeadas" and "Household Patrones."

47 In 1970 the district of San Felipe had a population of 68,106. In 1982, its population was 116,443 (INE, *Censo de población: Aconcagua, 1970, 1982,* [Santiago: INE, 1970, 1982]).

48 Steven Stern, *The Secret History of Gender: Women, Men, and Power in Late Colonial Mexico* (Chapel Hill: University of North Carolina Press, 1995).

49 During the 1960s female-headed households accounted for between 3 and 8 percent

of all rural households in Aconcagua (*Estudio de hogares*, INE, 1965; *Censo de población*, 1960 and 1970). After the return to democracy, Sernam estimated that the percentage of rural households head by women in the late 1980s was as high as 30 percent (quoted from Venegas, *Una gota al día . . . un chorro al año*).

50 Oral history of Raul Fuentes, Santa María, 15 November 1992.

51 Various oral sources. Of the 95 interviews conducted for this study, 15 were with women who had separated from their husbands. Five of these women claimed that they had left their spouses. Another two claimed that although their husband had abandoned them, they were emotionally better off without their spouse and had even welcomed their departure. I do not claim that these figures are statistically meaningful; however, even as anecdotal evidence, they suggest that there were a variety of ways that women came to head households and that, likewise, women had a variety of responses to assuming such positions.

52 In the 1950s and 1960s women who did not marry and/or live with wage-earning or land-owning men usually migrated to cities in search of employment as domestics.

53 Various oral histories including Rosa Toledo, Santa María, 11 October 1992; Padre Vicente, San Felipe, 14 November 1992; Daniel Sanfuentes, Santiago, 15 November 1992. Falabella, "Historia del Santa Maria sindicato inter-empresa"; Falabella, "Organizarse y sobrevivir"; X. Valdés, "Entre la crisis de la uva y la esperanza en crisis."

54 This assessment builds on the work of Temma Kaplan, "Female Consciousness and Collective Action: The Case of Barcelona, 1910–1918," *Signs* 7, no. 3 (1982): 545–63; and Maxine Molyneaux, "Mobilization *without* Emancipation: Women's Interests and the State in Nicaragua," *Feminist Studies*, 11, no. 2 (1985): 227–54.

55 Church activities during the dictatorship ranged from providing food through the Catholic aid program Caritas to protecting political refugees and documenting human rights abuses. During the 1980s many Catholic clergy, including members of the church hierarchy, as well as numerous priests in Aconcagua, outspokenly criticized the military regime for its political repression and failure to provide for the poor. Activities in Aconcagua included food distribution, vocational training workshops for the poor, Bible study groups, catechist organization, and meetings for families of the disappeared (various records from the Instituto Pastoral Rural, Santiago; Oficinia del Obizpo de San Felipe; Iglesia de Santa María; Casa Pastoral San Felipe).

56 Various oral histories including Rosa Toledo, Santa María, 11 October 1992; Padre Vicente, San Felipe, 14 November 1992; Daniel Sanfuentes, Santiago, 15 November 1992. Also, Falabella, "Historia del Santa María sindicato inter-empresa"; Falabella, "Organizarse y sobrevivir"; X. Valdés, "Entre la crisis de la uva y la esperanza en crisis."

57 In central Chile, many church-sponsored educational and recreational events were initiated by the Instituto Pastoral Rural (Inpru), a Catholic non-profit organization run by progressive clergy and laypeople, including former labor movement leaders and members of center and leftist political parties.

58 Oral histories of Pati Muñoz and Rosa Toledo, Santa María, 11 October 1992; María

Galdámez, Santa María, 22 November 1992; Padre Vicente, San Felipe, 14 November 1992.

59 Oral history of Sonia Gutiérrez, Santa María, 14 June 1993.

60 Falabella, "Historia del Santa María sindicato inter-empresa"; Falabella, "Organizarse y sobrevivir"; X. Valdés, "Feminización del mercado de trabajo"; X. Valdés, "Entre la crisis de la uva y la esperanza en crisis."

61 Santa María Sindicato Inter-Empresa de Trabajadores Permanentes y Temporeros, "Registro de socios." The Santa María union was an "inter-empresa" (cross-enterprise) union, involving workers employed by various employers. As such, under the dictatorship's Labor Code, the union was not permitted collective bargaining or strike rights.

62 As Veronica Schild has eloquently written in her study of Chilean poblaciones, it is crucial to conceptualize "politics" as including not only struggles for resources within the structural constraints of state-employer-worker relationships, but also as involving what she calls "struggles for subjectivities"—struggles that challenge power relations more broadly, especially relations that limit how people define themselves and their level of participation (Veronica Schild, "Recasting Popular Movements: Gender and Political Learning in Neighborhood Organizing in Chile," *Latin American Perspective* 21, no. 2 (1994): 59–80.

63 Gonzalo Falabella and Manuel Barrera, eds., *Sindicatos bajo regimes militares: Argentina, Brasil, Chile* (Santiago: CES, 1990); Paul Drake and Iván Jaksíc, *The Struggle for Democracy in Chile* (Lincoln: University of Nebraska Press, 1992).

64 James Petras, *Democracy and Poverty in Chile: The Limits of Electoral Politics* (Boulder: Westview Press, 1994); Cathy Schneider, *Shantytown Protests in Pinochet's Chile* (Philadelphia: Temple University Press, 1995).

65 In 1984 and 1986 the Confederación Nacional de Campesinos, an umbrella organization of Chile's five major campesino confederations, held national meetings on the importance of organizing rural women and temporeras.

66 Adding to the political urgency for worker mobilization, in 1989 fruit workers faced particular hardship when U.S. allegations that a grape imported from Chile contained cyanide resulted in a U.S. ban on Chilean fruit and consequent unemployment for temporeras/os. The military regime's inability to successfully resolve this crisis only added to its illegitimacy. Falabella, "Historia del Santa María sindicato inter-empresa."

67 The nonprofit organization La Casa del Temporero was a worker education project funded by the Inter-American Foundation and directed by Gonzalo Falabella, a member of the Pro-Democracy Party, a "reformed" off-shoot of the Allende-era Socialist Party.

68 Falabella, "Historia del Santa María sindicato inter-empresa"; Falabella, "Organizarse y sobrevivir"; interview with Gonzalo Falabella, Santiago, March 1992; interview with Padre Vicente, San Felipe, 14 November 1992; Santa María Sindicato Inter-Empresa de Trabajadores Permanentes y Temporeros, "Registro de miembros de la directiva."

69 Falabella, "Historia del Santa María sindicato inter-empresa"; Falabella, "Organizarse y sobrevivir."

70 Various oral interviews, including Sonia Gutiérrez, Santa María, 14 June 1993; María Galdámez, Santa María, 22 November 1992; Elena Muñoz, Santa María, 22 November 1992; Anita Hernández, Santa María, 4 October 1992; author's notes from meetings of the union executive committee, June and July 1991; February–December 1992.

71 In 1999, the official monthly minimum wage in Chile was 84,000 pesos or $162. Temporera piece rates are tied to the minimum wage, and, since working overtime is the norm, temporeras often make above the minimum wage during the two–three month harvest season. In 2002 the minimum wage was set at 111,000 pesos or $159 a month. Temporeras in Aconcagua told Peter Winn that they could earn monthly wages as high as 200,000 pesos ($286).

72 Since 1990 state-sponsored housing programs have encouraged home ownership. Applicants for housing put down a given sum of money (based on the size of the lodging and family income) and are awarded a state subsidy with which to purchase a home, which is built either directly by state agencies or, as is more common, by private contractors working with the state. According to government records, between 1990 and 1998 the state allotted over 500,000 such housing subsidies in rural and urban areas and directly built 120,000 new units (Chile: Balance, 1998, Secretary of Communication and Culture, Ministry of Government, Santiago, 1998).

73 Nuevo Codigo de Trabajo (Santiago: Ediciones Publiley, 1991, 1993).

74 Interview with Oscar Valladares and Daniel San Martín, officers of the confederation Unidad Obrero Campesino, Santiago, 20 July 1999.

75 In 2002 temporeros reported that the minimum wage was 111,000 pesos per month, while some temporeras reported earning as much as 200,000 pesos monthly. I thank Peter Winn for sharing with me his July 2002 interviews with Aconcagua temporeras.

76 In 1999 newspapers reported official unemployment rates in the Fifth Region (including the Aconcagua Valley) at hovering between 13 percent and 18 percent, the highest in the country. This crisis affected not only agriculture but also industries and port-related services in Valparaíso (El Mercurio, 14 July 1999, 4; La Nación, 14 July 1999, 3).

77 Sucro's more independent line stems from the Communist party's refusal to join the Concertación and its self-positioning as a loyal but critical opposition on the left.

78 Author's notes from "El Primer Encuentro Nacional de la Mujer Temporera," sponsored by the Comisión Nacional Campesina at Canelo de Nos, Santiago, Chile, 6–8 June 1993.

79 Author's notes from the National Congress of the United Chilean Campesino and Ethnicities Movement (Mucech), Santiago, September 1997.

80 In addition to the high profile enjoyed by the Santa María union at events sponsored by the labor movement, it is frequently the subject of occasional journalistic reports on the fruit industry. See La Tercera, 4 January 1998, 10–12; La Cuarta, 31 October 1997, 11; La Cuarta, 20 October 1997.]

81 Interview with Daniel San Martín, UOC, Santiago, 5 September 1997.

82 Interview with Olga Gutiérrez, Mucech, Santiago, 8 September 1997.

83 Several authors have argued that, although women had a significant presence in South American prodemocracy movements of the 1980s, following the transition to civilian rule, the political parties marginalized women's issues and failed to support significant female leadership within political parties and the government following the return to civilian rule. See various articles on Chile and other countries in Jane Jaquette, ed., *The Women's Movement in Latin America: Feminism and the Transition to Democracy* (Boston: Unwin and Hyman, 1989); and Jane Jaquette, ed., *The Women's Movement in Latin America: Participation and Democracy* (Boulder: Westview Press, 1994).

84 For the most recent evaluation of rural gender roles and temporeras' subjectivities in the 1990s, see Ximena Valdés, *Vida privada: Modernización agrícola y modernidad* (Santiago: CEDEM, 1998).

RACHEL SCHURMAN

Shuckers, Sorters, Headers, and Gutters: *Labor in the Fisheries Sector*

Angélica Rivera's story

It was still dark outside. Angélica rolled over in her warm bed, listening to the raindrops hit the tin roof of her three-room house on the island of Chiloé. Slowly, she dragged her tired, 52-year-old body out of bed. "It's time to get up," Angélica called to her children, as she searched for dry wood for the stove. She was trying to ignore the pain in her legs from being on her feet all week, filleting thousands of pounds of fish. At least tomorrow was Sunday, and she would have a day of rest.

As she heated water for coffee, her two daughters, Julia and Inés, came out of the bedroom, dressed in thick, handknit sweaters and several pairs of wool socks—their only protection against the cold and humidity of the plant. "Are you ready, vieja?" Julia asked her mother, worried about the time. Every morning at six, they would walk down the hill from Fátima, the biggest shantytown in Ancud, to wait for the bus. Missing it would mean losing half their monthly "attendance bonus," a hefty chunk of their salaries.

Life was so different now, Angélica thought to herself as she hurried out the door after her daughters. Both she and her husband, Juan José, had been born on a small island a few hours away by boat. Their families had had small farms, where they grew potatoes, wheat, and oats, and raised a few animals, both for themselves and for the market. But it wasn't really worth producing anything to sell anymore after the dictatorship got rid of the cooperatives and cut back all support to small farmers. Prices were so bad there was no reason to bother. Now the only way to survive was to try to find a job as a fisherman or in a "pesquera."

The screeching brakes of the bus brought Angélica back to reality. Soon, she would file into the plant with two hundred other compañeras, pick up her mask, knife, and apron, and take her place at the conveyer belt. With a sigh, Angélica stopped daydreaming. Last time she let her mind wander, she had almost lost a finger.[1]

During the Pinochet period, the Chilean fishing industry experienced a dramatic boom. Encouraged by changes in government policy, scores of savvy capitalists came into the fresh and frozen seafood sector and began shipping fish and shellfish to consumers in East Asia, Western Europe, and North America. Others invested in the fishmeal industry, renovating existing processing plants or building new ones. Between the mid-1970s and the mid-1990s, the number of fish-processing plants in the country grew from about 75 to well over 400,[2] with seafood exports coming to account for 12 percent of the country's total export earnings. As processing plants sprung up from Arica in the north to Punta Arenas in the south, some 32,000 people went to work as clam shuckers and sorters and fish headers and gutters, and even more went to work as fishermen.[3] According to a recent estimate, the fishing sector now provides about 200,000 direct jobs.[4]

One of these new fishery sector workers was Señora Rivera. Upon entering a fish-processing plant, she became part of the new export-oriented workforce in Chile—a group comprised heavily of women, residents of small cities and towns, and former campesinos and agricultural workers. Pulled out of their homes (if they were women) and pushed out of traditional agriculture and other economic activities (if they were men) by the widespread changes taking place in the economy, these workers and their families became economically dependent on jobs in the rapidly growing fisheries export industry.[5]

This chapter describes the conditions and changing situation of three groups of fisheries sector workers—fishermen, seafood-processing workers, and salmon farm workers—in the Lakes Region of the country. Located in the south-central part of Chile, some 700 miles south of Santiago and approximately the same distance north of Tierra del Fuego, the Lakes Region is one of Chile's primary shellfish- and fish-producing regions. At the beginning of the 1990s, it contained 30 percent of the nation's seafood-processing plants, was home to approximately 22,000 fishermen and seafood-processing plant workers, and produced virtually every kind of fisheries export available in Chile, with the exception of fish oil.[6] Originally based on wild fisheries, an increasing share of the industry is now accounted for by salmon aquaculture.

To understand the fate of these different industry workers during and after the dictatorship, it is necessary to closely examine the political economy and ecology of the industry.[7] At different moments in the industry's history, fishermen, seafood-processing workers, and salmon farm workers fared better or worse, depending on the abundance of natural resources, the balance of power between labor and capital and the specific relations of production in each subsector, state policies governing the labor market, and industry conditions at the international level. In the initial phase of the boom (circa 1975–87), draconian labor market policies, a weak economy, and a repressive state combined to create a situation in which processing plant owners could take extreme advantage of their workers. From the mid-1970s until the end of the 1980s, workers in the processing plants earned miserably low wages, toiled under conditions reminiscent of the industrial revolution, and were hired and fired at will, depending on their employers' needs and the availability of raw material. Despite the fact that many firm owners in the processing sector were earning huge profits, they shared little with the workers in their factories.

The economic situation of those who harvested raw material for the industry—that is, fishermen and shellfishermen—was considerably better, because of the relations of production that existed in this subsector. Fishermen and shellfishermen were independent workers who merely sold their catch to the processing plants; this meant that the incomes they earned, and the conditions they worked under, were largely determined by the availability of resources and the market for raw material supplies rather than by the processing plants. In the initial phase of the boom, when wild fishery stocks were abundant and competition for raw material among processing plants was fierce, resource harvesters were able to capture a portion of the resource rents in the industry, which bolstered their incomes. Their working conditions were comparatively good because there were still so many fish and shellfish in the sea.

Toward the end of the 1980s conditions in both the industry and the country as a whole changed substantially. General Pinochet lost his grip on power, workers began to organize, and the economy started to grow rapidly. The last of these phenomena created a situation of tight labor markets, which slightly shifted the balance of power away from processing plant owners and toward processing plant workers. In this second phase of the industry's development, plant workers succeeded in improving their wages and working conditions. Yet at this very same moment, two unanticipated problems appeared. One was a crisis in international markets, which put a downward pressure on seafood prices. The second was resource degradation. Virtually uncontrolled exploitation of the natural resource base for over a decade had seriously reduced the stocks of the region's key commercial species, leading to falling catches for fishermen and rising costs for fishermen and for seafood processors. As the earnings of both groups fell, many fishermen left the sector and processing plants went out of business. If not for the fact that the wild fisheries sector happened to be located where another new industry—salmon aquaculture—was just getting under way, thousands of seafood-processing workers also would have been out of job. Fortunately for the latter group, the growth of the aqua-culture sector acted as a life preserver.[8]

The third phase of the industry's development, which began around 1992 and has continued to the present, has been marked by the decline of the wild fisheries and the rapid growth of salmon aquaculture. Salmon aquaculture is not subject to the same sort of resource limitations that wild fisheries are and thus has the potential to be more sustainable, at least in terms of resource supply. And to a large degree, the salmon industry *has* provided a more stable employment alternative to the wild fisheries, at least for processing plant work-ers and those hired to work in the region's new salmon farms. But as we move into the 21st century, the future of even *these* workers has begun to look less secure and promising, as the salmon industry has revealed its own vulnerabili-ties to a multifaceted set of structural and conjunctural pressures. One struc-tural threat derives from the remarkable growth that salmon aquaculture has experienced globally over the last 10 years—a trend to which the Chilean sal-mon industry has contributed heavily. As Chilean salmon producers doubled, trebled, and then quadrupled their production, salmon and trout exports from Chile helped to create a serious glut on world markets—a glut that has driven down prices and increased competition for all participants in the global sal-mon market. Moreover, Chile's meteoric rise as a salmon producer has elicited a highly negative reaction from other national salmon industries, several of which have responded by bringing expensive and industry-damaging "anti-dumping" suits against Chilean producers. A third source of threat to the industry is environmental. While the development of aquaculture effectively loosened one environmental constraint on the fisheries sector (that of limited resource supply), it simultaneously exposed the industry to another—namely, the problem of infectious diseases, organic "pollution," and other environ-mental risks associated with large-scale industrial monoculture. Although the industry has yet to be devastated by disease or ecosystemic changes, it has suffered some acute mortality losses due to diseases and algae blooms and will inevitably experience new challenges in the future. All of these pressures and threats throw into question the long-term fate and security of Chile's aqua-culture sector workers.

A typical day in the Lakes Region begins with a light drizzle, works its way up to a steady rain that bounces off the rooftops like an infinite succession of tiny pebbles, pauses for a time while the sky looms solemn and gray, and then starts to downpour just as one decides that the coast is clear enough to go out. When the weather finally does break (it may be weeks, in the winter), the clouds lift to reveal a chain of snowcapped volcanoes and the Andes mountains to the east, and the Pacific Ocean to the West. The air at such moments is cool and fresh, and the skies, a celestial shade of blue. Rolling hills, once covered by dense redwood, oak, and cedar forests, mark the countryside, and cows graze idly, enjoying the cool, moist air and lush green grass that blankets the hills. The deep blue sea extends as far as the eye can see, filling the lungs, heart, and soul.

The fishing boom in the Lakes Region was concentrated around the city of Puerto Montt and the archipelago of Chiloé, an area that houses some of the richest shellfishing and fishing grounds in the country. Protected to the north by southern Llanquihue province, to the east by the grand island of Chiloé, and to the west by continental Chiloé, locos (a carnivorous gastropod sold as a substitute for abalone), a large variety of clam, mussel, and crab species, sea urchins, scallops, oysters, and a giant barnacle called the picoroco populate the calm interior waters of the Reloncavi Sound and the Gulfs of Ancud and Corcovado. Numerous species of bottom fish, including conger eel, several kinds of hake, rock cod, and sea bass, also swim near the ocean floor. Although local fishermen have exploited some of these species commercially for over a century (and they have represented a source of subsistence for local dwellers for many more), it was only in the 1980s that their harvest and trade became a major source of foreign exchange for Chile, connecting the once isolated archipelago of Chiloé with some of the largest commercial centers (Tokyo, Madrid, New York) in the world.

The boom in the export-oriented seafood industry commenced in the mid-1970s, largely in reaction to a new set of state policies.[9] Among the most important was the "apertura," or the dismantling of the country's tariff and nontariff trade barriers. The apertura ended the protection of the domestic economic sector, which reduced the profitability of firms producing for the national market. Soon after seizing power, the Pinochet government also initiated a series of currency devaluations that drove the real value of the peso substantially below its predictatorship levels, making Chilean exports significantly more competitive on international markets.[10] In the context of the apertura and strong international demand for Chile's products, this exchange rate devaluation created enormous profit-making opportunities in the export sectors, since labor and raw material could now be acquired very cheaply with pesos, and transformed into commodities that sold at high prices to customers with yen, franks, and dollars. The new economic opportunities that resulted—both real and perceived—served as a strong inducement to investors.

One of the first groups to establish a seafood-processing company in the area was the Infante family, headed by a father-and-son team of civil engineers from Santiago. As Eduardo Infante tells the story, he and his father firmly believed there were a lot of opportunities in the area.

> There was labor, there was financing, there was raw material . . . everything but good investment ideas. That year [1975] there was an export opening which was being promoted by the government. But we still had a bad financial situation, and . . . interest rates were high. Most people were gambling with the short-term financial markets, and there wasn't a lot of interest in productive projects. We began to offer our ideas, but no one was interested. So in the end we did it ourselves, with the little capital that we had. We began to form some companies and get involved in our projects as businessmen.

Joining them was Carlos Castaing, the owner of a small construction company from neighboring Osorno, and Luis Ritter, a doctor in the area. Both knew a good deal when they saw it and quickly moved to set up seafood-exporting companies in Puerto Montt. By their own accounts, none of these entrepreneurs knew anything about the business when they started. What they *did* know was that buying, processing, and selling seafood overseas would prove to be a very profitable endeavor.[11]

Shortly after these early entrants made their debut in the business, scores of others followed suit. In fifteen years' time the number of plants authorized to process fish and shellfish in the region rose from 12 to 112, an increase of over 800 percent. The growth in processing plants (*pesqueras*) had a powerful effect on the demand for fish and shellfish, as well as on the need for labor. With the explosion of new seafood-exporting businesses, the number of fishermen quadrupled and the number of plant workers rose from fewer than 650 workers in 1968 (the last preboom year for which data are available) to over 6,600 in 1989.[12] The seafood-processing industry became one of the largest industrial employers in a booming region, engaging one out of every three industrial workers.[13]

The Workers

Who were the people that met the needs of these seafood-processing and exporting enterprises? In the case of the harvesting sector, some came from families that engaged in shellfishing or fishing for all or part of their living. In the decades before the boom, their fathers would sell their catch to the handful of local shellfish canneries in Calbuco or to seafood merchants from Santiago. Another large group came from the traditional agriculture sector, which had experienced two major upheavals in the preceding twenty years.

The first took the form of a radical land reform program implemented by the Frei and Allende governments in the 1960s and early 1970s. During land reform, most of the country's big agricultural estates were expropriated, which "freed" a large number of landless agricultural laborers from the land. Those who did not receive land moved into nearly villages and towns to become part of the agricultural proletariat that eventually found its way into the fishing sector.[14] An agricultural support program to help the country's small-scale producers accompanied land reform. Among other things, this program extended technical assistance and a subsidized credit system to small farmers and created a state marketing board to buy their output.

When the Pinochet government came to power, however, it reversed the land reform and dismantled the agricultural support system on the grounds that these policies were inefficient. In this second major upheaval, the withdrawal of government support from small-scale farmers pushed these farmers back into subsistence farming or into other economic activities, such as fishing.

Children of the urban proletariat represented the third major source of new fishermen and shellfishermen. Among this group were sons of carpenters, woodcutters, furniture makers, public servants, mattress makers, night watchmen, daily laborers, painters, sales clerks, barbers, bakers, sailors, and others. If their mothers also worked outside the home, it was most often as domestic servants, although a few had mothers who were secretaries or teachers.[15] This group was attracted to fishing by the promise of a higher income, fueled by a few exaggerated success stories of those who had made a (small) fortune.

Workers in the processing plants had similar social origins. The majority came from the urban proletariat and from agriculture, particularly if they were from Chiloé (see table 1). About two-thirds were women. Of these, over half had not been in the labor force during the previous five years but instead had worked at home, raising their families (see table 2). They came out of their homes because their families were in dire economic need.

Such was the case with Nancy Torres Sanhueza. From the time she was

Table 1. Social Origins of Plant Workers in the Lakes Region (% distribution)

Social Origins	Total	Chiloé	Mainland
Proletarian/subproletarian	45.3%	31.2%	59.2%
Peasantry with land	28.6	42.5	14.8
Peasantry without land	9.9	12.5	7.4
Artisan or trades	6.2	5.0	7.4
Petty bourgeoisie	5.0	3.8	6.2
Fishermen	2.5	3.8	1.2
Professional	0.6	0.0	1.2
Unknown	1.9	1.2	2.5
TOTAL	100.0%	100.0%	99.9%

Source: Author survey of 161 plant workers in the Lakes Region, conducted in 1991.

seventeen, Señora Torres worked as a domestic for a Puerto Montt family. In 1964, at age 31, she got married and quit her job so she could take care of her new baby. For the next decade and a half she stayed at home, raising seven children. But in 1980 her husband, an independent carpenter, lost his steady job, and could not find another. She returned to the workforce and was still there in the early 1990s, when I met her. Of the 11 persons in her household (three of whom are men), Señora Torres was the primary breadwinner. This process of women entering the labor force because their partners were unable to earn a living wage was generalized throughout Chile, as studies of the fruit sector also reveal.[16]

Women such as Señora Torres perceived their incorporation into the seafood industry in positive as well as negative terms.[17] On the one hand, they saw the pesqueras as a relatively attractive new source of employment. It offered more pay and more respect than their main alternative, domestic service, and increased their sense of autonomy from husbands, fathers, and boyfriends. As one woman worker reflected, "Now I have my own money, and I can buy things for myself, and my children. I decide what to do with my own money. I do not have to be asking him [her husband] for money. Before when I asked him . . . there was sometimes no problem, but you know, you feel better when you know he is not maintaining you."[18]

In the words of another: "A woman [today] will not allow herself to be slapped or anything like that, because one has one's work and can live from

Table 2. Prior Occupation of Seafood-Processing Plant Workers (% distribution)

	Women (n = 124)	Men (n = 37)
Not in labor force	57.3%	24.3%
Ever before	37.9	24.3
In previous 5 years	19.4	0.0
In labor force	42.7	75.6
As maid	24.2	0.0
As hotel/restaurant worker	6.5	2.7
As salesperson	5.6	13.5
In government public works program	4.0	8.1
Unemployed	0.0	10.8
Fishermen	0.0	8.1
Construction	0.0	5.4
Transport	0.0	5.4
Other	2.4	21.6
TOTAL	100.0%	99.9%

Source: Author survey of 161 plant workers in the Lakes Region, conducted in 1991.

one's work. You see that on your own you can move up and have a better life. It's better to be alone than to be fighting."[19]

But while women clearly enjoyed some benefits from going to work in a seafood plant, they also paid a high price for increased economic independence and "freedom." The responsibility for childrearing, grocery shopping, meal preparation, laundry, and housework fell almost exclusively on their shoulders, a situation that did not change significantly when they entered the paid labor force. Carrying out all these tasks successfully and working a 10- to 12-hour day was simply impossible for most. Something had to give, be it maintenance of the household, one's relationship with one's compañero, or time with children. The guilt associated with failing to meet all these responsibilities only added to their burden. In short, these women experienced the same kind of contradictory and complex effects of capitalist industrial development that Aihwa Ong, Helen

Safa, and Diane Wolf identify in their respective studies of women factory workers in Malaysia, the Dominican Republic, and Indonesia.[20] While gaining a certain degree of freedom, autonomy, and respect (both from themselves and from others) as a result of their jobs, adding a second shift brought new pressures, stress, and physical and emotional exhaustion into their lives. Moreover, it in no way countered the fact that they (like men) were extremely exploited by their employers, as we will see below.

Winners and Losers

Throughout the years of the boom, the biggest winners were without doubt the owners of the seafood-processing plants. Although there is no way to directly measure the income shares going to firm owners, independent fishermen, and seafood-processing plant workers, several data sources provide us with a sense of how well different groups fared. According to interviews with seafood-processing plant owners in the early 1990s, annual returns on investments in loco and southern hake exports were on the order of 50 percent or higher during the early years. Several processing plant owners proudly revealed that they had built and equipped their large, modern plants with a year or two's worth of profits from loco sales, and one individual confessed that he had recouped his $200,000 investment "in a week," thanks to his good timing in establishing a processing plant. Others compared the experience to "ganando la Polla Gol," or winning the lottery—a telling statement, by any measure. Although latecomers did not realize such handsome returns, this group as a whole enjoyed the lion's share of the income generated by the industry.

One of the largest hake processor-exporters in the region, Jorge Miragallo, explained what made his business so profitable in the mid-1980s.[21] At the time (in 1983), the price of raw material (fresh hake) was about $1.00 per kilo, while his sales prices averaged about $4.00 per kilo. Labor, packaging, and other processing costs typically added another 60 cents per kilo, bringing total variable costs to about $1.60 per kilo. From the remaining $2.40, fixed costs of overhead, debt, and administration, which represented about 20 percent of the sales price, had to be subtracted. This yielded a profit rate of about 40 percent.

Even in 1987, although on their way down, hake exports were still generating significant profits for firm owners, as the information provided by another company, SeaHorse Exports, suggests.[22] Total direct costs of production for SeaHorse Exports in 1987 for two types of hake preparations were $1.07 per kilo and $1.40 per kilo respectively, for products that fetched $1.79 and $2.65 on the market. This yielded margins over direct costs of 41 percent and 47 percent.

Table 3. Annual Net Earnings of Shellfishermen in the Lakes Region, by Port and Year (in U.S. dollars of each year)

Job and Port	1985	1986	1987	1988	1989	1990	1991
Boat and gear owners							
Carelmapu	3,285	2,560	5,924	3,063	2,113	3,121	2,865
Ancud	2,061	2,145	6,343	2,369	1,541	2,083	2,124
Divers							
Carelmapu	1,643	1,280	2,962	1,531	1,056	1,561	1,432
Ancud	1,030	1,073	3,172	1,184	770	1,042	1,062
Divers' assistants							
Carelmapu	1,095	853	1,975	1,021	704	1,040	955
Ancud	515	536	1,586	592	385	537	·531

Source: Corfo/Ifop, Diagnóstico de las principales pesquerías nacionales bentónicas, III–IV y X Región, 1988.

This particular company had high indirect costs, however, which included an extremely well-paid management. Once these indirect costs were factored in, net profits for these products fell considerably, but SeaHorse Exports still managed to earn a total of more than $1.7 million in profits, indicating an average profit margin of 18 percent over sales.

A second group that benefited economically from the seafood sector's growth was fishermen. Fishermen managed to do well because they were independent operators who owned their own boats and gear (or shared ownership with a partner) and sold their catch to the processing companies. Thus, whenever their costs were lower than their revenues, they were able to turn a profit.

This was the case throughout most of the eighties, for two reasons. One was that at the beginning of the boom, fish and shellfish were plentiful, which meant that catches were high. Added to this was the fact that the market for fish and shellfish was competitive and became more so over time as additional processing firms entered the sector. Competition worked to the benefit of fishermen because the more processing firms there were trying to buy raw material, the higher was the price that fishermen could charge for their catch. In effect, the presence of such competition shifted the resource rent away from the processors and toward the fishermen. Even fishermen who did not own a boat

Table 4. Comparative Annual Income from Alternative Sources

Average earnings in agriculture (assuming 6–7 months of work per year)

1987	$392
1988	$462
1989	$574
1990	$623

Official minimum wage (annualized)

1985	$504
1986	$480
1987	$564
1988	$636
1989	$756
1990	$888
1991	$1,032

Sources: Ignacio Molina, "X Region: 1989." *Informes de Coyuntura.* No. 2. Grupo de Investigaciones Agrarias: Santiago, 1990; Instituto Nacional de Estadísticas.

and its gear but simply worked as crew members fared well because their pay system was based on the system of shares.[23]

Data collected by the national Fisheries Development Institute (Ifop) provide evidence that the region's fishermen made a comparatively good income from fishing. According to these data, the incomes earned by people who owned a shellfishing boat and equipment ranged from $2,113 to $5,924 in the port of Carelmapu, and from $1,541 to $6,343 in the port of Ancud, depending on the year (see table 3). If that same individual was also a diver or diver's assistant, which was typically the case, he would receive an additional income share. In the case of a shellfish boat owner-diver working out of Ancud in 1988, for example, earnings would have been about $3,500 for the year. That same year, the average annual earnings of an agricultural worker in the region were about $462, while the official minimum wage was $636 (see table 4).

Although the seafood sector was extremely profitable for processing plant owners and generated a relatively good living for fishermen, the wages of workers in the processing plants did not reflect the tide of industry prosperity. By all accounts, the earnings of these workers were uniformly abysmal. As late as 1987, for example, the wage for an unskilled worker was still only about $85.00 a month (or $1,020 a year) and that included overtime.[24] A kilo of bread cost about 50 cents at the time; a kilo of lamb chops, about $2.00; a large can of

Nescafé, $3.75; and a cheap pair of children's shoes, about $10.00.[25] If a family of six with two income earners bought the necessary 45 kilos of bread for the month, four kilos of meat (one per week), two cans of coffee, and one pair of children's shoes, it would have had only $75.00 left over to pay for the rest of its food, housing, electricity, and clothes each month. Clearly, most seafood work-ers' wages did not come close to approaching the cost of living.

Even employers in the sector readily admitted the insufficiency of their work-ers' wages. In the course of our conversations, seafood plant owners frequently told me, "La mano de obra no cuesta na' en Chile" (Labor doesn't cost anything in Chile.)[26] Despite this admission, employers showed no interest in trying to improve their workers' salaries.

The Source of Low Wages

Wages were low for a number of reasons. The most obvious was the fact that workers had no bargaining power to command higher wages from their em-ployers. State repression of labor unions following the 1973 coup was severe, and workers in the seafood sector, as in the rest of the country, were afraid to organize in such a hostile climate. Although a couple of plants were organized in the early eighties, these were the exceptions rather than the rule. "There used to be a union here, but the plant owner threw the union organizer out and the union disappeared," confided one worker from a plant in Chiloé. "Nobody complains now because we would be fired."

The terrible economic situation at the time added to workers' sense of fear and insecurity. While stimulating considerable investment in the export-oriented fishing, forestry, and fruit sectors, the apertura had a highly contractionary effect on other parts of the economy. Hundreds of manufacturing and other firms closed down in the late 1970s when the economy was opened up, which greatly reduced people's chance of finding employment.[27] The recessions of 1975 and 1982–83 exacerbated the apertura's negative employment impacts. National unemployment rates climbed from less than 5 percent in 1973, to 14 percent in 1975, to over 19 percent in 1982. Not until 1988 did they come back down below 10 percent.[28]

Reflecting these political and economic phenomena, almost no one in the sector dared organize. Indeed, as late as 1997, union organizers in the seafood-processing sector complained that it was hard to get workers to fight for their rights. As one lamented, "We've got 17 years of dictatorship weighing on us. The people are afraid and they don't [want to] say anything [about their conditions]."[29]

Even if more workers had been willing to run the risk of organizing, there were institutional obstacles to doing so. The labor law put in place by the Pinochet government effectively discouraged unionization. The 1979 Plan Laboral, the centerpiece of the new legislation, allowed four different types of unions to form (firm-level unions, interfirm unions, unions of independent workers, and unions of construction workers), but of these, only firm-level unions could negotiate legally on their members' behalf. Sector-level collective bargaining was expressly prohibited, and the labor law excluded certain groups—most importantly, temporary workers—from collective bargaining altogether.[30] Until the mid-1980s, temporary workers represented a large proportion of the seafood-processing workforce.

For a short period, the new labor laws permitted employers to pay their workers only for the hours they worked, which also served to hold down workers' wages. Under the new regime, which prioritized "labor market flexibility," employers could shift the risk of bad weather or a bad catch onto workers by calling on them when they needed them, and sending them home without pay when they did not.[31] As one plant manager noted,

> We started processing only locos [in 1983] . . . and were able to get by for a year or two without any problem just doing that, because the labor law wasn't fixed. What would happen is that if they [the government] placed a ban on locos, we wouldn't pay anyone; we'd throw everybody out: 'Go home,' we'd say. 'You had a job until yesterday.' But then the law began to change, giving the workers more stability, which is logical. If I contract you, I can't say, 'One day yes, one day, no, and the next day, maybe.' I can't do it, not if you depend on me. But that's what we used to do, because the law allowed it.[32]

Other empresarios admitted that this was a common practice. "It's not like before, when you could contract people by the hour," lamented the owner of a large sea urchin concern in Puerto Montt, referring to the mid-1980s. "When there was raw material, people worked, and when there wasn't, you didn't pay them."[33]

Such laws, together with the clear antilabor political climate in the country, weakened plant workers in their dealings with employers. Chilean empresarios knew who was in the driver's seat during the Pinochet era. In the words of one seafood-processing firm owner, "We were put on a level that was almost superhuman. In this country there was nothing that the private businessman couldn't do; nothing that wasn't within [our] reach. To touch a sensitive chord of the entrepreneur was contradictory; because thanks to the push that we have given him, Chile is what it is today, from an economic point of view." Several others claimed that they never would have begun a business if "their president" had not been in power, ready to support them.[34]

Working Can Be Bad for Your Health[35]

Other than the smell, the first thing you notice when you walk into a seafood-processing plant is the temperature of the air. Low temperatures are vital for keeping the fish and shellfish from decaying too fast, and most phases of the production process must be done in what feels like a giant refrigerator. Part of the work involves frequent contact with cold running water, used to wash off blood and waste and to clean the raw material. These requirements of the labor process meant that many seafood sector workers spent their workday in a cold, wet atmosphere. This led to physical discomforts and in some cases, serious health problems, such as eye trouble or kidney disease.[36]

In most seafood-processing plants, workers stand on their feet all day carrying out repetitive motions, usually at breakneck speed. As Priscilla Délano notes in her study, in those seafood-processing plants that have semiautomated production lines, "women [have] to perform different tasks at [such] great speed . . . they can hardly blink."[37] This caused them to suffer from various physical ills. "We don't even feel our feet until we get home," one seafood worker lamented, "and then they are completely swollen."[38] Some workers complained that their backs started hurting before the week is halfway over. This was especially true for men whose jobs required heavy lifting.

Management carefully monitored workers' speed and productivity in most processing plants. Part of the monitoring took place through the piece rate system, which rewarded workers for the number of kilos, cans, or fillets of fish and shellfish they processed. Monitoring was also facilitated by the physical layout of the workplace. Workers typically stood in long lines or around large tables, with a "capataz" standing by and watching them closely. In the event that they were found to be "too slow," they would be publicly admonished—a practice many found humiliating.[39] In a space reminiscent of Foucault's panopticon, plant managers and foremen typically had their offices built high above the shop floor, where they could watch workers through large plate glass windows. Even when the foreman or boss wasn't looking, workers felt as if they were under constant surveillance. This sense of being monitored, both real and perceived, created a tremendous amount of stress among workers.

As specified by Chilean law, the official schedule in the industry was a six-day, forty-eight-hour work week. During the 1970s and most of the 1980s, however, most people worked more when there *was* work, either because they had to in order to make ends meet or because they feared losing their jobs if they didn't. Twelve-hour days were not uncommon in the industry, especially during high season, when large deliveries of raw material would arrive regularly. Whenever this happened, most production managers insisted that all the raw material be processed before their workers went home, since failure to quickly process these highly perishable goods could lead to economic losses.

Workers who did not want to stay were often pressured to do so, under threat of losing their jobs. In one sea urchin–processing plant in the town of Quellón, workers described how their manager used to lock them inside the plant overnight, forcing them to work around the clock so the urchins would not spoil.[40] "At night they would come looking for me to come back to the plant, after I had already worked for 10 hours," said one 22-year-old worker. "I only went back to work to avoid problems with the bosses, not for the money. If you didn't do them the 'favor,' they would treat you badly."

Many workers recounted the seemingly endless workdays they put in when the loco fishery boomed. One young woman described walking to work in the dark from her neighborhood on one side of the city of Ancud, to the plant on the other, only to return in the dark some 14 hours later:

> We'd get up at six in the morning—my sister, brother, mother, and I—so we could get to the plant by eight. Then we would come home at 11 or 12 at night, on foot. They gave us permission to leave at 10 P.M. because if we left at midnight, we wouldn't have gotten home until one or two in the morning, and the next day we had to get up at six again. [It wasn't until] the next year [1987] that they gave us transportation. (Interview, Ancud, 1992)

Working such long hours, day after day, left people exhausted. Many workers described arriving at their homes absolutely exhausted, only to have to repeat the experience the next day.

Seasonal Labor Demand and Temporary Employment

Unlike most manufacturing and service-oriented industries, in which production is carried out more or less continuously, production in the seafood sector (as in many other nature-based industries) is inherently uneven because of its direct dependence on nature. Labor needs vary by season, as well as on a short-term and less predictable basis, depending on the weather, the size of the catch, and the luck of the fishermen.

This characteristic of fishing translated not only into the long hours of work just described, but also into a large number of seasonal jobs in the industry.

Most fishermen worked mainly in spring, summer, and fall when the fishing weather is best, and took a lot of time off in the winter, when the weather is far less hospitable. Workloads in the processing plants followed this seasonal rhythm.

Again, changes in the country's labor laws facilitated these particular work patterns.[41] Before 1973 several pieces of labor legislation had discouraged the use of temporary workers. Under legislation passed in the mid-1960s by the Frei government, for example, employees could not be fired without due cause, and when a worker *was* let go (justly or unjustly), significant severance costs had to be paid. Moreover, if a firm wanted to lay off more than ten workers in a single month, it had to obtain authorization from the Ministries of Labor and the Economy. Failure to do so resulted in the imposition of a fine and entitled workers to double the severance pay they would have received if the correct procedures had been followed.[42] When the Pinochet government came to power, it eliminated most of the financial disincentives associated with hiring temporary workers. For example, under a law known as D.L. 2200, it extended the maximum length of a temporary contract from six months to two years.[43] This same law also allowed employers to dismiss workers without statement of cause or appeal if the firm paid the worker the equivalent of one month of salary for each year worked (up to a maximum of five months)—another aspect of the prized "labor market flexibility."[44] The effect of these changes was to encourage the hiring of workers on a temporary basis.

The predominance of temporary contracts was not the only employment problem seafood-processing workers faced. Violations of the intent (and often the letter) of the labor law were also common. For example, even though D.L. 2200 was modified in 1981 so that temporary contracts could be renewed only once within a two-year period, many employers simply broke the law and hired workers on a "provisional" basis that lasted indefinitely. When it came time that the firm was legally obliged to make them into permanent workers, the worker would be fired, only to be rehired by the same plant a month later.[45] Employers' preference for temporary contracts translated into an extreme level of job instability and insecurity for seafood-processing workers during the Pinochet years.

In the latter part of the 1980s labor's fortunes in the seafood-processing plants started to change for the better. Between 1988 and 1992 real wages for seafood-processing plant workers rose 55 percent.[46] Other working conditions also improved as the decade began. Workers gained additional legal rights; employers became more reluctant to flagrantly violate labor laws; and certain unjust employment practices (e.g., intimidating workers into working overtime) became less common.[47] What led to these improvements?

Several factors were responsible. By far the most significant was the condition of the labor market. With the continued expansion of the fishing industry, local labor markets became increasingly tight. This was particularly true during the summer season, when labor demand was at its peak. Tight labor markets gave workers more bargaining power vis-à-vis their employers. If a firm wanted to attract and retain good workers, it had to offer better wages and working conditions. Workers began to base their decisions about where to work on the different working conditions firms offered.[48] The fact that they had a choice was indicative of the improved condition of the labor market.

Had the local labor market been the only one to expand, workers' situations might not have changed that much, since migration by workers from other regions who were looking for jobs probably would have grown to fill the demand. But this phenomenon was generalized throughout the country. Beginning in 1984 the Chilean economy entered into a period of rapid expansion that would last for 14 years. Virtually every sector of the economy grew, with the fastest growth rates in transport and communications, business, hotels and restaurants, and construction. The economy's new core productive sectors— fishing, forestry, fruit, and mining—stimulated a large group of linked activities, including input-supplying industries, industries based on the processing of primary products, and industries providing a wide variety of supporting services. Extensive forward and backward linkages developed around Chile's new export sectors to form a group of natural resource-based "production complexes" that rivaled the complexity of many consumer goods manufacturing sectors.[49]

The growth of the economy in general, and the development of these natural resource-based production complexes in particular, powerfully affected the demand for labor. Nationwide, employment rose almost 50 percent between 1985 and 1996, from 3.5 million workers to 5.3 million workers.[50] Over this same

Table 5. Unionization of Seafood-Processing Plants in the Lakes Region

Firm Name	Date Union Constituted	Number of Union Members
American Seafoods (Plant no. 1)	1987	150
Queitao Limitada	1987	43
Promex	1989	46
Pesquera Unichile	1989	120
Multiexport (Plant no.1)	1989	60
Conservamar	1990	72
Multiexport (Plant no. 2)	1990	61
American Seafoods (Plant no. 2)	1990	25
Pesquera Aguamar	1990	28
Pesquera Agroindustrial Santa Cruz	1990	37
Pesquera Unimarc	1991	63
Salmo Alimentos	1991	25
Pesquera Mares Australes	1991	182
Messamar	1991	226
Conservera Dalcahue	1992	25
Soc. de Alimentos Maritimos Avalos	1992	28
Pacifico Austral	1993	30

Source: Data provided to author by Señor Luís Rey, Dirección de Trabajo, Puerto Montt, Chile, 1994.

period, agriculture and fishing absorbed some 230,000 new workers; industry, another 373,600 workers; commerce, 279,500 workers; and services, 380,000 workers.[51] In 1992 national unemployment hit its lowest rate since the early seventies, a remarkable 4.4 percent.

While tight labor markets were the chief source of better wages and working conditions, they were not the only one. Emboldened by the new political space that opened up as the country neared its national plebiscite on whether General Pinochet should continue on as the head of state,[52] seafood-processing workers in the Lakes Region waged—and won—critical battles to form labor unions. As late as 1987 workers had only managed to organize themselves in two plants in the region; by 1991 however, workers had organized unions in 14 plants, and were in the process of organizing several more (see table 5).

Although the labor movement in the seafood-processing sector did not attain much real strength, it did bring tangible benefits to industry workers.[53] Among them was the shift to voluntary instead of forced overtime. While some managers in unionized plants still sought to intimidate workers into working overtime, unions managed to eradicate this practice in most plants. Unions also demanded an end to arbitrary firings and a more respectful treatment of workers. Finally, they managed to push up wages. While no union achieved glowing success in this regard, the average, non-overtime wage in unionized plants was about 12 percent higher than the wage in nonunionized plants.[54]

Another important factor that led to improved labor conditions was the decision of the Aylwin government in 1991 to make some small changes in the country's labor laws that contributed to better wages and working conditions. Although the central orientation of the labor market regime established by Pinochet was left intact—including its emphasis on "flexibility"[55]—the Aylwin government did reinsert a small modicum of worker protection against arbitrary dismissals into the law.[56] Other legal changes opened up the space for bargaining over a wider range of issues, gave unions the right to obtain information pertaining to the financial condition of the company, and augmented the legal sources of union funding.[57] Finally, Aylwin increased the real minimum wage by nearly 10 percent within a few weeks of assuming office. While most seafood-processing workers were already earning more than this, this gesture clearly had symbolic importance.

Not Enough Fish in the Sea

As anyone who works in the wild fisheries sector knows all too well, the long-term environmental—and economic—sustainability of this extractive activity depends on the continued abundance of fish. If fish or shellfish stocks are fished too hard, catches decline and costs of production rise. This is exactly what happened in the Lakes Region at the end of the eighties. Behind this phenomenon was the Pinochet government's decision to liberalize trade in the context of an open access resource and strong international demand. When trade barriers were lifted, it became so profitable to export fisheries products that too many fishermen and too many firms rushed in.

One piece of evidence that certain wild fishery stocks had been overfished came in the form of smaller catches in the best fishing locations. Fishermen who once enjoyed abundant catches of southern hake in the interior waters of the Reloncaví Sound found that they had to go farther and farther out to sea to keep their catch rates up. Many noticed the average size of the fish becoming smaller, another common indication of overfishing.[58]

Empirical studies conducted by the Fisheries Development Institute (Instituto de Fomento Pesquero, or Ifop) confirmed that local fish stocks were being overharvested as a result of the huge increase in fishing activity. According to two Ifop studies published in the early nineties, the biomass of southern hake (the most important fish species exploited in the region) fell by two-thirds between 1981 and 1991, from an estimated 525,000 tons to 178,000 tons.[59] Reflecting this decline (as well as growing demand in the exterior), raw materials prices for southern hake rose from 20 pesos per kilo in July 1980, to 140 pesos per kilo in 1987, to 220 in 1989, to over 630 pesos per kilo in September 1990. Even after adjusting these figures for inflation, the increase in hake prices paid by processors was on the order of 350 percent.[60]

A similar phenomenon occurred in the shellfish sector. In the first half of the eighties, the main extraction sites for shellfish were at 10 to 20 meters below the surface. At such shallow depths, almost anyone could don the requisite gear and, with a little bit of guts and practice, could make a good living. By the early nineties, however, these easily accessible shellfish banks were virtually exhausted. To catch enough to make the activity worthwhile, divers had to dive 30 to 50 meters below the surface to find banks that had not been severely exploited.[61]

Again, scientific studies conducted by Ifop confirmed the lived experience of shellfish divers. In 1991 Ifop researchers estimated that stocks of the clam known as *Venus antiqua*—one of the most heavily exploited shellfish species in the region—had fallen by over half in the Bay of Ancud between 1988 and 1990 (from 63,000 tons to 30,000 tons).[62] Stocks of other shellfish species were also shrinking. According to Ifop, the productivity of shellfishermen exploiting four out of five of the region's key shellfish species (sea urchins, hard clams, macha clams, and razor clams) fell during the second half of the 1980s.[63] Locos, the most heavily exploited shellfish resource in the region, were so seriously depleted in the 1980s that the Chilean government had to impose a complete ban on loco fishing.[64]

Resource degradation affected fishermen in several ways. As already noted, overfishing forced fishermen to go farther out to sea to make a good catch. This raised their costs and reduced their earnings, since now they had to pay more for fuel, oil, and other supplies. Longer trips translated into longer hours away from home and from their families. Fishing farther out at sea also made the work more dangerous, since fishermen were exposed to more inclement weather. It was difficult to get home quickly when the weather changed for the worse, which it often did. Shellfish divers began to dive deeper and deeper. At greater depths, the probability of "the bends" increased, since many threw caution to the wind in the scramble to keep yields up and did not take the time to allow their bodies to readjust to the changing pressure. As one 25-year-old diver from Chiloé described the dilemma, "Everybody knows you are supposed to wait ten minutes at each stage [every 10 meters], but if you wait this much time, and you are down fifty meters, it can take almost an hour to rise to the surface. Then you could only make two trips a day. So nobody does it."

On the docks it became common to see young men partially incapacitated from a bad diving experience; others had just died. Indeed, one of the most important acquisitions of the Ancud hospital in the 1980s was a decompression chamber for divers.

Exacerbating the problem of low catches for fishermen was a decline in the wholesale price of fish and shellfish. Typically when there is overfishing, dockside fish prices rise, as supply falls but demand stays the same. (Dockside prices are the prices received by fishermen.) Although this did occur for a short time, as noted above, higher prices didn't last. As it turned out, there was a recession and currency devaluation in Spain at the end of the 1980s, which was one of Chile's largest seafood markets. This meant that there were fewer consumers. At the same time, South Africa and Namibia greatly increased their supply of bottom fish to the market, which increased competition for customers.[65] Together, these two phenomena caused the wholesale price of shellfish and hake to fall in the early 1990s, to the detriment of fishermen's incomes. In the face of falling incomes, some fishermen decided to abandon fishing and look for another way to make a living.[66] Others stuck it out, waiting for their fortunes to improve. To date, they still have not done so.

PHASE THREE: THE RISE OF SALMON AQUACULTURE
(1992–PRESENT)

Under most scenarios, those who worked in the region's seafood-processing plants would also have been negatively affected by resource depletion, as fishermen started leaving the sector, and low or even negative profits led some processors to close their doors.[67] But processing plant workers in the Lakes Region were fortunate. Just when the wild fisheries sector entered a crisis, the salmon aquaculture industry appeared to save their jobs.

If the growth of the wild fisheries sector was impressive, the growth of the salmon industry was phenomenal—"dizzying" might be a better word to describe it. In the mid-1980s hardly any Chileans had heard of salmon farming, let alone considered investing in it.[68] Yet by 2001 Chile's farmed salmon and trout exports were worth $964 million, or over 5 percent of the country's total export earnings. The vast majority of salmon came from the Lakes Region, where a propitious combination of geographical features—deep glacial lakes, clean and protected inland seas, and perfect water temperatures—created some of the best salmon farming conditions anywhere in the world.

The boom in salmon production is reflected in available statistics on the volume of salmon exports. From a mere 1,645 tons in 1986, the Chilean salmon industry increased its export volume nearly 400 percent (to 8,000 tons) by 1989. Exports rose another 660 percent, to 61,000 tons, by 1993, and slightly more than doubled (to 135,000 tons) by 1996.[69] By 2001 total Chilean salmon and trout exports reached over 264,000 tons, making it the second largest salmon producer in the world.[70] The vast majority of Chile's salmon were farmed and processed in the Lakes Region.

As more and more firms began raising and processing salmon, the demand for labor rose. Workers who had been employed in plants dedicated to processing wild fish and shellfish easily made the switch to processing salmon and trout. In some cases, the move was a physical one—from a plant that had closed or cut back its production levels, to another that was expanding and adding production shifts to process more salmon. In other cases, workers stayed in the same plant and even worked for the same company, only now the company sold its processing services to the salmon industry. In a third group, the processing plant was taken over by a salmon company, and its workers were kept on. The salmon farms themselves, which came to number more than 100, also came to represent an important new source of jobs. Employment in the industry continued to grow, with salmon providing the impetus for expansion.

The Price of Success

Up until the late 1980s most of the world's salmon supply came from wild salmon fisheries located in Alaska, the Pacific Northwest, Canada, and Japan. Salmon supplies were limited by what could be caught during fishing season, which helped give salmon its luxury status and its correspondingly high price. But during the decades of the eighties and nineties, firms in Norway and Scotland, and later Chile and the United States, achieved enormous success with salmon farming and managed to raise their output dramatically. This massive increase in farmed salmon production produced a serious glut in world salmon markets, with negative implications for everyone involved.

The problem of market saturation was clearly reflected in the behavior of wholesale salmon prices. The wholesale price for coho salmon in Chile, which averaged $6.50 a kilo at the beginning of the 1990s, fell to about $4.00 in 1994. By the 1998 season, prices had fallen to $2.80 per kilo—or less than half of what they were in the second half of the 1980s.[71] Many accused the Japanese of purposely manipulating the market, which may have been true for this particular price fall, but the fact of the matter was that world salmon supplies were simply rising faster than demand, which favored buyers over sellers.

On the home front, Chile's salmon firms also had to contend with rising costs of production, an appreciating exchange rate, and a new "dumping" tariff imposed by the United States, the second largest importer of Chilean salmon.[72] During the 1990s, costs of production rose on virtually every front. The biggest concern for salmon producers was the rising price of salmon feed—the lion's share of a salmon farm's expenses. In Chile, salmon feed averages about 50–60 percent of production costs.[73] Although labor represented a much smaller fraction of costs, probably on the order of 10–15 percent, it too became progressively more expensive throughout most of the 1990s because of the pressure exerted by tight labor markets, changes in state policy, and a modicum of unionization in the seafood-processing industry. Capital costs were driven up by increased competition from other economic sectors and the country's burgeoning stock market.

Making matters worse, the Chilean salmon industry grew so fast and furiously that it started to be perceived as a major threat by salmon producers in other countries. Producers in the state of Maine and Washington were so affected by the new salmon supplies pouring into the country from Chile that they accused it of "dumping" its product on the U.S. market. In response, the U.S. Department of Commerce placed a countervailing duty on U.S. imports of Chilean Atlantic salmon, which in 2002, stood at 5 percent.[74] In fall 2002 Chilean producers were faced with the threat of a second antidumping suit, this time from European producers. If that lawsuit proceeds and is found in favor of the European Union, Chilean salmon producers could be facing a much larger tax on their exports to Europe, possibly reaching as high as 32 percent.[75] Even if that suit is not carried out, it is likely to impose high legal and public relations costs on the industry, as was the case for the previous antidumping suit, and for other unfair trade suits brought against Chile's "overly successful" new agro-food exporters.[76]

In the mid-1990s falling market prices, rising production costs, an appreciating peso, and new tariff barriers combined to create a serious "cost-price squeeze" in the industry. Although Chilean salmon farmers earned excess profits during the early years of the industry's existence, profits bottomed out around 1996 and never fully recovered.[77] This situation only grew worse during the Asian economic crisis, which seriously dampened demand for several years and then was followed by a more generalized worldwide economic recession. "We are down to the point where just a few cents makes all the difference, on the cost as well as the selling [price] side," observed the general manager of a large salmon firm. "In the old days, the margins were really quite big— everybody could make money, even if you were relatively inefficient. That is no longer the case. Our margins are very tight now."[78]

Economic Restructuring in the Salmon Sector

Beginning in 1996, in an effort to restore profits, Chilean salmon farmers began to change key aspects of their operations.[79] Both individually and collectively, they sought to raise demand for their products in the hopes of shoring up falling prices. Out of necessity, they transformed themselves into aggressive global marketers, traveling far and wide to seek out potential buyers. "In the past you sat here in your office, you produced your fish, you waited for people to come to buy, and you would deliver it," observed one salmon firm manager. "But today, Chilean producers all go to Japan to talk to their clients, to visit their facilities, to see what they do with their fish."[80] The industry also tried to stimulate demand within Chile, by increasing salmon shipments to Santiago and other national markets. While these efforts had some impact, national and world salmon supplies continued to rise far faster than demand, keeping a lid on prices.

Salmon firms also turned their attention to the production side, trying to cut costs in a variety of ways. Virtually all tried to increase their "feed conversion ratios"—the amount of salmon that can be produced with a set amount of salmon feed. As one firm manager described it, "Feed has a very significant impact on our costs. Before, if you had a conversion rate of two [two pounds of feed to one pound of salmon] you were satisfied. But today you have to get a conversion rate of 1.5 or less or you won't be happy." Toward the goal of wasting less feed, a few firms replaced manual with automatic feeding systems. Others attempted to make their operations more efficient by computerizing inventories and mechanizing parts of the production line, for example, by installing automated conveyor belts in the plants. Some bought machines that would clean and "deparasite" fish, or that could remove their scales and skins. As I argue below, such changes had mixed implications for labor.

Firms' efforts to lower production costs also took the form of exercising more careful control over the size and quality of the labor force. In the processing plants, managers sought to increase productivity by relying more heavily on piece rate systems, which tied worker productivity directly to earnings. By paying a worker for each salmon fillet she processes, the piece rate system encouraged workers to exert themselves more. Although there are no specific data for the salmon-processing industry, data for the seafood-processing sector as a whole indicate that productivity rose 38 percent between 1993 and 1995, providing strong evidence that industry workers were working harder even before the current crisis hit. (Real wages for this same period, by contrast, rose only 4 percent.)[81]

Managers in some plants also cut back on the number of workers they hired. "This year we are going to produce 20 percent more with 30 percent fewer workers," boasted the director of a large salmon farming company I interviewed in Puerto Montt in mid-1997. As they cut back, they took pains to identify and keep the most skilled and productive of their workers. "We can't keep saying to ourselves, 'I have one hundred manual laborers, and with those workers I am going to produce one thousand tons,' " claimed another salmon company manager. "You can't do it anymore because the price of salmon doesn't permit such a [high] level of inefficiency." This same individual explained that rather than hiring a lot of laborers to work in his company's aquaculture operations, his management strategy was to hire a smaller number of more qualified workers, even if he had to pay them more. "I can't give responsibility for [handling] 1,000 tons of fish to some unskilled worker," he noted. Managers of other companies expressed similar feelings.

Firms also sought to lower their costs by achieving greater economies of scale. Some companies bought out smaller processing plants and salmon farms, while others expanded production in their existing facilities.[82] By spreading their fixed costs over a greater quantity of production, these companies sought to reduce their unit costs of production. But while this solution made sense from an *individual* producer's perspective, it was irrational from an industry perspective because it led to *more* rather than less output. Such behavior only exacerbated the problem of declining prices and put the industry on a downward price spiral.[83]

Finally, firms made a major effort to increase the value they added to their products by selling processed salmon fillets, sushi cuts, and hand-processed smoked salmon to high-end, niche markets. Reflecting the success of this strategy, these "value added" products rose from a mere 5 percent of salmon exports in 1990 to 39 percent in 1996,[84] and have grown steadily since. In this sense, the salmon industry defies a major critical "structuralist" critique of natural resource exports, which is that natural resource-based activities are invariably low-productivity activities with limited potential for industrialization. (See, for instance, the arguments put forth by Raul Prebisch and his Cepal colleagues in the 1940s and 1950s.) Indeed, as I have argued elsewhere, the experience of the Chilean salmon industry suggests that natural resource industries can indeed be highly dynamic, and that the distinction between "stagnant" primary industries and "dynamic" secondary (manufacturing) industries has been seriously overdrawn.[85] This does not mean, of course, that nature-based activities do not present their own set of problems, as we will see shortly.

Implications for Fishery Sector Workers

The industrial restructuring processes described above have not brought many positive changes for salmon sector workers. Although employment in the industry as a whole has not exhibited any obvious decline (and may even have risen slightly, because of firms' efforts to resolve their problems by growing larger), the economic situation at the firm level has become much more competitive, causing companies to become much more concerned about productivity and wages, as noted earlier. The Lakes Region's salmon companies have been aided in their efforts to squeeze more out of their workers by prevailing economic conditions since the late 1990s. After the Asian market crashed in 1997, the outwardly oriented Chilean economy fell into a serious slump, resulting in a significant loosening of the labor market.[86] Unemployment went from 5 percent in the mid-1990s to 9 percent in 1999, where it has more or less remained to the time of this writing.[87]

Reflecting both of these phenomena—firms' greater sensitivity to production costs and a rise in national unemployment rates—workers' wages in the seafood-processing sector have leveled off. According to available data, the average monthly earnings of a Lakes Region processing plant worker in 2001 was about 120,000 pesos, compared to about 100,000 in 1997.[88] When adjusted for inflation, the real value of a worker's wage grew only 6 percent over the entire five-year period, or about 1.2 percent per annum.[89] (Recall that over this same period, the industry's output nearly doubled.) The general trend toward better working conditions and greater bargaining power have been similarly affected: compared to a period of small but significant improvements at the beginning of the decade, workers are again afraid to fight for their rights and to organize.[90]

Efforts to increase the productivity of labor by paying piece rates and/or simply increasing the pace of work have had mixed effects on workers. Paying workers by the piece has enabled some workers to significantly raise their take-home pay by working harder. Yet these workers have paid dearly with their bodies. As one processing plant worker put it, "You're earning money against your body, but after a while, your body collapses."[91] In industries that rely on assembly line production, as the seafood-processing industry does, increasing the work pace invariably has a negative impact on worker health and safety. Working with sharp knives at increasingly fast speeds has only made an already dangerous job even more dangerous.

Only skilled workers, for whom the labor market remains fairly tight, seem not to have been harmed by the industry's restructuring and may even have received a boost as the sector has grown in size and international stature. But the size of this group is small and promises to remain so in the future. The most highly "skilled" jobs in the salmon aquaculture industry are in management, finance, and disease eradication, and these jobs are limited in number.[92] Moreover, even as many salmon companies move toward staffing their grow-out operations with more highly skilled workers (as my interviews suggest they are doing), the salmon farms themselves do not employ that many people.[93] The bulk of the sector's employment is in fish processing, where unskilled workers outnumber their skilled counterparts by seven to one. Moreover, the limited historical data available on the seafood-processing industry suggest that there has been *no* trend toward using a more skilled workforce over time—an observation that also characterizes the forestry sector, as Thomas Klubock argues in his chapter in this volume.[94]

"Nature's Agency": New Environmental Threats
and the Salmon Industry

Although the shift to salmon aquaculture effectively resolves for seafood processor-exporters the problem of limited raw material supplies, the salmon industry's direct and continued dependence on a living biological resource renders it vulnerable to other environmental threats that will remain a continuing challenge for the sector. These include the industry's susceptibility to changes in environmental conditions and a wide variety of animal health risks. As the number of salmon farms and their production capacity and output have grown, the industry itself has profoundly affected the environment on which it depends to raise a healthy salmon "crop." One serious concern is the large amount of unconsumed food and salmon feces that have collected underneath the salmon pens, altering the oxygen content of the lakes in which the industry's grow-out operations are based, and potentially threatening farm productivity. According to one recent report, water quality is declining, which is in turn affecting the health of the fish.[95] Another major concern for the industry is algae or other plankton blooms, which reduce the oxygen content of water as they die, and can be fatal to fish. In the spring of 2002 a toxic algae bloom around the archipelago of Chiloé resulted in an estimated loss of 4 million pounds of salmon, worth several million dollars.[96]

Like any system of monocropping, salmon aquaculture is also vulnerable to the threat of pests and diseases, another expression of what William Cronon has referred to as "nature's agency."[97] Such pests and diseases can rapidly move through a farmer's (or even a whole region's) salmon pens, decimating part or all of the crop. In recent years the Chilean salmon industry has been afflicted by several major salmon diseases, including rickettsia (a disease that is specific to Chile), infectious pancreatic necrosis (IPN), and furunculosis.[98] In 1998 it appeared that a harmful new bacterium causing infectious salmon anemia (ISA) had entered the industry, possibly through salmon egg imports. At the time, an article in El Mercurio, Chile's leading newspaper, reported that more than 10 percent of the salmon population in southern Chile had been afflicted with ISA, which causes abdominal distension, internal hemorrhaging, physical deformities, and eventually, the death of the fish.[99] If this or any other disease were to spread rapidly, it could devastate the industry, and hence, employment in the sector, at least on a temporary basis.[100]

Although the Chilean salmon industry is no more vulnerable to the vagaries of nature than any other salmon industry elsewhere in the world, all nature-based industries face risks, surprises, and vulnerabilities that arise from their direct dependence on nature.[101] When these environmental risks and vulnerabilities are added to the already challenging economic conditions and low profit margins experienced by salmon producers worldwide, they create a situation of considerable risk and uncertainty, in which no company or industry can be said to be stable or even necessarily viable in the long term. Chile's "successful" integration into the new global economy on the basis of its natural resources has certainly had advantages for many entrepreneurs and workers, but it has also generated important new sources of vulnerability, deriving from exposure to world market competition, rapid price and market changes, and uncontrollable and unpredictable environmental threats, both alone and in combination. In countries in which labor is fully exposed to the market and cannot depend on the state for protection against such "natural" industry swings, we can expect workers to bear the brunt of these risks and vulnerabilities.

The last 25 years have been years of significant change for the workers in Chile's new export-oriented seafood industry. Due to tremendous structural changes in the economy, people were pushed out of one set of productive activities and pulled into another. For most workers in the industry, movement into the seafood sector was made not by choice, but by necessity. This did not mean that their situations did not improve with this occupational shift, for in some cases they did, and quite substantially. Those who benefited most from the change, at least in the short term, were independent fishermen and shellfishermen. While the resources were there and the demand for the catch was high, fishermen actually enjoyed quite a good living from fishing. Women also benefited in certain important ways from their access to new job opportunities and a new source of income.

Workers' fortunes in the industry rose or fell depending on the political economy and ecology of fishing, seafood processing, and later, salmon farming. The distinct experiences of different groups of workers were conditioned by their particular location in the industry, the ecological health of the fisheries, and conditions in the wild seafood and salmon aquaculture industries. The state of the Chilean economy also affected workers' experiences. During the first phase of the industry's development (the boom years), it was fishermen who enjoyed better salaries and working conditions; in the second phase and part of the third, it was seafood-processing workers.

State policies and practices on a number of different levels affected workers' fates in the industry. By opening the Chilean economy up to external trade, the macroeconomic policies of the Pinochet government both provoked the growth of the fishery sector (along with the fruit, forestry, and mining sectors) and helped contribute to the demise or restructuring of other productive sectors. By stimulating the export sectors, these policies tied the national economy much more closely to the global economy and to conditions in these global industries. In virtually every one of Chile's new export sectors, conditions became more competitive as new suppliers entered the market and world output grew.[102] This was clearly true in wild fisheries as well as in salmon aquaculture. After a brief period during which Chilean seafood-processing and salmon firms enjoyed immense comparative advantages (deriving from pristine environmental conditions and the low cost of labor), demand for their products fell and/or world markets become flooded and firms had to cut their costs and improve their efficiency in order to survive. These changes, which have taken a variety of forms and are still in the making, offered mixed results for seafood industry workers. The radical changes the Pinochet government made in Chile's labor market regime powerfully influenced the way industry workers experienced—and will continue to experience—these new local/global relations. Labor market flexibility, the central organizing principle of this new regulatory framework, was highly detrimental to seafood-processing workers. It allowed employers to impose the rhythms and shift the risk of nature-based production on to processing plant workers. Other elements of the new legislation made it far more difficult for workers to organize labor unions than in the past and thus to advance their own interests. Although the situation of organized labor improved after the transition to formal democracy, Chile's successive civilian governments did not reverse the laws that gave employers a high degree of flexibility. Perhaps even more important, just as the neoliberal architects of this legislation envisioned, neither the state nor labor unions are in a position to protect workers from changes in global industry conditions. In the case of Chile's natural resource industries—even those that might seem to be the most "sustainable"—nature's agency also plays a role in workers' increased economic vulnerability.

NOTES

1 Angélica Rivera is a fictional character whose story is a distilled collective biography of many of the women I interviewed for this study. For more on data and methods, see note 7.

2 Servicio Agrícola y Ganadero, *Anuario estadístico de pesca*, 1976 (Santiago: Ministry of Agriculture, 1976); Sernapesca (Servicio Nacional de Pesca), *Anuario estadístico de pesca*, 1995 (Santiago: Republic of Chile, 1996), 4. According to Sernapesca, there were 433 processing plants in Chile in 1995. My experience working with these data on a regional level suggests that these figures probably overestimate the real number of plants in operation by about 10 percent, when inoperative plants are discounted.

3 Employment in the fish-processing industry rose from 6,400 workers in 1975 to 17,400 in 1990, to 24,700 in 1995. By 1997, according to the Encuesta Nacional de la Industria Manufacturera, seafood-processing employment increased to 32,000 workers. The former figures include fishmeal and fish oil processing plants, and come from Instituto Nacional de Estadísticas (INE), *Anuarios de industrias manufactureras* (Santiago: INE, 1975, 1990, 1995). Data for 1997 are reported in Celina Carrasco et al., "Cultivando el mar: Para la calidad de las condiciones de trabajo," Cuaderno de investigación 13 (Organización Internacional del Trabajo: diciembre 2000), 29. The number of artisanal fishermen, which is the largest group of fishermen, increased from about 17,000 in 1975 to just under 39,000 in 1995 (Eduardo

Bitran, "Desarrollo y perspectivas del sector pesquero en Chile," working paper 7 [Santiago: Centro de Estudios de Desarrollo, October 1983]; and Sernapesca, *Anuario estadístico de pesca*, 1995, 2). I use the gendered term "fishermen" throughout this chapter because the vast majority of the people who work at sea are male.

4 Beatriz Corbo, "Cuotas pesqueras," op-ed column, El Mercurio, 12 July 1999, A-2.

5 The structural changes to which I am referring occurred between 1975 and 1985, and were the result of the "apertura," or opening up of the economy, and changes in government policy toward agriculture. These are discussed in more detail below. See also Klubock, this volume, for a more detailed discussion of how the rural peasantry was expelled from the countryside by the forestry policies of the dictatorship.

6 Sernapesca, *Anuario Estadístico de Pesca*, 1992 (Santiago: Republica de Chile, 1993); Corfo/Ifop (Corporación de Fomento/Instituto de Fomento Pesquero), *Diagnóstico de las Principales Pesquerías Nacionales: Pesquerías Bentónicas, III, IV y X Región* (Santiago: (Corfo/Ifop, 1991). The Lakes Region is Chile's largest producer of fresh-frozen and frozen seafood, and its third largest producer of canned seafood.

7 The bulk of the data for this study come from fourteen months of fieldwork carried out between 1990 and 1992, as part of my doctoral dissertation research. In the course of my fieldwork, I visited approximately 25 seafood-processing plants operating in the region (over a fifth of the total), surveyed 160 processing plant workers and over 300 shellfishermen, and interviewed some 35 empresarios and processing plant administrators. These data were updated during two additional visits to the region, one in the spring of 1994, and the other in the spring of 1997.

8 The same was not true for seafood-processing workers in other parts of the country, where salmon aquaculture was not established.

9 See Rachel Schurman, "Chile's New Entrepreneurs and the 'Economic Miracle': The Invisible Hand or a Hand from the State?" *Studies in Comparative International Development* 31, no. 3 (1996): 83–109. In this essay I argue that both state policy changes and the ideological practices of the Pinochet government had a major influence on the emergence of a new entrepreneurial class in the export sectors.

10 Although estimates of the devaluation effect vary, Corbo and Fischer suggest the real exchange rate rose almost two and half times between 1973 and 1990. (The real exchange rate refers to the nominal exchange rate corrected for internal and external inflation.) See Vittorio Corbo and Stanley Fischer, "Lessons from the Chilean Stabilization and Recovery," in *The Chilean Economy: Policy Lessons and Challenges*, ed. Barry Bosworth, Rudiger Dornbusch, and Raúl Labán (Washington, D.C.: Brookings Institution, 1994), 32–33.

11 For a more detailed analysis of the new entrepreneurial class that developed this industry, see Schurman, "Chile's New Entrepreneurs."

12 More specifically, the number of fishermen, shellfishermen, and auxiliary workers in the industry rose from 4,662 in 1975 to 16,036 in 1989. Calculated from Corfo/Ifop, "Analisis de la actividad pesquera extractiva nacional, I–III" (Santiago: Corfo/Ifop, 1990), table 5. The estimates of plant workers come from INE, *Anuario de industrias manufactureras* for 1971 and 1989.

13 Calculated from IN E, XVI Censo Naciónal de Población y V de Vivienda (Santiago: IN E, 1992), and IN E, *Anuario de industrias manufactureras, 1989* (Santiago: IN E, 1989).

14 The literature on Chile's agrarian history and its land reform is rich, and too extensive to cite here. For an entrée into this literature, see the work of Jose Bengoa, Rafael Baraona, Solon Barraclough, Cristobal Kay, Brian Loveman, and Lovell Jarvis.

15 These observations are based on two surveys, one of which I carried out with Nancy Barahona of the Instituto de Fomento Pesquero (Ifop), of 302 shellfishermen in Chiloé province in 1992. The other was an unpublished survey of 122 fishermen and shellfishermen in the Lakes Region, conducted by Ifop in 1989.

16 See, for instance, Silvia Venegas, *Una gota al dia . . . Un chorro al año: El impacto social de la expansion fruticultura* (Santiago: G EA [Grupo de Estudios Agrarios], 1992); and the collection of articles in *Sinopsis de una realidad ocultada: Los trabajadores del campo*, ed. Ximena Valdes, Veronica Riquelme, Julia Medel, et al. (Santiago: C E M [Centro de Estudios de la Mujer], 1987).

17 This discussion is based on my own interviews, as well as upon Priscilla Délano's dissertation, "Women and Work in Chile: A Case Study of the Fish-Processing Industry on the Island of Chiloé," Ph.D. diss., University of Cambridge, 1993. See also Priscilla Délano and David Lehmann, "Women Workers in Labor Intensive Factories: The Case of Chile's Fishing Industry," *European Journal of Development Research* 5, no. 2 (1993): 43–67, and Heidi Tinsman's contribution to this volume.

18 Quoted in Délano, "Women and Work in Chile," 264.

19 Quoted in Délano, "Women and Work in Chile," 279.

20 Aihwa Ong, *Spirits of Resistance and Capitalist Discipline: Factory Women in Malaysia* (Albany: State University of New York Press, 1987); Helen Safa, "Women, Production, and Reproduction in Industrial Capitalism: A Comparison of Brazilian and U.S. Factory Workers," in *Women, Men, and the International Division of Labor*, ed. Sharon Stichter and Jane L. Parpart (Philadelphia: Temple University Press: 1990), 72–97; Diane Wolf, *Factory Daughters: Gender, Household Dynamics, and Rural Industrialization in Java* (Los Angeles: University of California Press, 1992).

21 Interview, 1991. Sr. Miragallo is not this individual's real name.

22 This name is fictitious, though the data are not.

23 Under the share system, a boat's owner(s) and crew members receive a proportion of the revenues generated by the catch, after the boat's costs (e.g., fuel, supplies) are netted out. The share system is very common in artisanal fisheries. In southern Chile, the size of these shares varies by port. Typically, the owner's share ranges between 33 and 40 percent of the boat's revenues. He then receives another (smaller) share if he is a member of the crew. Crew members earn 10–15 percent of the boat's net revenues, depending on the number of people comprising the crew.

24 Unfortunately, it is difficult to get historical data on wages in the seafood processing industry, since firm owners are unwilling to part with any financial information in this highly competitive industry. These figures come from a very large plant in the region, with over six hundred workers. All figures are expressed in their U.S. dollar equivalent of the time.

25 Price estimates for bread and shoes come from Daniel Rodríguez and Silvia Venegas,

De praderas a parronales (Santiago: GEA [Grupo de Estudios Agrarios], 1989), 163–64, and those for lamb chops and Nescafé, from INE's *Anuario de precios* (Santiago: INE, 1987). The exchange rate used to convert these figures is 219.4 pesos to U.S.$1.00, and is published by the Central Bank, in its *Boletín Mensual*.

26 Interviews in the sector, 1990 and 1991.

27 See Jaime Gatica, *Deindustrialization in Chile* (Boulder: Westview Press, 1989); and Oscar Muñoz Goma, *Crisis y reorganización industrial en Chile*, Notas técnicas Cieplan 123 (Santiago: Cieplan, 1988).

28 These official figures originally come from INE-Odeplan and are reprinted in the Programa de Economía del Trabajo (PET), *Informe anual, 1990–1991*, cuadro 6. They exclude people in the government's emergency employment programs, known as the Programa de Empleo Minimo (PEM), and the Programa Ocupacional de Jefes de Hogar (POJH). If those inscribed in the government's emergency unemployment programs are included, unemployment rates for 1975 and 1983 rise to 17 percent and 26 percent respectively.

29 Interview with a member of the Women's Department of the Federación de Sindicatos de Trabajadores de Industrias Pesqueras, Puerto Montt, 4 April 1997.

30 Jaime Ruíz-Tagle, *El sindicalismo chileno después del Plan Laboral* (Santiago: PET, 1985); Pilar Romaguera, Cristian Echevarria, and Pablo Gonzalez, "Chile," in *Reforming the Labor Market in a Liberalized Economy*, ed. Gustavo Márquez (Baltimore: Johns Hopkins University Press, 1995), chap. 3.

31 For a description and critique of labor market flexibility, see Fernando Ignacio Leíva and Rafael Agacino, *Mercado de trabajo flexible: Pobreza y desintegración social en Chile, 1990–1994* (Santiago: Universidad Arcis, 1994). Labor market flexibility is also discussed by Ruíz-Tagle, *El sindicalismo chileno después del Plan Laboral*, and Romaguera, Echevarría, and Gonzalez, "Chile."

32 Interview with fish-processing plant manager, Ancud, Chiloé, 1991.

33 Interview, Puerto Montt, 1991.

34 Interviews with empresarios who were promised anonymity.

35 What I am about to describe represents the general case of workers in the industry. Some firms in the sector had considerably better labor practices than these. The important point is that many of these practices were formally or informally sanctioned by the law and the state during this period.

36 Délano, "Women and Work in Chile."

37 Délano, "Women and Work in Chile."

38 Interview in the seafood-processing sector, Puerto Montt, 1991.

39 This was one of the biggest complaints I heard from industry workers. When asked what they would like to change about their jobs, the second most common response referred to this issue of respect. The most common answer to this question was wages. (This survey included 161 workers from 17 different processing plants.)

40 Interviews with workers, Quellón, Chiloé, 1991.

41 In theory, there are three possible options for who will bear the cost of the uneven labor demand in nature-based industries: either the firm can bear these costs, by maintaining an adequately sized labor force throughout the year; or the state can

bear them, by offering unemployment insurance or some other form of economic support, such as public work programs; or workers can bear them, in the form of sporadic and/or seasonal unemployment and underemployment at certain times of the year and overemployment at others. In the Chilean case, the labor market regime was such that workers bore the full cost of these fluctuations in labor demand.

42 Ruíz-Tagle, El sindicalismo chileno, 62.

43 In 1981, this law was modified so that temporary contracts could only be renewed once; if renewed a second time, they were automatically converted into indefinite contracts, meaning that the worker would become a "permanent" rather than "temporary" employee (Ruíz-Tagle, El sindicalismo chileno, 64). However, even with this more labor-friendly modification, the reality was that a worker could be hired under temporary contract for up to two years.

44 See Romaguera, Echevarría, and Gonzalez, "Chile."

45 Interviews with workers in the seafood-processing sector.

46 This figure represents a weighted average of real wage increases in large firms (those with 50 or more employees) and small firms (those with between 10 and 49 workers). These figures were calculated on the basis of data provided in INE's Anuario de industrias manufactureras (various years), and were price deflated using the Central Bank's consumer price index. It should be noted that these estimates are based on wages per worker. Thus, to the extent that average hours per worker have grown, these figures will be biased upward.

47 These observations are based on interviews in the seafood-processing industry, April 1994.

48 Interviews with seafood-processing workers, 1991.

49 See also Rachel Schurman, "Uncertain Gains: Labor in Chile's New Export Sectors," Latin American Research Review 36, no. 2 (2001): 3–29.

50 Data come from the Instituto Nacional de Estadísticas, and represent the third trimester of each year. Reprinted in PET, Informe anual, 1997–1998, cuadro 7 (Santiago: PET, 1998).

51 The rates of employment growth in each of these sectors were 39 percent, 77 percent, 43 percent, and 28 percent respectively. Although these figures obviously include all workers and not just export sector workers, there is a broad scholarly consensus that it was the continued, indeed accelerated, growth of the export sectors that was driving this employment boom. Note that "services" includes financial as well as other kinds of services.

52 As specified by his own 1980 Constitution, Pinochet was forced to put his popularity to the test in 1988 in a national plebiscite on whether or not he should continue as president for the next eight years. To his surprise, the "no" vote won, meaning that a presidential election would take place in 1989. Patricio Aylwin, the candidate of a center-left coalition of political parties known as the Concertación, took the election with a strong majority, sending out a clear signal that the political pendulum had swung away from the authoritarian right.

53 The following observations are based on interviews with union organizers and workers in the sector, 1991, 1992, 1994, and 1997.

54 This estimate is based on self-reported workers' earnings from my 1991 survey of 167 plant workers in seventeen processing plants. Overtime earnings, which are harder to compare because of differences in the amount of overtime worked, showed a much smaller difference (only 3 percent).

55 See Leíva and Agacino, *Mercado de trabajo flexible*; Alejandra Mizala and Pilar Romaguera, "Flexibilidad del mercado de trabajo: El impacto del ajuste y los requisitos del crecimiento económico," *Colección Estudios Cieplan*, no. 43 (September 1996): 15–48.

56 Under the new Contract Termination and Employment Stability Law (Law 19,010) of November 1990, employers could no longer fire a worker without identifying a cause (although the needs of the firm to rationalize or modernize its operations, and/or to respond to changing market conditions, were considered acceptable motives). Law 19,010 also protected union organizers, pregnant women, and workers who were in the process of collective bargaining from being fired (Leíva and Agacino, *Mercado de trabajo flexible*, 18).

57 Leíva and Agacino, *Mercado de trabajo flexible*, 19.

58 Interviews with fishermen and managers at the Puerto Montt fisheries complex, 1991.

59 These data pertain to the entire southern Austral fishing zone, which extends from the Lakes Region in the north, to Tierra del Fuego in the south. See Corfo/ Ifop, *Diagnostico de las principales pesquerias nacionales: Estado de situacion y perspectivas del recurso pesquerias demersales "Peces" zona sur austral, 1990* (Corfo/Ifop: Santiago, 1991); Corfo/ Ifop, *Diagnostico de las principales pesquerias nacionales: Estado de situacion y perspectivas del recurso pesquerias demersales "Peces" zona sur austral, 1991* (Corfo/Ifop: Santiago, 1992).

60 These prices correspond to the prices received by fisherman at dockside. I thank Hector Vera for his help in obtaining these data from processors.

61 Interviews with divers and Ifop fisheries experts, Ancud, Chiloé, March 1992.

62 The Bay of Ancud has historically been the most important clam extraction area in the region.

63 This observation is based on my own analysis of data on catch per unit of fishing effort, collected and published by the Instituto de Fomento Pesquero in various annual reports on the state of the benthic fisheries.

64 This ban was initiated in 1989 and was lifted only once between 1989 and the end of 1993.

65 See Eduardo Infante, "1993: El difícil mercado del sector pesquero," *Chile pesquero*, no. 78 (1993): 67–69.

66 Another factor that pushed many fishermen out of the sector was the passage of a new fisheries law in 1991. Although the new law did not force anyone to leave the sector, it did represent a serious regulatory effort and imposed certain fees, registration, and other requirements on fishermen.

67 According to Enrique Moretti, owner of Pesquera Quehui, of the 30 firms that exported fresh hake to Spain in the 1980s (of which his company was one), only five managed to survive into the 1990s (interview, Puerto Montt, April 1994). And in 1991 the newspaper El Mercurio reported that three of the region's largest seafood-

processing plants had closed down, temporarily putting an estimated 2,000 people out of work (see El Mercurio, 3 May 1991, 3b).

68 The best early history of the salmon industry in Chile is Ricardo Méndez and Clara Munita, La salmonicultura en Chile (Santiago: Fundación Chile, 1989).

69 APST (Asociación de Productores de Salmon y Trucha de Chile), "Exportaciones de salmón y trucha: El creciente mercado regional," Salmonotícias: Medio Oficial de la Industria Salmonera de Chile, APST (January 1997): 15.

70 "November Black Month for Chilean Salmon Companies," IntraFish, 9 January 2002. These figures come from the APST, and correspond to the period from January to November.

71 El Mercurio, 12 April 1998, 6. Prices for Atlantic salmon have also fallen significantly. Atlantic salmon is mainly sold in the U.S. market, rather than in Japan. (Interview with a senior manager of Marine Harvest International, April 1997.)

72 The United States accounts for over 40 percent of salmon and trout exports; only Japan imports more. See Corfo/Ifop, Estado de situación de la acuicultura en Chile (Valparaiso: Corfo/Ifop, 1998), 44.

73 Ironically, feed costs were going up in part because of overfishing. Fishmeal is the main food fed to farmed salmon, and as stocks of Chile's pelagic fish species fell due to overfishing, among other things (e.g., climate change), the cost of fishmeal rose.

74 Originally, the tariff promised to be far more onerous (on the order of 42 percent), but after the Department of Commerce carried out its investigation, the dumping charges were found to be largely without merit. (SalmonChile, "Commerce Dept. Rejects U.S. Salmon Farmers' Allegations," at http://www.fis.com/salmonchile/finmix2.htm). Accessed 2 June 1998.

75 "Chilean Salmon Could Face 32% Tax in EU," Intrafish, 25 June 2002.

76 See, for example, "Chile Prepares Defence [sic] against Dumping Charges," Intrafish, 27 June 2002. To date, antidumping suits have been lodged against Chilean producers of raspberries, mushrooms, and wine. In the case of the mushroom producers, one accused producer was forced into bankruptcy by the high cost of defending himself against the unfair trade allegations.

77 "Excess profits" refers to profits that are above the "normal" rate of return in an industry; excess profits accrue when a firm or group of firms enjoy production costs that are substantially below the industry average. In the early years of the industry's existence, Chilean salmon farmers enjoyed unusually low production costs because of the low costs of labor, locally produced feed, locally built salmon pens, and cheap access to sites.

78 Interview with the director of one of the region's largest salmon firms, Puerto Montt, April 1997.

79 This discussion and the quotations that follow are based on interviews conducted with approximately a dozen salmon farm managers in Puerto Montt during 1994 and 1997.

80 Interview with the manager of a large salmon company in Puerto Montt, April 1997.

81 This productivity figure corresponds to firms with fifty or more employees, and is measured as value added per worker, where value added is expressed in real terms.

Both productivity and wage figures were calculated from the INE, *Anuarios de industrias manufactureras*, 1993 and 1995.

82 There has been a strong trend toward economic concentration and vertical integration in the industry, as large firms have bought out smaller ones, and some firms have merged together. These processes have been meticulously documented by Estrella Díaz, in her useful study, *Mejoramiento de Estandares Laborales en la Industria Processadora de Salmonidos* (Santiago: Hexagrama Consultoras, October 2001).

83 The salmon industry appears to be following the model of the poultry industry in the United States, which is characterized by enormous economic concentration and domination by a handful of megaproducers. These firms, such as Tyson's and Perdue, operate on the basis of very small profit margins and large volumes. What occurred in poultry was that small and medium-size firms could not compete against the enormous scale economies and low production costs achieved by large firms in the industry and were eventually forced out of business.

84 See APST, "Salmonideos generaron el 30.3% de los ingresos."

85 I develop this argument in more detail in "Uncertain Gains."

86 In 2001, 28 percent of Chile's gross domestic product was generated from exports.

87 These data come from the Banco Central de Chile Web site, at *www.bcentral.cl.indicadores/htm/empleo__desocupacion__INE*.htm. Accessed 25 September 2002.

88 Data for 2001 come from Díaz, *Mejoramiento de estandares laborales*, 39. Data for 1997 come from my interviews in the sector.

89 Interviews in the sector, April 1997. At that time, the exchange rate was 414 pesos to one U.S. dollar.

90 See the discussion in Díaz, *Mejoramiento de estandares laborales*, esp. 33–39.

91 Interview in the seafood-processing sector, Chiloé, 1991.

92 I put the term "skilled" in quotes because anyone who has tried to gut, clean, skin, and fillet salmon rapidly knows what enormous skill this job requires. Unfortunately, the labor market does not value this set of skills very highly.

93 The tendency among salmon firm owners in Chile seems to be not to try to follow the path of Norway or the United States by hiring a very reduced number of highly skilled workers but to follow a "middle path" that involves employing a larger number of less skilled workers. The low cost and high availability of unskilled labor in Chile makes this strategy possible. Whether or not this strategy is viewed as something positive depends on one's perspective.

94 The seven-to-one figure corresponds to all seafood-processing firms in the country and is not specific to those that process salmon. It is based on data collected and published by INE in its 1995 *Anuario de industrias manufactureras* (code 3114). This same data source suggests that between 1986 and 1995, there was no clear trend in the ratio of obreros to empleados, which fell slightly between 1986 and 1992 (from 7.7 to 5.9) and then began to rise through 1994 (to 7.6). In 1995, the last year for which data are available, the ratio fell again, from 7.2 to 1.0. (Calculated from INE, *Anuario de industrias manufactureras*, various years.)

95 See Gonzalo García, "Se deforman los salmones," *El Mercurio*, 14 July 1999, C-1.

96 Aslak Berge, "Lack of Candour on Chilean Algae Problems," *Intrafish*, 11 April 2002.

Berge estimated that the industry lost $7 million, but his figures are disputed by the Association of the Chilean Salmon Industry, which claims that the industry suffered a smaller financial loss. Algae blooms are not specific to Chile, of course, but plague salmon farming worldwide.

97 See William Cronon, *Changes in the Land: Indians, Colonists and the Economy of New England* (New York: Hill and Wang, 1983), and his later book, *Nature's Metropolis: Chicago and the Great West* (New York: W. W. Norton, 1991). The work of environmental historians Donald Worster and Caroline Merchant also pointed early on to the significance of "nature's agency." See William Boyd, Scott Prudham, and Rachel Schurman, "Industrial Dynamics and the Problem of Nature," *Society and Natural Resources* 14, no. 7 (2001): 555–70 for an effort to explore the significance of nature's agency in the context of nature-based industries.

98 Bent-Are Jensen, "Chilean Salmon Mortality Rate Almost 30 Per Cent," *Intrafish*, 10 June 2002.

99 García, "Se deforman los salmones."

100 Another potential problem is infestation from sea lice, which are associated with a high rate of salmon mortality. Although sea lice have yet to become an issue for salmon farmers in the Pacific, this situation could change very quickly.

101 See Boyd, Prudham, and Schurman, "Industrial Dynamics and the Problem of Nature."

102 See Schurman, "Uncertain Gains."

THOMAS MILLER KLUBOCK

Labor, Land, and Environmental Change
in the Forestry Sector in Chile, 1973–1998

On 31 December 1983, Chile's military dictator, General Augusto Pinochet, addressed the nation in his annual New Year's Eve speech. The country had suffered a year of devastating recession, and Pinochet struggled to find some glimmer of hope for an economy battered by the world recession and the radical neoliberal economic restructuring of the regime's economists, "the Chicago Boys." The general pointed to the forestry industry as the military government's major success story, boasting that the regime's free-market policies had led to a "forestry boom" in exports as well as the forestation of 1 million hectares of land.[1] During the late 1970s, the forestry sector had grown at double the annual rate of national economic growth, making forestry products a major source of export revenues, third behind mining and industry by the early 1980s.[2] The reality behind the "forestry boom" was, however, somewhat different from the rosy picture painted by Pinochet. The rapid expansion of the forestry sector during the late 1970s and 1980s, frequently cited by regime loyalists as a shining example of the Chilean economic "miracle," owed little to the Chicago Boys' neoclassical economic policies. Rather, reforestation and the growth in the export of forest products was a result of state planning and investment in both pine tree plantations and the lumber, paper, and wood pulp industries since the 1940s.

Pinochet's boast also concealed the harsh social costs that had accompanied the forestry boom of the 1970s. Behind the flattering statistics, the wholesale reorganization of social relations in the countryside following the 1973 military coup rendered the rural zones dedicated to the production of forest products among the poorest in the country, with unemployment rates that exceeded the national average of over 20 percent (in some zones approaching 50 percent) and a ballooning population of landless peasants who lived in rural *poblaciones* (shantytowns) along the sides of roads and highways. Workers in the forestry sector suffered the lowest wages and worst working conditions in the country, laboring on a temporary basis for numerous subcontractors. Finally, Pinochet's promise that the forestry boom would provide a model for private sector-led growth ignored the tremendous ecological costs of this particular version of export-oriented economic development. The expansion of pine tree plantations throughout southern Chile and the destruction of Chile's unique temperate rain forests provoked profound changes in the environment that rendered precarious the long-term prospects of forestry exports and had a devastating impact on local rural society, undermining the basis of the agricultural economy and ecological biodiversity that had sustained a significant population of peasant smallholders (campesinos) and estate laborers (inquilinos) before 1973.

In the 1990s the neoliberal model of export-led development in Chile met its most serious challenge from Mapuche communities who contested the authority of the large conglomerates and transnational corporations that had presided over the expansion of commercial monocultural forestry production after 1973. Mapuche organizations drew on a revitalized sense of ethnic identity and traditions of rural struggle to demand the return of lands usurped by large landowners and the state since the nineteenth century and an end to the commercial forestry industry's monopoly of forests in southern Chile.[3] While the labor force in logging camps and sawmills composed one of the most exploited and impoverished in all Chile, it was unable to mount a similar challenge to the authority of large forestry companies. The rural labor movement in forestry zones that had emerged during the 1960s was decimated by military repression and the restructuring of land and labor relations after 1973. Unions were weak, and most workers, because they were seasonal or temporary, had no legal right to collective bargaining according to the prescriptions of the military regime's 1979 Labor Code. In addition, most forestry workers were former peasants who had been deracinated from rural communities and expelled from their lands and thus lacked the social networks that might provide the foundation of a reinvigorated labor movement. This chapter examines the changes in the conditions of labor and land ownership in the forestry industry to ask why these workers, unlike indigenous communities, have not been able to launch a successful challenge to the organization of work, the arrangements of land ownership, and the strategies of forest exploitation employed by logging companies.[4]

In addition, this chapter seeks to uncover the connections between the labor history of the forestry industry and the environmental history of Chile's southern woods. The forestry sector provides one of the most acute examples of the depredatory nature of free-market capitalism as it developed in authoritarian and postauthoritarian Chile after 1973. The massive destruction of native forests and their replacement by pine and eucalyptus plantations have eroded the crucial biodiversity of southern forest ecosystems while it has transformed rural labor relations by making former peasants into a population of landless and itinerant part-time laborers, with neither access to land nor the benefits of permanent wage work and unionization. The effects of forestry development on the environment and on rural labor are interrelated. The destruction of rural ecosystems has been a major factor in the demise of the peasant economy and the conversion of rural workers—who at one time combined forestry work with both subsistence and commercial agricultural production—into temporary wage laborers. The expansion of commercial monocultural forestry production for export has been predicated both on the availability of land and cheap forest resources and on the availability of an inexpensive labor force. These two facts are connected dialectically: the expulsion of resident estate laborers and small-holders by large commercial forestry companies made available agricultural lands and forests that could be cleared, often with fire, and planted with pine plantations. At the same time, the expansion of the plantations undermined regional ecosystems that had sustained peasant agriculture and forced peasants to sell their lands and join a floating population of migrant temporary workers in shantytowns throughout the countryside.

THE DEVELOPMENT OF THE FORESTRY INDUSTRY BEFORE 1973

Despite Pinochet's claims that the expansion of forestry production and exports during the 1970s was a result of the military regime's free-market policies, the industry had developed, after slow growth during the beginning of the early 20th century, under the developmentalist policies of a series of governments from the Popular Front coalitions of the 1940s to the Christian Democratic government of Eduardo Frei (1964–70) and the Socialist government of Salvador Allende (1970–73). Since the late 19th century, foreign travelers and local observers had seen potential riches in the forests of Chile's southern frontier. Following the military defeat of the Mapuche during the 1880s, the government initiated colonization schemes designed to populate the regions south of the Bío-Bío river with European immigrants and mestizo farmers from central Chile and to promote the development of agricultural production, mainly of wheat and livestock. The state granted land to individual farmers and to colonization companies that pledged to clear forest lands and make the southern territories agriculturally productive. In the process, the Chilean state created forest reserves and licensed individuals and companies to extract wood from both public and private lands. Initially, landowners used fire to clear virgin forests for agriculture and grazing. By the turn of the century, however, many brought in small portable mills and employed agricultural workers, inquilinos and *peones* (landless laborers) to log forests and work in mills during the off-seasons, beginning in autumn. The use of fire to clear land, both for cutting and for agricultural purposes, led to the mass destruction of native hardwood forests during the first two decades of the 20th century. The state developed a contradictory forestry policy that sought both to protect southern forests from deforestation in order to maximize the potential revenues from publically owned woods and to promote private colonization and agricultural development in the south, which entailed the massive clearing of forested lands.[5] Chilean governments began to develop a policy toward the country's forests mainly in terms of efforts to conserve native forests on state-owned lands from private exploitation in order to guarantee state control of the profits of logging. Because of the weak presence of the state on the southern frontier, however, efforts to limit the destruction of forests and exert control over logging profits were largely futile, and millions of hectares of Chile's unique hardwood species—raulí, roble, araucaria, coigues, tepas, mañio, lingue, and alerce—were destroyed.[6]

During the same period, in the province of Concepción, coal-mining companies planted the first plantations of pine trees imported from North America to replace the exhausted forests that had supplied wood and fuel to the mines of Lota. Between 1902 and 1920 coal companies planted eight hundred hectares of Monterey pine (*Pino insigne*). While pine proved to be too soft for use in reinforcing mine shafts and unsuitable as fuel wood, the plantations demonstrated that the species grew three times as fast in Chilean soil as in its native North America soil, reaching a harvestable size within twenty years.[7] State efforts to promote the forestry industry and reforestation turned to developing plantations of North American pine, rather than the conservation or management of native forests. In 1931 the Ley de Bosques (Forestry Law) compiled a series of laws passed since 1925 designed to promote pine plantations primarily to reforest the denuded agricultural lands surrounding Concepción. During the 1940s the Ministerio de Tierras y Colonización (Ministry of Lands and Colonization) auctioned off provisional land grants to private individuals and companies.[8] Definitive titles and tax exemptions were granted when the owners had demonstrated that they had planted significant numbers of pine trees.[9] By 1951, under the Ley de Bosques, 200,000 hectares of pines had been planted throughout southern Chile, most in what is now the Eighth Region, comprising the provinces of Ñuble, Concepción, Arauco, and Bío-Bío.[10] By the 1950s hundreds of small portable sawmills worked native forests and pine plantations on privately owned and public lands south of the Bío-Bío in the Cordillera de los Andes and the smaller Cordillera de la Costa, providing wood to domestic markets. In 1948, 800 small sawmills employed 22,000 workers who produced wood for the construction industry and for factories that manufactured furniture, boxes, doors and windows, matches, pulp, and sheds.[11] These workers were joined by thousands of agricultural workers who engaged in logging and milling on large estates during off-seasons.

Through the 1960s most forestry workers were contracted by privately and publically owned estates as either inquilinos or peones, even if they worked in sawmills or wood factories on the estates, allowing landowners to pay lower wages and avoid labor laws that provided the framework for the unionization and benefits of industrial workers.[12] Despite land- and mill owners' classification of logging and mill industries as "agricultural" and forestry workers as "campesinos," most workers combined agricultural and industrial forms of labor. Estate residents tended plots of land and pastured cattle, as well as logging forests and working in mills and wood factories. Nonetheless, because most forests and mills, and even some factories, were located on private estates, workers were enmeshed in the system of land and labor relations that characterized most of rural Chile. Their legal status as agricultural workers, while as much a ploy by patrones to keep down wages and benefits and prevent unionization, reflected a system of labor relations defined by the traditional system of inquilinaje and landlord-tenant farmer relations. In addition to their salaries, workers were provided small parcels of land to grow vegetables and pasture animals. Landowners often paid workers with tokens that could be redeemed at a company store on the estate (pulpería), or deducted the price of goods from workers' salaries. Most equipment and animals on estates—tractors, donkeys, firewood, and wood for building houses—was owned by the landowner and provided to workers as part of their contracts. This system allowed the landowner to exercise powerful paternalistic control over labor relations and cement the dependency of the labor force on forestry estates. Landowners prevented unionization of their workforces, barring entrances and exits to estates, calling on carabineros [the police] to arrest troublesome workers, and setting the hours of work and pay, often forcing workers to work "extra" unpaid hours and cheating them on wages.[13]

Through the 1940s logging and sawmill activities on large private estates were secondary to agricultural production. Logging was often viewed as a corollary to clearing land for planting and as a way to employ resident laborers during off-seasons. Investments in roads and machinery were minimal, and the use of antiquated and primitive equipment, combined with the use of fire for clearing land, contributed to the inefficient exploitation and destruction of forest resources. Workers used axes to fell trees and chop logs and transported logs to mills in ox-drawn carts. Mills were fueled by wood and produced low-quality lumber. As a report by the United States Forest Service noted, "The entire small mill operation is a model of inefficiency. . . . Its defects are . . . inadequate supervision and equipment resulting in excessive waste, inefficiency, higher operating costs, and inadequate financing."[14] However, as the report also observed, this system had its advantages: small portable mills involved only small amounts of capital and risk and could be moved easily between forest stands. The low cost of labor compensated for the lack of mechanization. In addition, the use of small mills allowed campesinos with farms of only a few hectares to log their own properties or to contract out to larger landowners during off-seasons. In forest regions, many small landowners operated their own portable mills, employing family labor and contracting with hacienda owners to log their forests and produce wood. Many villages in forestry zones had their origins in the installation of sawmills near forests on privately owned farms and estates. Sawmill and forestry workers built houses and established permanent residences in small towns and on estates in areas dedicated to the timber industry. Campesinos, like inquilinos, combined lumbering with agricultural production and raising livestock.

During the 1940s the Popular Front center-left governments (1938–52) looked to develop modern wood industries that would supply domestic markets, particularly in the construction of low-income housing for the burgeoning urban population, through the Corporación de Fomento (Development Corporation—Corfo). From the late 1800s through the first half of the 20th century, only a couple of major industrial enterprises had developed in the forestry sector. By the 1950s only one company, the Compañía Manufacturera de Papeles y Cartones (CMPC), or "la Papalera" as it is still known, produced 90 percent of Chile's paper.[15] The Popular Front governments, following the blueprint provided by the U.S. Forest Service in 1946, sought to promote the establishment of modern mechanized sawmills, paper factories, and pulp plants.

During the 1950s and 1960s, under the direction of Corfo, the cellulose (wood pulp) and paper industries grew rapidly. A combination of state and private investments founded a number of large companies that worked with both native and exotic species. During the government of Christian Democrat Eduardo Frei (1964–70), the state became an active associate of private capital, making large investments with already established companies and using credits from multilateral lending institutions such as the World Bank to fund the establishment of paper and pulp factories. The goal of Corfo's forestry policy was to promote the formation of diverse industrial activities, primarily the production of pulp and paper in combination with more traditional wood industries. For the most part, these new cellulose and paper plants were supplied by pine plantations established by Corfo on both public and privately owned lands. During this period (1946–70), the state financed reforestation of both public and private lands. Numerous agreements were made in which private landowners provided their land and the state forested it and managed the plantations.[16] In addition, a number of state institutions, such as the Social Security Service and parastate retirement funds (cajas) purchased estates that they planted with pine.[17] This state-directed growth also stimulated an increase in the exports of forest products. While until the late 1960s most industrial production was oriented toward internal markets, exports increased significantly after 1968 as cellulose replaced lumber and paper as Chile's major forest-based export, according to the program established by the World Bank and the Frei government.[18]

This process of state-directed development accelerated under the government of Salvador Allende's Unidad Popular (Popular Unity—UP) coalition, which attempted to create greater horizontal integration of forestry production by establishing large, centrally administered forestry complexes that united the diverse steps in the production process, from planting and logging in the forests and producing lumber in sawmills, to industrial processing in large cellulose and paper factories. A large number of plantations were founded on state-owned lands in the south or on lands within the area expropriated under the agrarian reform. Through the intensification of the agrarian reform initiated under the Frei government during the 1960s, the UP sought to bring native forests owned by private estates under state management and to meet the demands of the increasingly radical rural labor movement by distributing lands to both campesinos and inquilinos.

In 1972 the UP embarked on a program to expropriate 1.5 million hectares of southern forest lands in order to establish the sustainable exploitation of native forests. Land expropriations would both meet the needs of peasants, resident laborers, and the unemployed rural poor and "bring into the social and mixed property areas the estates that were traditionally responsible for the elimination of native forests, the impoverishment of the soil, the exhaustion of pine reserves, and the erosion of Chilean soil."[19] In a 1971 speech to workers in Cautín, Allende described the combined goals of redistributing lands to peasants, protecting native forests from private exploitation, and developing a modern forestry industry:

Over the last months we have dictated a decree of extraordinary importance. It creates a frontier zone in order to expropriate not only 270 thousand hectares of agricultural estates, but also fundamentally forested estates near the cordillera at the frontier with Argentina. We have done this in order to preserve the reserves of native forests that have been implacably exploited for private profit. . . . [W]e will create sawmills, we will implement a policy of reforestation, and we will install a cellulose plant to provide jobs in this zone . . . in order to put an end to the misery, hunger, and lack of culture of the Chileans who work in sawmills and logging, a profound drama, even more serious than the drama of the campesinos.[20]

By 1973 the state had become the major owner and administrator both of plantations and the industrial processing of forest products. The UP installed modern sawmills in order to stimulate wood production in the agrarian reform sector and planned the construction of new pulp and paper plants.

State ownership of plantations, sawmills, and forestry industries during the 1960s and early 1970s was also propelled by an increasingly militant rural labor movement. Campesino unions in forestry regions pushed the government to expropriate estate lands and establish new industries to provide jobs. Under the Christian Democratic Frei government, especially after the 1967 law legalizing peasant unions, forestry workers, estate residents, and smallholders organized militant unions and choreographed numerous land invasions and strikes. An important example of the trajectory of the labor movement in the forestry sector is the case of the Buena Esperanza hacienda in the Nahuelbuta Cordillera, a center of logging activity in the southern native forests. The establishment of rural unions in the region began in 1961 when 18 inquilino families on a nearby estate, Mundo Nuevo, left after their struggle to win rights to *parcelas* (small plots of land) on the estate was defeated. A number of inquilinos moved to the Buena Esperanza estate, owned by the Caja de Empleados Públicos y Periodistas (a parastate social insurance institution) and formed a committee to begin organizing a union. Because the law required unions to have a minimum of 100 workers, members of the Buena Esperanza committee traveled around the area organizing workers on neighboring estates into the "Sindicato Nahuelbuta." As the former union leader Filadelfo Guzmán remembered in 1983, "At times I walked five or six hours to go to meetings in Curañanco or Curihuillín." By 1964 Buena Esperanza's workers had established a settlement with 112 families and 263 workers. This preliminary union gave rise to a militant regional labor movement of campesinos and forestry workers: "The Sindicato Nahuelbuta had around 500 members, spread out in Curihuillín, Troncalo, Curañanco, and other locations. Struggling for our rights we were able to organize strikes on a number of estates. But most important was that we organized workers who didn't know anything, didn't know what collective bargaining was." The Sindicato Nahuelbuta then became part of the larger Federación Campesina Caupolicán based in Cañete and the left-wing Confederación Nacional Campesina e Indígena "Ranquil" (National Federation of Peasants and Indigenous Peoples "Ranquil"), and Don Filadelfo became a leader of the regional federation. By the 1970s the Buena Esperanza union had won from the Caja the infrastructure of a permanent settlement: a primary school, a medical clinic, transportation, electricity, a union hall, and a community center.[21]

The organization of the unions and the federation of inquilinos on estates dedicated to forestry production in the Nuhuelbuta Cordillera mirrored the development of the rural labor movement in Chile's southern provinces and forestry zones. Workers organized the first major union federation, the Federación de Trabajadores del Bosque "Liberación" (Federation of Forestry Workers "Liberation") in Concepción in 1967, shortly after congress passed the Ley de Sindicalización Campesina (Peasant Unionization Law), legalizing unions of peasants and rural workers.[22] In 1967 there were only 24 agricultural and forestry workers' unions in Chile. By 1970 there were 400. The Catholic Church–based "Liberación" Federation grouped together five unions of forestry workers with 12,000 members in the region surrounding Concepción: Aurora de Chile in Coelemu, Pedro Soto Rodríguez in Ranquil, La Esperanza in Tomé, Unidad Campesina in Talcahuano, and Lautaro in Coronel. By 1970 union militants had founded an interregional federation that linked 16 forestry workers' unions. Two years later this federation joined with the campesino unions Los Valientes de Concepción and the national Christian Democratic party confederation El Triunfo Campesino to present a common set of demands to 250 agricultural and forestry employers. The move was successful, and workers won a 42 percent wage hike, company-run health clinics, work security systems, education bonuses for their children, and bonuses for births, marriages, and funerals.[23] Workers on state-owned forestry lands also organized during this period. In early 1970 Ranquil, the bulletin of the Confederación Ranquil, noted that 1,000 agricultural and forestry workers in the province of Arauco, a center of forestry activity, were engaged in strikes against landowners, including the large company Forestal Pilpilco, as well as with administrators of estates owned by Corfo and parastate organizations such as the Caja de Empleados Públicos y Periodistas.[24]

Beyond forming labor unions, resident workers on rural estates devoted to forestry participated in the wave of land invasions under the UP that intensified the process of agrarian reform. In late 1970 and early 1971 outside Valdivia in Panguipulli, 2,600 workers invaded 22 estates, with support of militants of the

Revolutionary Movement of the Left (MIR) and the Socialist party and pressured the state to expropriate the forestry lands, two factories, and a sawmill and to create a large worker-run forestry complex with over 320,000 hectares of land.[25] Panguipulli became the country's largest forestry-wood complex with a modern sawmill, a plywood factory, and a planned cellulose plant. The Complejo Maderero Panguipulli was organized eventually to support 9,000 campesino families. Invasions and expropriations of forestry estates spread to other provinces as well. In one exemplary case in the province of Talca, inquilinos invaded the Agua Fría forestry estate and demanded its expropriation. The workers complained that the landowner ruled like a feudal lord. Like other landowners, he required his resident laborers to sell him the animals they raised on their small plots at prices he determined, neglected to pay their social security contributions, and, as one worker noted, "No one was allowed to read newspapers, listen to the radio, or even own a watch, because the only time was the patrón's time."[26]

The result of the UP's forestry policy and the strikes and land invasions by peasants and forestry workers was the consolidation of state control over factories, large mills, and plantations and the bolstering of a peasant economy that mixed wage labor on plantations and in mills and factories, commercial and subsistence agricultural production, and the exploitation of native forests for seeds, fuel, mushrooms, and wild game and for wood to be sold in local and regional markets. The UP's forestry strategy sought to preserve native forests from deforestation by private estates and logging companies and to manage sustainable exploitation to meet the needs of campesinos through Conaf (Corporacíon Nacional Forestal). In addition, in regions like Concepción where deforestation was already a fact, the UP planned reforestation with pine plantations. Under Allende, the state attempted a complicated juggling act of potentially competing goals in which it promoted reforestation with pines in already deforested areas, as well as the management and protection of native forests, state-administered forestry industries, and a campesino economy that depended both on access to native forests as part of subsistence and commercial agricultural strategies and access to wage labor in mills and wood factories. Most important, by establishing state management of both plantations and native forests, the UP braked the unregulated private exploitation of forests and initiated state management of Chile's forest resources for the first time. In addition, by addressing the demands of the rural labor and campesino movement, the UP lent its support to a peasant economy that combined exploitation of native forests with agricultural activities.

The 1973 military coup led to the complete restructuring of the forestry sector. The military junta viewed the state-run plantations and wood, pulp, and paper industries and the militant rural labor movement in the forestry sector as symptomatic of the policies of the UP and sought to promote an entirely different model of forestry development based on the radical free-market policies of the Chicago Boys. Privatization, the operation of market forces, and the promotion of forest exports would stimulate the modernization and development of the forestry industry. In forestry regions, as in other rural areas, the regime rolled back the agrarian reform. Forest lands that had been transferred to Conaf by Corfo were auctioned off, as were lands owned by state organizations such as the Social Security Service. Public lands were also sold, and lands expropriated under the agrarian reform were returned to their previous owners.[27] Corfo began to sell off industries, plantations, and forests at bargain prices to well-connected financial groups, including the three major companies Forestal and Celulosa Arauco, Forestal and Celulosa Constitución (Celco), and Industrias Forestales (Infor) and to the smaller Forestal Pilpilco, Forestanac, Bima, Esmail, and Ralco, among others. Chile's major forestry company, Forestal Arauco, was sold to Copec (owned by the Cruzat-Larraín financial group) for $35 million, with $8 million paid upon purchase and the rest to be paid in quotas over the next eight years. By 1988 it was still unclear whether any of the quotas had ever been paid. In 1973 Forestal Arauco's cellulose plant, which had begun production in 1972 as a state-financed project, was one of the most profitable and efficient state-owned businesses.[28] At the time of the sale, Forestal Arauco had $85 million in cash, $45 million in liabilities, financial reserves of $39 million, and assets worth $40 million. In 1979 Copec also acquired Celco, the most modern cellulose plant in Chile, constructed and financed by the state in Maule, for $58 million with 25 percent down and the rest to paid over eight years. Inforsa (Industrias Forestales, S.A.), developed by foreign capital in association with Corfo during the 1960s, was sold to the Compañía Industria Indus (controlled by the Vial financial group) for $40 million.[29] Despite the military regime's commitment to the free play of market forces, all these sales were made at well under the value of the enterprises' properties and assets to financial groups that had cultivated close relations with the regime.

In 1974 the military junta declared the Decree-Law 701 in order to stimulate the privatization and growth of the forestry sector. The law established 20-year credits to cover the costs of forestation of lands, including the costs of managing forests (pruning, thinning, and administrative costs). The decree-law also dictated a subsidy of 75 percent of the value of forestation, exempted land devoted to forestry from the taxes that applied to most agricultural properties, and established lines of credit from the Central Bank, channeled through commercial banks, to foment forestation. A final clause made forested lands legally inexpropriable. A second decree-law in 1975 allowed the exportation of forestry products in any stage of elaboration, creating the possibility of exporting logs without any value-added processing.[30] Large companies, stimulated by the incentives in Decree-Law 701 and the guarantee against expropriation, as well as the low prices at which public land was auctioned off, began to accumulate vast tracts of lands. Planting pine became profitable in and of itself, and the hectares planted soon outpaced the demands of the companies' industrial plants. By monopolizing lands and devoting them to pine plantations, large forestry companies began to squeeze out alternative agricultural activities and the small landholders and resident estate laborers these activities sustained in forestry zones, particularly in the Eighth Region. Forestry companies began to expel inquilinos from the private estates they purchased and to buy land from campesinos at low prices, establishing a monopoly over forests. They then earned credits and subsidies from the state by planting pines, which in turn drove up the price of land. The control of land in forestry zones also ensured forestry companies a cheap source of labor, since former agricultural workers and peasants, deprived of access to agricultural lands, turned to wage labor in logging camps and sawmills.

Thus the reality behind Pinochet's boast in 1983 was somewhat different. While the military had indeed presided over the planting of 1 million hectares of pines, in reality this had been accomplished both through direct state action, state subsidies and credits, and pre-1973 investments in developing the forestry sector. The operation of market forces and private investments had played a relatively small role in the expansion of plantations and exports. Of the one million hectares planted between 1974 and 1980, Conaf was responsible for planting 37.5 percent and for financing with subsidies and credits another 39.4 percent. This was in accordance with plans laid out by Corfo before 1970 to plant 100,000 hectares a year in pine plantations. Private capital financed and planted only 23.1 percent of the pine plantations during this period.[31] In 1977 state investments in forestation totaled $8.5 million, while private sector investments came to only $1 million. In 1980, the state invested $6.5 million and the private sector less than $1 million.[32] In addition, as analysts pointed out at the time, of Pinochet's heralded "one million hectares of forestation," over 80 percent had trees that were 10 years old or less and would only be ready for production over the next ten years. The wood exploited and exported during the 1970s and early 1980s had, in fact, been planted before 1973 as part of the state-directed program of developing the forestry industry under the Frei and Allende governments. The three largest economic groups, which controlled 60 percent of the subsidized plantations, took in $12.8 million in incentives. As analysts pointed out following Pinochet's New Year's speech, the pine plantations had been funded almost entirely by the state, even though the vast majority were privately owned and private investors reaped the profits.[33]

The factories that processed trees into lumber, pulp, and paper had also been founded with state input during the period before the 1973 coup. In 1989 Chile had basically the same number of industrial plants in operation for producing cellulose, paper, fiber board, particle board, plywood, and lumber as it had before 1973, since private investment was directed at expanding existing plants rather than new enterprises.[34] Between 1960 and 1974 production in the forestry sector grew at an average annual rate of 9.9 percent. Between 1974 and 1986, however, production increased at an annual rate of 8.4 percent, a rate lower than average productivity for the period between 1959 and 1986.[35] The "boom" in exports of forestry products from $42.5 million in 1971 (4.1 percent of all exports) to $362.2 million in 1983 (8.4 percent of all exports) was composed to a significant degree of the export of logs that had, before 1973, been used in the production of lumber, limiting the value added through industrial elaboration.[36] Exports of forestry products increased as internal demand, mostly from the construction sector, contracted due to the recessionary crisis that accompanied economic restructuring.

While small and medium-size land and mill owners had played a significant role in the forestry industry in partnership with the state before 1973, by 1984 three major financial groups, Cruzat-Larraín, Matte-Alessandri, and Vial, had come to dominate the industry. Two companies alone, Copec (Cruzat-Larraín) and CMPC (Matte-Alessandri) controlled 50 percent of pine plantations and 100 percent of the cellulose industry.[37] Combined the three financial groups owned 75 percent of plantations, 78 percent of industrial production, and 73 percent of exports and received 85 percent of the state subsidies and credits for forest cultivation and management.[38] Yet the paper and cellulose plants they operated and that supplied 58 percent of the export value of forestry products had been started during the 1960s and early 1970s under the direction of the state. While they exercised monopoly control over the industry, the three financial groups invested little in new projects or in the expansion of the industrial enterprises begun before 1973. Rather, they profited by purchasing already existing companies at bargain prices and by accumulating lands for planting pines for which they received state subsidies and access to cheap credit.

The abrupt transfer of forest lands and forestry industries from the state sector and peasant smallholders to a few major financial groups required the repression of the militant rural labor movement that had emerged during the 1960s. Economic restructuring in the forestry sector entailed both the reversal of the agrarian reform and the dismantling of campesino unions. The rural labor movement in the forestry sector was "only in diapers" in 1973, as one union leader put it in an oral history.[39] However, the militancy of rural unions provoked ferocious repression following the military coup. As with campesino unions, forestry workers' organizations were shut down, their leaders arrested, and their properties confiscated. In the Federación Liberación, of 17 union leaders, only three remained unscathed by repression. The president of the union, Mario Ruiz, was detained in a concentration camp for four years; a number of the union's leaders were simply disappeared, and, as a union leader noted, "We never heard what happened to them."[40] On three forestry estates in Mulchén, "El Morro," "El Carmen-Maitenes," and "Pemehue," 18 forestry workers employed by Conaf were detained in the days following the military coup. In 1979 their bodies were found in a mass grave.[41] Perhaps the most devastating example of the repression of peasant families and communities in the forestry sector was the Complejo Maderero Panguipulli. After 1973 the complex was shut down (to be broken up and the expropriated estates returned to their owners or auctioned off in the late 1970s and 1980s), and a large number of members of the community of workers who had joined the parties of the UP, the MIR, and the radical rural labor movement in the region were detained by the military. Forty-four workers from the farms Neltulme, Chihuío, Futrono, Llifén, Arquilhue, Curriñe, Chabranco, and Liquiñe within the Complejo were detained, executed, and buried in mass clandestine graves.[42] Many of the survivors of the repression abandoned the closed complex and migrated to settlements on the outskirts of Valdivia.[43]

The repression of the rural labor movement and communities of forestry workers through military violence enabled the financial groups that had taken control of the forestry sector to reorder land and labor relations in the rural regions of southern Chile. Thousands of former inquilinos were expelled from estates acquired by large forestry companies, and campesinos were forced to sell their small parcelas through indirect pressures.[44] Rural communities that had been formed on forestry estates or in areas devoted to forestry production by smallholders were broken up as forestry companies extended their control of forested lands to supply their modern sawmills, factories, and industrial plants. Small landholders and resident estate workers lost their access to land and left farms and estates behind to migrate either to cities or semiurban squatter settlements along the sides of roads in agricultural zones. Male peasants came to constitute a mobile and flexible supply of cheap wage labor to estates, plantations, and industries, laboring for low wages, without benefits, on a temporary basis for subcontractors, while women and children remained behind in rural shantytowns, deprived of access to the agricultural lands that had been central to the rural household economy.

After 1973 government incentives stimulated large companies to expand their land holdings in forestry regions in order to plant pine by purchasing large estates and small farms. By the early 1980s these estates planted pine trees where they had once cultivated wheat and corn or pastured animals, pushing out resident agricultural laborers. Few small landowners could compete with large forestry companies as the push to plant pine plantations consumed rural areas in the Eighth Region. Campesinos could not afford to plant pine and then wait 17 to 25 years for their lands to produce since they depended on their parcelas for subsistence. Nor did smallholders have access to the credits and state subsidies enjoyed by the large companies. As a leader of the Conaf workers union, the Federación Nacional de Sindicatos de Conaf (Fenasic) pointed out, noting the demise of small holdings in the forestry sector: "The state doesn't provide incentives or subsidies for the small producers. Only the large companies receive credits and incentives."[45] Planting pine required long periods for the trees to maturate, large extensions of land, and an intensive use of capital.[46] In addition, large companies' monopoly of sawmills and factories enabled them to purchase wood from smallholders at low prices. As another Fenasic leader pointed out, "The large monopolistic companies like Celulosa Arauco and Celulosa Celco" drove campesinos out of forestry zones by "fixing low prices [for the wood of] of small producers."[47]

Nor could campesino smallholders who operated their own rudimentary sawmills compete with the modern plants owned by forestry companies. Large companies used their control of land and of pine plantations to produce cheap and high-quality pine boards for the construction sector and for export. Small producers, who worked native forests and employed antiquated machinery in their family-operated mobile mills, could not compete with the technologies used by the modern sawmills owned by the forestry companies, which enjoyed access to rapidly and inexpensively grown pine trees, economies of scale, and a monopoly over land. As a leader of the Confederación de Trabajadores Forestales (CTF) noted, "There were many small landholders who, sadly, could not compete, who lacked the resources, and it was easier for them to sell off their lands. . . . They were smallholders who had small woods that they exploited, but they didn't have the resources to make an adequate investment, to buy the plants, to contract a technician . . . . They lacked the training and the capital . . . and so the smallholders began to disappear. . . . Many stayed on working for the same businesses that had purchased their lands."[48] Similarly, a Federación Liberación leader observed that in the zones around Concepción, "Forestal Arauco displaced small businesses producing wood for the construction sector, the internal market, particularly the campesinos who had saws, sawmills, were closed down."[49] According to union leaders, the lack of state support for small producers and the monopoly of land, mills, and industries exercised by large forestry companies led to deepening rural poverty and stimulated peasants to migrate to the outskirts of rural towns and cities, "where they live in shanty towns on belts of poverty."[50]

The dispossession of campesinos in forestry zones was accompanied by the expulsion of resident laborers from estates dedicated to forestry production. As landowners sold their estates to the big forestry companies or turned to planting pines themselves, they began to evict permanent workers and their families. Where rural estates had once engaged in agricultural production that had sustained a significant population of inquilinos, they now substituted both agricultural crops and resident laborers with pine trees. Estates began to fire resident laborers and replace them with temporary workers hired by subcontractors. In 1978, for example, the 3,500-hectare estate Fundo "Penuchas," owned by Corfo, was sold to private owners, who proceeded to expel the inquilinos and their families, leaving 360 laborers without work and their families homeless.[51] On the Totoral estate in Coelemu, a disagreement over work hours between 20 workers and the estate's manager led to the workers' immediate dismissal. Shortly afterward, the estate was sold to a large forestry company that destroyed the former workers' houses (ranchas) and evicted the resident laborers. The workers and their families, most of whom had lived on the estate from twenty to thirty years, found themselves in a rural settlement on the side of a highway "without electricity, without water."[52] This case was repeated throughout the region. As the publication of the Archbishop's Pastoral Obrera (Workers' Pastoral Vicariate) in Concepción, El Pino Insigne, noted: "In Ranquelmo the Magosa [estate] joined the show and fired forty workers, not coincidentally the oldest. . . . And the Magaluf, [estate] with more than one hundred workers is shutting down this month. The Puchacay estate. They shut down here, they shut down there, dismissals, unemployment, problems, debts, vices, no union organization. This is the scene in Coelemu for the hard winter ahead."[53]

In Buena Esperanza, where Don Filadelfo Guzmán had helped to organize the Sindicato Nahuelbuta and then the Federación Campesina Caupolicán, the estate was sold in 1979 to Forestal Arauco, which then proceeded to expel the workers and their families. As Don Filadelfo recalled in a 1983 interview with *Pino Insigne:* "So then everything changed. The Forestal threw us all out and kept the forest that we had planted and that now is 33 years old."[54] One hundred and three workers and their families, who had lived on the estate from 15 to 40 years, were accused of being "revoltosos" for resisting the expulsion and were forced by carabineros to leave the estate and watch as trucks brought temporary workers hired by private contracting firms to work the forests.[55] The eviction brought an end to both the peasant community and the union that had been formed on Buena Esperanza during the early 1960s. For smallholders, as well as resident laborers, in the region, the expansion of Forestal Arauco also spelled disaster. Campesinos in the neighboring villages of Colico Norte and Temuco Chico who had not already sold their parcelas remained surrounded by the company's pine plantations. The only roads in the region were built for the company's trucks, and campesinos were prohibited access since the company alleged that their carts damaged the roads. In addition, campesinos were forbidden from entering the forests to collect firewood from fallen branches or to collect mushrooms, seeds, and cones, and Forestal Arauco installed private guards to expel those who entered. Campesinos from the neighboring Mundo Nuevo and Buena Esperanza villages wound up selling their lands to the company.[56]

The expulsion of the rural labor force from forestry areas was intensified by changes in regional ecosystems and strategies of land use. Traditional patterns of rural residence posed a threat to the extension of pine plantations, and large companies sought to displace smallholders and resident laborers from the margins of their expanding estates by establishing security zones protected by private guards on the outskirts of plantations. Forestry companies feared forest fires as a danger to their plantations and viewed campesinos, who relied on fire for fuel, heat, and clearing land, as a risk to their investments. Large pine plantations began to encircle campesinos' small plots and cut off their access to water, forests, and transit, making peasant production for subsistence increasingly untenable. As a union leader from the Federación Forestal Liberación noted: "In the province of Concepción there were a lot of smallholders [*pequeños propietarios*] with five to even 20 hectares of land. The holding companies that arrived [during the 1970s], Arauco, Mininco . . . surrounded and isolated the smallholders, provoking problems like today with the Mapuche. They had them trapped and didn't let them leave their lands. They couldn't raise animals since animals damage young pines. The campesinos were pressured off their lands and forced to leave for the city."[57] This assessment echoed a 1986 report by the Economic Commission on Latin America (CEPAL): "The sale of small farms increases in the zones where the large [forestry] companies operate. First, when they buy large amounts of land the companies close off the roads, putting obstacles in front of campesinos, forcing them to sell."[58]

Not only did the forestry companies interfere with traditional access to forest resources, they also damaged the environment for the peasants who remained. The testimony of a campesino printed in 1983 in *El Pino Insigne* described the disruption of peasant agriculture as native forests were replaced by pine plantations in the mountains. During the winter, the source noted, peasants would go into the mountains with their carts to bring back firewood for fuel and heat during the cold months. In addition, they would collect piñones (seeds from the cones of the *Araucaria araucana* tree) to be used as a substitute for flour, which was scarce in many rural areas. Peasants brought their livestock up into mountain forests for the winter, where the animals would be protected by trees and feed on tender bamboo shoots until they could return in the spring to pasture on grass in the valleys. Mountain streams provided water for peasants' small plots and at times trout for fishing. Peasants also hunted small game and birds in the forests:

> Nobody claimed the forests in the cordillera; everyone depended on them and used their products, but they didn't belong to anyone. . . . But if someone sets fire to the woods or if an ambitious forestry company destroys them, everyone ends up damaged because the rivers become muddy like chocolate and those who live below are left with no water; the birds [*choroyes*] take off and fly further south and no one can collect cones anymore or take animals up to pasture in the winter. . . . In our region we see that the plantations are fenced off, the roads are barred, the waters of the Andalién, Bío-Bío and Trongol rivers are contaminated because the landowners exploit the forests that grow on the banks of the watersheds and they don't care who uses the water below.[59]

Forestry companies replaced the native forests that had been the staple of the peasant economy with pine plantations that eroded the regional ecological biodiversity. In 1983 El Mercurio described the scene as forestry companies burned native forests in the cordillera in order to plant pines:

> The day was strange, Quilleco's sky [near Los Angeles, toward the cordillera] was lead gray and half pink, in spite of the fact that there were no clouds. . . . But, as you looked toward the mountains you saw what was happening: huge columns of smoke were rising from the hills. Fat raulíes with their yellow autumn leaves burned along with gigantic coigües more than thirty meters tall; secondary growths of robles, avellanos, and lingues were rapidly consumed by the flames. A small pudú [forest deer] jumped among the branches covered in flame looking for a stream to throw itself into. Torcazas and choroyes flew away toward somewhere where the pine hasn't yet arrived. The fire embraced the estates of Las Lumas, Olvillo, Manzanares, and Los Cuartos, whose lands covered three thousand hectares. Nothing was to be left alive, so that next winter Forestal Mininco could plant its pines. . . . They had to be planted in order to earn the forestation subsidy. . . . The business wasn't bad: you could get from the state around 25 million pesos [($9,600)] for each hectare planted.[60]

One hundred and twenty people lived and worked as resident laborers on the Los Cuartos estate, making poles of pellín and coal, selling firewood and hazelnuts, and raising animals. But when the estate was bought by Forestal Mininco, the inquilinos were expelled and a private guard was put in place to prevent access to the forests. As El Pino Insigne noted, "These events are repeated every year in our region. Who hasn't seen the pink clouds rising above the Nahuelbuta cordillera in burning season . . . or in Cayucupil, or Trongol, or Coihuesco, or Antuco? . . . Every year the companies burn between seven and ten thousand hectares of Chilean mountain forests in this region."[61] In effect, the state was paying private forestry companies to burn Chile's unique temperate rainforests and replace them with monocultural pine plantations.[62]

Pine plantations' corrosive effects on the regional rural ecology undermined the viability of campesino agricultural production. The extensive plantations caused the desiccation of topsoil and diminished the amount of water in the valleys at the feet of planted hillsides, leading to the deterioration of the conditions of agricultural production upon which peasants depended for their subsistence. Pine trees retain water in their needles, facilitating evaporation before water hits the soil, and pine plantations lack the low plants and bushes that grow in Chile's native forests and that help to conserve rainwater and humidity in the soil. In addition, the very concentrated nature of pine plantations—their biomass—means that they absorb several times the amount of water consumed by native forests. As one campesino noted in an early 1980s study, "In the zone of Maule any campesino can tell you that the watersheds are drying out, that the streams are exhausted. Now there are abandoned houses because of the lack of water. . . . Nobody can live in the middle of a [pine] forest."[63] Similarly, the wife of a forestry worker in the Eighth Region outside Concepción described in 1981 how "there is great poverty in the countryside. . . . There is no longer any water. . . . You have to go out in the world to look for water, far from the estuary. The pines suck up all the water that ran by here. . . . Before the plantations were here I remember that I had more than enough water for my garden."[64] She observed that peasant families who owned small parcelas had seen their livelihoods threatened by the drying-up of rivers and watersheds. The lack of water prevented the irrigation of the garden plots that campesino women cultivated and from which their families obtained an important part of their sustenance and a few pesos from what they marketed.

Lack of water, combined with diminished sunlight in densely planted plantations, also leads to a decline in the decomposition of organic materials and thus prevents the formation of a layer of nutrient-rich humus. As opposed to native forests, which maintain a thick layer of humus filled with nutrients from decayed vegetation, the soils of pine forests stay dry even during rainy winter months. While native forests have old and decayed trees that replenish the soil with nutrients during rains, plantation pines are harvested once they mature. Because pine plantation owners in Chile do not use fertilizers, after one or two plantings the soil becomes drained of its nutrients. Campesinos in areas dominated by plantations also complained that pines created excessive soil acidity, contaminating groundwater and poisoning wells and streams used for irrigation.[65]

Monocultural agricultural production in the form of pine plantations rendered southern forests and the forestry industry vulnerable to new pests and diseases. In 1953 there were eight known insects associated with pine plantations in Chile. By the 1990s over 50 species of insects fed on pine trees and posed a serious threat to their fragile ecosystems. In addition, pine plantations were plagued by rodents and rabbits that fed on the bark of the trees and the tops of young saplings. New fungi also attacked the trees and posed a serious threat to the plantations. In order to combat the spread of insects, fungi, and animals forestry companies sprayed pesticides and fungicides in areas inhabited by campesinos, often contaminating streams and the groundwater. The chemicals had a disastrous effect on the health of local peasant populations and on their farm animals and crops, in one case killing a child who drank contaminated water, and this danger to people's health contributed to the exodus from rural forestry zones.[66]

The fumigation of the pine plantations also contributed to the decimation of the population of wild game (rabbits, *liberes* [hares], and *perdices* [partridges]) that had provided an important supplement to peasants' diets, as well as the deaths of farm animals. Defoliants and herbicides aimed at destroying the native species that could compete with the pines and destroy the plantations also damaged crops on lands near plantations and contaminated groundwater. In 1986 CEPAL found that one of the principal factors in the exodus of campesinos from the countryside was "the difficulty that the small landowners confront in the poison used by the large forestry companies' plantations that is highly damaging to livestock."[67]

Peasants who had depended on forests for water, small game, and firewood now faced a threat to their subsistence as pesticides, herbicides, and defoliants made life and labor on the margins of the plantations impossible.[68] As a union leader and forestry worker observed, "In this zone [Concepción] that was a zone of campesinos, the smallholder produced everything he needed, potatoes, wheat, cereals. . . . He stayed in the forest. But everything changed. There is no longer any agricultural production in the countryside. There is no water for agriculture because the pines require a lot of irrigation. This region produced a lot of wine; there were numerous vineyards on the lands of smallholders. Almost everyone had vines, but now everything is over because of the lack of water, the fumigations. The forest blocks out the sun that the grapes need to grow."[69] A leader of the CTF similarly described the transformations in agricultural production wrought by the expansion of pine plantations:

> Where there were plantations there were no longer the things [campesinos] lived on, for example, forest animals. They could no longer hunt rabbits for food. They no longer had natural fruits like seeds that they could consume. They lost the biodiversity that there had been before because there was only pine and eucalyptus, and as we all know these are species that don't allow other kinds of life within the forest. The native forest allowed rabbits and other species to live there, while the other forests destroyed this biodiversity. As a consequence campesino families were surrounded and lost a great deal of space.[70]

Faced with low prices for agricultural goods and forest products, lack of credit, and the erosion of the regional ecosystem during the early 1980s, young campesino men looked to employment in government public works programs designed to alleviate unemployment, abandoning their fields. One 1983 press report noted that the Eighth Region was now "heavily forested" and that in areas traditionally dominated by a balance between pine plantations and small-holders who owned parcelas of four to eight hectares, most peasants had left and sold their lands. In campesino communities throughout the region, the report noted, it was common to see 300 to 400 young men working in government programs for the unemployed cleaning streets rather than working their fields.[71] The head of the Archbishop of Concepción's Departamento Campesino observed that "today you see something that never before occurred in the countryside. The campesinos are coming to the cities to work in the PEM (Programa de Empleo Mínimo) and they no longer cultivate the land or work in the forests."[72]

The displacement of peasant smallholders and estate laborers was exacerbated by the restructuring of the forestry industry. The reorientation of the industry away from the internal market for elaborated wood products and lumber to export markets for logs, wood pulp, and paper led to the firing of thousands of sawmill and factory workers. While exports of pulp and logs grew, employment in wood industries declined. Lino Lira, the president of the forestry workers' Federation Liberación, noted in 1983 that since the transition to the export of logs, the permanent labor force in industrial activities related to forestry had dropped by 70 percent and had been replaced by subcontracted temporary workers (temporeros).[73] Another union leader linked the growth in exports of unprocessed logs to forestry companies' focus on short-term profits and the low costs of planting and harvesting pine:

> A number of industries that produced goods for the domestic market closed down because they had to look to other markets. For us, it's a contradiction that businesses earned so much money exporting prime materials because in exporting logs, they shipped out the primary material that could have been used in our industries. . . . They only exported logs and why? Because they had the guarantee that they had huge amounts of forests for plantations. They planted exotic species that grew rapidly, that in Chile gave a very good result; in 25 years you could harvest what was planted and in other countries it could take 40 years. . . . They also need fewer workers for exporting logs, just for cutting down the trees and transporting them. They work the forests rapidly and earn profits fast too. Exploiting forests with other goals, with value added, requires more investment, more machinery, more workers . . . and the results take longer. It was easier and quicker [to grow pine and export logs].[74]

As the union leader noted, pine plantations and the export of unprocessed logs had lower labor costs and produced more immediate profits than the wood industries based on the exploitation of native forests. In 1983 El Pino Insigne noted that "the workers who labored in the wood factories of Antihuala, in the box factories in Escuadrón are unemployed. 'Forestry development' forced them to close because it was more profitable to export logs than sawed wood or than to make boxes. They worked 10, 16, or more years. Now they wait for some *contratista* [subcontractor] who works for Forestal Arauco to work in the forests for a piece rate."[75] In 1974 Chile exported no unprocessed tree products. Between 1976 and 1980 log exports grew from 17,000 cubic meters to 1,052,400 cubic meters. By 1988 this figure had reached 2,801,300 cubic meters.[76]

The large forestry companies also displaced small sawmills and wood factories and monopolized the internal market for wood products, substituting inexpensively grown pine products for the native woods worked by smaller mills and factories. Lino Lira observed in 1983 that "before in Concepción there were around 2,000 [small mobile] sawmills. Today there are no more than 15 [large mills], which has aggravated the situation of workers who work with axes and chainsaws."[77] Similarly, CEPAL found that "the emigration from the rural sector in areas with a large proportion of plantations has been produced fundamentally by the closing down of small sawmills that were absorbed by a few highly mechanized and capitalized mills."[78] Forestry companies' control of inexpensive raw materials (pine plantations) and access to modern technology and a cheap labor force of former rural workers and peasants allowed them to drive smaller mills and factories out of business and to dominate the internal market for wood products, as well as export markets for lumber, pulp, and paper. The replacement of native forests with pine plantations, native wood with pine, industrial wood products with exports of logs, and peasants with temporary wage laborers went hand in hand as forestry companies, unchecked, redrew the social and ecological landscape of southern Chile.

RESTRUCTURING AND THE LABOR FORCE

Unemployment caused by the expulsion of agricultural workers and peasants from forested lands and the decline in the industrial processing of wood products was exacerbated by the spread of subcontracting in the forestry industry. Forestry companies, unhindered by labor legislation or the presence of unions, began to dismiss their permanent labor forces and to replace them with workers employed by subcontracting firms during the 1970s. This process accelerated after the 1979 Labor Code made it possible for employers to fire permanent workers and to hire workers on a temporary basis without paying them benefits or negotiating collective contracts. Before 1973, 60 percent of forestry workers were permanent. The remaining 40 percent were hired on a seasonal basis from the population of peasant smallholders in forestry regions. In 1982 75 percent of forestry workers labored for less than six months for one employer, and 50 percent lasted two months at one job. Twenty percent changed jobs every month or two weeks.[79] In 1972 Forestal Arauco had employed 3,000 permanent workers. By 1978 it had cut this workforce by one-third, and in 1982 it fired the last 70 workers, transferring all its operations to subcontractors.[80] In 1984 the largest forestry companies, Forestal Arauco, Forestal Mininco, Crecex (Inforsa), and Celso had almost no permanent workers.

Workers in wood industries, sawmills, and logging camps had enjoyed job stability and a living wage that allowed them to support their families. When sawmills moved from forest to forest they brought their entire workforces with them, rather than shutting down, firing their workers, and rehiring workers from different regions. Companies moved entire families and their belongings and provided a basic infrastructure that allowed workers and their families to live a decent life. They were allowed access to the forests to collect wood and hunt and were given small patches of land to pasture animals and grow vegetables.[81] Forestal Arauco, under state management, had established three health clinics, housing, and schools for its 3,000 workers and their families. These were closed down when the company was privatized and the labor force shifted to subcontractors.[82]

Contratistas callampas (fly-by-night subcontractors) spread at an expanded pace after 1976. The contratistas competed for jobs from large forestry companies by lowering their costs at the expense of workers' salaries and work conditions. Often these subcontactors were former foremen, consultants, or technicians who had worked for large companies. In fact, many companies offered to give subcontracted jobs to their foremen and supervisors if they agreed to resign and start contracting firms.[83] Many of these small firms were undercapitalized and possessed no trucks, machinery, or tools. They hired workers on a temporary basis according to jobs contracted with the large forestry companies and covered their preliminary expenses with advances. The contratistas callampas had an ephemeral existence, often lasting a short time until being driven out of business. Until the mid-1980s, these companies frequently took on jobs, hired workers with the promise of a steady wage, operated until they received advances from the forestry companies or until they were paid for a portion of what they had produced and then closed down, abandoning their workers without pay when they realized they could not cover their debts or costs.

Many workers received no pay or only a part of their wages for their weeks of labor in logging camps. In 1983 a forestry worker described to El Pino Insigne how about 40 workers were hired by a contratista to cut wood on the "El Roble" estate:

We worked three months for the contratista who only paid us in vouchers. After two months we began to complain a little since we hadn't seen any cash. He promised us "the earth and sky," but when pay day came there was always another excuse. We were almost finished when one day we found out that the contratista had left. *Se echó el pollo* [he took off], as we say. So then we began proceedings in the courts. . . . We had a lawyer. There were judicial summonses, and we waited in the street for him [the contratista] for days to show up. Finally they located the contratista, but no one took responsibility for bringing him to the courts. . . .Three months almost given away for nothing to a contratista and with the wife and kids at home complaining [of hunger].[84]

That year the Departamento Campesino of the Archbishop of Concepción estimated that forestry subcontractors owed workers in the Eighth Region over 1 million pesos.[85]

Subcontractors survived by winning advances and credits and recruiting a low-wage temporary labor force from the large population of landless young men in the countryside. Far from urban centers, with little oversight from the Dirección del Trabajo (Labor Inspectorate), and facing no challenge from a moribund rural labor movement, contratistas reproduced 19th-century work conditions in their camps in order to reduce their expenses and compete for contracts. Contratistas used the remote locations of logging camps and private guards to cement workers' dependence on the job, prevent organizing, and avoid oversight by government inspectors. Because the camps were located in the mountains far from rural settlements and cities, most workers traveled to see their families between once every 15 days and once every four months. The small firms provided no transportation to and from the isolated camps and frequently recruited workers from other provinces to increase the isolation and dependence of the labor force. Contratistas offered no benefits and paid wages by the quantity of wood logged. Working by piece rate, workers frequently made less than the legal minimum wage. In 1980, for example, workers earned on average two dollars a day (60–70 pesos). Contratistas frequently undercounted the amount of wood cut by workers in order to reduce their pay and failed to pay social security contributions. Workers were forced to provide their own tools, boots, gloves, and helmets and lived in rudimentary huts, *rucos*, often sleeping on straw. The camps had no kitchens or formal cooking spaces, and workers were responsible for feeding themselves with food they brought from outside or purchased at artificially inflated prices at company concessions. Often they were paid in tokens that could only be redeemed at pulperías which often failed to list prices and discounted workers' debts from their wages. To save money workers frequently brought bread, chile peppers, and instant soups with them for their two-week to four-month stints in the camps. They survived on diets that barely allowed them to endure the arduous conditions of the camps and the physically difficult and dangerous labor of logging. During the early 1980s the average meal for most workers consisted of a piece of bread and broth made of boiled water, a chile, a couple of potatoes, and some noodles.[86]

Despite this diet, workers toiled in the forests for hours that often exceeded the maximum allowed by law. In 1982 a third of all forestry workers worked 56-hour weeks.[87] Because contratistas looked for unemployed and uneducated younger men with little experience in logging (the illiteracy rate among forestry workers was 30 percent, even higher than among campesinos) and provided no security equipment, the forestry industry had the highest number of accidents in the country, surpassing even the construction industry.[88] In 1983 union leader Lino Lira pointed out that accident rates were high in the forestry sector because "the owners don't even provide minimal systems of security on the job, since they don't provide helmets, boots, gloves, or adequate clothing."[89] In an extended 1984 interview with the bulletin Noticiero de la Realidad Agraria, Don Eliodoro, an old-time worker employed by a contratista working a farm near Concepción owned by the giant Forestal Mininco, provided vivid descriptions of work conditions in logging camps during the early 1980s:

> At times I have seen branch strippers who earn 5,000 or 6,000 pesos [a month] and have to support eight people. It's painful to see these guys: coffee in the morning, coffee at noon, and coffee at night. At the most a piece of bread. I've seen them in my own cuadrilla [work team]. . . . They work all day without eating. . . . At times even the branch strippers wind up soaked. I have seen them fainting from hunger. . . . We get up at seven . . . we have breakfast, coffee and bread, that we ourselves bring and prepare. The same with lunch. The lunch we prepare the night before. After work each of us cooks, eats, and keeps what's left over for lunch the next day. . . . Sometimes I go for an entire month eating nothing but beans. I also make a broth of potatoes. There are no eggs or meat. . . . Every 15 days more or less I go down to leave some money with my wife. We're 12 at home, including a grandchild and unemployed son-in-law . . . in a three-room house in a población in Concepción on land taken in an invasion.[90]

Don Eliodoro, a skilled worker who operated a chainsaw, earned 34 pesos for a metro ruma[91] and could earn up to 680 pesos a day "working himself to death."

In regions dedicated to the exploitation of native forests, rather than pine plantations, mostly located outside Valdivia in the Tenth Region, conditions for workers also deteriorated after 1973. Unlike the pine plantations, which provided wood for cellulose and paper plants, sawmills processing native woods supplied factories producing furniture, wood for construction, cardboard, moldings, veneers, and particle board. Until the 1990s, however, the native wood industry was dominated by small producers.[92] In part this was because both the Chilean state and international development agencies focused on the production of pine to supply the cellulose and paper industries after the 1940s, a development philosophy maintained by the military regime. World Bank loans in 1966 and 1975 funded an expansion of pine plantations and the installation of paper and pulp/cellulose plants. From an environmental perspective, the forestry strategy developed by the Chilean state during the 1940s, with the advice and assistance of the North American government and multilateral lending institutions, was to reproduce the environmental conditions of North America and to apply the technologies and systems of knowledge developed there in order to produce a profitable forestry industry. (In 1992, Conaf estimated that there remained only 250,000 hectares of native forest in the Eighth Region.)[93] As a Fenasic union leader noted of Conaf's forestry service, "On the pine plantations and the sawmills we have the most modern technologies and systems of production, just like in the United States, Europe, Japan, Canada. We have studies and detailed knowledge about everything having to do with pine and eucalyptus. But we know very little about managing native forests." He pointed out that the state and Conaf had invested little in studying the sustainable management and exploitation of Chile's native forests.[94]

In effect, it was cheaper to exchange natural environments, the forest and natural resources of Chile, for imported forests, technologies, and forms of exploitation than to develop a forestry industry based on the sustainable exploitation of Chile's native forests. The mountainous topography of the Tenth Region made growing pine and eucalyptus more difficult, since the trees grew at a slower rate at altitudes above 600 meters.[95] The result was that forestry policy tended to ignore the native forests of the Tenth Region, allowing a certain space for smallholders to continue their activities extracting wood and processing it through rudimentary sawmills for limited local and regional markets. As an Infor report observed in 1991: "The country has achieved the significant development of the forestry sector based on its plantations, which have impelled a dynamic and internationally competitive industry. However, in terms of its native forest resources, it has not known how to take advantage of the potential that these have as a source of primary materials and industrial growth." The report proposed the creation of programs to assist small producers in developing the sustainable exploitation of the Tenth Region's woods, which constituted nearly half (47.4 percent) of the country's native forests and 83 percent of the region's forest resources (pine composed only 6.9 percent of forests in the Tenth Region).[96]

Conditions for the small "artisan" mill owners who exploited native forests were often only marginally better than in the rest of the industry. Most businesses were owned by families, and most operators of small sawmills learned the job working with their fathers or as apprentices without a wage. These small sawmills employed four to nine people, almost always family members, in remote rural zones in the mountains, felling trees, cutting logs, and sawing lumber. During the late 1980s a third of mill owners gained access to wood by signing contracts with private landowners, 45 percent owned small farms with woods, and 22 percent purchased logs from third parties. Sawmill owners had little capital, worked on a seasonal basis during summers when the price of wood was high, depended on private landowners for access to forests, and had no access to credits or loans or to national market networks. Their equipment was rudimentary, often powered by energy from rivers or from burning firewood. As a CTF leader noted:

> In the south there are a large number of small sawmills without the technology of the modern sawmills, as in Coronel, which has the latest technologies . . . . They produce energy [for the mill] with firewood. They're small businesses who produce boards and exploit small woods; generally they only work when the weather is good because . . . they work without a roof—their mills are installed in the middle of the countryside, near a river because they need water for the engine, and they have no roof. They can't provide any kind of camp, bathroom; they work in conditions that are pretty artisanal and precarious.[97]

Because they lacked financing and credit and employed tools and machinery that were obsolescent, these mills produced low-quality wood suitable only for limited local markets. In addition, the production process was inefficient, leading to low production levels and the waste of woods. Small producers, saddled with debt and scratching to make a living, minimized their costs by employing unpaid family labor and apprentices and by extracting native woods from forests with little concern for the regeneration of forest resources.[98]

TRANSFORMATIONS IN HOUSEHOLD ECONOMIES AND THE BREAKDOWN OF RURAL COMMUNITIES

The restructuring of the forestry industry led to the transformation of the spatial organization of the countryside through the erosion of peasant household economies and changing patterns of residence and labor. In the Eighth Region, urban industries had traditionally provided an alternative for agricultural workers and peasants who maintained a steady flow of migration to Concepción, following family and village networks. After 1973, however, economic "shock" produced stagnation and unemployment in the urban sector as industries began to close their doors and cities no longer provided employment possibilities for displaced peasants. Concepción, a major center of national industrial activity, experienced a devastating economic crisis that drove regional unemployment levels far above already high national averages. By 1983 the Huachipato steel plant, which had employed 7,000 workers in 1972, had cut its workforce to 4,200. In Penco and Tomé, former centers of textile production, every plant had closed down except for the Bellavista factory, which operated at minimum capacity. In addition, the production of the region's coal mines continued to decline. In the Eighth Region unemployment reached 40 percent with 11 percent employed in the Programa de Empleo Minimo (PEM—Minimum Employment Program).[99] Former peasants migrated to squatter settlements throughout the countryside, usually on the sides of roads and highways, or to shantytowns in towns and small cities. There they constituted an easily available, inexpensive, and vulnerable temporary labor force for estates devoted to producing fruit and forest products for export markets.

The rural poblaciones that mushroomed throughout the south from Concepción to Valdivia after 1973 existed on the margins of urban society. They often lacked electricity, drinkable water, and sewage systems. In 1981 one report noted that "one can see along the roads running into the Pan-American Highway where before there had only been fields and copses, today there are groups of little multicolored houses. The same as in the poblaciones *marginales* of the big cities."[100] Few had medical clinics and pobladores had to travel long distances to other villages and towns to seek medical attention. Families survived on the meager wages earned by male temporeros and suffered the insecurity of living as illegal squatters.[101]

Life in squatter settlements contributed to changes in family relations and the household economy. Men were absent for long stretches of time as they followed jobs in areas of forestry activity, leaving their wives and families behind to fend for themselves. Often they returned for weekends with only small amounts of money, which failed to cover their families' expenses. As one woman noted in a 1983 study, her husband could only find work between the spring and summer months of September and January, traveling to different zones: "He's become an itinerant *jornalero* who, when he can find work, goes up to the forests and can only return home after a couple of weeks. . . . They offer him a wage and benefits and then later they don't pay anything and he has to come home without work, without money, worse off than before. Other times they pay him with the pulpería and he doesn't get another peso. And all this effects how he treats his wife and children."[102] In stark contrast to the conservative profamily rhetoric of the Pinochet regime, the changes introduced by the military government rendered family relations in the countryside increasingly unstable as the economic basis of rural household economies was undermined by new patterns of labor and residence.[103]

Women confronted a shrinking horizon of possibilities. If they had held on to small plots of land in plantation zones, these no longer produced crops to feed their families because of the lack of water, and if they lived in rural settlements they often had no land at all. One woman described how in the rural poblaciones women could no longer grow vegetables to feed their families as they had done before: "Here what can grow? . . . A small piece of land is filled up by a couple of tiny potatoes." Instead of the wheat, lentils, navy beans, green beans, lima beans, tomatoes, onions, cilantro, and parsley that women grew in the countryside, "here one has a nothing of a parcel of land to cultivate."[104] A forestry workers union leader similarly described how the spread of plantations had transformed women's lives:

> Before women irrigated land, cultivated their gardens, and the children also worked; they collected things in the forest like seeds, and with the change to the forestry industry they were isolated in their little houses in any place [they could go], in small settlements anywhere they could, very isolated, and women only stayed inside the house, preparing food for the children, but there were no longer any other possibilities for earning money.[105]

The breakdown in the rural household economy described in these interviews reflected the more general fragmentation of campesino communities throughout the countryside and the separation of workplace from residence that accompanied the process of descampinización or proletarianization after 1973. A union leader noted that the dispersal of the rural population was due both to the peregrinations of men throughout the forestry economy and the lack of income and resources that could support families and allow the maintenance of permanent communities: "The peasants can't live in a permanent community anymore—to form a permanent community they need income to support it. If there's no work, there's no community. They've been transformed into permanent migrants who travel to Concepción, Temuco, Valdivia, looking for work, knocking on doors."[106] The same union leader noted the abrupt changes in rhythms of work and time as campesinos were converted into temporary forestry workers: "Now they're realizing that . . . life in the countryside was much less difficult in terms of the hours they worked. In the industries they have to work on the basis of productivity and quantity. There is more pressure in terms of your work responsibilities. Everyday you have the uncertainty of whether your job will end."

For women in forestry zones, the changes introduced by the expansion of plantations and agro-industry were particularly acute. Unlike in Chile's central valleys, where fruit plantations began to hire women in large numbers as temporeras, until the mid-1990s forestry work in all stages of the production process—collecting and planting seeds, thinning and pruning, logging, transportation, industrial work in saw mills, wood factories, and paper and pulp plants—was defined as a masculine domain.[107] In the case of the forestry sector, the erosion of the peasant household economy did not contribute to a reorganization of rural patriarchy within communities or families or to opening new social spaces for women. Rather, the transformation of male campesinos and former inquilinos into migrant temporeros was accompanied by women's increased subordination to men and a reaffirmation of patterns of patriarchy, even as households and families were thrown apart by the spatial reorganization of patterns of work and residence.

THE LABOR MOVEMENT UNDER MILITARY RULE

Military repression, the restructuring of the forestry industry, and the reordering of rural labor and land relations provoked an abrupt decline in union activity. As forestry unions struggled to survive during the 1970s, union leaders faced dismissal, arrest, and internal exile. Many unionized companies replaced their workforces with nonunionized temporary workers or simply closed down and moved to other regions where they opened up under different names. The campesino unions that had been organized at the level of *comunas* and on rural estates completely disappeared after 1973, decimated by repression and by the break-up of rural communities with the restructuring of the forestry industry. By the early 1980s, however, following the reemergence of the national labor movement and a reinvigorated grassroots struggle for democracy in urban poblaciones, forestry workers began to rebuild their unions. In August 1984, forestry workers employed by three subcontracting firms in Cerro Alto and Los Álamos, outside Concepción, formed the first interindustry union, the Sindicato Interempresa "El Araucano," with a seat located in the coal miners' union hall. After two months the union had 150 members. In October of the same year, a group of 10 forestry, wood, and paper unions with more than 1,500 members founded a regional federation in Concepción.[108] These new unions reflected efforts by labor activists to organize and negotiate contracts by region, rather than company, and rebuild the kinds of region and industry-wide organizations that had characterized the pre-1973 labor movement. Organizing workers employed by contratistas in regional unions gave temporary workers more clout and raised the possibility of negotiating regional contracts with employers. In addition, by linking forestry workers' unions to the unions of industrial workers in cellulose, wood, and paper plants, the new regional federation made it possible for unions to negotiate with employers, like Forestal Arauco, whose activities spanned the gamut of these activities, even if their operations were divided among a variety of subsidiaries. Regional labor organizations created the possibility for workers to overcome the structural and geographical obstacles presented by the dispersal of the workforce and the fragmentation of the industry. However, workers continued to confront legal obstacles to unionization at regional levels since the 1979 Labor Code neither recognized the legal status of industry-wide or regional unions nor required employers to bargain with temporary workers. Subcontractors were under no obligation to bargain with workers and could use the temporary nature of work to fire labor activists and impede the unionization of their labor force. Until the early 1990s these new unions were unable to organize strikes or win significant concessions from employers.

The Catholic Church played an important role in the reanimation of the labor movement among forestry workers. In Concepción, the church's Vicaría Pastoral Obrera organized classes for workers on how to organize unions and offered training and education for union leaders. Workers held meetings in the Vicaría's offices as they attempted to build new union networks. In addition, the Vicaría published a clandestine newsletter, El Pino Insigne, that documented work conditions and labor conflicts in the forestry sector. The newsletter interviewed workers and union leaders and provided updates on organizing campaigns, strikes, and dismissals. El Pino Insigne also provided accounts of the history of the forestry sector and rural labor and land relations in the region. The Vicaría organized social assistance programs in the new rural poblaciones, creating small projects to earn residents income and providing classes on how to make do with the resources at their disposal. During strikes workers held assemblies, cultural acts, and organized soup kitchens in the Vicaría. In addition, the Vicaría provided legal aid to workers. In 1983, for example, the Vicaría helped bring lawsuits on behalf of 180 workers against 12 subcontracting companies for failing to pay workers' salaries.[109] Union leader and cofounder of the CTF, Caupolicán Pavez, observed: "I don't believe that there is a union or a federation, in any sector of the economy, that didn't receive the support of the

Vicaría [in Concepción]. We held union meetings at the Vicaría, and even today the old union leaders keep meeting there."[110] Under military dictatorship the Vicaría provided one of the few places where union leaders and workers could hold meetings.

Despite the rebuilding of forestry workers' unions after 1983, repression by the dictatorship and the structural conditions of the industry imposed limits on organizing. The military regime responded to the reemergence of rural unions in Concepción by jailing and sending union leaders into internal exile. On 4 February 1985, Lino Lara Valenzuela, president of Federación Campesina Liberación, and Carlos López López, president of Sindicato Agrícola Manuel Rodríguez and vice president of the Federación Liberación, along with four other regional union leaders, were arrested at five in the morning and sent to the Campamento Militar de Conchi in the Atacama Desert for four months, where they were joined by more than 20 other union leaders from Santiago and Valparaíso. They were then relegated for three more months to distant villages in the north such as Pisagua, site of a concentration camp since the 1940s.[111] Workers' efforts to rebuild the labor movement in the forestry sector were also hampered by the 1978 Labor Code and the post-1973 restructuring of the industry. Almost three-quarters of all forestry workers labored for small subcontractors on a temporary basis and thus could not legally bargain collectively. In addition, the transience of this labor force made it extremely difficult to organize. Workers moved from work site to work site, employer to employer, region to region on an almost monthly basis. In logging camps, workers remained isolated and dependent, cut off from communication with the outside world. The expulsion of rural workers from farms, estates, and parcelas led to the dispersal of forestry families throughout rural areas and the breakup of local communities that had provided the foundation of the militant rural labor movement of the 1960s.

In 1989, as it contemplated labor strategies for the transition to democracy, the recently organized Confederación de Trabajadores Forestales noted the importance of organizing new unions and federations of new "modern" workers in the agro-industrial sector. The CTF observed that campesinos and campesino unions had been replaced by a largely nonunionized wage-earning work force of former campesinos. Owing to repression, the expulsion of inquilinos and campesinos from the countryside, and the regime's labor code, the campesino unions that had been the backbone of the rural labor movement before 1973, such as the Confederación Ranquil, had disappeared.[112] A 1998 CTF report echoed the conclusion that the nature of the forestry labor force had been transformed by proletarianization or descampinización: "The appropriation of land by transnationals has meant the conversion of thousands of former campesinos into modern forestry and wood workers."[113] The transformation of campesinos and inquilinos into rural proletarians, temporary wage workers with no access to land, was the major impediment confronting the labor movement in the forestry sector. Proletarianization had undermined the bases of the once powerful rural labor movement without creating the conditions for new union organizations. In 1989 only 11,000 workers, around 10 percent of the forestry labor force, were organized in three unions: the Federación Liberación in the Eighth Region; the Federación Nacional de la Madera in the Eighth, Ninth, and Tenth regions; and the Federación Forestal Maule. These three unions formed the Confederación de Trabajadores Forestales in 1988.

The case of 40 forestry workers employed by the contratista Empresa "Sociedad Agrícola y Forestal CEP, Concepción during the 1980s illustrates the constraints on labor activism. In late 1983 workers engaged in a work stoppage and sued the company for failing to pay wages and benefits and for "continually harassing and humiliating workers": "They often made us wait until late, deceiving us that the money, the salary, was on the way; then they ordered a change of site and left us waiting in the meantime. On three occasions, because some compañeros dared to complain, they sent carabineros." As the court case and strike dragged on, workers and their families organized a soup kitchen (olla común) in the Vicaría Pastoral Obrera for three months. Through the Vicaría they received legal assistance and financial support from unions in the region that provided their children food and dental and medical care. The Vicaría also served as a center for meetings and legal proceedings. Workers held a raffle and cultural events to raise money, in which they "denounced the violations of our rights by the employers and the impotence of the workers to gain their rights." After three months the courts found in the workers' favor, but the contratista had disappeared and the workers never received their wages.[114]

Beyond employers' ability to intimidate workers, dismiss union activists, and move to other regions and the legal constraints imposed by labor law, union organizers confronted the effects of military repression and economic insecurity on workers. One founder of the CTF noted, for example, that it had been extremely difficult to reorganize unions during the early 1980s. He had had to travel throughout the countryside, going into the forests to talk to old workers. To win their trust he often was accompanied by old-time union leaders who were known in the region. He noted that forestry workers had their own culture, which marked them as different even from other workers (even from the same regions) and were suspicious of outsiders. This lack of trust was exacerbated by repression: "They are still afraid. They saw union leaders killed after 1973 and think, 'Maybe there will be another coup and I'll be killed.' "[115] Only between 10 and 12 percent of forestry workers were organized since, "often for fear of losing their jobs, they prefer not to participate in the union and accept the bosses' conditions."[116] It was hard to find workers willing to take on the responsibilities of organizing unions because of this fear of losing their jobs or their lives. In addition, union leaders were unpaid, and the union job constituted for them a second shift. Forestry workers' unions had little financial base since few workers could afford to pay dues and could rarely pay union leaders who could only tend to union business when they were off work. This left little time for organizing, which required a great deal of travel from work site to work site as union leaders attempted to communicate with the transient labor force.

Despite the resurgence of unionization during the early 1980s and the organization of some regional union federations and the CTF, forestry workers approached the transition to democracy in a weakened position. The CTF's 1989 "Proposal for Democracy" reflected workers' sense that only profound changes in labor legislation and state regulation of the forestry sector and intervention in labor-capital relations would improve work conditions and the possibilities for building a strong labor movement. The "Proposal" also indicated the unions' efforts to reverse the social and ecological changes that had provoked the descampinización of the countryside. In many ways, the CTF "Proposal" called for a return to pre-1973 conditions when small landholders and mill owners played a significant part in the forestry industry and the state promoted the development of industries and regulated reforestation and the management of native forests.[117]

Beyond basic demands for the elimination of subcontractors and temporary work, the institution of an eight-hour day, partial employer financing of unions, and national and sectoral contracts negotiated by the CTF and the regional federations, the CTF critiqued the neoliberal model of development and proposed state intervention to support small and medium-size landowners and industries that produced wood products for the domestic market. Rather than the export of forestry products with little added value, the CTF advocated the transfer of technology and technical assistance to small producers in order to "incorporate the maximum value added to forestry products." The CTF called on the state to promote internal markets for industrialized wood commodities produced by small and medium businesses. The "Proposal" asked for a revision of the subsidy structures in D.L. 701 in order to "direct its benefits to small and medium proprietors, subsidizing and assigning state financing according to scales of production. . . . A strong credit incentive is necessary for small and medium companies, creators of large number of jobs . . . [along with] technical support, technology, and marketing to supply the domestic, not the external, market."

The CTF proposed, in effect, that the state intervene to reproduce the developmentalist programs and policies of the pre-1973 period and reestablish the social arrangements that had characterized the pre-1973 forestry industry. Thus the CTF urged the state to establish incentives for the small landowners with forests, "with the objective of . . . integrating agricultural cultivation, forestry, and the pasture of animals on their farms" in order to rebuild the vanishing campesino economy. In addition, the CTF proposed subsidies and credits for small sawmill owners, as well as training for workers and owners in order to make small wood producers' use of forests more efficient and ecologically viable. The CTF argued that "credit and technical assistance to campesinos with native forests and the promotion of marketing cooperatives" would "ensure the management of forest resources and the price of wood." The CTF also called for a "revision and redefinition of the transfer of lands from indigenous communities to private companies and an inventory of forests on indigenous lands."

The CTF proposal hinged on a reevaluation of the social ecology of forestry development. It explicitly linked the post-1973 reorganization of the forestry industry and the restructuring of agrarian labor and land relations to destructive environmental changes. The CTF noted the ecological precariousness of a development model rooted in monocultural export agriculture and the effects of ecological transformations on campesinos and workers. Diversification within the forestry sector would not just involve the establishment of a variety of industrial forestry activities oriented toward the internal market; it would also depend on ecological diversification. By promoting the sustainable exploitation of native forests, the CTF plan would prevent the wholesale destruction of these diverse ecosystems and their replacement by pine and eucalyptus plantations. Thus the CTF proposed that the native forests of the precordillera be incorporated into regional economies "through the production of wood, firewood, honey, hazelnuts, prohibiting their complete transformation into wood chips, which will ensure, among other things, that they not be replaced with pines." The CTF noted that its proposals for reforms of the forestry sector were directed at promoting "the preservation of species and natural environments for the future generations." To this end the CTF advocated a return to the pre-1973 system of state regulation of forestry exploitation and curbs on the substitution of pine plantations for native forests: "We propose that our native forests be submitted to the tutelage of the state to ensure their preservation and to prevent the substitution of the species that we observe today."

The CTF's proposal represented a combination of the concerns of environmentalists and the labor movement. While it acknowledged that pine plantations were an established economic and ecological fact, the CTF linked the spread of the plantations to the social and economic changes that had redefined the terms of labor and land relations and allowed the domination of the industry by a few large companies oriented toward export markets. The CTF recognized the expansion of plantations as a menace to native forests and to the jobs and work conditions of forestry workers. The union's vision was not narrowly conservationist but provided a program for combining commercial and subsistence agricultural production, forests and agricultural crops, pine plantations and native forests in order to satisfy the demands of workers and peasants who depended both on native forests for subsistence and the commercial exploitation of native forests by wood industries.

THE LABOR MOVEMENT IN THE FORESTRY SECTOR DURING THE 1990S

Under the governments of the Concertación the forestry sector continued to expand at rates exceeding levels of national economic growth. By 1997 exports of forest products accounted for 11 percent of Chile's export revenues, third behind mining (51 percent) and industry (30 percent), and had nearly tripled in value from $771.2 million in 1989 to $1,920.7 million in 1997. Exports of wood chips, pulp, and logs continued to expand under the governments of the Concertación with pulp accounting for 38 percent of forestry export earnings.[118] The major change in the industry was a significant increase in foreign investment beginning in the late 1980s, before the transition to democracy, and increasing during the 1990s. Following the 1982–85 economic crisis and the bankruptcy of a number of large financial groups, foreign investment flooded into the forestry sector. In 1985 foreign investment amounted to $350 million. By 1989 this figure had reached just under $800 million and in 1993 $1,200 million.[119] Transnational logging companies from Canada, the United States, Switzerland, New Zealand, and Japan, often in joint ventures with Chilean capital, began to purchase plantations and native forests and install wood chip and cellulose plants.[120] While in 1986 Chile exported no wood chips, in 1991 it exported 3,066,000 tons, and in 1995, 4,076,500 tons.[121] In 1992 Japan purchased 80 percent of the world production of wood chips (used for making computer and fax paper), and Chile was Japan's third largest supplier.[122] The explosion of the wood chip industry led to the intensified exploitation of native forests in the Tenth Region by Japanese, United States, and Chilean companies. At the same time, these companies also began to cultivate eucalyptus plantations to supply their factories, and tree plantations began to replace native forests in the Tenth Region. Eucalyptus was attractive to transnationals since it produced wood apt for high-quality paper products and thus earned higher prices than pine.[123] Between 1989 and 1998 Chilean and transnational companies planted fifteen thousand hectares of pine and eucalyptus—the majority eucalyptus—annually in the Tenth Region for cellulose and chip production.

Despite growth in investment, production, and exports in the forestry sector and the CTF's ambitious program of reform for the forestry industry, the transition to democracy failed to meet forestry workers' expectations. For workers, conditions in some logging camps improved due to pressure from the unions and increased state regulation, but in many camps run by subcontractors conditions remained the same. Following the 1983 recession, many of the small contratistas had gone bankrupt, leaving a smaller number of bigger companies that were able to guarantee better work conditions. In addition, through bringing cases to the Inspección del Trabajo during the 1990s, unions were able to force a number of contratistas to improve conditions in the camps and pay workers' salaries.[124] A union leader noted that "in the large companies and consortiums, like the COPEC group, the Shell group, we know that they are pressuring the contratistas to improve work conditions." "On the other hand," he continued, "if we go into the Nahuelbuta Cordillera we see really miserable conditions, where forestry workers still live in huts and depend on a pulpería, that in the majority of cases, belongs to the contratista. The contratista contracts people for one month, two months, three months sometimes; and no one regulates him. . . . There are contratistas that have beaten workers for the sole fact of demanding their wages, demanding their rights." Union leaders noted that often in the worst cases, contratistas preferred to go to courts, where cases could take years, and then pay small fines to changing conditions in the camps.[125] As late as 1996, despite improvements under the governments of the Concertación, 82 percent of forestry workers lived beneath the poverty line and 18 percent received less than the minimum wage (in the Eighth Region this figure rose to 27 percent).[126]

Under the governments of the Concertación workers continued to confront serious obstacles to organizing due to the labor legislation implemented under the dictatorship, the restructuring of the forestry industry, the legacy of fear left by years of repression, and the intransigence of employers. In 2000 one union leader wondered, "How are we to organize workers who have two-month contracts? . . . When workers try to negotiate with employers extralegally [since the labor code does not require employers to bargain with temporary workers], they simply dismiss the workers. We have almost no possibility of bargaining collectively and the majority of the workers aren't organized. There is still persecution of union leaders. If we try to organize a work site, after two months they close down the work site, fire the guys, and then the next month they call the same workers and sign them to new contracts, without the union, and at lower wages."[127] The union leader observed that few workers had any familiarity or experience with unions, and that most had no job stability and continued to fear repression: "No one wants to participate in the union because of fear. Right now we're trying to negotiate contracts in two companies, but what's the point if in four months they shut down and there is no work? The union has little credibility and legitimacy among the workers. The workers want to demand wage increases, immediate benefits, but the union is trying to protect their jobs. Owners offer them incentives not to join the union: 'We'd give you raises or bonuses, but you're unionized.' On a large estate of 30,000 hectares there could be thirty different contratistas, so the workers are divided by activity and company." For union leaders, the lack of resources for unions also limited their capacity to organize workers: "It is difficult for the unions to get to the camps. They have few resources. You have to go in personal vehicles, you have to rent a car, or convince a friend to take you. There are workers in camps that are very distant from any human settlement."[128]

In 1998 the CTF pointed out, "Our union movement is in decline for many reasons. . . . There still is a great deal of fear, as much of the military as of the bosses."[129] The weak unions of forestry workers were able to launch few strikes during the 1990s because they were hampered by labor legislation inherited from the dictatorship. As another union leader noted: "The truth is that the strike hasn't been used much in the forestry sector because we haven't had very good experiences of strikes, because we have lost more than we have won. . . . The companies are allowed to hire strike breakers, and that undermines the movement. If the compañeros are on strike, they have to return to work for whatever the bosses want to give them."[130] The weakness of the labor movement in the forestry sector led workers to be increasingly skeptical about joining unions. Union leaders noted that memberships had dropped during the late 1980s and 1990s, precisely during the transition to democracy, because a new generation of younger workers neither shared the union experiences of older workers nor viewed unions as effective tools for improving work conditions and wages. A regional labor organizer in Concepción contrasted the well-organized and militant Mapuche movement of the 1990s that challenged the rights of forestry companies to forest lands and the weak labor movement among forestry workers.[131] He noted that the Mapuche movement was rooted in a strong sense of community and cultural identity that relied on a powerful historical memory—memory of struggles over land, ethnic conflicts, and family histories. Forestry workers no longer resided in communities with long-standing traditions, and they worked for only short stints at the same job. An entire generation separated them from the land conflicts and labor actions prior to the military coup, and the breakup of communities after 1973 had fragmented the historical memory that might have served as a vehicle for political identity and collective action. By the late 1980s and 1990s most forestry workers were young men. And, as the union organizer observed, these workers had little experience with strikes or unions and had been thrown into the workforce following the erosion of campesino communities. A 1998 CTF report noted the problem of generation, memory, and the transformation of the forestry labor force through proletarianization: "It is a working class that is young and that doesn't have a meaningful experience of strikes and that has, for the same reason, a high grade of identification with the company."[132]

In an oral history interview, a CTF leader noted problems of generation in organizing forestry workers: "There were 17 years in which they cultivated fear . . . and this was important because the youth are no longer 'with it' [no está ni allí]. . . . You speak to them about unionization and they say, 'Ah, I'm not into that, I like to go to bars, to hang out.' They have other concerns, and the older workers are still afraid of the dictatorship that also launched a campaign to delegitimize unions. They say, 'The guy who gets involved with the union is a communist.' They speak worse of the unions than the businesses."[133] For this worker, one of the legacies of the dictatorship was "apoliticism" and a lack of political culture, a rejection of political parties and the role of parties in the unions. Workers frequently viewed union leaders as "haciendo política" (politicking), rather than fighting for their interests since unions could provide little in the way of material benefits for workers because they were hindered by labor legislation that precluded collective bargaining and made strikes ineffective.

In 1992 CTF leaders who had worked with and supported the Concertación de Partidos por la Democracia (Coalition of Parties for Democracy) noted their disillusion with the coalition democratic governments. According to union leaders, as soon as the elections were over members of the governing parties lost interest in meeting with union leaders or responding to workers' demands. A former CTF leader described how union leaders had met with delegations from the Concertación "to discuss the future of forestry that, in our opinion, is in the industrialization of wood. It doesn't serve the country to keep exporting logs or mountains of chips, its necessary to add value to production, to develop an industrial complex of wood." However, "When the regional branch of the CUT in Concepción convoked a forum with the participation of senators and deputies, only two came and one left immediately, because maybe they were afraid of confronting union leaders."[134] This situation had only deteriorated from the forestry workers' point of view at the end of the decade. The same union leader noted in 1998 that "once democracy arrived . . . the politicians didn't even meet with union leaders after the first two or three years. . . . I don't see any fluid dialogue between the unions and the government as existed before during the dictatorship. . . . In those days we were 'good friends,' but the other day I was in a meeting in Concepción with union leaders and we had invited five deputies from this zone and not one came."[135]

By 1998 the CTF leadership had become even more critical of the Concertación. Headed by militants of the Communist party, the CTF adopted a militant posture both toward the CUT and the government. In its report for 1998 the CTF argued that organizing in the forestry sector had been hampered by the lack of support from the government, the CUT's compliance with the policies of the Concertación, and the labor movement's adherence to the 1978 Labor Code.[136] In addition, the CTF argued that the federation of forestry workers, like other union structures, had been organized out of legal compliance with the labor code and not out of organizing at the grassroots level. Following the dictates of the code had, the CTF asserted, limited the union's scope of activity and impeded strengthening the organization "because we are legalistic in the extreme and we don't take a step if it is not laid out in the Labor Code. In this terrible code it is established that collective bargaining is a privilege for those who have permanent contracts and collective negotiation is tied to the union by company . . . and this produces the marginalization of thousands of workers from the right to organize. . . . On the other hand, we ourselves have not been capable of mentally freeing ourselves and creating our own system of organization." The CTF report argued that because unions had stuck too closely to the letter of the law and lent their unconditional support to the Concertación, they had lost the strength that came from organizing at the base. "In our best moment [1989–90] we brought together 67 unions and nearly 10,000 workers; today we have no more than 40, and we barely represent 6,000 workers."[137] Union membership in the forestry sector had actually declined during the 1990s. The CTF looked to the example of the regional union of temporary workers, the Sindicato La Araucaría in Arauco, as a model of a new kind of organizing that bypassed the limitations of the labor code by operating at a sectoral and regional level and by placing pressure on the state, rather than negotiating on a plant-by-plant basis with individual employers. The CTF imagined unions organized by locality rather than workplace or employer in which the union "represents all the workers and their families . . . and leads mobilizations directed at provincial and communal authorities."

Despite the CTF's more militant stance at the end of the 1990s, the labor movement in the forestry sector made little headway in the struggle to build strong unions, improve work conditions and wages, and deter the expansion of plantations and elimination of native forests. The governments of the Concertación remained wedded to an economic model that prioritized export-oriented commercial agriculture and foreign investment and made little effort to regulate commercial logging or to expand state management of native forests. In addition, at the end of the decade no significant amendments to the labor legislation handed down by the Pinochet dictatorship had been passed in a Congress where "appointed" senators blocked the Concertación's proposed labor reforms. As the CTF understood in 1998, only extralegal forms of organizing by region and a more independent and confrontational posture toward the Concertación would allow workers to rebuild unions and challenge the authority of the forestry companies. CTF leaders perceived that they would receive little help from the state in attempting to overcome the obstacles presented by the restructuring of the forestry industry and the reorganization of labor and land relations in the countryside. It would take new forms of grassroots organizing, rooted in rural communities rather than work sites, and a new understanding of what it meant to be a worker for a new generation of proletarianized but temporary seasonal laborers whose ties to the world of the campesino economy had been severed.

In 2002 I traveled around Lago Panguipulli into the Cordillera de los Andes to the town of Neltume, a large landed estate until it was expropriated and incorporated into the socialist Complejo Maderero Panguipulli in 1971. On the trip up the dirt roads into the high-altitude Andean forests I was able to appreciate the marks of history on the mountain landscape. Huge swaths of cleared native forest scarred mountain sides and tree plantations, many of pine, dotted the hills, designated to supply the companies lumbering the region in accordance with new legislation, passed under the Concertación and enforced for the first time by Conaf in the late 1990s, that required companies to reforest cleared lands. In 1997 the French company logging Neltume had been fined 800 million pesos for destroying native forests, and despite commitments to Conaf it continued to ignore prescribed forest management plans.[138] At the entrance to

Neltume is a memorial to the many forestry workers assassinated or disappeared by the military dictatorship: a statue of a bare-chested worker with a plaque with the names of the Complejo workers who perished after 1973. Many of the estates that belonged to the Complejo had been either returned to their former owners or auctioned off during the 1980s. For a time during the late 1970s the Complejo was run by General Pinochet's son-in-law, Julio Ponce, who lined his own pockets by selling off the Complejo's assets undercover to the armed forces. Today, many of the estates are moribund as their owners wait for a new cellulose plant to be established in the region, but Neltume is owned by the French company, Forestal Neltume Carranco S.A.[139]

Neltume has the air of a desolate company town, isolated in the mountains and guarded by a carabineros station at the entrance to town. Most of the residents work for the logging company, but few are actual employees. Instead they labor for small contratistas who compete for logging jobs. Like the contratistas in the mountains outside Concepción during the 1980s and early 1990s, the subcontractors are often former employees of the company or fellow workers. They bid on jobs, and workers pay the price in low wages, lack of benefits, no overtime, no insurance against accidents, no social security or health care, and no job security. Workers supply their own gear and tools. Often contratistas pay them with chits that can be used to purchase goods at one of the few stores in town, and often store owners operate as contratistas. The subcontractors hire fewer than 25 workers in order to prevent unionization, and labor inspectors never make it to this isolated mountain region near the frontier with Argentina. Workers who seek legal remedies or complain about abuses to the company are frequently fired and face unemployment. A young worker I interviewed, the son of a forestry worker from the region and brother of one of the workers killed by the army after 1973, has worked for over 20 separate contratistas over the last decade. In each case, he and his fellow workers logged the mountains for anywhere from one month to six months until the pay checks, always late in coming, began to disappear. After working for a month or so without pay, they would quit and look for work with another contratista who could pay, giving up on their lost wages. And the cycle would begin again. In Neltume it is hard to see how over a decade of democratically elected governments have made much of a difference.

During the almost three decades following the military coup, the forestry sector became Chile's third most important source of foreign earnings. Decades of state investments in plantations and industrial plants producing cellulose, paper, and wood after 1946 laid the basis for the "boom" in forestry exports and reforestation of the 1970s and 1980s. Under the governments of the

Concertación this growth continued at an even more rapid rate as foreign investment poured into new enterprises that planted pine and eucalyptus and exported logs, wood chips, and pulp. While the transition democratic governments have presided over impressive annual increases in forestry exports, they have not addressed the profound ecological and social dislocations caused by the spread of monocultural plantations and the monopoly of forest lands by commercial logging companies. The coalition governments have failed to elaborate an environmental policy that would establish the sustainable management of what remains of Chile's temperate rain forests. In addition, they have done little to improve labor relations and social conditions in the forestry sector, where workers suffer some of the worst working conditions in Chile. As the labor movement rebuilds, it offers an important critique of the links between the spread of plantations and destruction of forests and the social changes in the countryside since 1973. Forestry workers' unions have articulated an alternative vision of how the forestry industry might sustain both the ecological biodiversity of Chile's native forests and improved work conditions for workers and campesinos. The unions' growing understanding of the close ties between the natural worlds of forests and the social worlds in which labor and land are, like rare native hardwoods, transformed into commodities, bridges the concerns of union and environmental activists and provides an important alternative to the widely accepted view that the market is the best regulator of both labor relations and the environment.

NOTES

This essay is based on research I have done for a project on labor and the environment in Chile's southern forests from the late 19th to the late 20th century. I would like to thank Peter Winn for his insightful comments and my research assistant in Chile, Alberto Harambour, for his invaluable contributions to this project. I would also like to thank the Departamento de Pastoral Obrera of the Arzobispado de Concepción, specifically Jaime Torres and Eduardo Mora, union leaders from the Confederación de Trabajadores Forestales (CTF) and the Federación Liberación, and Caupolicán Pavez, a former head of the CTF.

1 GIA (Grupo de Investigaciones Agrarias), *Noticiero de la realidad agraria*, no. 15 (January 1984).
2 Instituto Forestal (Infor), "Boletín Estadístico," no. 61. *Estadísticas Forestales*, 1997.
3 Mapuche communities are organized in a variety of organizations with varying approaches to confrontations with forestry companies and the state: the Coordinadora

de Comunidades en Conflicto de Arauco y Malleco; the Asociación Comunal Ñanku-cheu de Lumako; and the Consejo de Todas las Tierras. For a discussion of these groups and "the Mapuche conflict," see *Punto Final*, 19 March–2 April 1999.

4 Despite the contention by most observers that the Mapuche movement represents a struggle for land and ethnic rights, the Mapuche organizations have important ties to the rural labor movement. Thus the Coordinadora de Comunidades en Conflicto de Arauco y Malleco held its founding meeting in the union hall of the CTF in Concepción with support from the forestry workers unions. Forestry workers and Mapuche communities share a history of the pre-1973 union movement and land invasions and a common enemy in the large forestry companies that dominate the southern agricultural economy. In addition, many forestry workers have ties to Mapuche communities. Interviews with labor leaders from the CTF and the Federación Liberación, Concepción, April 2000.

5 For an important statement on the need of the state to promote the sustainable exploitation of forest resources on both private and public lands in the face of growing deforestation, see Victorino Rojas Magallanes, *Informe sobre bosques presentado al Ministerio de Industria y Obras Públicas* (Santiago: Imprenta Litografía y Encaudernación Barcelona, 1902). For travelers who saw in Chile's southern forests tremendous untapped commercial potential, see Robert E. Mansfield, *Progressive Chile* (New York: Neale Publishing, 1913) and L. E. Elliott, *Chile: Today and Tomorrow* (New York: MacMillan, 1922). In *My Native Land* (London: Ernest Bean, 1928), Agustín Edwards both noted the encroaching deforestation in southern Chile and the region's potential forestry riches.

6 For state forestry policy during this period see the archives of the Departamento de Bosques (Forestry Department) of the Ministerio de Tierras y Colonización, the Ministerio de Propriedad Austral, and the Ministerio de Agricultura in the Archivo Siglo XX, Santiago. Also see U.S. Department of Agriculture, Forest Service (hereafter U.S. Forest Service), *Forest Resources of Chile as a Basis for Industrial Expansion* (1946).

7 Grupo de Investigaciones Agrarias, "Región forestal: Empresas y trabajadores" (Santiago: Grupo de Investigaciones Agrarias, Academia de Humanismo Cristiano, n.d.), 11–14. On forestation with pines, see the reports by Federico Albert, head of the Sección Aguas y Bosques, Ministerio de Industria y Obras Públicas, "Pino Monterey" (n.d.), "Siete arboles muy recomendables para el País" (1909), "Los bosques en el País" (1901–3).

8 Jorge Morales Gamboni, "El estado y el sector privado en la industria forestal: El caso de la región de Concepción," *Boletín de Estudios Agrarios*, no. 24 (August 1989).

9 To cite one of numerous examples found in the ministry's archives, on 18 August 1945 the owner of the estate Los Pinos in Mulchén in the province of Bío-Bío, Don Alberto Heck, was granted by the ministry's Departamento de Bosques tax exemptions for the land granted to the estate in 1939 and official status as a "fundo forestal" (forestry farm). By 1945 Heck had planted 273.3 hectares with over 1,119,184 pine trees. Heck was fairly typical of those medium and large landowners who

received tax exemptions from the state in exchange for planting pine plantations during this period. Ministerio de Tierras y Colonización, Providencias, 5–121 (1946), Archivo Siglo XX.

10 *Revista Forestal Chilena*, no. 1 (May 1951). The regions in which the forestry industry has historically been concentrated are the Seventh (Curicó, Talca, Linares, and Cauquenes provinces), Eighth, Ninth (Malleco and Cautín provinces), and Tenth (Valdivia, Osorno, Llanquihue, Chiloé, and Palena provinces). Pine plantations are mostly located in the Eighth Region, whereas logging operations of native forests are mostly located in the Tenth.

11 Evaristo Figueroa de la Fuente, "La industria maderera en Chile" (Santiago: Thesis, Universidad de Chile, 1948), 20. U.S. Forest Service, *Forest Resources of Chile as a Basis for Industrial Expansion*.

12 See, for example, the description of the company Forestal Colcura owned by the coal company Compañía Carbonífera de Lota, which employed 700 workers logging pine plantations and producing wood in a sawmill and which classified itself as an agricultural rather than industrial enterprise, in *El Siglo*, 31 December 1959.

13 For an excellent description of labor relations and life on a forestry estate, see the interviews with former workers on the Neltume hacienda in Panguipulli cited in Victor Espinoza Cuevas, Paz Rojas Baeza, and María Luisa Ortiz Rojas, *Derechos humanos: Sus huellas en el tiempo*, Serie Verdad y Justicia (Santiago: Codepu, 1999). For descriptions of life and labor on other estates that later made up the Complejo Maderero Panguipulli, see *Punto Final*, 8 March 1971, cited in Codepu (Comite de Defensa de los Derechos del Pueblo), *Chile: Recuerdos de la guerra. Valdivia, Neltume, Chihuio, Liquiñe*, Serie Verdad y Justicia (Santiago: Codepu, n.d.).

14 U.S. Forest Service, *Forest Resources of Chile as a Basis for Industrial Expansion*, 87–90.

15 Grupo de Investigaciones Agrarias, "Región forestal," 23–31; U.S. Forest Service, *Forest Resources of Chile as a Basis for Industrial Expansion*.

16 U.S. Forest Service, *Forest Resources of Chile as a Basis for Industrial Expansion*, 18.

17 The basis for the development of forestry industries in Chile during the postwar period was the 1946 study by the U.S. Forest Service sponsored by Corfo, *Forest Resources of Chile as a Basis for Industrial Expansion*. In the case of Papelera Nacimiento, the business was created out of a project designed by the Canadian company Sanwell International for the Chilean company Inforsa (founded in 1956 by private capital but controlled by Corfo in 1964 when the agency purchased a majority of its stock), which invested only 34 percent of the capital. The rest was covered by credits from the Export-Credit Corporation of Canada (60 percent) with a guarantee from the state and funds from Corfo (6 percent). Celulosa Arauco was created in 1968 with an 80 percent investment by Corfo with the rest made up by the North American company Parson and Whittmore, whose 20 percent was purchased by Corfo in 1972. Forestal Arauco was founded and financed entirely by Corfo in 1969 to provide pine plantations for Celulosa Arauco. In a final example, Celulosa Constitución was initiated in 1971 by Corfo in combination with a French consortium and the Fundación para el Desarrollo of the archbishop of Talca. Corfo also started Forestal Celco

to provide pines for Celulosa Constitución (Grupo de Investigaciones Agrarias, "Región forestal," 37–40).

18 Infor (Instituto Forestal), "Boletín Estadístico no. 61," *Estadísticas Forestales*, 1997.
19 *Poder Campesino*, no. 22, n.d., 1972.
20 *Poder Campesino*, no. 6, 15–30 March 1971.
21 This account is taken from the interview with Filadelfo Guzmán in *El Pino Insigne*, August 1983. *El Pino Insigne* was a clandestine pamphlet produced and distributed by the Vicaría Pastoral Obrera in Concepción as part of its efforts to lend support to unions in the region,
22 "Primer taller forestal," *Boletín de Estudios Agrarios*, no. 22, May 1988.
23 *Periódico Forestal* (CTF), no. 1, October 1992; "Primer taller forestal."
24 *Ranquil* (Confederación Nacional Campesina e Indígena "Ranquil"), no. 9, April–May 1970.
25 For an account of the land invasions in Panguipulli, see *El Rebelde*, no. 7, 5 November 1971, and no. 17, 15–22 February 1972; *Poder Campesino*, no. 2, 15–30 January 1971, and no. 7, April 1971.
26 *Poder Campesino*, no. 4, 15–20 February 1971.
27 Marlene Gimpel Madariaga, "El sector forestal ante la apertura económica: Exportaciones y medio ambiente," in *El tigre sin selva: Consecuencias ambientales de la transformación económica de Chile*, ed. Rayén Quiroga Martínez (Santiago: Instituto de Ecología Política, 1994), 310.
28 Morales Gamboni, "El estado y el sector privado en la industria forestal." There is little available information about whether these payments were ever made.
29 Morales Gamboni, "El estado y el sector privado en la industria forestal."
30 Francisco Reusch, "La política forestal del gobierno y la concentración económica en el sector forestal," *Boletín de Estudios Agrarios*, 7 March 1981.
31 *Noticiero de la Realidad Agraria* (GIA), no. 5 (January 1984).
32 Grupo de Investigaciones Agrarias, "Región forestal," 19.
33 Grupo de Investigaciones Agrarias, "Región forestal," 20–23.
34 Morales Gamboni, "El estado y el sector privado en la industria forestal."
35 Patricio Escobar and Diego López, *El sector forestal en Chile: Crecimiento y precarización del empleo* (Santiago: PET, 1996), 80.
36 Infor, "Boletín Estadístico no. 61," *Estadísticas Forestales*, 1997; Escobar and López, *El sector forestal en Chile*, 82.
37 Cruzat-Larraín controlled Forestal Arauco, Celulosa Arauco, Celulosa Constitución, Forestal Celco, and Forestal Chile; Matte-Alessandri owned CMPC with plants in Puente Alto, Laja, Bío-Bío, and Valdivia, Laja Crown, Forestal Mininco with 150,000 hectares of plantations, Fábrica Chilena de Moldeados, Aserradero San Pedro, and Sociedad Recuperadora de Papel; finally, the Vial group, through the Banco Hipotecario y de Fomento de Chile (BHC), had Inforsa with its pulp plant and two paper factories, the Forestales Rio Vergara, CRECEX, Georgia Pacific CRECEX, and Maderas Nacimineto, Papelero Sud America, and Maderas y Paneles (Mapal) (Grupo de Investigaciones Agrarias, "Región forestal," 38–45).

38 Luis Otero, "El problema social detrás de los bosques" (Concepción: Vicaría de la Pastoral Obrera, 1984).

39 Union leader, Federación Forestal Liberación, Concepción, interview of 19 April 2000.

40 Union leader, Federación Forestal Liberación, Concepción, interview of 19 April 2000.

41 El Pino Insigne, October 1984.

42 Two very important histories of the events in Panguipulli preceding the military coup and of the violation of human rights, including detentions and disappearances, after the coup are Codepu, Chile: Recuerdos de la guerra and Espinoza Cuevas, Rojas Baeza, and Ortiz Rojas, Derechos humanos.

43 Codepu, Chile: Recuerdos de la Guerra; and Cuevas, Baeza, and Rojas, Derechos humanos.

44 Codepu, Chile: Recuerdos de la Guerra; and Cuevas, Baeza, and Rojas, Derechos humanos.

45 Union leaders, Federación Nacional de Sindicatos de Conaf (Fenasic), Santiago, interview of 14 April 2000.

46 Sergio Gomez, "Forestación y campesinado," document no. 19 (Santiago: Instituto de Desarrollo Agropecuario, January 1994).

47 Union leaders, Federación Nacional de Sindicatos de Conaf (Fenasic), Santiago, interview of 14 April 2000.

48 Union leader, CTF, Concepción, interview of 17 April 2000.

49 Union leader, Federación Forestal Liberación, Concepción, interview of 19 April 2000.

50 Union leaders, Federación Nacional de Sindicatos de Conaf (Fenasic), Santiago, interview of 14 April 2000.

51 Páginas Sindicales, no. 14, December 1978.

52 El Pino Insigne, 2, n.d.

53 El Pino Insigne, 2, n.d.

54 El Pino Insigne, August 1983.

55 El Pino Insigne, 11, n.d.

56 El Pino Insigne, August 1983.

57 Union leader, Federación Forestal Liberación, Concepción, interview of 19 April 2000.

58 Cepal, "El desarrollo frutícola y forestal y sus derivaciones sociales," Estudios e Informes de la CEPAL no. 57 (Santiago: Cepal, 1986), 184.

59 El Pino Insigne, December 1983.

60 El Mercurio, 17 July 1983, quoted in El Pino Insigne, December 1983.

61 Ibid.

62 For a discussion of the policy of replacing native forests with plantations, see Gimpel Madariaga, "El sector forestal ante la apertura económica." A 1993 study of the province of Valdivia found that of 100,000 hectares of plantations in the Cordillera de la Costa 45 percent had replaced native forests. In the Eighth Region, between 1978 and 1986, 31 percent of the native forests in the Cordillera de la Costa were burnt and replaced with plantations (Rayén Quiroga Martínez and Saar Van Hauwermeiven, Globalización e insustentabilidad: Una mirada desde la economía ecológica [Santiago: Instituto de Ecología Política, 1996], 67).

63 Quoted in GIA, "Región forestal," 60.

64 Quoted in *Noticiero de la Realidad Agraria* (G I A), no. 19, June 1981.

65 Alejandro Cerda, New York, interview of 6 June 2000.

66 Quiroga Martínez and Van Hauwermeiven, *Globalización e insustentabilidad*, 69–70.

67 Cepal, "El desarrollo frutícola y forestal," 184.

68 Rigoberta Rivera and M. Elena Cruz, *Pobladores rurales* (Santiago: Grupo de Investigaciones Agrarias/Academia de Humanismo Cristiano, 1984), 131–38.

69 Union leader, Federación Forestal Liberación, Concepción, interview of 19 April 2000.

70 Union leader, C T F, Concepción, interview of 17 April 2000.

71 *Análisis*, January 1983.

72 *Páginas Sindicales*, no. 55, 15 May 1983.

73 *Noticiero de la Realidad Agraria* (G I A), no. 3, January 1983.

74 Union leader, C T F, Concepción, interview of 17 April 2000.

75 *El Pino Insigne*, August 1983.

76 Infor, "Volumen exportaciones principales productos forestales."

77 *Noticiero de la Realidad Agraria* (G I A), no. 3, January 1983.

78 Cepal, "El desarrollo frutícola y forestal," 213.

79 Otero, "El problema social detrás de los bosques," 16.

80 Ibid.

81 Ibid.

82 "Primer taller forestal."

83 Luis Otero, "Los trabajadores y el sistema de contratistas en el sector forestal," *Boletín de Estudios Agrarios*, 7 March 1981.

84 *El Pino Insigne*, 11, 1983. Also see a description of problems on the estate in *Páginas Sindicales*, no. 43, 9 December 1981.

85 *Páginas Sindicales*, no. 55, 15 May 1983.

86 Hoy, no. 165, 17–23 September 1980; Luis Otero, "El problema social detrás los bosques"; "Primer taller forestal."

87 Otero, "El problema social detrás de los bosques," 17.

88 Ibid., 24.

89 *Noticiero de la Realidad Agraria* (G I A), January 1983.

90 *Noticiero de la Realidad Agraria* (G I A), 15 January 1984.

91 In Chilean forestry a metro ruma is a pile of 2.44 meter-long logs 1.0 meter high and 1.0 meter wide.

92 *Sinopsis del sector forestal maderero* (Concepción, Universidad del Biobio, 1983), 16; *Análisis*, no. 20, July 1992.

93 *Análisis*, no. 20, July 1992.

94 Union leaders, Federación Nacional de Sindicatos de Conaf (Fenasic), Santiago, interview of 14 April 2000.

95 Union leader, C T F, Concepción, interview of 17 April 2000.

96 Infor, *La pequeña empresa madera de bosque nativo: Su importancia, perspectiva y una propuesta para su desarrollo*, technical bulletin 128 (Santiago: Infor, 1991).

97 Union leader, C T F, Concepción, interview of 17 April 2000.

98 Infor, *La pequeña empresa madera de bosque nativo; Sinopsis del sector forestal maderero*, 24.

99 *Análisis*, January 1983.

100 *Noticiero de la Realidad Agraria* (GIA), no. 4, February 1982.

101 Rivera and Cruz, *Pobladores rurales*, 131–38.

102 Quoted in *Noticiero de la Realidad Agraria* (GIA), no. 19, June 1981.

103 For an extended analysis of this contradiction and changes in household patriarchy in rural areas devoted to fruit production, see the chapter by Heidi Tinsman in this volume.

104 Quoted in Kirai de León, "La mujer en las pueblas forestales," *Boletín de Estudios Agrarios*, no. 13, October 1982. See also the interviews by Kirai de León in Ximena Valdés, Sonia Montecino, Kirai de León, Macarena Mack, *Historias testimoniales de mujeres del campo* (Santiago: Programa de Estudios y Capacitación de la Mujer Campesina e Indígena, 1986), and in Kirai de León, *Andar andando: Testimonio de mujeres del sector forestal* (Santiago: CEM [Centro de Estudios de la Mujer]/Pehuén, 1986).

105 Union leader, CTF, Concepción, interview of 17 April 2000.

106 Union leader, Federación Forestal Liberación, Concepción, interview of 19 April 2000.

107 See the chapter by Heidi Tinsman in this volume.

108 *El Pino Insigne*, October 1984.

109 *Páginas Sindicales*, no. 55, 15 May 1983.

110 Caupolicán Pavez, Concepción, interview of 18 April 2000.

111 *El Pino Insigne*, n.d.

112 CTF, Grupo de Estudios Agro-Regionales, Centro para el Desarrollo Forestal, "Propuestas forestales y laborales para la democracia" (Concepción, October 1989).

113 CTF, "Propuestas forestales y laborales"; "Informe central al Quinto Congreso Nacional Elecicionario de la Confederación Nacional de Trabajadores Forestales de Chile C.T.F." (Constitución, 5–6 June 1998).

114 *El Pino Insigne*, no. 2, n.d.

115 Caupolicán Pavez, Concepción, interview of 19 April 2000.

116 Interview with Caupolicán Pavez, in Fernando Echeverría and Jorge Rojas Hernández, *Añoranzas, sueños, realidades: Dirigentes sindicales hablan de la transición* (Santiago: Ediciones SUR, 1992), 137–43.

117 CTF, "Propuestas forestales y laborales."

118 Infor, "Exportaciones chilenas por sectores de la economía" and "Volumen exportaciones principales productos forestales," *Estadísticas Forestales*, 1997.

119 Gimpel Madariaga, "El sector forestal ante la apertura económica," 313.

120 Escobar and López, *El sector forestal en Chile*, 56.

121 Infor, "Volumen exportaciones principales productos forestales, 1962–1997."

122 *Análisis*, no. 20, July 1992.

123 Gomez, "Forestación y campesinado."

124 Union leader, CTF, Concepción, interview of 17 April 2000.

125 Interview with Caupolicán Pavez, in Echeverría and Rojas Hernández, *Añoranzas, sueños, realidades.*

126 Escobar and López, *El sector forestal en Chile*, 126.

127 Union leader, Federación Forestal Liberación, Concepción, interview of 19 April 2000.

128 Union leader, CTF, Concepción, interview of 17 April 2000.

129 "Informe Central al Quinto Congreso Nacional Eleccionario de la Confederación Nacional de Trabajadores Forestales de Chile C.T.F."

130 Union leader, CTF, Concepción, interview of 17 April 2000.

131 Former textile union leader and regional labor organizer, Departamento Pastoral Obrera, Concepción, interview of 18 April 2000.

132 "Informe central al Quinto Congreso Nacional Eleccionario de la Confederación Nacional de Trabajadores Forestales de Chile C.T.F."

133 Union leader, CTF, Concepción, interview of 17 April 2000.

134 Interview with Caupolicán Pavez, in Echeverría and Rojas Hernández, *Añoranzas, sueños, realidades.*

135 Caupolicán Pavez, Concepción, interview of 18 April 2000.

136 "Informe Central al Quinto Congreso Nacional Eleccionario de la Confederación Nacional de Trabajadores Forestales de Chile C.T.F."

137 The number of workers in the forestry sector is difficult to determine given the transience of the labor force. Many estimates put the figure at over 100,000 (with 47,000 alone in the Eighth Region) during the 1980s and 1990s. See, for example, *Periódico Forestal* (CTF), no. 2, December 1992.

138 ¿Qué Pasa? 3 January 2000. See also *La Tercera,* 3 April 1999 for a discussion of Neltume Carranco's failure to comply with forest management plans elaborated by Conaf.

139 I interviewed a number of forestry workers and Neltume residents with journalist Mauricio Durán in March 2002. I do not include their names here in order to protect their anonymity. Also see an investigative report on Neltume in *Punto Final,* 1 April 1999.

Abramo, Lais, and Alberto Cuevas, eds. *El sindicalismo latinoamericano en los noventa: Negociación colectiva y sindicatos*. Santiago: CLACSO, 1992.

Acuña, Eugenio, and Mario Albuquerque. "Algunas hipótesis sobre modernización de las relaciones laborales en las empresas chilenas." *Estudios de Administración* (Universidad de Chile, Facultad de Ciencias Económicas y Administrativas, Departamento de Administración) 3, no. 2 (spring 1992): 105–42.

Affonso, Almino, Sergio Gómez, Emilio Kline, and Pablo Ramírez. *Movimiento campesino chileno*. 2 vols. Santiago: ICIRA, 1970.

Agacino, Rafael. "Cinco ecuaciones 'virtuosas' del modelo económico chileno y orientaciones para una nueva política económica." *Economía y Trabajo: Informe anual, 1995– 1996*. Santiago: PET, 1996: 57–84.

———. *Evolución económica reciente de los sectores textil y del vestuario, 1986–1990*. Santiago: PET, 1991.

Agacino, Rafael, and Mario Echeverría, eds. *Flexibilidad y condiciones de trabajo precarias*. Santiago: PET, 1995.

Agacino, Rafael, Cristián González, and Jorge Rojas. *Capital transnacional y trabajo: El desarrollo minero en Chile*. Santiago: PET/LOM, 1998.

Albuquerque, Mario, Fernando Echeverría, Oscar MacClure, and Eugenio Tironi. "La acción sindical en los sectores metalmecánico y cuprífero: Informe de investigación." Working paper. Santiago: Sur-Cedal, 1987.

Albuquerque, Mario. *El sindicalismo en el primer año de gobierno democrático*. Serie documentos Ciasi (Centro de Investigación y Asesoría Sindical) 9. Santiago: Ciasi, 1991.

Albuquerque, Mario, and Eugenio Rivera. "El debate en torno a la concertación social y económica." *Proposiciones* 18 (1990): 85–110.

Allamand, Andrés. "Las paradojas de un legado." In *El modelo chileno: Democracia y desarrollo en los noventa*, edited by Paul W. Drake and Ivan Jáksic. Santiago: LOM, 1999.

Angell, Alan. *Politics and the Labour Movement in Chile*. London: Oxford University Press, 1972.

———. "Unions and Workers in Chile During the 1980s." In *The Struggle for Democracy in Chile, 1982–1990*, edited by Paul W. Drake and Iván Jáksic. Lincoln: University of Nebraska Press, 1991.

Aninat, Augusto, et al. *La industria chilena: Cuatro visiones sectoriales*. Santiago: Centro de Estudios de Desarrollo, 1986.

Appadurai, Arjun. *Modernity at Large: Cultural Dimensions of Globalization*. Minneapolis: University of Minnesota Press, 1996.

Arrieta, Adolfo. "Discusión del movimiento sindical sobre remuneraciones e ingreso minimo." Unpublished document. CUT Comite Ejecutivo. April 1996.

APST (Asociación de Productores de Salmon y Trucha de Chile). "Exportaciones de salmón y trucha: El creciente mercado regional." *Salmonotícias: Medio Oficial de la Industria Salmonera de Chile*, APST, (January 1997): 15.

———. "Salmonideos generaron el 30.3% de los ingresos de las exportaciones pesqueras." *Salmonotícias*. Santiago: APST, 1997.

Baldez, Lisa. *Why Women Protest: Women's Movements in Chile*. Cambridge: Cambridge University Press, 2002.

Banco Central de Chile. *www.bcentral.cl.indicadores/htm/empleo__desocu pación__INE.htm*. Accessed 25 September 2002.

Barber, Benjamin. *Jihad vs. McWorld: How Globalism and Tribalism Are Reshaping the World*. New York: Ballantine, 1995.

Barrera, Manuel. *Consideraciones acerca de la relación entre política y movimiento sindical*. Santiago: Centro de Estudios Sociales, 1988.

Barrera, Manuel, and Gonzalo Falabella. *Sindicatos bajo regimenes militares: Argentina, Brasil, Chile*. Santiago: Centro de Estudios Sociales, 1990.

Barrera, Manuel, Helia Henriquez, and Teresita Selamé. *Sindicatos y estado en el Chile actual*. Santiago: Centro de Estudios Sociales, 1985.

Barrera, Manuel, and J. Samuel Valenzuela. "The Development of Labor Movement Opposition to the Military Regime." In *Military Rule in Chile: Dictatorship and Oppositions*, edited by J. Samuel Valenzuela and Arturo Valenzuela. Baltimore: Johns Hopkins University Press, 1986.

Barrett, Patrick. "Labour Policy, Labour-Business Relations, and the Transition to Democracy in Chile." *Journal of Latin American Studies* 33 (2001): 561–97.

Bartell, Ernest. "Business Perceptions and the Transition to Democracy in Chile." Working paper 184. Notre Dame: Helen Kellogg Institute for International Studies, University of Notre Dame, 1992.

Bender, Daniel. "Sweatshop Subjectivity and the Politics of Description and Exhibition." *International Labor and Working-Class History* 61 (spring 2002): *Sweated Labor: The Politics of Representation and Reform*, 13–23.

Berge, Aslak. "Lack of Candor on Chilean Algae Problems." *Intrafish*, 11 April 2002.

Bitar, Sergio, and Crisostomo Pizarro. *La caída de Allende y la huelga de El Teniente*. Santiago: Ediciones del Ornitirrinco, 1986.

Bitar, Sergio. "¿Es posible la democracia con el neoliberalismo?" *Carta Mensual: Chile VeintiUno* 3, no. 20, 1996.

Bitran, Eduardo. "Desarrollo y perspectivas del sector pesquero en Chile." Working paper 7. Santiago: CED (Centro de Estudios de Desarrollo), 1983.

Bongcam, Carlos. *Sindicalismo chileno: Hechos y documentos, 1973–1983*. Spanga: CELA, 1984.

Bonifaz, Rodolfo. "Comentarios de los actores sociales al proyecto de ley que modifica el codigo del trabajo en materias de negociacíon colectiva y otras." Unpublished document. 1996. Chapter author has photocopy.

Bosworth, Barry, Rudiger Dornbusch, and Raúl Labán, eds. *The Chilean Economy: Policy Lessons and Challenges.* Washington, D.C.: Brookings Institution, 1994.

Bourdieu, Pierre. *Distinction: A Social Critique of the Judgment of Taste.* Cambridge: Harvard University Press, 1984.

Boyd, William, Scott Prudham, and Rachel Schurman. "Industrial Dynamics and the Problem of Nature." *Society and Natural Resources* 14, no. 7 (2001): 555–70.

Bresser-Pereira, Louis Carlos, Jose María Maravall, and Adam Przeworski. *Economic Reforms in New Democracies: A Social Democratic Approach.* New York: Cambridge University Press, 1993.

Burawoy, Michael, et al. *Global Ethnography: Forces, Connections, and Imaginations in a Postmodern World.* Berkeley: University of California Press, 2000.

Bustos, Manuel. Letter to M. Feliu. Photocopy. Santiago: Ciasi, 1988.

Bustos, Manuel, Diego Olivares, and Arturo Martínez. *El movimiento sindical y las relaciones laborales.* Serie documentos 8. Santiago: Ciasi, 1993.

Cáceres, Gonzalo, and Lorena Farías. "Efectos de las grandes superficies comerciales en el Santiago de la modernización ininterrumpida, 1982–1999." *Ambiente y·Desarrollo* 15, no. 4 (1999): 36–41.

Cámara de Comercio de Santiago. *Deudas de consumo consolidadas por estrato socioeconomico.* Photocopy. Santiago: Departmento de Estudios Económicos/Cámara de Comercio de Santiago, 1996.

Campero, Guillermo. "Los actores sociales y la clase política." Serie documentos, unnumbered. Santiago: ILET, 1989.

———. *Los empresarios chilenos en el regimen militar y el post plebiscito.* Santiago: ILET, 1989.

———. "El movimiento sindical: Situación y perspectivas." In *Añoranzas, sueños, realidades: Dirigentes sindicales hablan de la transición,* edited by Fernando Echeverría and Jorge Rojas. Santiago: Sur, 1992.

———. "¿Es posible y necesario concertarse en la empresa hoy?" Working paper 63. Santiago: Vicaría de Pastoral Obrera, Arzobispado de Santiago, 1986.

Campero, Guillermo, and René Cortázar. "Logics of Union Action in Chile." Working paper 85. Notre Dame: Kellogg Institute for International Studies, University of Notre Dame, 1986.

Campero, Guillermo, and José A. Valenzuela. *El movimiento sindical en el regimen militar chileno, 1973–1981.* Santiago: ILET, 1984.

Campero, Guillermo, and Julio Valenzuela. *El movimiento sindical chileno en el capitalismo autoritario.* Santiago: ILET, 1981.

Carrasco, Celina, et al. "Cultivando el mar: Para la calidad de las condiciones de trabajo." Cuaderno de investigación 13 (Organización Internacional del Trabajo: diciembre 2000), 29.

Castillo, Mario, and Raúl Alvarez. "El liderazgo en las grandes empresas en Chile." In *Grandes empresas y grupos industriales latinoamericanos,* edited by W. Péres. Mexico City: Siglo XXI, 1998.

Castillo, Mario, et al. "Reorganización industrial y estrategias competitivas en Chile." In *Estabilización macroeconómica, reforma estructural, y comportamiento industrial*, edited by J. Katz. Buenos Aires: Cepal, 1996.

CERC (Centro de Estudios de la Realidad Contemporanea). *Barómetro CERC*. Reports for March, July, September, and December 1999. Santiago: CERC, 1999.

"Chile Prepares Defense against Dumping Charges." *Intrafish*, 27 June 2002.

"Chilean Salmon Could Face 32% Tax in EU." *Intrafish*, 25 June 2002.

Ciasi (Centro de Investigación y Asesoría Sindical). "Memorandum de discusión con el gobierno sobre participación sindical." Memorandum, dated August 1991.

——. "Memorandum de la Comisión de Trabajo." Memorandum, dated 15 December 1992.

——. "Memorandum sobre el documento CUT en materia participación." Memorandum, July 1991.

——. "Minuta de discusión con el gobierno sobre participación sindical." Meeting notes, July 1991.

——. *Negociación colectiva*. Serie documentos 11. Santiago: Ciasi, 1995.

——. "Notas de jornada de análisis entre dirigentes de la CUT y diversos ministros de gobierno." Meeting notes, 17 December 1991.

CIREN. *Directorio agro-industrial fruticola de Chile*. Santiago: CIREN, 1979, 1983, 1984, 1988, 1993.

Codepu (Comite de Defensa de los Derechos del Pueblo). *Chile: Recuerdos de la guerra. Valdivia-Neltume-Chihuio-Liquine*. Santiago: Codepu, [1999].

Collier, Ruth Berins, and David Collier. "Inducements versus Constraints: Disaggregating 'Corporatism.'" *American Political Science Review* 73, no. 4 (December 1979): 967–986.

——. *Shaping the Political Arena: Critical Junctures, Trade Unions, and the State in Latin America*. Princeton: Princeton University Press, 1991.

Colloredo-Mansfeld, Rudi. *The Native Leisure Class: Consumption and Cultural Creativity in the Andes*. Chicago: University of Chicago Press, 1999.

Constable, Pamela, and Arturo Valenzuela. *A Nation of Enemies: Chile under Pinochet*. New York: W. W. Norton, 1991.

Consumers International. *Cambios en los patrones de consumo y sustenabilidad en Chile*. Santiago: Consumers International, 2000.

Cook, Maria Lorena. "Toward Flexible Industrial Relations? Neo-liberalism, Democracy, and Labor Reform in Latin America." *Industrial Relations* 37, no. 3 (1998): 311–37.

Corbo, Beatriz. "Cuotas pesqueras." *El Mercurio*, 12 July 1999, A-2.

Corbo, Vittorio, and Stanley Fischer. "Lessons from the Chilean Stabilization Recovery." In *The Chilean Economy: Policy Lessons and Challenges*, edited by Larry Bosworth, Rodiger Dornbusch, and Raul Laban. Washington, D.C.: Brookings Institution, 1994.

Corfo/Ifop (Corporación de Fomento de la Producción/Instituto de Fomento Pesquero). "Diagnóstico de las principales pesquerías nacionales bentónicas, III, IV, y X región." Santiago: Corfo/Ifop, 1991.

——. "Diagnóstico de las principales pesquerías nacionales: Estado de situación y perspectivas del recurso pesquerías demersales 'Peces' Zona Sur Austral, 1990." Santiago: Corfo/Ifop, 1991.

———. "Diagnóstico de las principales pesquerías nacionales: Estado de situación y perspectivas del recurso pesquerías demersales "Peces" Zona Sur Austral, 1991." Santiago: Corfo/Ifop, 1992.

———. "Análisis de la actividad pesquera extractiva nacional, I–III." Santiago: Corfo/Ifop, 1990.

———. "Estado de situación de la acuicultura en Chile." Valparaiso: Corfo/Ifop, 1998.

Cortázar, René. *Política laboral en el Chile democrático: Avances y desafíos en los noventa.* Santiago: Dolmen, 1993.

Cortázar, René, and Joaquín Vial, eds. *Construyendo opciones: Propuestas económicas y sociales para el cambio de siglo.* Santiago: Dolmen, 1998.

Coward, Jefferson. "A Century of Sweat: Subcontracting, Flexibility, and Consumption." *International Labor and Working-Class History* 61 (spring 2002): *Sweated Labor: The Politics of Representation and Reform*, 128–40.

Concertación de Partidos por la Democracia. *Compromiso económico y social de la campaña por el no.* Santiago: CPD, 1988.

———. *Programa de gobierno.* Santiago: CPD, 1989.

Crispi, Jaime. "Neo-liberalismo y campesinado en Chile." Working paper 5. Santiago: GIA, 1981.

Crisol. Sindicato No. 1 Madeco 1992–1997. Santiago: Madeco, 1998.

Cronon, William. *Changes in the Land: Indians, Colonists, and the Ecology of New England.* New York: Hill and Wang, 1983.

———. *Nature's Metropolis : Chicago and the Great West.* New York: W. W. Norton, 1991.

Crummett, María de los Angeles. "El *poder feminino:* The Mobilization of Women against Socialism in Chile." *Latin American Perspectives* 4, no. 4 (1977): 103–14.

Cruz, María Elena, and Cecilia Leiva. *La fruiticultura en Chile después de 1973: Una area privilegiada de expansion del capitalismo.* Santiago: GIA, 1987.

CUT (Central Unitaria de Trabajadores). "Bases para una estratégia de desarrollo nacional: Propuesta para el Primer Congreso." Photocopy. Santiago: CUT, October 1991. Memorandum.

———. "Carta del Presidente de la Republica a la Central Unitaria de Trabajadores (CUT)." Mimeo. Santiago: CUT, 9 March 1992.

———. *La CUT frente a la situación política del país.* Santiago: CUT, 1990.

———. *Estadísticas laborales 2002.* Santiago: CUT, 2003.

———. "Nuevas orientaciones para la acción sindical de la CUT: Propuesta para el Primer Congreso." Mimeo. Santiago: CUT, 1991.

———. "Orientaciones para el fortalecimiento y desarrollo orgánico de la CUT: Propuesta para el Primer Congreso." Mimeo. Santiago: CUT, October 1991.

———. "Reglamiento de funcionamiento del colegio electoral nacional." Santiago: CUT, 1998.

———. *Las reformas laborales: Un desafío para los trabajadores.* Pamphlet. Santiago: CUT, 2001.

———. *Propuesta de la CUT para la transición a la democracia.* Santiago: CUT, 1989.

——. *Union y trabajo*. Informativo de la Central Unitaria de Trabajadores, nos. 1–22 (March 1990–April 1992).

CUT, Comité Ejecutivo (Executive Committee). "Discusión sobre el movimiento sindical." Santiago: CUT, 1996.

CUT and CPC (Confederación de la Producción y de Comercio). *Marco de referencia para el diálogo*. Santiago: CUT, January 1990.

CUT, CPC, and Government of Chile. *Acuerdo Marco*. Santiago: CUT, May 1990.

——. *Acuerdo Marco*. Santiago: CUT, April 1991.

Dahse, Fernando. *Mapa de la extrema riqueza: Los grupos económicos y el proceso de concentración de capitales*. Santiago: Aconcagua, 1979.

de Castro, Sergio, ed. *El ladrillo: Bases de la política económica del gobierno militar chileno*. Santiago: CEP, 1992.

de Laire, Fernando. *La trama invisible o los claroscuros de la flexibilidad: Producir, construir y proveer servicios bajo jornadas excepcionales en la minería privada y en sus eslabonamientos de subcontratación*. Cuadernos de Investigación 8. Santiago: Dirección del Trabajo, 1999.

de León, Kirai. *Andar andando: Testimonio de mujeres del sector forestal*. Santiago: CEM (Centro de Estudios de la Mujer)/Pehuén, 1986.

——. "La mujer en las pueblas forestales." *Boletín de Estudios Agrarios*, no. 13, October 1982.

Deere, Carmen Diana, and Magdalena Leon, eds. *Rural Women and State Policy: Feminist Perspectives on Latin America*. Boulder: Westview Press, 1987.

Délano, Priscilla. "Women and Work in Chile: A Case Study of the Fish-Processing Industry on the Island of Chiloé." Ph.D. diss., University of Cambridge, 1993.

Délano, Priscilla, and David Lehmann. "Women Workers in Labour-Intensive Factories: The Case of Chile's Fishing Industry." *European Journal of Development Research* 5, no. 2 (1993): 43–67.

Derby, Lauren. "Gringo Chickens with Worms: Food and Nationalism in the Dominican Republic." In *Close Encounters of Empire: Writing the Cultural History of U.S.-Latin American Relations*, edited by G. Joseph, C. LeGrand, and R. Salvatore. Durham: Duke University Press, 1998.

Díaz, Alvaro. "Chile: Dinámica de largo plazo en el cambio tecnológico de una empresa metalmecánica." Working paper 135. Santiago: Sur, 1992.

——. "Restructuring and the Working Classes in Chile: Trends in Waged Employment, Informality, and Poverty, 1973–1990." Discussion paper 47. Geneva: UNRISD (United Nations Research Institute for Social Development), 1993.

Díaz, Estrella. *Mejoramiento de estandares laborales en la industria procesadora de salmonidos*. Santiago: Hexagrama Consultoras, October 2001.

Díaz, Eugenio. *El proceso de calidad total: Nociones fundamentales*. Serie documentos Ciasi 10, Santiago: Ciasi, 1993.

Díaz, Ximena, and Norah Schlaen. *La salud ignorada: Trabajadores de la confección*. Santiago: CEM, 1994.

Díaz, Ximena, and Sonia Yáñez. "La proliferación del sistema de subcontrataciones en la industria del vestuario en Chile como fuente de la precarización del empleo femenino." Santiago: CEM, 1998.

Díaz, Ximena, Julía Medel, and Norah Schlaen. *Mujer, trabajo y familia: El trabajo a domicilio en Chile.* Santiago: CEM, 1996.

Dinges, John, and Saul Landau. *Assassination on Embassy Row.* New York: Pantheon, 1980.

Dirección del Trabajo (Ministry of Labor). *Como operan las normas de negociación colectíva y de organizaciones sindicales.* Cuaderno de Investigación 1. Santiago: Dirección del Trabajo, 1995.

——. *¿Empresas sin trabajadores? Legislación sobre las empresas de trabajo temporal.* Cuadernos de Investigación 10. Santiago: Dirección del Trabajo, 1999.

——. *Informes de conflictividad. Serie años 1989–2000 huelgas legales en negociacíones colectivas.* Santiago: Dirección del Trabajo, 2002.

——. *ENCLA 98: Encuesta Laboral Informe Ejecutivo.* Santiago: Dirección del Trabajo, Departamento de Estudios, 1998.

——. *Informativo del Departamento de las Relaciones Laborales de la Dirección del Trabajo para organizaciones sindicales, empresas y usuarios en general.* Santiago: Dirección del Trabajo, 1998.

——. *Informe Estadístico Trimestral de Negociación Colectiva.* Santiago: Dirección del Trabajo, 1994.

——. *Informes de conflictividad: Serie años 1989–2000, huelgas legales en negociaciones colectivas.* Santiago: Dirección del Trabajo, Departamento de Estudios, 2002.

——. *Sindicalismo en la empresa moderna: Ni ocaso, ni crísis terminal.* Cuaderno de Investigación 4. Santiago: Dirección del Trabajo, 1997.

——. *Temas Laborales:* 1, no. 1 (September 1995); 1, no. 2 (January 1996); 1, no. 3 (May 1996); 1, no. 4 (September 1996); 2, no. 5 (January 1997).

——. *Tendencias sindicales: Análisis de una década.* Cuaderno de Investigación 2. Santiago: Dirección del Trabajo, 1996.

Drake, Paul. *Labor Movements and Dictatorships: The Southern Cone in Comparative Perspective.* Baltimore: Johns Hopkins University Press, 1996.

Drake, Paul, and Iván Jáksic, eds. *The Struggle for Democracy in Chile, 1982–1990.* Lincoln: University of Nebraska Press, 1991.

——, eds. *El modelo chileno: Democracia y desarrollo en los noventa.* Santiago: LOM, 1999.

Echeverría, Fernando. "Transición democrática: Sindicalización y cambios laborales." In *Añoranzas, sueños, realidades: Dirigentes sindicales hablan de la transición,* edited by Fernando Echeverría and Jorge Rojas. Santiago: Sur, 1992.

Echeverría, Magdalena, and Gonzalo Herrera. "Innovaciones en la empresa y situación del trabajo: La visión sindical." Working paper 97. Santiago: PET, 1993.

Echeverría, Magdalena , Valeria Solis, and Verónica Uribe-Echevarría. *El otro trabajo: El suministro de personas en las empresas.* Cuadernos de Investigación 7. Santiago: Dirección del Trabajo, 1998.

Edwards, Agustín. *My Native Land.* London: Ernest Bean, 1928.

Edwards, Sebastián, and Alejandra Cox. *Monetarism and Liberalization: The Chilean Experiment.* Cambridge, Mass.: Ballinger, 1987.

Elam, Mark. "Puzzling Out the Post-Fordist Debate: Technology, Markets, and Institutions." In *Post-Fordism: A Reader,* edited by A. Amin. Oxford: Blackwell, 1994.

Elliott, L. E. *Chile: Today and Tomorrow.* New York: MacMillan, 1922.

Epstein, Edward. "Labor and Political Stability in the New Chilean Democracy: Three Illusions." *Revista de Economía y Trabajo* 1, no. 2 (July–December, 1993): 45–64.

Errazuriz, Enrique, et al. *Huachipato, 1947–1988: De empresa pública a empresa privada.* Santiago: PET, 1990.

Escobar, Patricio. *Trabajadores y empleo en el Chile de los noventa.* Santiago: LOM, 1999.

Escobar, Patricio, and Diego López. *El sector forestal en Chile: Crecimiento y precarización del empleo.* Santiago: PET, 1996.

Espinoza Cuevas, Victor, Paz Rojas Baeza, and María Luisa Ortiz Rojas. *Derechos humanos: Sus huellas en el tiempo.* Serie Verdad y Justicia. Santiago: Codepu, 1999.

Espinosa, Malva, and Laís Abramo. *Los empresarios en la transición democrática.* Santiago: ILET, 1992.

Espinoza, Mario. *A propósito de las reformas laborales: Politizar el debate para desideologizar las posiciones.* Serie Publicaciones Analisis Laboral 1. Santiago: Fundación Friedrich Ebert, 1996.

Falabella, Gonzalo. "Historia del Santa María sindicato inter-empresa de trabajadores permanentes y temporero." Unpublished paper. Santiago: Mancomunal, 1990.

———. "La diversidad en el movimiento sindical chileno bajo el régimen militar." In *Sindicatos bajo regimenes militares: Argentina, Brasil, Chile.* Edited by Manuel Barrera and Gonzalo Falabella. Santiago: CES, 1990.

———. "Organizarse y sobrevivir: Democracia y sindicalización en Santa Maria." Paper presented at the 47th American Congress, New Orleans, July 1991.

———. "Reestructuración y respuesta sindical: La experiencia en Santa Maria, madre de la fruta chilena." *Economia y Trabajo* 1, no. 2 (1993): 239–61.

———. "Trabajo temporal y desorganizacion social." *Proposiciones* 18 (1988): 251–68.

Falabella, Gonzalo, and Manuel Barrera, eds. *Sindicatos bajo regimenes militares: Argentina, Brasil, Chile.* Santiago: CES, 1990.

Fazio, Hugo, *La transnacionalización de la economía chilena: Mapa de la extrema riqueza al año 2000.* Santiago: LOM, 2000.

Feres, Maria Ester. "Algunas consideraciones sobre el derecho del trabajo y la acción sindical." *Cuadernos de la Realidad Nacional,* no. 8 (1971): 54–69.

Ffrench-Davis, Ricardo. *Entre el neoliberalismo y el crecimiento con equidad: Tres décadas de política económica en Chile.* Santiago: Dolmen, 1999.

Ffrench-Davis, Ricardo, and Barbara Stallings, eds. *Reformas, crecimiento y políticas sociales en Chile desde 1973.* Santiago: LOM, 2001.

Fine, Ben, and Ellen Leopold. *The World of Consumption.* London: Routledge, 1993.

Flaño, Nicolas, and Gustavo Jiménez. *Empleo, política económica y concertación: ¿Que opinan los empresarios?* Santiago: ICHEH, 1987.

Flisfisch, Angel. *Consenso, pacto, proyecto y estabilidad democrática.* Documento de Trabajo 4. Santiago: CED, 1984.

Fontaine Aldunate, Arturo. *Los economistas y el presidente Pinochet.* Santiago: Zig-Zag, 1988.

Foxley, Alejandro. "Algunas condiciones para una democratización estable: El caso de Chile." *Colección Estudios Cieplan,* no. 9 (1982): 139–70.

———. "Bases para el desarrollo de la economía Chilena: Una visión alternativa." *Colección Estudios Cieplan,* no. 26 (1989): 175–86.

——. *Chile y su futuro: Un país posible.* Santiago: Cieplan, 1987.

——. *Experimentos neoliberales en América Latina.* Mexico: Fondo de Cultura Económica, 1988.

——. "Formas de la política después del autoritarismo." *Colección Estudios Cieplan,* no. 15 (1984): 203–210.

——. *La economia política de la transición: El camino al dialogo.* Santiago: Dolmen, 1993.

——. *Latin American Experiments in Neoconservative Economics.* Berkeley: University of California Press, 1983.

Frank, Volker. "The Elusive Goal in Democratic Chile: Reforming the Pinochet Labor Legislation." *Latin American Politics and Society* 44, no. 1 (2001): 35–68.

——. "The Labor Movement in Democratic Chile, 1990–2000." Working paper 298. Notre Dame: Helen Kellogg Institute for International Studies, University of Notre Dame, 2002.

——. "Plant-Level Leaders, the Union Movement, and the Return to Democracy in Chile." Ph.D. diss., University of Notre Dame, 1995.

Frías, Patricio. *Desafíos de modernización de las relaciones laborales: Hacia una nueva cultura y concertación empresarial.* Santiago: LOM, 2001.

——. "Desarrollo del sindicalismo chileno, 1995–96." In *Economia y Trabajo: Informe anual, 1995–1996.* Santiago: PET (1996): 203–22.

——. *El movimiento sindical chileno en la lucha por la democracia.* Santiago: PET, 1989.

——. "Perspectiva del estado de las relaciones laborales en Chile: Del gobierno autoritario a la transición democratica." Santiago: Dirección del Trabajo, Departamento de Relaciones Laborales, 1998.

——. "Perspectivas de redefinición de la acción sindical." In *Economia y Trabajo: Informe anual, 1992–1993.* Santiago: PET (1993): 91–114.

——. "Sindicalismo y desarrollo de acción contestataria." In *Economía y Trabajo: Informe anual, 1994–1995.* Santiago: PET (1995): 57–74.

——. "Sindicatos en la transición: En la busqueda de una nueva identidad." In *Economia y Trabajo: Informe anual, 1993–1994.* Santiago: PET (1994): 55–73.

Frías, Patricio, Magdalena Echevarría, Gonzalo Herrera, and Cristian Larraín. *Industria textil y del vestuario en Chile.* 3 vols. Santiago: PET, 1987.

Frigolett, Hernán, and Alejandra Sanhueza. *Evolución del gasto del consumo de los hogares en Chile, 1985–1995.* Santiago: Mideplan, 1999.

Fuentes, Claudio. "Partidos y coaliciones en el Chile de los '90: Entre pactos y proyectos." In *El modelo chileno democracia y desarrollo en los noventa,* edited by Paul W. Drake and Ivan Jáksic. Santiago: LOM, 1999.

García, Gonzalo. "Se Deforman los Salmones." *El Mercurio,* 14 July 1999.

Garcia-Canclini, Néstor. 2001. *Consumers and Citizens: Globalization and Multicultural Conflicts.* Translated by George Yúdice. Minneapolis: University of Minnesota Press, 2001.

Garretón, Manuel Antonio. *Hacia una nueva era política: Estudio sobre las democratizaciones.* Mexico City: Fondo de Cultura Economica, 1995.

Garrett, Patricia. "Growing Apart: The Experiences of Rural Men and Women in Central Chile." Ph.D. diss., University of Wisconsin-Madison, 1978.

Gatica, Jaime. *Deindustrialization in Chile.* Boulder: Westview Press, 1989.

Gaviola, Edda, Lorella Lopresti, and Claudia Rojas. "Los centros de madres: Una forma de organización para la mujer rural." Unpublished manuscript. Santiago: ISIS, 1988.

Geller, Lucio, and Claudio Ramos. "Chile: Innovaciones en la empresa industrial metal-mecánica, 1990–1995: Programas y resultados de la gestión de productividad." Working paper 54. Lima: OIT, 1997.

Gereffi, Gary, David Spener, and Jennifer Bair, eds. *Free Trade and Uneven Development: The North American Apparel Industry after NAFTA*. Philadelphia: Temple University Press, 2002.

GIA (Grupo de Investigaciones Agrarias). *Noticiero de la realidad*. No. 15 (January 1984).

——. "Región forestal: Empresas y trabajadores." Santiago: Grupo de Investigaciones Agrarias, Academia de Humanismo Cristiano, n.d.

Giddens, Anthony. *Runaway World: How Globalization Is Reshaping our Lives*. New York: Routledge, 2000.

Gimpel Madariaga, Marlene. "El sector forestal ante la apertura económica: exporta-ciones y medio ambiente." In *El tigre sin selva: consecuencias ambientales de la transforma-ción económica de Chile*, edited by Rayén Quiroga Martínez. Santiago: Instituto de Ecolo-gía Política, 1994.

Gomez, Sergio. *Forestación y campesinado*. Document 19. Santiago: Instituto de Desarrollo Agropecuario, January 1994.

——. *Politicas estatales y campesinado en Chile, 1960–1989*. Santiago: FLACSO, 1989.

Gómez, Sergio, and Jorge Echenique. *La agricultura chilena: Dos caras de la modernización*. Santiago: CIREN, 1988.

Gonzáles, Cristián. "Notas sobre empleo precario y precarización del empleo en Chile." In *Economía y Trabajo: Informe Anual, 1997–1998*. Santiago: PET (1998): 51–58.

Guillén, Mauro. "Is Globalization Civilizing, Destructive, or Feeble? A Critique of Five Key Debates." *Annual Review of Sociology* 27 (2001): 235–260.

Hachette, Dominique. "Privatizaciones: Reforma estructural, pero inconclusa." In *La transformación económica de Chile*, ed. Felipe Larraín and Rodrigo Vergara. Santiago: CEP, 2000.

Harrison, Bennett. *Lean and Mean: The Changing Architecture of Corporate Power in the Age of Flexibility*. New York: BasicBooks, 1994.

Held, David, Anthony McGrew, David Goldblatt, and Jonathan Perraton. *Global Transfor-mations: Politics, Economics, and Culture*. Stanford: Stanford University Press, 1999.

Henriquez Riquelme, Helia. "Las relaciones laborales en Chile: Un sistema colectivo o un amplio espacio para la dispersión?" In *El modelo chileno: democracia y desarrollo en los noventa*, edited by Paul W. Drake and Iván Jáksic. Santiago: LOM, 1999.

Herrera, Gonzalo. "Tendencias del cambio tecnológico en la industria chilena." In *Econ-omía y Trabajo: Informe Anual, 1994–1995*. Santiago: PET (1995): 75–94.

Howes, David, ed. *Cross-Cultural Consumption: Global Markets, Local Realities*. London: Rout-ledge, 1996.

Huber, Evelyn, and Sergio Berensztein. "The Politics of Social Policy in Chile, Costa Rica, and Mexico: Crisis and Response." Paper presented at the 19th Latin American Studies Association (LASA) Congress, Washington, D.C., 28–30 September 1995.

Huneeus, Carlos. *Malestar y desencanto en Chile: Legados del autoritarismo y costos de la transi-ción*. Working paper. Santiago: PEP, Corporación Tiempo 2000, 1998.

——. "La nueva derecha en el postautoritarismo en Chile: La unión democrata independiente (UDI)." Working paper 285. Notre Dame: Helen Kellogg Institute for International Studies, University of Notre Dame, 2000.

——. El régimen de Pinochet. Santiago: Sudamericana, 2001.

Hutchison, Elizabeth Quay. Labors Appropriate to Their Sex: Gender, Work, and Politics in Chile.
Durham: Duke University Press, 2001.

——. "El fruto envenenado del arbol capitalista: Women Workers and the Prostitution of
Labor in Urban Chile, 1896–1925." Journal of Women's History 9, no. 4 (1998): 131–52.

INE (Instituto Nacional de Estadísticas). Anuario de industrias manufactureras, 1975. Santiago: INE, 1975.

——. Anuario de industrias manufactureras, 1989. Santiago: INE, 1989.

——. Anuario de industrias manufactureras, 1990. Santiago: INE, 1990.

——. Anuario de industrias manufactureras, 1995. Santiago: INE, 1995.

——. Anuario de precios. Santiago: INE, 1987.

——. Compendio estadístico, 1995. Santiago: INE, 1995.

——. Vencuesta de presupuestos familiares, 1996–1997. Summary. Santiago: INE, 1999.

——. XVI censo nacional de población y V de vivienda. Santiago: INE, 1992.

Infante, Eduardo. "1993: El difícil mercado del sector pesquero." Chile Pesquero, no. 78
(1993): 67–69.

——, ed. La calidad del empleo: La experiencia de los países latinoamericanos y de los Estados
Unidos. 2d ed. Santiago: OIT, 2000.

Infor (Instituto Forestal). "Boletín Estadístico," no. 61. Estadísticas Forestales, 1997.

——. La pequeña empresa madera de bosque nativo: Su importancia, perspectiva y una propuesta
para su desarrollo. Technical bulletin 128. Santiago: Infor, 1991.

Jacoby, Sanford, ed. The Workers of Nations: Industrial Relations in a Global Economy. New
York: Oxford University Press, 1997.

Jaquette, Jane. ed. The Women's Movement in Latin America: Feminism and the Transition to
Democracy. Boston: Unwin and Hyman, 1989.

——. The Women's Movement in Latin America: Participation and Democracy. Boulder: Westview Press, 1994.

Jarvis, Lovell. Chilean Agriculture under Military Rule. Berkeley: University of California
Press, 1985.

Jensen, Bent-Are. "Chilean Salmon Mortality Rate Almost 30 Per Cent." Intrafish, 10 June
2002.

Junta de Gobierno. Primer año de la reconstruccion nacional. Santiago: Government of Chile,
1974.

Katz, Jorge, and Héctor Vera. "Evolución histórica de una planta metalmecánica
chilena." Paper presented at the conference "Productividad, cambio tecnológico, y
sistemas innovativos en América Latina en los años 90," sponsored by
CEPAL/Comisíon Económica para América Latina, Naciones Unidas, Marbella,
Chile, 1995.

Kay, Cristobal, and Patricio Silva, eds. Development and Social Change in the Chilean Countryside. Amsterdam: CEDLA, 1992.

Keck, Margaret. "The New Unionism in the Brazilian Transition." In Democratizing Brazil:

Problems of Transition and Consolidation, edited by Alfred Stepan. New York: Oxford University Press, 1989.

Kingsolver, Barbara. *Holding the Line: Women in the Great Arizona Mine Strike of 1983*. Ithaca: ILR Press, 1989.

Klubock, Thomas Miller. *Contested Communities: Class, Gender, and Politics in the Chilean Copper Mines, 1904–1951*. Durham: Duke University Press, 1998.

Kochan, Thomas, Russell Lansbury, and John MacDuffie, eds. *After Lean Production: Evolving Employment Practices in the World Auto Industry*. Ithaca: Cornell University, ILR Press, 1997.

Kornbluh, Peter. "Chile and the United States: Declassified Documents Related to the Military Coup of September 11, 1973." National Security Archive, Electronic Briefing Book no. 8, http://www.gwu.edu/7Ensarchiv/latin__america/ chile.htm.

——, ed. *The Pinochet File: A Declassified Dossier on Atrocity and Accountability*. New York: New Press, 2003.

Kumazawa, Makoto. *Portraits of the Japanese Workplace: Labor Movements, Workers, and Managers*. Boulder: Westview, 1996.

Lago, María Soledad, and Carlota Olavarria. *La participacion de la mujer en las economias campesinas: Un estudio de casos en dos comunas fruticolas*. Santiago: GIA, 1981.

Lagos, Ricardo. "Effects of Extreme De-regulation of the Labour Market: Chile 1974–1990." Santiago: OIT, 1995.

Larraín, Felipe, and Rodrigo Vergara, eds. *La transformación económica de Chile*. Santiago: CEP, 2000.

Larrañaga, Osvaldo. "Distribución de ingresos: 1958–2001." In *Reformas, crecimiento y políticas sociales en Chile desde 1973*, ed. Ricardo Ffrench-Davis and Barbara Stallings. Santiago: LOM/Cepal, 2001.

Leíva, Fernando Ignacio, and Rafael Agacino. *Mercado de trabajo flexible, pobreza y desintegración social en Chile,1990–1994*. Santiago: Universidad Arcis, 1994.

Linz, Juan, and Alfred Stepan. *Problems of Democratic Transition and Consolidation: Southern Europe, South America, and Post-Communist Europe*. Baltimore: Johns Hopkins University Press, 1996.

Lopez Diego. "El proyecto de reforma laboral: Avances y desafios." In *Economía y Trabajo: Informe anual, 1994–1995*. Santiago: PET (1995): 95–114.

Louie, Mariam Ching Yoon. *Sweatshop Warriors: Immigrant Women Workers Take On the Global Factory*. Cambridge, Mass.: South End Press, 2001.

Loveman, Brian. *Chile: The Legacy of Hispanic Capitalism*. 3d ed. New York: Oxford University Press, 2001.

——. *Struggle in the Countryside: Politics and Rural Labor in Chile*. Bloomington: University of Indiana Press, 1976.

Loyola, Manuel, and Jorge Rojas, eds. *Por un rojo amanecer: Hacia una historia de los comunistas chilenos*. Santiago: Valus, 2000.

MacClure Hortal, Oscar, and Ivan Valenzuela Rabi. "Conflictos en la gran minería del cobre, 1973–1983." Working paper. Santiago: Cedal, May 1985.

Mansfield, Robert E. *Progessive Chile*. New York: Neale Publishing, 1913.

Manufacturas de Cobre, S.A. (Madeco). *Memoria anual*. Santiago: Madeco, S.A., 1944–1998.

Martínez, Javier, and Alvaro Díaz. *Chile: The Great Transformation*. Washington, D.C.: Brookings Institution/Geneva: U.N. Research Institute for Social Development, 1996.

Maturana, Victor. "Primer semestre 1991: Más huelgas, pero más cortas." Unpublished paper. Santiago: Ciasi, 1991.

———. "Y los trabajadores . . . ¿cuando?" *Revista Cambio*, no. 7 (September–October 1987): 18–23.

Medel, Julia, Soledad Olivos, and Verónica Riquelme. *Las temporeras y sus visiones del trabajo*. Santiago: CEM, 1989.

Meller, Patricio. "Pobreza y distribución del ingreso en Chile (década de los noventa)." In *El modelo chileno: Democracia y desarrollo en los noventa*, edited by Paul W. Drake and Iván Jáksic. Santiago: LOM, 1999.

———. *Un siglo de economía política chilena (1890–1990)*. Santiago: Andrés Bello, 1996.

Mendez, Ricardo, and Clara Muñita. *La salmonicultura en Chile*. Santiago: Fundación Chile, 1989.

Mideplan (Ministerio de Planificación y Cooperación). *Empleo y remuneraciones, 1995*. Documentos/Económicos. Santiago: Mideplan, 1996.

Miller, Daniel. *Capitalism: An Ethnographic Approach*. New York: Berg, 1997.

———. *Modernity: An Ethnographic Approach. Dualism and Mass Consumption in Trinidad*. Oxford: Berg, 1994.

Ministerio de Economía, Fomento y Reconstrucción. *Chile: Centro Nacional de la Productividad y la Calidad*. Santiago: Ministerio de Economía, Fomento y Reconstrucción Minkcon, 1997.

Ministerio de Trabajo (MinTrab). *Nuevo Código del trabajo*. Santiago: Jurídica de Chile, 1971.

———. *Codigo del trabajo*. Santiago: Editora Jurídica Publigráfica, 1992.

———. *Nuevo Código del Trabajo*. Santiago: Publiley, 1991, 1992, 1993.

Ministry of Agriculture (MinAgro), Servicio Agrícola y Ganadero (SAG). *Anuario estadístico de pesca, 1976*. Santiago: MinAgro, 1976.

Mizala, Alejandra, and Pilar Romaguera. "Flexibilidad del mercado de trabajo: El impacto del ajuste y los requisitos del crecimiento económico." *Colección Estudios Cieplan*, no. 43 (September 1996): 15–48.

Molina, Ignacio. "X Region: 1989." *Informes de Coyuntura*. No. 2. Grupo de Investigaciones Agrarias: Santiago, 1990.

Montero, Cecilia. "La evolución del empresario chileno ¿Surge un nuevo actor?" *Colección Estudios Cieplan*, no. 30 (1990): 91–122.

Montero, Cecilia, Lovell Jarvis, and Sergio Gómez, eds. "El sector frutícola en la encrucijada: Opciones para una expansión sostenida." Working paper 112. Santiago: Cieplan, 1992.

Morales Gamboni, Jorge. "El estado y el sector privado en la industria forestal: El caso de la región de Concepción." *Boletín de Estudios Agrarios*, no. 24 (August 1989).

Moreira Alves, Maria Helena. (1989). "Trade Unions in Brazil: A Search for Autonomy and Organization." In *Labor Autonomy and the State in Latin America*, edited by Edward Epstein. Boston: Unwin Hyman, 1989.

Moulian, Tomás. *Chile actual: Anatomía de un mito*. Santiago: LOM, 1997.

———. *El consumo me consume*. Santiago: LOM, 1988.

———. "Desarrollo político y estado de compromiso: Desajustes y crisis estatal en Chile." Colección Estudios Cieplan, no. 8 (1982): 43–53.

Muñoz Goma, Oscar. *Crisis y reorganizacion industrial en Chile*. Notas tecnicas 123. Santiago: Cieplan, 1988.

Newman, Constance. "How Are Piece Rates Determined? A Micro-Level Analysis of Piece Rates in Chilean Table Grape-Packing Sheds." Ph.D. diss., University of California-Davis, 1994.

"November Black Month for Chilean Salmon Companies." *Intrafish*, 9 January 2002.

O'Donnell, Guillermo. "Teoria democratica y política comparada." *Desarrollo Económico: Revista de Ciencias Sociales* 39, no. 156 (2000): 519–570.

———. "Transitions, Continuities, and Paradoxes." In *Issues in Democratic Consolidation*, edited by Scott Mainwaring, Guillermo O'Donnell, and J. Samuel Valenzuela. Notre Dame: Notre Dame University Press, 1992.

O'Donnell, Guillermo, Philippe Schmitter, and Laurence Whitehead, eds. *Transitions from Authoritarian Rule*. 4 vols. Baltimore: Johns Hopkins University Press, 1986.

Ong, Aihwa. *Spirits of Resistance and Capitalist Discipline: Factory Women in Malaysia*. Albany: State University of New York Press, 1987.

Ortega-Frei, Eugenio. *Historia de una alianza. El Partido Socialista de Chile y el Partido Democrata-Christiano, 1973–1988*. Santiago: CED-CESOC, 1992.

Otero, Luis. "El problema social detrás de los bosques." Concepción: Vicaría de la Pastoral Obrera, 1984.

———. "Los trabajadores y el sistema de contratistas en el sector forestal." *Boletín de Estudios Agrarios* (7 March 1981): 52–88.

Oxhorn, Philip. *Organizing Civil Society: The Popular Sectors and the Struggle for Democracy in Chile*. University Park: Pennsylvania State University Press, 1995.

Oxmán, Veronica. *La participación de la mujer campesina en organizaciones*. Santiago: ISIS, 1983.

PET (Programa de Economía y Trabajo). *Informe anual*. Annual issues, 1991–1998. Santiago: PET, 1991–1998.

Petras, James, Fernando I. Leiva, and Henry Veltmeyer. *Democracy and Poverty in Chile: The Limits to Electoral Politics*. Boulder: Westview Press, 1994.

Piore, Michael, and Charles Sabel. *The Second Industrial Divide: Possibilities for Prosperity*. New York: Basic Books, 1984.

Pizzorno, Alessandro. "Political Exchange and Collective Identities in Industrial Conflict." In vol. 2 of *The Resurgence of Class Conflict in Western Europe since 1968: Comparative Analysis*, edited by Alessandro Pizzorno and Colin Crouch. New York: Holmes and Meier, 1968.

Power, Margaret. "Right-Wing Women and Chilean Politics, 1964–1973," Ph.D. diss., University of Illinois-Chicago, 1997.

——. *Right-Wing Women in Chile: Feminine Power and the Struggle against Allende, 1964–1973.* University Park: Pennsylvania State University Press, 2002.

Quinteros Tamayo, Domingo. *Memoria testimonial: Año 1991.* Rancagua, January 1992.

Quiroga Martínez, Rayén, and Saar Van Hauwermeiven. *Globalización e insustentabilidad: Una mirada desde la economía ecológica.* Santiago: Instituto de Ecología Política, 1996.

Quiroga, Rayén, and Saar von Hauwermeiren, eds. *The Tiger without a Jungle: Environmental Consequences of the Economic Transformation of Chile.* Santiago: Instituto de Ecología Política, 1996.

Quiroz, César. "La política de la rebelión popular de las masas." In *Por un rojo amanecer: hacia una historia de los comunistas chilenos,* ed. Manuel Loyola and Jorge Rojas. Santiago: Valus, 2000.

Raczynski, Dagmar. "Políticas sociales en los años noventa en Chile: Balance y desafío." In *El modelo chileno democracia y desarrollo en los noventa,* edited by Paul Drake and Iván Jáksic. Santiago: LOM, 1999.

Raskill Information Services. *The Economics of Copper.* 3d ed. London: Raskill, 1984.

Razeto, Manuel. "El proceso de reformas laborales: Itinerario, enseñanzas y propuestas para el mundo sindical." *Revista de Economía y Trabajo* (Santiago: PET, 2000): 177–225.

Reinecke, Gerhart. "Inside the Model: Politics, Enterprise Strategies, and Employment Quality in Chile." Ph.D. diss., University of Hamburg, 2000.

Reinecke, Gerhart, and Raymond Torres. *Chile: Social Dimensions of Globalization.* Geneva: ILO, 2001.

Reusch, Francisco. "La política forestal del gobierno y la concentración económica en el sector forestal." *Boletín de Estudios Agrarios,* no. 7 (March 1981): 25–51.

Ritzer, George. *The McDonaldization Thesis: Explorations and Extensions.* London: Sage, 1998.

Rivera, Rigoberta, and M. Elena Cruz. *Pobladores rurales.* Santiago: Grupo de Investigaciones Agrarias/Academia de Humanismo Cristiano, 1984.

Rodríguez, Daniel, and Silvia Venegas. *De praderas a parronales.* Santiago: GEA (Grupo de Estudios Agrarios), 1989.

Rojas Magallanes, Victorino. *Informe sobre bosques presentado al Ministerio de Industria y Obras Públicas.* Santiago: Imprenta Litografía y Encaudernación Barcelona, 1902.

Romaguera, Pilar, Cristían Echevarría, and Pablo González. "Chile." In *Reforming the Labor Market in a Liberalized Economy,* edited by Gustavo Márquéz. Baltimore: Johns Hopkins University Press, 1995.

Roseberry, William. "Americanization in the Americas." In *Anthropologies and Histories: Essays in Culture, History and Political Economy,* by William Roseberry. New Brunswick: Rutgers University Press, 1991.

Rosemblatt, Karin Alejandra. *Gendered Compromises: Political Cultures and the State in Chile, 1920–1950.* Chapel Hill: University of North Carolina Press, 2002.

Rosenbaum, Jonathan D. *Copper Crucible: How the Arizona Miners' Strike of 1983 Recast Labor-Management Relations in America.* Ithaca: ILR Press, 1995.

Rueschemeyer, Dietrich, John Stephens, and Evelyn Huber. *Capitalist Development and Democracy.* Chicago: University of Chicago Press, 1992.

Ruíz-Tagle, Jaime. "Desarrollo social y políticas públicas en Chile, 1985–1995." In *Economía y Trabajo: Informe Anual, 1995–1996.* Santiago: PET (1996): 7–56.

———. *El sindicalismo chileno después del Plan Laboral.* Santiago: PET, 1985.

Sáez, Arturo. *El empresario fruticola chileno, 1973–1985: Uvas y manzanas, democracia y auto-ritarismo.* Santiago: Sur, 1986.

Safa, Helen. "Women, Production, and Reproduction in Industrial Capitalism: A Comparison of Brazilian and U.S. Factory Workers." In *Women, Men, and the International Division of Labor,* edited by Sharon Stichter and Jane Parpart. Philadelphia: Temple University Press, 1990.

Salinas, Luís. *Trayectoria de la organizacíon campesina.* Santiago: AGRA, 1985.

SalmonChile. "Commerce Dept. Rejects US Salmon Farmers' Allegations." http://www.fis.com/salmonchile/finmix2.htm, 1998. Accessed 2 June 1998.

Salomon Brothers, et al. "Prospectus: 3,937,500 Depositary Shares, Representing 30,375,000 Shares of Common Stock: Madeco, S.A." New York: Salomon Brothers, et al. 7 May 1993.

Schedler, Andreas. "Condiciones y racionalidades de la concertación social." Working paper 23. Santiago: FLACSO, 1992.

Schild, Veronica. "Recasting Popular Movements: Gender and Political Learning in Neighborhood Organizing in Chile." *Latin American Perspectives* 21, no. 2 (1994): 59–80.

Schkolnik, Mariana. *Transformaciones en las pautas de consumo y políticas neoliberales: Chile: 1974–1981.* Santiago: PET, 1983.

Schmitter, Philippe. "Modes of Interest Intermediation and Models of Societal Change in Western Europe." In *Trends toward Corporatist Intermediation,* edited by Philip Schmitter and Georg Lehmbruch. London: Sage, 1979.

Schneider, Cathy. "Radical Opposition Parties and Squatter Movements in Pinochet's Chile." In *The Making of Social Movements in Latin America,* edited by Sonia Alvarez and Arturo Escobar. Boulder, Westview, 1992.

———. *Shantytown Protest in Pinochet's Chile.* Philadelphia:Temple University Press, 1995.

Schurman, Rachel. "Chile's New Entrepreneurs and the 'Economic Miracle': The Invisible Hand or a Hand From the State?" *Studies in Comparative International Development* 31, no. 3 (1996): 83–109.

———. "Uncertain Gains: Labor in Chile's New Export Sectors." *Latin American Research Review* 36, no. 2 (2001): 3–29.

Segundo Gobierno de la Concertación (Government of President Eduardo Frei [Jr.]). "Un gobierno para los nuevos tiempos: Bases programáticas del Segundo Gobierno de la Concertación." Santiago: [Concertación, 1993].

Sernapesca (Servicio Nacional de Pesca). *Anuario estadístico de pesca, 1992.* Santiago: Sernapesca, 1993.

———. *Anuario estadístico de pesca 1995.* Santiago: Republic of Chile, 1996.

Shaiken, Harley. "Advanced Manufacturing and Mexico: A New International Division of Labor?" *Latin American Research Review* 29, no. 2 (1994): 39–71.

Silva, Eduardo. *The State and Capital in Chile: Business Elites, Technocrats, and Market Economics.* Boulder: Westview Press, 1996.

Silva, Patricio. "The State, Politics, and Peasant Unions in Chile." *Journal of Latin American Studies,* no. 20 (n.d.): n.p.

Sindicato No. 1, Madeco. "Asamblea general de socios/Asamblea extraordinaria de socios." Minutes of union meetings. Santiago, 1988–1998.

Sindicato No. 1, Madeco-Madeco, S.A. "Convenio colectivo Sindicato no. 1. Vigencia: 1 de noviembre 1998–31 de enero 2002." Santiago.

Sklair, Leslie. *Sociology of the Global System*. 2d ed. Baltimore: Johns Hopkins University Press, 1995.

Smith, William, Carlos Acuña, and Eduardo Gamarra, eds. *Democracy, Markets, and Structural Reform in Latin America*. New Brunswick: Transaction Books, 1994.

Stepan, Alfred. *Rethinking Military Politics: Brazil and the Southern Cone*. Princeton: Princeton University Press, 1988.

Stern, Steven. *The Secret History of Gender: Women, Men, and Power in Late Colonial Mexico*. Chapel Hill: University of North Carolina Press, 1995.

Stiglitz, Joseph E. *Globalization and Its Discontents*. New York: W. W. Norton, 2002.

Stillerman, Joel. " 'Dando la pelea hasta el final.' Metal Workers' Resistance in Authoritarian Chile, 1976–1983." Paper presented at the 13th annual Latin American Labor History Conference, Duke University, Durham, N.C., 1996.

———. "From Solidarity to Survival: Transformations in the Culture and Styles of Mobilization of Chilean Metalworkers under Democratic and Authoritarian Regimes, 1945–1995." Ph.D. diss., New School for Social Research, New York, 1998.

———. "Gender, Class, and Generational Contexts for Consumption in Contemporary Chile." *Journal of Consumer Culture* 4, no. 1 (2004).

———. "Militant Trade-Unionist or Happy Consumer? The Ambiguities of Working-Class Identity in Post-Pinochet Chile." Paper presented at the 20th International Latin American Studies Association (LASA) Conference, Guadalajara, April 1997.

———. "The Paradoxes of Power: The Unintended Consequences of Military Rule for Chilean Working-class Mobilization." *Political Power and Social Theory* 12 (1998): 97–139.

Streek, Wolfgang. "Organizational Consequences of Neo-Corporatist Co-operation in West German Labour Unions." In *Patterns of Corporatist Policy-Making*, edited by Philippe Schmitter and Georg Lehmbruch. Beverly Hills: Sage, 1982.

Tardanico, Richard, and Rafael Menjívar, eds. *Global Restructuring, Employment, and Social Inequality in Urban Latin America*. Coral Gables, Fla.: North-South Press, 1997.

Tinsman, Heidi. "Esposas golpeadas: Violencia domestica y control sexual en Chile rural, 1958–1988," In *Disciplina y descato: Estudios de género en la historia de Chile, siglos XIX y XX*, edited by Lorena Gody, Elizabeth Hutchison, Karin Rosemblatt, and Soledad Zárate. Santiago: Sur/CEDEM, 1995.

———. "Household Patrones: Wife Beating and Sexual Control in Rural Chile." In *The Gendered Worlds of Latin American Women Workers*, edited by Daniel James and John French. Durham: Duke University Press, 1997.

———. *Partners in Conflict: The Politics of Gender, Sexuality, and Labor in the Chilean Agrarian Reform, 1950–1973*. Durham: Duke University Press, 2002.

———. "Unequal Uplift: The Sexual Politics of Gender, Work, and Community in the Chilean Agrarian Reform." Ph.D. diss., Yale University, 1996.

Tironi, Eugenio. *El cambio está aquí*. Santiago: La Tercera/Mondadori, 2002.

Tomaney, John. "A New Paradigm of Work Organization and Technology?" In *Post-Fordism: A Reader*, edited by A. Amin. Oxford: Blackwell, 1994.

Tortora, Alicia, and Susana Vilacura. "Sistematización de práctica efectuada en Manufacturas de Cobre, S.A. Madeco." B.A. Practicum Report. Departmento de Trabajo Social, Universidad Católica de Chile, Santiago. October 1974.

U.S. Senate Committee on Intelligence. 94th Congress, 1st Session. *Covert Action in Chile, 1963–1973*. Staff report. 1975.

Valdés, Juan Gabriel. *Pinochet's Economists: The Chicago School in Chile*. Cambridge: Cambridge University Press, 1995.

Valdés, Teresa, and Enrique Gómez, coordinators. *Latin American Women: Compared Figures*. Santiago: FLACSO, 1995.

Valdés, Teresa, María Weinstein, María Isabel Toledo, and Lilian Letelier. "Centros de madre, 1973–1989: Solo disciplinamiento?" Working paper 416. Santiago: FLACSO, 1989.

Valdés, Ximena. "Entre la crisis de la uva y la esperanza en crisis." Paper presented at the 47th American Congress, New Orleans, July 1991.

——. "Una experiencia de organización autónoma de mujeres del campo." In *Cuadernos de la mujer del campo*. Santiago: GIA, 1983.

——. "Feminización del mercado de trabajo agrícola: Las temporeras." In *Mundo de mujer: Cambio y continuidad*. Santiago: CEM, 1988.

——. *La posicion de la mujer en la hacienda*. Santiago: CEM, 1988.

——. *Mujer, trabajo, y medio ambiente: Los nudos de la modernización agraria*. Santiago: CEM, 1992.

——. *La posición de la mujer en la hacienda*. Santiago: CEM, 1988.

——. *Sinopsis de una realidad oculta: Las trabajadoras del campo*. Santiago: CEM, 1987.

——. *Vida privada: Modernización agrícola y modernidad*. Santiago: CEDEM, 1998.

Valdés, Ximena, Sonia Montecino, Kirai de León, Macarena Mack. *Historias testimoniales de mujeres del campo*. Santiago: Programa de Estudios y Capacitación de la Mujer Campesina e Indígena, 1986.

Valdés, Ximena, Veronica Riquelme, Julia Medel, et al. *Sinopsis de un Realidad Ocultada: Las Trabajadoras del Campo*. Santiago: CEM [Centro de Estudios de la Mujer], 1987.

Valdivia, Veronica. *El golpe despúes del golpe: Leigh vs. Pinochet, 1960–1980*. Santiago: LOM, 2003.

——. "Estatismo y neoliberalismo: Un contrapunto militar, Chile, 1973–1979." *Historia* (Santiago) 34 (2001): 194–214.

Valenzuela, Arturo. *The Breakdown of Democratic Regimes: Chile*. Baltimore: Johns Hopkins University Press, 1978.

Valenzuela, Arturo, and J. Samuel Valenzuela, eds. *Military Rule in Chile*. Baltimore: Johns Hopkins University Press, 1986.

Valenzuela, J. Samuel. "The Chilean Labor Movement: The Institutionalization of Conflict." In *Chile: Politics and Society*, edited by Arturo Valenzuela and J. Samuel Valenzuela. New Brunswick: Transaction Books, 1976.

——. "Democratic Consolidation in Post-Transitional Settings: Notion, Process, and Facilitating Conditions." In *Issues in Democratic Consolidation*, edited by Scott Mainwaring, Guillermo O'Donnell, and J. Samuel Valenzuela. Notre Dame: Notre Dame University Press, 1992.

———. "Los escollos de la redemocratización chilena." *Boletín SAAP* 5, no. 9 (1999): 111–28.

———. "Labor Movement Formation and Politics: The Chilean and French Cases in Comparative Perspective." Ph.D. diss., Columbia University, 1979.

———. "Labor Movements in Transitions to Democracy: A Framework for Analysis." *Comparative Politics* 21, no. 4 (1989): 445–472.

———. "Recasting State-Union Relations in Latin America." In *Redefining the State*, edited by Colin Bradford Jr. Paris: OECD, 1994.

———. "Sindicalismo, desarrollo económico y democracia: Hacia un nuevo modelo de organización laboral en Chile." *Economía y Trabajo* 1, no. 2 (1993): 67–97.

Varas, Augusto. *Los militares en el poder: Régimen y gobierno militar en Chile, 1973–1986.* Santiago: FLACSO, 1987.

Velasquez, Mario. *Reformas y flexibilidad laboral.* Serie Publicaciones Análisis Laboral 1. Santiago: Fundación Friedrich Ebert, 1996.

Venegas, Silvia. *Una gota al día . . . un chorro al año: El impacto social de la expansión fruticultura.* Santiago: GEA, 1992.

Vergara, Pilar. *Auge y caída del neoliberalismo en Chile.* Santiago: FLACSO, 1985.

Vilas, Carlos. "Forward Back: Capitalist Restructuring, the State, and Working Class in Latin America." In *Whither Marxism? Global Crises in International Perspective*, edited by Bernd Magnus and Stephen Cullenberg. New York: Routledge, 1995.

Watson, James L., ed. *Golden Arches East: McDonalds in East Asia.* Stanford: Stanford University Press, 1997.

Weyland, Kurt. " 'Growth with Equity' in Chile's New Democracy." *Latin American Research Review* 32, no. 1 (1997): 37–68.

———. "La política económica en la nueva democracia chilena." In *El modelo chileno: democracia y desarrollo en los noventa*, edited by Paul W. Drake and Iván Jáksic. Santiago: LOM, 1999.

Whelan, Carmen Teresa. "Sweatshops Here and There: The Garment Industry, Latinas and Labor Migration." *International Labor and Working-Class History* 61 (spring 2002): *Sweated Labor: The Politics of Representation and Reform*, 45–68.

Wilk, Richard. "Food and Nationalism: The Origins of 'Belizean Food.' " In *Food Nations: Selling Taste in Consumer Societies*, edited by W. Bellasco and P. Scranton. New York: Routledge, 2002.

Winn, Peter. *Americas: The Changing Face of Latin America and the Caribbean.* 2d ed. Berkeley: University of California Press, 1999.

———. *Weavers of Revolution: The Yarur Workers and Chile's Road to Socialism.* New York: Oxford University Press, 1986.

Winn, Peter, and Maria Angélica Ibáñez. "Textile Entrepreneurs and Workers in Pinochet's Chile, 1973–1989." Institute for Latin American and Iberian Studies, Papers on Latin America 15. New York: Columbia University, 1990.

Wolf, Diane. *Factory Daughters: Gender, Household Dynamics, and Rural Industrialization in Java.* Los Angeles: University of California Press, 1992.

Womack, James P., Daniel Roos, and Daniel Jones. *The Machine That Changed the World*. New York: Rawson Associates, 1990.

Yanes, Lara Hugo. *Las comisiones tripartitas*. Serie documentos 4. Santiago: Ciasi, 1990.

Zapata, Francisco. "The Chilean Labor Movement under Salvador Allende, 1970–1973." *Latin American Perspectives* 3, no. 1 (winter 1976): 85–97.

——. "The End of the Honeymoon: The Chilean Labor Scene." *Latin American Labor News* 5 (1992): 9.

Contributors

PAUL DRAKE is dean of the Division of Social Science, professor of Political Science, and adjunct professor of History and of IRPS at the University of California, San Diego. He is the author of *Labor Movements and Dictatorships: The Southern Cone in Comparative Perspective*; *The Money Doctor in the Andes: The Kemmerer Missions, 1923–1933*; and *Socialism and Populism in Chile, 1932–1952*. He is also the coeditor of *The Origins of Liberty: Political and Economic Liberalization in the Modern World*; *The Struggle for Democracy in Chile*; *Money Doctors, Foreign Debts, and Economic Reforms in Latin America from the 1890s to the Present*; *The Struggle for Democracy in Chile, 1982–1990*; and *Elections and Democratization in Latin America, 1980–1985*.

VOLKER FRANK is an associate professor of Sociology at the University of North Carolina, Asheville. His research interests include labor movements, democratization and labor parties.

THOMAS MILLER KLUBOCK is an associate professor of History at the State University of New York, Stony Brook. He is the author of *Contested Communities: Class, Gender, and Politics in Chile's El Teniente Copper Mine, 1904–1951*.

RACHEL A. SCHURMAN is an assistant professor of Sociology at the University of Illinois, Champaign-Urbana. Her research interests include labor in the global economy, Latin American development and the political economy of agrofood systems.

JOEL STILLERMAN is an assistant professor of Sociology at Grand Valley State University. His recent publications on labor and consumer culture in Chile and North America appear in *Mobilization: An International Journal*, *Social Science History* and *Journal of Consumer Culture*.

HEIDI TINSMAN is an associate professor of History at the University of California, Irvine. She is the author of *Partners in Conflict: The Politics of Gender, Sexuality, and Labor in the Chilean Agrarian Reform, 1950–1973*.

PETER WINN is a professor of History and the director of Latin American Studies at Tufts University. He is the author of *Americas: The Changing Face of Latin America and the Caribbean* and *Weavers of Revolution: The Yarur Workers and Chile's Road to Socialism*.

Bush, George W., and Chilean textile industry, 149–150

Business community, in 1990s, 54–55

Bustos, Manuel, 37, 113; on Mining Law, 233; targeting and detainment of, 22, 47, 137, 237

Cafeteria protests, 193, 222

Caja de Empleados Publicos y Periodistas, 344

Calderón, Marcelo, 145

Campero, Guillermo, 35

Campesinos (peasants), 261; and forestry industry, 351–352, 354, 356–358, 366–367. *See also* Men, rural; Women, rural

Capitalism, and wage work, 268–269

Capital-labor relations, under Aylwin rule, 84–86

Capital markets, deregulation of, 40–41

"Caravan of Death," 19

Carter, Jimmy, 29, 31–32

Castaing, Carlos, 303

Catholic Church, 44; and forestry workers, 368; and rural women, 278–279

Cauas, Jorge, 26–27

CEAT International, 167

Center for National Intelligence (CNI), 236, 238

Central Bank, and Pinochet, 40, 143

Central Unica de Trabajadores (CUT). *See* CUT

Chacarillas Plan, 29

Chain stores, and textile industry, 146

"Chicago Boys": and Chilean economy, 41; and forestry industry, 337; and neoliberalism, 25–29; and textile industry, 128. *See also* Friedman, Milton

Chiguyante, workers at, 153

Children, of El Teniente miners, 220, 225

Chile Actual (Moulian), 4–5

Chilean Labor Directorate (DT), 100

Chilean "miracle," term defined, 1

"Chilean Road to Socialism," and Allende, 16–19

"Chilean Tiger," Madeco as, 173–178

Chinese textile industry, and Chilean textile industry, 144–145

Christian Democrats: and labor reform, 31–31, 97; leaders, 23–24; versus Popular Unity, 18; and unions, 225

Chuquicamata, miners of, 237–238

City dwelling, versus mining camps, 247–248, 253

Class, working, and elites, 185–186

Class conflicts, and democracy, 80–81

Class identity, 253; and consumerism, 181 (*see also* Consumerism); of copper miners, 255; and cultural life, 248–249; and union activists, 186. *See also* Identity, worker

Clothing workers. *See* Textile workers

CMPC (Compañía Manufacturera de Papeles y Cartones), 342

CMPC (Matte-Alessandri), 349

CNI (Center for National Intelligence), 236, 238

CNS (Coordinadora Nacional Sindical): and Concertacíon, 37; formation of, 23–24; leftist groups within, 37; and Mining Law, 233; in 1970s, 37; and textile workers, 140

CNT (Central Nacional de Trabajadores), 23–24, 43, 140

Coalition of Parties for Democracy. *See* Concertacíon government

Cocesa (Cobre Cerrillos, Sociedad Anónima), 172

Codeju (Youth Defense Committee), 232

Codelco (Corporación del Cobre), mines owned by, 211–212, 242–243; and Asian economic crisis, 252; conditions at, 220–221, 254–255; unionization of, 221; workers at, 7, 217–218

Collective bargaining, 73; and D.L. 2758, 33–34; and economic gains, 103–109; in El Teniente, 233–235; under Frei, 88; laws on, 77–79; under Plan Laboral, 93–94; pros and cons of, 108; and right

to strike, 103–104; and temporary
workers, 102; and transitory unions, 88
Comando Provincial de Trabajadores
Cachapoal, 232
Commerce industry, union affiliation in,
100–101
Communist party (PC), 44, 45, 212;
unions of, 225
Community, and restructuring of forestry
industry, 364–367
Community, business, economic model
of, 54–55
Community, mining: changes in, 247; in
El Teniente, 212–213; in 1990s, 246
Community, working-class, effects of dic-
tatorship on, 210
Company unions, and blue-collar unions,
194
Compensation, worker, 173. *See also*
Wages
Competition, amongst workers, 176–177
Complejo Maderero Panguipulli, 350, 379
Conaf, 347–348
Concepcíon, forest industry in, 340
Concertacíon government: and Acuerdo
Marco, 76, 77; and CNS, compared,
37; and consensus, 99–100; and CTF,
376–378; and CUT, 113; and economy,
52–53, 91–92; and environment, 55;
after Pinochet, 49–50; program for
change, 81–82; and workers, 59–60
Concertación por el No, 46–47
Conditions, working. *See* Working
conditions
Confederacion de Trabajados Forestales
(CTF), 369–337, 376–378
Coñomon, Patricia, 12, 155
Consensus: as ideal, 80–81; and labor
reform, 98–100; and union leadership,
110–111
Constitution: 1925, 30; 1980, 30, 43–44;
after 1988 plebescite, 49
Construction industry, union affiliation
in, 102

Consumerism: under Allende, 17; and
debt, 183; and identity, 10, 181, 186,
249, 253–254; in 1990s, 180; and union
members, 185, 249; and women's wage
work, 271; and work, 178–186, 198–
199; of workers, 178–179, 197
Contevech (Confederation of Textile and
Clothing Workers), 138, 140
Contextil (Confederation of Textile
Workers), 140, 154
Contract: labor force not under, 102–103;
termination of, 77–78
Contratistas callampas ("fly-by-night"
subcontractors), 360. *See also* Temporary workers
Coordinadora Nacional Sindical. *See* CNS
Copec (Cruzat-Larraín), 349
Coporarción del Cobre (Codelco). *See*
Codelco
Copper industry, 237, 250
Copper miners, 6–7; impact of technol-
ogy on, 219; and May 1983 protest, 209,
229; under Pinochet, 209–255, 251;
portrayed as elites, 239–240; resistance
actions of, 22–23, 222–223, 235, 237–
238; and transition to democracy, 209–
255; unions of, 232
Copper mines: under Frei, 212–213; and
neoliberalism, 214–222; strikes in,
230–231
Cordones industriales, 18
Corfo (Corporación de Fomento), 27,
342–343, 345, 347–348
Cortázar, René, 98, 104
CPC, 75, 86
Credit, and consumption, 180–181, 183–
184, 186, 197–198. *See also*
Consumerism
Cronon, William, 326
Cruzat-Larraín, 349
CTC: and plebsicite, 236–237; and pro-
tests, 228–230
CTF (Confederacion de Trabajados Fore-
stales), 369–373, 376–378

Cultural life: and class identity, 248–249; in 1990s, 51–52

Cussen, Albert, 196

CUT (Central Unica de Trabajadores), 21; and Acuerdo Marco, 109; and Aylwin, 75, 82–83, 110–113; in 1990s, 57; and political parties, 47–48; and textile workers, 140

Dall'Ollio, Tiberio, 171, 196

Debt, and consumerism, 183, 185. See also Consumerism

Debts, private, socialization of, 40

De Castro, Sergio, 26–29, 38, 40, 42

Decree-Law, 22. See also specific Decree-Laws (i.e. D.L. 600, etc)

Deindustrialization, 39

Deischler, Jaime, 168, 187, 195, 196

Délano, Priscilla, 312

Democracy, in Chile: and consensus, as ideal, 80–81; and labor movement, 100; and social concertation, 19, 52, 57–60, 79–82; transition to, 46–47, 97–98, 104, 113

Department stores, impact on textile industry, 146

Deregulation, of markets, and economy, 40–41

Díaz, Nicanor, 24

DINA (Direccíon de Inteligensia Nacional), 19–21

Dirección de Trabajo, 35, 103

Dirección General del Trabajo, 236

Disputada de Las Condes, 242, 245

D.L. 600, 241–242

D.L. 701, 347–348, 371

D.L. 2200, 32, 314

D.L. 2578, 34–35

D.L. 2756, 33

D.L. 2758, 33–34

D.L. 3355, 33

D.L. 3648, 35

Dole, employment of women workers, 263

Duration, strike, under 1991–2 labor laws, 79

Economic boom, in Chile: consumption after, 197; and economic crisis abroad, 12; and workers, 1–2

Economic crisis, 1980s, 3, 38–48, 228–233

Economic gains, and collective bargaining, 103–109

Economic model, neoliberalism as, 27–28

Economic policies, 51, 142. See also Neoliberalism

Economy: and Concertacion, 52–53, 91–92; and democracy, 81; and neoliberalism, 52; present, 59; during "Program of Economic Recovery," 28–29

Ecosystems, changes in, and forestry industry, 353–354

Education levels, of workers, 168–169, 172

Eliodoro, Don, 362

Elites: and economic development, 114–115; portrayal of copper workers as, 239–240; and working class, 72–73

El Teniente, management at, 245

El Teniente, miners of, 6–7; children of, 220; and collective action, 233–235; and Concertación, 238–239; and job security, 230; and Labor Code, 218–219; and labor movement, 236; and mechanization, 245–246; and modernization, 251; and 1973 coup, 212–214, 217; and Pinochet rule, 210–212; and privatization, 220; protest actions of, 222–228; and "Reconversión Laboral," 245; solidarity of, 213–214; strikes by, 209, 237; during transition to democracy, 211

El Teniente, white-collar workers at, 214–215

Employers: and Acuerdo Marco, 77; and collective bargaining, 78; and government praise, 114–115; and labor reform, 95–96, 99–100, 114; and Plan Laboral, 35–36, 94; rights about strikes, 92–93; and social concertation, 86; and strikers, 92, 108; and unions, 89, 187–198

Employment: flexibility of, 73; in 1980s and 1990s, 315–316; of salmon workers, 323

Entrepreneurs: inexperience of, 41; during Pinochet era, 5–6; in textile industry, 126–129, 140–142

Environment: degradation of, 10, 55; and fishing industry, 301, 325–326, 328; and forestry industry, 338–339, 354, 363; and neoliberalism, 8; and rural social relations, 350–359

Equality, under Allende, 56

"Equal Opportunity Program for Women," 286

Estates, rural forestry, 345–346

Estrada, Nicanor Díaz, 23, 215

Ethnic groups, and rural unions, 285

Europe, worker relations in, 98

European Union, and textile industry, 149–150

Export industries, and workers, 5, 9–10

Falabella, Gonzalo, 279

Family planning, 270, 274

Family relations, rural: and forestry industry, 365–366; in 1990s, 286–287; and women's wage work, 265, 271–272

Fear: of illness, 139; of job loss, 154; in mining industry, 216–217; of repression, 368–371; in seafood-processing plants, 310; in textile industry, 133–134

Federación Forestal Liberación, 354

Federación Liberación, 350

Federación Minera, 37

Fernández, Sergio, 24, 27

Ffrench-Davis, Ricardo, 41

Filadelfo, Don, 345

Financial markets, deregulation of, 40–41

Fisheries, wild, and economic boom, 302–314

Fisheries Development Institute (Instituto de Fomento Persquero), 318

Fishermen: economic situation of, 300; gains of, 308–309; impact of overfishing on, 318–319; wages of, 309–310; working conditions for, 299

Fishing industry, 5; boom in, 302–303, 308–309; labor in, 298–320; and land reform program, 304; and neoliberalism, 9; and overfishing, 317–319; and Plan Laboral, 311; seasonal labor in, 313–314; workers in, 7–8, 304–305, 324–325; and work hours, 312–313; working conditions, 315–319. See also Seafood-processing: industry and plants

Ford, Gerald, 31

Foreign investment: and copper miners, 232; and fruit industry, 262; and seafood industry, 327

Forestal and Celulosa Arauco, 347

Forestal and Celulosa Constitución (Celco), 347

Forestry companies, practices of, 354–355, 359

Forestry development, and CTF, 371–373

Forestry industry, 5, 8, 337–380; before 1973, 339–346; boom in, 337–338, 379–380; and Chilean government, 340; development of, 343; and D.L. 701, 347–348; and environment, 350–359; and labor movement, 344–345, 373–380; ownership in, 351–352; restructuring of, 347–350, 364–367; unemployment in, 359; workers in, 337–338

Forestry unions, 367–369, 374–377, 379–380

Forestry workers, 351–352, 358–364; and Catholic Church, 368; and neoliberalism, 9; and repression, 368–370; and subcontracting, 100; and transition to

Profit sharing, at Madeco, 169–170,
189–195
"Program of Economic Recovery," 28–29
"Proposal for Democracy," CTF, 371–373
"Protected democracy," Pinochet, 29–30
Public employees' associations, as
unions, 88
Puentes, Samuel, 148, 149
Puerto Montt, fishing industry in, 302

Quality of life, for workers, 114
Quebrada Blanca, 242

Rancagua (union), 231
Reagan, Ronald, 30
"Real men," union members as, 182. See
also Identity, worker
Recession, in 1990s, 54–55
"Reconversión Laboral," 245
Reform, agrarian. See Agrarian reform
Reforms, labor law. See Labor laws; Labor
reform
Resistance, of workers, 11–12, 15, 22–23,
187. See also Union activism
Right, political, and labor reform, 96–97,
100
Ritter, Luis, 303
Rivera, Angelica, 298–299
Rodríguez, Luis, 1
Rollbacks, and miners strikes, 10
Romo, Osvaldo, 168
Ruiz, Mario, 350
Rural communities, 277–278, 364–367
Rural labor movement, 344–345, 350–351
Rural men, 266–267, 270, 276
Rural social relations, and environment,
350–359
Rural unions, 284–285
Rural women. See Women, rural

Saéz, Raul, 25
Safa, Halen, 306–307
Salmon farm workers, conditions for, 299
Salmon industry, 300–301, 319–327, 320
Salomen Smith Barney, 196

Sandinista, overthrow in Nicaragua, 44
Sanhuenza, Nancy Torres, 304–305
Santa María union, 280–281, 285–286
Santana, Guillermo, 215
Sawmills, and processing plants, 341–
342, 362–363
Scheider, René, 20
Schmitter, Philip, 75
Schurman, Rachel, 7–9, 12, 58–59
Seafood industry. See Fishing industry
Seafood-processing: industry and plants,
303, 307–313, 316, 327; workers, 299,
304–307
SeaHorse Exports, 307–308
Seasonal labor, in fishing industry, 313–
314. See also Temporary workers
Secret police (DINA), 21
Security, job. See Job security
Seguel, Rodolfo, 230
Sexual harassment, of women workers,
273–274
Sexuality, of women, perceptions of, 274–
275. See also Identity, of women
Sexual promiscuity, fear of, 272, 273
Shellfish, overfishing of, 318–319
Shellfishermen, economic situation of,
300
"Shock treatment," economic, 26
Silicosis, 239–240
Simonetti brothers, 167
Sinami (union), 221
Sindicato Industrial Caletones, 236
Sindicato Industrial Sewell y Mina,
231–232
Sindicato Naheulbuta, 345
Siteco (Sindicato Interempresa de Traba-
jadores Contratistas del Cobre), 221
Skilled workers, in seafood industry, 325
Skills, of copper miners, 244
Small landholders, in forestry industry,
351–352, 357–358
Social concertation: failure of, 71–115;
and labor movement, 86, 109–113;
origins of, 80; and workers, 74

177; and Concertacion, 59–60; and democracy, 114; and economic crisis, 41–42; and globalization, 9–10; job security of, 84; and 1973 coup, 21–22; during Pinochet rule, 1–2, 5–6, 15; right to strike, 92–93; role in transition to democracy, 46–47; and social concertation, 74; and socialism, 16–17; as victims, 10–11; without contract, 102–103. See also specific industries (i.e. Textile workers, Forestry workers, etc.)

Worker solidarity. See Solidarity, worker

Working class: and consumerism, 180–181, 249; and elites, 72–73; in 1990s, 57–58; solidarity of, 165

Working conditions: in agricultural industry, 262; and Codelco, 220–221; in fishing industry, 299; in forestry industry, 360–362; in fruit industry, 283; in mining industry, 238, 254–255; in 1990s, 156; for rural men, 267; in sawmill processing plants, 362–363; in seafood industry, 315–319; at Tejidos Lopez, 137–138; for temporary workers, 263; in textile industry, 152, 157–158; workers' participation in shaping, 156

Younger workers, and class consciousness, 253. See also Older workers

Library of Congress Cataloging-in-Publication Data

Victims of the Chilean miracle : workers and neoliberalism in the Pinochet era, 1973–
2002/edited by Peter Winn.
p. cm.
Includes bibliographical references and index.
ISBN 0-8223-3309-0 (cloth : alk. paper)—ISBN 0-8223- 3321-X (pbk. : alk. paper)
1. Working class—Chile—History—20th century. 2. Chile—Economic policy. 3. Industrial
relations—Chile—History—20th century. 4. Liberalism—Chile—History—20th century.
5. Chile—Politics and government—1973—I. Winn, Peter.
HD8296.5.V53 2004
331'.0983'09045—dc22   2004001304